# FOOTBALL
# IN
# EUROPE

**1990-91**

A complete record of the

1990/91 season in Europe.

**Compiled by**
**DAVID CLAYTON**
and
**JAN BUITENGA**

SOCCER BOOK PUBLISHING LIMITED

## ACKNOWLEDGEMENTS

The Authors wish to express their thanks for assistance with the compilation of this book to the correspondents for each country as itemised and to the following people:-

Sabri Kenan Bagci
Johannes de Boer
Tamás Dénes
VV Drechtstreek
Fer van Dijk
Geveke BV, Papendrecht
Olafur Brynjar Halldórsson
Mike Hammond
Irish League
J.W.S. de Jong
M & D de Jong
Kazimlerz Oleszek
John Robinson
Michael Robinson
Henk van der Sluis
FA of Switzerland
(Beatrix Luginbühl)
Mel ap Ior Thomas
FA of Wales

British Library Cataloguing in Publication Data
Buitenga, Jan
  Football in Europe : season 1990/91.
  I. Title II. Clayton, David
  796.334094

ISBN 0947808175

Voetbal in Europa 1990/1991 : ISBN 90.252.9387.5

Printed in Great Britain by
ADLARD PRINT & TYPESETTING SERVICES, RUDDINGTON, NOTTINGHAM
Photographs supplied by
ACTION IMAGES SPORTS PHOTOGRAPHY.

# INTRODUCTION

We are pleased to present "FOOTBALL IN EUROPE 1990/91", documenting the game in each country during the recently completed season.

The information provided in this book has been acquired from the countries of origin, experience having shown us that there is no other way of ensuring it's reliability. Our most grateful thanks therefore go out to our network of correspondents, whose loyalty and co-operation have made this publication possible.

Due to its largely statistical content "FOOTBALL IN EUROPE" will cross language barriers and we feel sure that our publication will be welcomed throughout Europe, being ideally suited to the increasing demand for information concerning the International game.

We have every reason to believe that the two previous editions of "FOOTBALL IN EUROPE" were very well received and look forward to the compilation of further volumes for many years to come.

**David Clayton & Jan Buitenga**

## INDEX

*Further copies of this book may be obtained directly from the publishers: Soccer Book Publishing Limited, 72 St. Peters Avenue, Cleethorpes, DN35 8HU, England — priced £9.99 per copy — post free.*

# ALBANIA  Correspondent : GEZIM NUSHI

**ALBANIA 1st Division — Season 1990/91**

| Team | DINAMO | PARTIZANI | FLAMURTARI | 17 NËNTORI | VLLAZNIA | APOLONIA | LUFTËTARI | BESA | TOMORI | LOKOMOTIVA | LABINOTI | KASTRIOTI | SKENDERBEU | TRAKTORI |
|---|---|---|---|---|---|---|---|---|---|---|---|---|---|---|
| DINAMO TIRANË | ■ | 2-3 | 0-1 | 1-1 | 3-0 | 1-0 | 2-0 | 2-0 | 1-1 | 4-0 | 1-0 | 6-1 | 2-2 | 2-0 |
| | ■ | | | 1-5 | | 1-1 | | 2-0 | 1-1 | | 2-0 | 2-3 | 1-1 | 1-0 |
| PARTIZANI TIRANË | 2-3 | ■ | 0-0 | 1-0 | 1-1 | 1-0 | 1-0 | 1-1 | 3-1 | 1-0 | 2-0 | 6-2 | 2-1 | 3-0 |
| | 0-0 | ■ | | | 1-0 | 4-1 | 2-0 | | 2-1 | | | 2-1 | | 1-0 |
| FLAMURTARI VLORË | 3-2 | 3-0 | ■ | 1-0 | 2-0 | 1-0 | 3-0 | 1-0 | 1-0 | 4-1 | 0-1 | 3-0 | 2-0 | 4-0 |
| | 1-0 | 1-0 | ■ | 3-1 | 5-2 | 4-1 | | 2-1 | | | | | 0-0 | |
| 17 NËNTORI TIRANË | 1-1 | 2-3 | 1-2 | ■ | 1-1 | 1-0 | 3-1 | 1-0 | 3-1 | 2-2 | 1-0 | 4-1 | 1-1 | 3-1 |
| | 2-1 | | | ■ | 3-1 | | 1-1 | 2-1 | 2-1 | 2-1 | | | 0-2 | |
| VLLAZNIA SHKODER | 2-1 | 0-0 | 1-0 | 2-0 | ■ | 1-1 | 1-0 | 3-2 | 5-2 | 2-0 | 0-0 | 2-2 | 1-1 | 1-0 |
| | 3-1 | | | 1-1 | ■ | 3-1 | | | 2-0 | | | 4-2 | 2-1 | 5-3 |
| APOLONIA FIER | 1-1 | 2-2 | 1-2 | 1-0 | 3-3 | ■ | 5-2 | 2-0 | 1-0 | 0-0 | 0-0 | 4-1 | 2-0 | 1-0 |
| | | | | | | ■ | | 1-0 | 2-1 | 0-0 | 0-0 | 2-1 | 4-1 | 1-1 |
| LUFTËTARI GJIROKASTËR | 0-1 | 2-1 | 0-1 | 2-1 | 0-1 | 2-1 | ■ | 2-1 | 1-1 | 2-0 | 0-0 | 2-1 | 2-1 | 1-0 |
| | 2-0 | | 2-1 | 0-0 | 1-0 | 2-1 | ■ | | | | | | | |
| BESA KAVAJË | 0-0 | 0-0 | 0-0 | 0-2 | 1-2 | 3-2 | 1-1 | ■ | 2-3 | 3-0 | 2-1 | 3-1 | 2-1 | 1-0 |
| | 2-1 | 3-1 | | 2-1 | | 3-0 | | ■ | | | 0-0 | | | 4-4 |
| TOMORI BERAT | 1-1 | 0-0 | 1-1 | 0-0 | 2-2 | 1-1 | 5-1 | 1-1 | ■ | 1-1 | 1-0 | 4-0 | 3-1 | 5-0 |
| | | | | 3-0 | 0-0 | | 1-0 | 3-0 | ■ | 2-0 | 5-0 | 6-5 | | |
| LOKOMOTIVA DURRES | 2-0 | 1-0 | 0-1 | 0-0 | 0-0 | 0-0 | 1-0 | 0-0 | 0-1 | ■ | 0-1 | 0-0 | 3-0 | 1-0 |
| | 2-1 | 1-0 | 3-2 | | 1-0 | | 1-0 | | | ■ | | | | 3-0 |
| LABINOTI ELBASAN | 1-1 | 1-1 | 1-3 | 1-0 | 3-2 | 0-3 | 3-0 | 1-1 | 1-0 | 2-0 | ■ | 0-0 | 1-0 | 0-0 |
| | | | 0-0 | | | 1-1 | 2-1 | | 1-1 | | ■ | 1-0 | | |
| KASTRIOTI KRUJË | 1-0 | 1-0 | 1-0 | 0-0 | 0-0 | 0-1 | 1-0 | 2-1 | 2-0 | 1-2 | 1-0 | ■ | 2-2 | 2-2 |
| | | 0-0 | 4-2 | | | 2-0 | 0-3 | 1-0 | | | | ■ | | 1-1 |
| SKENDERBEU KORCË | 1-1 | 2-2 | 2-0 | 2-2 | 0-0 | 2-0 | 1-0 | 4-0 | 1-1 | 2-1 | 2-1 | 1-0 | ■ | 3-0 |
| | | | 1-1 | 2-0 | | 1-1 | 0-0 | 0-2 | | | | | ■ | 2-2 |
| TRAKTORI LUSHNJË | 1-1 | 1-1 | 0-0 | 0-1 | 1-0 | 2-1 | 1-0 | 2-1 | 1-1 | 2-1 | 0-0 | 2-2 | 2-0 | ■ |
| | 0-1 | 3-2 | 1-0 | 2-1 | | 2-1 | | | | | | | | ■ |

## ALBANIA 1ST DIVISION 1990/91
### LEAGUE TABLE FINAL

| | P | W | D | L | F | A | Pts |
|---|---|---|---|---|---|---|---|
| Flamurtari Vlorë | 39 | 24 | 6 | 9 | 63 | 32 | 54 |
| Partizani Tiranë | 39 | 18 | 12 | 9 | 52 | 35 | 48 |
| Vllaznia Shkoder | 39 | 16 | 13 | 10 | 57 | 47 | 45 |
| 17 Nëntori Tiranë | 39 | 16 | 12 | 11 | 52 | 40 | 44 |
| Tomori Berat | 39 | 13 | 14 | 12 | 62 | 47 | 40 |
| Dinamo Tiranë | 39 | 13 | 14 | 12 | 53 | 44 | 40 |
| Apolonia Fier | 39 | 13 | 12 | 14 | 49 | 47 | 38 |
| Lokomotiva Durres | 39 | 12 | 12 | 15 | 30 | 38 | 36 |
| Labinoti Elbasan | 39 | 11 | 14 | 14 | 29 | 37 | 36 |
| Skenderbeu Korcë | 39 | 10 | 15 | 14 | 46 | 55 | 35 |
| Besa Kavajë | 39 | 11 | 12 | 16 | 45 | 50 | 34 |
| Kastrioti Krujë | 39 | 12 | 10 | 17 | 41 | 62 | 34 |
| Traktori Lushnjë | 39 | 10 | 12 | 17 | 39 | 60 | 32 |
| Luftetari Gjirokastër | 39 | 12 | 6 | 21 | 31 | 55 | 30 |

Champions : - Flamurtari Vlorë
Relegated : - Luftetari Gjirokastër
League to be increased to 16 clubs for Season 1991/92

### NAME CHANGE FOR SEASON 1991/92
17 Nëntori Tiranë to SK Tiranë

### TOP SCORERS
1. Bozgo (Tomori Berat) — 29
2. Raklli (Besa Kavajë) — 27
3. Kepa (Vllaznia Shkoder) — 16
4. Tahiri (Dinamo Tiranë) — 14
5. Kushta (Flamurtari Vlorë) — 13
   Kacaci (Partizani Tiranë) — 13
   Majaci (Apolonia Fier) — 13
8. Voda (Tomori Berat) — 12
   Dosti (Kastrioti Krujë/Partizani) — 12
10. Alimehmeti (17 Nëntori Tiranë) — 11

## ALBANIA 2ND DIVISION A 1990/91
### LEAGUE TABLE FINAL

| | P | W | D | L | F | A | Pts |
|---|---|---|---|---|---|---|---|
| Industriali Lac | 24 | 18 | 2 | 4 | 45 | 14 | 38 |
| Korabi Peshkopi | 24 | 14 | 4 | 4 | 41 | 14 | 32 |
| Dajti Tiranë | 24 | 15 | 1 | 8 | 34 | 14 | 31 |
| Shkumbini Peqin | 24 | 14 | 2 | 8 | 32 | 14 | 30 |
| 31 Korriku Burrel | 24 | 12 | 5 | 7 | 41 | 26 | 29 |
| Përparimi Kukës | 23 | 12 | 4 | 7 | 35 | 23 | 28 |
| Veleciku Koplik | 23 | 9 | 6 | 8 | 31 | 23 | 24 |
| Volbana Bajram Curri | 23 | 9 | 6 | 8 | 27 | 24 | 24 |
| Erzeni Shjiak | 24 | 10 | 4 | 10 | 21 | 20 | 24 |
| 8 Nentori Sukhti | 24 | 6 | 7 | 11 | 23 | 39 | 19 |
| Tërbuni Puke | 23 | 5 | 4 | 14 | 18 | 47 | 14 |
| 18 Shkurti Bulqiza | 24 | 3 | 3 | 18 | 13 | 49 | 9 |
| Minatori Rreshën | 24 | 0 | 4 | 20 | 14 | 68 | 4 |

## ALBANIA 2ND DIVISION B 1990/91
### LEAGUE TABLE FINAL

| | P | W | D | L | F | A | Pts |
|---|---|---|---|---|---|---|---|
| 21 Shkurti Selenica | 22 | 15 | 1 | 6 | 71 | 25 | 31 |
| Naftëtari Qyteti St. | 22 | 14 | 3 | 5 | 57 | 19 | 31 |
| Punëtori Patos | 22 | 13 | 3 | 6 | 55 | 26 | 29 |
| Ballshi I Ri Ballsh | 22 | 11 | 5 | 6 | 27 | 29 | 27 |
| Besëlidhja Lezhe | 22 | 11 | 3 | 8 | 42 | 31 | 25 |
| Sopoti Librazhd | 22 | 10 | 5 | 7 | 27 | 20 | 25 |
| 5 Shtatori Surapar | 22 | 9 | 4 | 9 | 24 | 27 | 22 |
| Turbina Cërrik | 22 | 9 | 3 | 10 | 30 | 21 | 21 |
| 22 Tetori Policiani | 22 | 8 | 5 | 9 | 30 | 48 | 21 |
| Domosdova Prrenjas | 22 | 5 | 5 | 12 | 21 | 38 | 15 |
| Vullneti Rrogozhine | 22 | 5 | 5 | 12 | 13 | 47 | 15 |
| 10 Korriku Gramsh | 22 | 0 | 2 | 20 | 5 | 71 | 2 |

## ALBANIA 2ND DIVISION C 1990/91
### LEAGUE TABLE FINAL

| | P | W | D | L | F | A | Pts |
|---|---|---|---|---|---|---|---|
| Ylli I Kuq Pogradec | 22 | 16 | 2 | 4 | 40 | 19 | 34 |
| Butrinti Sarandë | 22 | 14 | 2 | 6 | 50 | 18 | 30 |
| Minatori Tepelenë | 22 | 13 | 3 | 6 | 41 | 21 | 29 |
| Minatori Memaliaj | 22 | 12 | 3 | 7 | 41 | 24 | 27 |
| Bistrica Delvinë | 22 | 11 | 3 | 8 | 37 | 22 | 25 |
| 24 Maji Përmët | 22 | 10 | 5 | 7 | 25 | 21 | 25 |
| Studenti Tiranë | 22 | 8 | 8 | 6 | 38 | 26 | 24 |
| Vetëtima Himare | 22 | 7 | 4 | 11 | 29 | 38 | 18 |
| Gramozi Erseke | 22 | 5 | 6 | 11 | 22 | 24 | 16 |
| Trebeshina Kelcyra | 22 | 4 | 5 | 13 | 22 | 43 | 13 |
| Devolli Bilishti | 22 | 3 | 6 | 13 | 19 | 57 | 12 |
| Melesini Leskoviu | 22 | 5 | 1 | 16 | 17 | 68 | 11 |

Promoted : -Industriali Lac
21 Shkurti Selenica
Ylli I Kuq Pogradec

# ALBANIA CUP 1990/91

## GROUP A

| | | | |
|---|---|---|---|
| Dinamo Tiranë | 6 | Terbuni Pukë | 0 |
| Erzeni Shjak | 4 | 18 Shkurti Bulqiza | 0 |
| Korabi Peshkopi | 0 | Industriali Lac | 0 |
| Erzeni Shjak | 5 | 18 Shkurti Bulqiza | 1 |
| Industriali Lac | 1 | Korabi Peshkopi | 1 |
| Terbuni Puke | 2 | Dinamo Tiranë | 0 |
| Dinamo Tiranë | 2 | Industriali Lac | 0 |
| Korabi Peshkopi | 3 | 18 Shkurti Bulqiza | 1 |
| Terbuni Puke | 0 | Erzeni Shjak | 0 |
| Erzeni Shjak | 3 | Industriali Lac | 1 |
| Korabi Peshkopi | 1 | Dinamo Tiranë | 4 |
| Industriali Lac | 3 | Terbuni Puke | 1 |
| Korabi Peshkopi | 0 | Terbuni Puke | 0 |

**LEAGUE TABLE FINAL**

| Team | P | W | D | L | F | A | Pts |
|---|---|---|---|---|---|---|---|
| Dinamo Tiranë | 5 | 4 | 0 | 1 | 18 | 2 | 8 |
| Erzeni Shjak | 5 | 3 | 1 | 1 | 8 | 2 | 7 |
| Industriali Lac | 5 | 2 | 1 | 2 | 5 | 11 | 5 |
| Terbuni Puke | 5 | 2 | 1 | 2 | 7 | 5 | 5 |
| Korabi Peshkopi | 5 | 1 | 0 | 4 | 4 | 12 | 2 |
| 18 Shkurti Bulqiza | 5 | 0 | 1 | 4 | 1 | 9 | 1 |

## GROUP B

| | | | |
|---|---|---|---|
| Domosdv. Prrenjas | 2 | Dajti Tiranë | 3 |
| 10 Korriku Gramsh | 0 | Partizani Tiranë | 3 |
| Skenderbeu Korcë | 1 | Studenti Tiranë | 0 |
| Partizani Tiranë | 1 | Dajti Tiranë | 1 |
| Studenti Tiranë | 4 | Skenderbeu Korcë | 4 |
| Dajt Tiranë | 2 | Studenti Tiranë | 2 |
| Domosdv. Prrenjas | 0 | Partizani Tiranë | 0 |
| Partizani Tiranë | 0 | Skenderbeu Korcë | 5 |
| 10 Korriku Gramsh | 5 | Dajti Tiranë | 1 |
| Dajti Tiranë | 0 | Domosdv. Prrenjas | 1 |
| Domosdv. Prrenjas | 1 | Studenti Tiranë | 2 |
| Studenti Tiranë | 2 | 10 Korriku Gramsh | 2 |
| Domosdova Prrenjas | 3 | 10 Korriku Gramsh | 3 |
| Partizani Tiranë | 7 | 10 Korriku Gramsh | 4 |
| Skenderbeu Korcë | 4 | | |

**LEAGUE TABLE FINAL**

| Team | P | W | D | L | F | A | Pts |
|---|---|---|---|---|---|---|---|
| Partizani Tiranë | 5 | 4 | 1 | 0 | 15 | 0 | 9 |
| Skenderbeu Korcë | 5 | 4 | 0 | 1 | 12 | 5 | 8 |
| Studenti Tiranë | 5 | 2 | 1 | 2 | 6 | 11 | 5 |
| Dajti Tiranë | 5 | 2 | 0 | 3 | 6 | 12 | 4 |
| Domosdova Prrenjas | 5 | 1 | 0 | 4 | 5 | 14 | 2 |
| 10 Korriku Gramsh | 5 | 0 | 1 | 4 | 3 | 14 | 1 |

## GROUP C

| | | | |
|---|---|---|---|
| Minatori Memaliaj | 0 | 24 Maji Përmët | 1 |
| Traktori Lushnjë | 1 | Minatori Tepelenë | 1 |
| Trebeshina Kelcyra | 5 | Flamurtari Vlorë | 1 |
| Flamurtari Vlorë | 1 | Minatori Tepelenë | 0 |
| 24 Maji Përmët | 6 | Trebeshina Kelcyra | 1 |
| Minatori Memaliaj | 0 | Traktori Lushnjë | 1 |
| Minatori Tepelenë | 3 | Flamurtari Vlorë | 2 |
| Minatori Memaliaj | 1 | Traktori Lushnjë | 2 |
| Trebeshina Kelcyra | 0 | Minatori Tepelenë | 1 |
| Flamurtari Vlorë | 5 | 24 Maji Përmët | 1 |
| Minatori Tepelenë | 1 | 24 Maji Përmët | 5 |
| Traktori Lushnjë | 1 | Trebeshina Kelcyra | 0 |

**LEAGUE TABLE FINAL**

| Team | P | W | D | L | F | A | Pts |
|---|---|---|---|---|---|---|---|
| Flamurtari Vlorë | 5 | 5 | 0 | 0 | 16 | 4 | 10 |
| 24 Maji Përmët | 5 | 4 | 0 | 1 | 6 | 6 | 8 |
| Traktori Lushnjë | 5 | 2 | 1 | 2 | 11 | 6 | 5 |
| Minatori Tepelenë | 5 | 1 | 2 | 2 | 7 | 5 | 4 |
| Trebeshina Kelcyra | 5 | 1 | 0 | 4 | 4 | 12 | 2 |
| Minatori Memaliaj | 5 | 0 | 1 | 4 | 1 | 9 | 1 |

## GROUP D

| | | | |
|---|---|---|---|
| Kastrioti Krujë | 2 | Butrinti Sarandë | 2 |
| 17 Nëntori Tiranë | 7 | Vullneti Rrogozhine | 1 |
| 21 Shkurti Selenica | 1 | Ballshi i Ri Ballsh | 0 |
| Butrinti Sarandë | 1 | 17 Nëntori Tiranë | 1 |
| Kastrioti Krujë | 1 | Butrinti Sarandë | 1 |
| 17 Nëntori Tiranë | 3 | 21 Shkurti Selenica | 1 |
| Kastrioti Krujë | 2 | Ballshi i Ri Ballsh | 3 |
| Ballshi i Ri Ballsh | 5 | Butrinti Sarandë | 1 |
| 17 Nëntori Tiranë | 1 | 21 Shkurti Selenica | 1 |

**LEAGUE TABLE FINAL**

| Team | P | W | D | L | F | A | Pts |
|---|---|---|---|---|---|---|---|
| Kastrioti Krujë | 5 | 4 | 1 | 0 | 16 | 1 | 9 |
| 17 Nëntori Tiranë | 5 | 4 | 0 | 1 | 6 | 6 | 8 |
| 21 Shkurti Selenica | 5 | 2 | 1 | 2 | 4 | 4 | 5 |
| Ballshi i Ri Ballsh | 5 | 2 | 0 | 3 | 7 | 10 | 4 |
| Butrinti Sarandë | 5 | 1 | 0 | 4 | 6 | 11 | 2 |
| Vullneti Rrogozhine | 5 | 0 | 1 | 4 | 3 | 12 | 1 |

## GROUP E

| | | | |
|---|---|---|---|
| 31 Korriku Burrel | 2 | Valbona Tropoja | 0 |
| Përparimi Kukës | 0 | Vllaznia Shkoder | 2 |
| Veleciku Koplik | 6 | Besëlidhja Lezhe | 0 |
| 31 Korriku Burrel | 0 | Veleciku Koplik | 1 |
| Valbona Tropoja | 0 | Besëlidhja Lezhe | 2 |
| Vllaznia Shkoder | 3 | Përparimi Kukës | 0 |
| Besëlidhja Lezhe | 2 | Valbona Tropo,a | 0 |
| Veleciku Koplik | 3 | Përparimi Kukës | 3 |
| Vllaznia Shkoder | 4 | 31 Korriku Burrel | 0 |
| Besëlidhja Lezhe | 5 | 31 Korriku Burrel | 1 |
| Përparimi Kukës | 1 | Veleciku Koplik | 4 |
| 31 Korriku Burrel | 1 | Vllaznia Shkoder | 3 |

**LEAGUE TABLE FINAL**

| Team | P | W | D | L | F | A | Pts |
|---|---|---|---|---|---|---|---|
| Vllaznia Shkoder | 5 | 3 | 2 | 0 | 16 | 9 | 8 |
| Veleciku Koplik | 5 | 3 | 1 | 1 | 9 | 5 | 7 |
| Besëlidhja Lezhe | 5 | 3 | 0 | 2 | 12 | 8 | 6 |
| 31 Korriku Burrel | 5 | 3 | 0 | 2 | 10 | 7 | 6 |
| Përparimi Kukës | 5 | 1 | 0 | 4 | 4 | 16 | 2 |
| Valbona Tropoja | 5 | 0 | 1 | 4 | 3 | 9 | 1 |

## GROUP F

| | | | |
|---|---|---|---|
| Apolonia Fier | 0 | Naftëtari Qyt. Stalin | 0 |
| Labinoti Elbasan | 1 | Sopoti Librazhd | 1 |
| Vetëtima Himare | 0 | Bistrica Delvinë | 1 |
| Apolonia Fier | 5 | Labinoti Elbasan | 0 |
| Naftëtari Qyt. Stalin | 1 | Bistrica Delvinë | 0 |
| Sopoti Librazhd | 2 | Vetëtima Himare | 2 |
| Bistrica Delvinë | 2 | Sopoti Librazhd | 0 |
| Labinoti Elbasan | 1 | Naftëtari Qyt. Stalin | 0 |
| Vetëtima Himare | 7 | Apolonia Fier | 1 |
| Apolonia Fier | 3 | Bistrica Delvinë | 0 |
| Labinoti Elbasan | 3 | Vetëtima Himare | 2 |
| Naftëtari Qyt. Stalin | 5 | Sopoti Librazhd | 2 |
| Bistrica Delvinë | 1 | Labinoti Elbasan | 3 |
| Sopoti Librazhd | 1 | Apolonia Fier | 3 |
| Vetëtima Himare | 1 | Naftëtari Qyt. Stalin | 0 |

**LEAGUE TABLE FINAL**

| Team | P | W | D | L | F | A | Pts |
|---|---|---|---|---|---|---|---|
| Apolonia Fier | 5 | 3 | 2 | 0 | 16 | 3 | 8 |
| Naftëtari Qyteti Stalin | 5 | 3 | 1 | 1 | 8 | 7 | 7 |
| Labinoti Elbasan | 5 | 3 | 1 | 1 | 8 | 6 | 7 |
| Vetëtima Himare | 5 | 2 | 1 | 2 | 10 | 8 | 5 |
| Sopoti Librazhd | 5 | 0 | 3 | 2 | 4 | 13 | 3 |
| Bistrica Delvinë | 5 | 1 | 0 | 4 | 3 | 12 | 2 |

## GROUP G

| | | | |
|---|---|---|---|
| Lokomotiva Durres | 2 | Gramozi Erseke | 2 |
| Luftëtari Gjirokastër | 4 | Devolli Bilishti | 0 |
| Ylli i Kuq Pogradec | 1 | 5 Shtatori Surapar | 0 |
| Devolli Bilishti | 2 | 5 Shtatori Surapar | 1 |
| Gramozi Erseke | 0 | Ylli i Kuq Pogradec | 0 |
| Luftëtari Gjirokastër | 2 | Lokomotiva Durres | 2 |
| Lokomotiva Durres | 2 | Devolli Bilishti | 0 |
| 5 Shtatori Surapar | 4 | Gramozi Erseke | 1 |
| Ylli i Kuq Pogradec | 1 | Luftëtari Gjirokastër | 1 |
| Devolli Bilishti | 0 | Ylli i Kuq Pogradec | 1 |
| Luftëtari Gjirokastër | 3 | Gramozi Erseke | 1 |
| Lokomotiva Durres | 1 | 5 Shtatori Surapar | 2 |
| Gramozi Erseke | 3 | Lokomotiva Durres | 2 |
| 5 Shtatori Surapar | 2 | Luftëtari Gjirokastër | 3 |
| Ylli i Kuq Pogradec | 3 | Devolli Bilishti | 0 |

**LEAGUE TABLE FINAL**

| Team | P | W | D | L | F | A | Pts |
|---|---|---|---|---|---|---|---|
| Luftëtari Gjirokastër | 5 | 4 | 0 | 1 | 13 | 5 | 8 |
| Ylli i Kuq Pogradec | 5 | 3 | 2 | 0 | 7 | 3 | 8 |
| Lokomotiva Durres | 5 | 2 | 2 | 1 | 7 | 5 | 6 |
| 5 Shtatori Surapar | 5 | 2 | 1 | 2 | 7 | 6 | 5 |
| Devolli Bilishti | 5 | 1 | 0 | 4 | 3 | 11 | 3 |
| Gramozi Erseke | 5 | 0 | 2 | 3 | 4 | 10 | 2 |

## GROUP H

| | | | |
|---|---|---|---|
| Minatori Rreshën | 1 | Besa Kavajë | 3 |
| Punëtori Patos | 0 | Turbina Cërrik | 3 |
| Tomori Berat | 4 | Shkumbini Peqin | 1 |
| Besa Kavajë | 1 | Tomori Berat | 1 |
| Minatori Rreshën | 2 | Turbina Cërrik | 1 |
| Shkumbini Peqin | 2 | Punëtori Patos | 1 |
| Punëtori Patos | 1 | Besa Kavajë | 2 |
| Tomori Berat | 7 | Minatori Rreshën | 3 |
| Turbina Cërrik | 1 | Shkumbini Peqin | 2 |
| Besa Kavajë | 3 | Shkumbini Peqin | 1 |
| Tomori Berat | 4 | Minatori Rreshën | 2 |
| Shkumbini Peqin | 0 | Punëtori Patos | 0 |
| Besa Kavajë | 2 | Punëtori Patos | 6 |
| Minatori Rreshën | 3 | Tomori Berat | 0 |
| Turbina Cërrik | 1 | | |

**LEAGUE TABLE FINAL**

| Team | P | W | D | L | F | A | Pts |
|---|---|---|---|---|---|---|---|
| Besa Kavajë | 5 | 4 | 1 | 0 | 11 | 4 | 9 |
| Tomori Berat | 5 | 3 | 2 | 0 | 15 | 2 | 8 |
| Shkumbini Peqin | 5 | 2 | 1 | 2 | 9 | 11 | 5 |
| Punëtori Patos | 5 | 2 | 0 | 3 | 9 | 10 | 4 |
| Turbina Cërrik | 5 | 1 | 1 | 3 | 8 | 8 | 3 |
| Minatori Rreshën | 5 | 1 | 0 | 4 | 4 | 21 | 2 |

Winners and Runners-Up of each group qualify for 18 Finals.

## INTERNATIONAL LINE-UPS 1990

| Date | Match | Venue | Referee | Competition |
|---|---|---|---|---|
| 30/5/90 | ICELAND 2 ALBANIA 0 | Reykjavik | McKnight (N.Ireland) | EuroCh.Q. |
| 5/9/90 | GREECE 1 ALBANIA 0 | Patras | Vutzaras (Greece) | Friendly |
| 17/11/90 | ALBANIA 0 FRANCE 1 | Tiranë | Galler (Switzerland) | EuroCh.Q. |
| 19/12/90 | SPAIN 9 ALBANIA 0 | Sevilla | Constantin (Belgium) | EuroCh.Q. |

**CAPS AT 31/12/90 / GOALS AT 31/12/90**

| Player | Caps |
|---|---|
| Foto Strakosha | 1 |
| Fatbardh Jera | 15 |
| Pjerin Noga | 3 |
| Artur Lekbello | 12 |
| Naum Kove | 1 |
| Rudi Vata | 1 |
| Mirel Josa | 24 |
| Lefter Millo | 10 |
| Sulejman Demollari | 25 |
| Eduard Abazi | 2 |
| Ylli Shehu | 7 |
| Roland Iljadhi | 4 |
| Arben Arberi | 3 |
| Sotir Shkurti | 4 |
| Genci Ibro | 3 |
| Skender Hodja | 21 |
| Rrapo Taho | 9 |
| Lorenc Leskaj | 2 |
| Eqerem Memushi | 1 |
| Ledio Pano | 3 |
| Hysen Zmijani | 21 |
| Alfred Ferko | 8 |
| Sokol Kushta | 9 |
| Eduard Kacaci | 9 |
| Ardian Suka | 1 |
| Ermal Tahiri | 2 |
| Ardian Barbullushi | 1 |
| Anest Arapi | 2 |
| Arjan Stafa | 3 |
| Kujtim Majaci | 3 |
| Gjergji Dëma | 1 |
| Bledar Kola | 1 |

## 1/8 FINALS

| | 1ST LEG | 2ND LEG | AGG. |
|---|---|---|---|
| Besa Kavajë v Erzeni Shijak | 3-0 | 0-1 | 3-1 |
| Dinamo Tiranë v 24 Maji Përmët | 3-0 | 0-1 | 3-1 |
| Flamurtari Vlorë v Tomori Berat | 4-0 | 2-0 | 6-0 |
| Kastrioti Krujë v Skenderbeu Korcë | 3-0 | 3-1 | 6-1 |
| Naftëtari Qyteti Stalin v Apolonia Fier | 3-1 | 1-4 (aet.) | 4-5 |
| Veleciku Koplik v Partizani Tiranë | 1-0 | 0-2 | 1-2 |
| Vllaznia Shkoder v 17 Nëntori Tiranë | 1-0 | 0-3 | 1-3 |
| Ylli I Kuq Pogradec v Luftëtari Gjirokastër | 1-1 | 0-2 | 1-3 |

## 1/4 FINALS

| | 1ST LEG | 2ND LEG | AGG. |
|---|---|---|---|
| Apolonia Fier v Luftëtari Gjirokastër | 2-0 | 0-0 | 2-0 |
| Flamurtari Vlorë v 17 Nëntori Tiranë | 2-0 | 0-1 | 2-1 |
| Kastrioti Krujë v Dinamo Tiranë | 2-1 | 1-3 | 3-4 |
| Partizani Tiranë v Besa Kavajë | 3-1 | 2-0 | 5-1 |

## SEMI-FINALS

Flamurtari Vlorë ...... 4    Dinamo Tiranë ...... 1
Partizani Tiranë ...... 1    Apolonia Fier ...... 0

## FINAL

Partizani Tiranë ......1    Flamurtari Vlorë ...... 1 (aet.)

Partizani : Musta, Berberi, Ocelli, Shulku, Sheta, Ndoci (Berisha 46), Muca, Kola, Fejzolli (Satko 106), Hasanpapa, Dosti.
Flamurtari : Arapi, Dema (Vito 91), Cipi, Taho, Iljadhi, Mehilli, Shaqiri, Ciruna (Memushi 65), Gjondeda, Daulija, Lutaj.
Referee : Plarent Kotherja

1-0   Berberi   9
1-1   Lutaj   22

PARTIZANI TIRANË WIN 4-3 ON PENALTIES.

## ALBANIA : ALL TIME RECORDS AS AT 31/12/90 - CAPS

1. Arben Minga (17 Nentori Tiranë) — 28
2. Sulejman Demollari (Dinamo Tiranë) — 25
3. Loro Boriçi (Vllaznia Shkoder/Partizani Tiranë) — 24
   Panajot Pano (Partizani Tiranë) — 24
   Mirel Josa (17 Nentori Tiranë) — 24
6. Muhedin Targaj (Dinamo Tiranë) — 23
7. Perlat Musta (Partizani Tiranë) — 22
   Skender Hodja (17 Nentori Tiranë) — 21
   Hysen Zmijani (Vllaznia Shkoder) — 21
10. Safet Benisha (Partizani Tiranë) — 20
    Muhamet Dibra (Vllaznia Shkoder/Partizani Tiranë) — 20

## ALBANIA : ALL TIME RECORDS AS AT 31/12/90 - GOALS

1. Qamil Teliti (?)
2. Loro Boriçi (Vllaznia Shkoder/Partizani Tiranë)
3. Llir Pernaska (Dinamo Tiranë)
4. (?)Mirashi (Vllaznia Shkoder)
5. (?)Gjinali (Dinamo Tiranë)
   Bedri Omuri (17 Nentori Tiranë)
   Muhedin Targaj (Dinamo Tiranë)
   Panajot Pano (Partizani Tiranë)
9. (?)Juka (?)
   (?)Kraja (Partizani Tiranë)
   (?)Zhega (Dinamo Tiranë)
   Sokol Kushta (Flamurtari Vlorë)
   Shkelqim Muca (17 Nentori Tiranë)
   Arben Minga (17 Nentori Tiranë)

# AUSTRIA  Correspondent : ERICH STEMPIEN

## AUSTRIA 1st Division — Autumn 1990

| | FC TIROL | FK AUSTRIA | RAPID | ADMIRA-W. | STURM | SALZBURG | ST.PÖLTEN | VIENNA | STEYR | WIENER SC | KREMS | DONAWITZ |
|---|---|---|---|---|---|---|---|---|---|---|---|---|
| FC TIROL | | 1-2 | 3-2 | 0-0 | 4-1 | 3-0 | 5-0 | 4-1 | 2-2 | 2-0 | 4-0 | 3-0 |
| FK AÜSTRIA WIEN | 1-1 | | 0-3 | 5-0 | 0-0 | 1-0 | 3-0 | 1-0 | 4-1 | 4-2 | 6-0 | 0-0 |
| SK RAPID WIEN | 1-2 | 2-0 | | 2-0 | 3-1 | 2-4 | 1-1 | 3-1 | 2-0 | 5-0 | 4-1 | 0-2 |
| FC ADMIRA-WACKER | 0-2 | 0-3 | 0-2 | | 1-0 | 1-2 | 2-1 | 1-0 | 0-3 | 1-0 | 2-0 | 1-1 |
| SK STURM GRAZ | 2-1 | 1-0 | 1-1 | 1-1 | | 4-0 | 3-0 | 4-1 | 3-4 | 3-0 | 0-0 | 6-1 |
| SV AUSTRIA SALZBURG | 0-1 | 3-2 | 2-0 | 1-1 | 0-1 | | 5-1 | 1-1 | 2-1 | 2-0 | 1-0 | 1-2 |
| VSE SANKT PÖLTEN | 0-0 | 1-4 | 1-0 | 2-1 | 2-2 | 1-2 | | 2-5 | 1-2 | 0-2 | 0-0 | 1-1 |
| 1 VIENNA FC WIEN | 0-0 | 2-6 | 0-2 | 2-1 | 1-0 | 3-2 | 3-1 | | 1-1 | 0-4 | 2-2 | 1-4 |
| SK VORWÄRTS STEYR | 3-3 | 0-2 | 1-2 | 0-0 | 1-3 | 1-0 | 1-3 | 3-0 | | 2-1 | 3-2 | 0-1 |
| WIENER SPORT-CLUB | 0-3 | 1-1 | 1-7 | 1-1 | 2-3 | 2-5 | 2-0 | 2-0 | 0-2 | | 2-0 | 1-0 |
| KREMSER SC | 3-2 | 2-2 | 0-3 | 0-0 | 2-1 | 0-1 | 2-0 | 1-2 | 1-1 | 0-1 | | 1-1 |
| DONAWITZER SV | 0-3 | 1-1 | 0-0 | 1-3 | 0-2 | 0-4 | 4-0 | 3-3 | 0-0 | 1-1 | 2-1 | |

## AUSTRIA Championship Section — Spring 1991

| | FC TIROL | FK AUSTRIA | RAPID | STURM | SALZBURG | STEYR | DONAWITZ | ADMIRA-W |
|---|---|---|---|---|---|---|---|---|
| FC TIROL | | 4-1 | 2-0 | 3-0 | 1-0 | 3-3 | 3-1 | 3-1 |
| FK AUSTRIA WIEN | 3-1 | | 2-1 | 2-0 | 1-0 | 1-0 | 0-1 | 4-0 |
| SK RAPID WIEN | 3-2 | 1-2 | | 0-1 | 4-2 | 0-2 | 4-0 | 1-0 |
| SK STURM GRAZ | 0-0 | 2-0 | 3-1 | | 3-1 | 1-1 | 2-1 | 0-0 |
| SV AUST. SALZBURG | 1-2 | 0-2 | 0-0 | 1-1 | | 5-0 | 3-2 | 1-1 |
| SK VORWÄRTS STEYR | 1-1 | 0-2 | 0-3 | 1-3 | 0-0 | | 3-1 | 2-3 |
| DONAWITZER SV | 2-1 | 0-2 | 2-0 | 0-2 | 2-5 | 1-1 | | 0-0 |
| FC ADMIRA-WACKER | 1-3 | 2-2 | 2-2 | 1-0 | 1-1 | 0-0 | 2-0 | |

## AUSTRIA 1ST DIVISION AUTUMN 1990

### LEAGUE TABLE 1ST STAGE FINAL

| | | | | | | | |
|---|---|---|---|---|---|---|---|
| FC Tirol | 22 | 13 | 6 | 3 | 49 | 18 | 32 |
| FK Austria Wien | 22 | 12 | 6 | 4 | 48 | 21 | 30 |
| SK Rapid Wien | 22 | 13 | 3 | 6 | 47 | 21 | 29 |
| SK Sturm Graz | 22 | 11 | 5 | 6 | 42 | 25 | 27 |
| SV Austria Salzburg | 22 | 12 | 2 | 8 | 38 | 28 | 26 |
| SK Vorwärts Steyr | 22 | 8 | 6 | 8 | 32 | 33 | 22 |
| Donawitzer SV | 22 | 6 | 9 | 7 | 25 | 33 | 21 |
| FC Admira-Wacker | 22 | 6 | 7 | 9 | 17 | 29 | 19 |
| Wiener Sport-Club | 22 | 7 | 3 | 12 | 25 | 42 | 17 |
| 1 Vienna FC Wien | 22 | 6 | 5 | 11 | 29 | 48 | 17 |
| Kremser SC | 22 | 3 | 7 | 12 | 18 | 40 | 13 |
| VSE Sankt Pölten | 22 | 3 | 5 | 14 | 18 | 50 | 11 |

### TOP SCORERS
1. Václav Danek (FC Tirol) — 20
2. Oliver Bierhoff (Aust.Salzburg) — 16
3. Jan Age Fjørtoft (SK Rapid) — 13
4. Peter Pacult (FC Tirol) — 12
5. Ralph Balzis (1 Vienna FC Wien) — 9
   Srecko Kurbasa (Aust.Salzburg) — 9
7. Heimo Pfeifenberger (SK Rapid) — 8
   Peter Stöger (FK Austria) — 8
   Arnold Wetl (SK Sturm) — 8
9. Slobodan Brankovic (Steyr) — 7
   Sigurd Kristensen (SK Sturm) — 7
   Andreas Ogris (FK Austria) — 7
   Dejan Stankovic (DSV) — 7

## AUSTRIA CHAMP'SHIP PLAY-OFFS SPRING 1991

### LEAGUE TABLE FINAL

| | | | | | | | |
|---|---|---|---|---|---|---|---|
| FK Austria Wien | 36 | 22 | 7 | 7 | 72 | 33 | 36 |
| FC Tirol | 36 | 21 | 9 | 6 | 78 | 35 | 35 |
| SK Sturm Graz | 36 | 18 | 9 | 9 | 60 | 37 | 32 |
| SK Rapid Wien | 36 | 18 | 5 | 13 | 67 | 41 | 27 |
| SV Austria Salzburg | 36 | 15 | 7 | 14 | 58 | 48 | 24 |
| FC Admira-Wacker | 36 | 9 | 14 | 13 | 31 | 48 | 23 |
| SK Vorwärts Steyr | 36 | 10 | 12 | 14 | 46 | 57 | 21 |
| Donawitzer SV | 36 | 9 | 11 | 16 | 38 | 61 | 19 |

Champions : - FK Austria Wien

### TOP SCORERS
1. Václav Danek (FC Tirol) — 29
2. Oliver Bierhoff (SV Austria Salzburg) — 23
3. Jan-Aage Fjørtoft (SK Rapid Wien) — 16
4. Christoph Westerthaler (FC Tirol) — 14
5. Peter Pacult (FC Tirol) — 13
6. Arnold Wetl (SK Sturm Graz) — 12
7. Ralph Hasenhüttl (FK Austria Wien) — 11

Top 8 clubs to form 1st Division Championship section, matches to played during Spring Season 1991. 1st Stage records carried forwards to 2nd Stage with half points total, where necessary half points being rounded upwards. Points totals carried forwards as follows : - FC Tirol 16, FK Austria Wien 15, SK Rapid Wien 15, SK Sturm Graz 14, SV Austria Salzburg 13, SK Vorwärts Steyr 11, Donawitzer SV 11, FC Admira-Wacker 10. Bottom 4 clubs, Wiener Sport-Club, 1 Vienna FC Wien, Kremser SC and VSE Sankt Pölten, to form promotion/relegation section with top 4 clubs from 2nd Division to decide 4 1st Division places for Autumn Season 1991. 1st Stage records not carried forward and matches to be played during Spring Season 1991.

## AUSTRIA 2nd Division — Autumn 1990

| | VÖEST | MÖDLING | GAK | SPITTAL/D | LASK | WATTENS | VÖSENDORF | KL'FURT | STOCKERAU | SALZBURG | DONAUFELD | WAC |
|---|---|---|---|---|---|---|---|---|---|---|---|---|
| VÖEST LINZ | | 3-1 | 1-0 | 3-1 | 0-1 | 6-0 | 0-0 | 2-0 | 2-2 | 3-2 | 2-1 | 3-1 |
| VfB MÖDLING | 7-0 | | 2-0 | 3-1 | 3-1 | 5-0 | 6-0 | 3-1 | 0-3 | 2-1 | 3-1 | 3-0 |
| GRAZER AK | 5-1 | 0-0 | | 1-2 | 0-0 | 3-1 | 1-0 | 0-0 | 2-0 | 5-0 | 4-1 | 0-0 |
| SV SPITTAL/DRAU | 2-2 | 2-2 | 2-2 | | 4-2 | 2-1 | 1-2 | 3-1 | 0-2 | 1-2 | 3-4 | 2-0 |
| LINZER ASK | 1-3 | 1-0 | 0-0 | 2-1 | | 2-2 | 3-1 | 2-1 | 2-2 | 1-2 | 5-1 | 4-1 |
| WSG WATTENS | 0-3 | 1-1 | 3-1 | 1-0 | 1-2 | | 1-1 | 6-1 | 1-1 | 4-1 | 1-0 | 1-0 |
| ASV AUSTRIA VÖSENDORF | 1-0 | 0-7 | 0-0 | 1-0 | 3-2 | 0-0 | | 0-0 | 1-2 | 3-2 | 2-0 | 2-0 |
| SK AUSTRIA KLAGENFURT | 1-3 | 1-2 | 0-1 | 0-0 | 0-3 | 4-3 | 2-1 | | 0-0 | 0-4 | 0-0 | 2-4 |
| SV STOCKERAU | 1-1 | 0-0 | 4-0 | 1-0 | 0-0 | 1-1 | 3-1 | 2-0 | | 2-1 | 2-0 | 3-2 |
| FC SALZBURG | 2-3 | 4-4 | 0-1 | 2-4 | 0-4 | 3-3 | 3-5 | 6-1 | 6-2 | | 5-2 | 2-0 |
| SV DONAUFELD | 2-1 | 1-1 | 1-1 | 0-0 | 0-1 | 2-2 | 6-2 | 0-0 | 3-0 | 0-3 | | 0-3 |
| WOLFSBERGER AC | 1-3 | 0-4 | 0-4 | 1-0 | 2-2 | 2-4 | 3-1 | 1-1 | 0-0 | 1-6 | 2-2 | |

## AUSTRIA Prom./Relegat. Section — Spring 1991

| | WIENER SC | VIENNA | KREMS | ST.PÖLTEN | MÖDLING | VÖEST | STOCKERAU | LASK |
|---|---|---|---|---|---|---|---|---|
| WIENER SPORT-CLUB | | 2-1 | 2-2 | 1-3 | 0-2 | 0-4 | 4-1 | 1-2 |
| 1 VIENNA FC WIEN | 2-1 | | 2-0 | 2-0 | 1-0 | 2-2 | 1-1 | 5-1 |
| KREMSER SC | 4-0 | 2-0 | | 2-0 | 0-0 | 0-0 | 3-1 | 3-1 |
| VSE SANKT PÖLTEN | 1-0 | 3-1 | 0-0 | | 3-1 | 0-0 | 0-0 | 3-0 |
| VfB MÖDLING | 1-0 | 0-0 | 0-1 | 1-1 | | 1-1 | 4-1 | 4-1 |
| VÖEST LINZ | 2-0 | 1-4 | 3-2 | 1-1 | 2-1 | | 1-0 | 1-2 |
| SV STOCKERAU | 0-2 | 1-3 | 1-2 | 0-2 | 1-0 | 2-2 | | 4-4 |
| LINZER ASK | 2-1 | 1-1 | 2-2 | 0-2 | 2-1 | 0-1 | 0-3 | |

## AUSTRIA 2ND DIVISION AUTUMN 1990
### LEAGUE TABLE 1ST STAGE FINAL

| | | | | | | | |
|---|---|---|---|---|---|---|---|
| VfB Mödling | 22 | 13 | 5 | 4 | 59 | 22 | 31 |
| VÖEST Linz | 22 | 13 | 4 | 5 | 45 | 32 | 30 |
| SV Stockerau | 22 | 10 | 9 | 3 | 34 | 23 | 29 |
| Linzer ASK | 22 | 11 | 6 | 5 | 41 | 27 | 28 |
| Grazer AK | 22 | 9 | 8 | 5 | 31 | 18 | 26 |
| ASV Austria Vösendorf | 22 | 8 | 5 | 9 | 27 | 42 | 21 |
| FC Salzburg | 22 | 9 | 2 | 11 | 57 | 51 | 20 |
| WSG Wattens | 22 | 6 | 8 | 8 | 36 | 42 | 20 |
| SV Donaufeld | 22 | 6 | 6 | 10 | 29 | 42 | 18 |
| SV Spittal/Drau | 22 | 6 | 5 | 11 | 31 | 36 | 17 |
| Wolfsberger AC | 22 | 4 | 5 | 13 | 24 | 49 | 13 |
| SK Austria Klagenfurt | 22 | 2 | 7 | 13 | 16 | 46 | 11 |

## AUSTRIA PROMOTION./RELEGATATION PLAY-OFFS SPRING 1991
### LEAGUE TABLE FINAL

| | | | | | | | |
|---|---|---|---|---|---|---|---|
| VÖEST Linz | 14 | 7 | 6 | 1 | 24 | 12 | 20 |
| Kremser SC | 14 | 7 | 5 | 2 | 23 | 12 | 19 |
| VSE Sankt Pölten | 14 | 7 | 5 | 2 | 19 | 9 | 19 |
| 1 Vienna FC Wien | 14 | 6 | 4 | 4 | 22 | 18 | 16 |
| VfB Mödling | 14 | 4 | 4 | 6 | 16 | 14 | 12 |
| Linzer ASK | 14 | 4 | 3 | 7 | 18 | 32 | 11 |
| SV Stockerau | 14 | 2 | 4 | 8 | 16 | 28 | 8 |
| Wiener Sport-Club | 14 | 3 | 1 | 10 | 14 | 27 | 7 |

VÖEST Linz, Kremser SC, VSE St.Polten and 1 Vienna FC Wien gain 1st Division places for Autumn Season 1991.

**NAME CHANGE FOR AUTUMN SEASON 1991 : -**
VÖEST Linz to FC Stahl Linz

Top 4 clubs VfB Mödling, FK VÖEST Linz, SV Stockerau and Linzer ASK to form promotion/relegation section with bottom 4 clubs from 1st Division to decide 4 1st Division place for Autumn Season 1991, 1st Stage results not carried forward and matches to be played during Spring Season 1991. Bottom 8 clubs to form 2nd Division relegation section, matches to be played during Spring Season 1991. 1st Stage records carried forward to 2nd Stage with half points total, where necessary half points being rounded upwards. Points totals carried forward as follows : - Grazer AK 13, ASV Austria Vösendorf 11, FC Salzburg 10, WSG Wattens 10, SR Donaufeld 9, SV Spittal/Drau 9, Wolfsberger AC 7, SK Austria Klagenfurt 6.

| AUSTRIA Relegation Section Spring 1991 | GAK | VÖSENDORF | SALZBURG | WATTENS | DONAUFELD | SPITTAL/D | WAC | KLAGENFURT |
|---|---|---|---|---|---|---|---|---|
| GRAZER AK | | 1-1 | 3-1 | 2-0 | 2-2 | 2-1 | 2-0 | 3-2 |
| ASV AUSTRIA VÖSENDORF | 0-1 | | 0-0 | 3-0 | 1-3 | 2-0 | 1-1 | 2-1 |
| FC SALZBURG | 4-2 | 2-0 | | 1-1 | 2-4 | 3-4 | 0-1 | 2-1 |
| WSG WATTENS | 0-0 | 1-0 | 4-1 | | 3-3 | 1-0 | 5-2 | 0-0 |
| SV DONAUFELD | 1-2 | 2-1 | 3-0 | 2-0 | | 1-1 | 4-1 | 0-0 |
| SV SPITTAL/DRAU | 1-1 | 3-0 | 3-2 | 0-2 | 4-2 | | 2-0 | 0-0 |
| WOLFSBERGER AC | 0-6 | 2-1 | 3-1 | 2-1 | 1-3 | 1-1 | | 1-1 |
| SK AUSTRIA KLAGENFURT | 1-0 | 2-1 | 1-0 | 1-1 | 1-0 | 1-1 | 2-0 | |

## AUSTRIA RELEGATION PLAY-OFFS SPRING 1991
### LEAGUE TABLE FINAL

| | | | | | | | |
|---|---|---|---|---|---|---|---|
| Grazer AK | 36 | 17 | 12 | 7 | 58 | 32 | 33 |
| SV Donaufeld | 36 | 13 | 10 | 13 | 59 | 61 | 27 |
| WSG Wattens | 36 | 11 | 13 | 12 | 55 | 59 | 25 |
| SV Spittal/Drau | 36 | 11 | 10 | 15 | 52 | 54 | 24 |
| SK Austria Klagenfurt | 36 | 7 | 13 | 16 | 30 | 57 | 22 |
| ASV Austria Vösendorf | 36 | 11 | 8 | 17 | 40 | 61 | 20 |
| FC Salzburg | 36 | 12 | 4 | 20 | 76 | 81 | 18 |
| Wolfsberger AC | 36 | 8 | 8 | 20 | 39 | 79 | 18 |

Relegated : - ASV Austria Vösendorf, FC Salzburg and Wolfsberger AC

## AUSTRIA 3RD DIVISION EAST 1990/91
### LEAGUE TABLE FINAL

| | | | | | | | |
|---|---|---|---|---|---|---|---|
| FavAC (Wien) | 30 | 19 | 7 | 4 | 51 | 23 | 45 |
| SV Oberwart | 30 | 19 | 6 | 5 | 45 | 20 | 44 |
| SV Sigless | 30 | 14 | 7 | 9 | 56 | 38 | 35 |
| SC Zwettl | 30 | 12 | 11 | 7 | 40 | 29 | 35 |
| SVg Wiener Neudorf | 30 | 13 | 6 | 11 | 48 | 45 | 32 |
| ASK Ybbs/Donau | 30 | 11 | 10 | 9 | 32 | 32 | 32 |
| EPSV Gmünd | 30 | 10 | 8 | 12 | 57 | 63 | 28 |
| SC Wiener Neustadt | 30 | 11 | 6 | 13 | 42 | 48 | 28 |
| SV Gols | 30 | 11 | 5 | 14 | 48 | 44 | 27 |
| ASK Bruck/Leitha | 30 | 9 | 9 | 12 | 35 | 45 | 27 |
| SV Schwechat | 30 | 8 | 10 | 12 | 30 | 33 | 26 |
| Badener AC | 30 | 5 | 16 | 9 | 39 | 49 | 26 |
| SK Slovan-HAC (Wien) | 30 | 9 | 7 | 14 | 39 | 44 | 25 |
| G FAC/Gr.Viktoria (Wien) | 30 | 6 | 13 | 11 | 32 | 43 | 25 |
| SC Eisenstadt | 30 | 7 | 11 | 12 | 29 | 40 | 25 |
| SC Red Star (Wien) | 30 | 7 | 6 | 17 | 32 | 59 | 20 |

Promoted : - Favoritner AC
Relegated : - SC Eisenstadt and SC Red Star

**PROMOTED FROM 4TH DIVISION : -**
East : ÖMV Stadlau (Wien), SV Horn and ASK Baumgarten
West : HSV Salzburg, SK Rum and FC Nenzing

## AUSTRIA 3RD DIVISION WEST 1990/91
### LEAGUE TABLE FINAL

| | | | | | | | |
|---|---|---|---|---|---|---|---|
| SC Rheindorf Altach | 26 | 17 | 4 | 5 | 57 | 26 | 38 |
| Salzburger AK 1914 | 26 | 15 | 3 | 8 | 58 | 35 | 33 |
| VfB Hohenems | 26 | 12 | 8 | 6 | 56 | 32 | 32 |
| FC Puch | 26 | 15 | 2 | 9 | 60 | 37 | 32 |
| FC Kufstein | 26 | 11 | -9 | 6 | 42 | 35 | 31 |
| FC Dornbirn | 26 | 12 | 7 | 7 | 47 | 41 | 31 |
| SV Hard | 26 | 11 | 8 | 7 | 42 | 27 | 30 |
| SC Austria Lustenau | 26 | 11 | 8 | 7 | 35 | 36 | 30 |
| ESV Saalfelden | 26 | 6 | 12 | 8 | 34 | 40 | 24 |
| SC Kundl | 26 | 9 | 5 | 12 | 44 | 46 | 23 |
| SV Hall/Tirol | 26 | 10 | 3 | 13 | 36 | 52 | 23 |
| SV Fügen | 26 | 5 | 7 | 14 | 32 | 48 | 17 |
| USK Anif | 26 | 5 | 7 | 14 | 31 | 57 | 17 |
| SV Axams | 26 | 0 | 3 | 23 | 19 | 81 | 3 |

Promoted : - SC Rheindorf Altach
Relegated : - SV Fügen, USK Anif and SV Axams

## AUSTRIA 3RD DIVISION MID 1990/91
**PROMOTION PLAY-OFFS** Played between Champions of the Districts Oberösterreich, Steiermark and Kärnten

| | | | |
|---|---|---|---|
| SV Ried.................... 3 | SVG Bleiburg ............ 1 |
| SCG Bleiburg ............ 3 | SV Flavia Solva ......... 1 |
| SV Flavia Solva ....... 1 | SV Ried.................... 0 |
| SVG Bleiburg ........... 1 | SV Ried.................... 2 |
| SV Flavia Solva........ 6 | SVG Bleiburg ............ 0 |
| SV Ried.................... 3 | SV Flavia Solva ........ 0 |

### LEAGUE TABLE FINAL

| | | | | | | | |
|---|---|---|---|---|---|---|---|
| SV Ried | 4 | 3 | 0 | 1 | 8 | 3 | 6 |
| SV Flavia Solva | 4 | 2 | 0 | 2 | 8 | 6 | 4 |
| SVG Bleiburg | 4 | 1 | 0 | 3 | 5 | 12 | 2 |

Promoted : - SV Ried/Innkreis

# AUSTRIA CUP 1990/91

### 1ST ROUND

SV Sankt Veit 2 – SAK Klagenfurt 4 (aet.)
SVG Bleiburg 2 – SV Rapid Lienz 1
SC Untersiebenbr'n 1 – ASK Bruck/Leitha 0
SV Wienerfeld 0 – Viktoria/FAC Wien 3
ASK Köflach 1 – SV Kindberg 0
Amateure Kufstein 2 – FC Kufstein 12
SC Wiener Neustadt 5 – FC Gottsdorf 0
Badener AC 0 – ASK Ybbs/Donau 0 (aet.)
Badener AC win 2-1 on penalties
SK Pinkafeld 0 – SV Sigless 3
SV Oberwart 0 – SV Gols 2
LAC Persil 0 – Favoritner AC Wien 5
SV Schwechat 0 – SK Slvn-HAC Wien 0 (aet.)
SV Schwechat win 6-5 on penalties
SK Feldbach 6 – FKL Wimmer 1
SV Flavia Solva 5 – TSV Hartberg 1
SV Grieskirchen 2 – ABV Steyrermühl 5
Amateure Steyr 8 – ASK Sankt Valentin 0
ASK Nettingsdorf 2 – SC Marchtrenk 1
SV Micheldorf 1 – SK Altheim 2
FC Zell-am-Zee 0 – FC Puch 4
ESV Saalfelden 0 – SV Fügen 1
SV Hall 4 – VfB Hohenems 3 (aet.)
FC Hard 0 – SC Rheindorf-Altach 0 (aet.)
SC Rheindorf-Altach win 2-4 on penalties

Villacher SV 2 – SV Wietersdorf 0
SV Feldkirchen 1 – Friesacher AC 1 (aet.)
SV Feldkirchen win 7-6 on penalties
LUV Graz 2 – Kapfenberger SV 1
SC Eisenstadt 2 – ASK Baumgarten 0
SC Zwettl 1 – EPSV Gmünd 1 (aet.)
SC Zwettl win 7-6 on penalties
SV Horn 1 – SVg Wiener Neudorf 2
ASV Hohenau 3 – SC ATSV Tulln 3 (aet.)
SC ATSV Tulln win 7-8 on penalties
SV Schattendorf 1 – UFC Purbach 0
SV Gerasdorf 1 – ÖMV Stadlau 4
SV Wienerberg 1 – Red Star/Auto Wien 1 (aet.)
SV Wienerberg win 4-2 on penalties
SV Ilz 0 – ASK Voitsberg 3
SK Deutschlandsbg. 3 – ATUS Bärnbach 0
Austria Tabak Linz 3 – SV Ried 1 (aet.)
ATSV Lenzing 2 – Union Esternberg 2 (aet.)
Union Esternberg win 3-5 on penalties
USK Anif 3 – Salzburger AK 1914 4
SK Bischofshofen 1 – SC Mittersill 3
SK Ebbs 0 – SC Kundl 3
FC Dornbirn 0 – SV Wolfurt 1

### 2ND ROUND

SV Schattendorf 0 – 1 Vienna FC Wien 4
ASK Köflach 1 – SV Spittal/Drau 2 (aet.)
FC Kustein 2 – SV Hall 0
SC Zwettl 0 – Wiener Sport-Club 6
SC Wiener Neustadt 2 – SV Stockerau 8
SC Untersiebenbr'n 0 – SV Donaufeld 0 (aet.)
SV Donaufeld win 10-11 on penalties
SV Wienerberg 0 – FC Admira-Wacker 7
Feldbach 1 – SK Sturm Graz 2
Salzburger AK 1914 0 – SK Aust. Klagenfurt 1
SK Deutschlandsbg. 2 – Wolfsberger AC 1 (aet.)
ASK Nettingsdorf 2 – Austria Tabak Linz 1
SV Flavia Solva 4 – Amateure Steyr 1
Union Esternberg 4 – LUV Graz 4 (aet.)
LUV Graz win 2-4 on penalties
SV Fügen 0 – WSG Wattens 6
FC Puch 7 – SC Mittersill 0
SK Altheim 3 – Grazer AK 4
SC Eisenstadt 2 – ÖMV Stadlau Wien 0

ATSV Steyrermühl 0 – Donawitzer SV 4
Badener AC 0 – SV Schwechat 0 (aet.)
Badener AC win 5-3 on penalties
SV Siegless 1 – SK Rapid Wien 5
SC ATSV Tulln 0 – ASV Aust.Vösendorf 3
Viktoria/FAC Wien 1 – FK Austria Wien 5
SV Gols 0 – VSE Sankt Pölten 1
Favoritner AC Wien 1 – VfB Mödling 0
ASK Voitsberg 0 – Linzer ASK 2
SVG Bleiburg 0 – SK Vorwärts Steyr 3
SV Feldkirchen 2 – SK VÖEST Linz 2 (aet.)
SK VÖEST Linz win 2-4 on penalties
Villacher SV 2 – SAK Klagenfurt 0
SC Rheindorf-Altach 5 – FC Salzburg 5 (aet.)
FC Salzburg win 3-4 on penalties
FC Wolfurt 1 – FC Tirol 8
SC Kundl 1 – SV Austria Salzburg 9
SVg Wiener Neudorf 2 – Kremser SC 1

### 3RD ROUND

Badener AC 0 – FC Admira-Wacker 2
SVg Wiener Neudorf 1 – SV Donaufeld 2
Favoritner AC Wien 3 – 1 Vienna FC Wien 0
Wiener Sport-Club 3 – FK Austria Wien 0
Villacher SV 1 – Grazer AK 2 (aet.)
SK Deutschlandsbg. 1 – Donawitzer SV 1 (aet.)
SK Deutschlandsberg win 5-3 on penalties

ASK Nettingsdorf 1 – ASV Aust.Vösendorf 1 (aet.)
ASV Austria Vösendorf win 3-4 on penalties
SV Stockerau 2 – VSE Sankt Pölten 0
SV Flavia Solva 1 – SK VÖEST Linz 4
LUV Graz 1 – SV Spittal/Drau 0
SK Aust. Klagenfurt 0 – SK Sturm Graz 5
Linzer ASK 3 – SK Vorwärts Steyr 2 (aet.)

FC Puch 1 – FC Salzburg 4
WSG Wattens 1 – FC Tirol 5

FC Kufstein 2 – SV Austria Salzburg 4 (aet.)
SC Eisenstadt 0 – SK Rapid Wien 5

### 4TH ROUND

SK Deutschlandsbg 1 – SK Rapid Wien 3
SV Donaufeld 1 – SK Sturm Graz 2
FC Tirol 2 – SV Austria Salzburg 3
ASV Aust.Vösendorf 1 – FC Salzburg 3

LUV Graz 1 – Linzer ASK 0
Wiener Sport-Club 3 – Grazer AK 2 (aet.)
SV Stockerau 3 – FC Admira-Wacker 2
Favoritner AC Wien 1 – SK VÖEST Linz 2 (aet.)

### 1/4 FINALS

FC Salzburg 1 – SK Rapid Wien 5
Wiener Sport-Club 1 – SV Austria Salzburg 0 (aet.)

LUV Graz 2 – SK Sturm Graz 1
SV Stockerau 3 – SK VÖEST Linz 1

### SEMI-FINALS

SV Stockerau 1 – Wiener Sport-Club 0

LUV Graz 0 – SK Rapid Wien 1

### FINAL 30/5/91 (at Praterstadion, Wien)

SV Stockerau 2 – SK Rapid Wien 1

Stockerau : Zajicek, Mazura, Keller, Wenzel, Wacek, Binder, Pospisil, Ostrowski, Weinhofer, Augustin, Marko (Wiktora 90).
SK Rapid : Konsel, Hatz (Poiger 55), Schöttel, Pfeifenberger, Keglevits, Hauptmann, Reiter, Herzog, Resch (Reisinger 56), Medford, Fjørtoft.

| | | |
|---|---|---|
| 0-1 | Reiter | 8 |
| 1-1 | Wenzel | 30 |
| 2-1 | Pospisil | 52 |

Referee : Kapl
Attendance : 12,000

## AUSTRIA : All Time International Records as at 31/12/90 - GOALS

| | | | |
|---|---|---|---|
| 1. | Hans Krankl (1 Vienna FC Wien/SK Rapid Wien/CF Barcelona) | (69) | 34 |
| 2. | Erich Hof (Wiener SC) | (36) | 28 |
| | Johann Jorvath (SC Simmering/SK Rapid Wien/SC Wacker Wien/FC Wien) | (46) | 28 |
| - 4. | Anton Schall (ESV Admira Wien) | (28) | 27 |
| | Matthias Sindelar (Amateure/FK Austria Wien) | (43) | 27 |
| 6. | Karl Zischek (SC Wacker Wien) | (40) | 24 |
| 7. | Walter Schachner (Donawitzer SV/FK Austria Wien/AC Cesena/AC Torino/SC Pisa/unattached/US Avellino) | (63) | 23 |
| 8. | Theodor Wagner (SC Wacker Wien) | (46) | 22 |
| 9. | Karl Decker (1 Vienna FC Wien) | (25) | 19 |
| 10. | Erich Probst (SK Rapid Wien) | (18) | 17 |
| | Ferdl Swatosch (SC Simmering/SK Rapid Wien/Amateure Wien/Kölner BC) | (23) | 17 |
| | Johann Studnicka (WAC) | (28) | 17 |
| | Ferdinand Wessely (SK Rapid Wien) | (41) | 17 |

# INTERNATIONAL LINE-UPS 1990

**Matches**

| Date | Result | Venue | Referee | Competition | Scorers |
|---|---|---|---|---|---|
| 28/2/90 | EGYPT 0 AUSTRIA 0 | Cairo | Bouillet (France) | Friendly | |
| 28/3/90 | SPAIN 2 AUSTRIA 3 | Malaga | D'Elia (Italy) | Friendly | (Hörtnagl, Polster, Rodax) |
| 11/4/90 | AUSTRIA 3 HUNGARY 0 | Salzburg | Hackett (England) | Friendly | (Artner, Ogris, Keglevits) |
| 2/5/90 | AUSTRIA 1 ARGENTINA 1 | Wien | Constantin (Belgium) | Friendly | (Zsak) |
| 30/5/90 | AUSTRIA 3 HOLLAND 2 | Wien | Rossner (DDR) | Friendly | (Pecl, Zsak, Pfeffer) |
| 9/6/90 | ITALY 1 AUSTRIA 0 | Roma | Wright (Brazil) | World Cup | |
| 15/6/90 | CZECHOSLOVAKIA 1 AUSTRIA 0 | Firenze | Smith (Scotland) | World Cup | |
| 19/6/90 | USA 1 AUSTRIA 2 | Firenze | Al Sharif (Syria) | World Cup | (Ogris, Rodax) |
| 21/8/90 | AUSTRIA 1 SWITZERLAND 3 | Wien | Longhi (Italy) | Friendly | (Ogris) |
| 12/9/90 | FAROER ISLANDS 1 AUSTRIA 0 | Landskrona | Nervik (Norway) | EuroCh.Q. | |
| 31/10 90 | YUGOSLAVIA 4 AUSTRIA 1 | Beograd | Schmidhuber (W.Germany) | EuroCh.Q. | (Ogris) |
| 14/11/90 | AUSTRIA 0 NORTHERN IRELAND 0 | Wien | Biguet (France) | EuroCh.Q. | |

**Line-ups (shirt numbers; substitutes in parentheses)**

| Player | 28/2 | 28/3 | 11/4 | 2/5 | 30/5 | 9/6 | 15/6 | 19/6 | 21/8 | 12/9 | 31/10 | 14/11 | CAPS | GOALS |
|---|---|---|---|---|---|---|---|---|---|---|---|---|---|---|
| Klaus Lindenberger | 1 | 1 | | | | | | | | | | | 41 | |
| Kurt Russ | 2 | (6) | | | | | | 5 | 3 | | | 2 | 24 | |
| Peter Schöttel | 3 | 8 | 8 | 2 | 7 | 4 | | 3 | | | 6 | | 16 | |
| Robert Pecl | 4 | 2 | 4 | | 2 | 4 | 3 | | | | | | 25 | 1 |
| Christian Keglevits | 5 | (9) | (9) | | (7) | 6 | | | | | 8 | | 16 | 3 |
| Peter Artner | 6 | 6 | 6 | | 6 | 6 | 6 | | | | | 5 | 25 | 1 |
| Manfred Linzmaier | 7 | (7) | 8 | 6 | 8 | 8 | | | | | | 7 | 23 | 2 |
| Andreas Herzog | 8 | (9) | 9 | 9 | 9 | 9 | 7 | (8) | | | | 7 | 22 | 3 |
| Alfred Hörtnagl | 9 | 7 | 7 | | | 10 | 9 | | | | | | 15 | 1 |
| Andreas Ogris | 10 | (10) | (10) | | | 9 | | (8) | 9 | 11 | 7 | 10 | 34 | 7 |
| Heimo Pfeifenberger | 11 | | | | | | | | | | | | 3 | 1 |
| Michael Konsel | (1) | | | | | 1 | 1 | | | | 3 | | 9 | |
| Ernst Aigner | (3) | 3 | 3 | | | 2 | 2 | 2 | | | | | 11 | |
| Josef Degeorgi | (5) | | | | | | | | | | | | 30 | |
| Andreas Reisinger | (10) | (8) | 9 | | (11) | | | 4 | 7 | (5) | (10) | | 10 | 1 |
| Anton Pfeffer | | (4) | 4 | | 3 | | 3 | (5) | (6) | | 4 | 6 | 24 | 1 |
| Manfred Zsak | | (6) | 7 | | | 7 | 6 | | 7 | | | | 31 | 5 |
| Toni Polster | | 11 | 11 | 11 | 11 | 11 | 10 | 11 | | 11 | | | 42 | 15 |
| Otto Konrad | | | | | | | | | | (1) | 1 | | 2 | |
| Michael Streiter | | (7) | | | | 8 | | | | 3 | | 11 | 13 | 1 |
| Gerhard Rodax | | 10 | | | | | | 3 | 11 | | | | 19 | 3 |
| Franz Wohlfahrt | | | 1 | | | | | | | | | (1) | 6 | |
| Michael Baur | | | | | | | | | (6) | | | | 2 | |
| Gerald Glatzmayer | | | | | | | | | | | (10) | | 6 | |
| Bruno Pezzey | | | | 2 | | | 5 | | 2 | | | | 84 | |
| Wolfgang Feiersinger | | | | | | | | | | | 5 | | 1 | |
| Peter Stöger | | | | | | | | | | 6 | | 11 | 8 | |
| Ralph Hasenhüttl | | | | | | | | | | 2 | | 11 | 2 | |
| Jürgen Hartmann | | | | | | | | | | | 5 | | 1 | |
| Heinz Peischl | | | | | | | | | | 6 | 7 | | 2 | |
| Gerald Willfurth | | | | | | | | (8) | 8 | | | 29 | | 3 |
| Peter Pacult | | | | | | | | | (9) | (10) | (10) | | 21 | 1 |
| Andreas Poiger | | | | | | | | | | | | 4 | 1 | |

## AUSTRIA : All Time International Records as at 31/12/90 - CAPS

1. Gerhard Hanappi (SC Wacker Wien/unattached/SK Rapid Wien) — 93
2. Karl Koller (1 Vienna FC Wien) — 86
3. Friedrich Koncilia (WSG Wattens/SW Innsbruck/RSC Anderlecht/FK Austria Wien) — 84
4. Bruno Pezzey (SW Innsbruck/SG Eintracht Frankfurt/SV Werder Bremen/FC Tirol/unattached) — 84
5. Herbert Prohaska (FK Austria Wien/Internazionale FC/AS Roma) — 83
6. Hans Krankl (1 Vienna FC Wien/SK Rapid Wien/CF Barcelona) — 69
7. Heribert Weber (SK Sturm Graz/SK Rapid Wien/SV Austria Salzburg) — 68
8. Walter Schachner (Donawitzer SV/FK Austria Wien/AC Cesena/ AC Torino/SC Pisa/unattached/US Avellino) — 63
9. Ernst Ockwirk (FAC/FK Austria Wien) — 62
10. Kurt Jara (SW Innsbruck/Valencia CF/MSV Duisburg/FC Schalke 04/Grasshopper Club) — 59

# BELGIUM Correspondent : SERGE VAN HOOF

## BELGIUM — Eerste Klasse — Season 1990/91

| | FC BRUGGE | ANDERLECHT | KVM | ANTWERP | STANDARD | AA GENT | KORTRIJK | BEERSCHOT | CERCLE | LIERSE | LOKEREN | FC LIÈGE | EKEREN | CHARLEROI | STVV | WAREGEM | RWDM | GENK |
|---|---|---|---|---|---|---|---|---|---|---|---|---|---|---|---|---|---|---|
| FC BRUGGE | ■ | 0-2 | 1-1 | 2-0 | 4-1 | 0-1 | 1-1 | 3-0 | 10-0 | 1-1 | 1-0 | 3-1 | 2-1 | 3-0 | 2-0 | 2-0 | 2-0 | 0-1 |
| RSC ANDERLECHT | 5-1 | ■ | 0-0 | 3-0 | 5-1 | 1-1 | 3-0 | 1-0 | 0-0 | 1-0 | 0-1 | 3-1 | 4-0 | 4-0 | 1-0 | 4-0 | 1-0 | 1-1 |
| KV MECHELEN | 1-1 | 1-1 | ■ | 2-2 | 1-3 | 1-0 | 3-2 | 1-0 | 3-2 | 1-0 | 0-0 | 2-0 | 2-1 | 0-0 | 4-0 | 1-0 | 4-0 | 6-0 |
| ROYAL ANTWERP FC | 0-0 | 1-0 | 0-0 | ■ | 4-0 | 4-1 | 2-2 | 3-0 | 2-2 | 2-0 | 0-0 | 2-2 | 0-1 | 1-1 | 2-2 | 1-0 | 1-1 | 6-2 |
| STANDARD CLUB LIÈGE | 0-0 | 1-2 | 0-1 | 2-1 | ■ | 2-0 | 1-0 | 7-1 | 3-2 | 0-0 | 3-1 | 2-2 | 2-2 | 2-1 | 1-1 | 1-0 | 1-0 | 3-1 |
| AA GENT | 1-1 | 1-1 | 2-1 | 0-1 | 1-1 | ■ | 2-1 | 1-0 | 3-0 | 5-1 | 5-1 | 1-0 | 2-0 | 1-1 | 6-3 | 4-0 | 1-2 | 6-1 |
| KV KORTRIJK | 2-2 | 1-7 | 0-4 | 4-1 | 0-2 | 1-2 | ■ | 1-3 | 3-0 | 1-2 | 0-1 | 2-0 | 0-0 | 2-1 | 0-1 | 2-0 | 2-0 | 5-0 |
| BEERSCHOT VAV | 2-4 | 0-2 | 2-2 | 1-2 | 1-2 | 2-3 | 0-4 | ■ | 3-2 | 3-0 | 2-0 | 0-1 | 0-1 | 0-2 | 4-0 | 1-1 | 1-3 | 1-1 |
| SV CERCLE BRUGGE | 0-1 | 1-3 | 0-2 | 1-1 | 0-0 | 1-2 | 2-0 | 3-0 | ■ | 0-0 | 3-1 | 1-1 | 3-2 | 1-0 | 0-4 | 3-0 | 1-1 | 3-1 |
| LIERSE SK | 1-1 | 0-4 | 0-4 | 2-1 | 0-0 | 0-1 | 0-1 | 3-0 | 4-0 | ■ | 0-2 | 1-1 | 0-2 | 2-1 | 0-0 | 2-0 | 2-1 | 2-0 |
| SC LOKEREN | 0-1 | 0-1 | 0-1 | 0-3 | 2-2 | 1-2 | 0-2 | 3-1 | 2-0 | 2-0 | ■ | 2-0 | 2-5 | 0-1 | 2-0 | 1-1 | 3-0 | 4-2 |
| FC LIÈGEOIS | 0-2 | 4-2 | 0-2 | 1-1 | 4-2 | 0-1 | 2-0 | 2-0 | 4-1 | 0-0 | 2-2 | ■ | 1-0 | 2-0 | 2-2 | 2-2 | 2-0 | 2-1 |
| GERMINAL EKEREN | 0-3 | 3-2 | 0-0 | 2-2 | 2-0 | 3-1 | 5-1 | 2-0 | 6-1 | 1-0 | 3-0 | 2-2 | ■ | 1-0 | 1-0 | 0-0 | 2-0 | 2-0 |
| CHARLEROI SC | 1-1 | 1-1 | 5-1 | 1-1 | 2-0 | 2-2 | 2-1 | 4-2 | 1-2 | 1-1 | 1-1 | 1-1 | 2-0 | ■ | 0-0 | 1-0 | 0-0 | 2-0 |
| ST.TRUIDEN VV | 0-2 | 1-2 | 0-3 | 5-2 | 0-1 | 0-0 | 1-0 | 1-1 | 0-1 | 2-0 | 0-2 | 1-1 | 1-1 | 0-0 | ■ | 3-1 | 0-2 | 0-1 |
| SV WAREGEM | 2-2 | 0-2 | 1-0 | 1-5 | 1-1 | 3-0 | 0-0 | 1-1 | 3-1 | 1-2 | 1-1 | 1-0 | 3-0 | 0-0 | 3-1 | ■ | 2-0 | 4-0 |
| RWD MOLENBEEK | 0-1 | 1-2 | 0-1 | 2-0 | 1-0 | 1-5 | 5-0 | 4-1 | 4-3 | 0-0 | 0-2 | 6-1 | 1-1 | 2-2 | | 0-0 | ■ | 2-0 |
| RACING CLUB GENK | 2-1 | 0-3 | 1-2 | 2-0 | 0-3 | 0-3 | 2-0 | 2-0 | 3-0 | 0-0 | 2-2 | 1-0 | 1-1 | 1-1 | 1-0 | 1-1 | 0-0 | ■ |

Note : The match Stade Leuven 2 Racing Jette Wavre 2 was later awarded Stade Leuven 0 Racing Jette wavre 5.

## BELGIUM — Tweede Klasse — Season 1990/91

| | BEVEREN | RCM | BOOM | ZW. LEEUW | LOMMEL | EEKLO | DIEST | GEEL | EISDEN | AALST | ST.NIKLAAS | R.JETTE | LEUVEN | TONGEREN | HARELBEKE | TURNHOUT |
|---|---|---|---|---|---|---|---|---|---|---|---|---|---|---|---|---|
| SK BEVEREN | ■ | 3-1 | 3-1 | 3-0 | 5-1 | 1-0 | 4-0 | 2-1 | 1-1 | 5-3 | 1-1 | 2-0 | 1-0 | 2-1 | 1-0 | 1-0 |
| RACING MECHELEN | 0-0 | ■ | 1-0 | 0-0 | 0-0 | 0-0 | 0-3 | 0-1 | 0-0 | 1-2 | 4-2 | 0-2 | 1-0 | 1-0 | 3-1 | 4-4 |
| BOOM FC | 1-3 | 4-0 | ■ | 1-0 | 1-1 | 2-1 | 3-0 | 7-1 | 3-1 | 4-1 | 1-1 | 3-3 | 1-1 | 2-1 | 1-1 | 2-0 |
| FC ZWARTE LEEUW | 0-5 | 0-0 | 3-3 | ■ | 1-1 | 1-2 | 0-0 | 2-2 | 0-3 | 2-0 | 1-2 | 2-1 | 1-1 | 0-0 | 1-1 | 3-0 |
| FC LOMMEL SK | 1-1 | 0-0 | 2-5 | 1-2 | ■ | 1-2 | 2-1 | 0-0 | 0-1 | 2-1 | 3-0 | 0-1 | 5-0 | 2-1 | | |
| FC EEKLO | 0-3 | 0-1 | 1-1 | 1-1 | 0-0 | ■ | 0-0 | 1-2 | 1-1 | 2-1 | 1-1 | 2-0 | 1-0 | 2-0 | 1-1 | 1-0 |
| TH DIEST | 2-0 | 0-0 | 1-0 | 1-1 | 0-3 | 2-1 | ■ | 4-1 | 2-1 | 0-1 | 1-5 | 1-0 | 2-2 | 2-1 | 0-1 | 0-0 |
| FC VERBROEDERING GEEL | 0-0 | 2-2 | 2-0 | 1-1 | 0-0 | 4-0 | 2-1 | ■ | 3-0 | 1-1 | 0-1 | 0-0 | 1-0 | 0-0 | 2-0 | 6-1 |
| PATRO EISDEN | 1-1 | 1-1 | 1-2 | 1-0 | 1-1 | 0-1 | 1-0 | 2-2 | ■ | 0-1 | 0-2 | 2-0 | 6-0 | 1-1 | 1-2 | 3-3 |
| SC EENDRACHT AALST | 0-0 | 4-1 | 0-1 | 1-0 | 2-0 | 0-1 | 4-4 | 2-0 | 1-1 | ■ | 0-4 | 2-1 | 2-1 | 5-2 | 1-1 | 0-2 |
| SK ST.NIKLAAS | 1-6 | 1-0 | 0-0 | 3-0 | 1-1 | 2-0 | 3-0 | 0-0 | 2-1 | 0-0 | ■ | 0-0 | 1-0 | 4-1 | 1-1 | 2-1 |
| RACING JETTE WAVRE | 1-3 | 1-0 | 0-0 | 1-0 | 1-1 | 4-1 | 0-0 | 1-0 | 1-1 | 2-2 | 0-1 | ■ | 1-0 | 1-0 | 1-1 | 2-3 |
| STADE LEUVEN | 0-3 | 0-1 | 0-1 | 1-3 | 0-0 | 0-2 | 2-2 | 3-1 | 0-1 | 0-3 | 0-3 | 2-2 | ■ | 2-2 | 1-1 | 3-3 |
| SK TONGEREN | 0-1 | 1-1 | 1-0 | 0-4 | 1-1 | 0-0 | 1-1 | 1-0 | 0-2 | 0-2 | 1-1 | 2-1 | 1-2 | ■ | 1-2 | 0-2 |
| RC HARELBEKE | 1-1 | 3-2 | 0-3 | 1-1 | 1-1 | 7-0 | 0-0 | 1-0 | 2-1 | 1-1 | 0-0 | 2-2 | 2-0 | 1-2 | ■ | 4-2 |
| FC TURNHOUT | 3-1 | 1-0 | 1-0 | 1-1 | 1-1 | 3-0 | 2-0 | 3-3 | 4-0 | 2-2 | 1-1 | 0-1 | 1-0 | 2-2 | 3-2 | ■ |

## BELGIUM EERSTE KLASSE 1990/91
### LEAGUE TABLE FINAL

| | | | | | | | |
|---|---|---|---|---|---|---|---|
| RSC Anderlecht | 34 | 23 | 7 | 4 | 74 | 22 | 53 |
| KV Mechelen | 34 | 20 | 10 | 4 | 59 | 24 | 50 |
| AA Gent | 34 | 20 | 7 | 7 | 67 | 37 | 47 |
| FC Brugge | 34 | 18 | 11 | 5 | 61 | 27 | 47 |
| Germinal Ekeren | 34 | 17 | 8 | 9 | 55 | 41 | 42 |
| Standard CL | 34 | 16 | 10 | 8 | 51 | 42 | 42 |
| Antwerp FC | 34 | 11 | 14 | 9 | 54 | 45 | 36 |
| Charleroi SC | 34 | 9 | 15 | 10 | 36 | 36 | 33 |
| SC Lokeren | 34 | 12 | 8 | 14 | 41 | 45 | 32 |
| FC Liègeois | 34 | 11 | 10 | 13 | 42 | 45 | 32 |
| Lierse SK | 34 | 9 | 11 | 14 | 26 | 41 | 29 |
| RWD Molenbeek | 34 | 10 | 8 | 16 | 40 | 45 | 28 |
| SV Waregem | 34 | 8 | 12 | 14 | 33 | 45 | 28 |
| Racing Genk | 34 | 9 | 8 | 17 | 31 | 66 | 26 |
| KV Kortrijk | 34 | 10 | 5 | 19 | 41 | 57 | 25 |
| SV Cercle Brugge | 34 | 9 | 7 | 18 | 40 | 73 | 25 |
| St.Truiden VV | 34 | 6 | 10 | 18 | 30 | 51 | 22 |
| Beerschot VAV | 34 | 5 | 5 | 24 | 33 | 72 | 15 |

Champions : - RSC Anderlecht
Relegated : - St.Truiden VV and Beerschot VAV

Note : In Belgium clubs finishing level on points are separated by number of victories gained.
Later, Beerschot were relegated to Derde Klasse due to financial malpractice. SK Tongeren to retain place in Tweede Klasse for Season 1991/92.

## TOP SCORERS

| | | |
|---|---|---|
| 1. | Erwin Vandenbergh (AA Gent) | 23 |
| 2. | Josip Weber (Cercle Brugge) | 20 |
| 3. | Luc Nilis (RSC Anderlecht) | 19 |
| 4. | Gunther Hofmans (Germinal Ekeren) | 18 |
| | Oliveira Barroso Luis (RSC Anderlecht) | 18 |
| 6. | Patrick Goots (KV Kortrijk) | 15 |
| | Nebosja Malbasa (FC Liègeois) | 15 |
| 8. | Jan Ceulemans (FC Brugge) | 14 |
| 9. | Foeke Booy (FC Brugge) | 13 |
| | Marc Degryse (RSC Anderlecht) | 13 |
| | Branko Karacic (Cercle Brugge) | 13 |
| | Francis Severeyns (KV Mechelen) | 13 |
| | Bruno Versavel (KV Mechelen) | 13 |
| | Willy Wellens (RWD Molenbeek) | 13 |
| 15. | Frank Farina (FC Brugge) | 12 |
| | Frans Van Rooy (Antwerp FC) | 12 |
| | Eric Viscaal (AA Gent) | 12 |
| 18. | Nico Claesen (Antwerp FC) | 11 |
| | Miklos Molnar (Standard CL) | 11 |
| | Ferenc Meszaros (SC Lokeren) | 11 |

## BELGIUM TWEEDE KLASSE 1990/91
### LEAGUE TABLE FINAL

| | | | | | | | |
|---|---|---|---|---|---|---|---|
| SK Beveren | 30 | 20 | 8 | 2 | 63 | 21 | 48 |
| SK St.Niklaas | 30 | 15 | 12 | 3 | 47 | 24 | 42 |
| Boom FC | 30 | 14 | 9 | 7 | 53 | 31 | 37 |
| SC Eendracht Aalst | 30 | 13 | 9 | 8 | 45 | 39 | 35 |
| FC Turnhout | 30 | 11 | 10 | 9 | 50 | 47 | 32 |
| RC Harelbeke | 30 | 9 | 14 | 7 | 42 | 36 | 32 |
| FC Lommel SK | 30 | 8 | 15 | 7 | 35 | 31 | 31 |
| FC Eeklo | 30 | 10 | 9 | 11 | 25 | 39 | 29 |
| FC Verbroedering Geel | 30 | 9 | 11 | 10 | 39 | 38 | 29 |
| Racing Jette Wavre | 30 | 9 | 10 | 11 | 33 | 34 | 28 |
| TH Diest | 30 | 8 | 11 | 11 | 29 | 41 | 27 |
| Patro Eisden | 30 | 7 | 12 | 11 | 35 | 37 | 26 |
| Racing Mechelen | 30 | 7 | 12 | 11 | 25 | 36 | 26 |
| FC Zwarte Leeuw | 30 | 6 | 14 | 10 | 31 | 38 | 26 |
| SK Tongeren | 30 | 4 | 10 | 16 | 23 | 50 | 18 |
| Stade Leuven | 30 | 3 | 8 | 19 | 20 | 53 | 14 |

Period Champions : - SK Beveren, SC Eendracht Aalst and SK St.Niklaas
Promoted : - SK Beveren and SC Eendracht Aalst
Relegated : - SK Tongeren and Stade Leuven

### PROMOTION PLAY-OFFS

| | | |
|---|---|---|
| SC Eendracht Aalst... | 1 | Boom FC .................. 0 |
| SK St.Niklaas ........... | 1 | FC Turnhout ............. 1 |
| Boom FC .................. | 0 | SC Eendracht Aalst ... 1 |
| FC Turnhout ............. | 1 | SK St.Niklaas ........... 1 |
| SC Eendracht Aalst... | 4 | FC Turnhout ............. 2 |
| Boom FC .................. | 3 | SK St.Niklaas ........... 4 |
| FC Turnhout ............. | 3 | Boom FC .................. 1 |
| SK St.Niklaas ........... | 0 | SC Eendracht Aalst ... 0 |
| SK St.Niklaas ........... | 3 | Boom FC .................. 1 |
| FC Turnhout ............. | 0 | SC Eendracht Aalst ... 1 |
| SC Eendracht Aalst... | 1 | SK St.Niklaas ........... 1 |
| Boom FC .................. | 6 | FC Turnhout ............. 1 |

### LEAGUE TABLE FINAL

| | | | | | | | |
|---|---|---|---|---|---|---|---|
| SC Eendracht Aalst | 6 | 4 | 2 | 0 | 8 | 3 | 10 |
| SK St.Niklaas | 6 | 2 | 4 | 0 | 10 | 7 | 8 |
| FC Turnhout | 6 | 1 | 2 | 3 | 8 | 14 | 4 |
| Boom FC | 6 | 1 | 0 | 5 | 11 | 13 | 2 |

## BELGIUM DERDE KLASSE A 1990/91
### LEAGUE TABLE FINAL

| | | | | | | | |
|---|---|---|---|---|---|---|---|
| Exc. Moeskroen | 30 | 20 | 7 | 3 | 66 | 24 | 47 |
| Berchem Sport | 30 | 17 | 7 | 6 | 56 | 29 | 41 |
| KV Oostende | 30 | 15 | 10 | 5 | 54 | 30 | 40 |
| SK Roeselare | 30 | 15 | 8 | 7 | 55 | 26 | 38 |
| OC Charleroi | 30 | 13 | 8 | 9 | 40 | 37 | 34 |
| Eendracht Wervik | 30 | 10 | 12 | 8 | 56 | 48 | 32 |
| Stade Wetteren | 30 | 11 | 9 | 10 | 45 | 48 | 31 |
| Union St.Gilloise | 30 | 10 | 10 | 10 | 31 | 30 | 30 |
| Franc Borains | 30 | 12 | 5 | 13 | 48 | 49 | 29 |
| AEC Mons | 30 | 8 | 12 | 10 | 37 | 48 | 28 |
| SC Menen | 30 | 7 | 13 | 10 | 26 | 34 | 27 |
| FC Eendracht Zele | 30 | 10 | 5 | 15 | 41 | 56 | 25 |
| AA La Louvière | 30 | 5 | 14 | 11 | 44 | 50 | 24 |
| FC Namur | 30 | 4 | 13 | 13 | 34 | 49 | 21 |
| Hoeselt VV | 30 | 7 | 5 | 18 | 29 | 53 | 19 |
| VK Ninove | 30 | 5 | 4 | 21 | 30 | 81 | 14 |

Promoted : - Excelsior Moeskroen
Relegated : - Hoeselt VV and VK Ninove

## BELGIUM DERDE KLASSE B 1990/91
### LEAGUE TABLE FINAL

| | | | | | | | |
|---|---|---|---|---|---|---|---|
| VK Tienen | 30 | 17 | 8 | 5 | 48 | 21 | 42 |
| FC Seraing | 30 | 17 | 8 | 5 | 51 | 25 | 42 |
| FC Tilleur | 30 | 12 | 14 | 4 | 48 | 27 | 38 |
| FC Poederlee | 30 | 13 | 10 | 7 | 44 | 24 | 36 |
| Hoogstraten VV | 30 | 13 | 9 | 8 | 30 | 24 | 35 |
| SC Hasselt | 30 | 11 | 12 | 7 | 32 | 23 | 34 |
| VO Aarschot | 30 | 10 | 12 | 8 | 34 | 31 | 32 |
| FC Heultje | 30 | 10 | 12 | 8 | 47 | 48 | 32 |
| Lyra TSV | 30 | 10 | 10 | 10 | 32 | 36 | 30 |
| Beringen FC | 30 | 9 | 12 | 9 | 32 | 33 | 30 |
| VV Looi Sport T. | 30 | 7 | 11 | 12 | 30 | 36 | 25 |
| VC Westerlo | 30 | 7 | 11 | 12 | 29 | 40 | 25 |
| SV Mol | 30 | 10 | 4 | 16 | 39 | 47 | 24 |
| FC Heist Sport | 30 | 8 | 8 | 14 | 24 | 35 | 24 |
| Aubel FC | 30 | 7 | 4 | 19 | 32 | 61 | 18 |
| Witgoor Dessel | 30 | 4 | 5 | 21 | 29 | 70 | 13 |

Promotion Play-Off : -
FC Seraing.....1   VK Tienen........0   (at Genk)
Promoted : - FC Seraing
Relegated : - Aubel FC and Witgoor Dessel

## BELGIUM VIERDE KLASSE A 1990/91
### LEAGUE TABLE FINAL

| | | | | | | | |
|---|---|---|---|---|---|---|---|
| FC Roeselare | 30 | 20 | 7 | 3 | 58 | 17 | 47 |
| KMSK Deinze | 30 | 19 | 7 | 4 | 52 | 19 | 45 |
| RC Heirnis Gent | 30 | 17 | 9 | 4 | 54 | 29 | 43 |
| SVD Handzame | 30 | 16 | 8 | 6 | 45 | 27 | 40 |
| FC Izegem | 30 | 12 | 10 | 8 | 31 | 24 | 34 |
| SK Torhout | 30 | 9 | 13 | 8 | 28 | 24 | 31 |
| Londerzeel SK | 30 | 12 | 5 | 13 | 38 | 43 | 29 |
| Evergem-Center | 30 | 10 | 7 | 13 | 37 | 43 | 27 |
| SC Wielsbeke | 30 | 9 | 9 | 12 | 26 | 33 | 27 |
| WSC Lauwe | 30 | 10 | 6 | 14 | 39 | 47 | 26 |
| Diegem Sport | 30 | 8 | 9 | 13 | 34 | 37 | 25 |
| VK Torhout | 30 | 7 | 11 | 12 | 30 | 42 | 25 |
| FC Strombeek | 30 | 7 | 10 | 13 | 35 | 47 | 24 |
| VV Eendracht Aalter | 30 | 7 | 7 | 16 | 36 | 59 | 21 |
| HO Merchtem | 30 | 6 | 8 | 16 | 27 | 47 | 20 |
| Wolvertem SC | 30 | 2 | 12 | 16 | 25 | 57 | 16 |

Promoted : - FC Roeselare
Relegated : - VV Eendracht Aalter, HO Merchtem Leest
and Wolvertem SC

## BELGIUM VIERDE KLASSE B 1990/91
### LEAGUE TABLE FINAL

| | | | | | | | |
|---|---|---|---|---|---|---|---|
| Kapellen FC | 30 | 19 | 8 | 3 | 46 | 10 | 46 |
| SV Bornem | 30 | 18 | 7 | 5 | 67 | 23 | 43 |
| Tub. Borgerhout | 30 | 16 | 9 | 5 | 54 | 31 | 41 |
| FC VW Hamme | 30 | 13 | 9 | 8 | 53 | 27 | 35 |
| FC Herentals | 30 | 12 | 8 | 10 | 35 | 34 | 32 |
| AV Dendermonde | 30 | 11 | 9 | 10 | 45 | 40 | 31 |
| Olsa Brakel | 30 | 11 | 9 | 10 | 36 | 33 | 31 |
| FC Dessel Sport | 30 | 10 | 11 | 9 | 41 | 37 | 31 |
| Oude Gold Sport | 30 | 10 | 10 | 10 | 38 | 39 | 30 |
| FC Rita Berlaar | 30 | 10 | 9 | 11 | 41 | 39 | 29 |
| FC Putte | 30 | 9 | 10 | 11 | 42 | 46 | 28 |
| Ver. Denderhoutem | 30 | 9 | 8 | 13 | 33 | 44 | 26 |
| FC Duffel | 30 | 9 | 7 | 14 | 46 | 55 | 25 |
| Wijnegem VC | 30 | 8 | 9 | 13 | 32 | 50 | 25 |
| VVOC Vorselaar | 30 | 4 | 6 | 20 | 22 | 73 | 14 |
| VV Leest | 30 | 2 | 9 | 19 | 23 | 73 | 13 |

Promoted : - Kapellen FC
Relegated : - Wijnegem VC, VVOC Vorselaar, VV Leest

## BELGIUM VIERDE KLASSE C 1990/91
### LEAGUE TABLE FINAL

| | | | | | | | |
|---|---|---|---|---|---|---|---|
| Avenir Lembeek | 30 | 20 | 7 | 3 | 49 | 18 | 47 |
| CS Brainois | 30 | 16 | 9 | 5 | 48 | 24 | 41 |
| AS Hemptinne | 30 | 16 | 9 | 5 | 41 | 20 | 41 |
| US Tournai | 30 | 13 | 11 | 6 | 47 | 31 | 37 |
| US Binche | 30 | 12 | 11 | 7 | 40 | 36 | 35 |
| RC Tournai | 30 | 11 | 11 | 8 | 43 | 26 | 33 |
| FC Hannuit | 30 | 10 | 10 | 10 | 41 | 41 | 30 |
| J.Rochefort | 30 | 10 | 10 | 10 | 40 | 40 | 30 |
| A.Marchienne | 30 | 10 | 7 | 13 | 41 | 42 | 27 |
| CS Andenne 60 | 30 | 10 | 7 | 13 | 31 | 38 | 27 |
| FC Farciennes | 30 | 9 | 9 | 12 | 33 | 38 | 27 |
| CS La Forestoise | 30 | 5 | 16 | 9 | 33 | 37 | 26 |
| Stade Borgworm FC | 30 | 8 | 9 | 13 | 37 | 42 | 25 |
| Union Huy FC | 30 | 5 | 17 | 4 | 42 | 64 | 21 |
| SC Eghezée | 30 | 6 | 7 | 17 | 36 | 58 | 19 |
| CS Condruzien | 30 | 3 | 8 | 19 | 21 | 68 | 14 |

Promoted : - Avenir Lembeek
Relegated : - Union Hutoise, SC Eghezée and CS Condruzien

# BELGIUM VIERDE KLASSE D 1990/91

## LEAGUE TABLE FINAL

| | | | | | | | |
|---|---|---|---|---|---|---|---|
| VV Overpelt Fabriek | 30 | 23 | 4 | 3 | 77 | 21 | 50 |
| Gerhees Oostham | 30 | 21 | 5 | 4 | 62 | 25 | 47 |
| Wellense SK | 30 | 11 | 13 | 6 | 51 | 36 | 35 |
| CS Verviers | 30 | 10 | 14 | 6 | 29 | 21 | 34 |
| Prayon FC | 30 | 12 | 8 | 10 | 46 | 30 | 32 |
| ESC Virton | 30 | 11 | 10 | 9 | 44 | 32 | 32 |
| SC Theux | 30 | 11 | 9 | 10 | 42 | 35 | 31 |
| L.Lorr.Arlon | 30 | 11 | 9 | 10 | 33 | 37 | 31 |
| SRU Verviers | 30 | 8 | 14 | 8 | 33 | 30 | 30 |
| Rapid Spouwen | 30 | 9 | 11 | 10 | 42 | 46 | 29 |
| Mechelen a/d Maas | 30 | 10 | 8 | 12 | 38 | 39 | 28 |
| AS Eupen | 30 | 9 | 9 | 12 | 40 | 37 | 27 |
| Melen-Micheroux | 30 | 7 | 10 | 13 | 30 | 53 | 24 |
| St.FC Andrimont | 30 | 6 | 7 | 17 | 23 | 55 | 19 |
| E.Bertrix | 30 | 5 | 7 | 18 | 27 | 73 | 17 |
| LC Bastogne | 30 | 4 | 6 | 20 | 19 | 66 | 14 |

Promoted : - VV Overpelt Fabriek

Relegated : - SFC Andrimont, E.Bertrix and LC Bastogne

# BELGIUM CUP 1990/91

## 1/32 FINALS

| | | | |
|---|---|---|---|
| Charleroi SC............4 | VV Eendracht Aalter..0 | VV Looi Sport Tess.....0 | Stade Leuven............5 |
| FC Turnhout............1 | Boom FC.................1 (aet.) | KV Mechelen.............5 | SK Kampenhout.........0 |
| Boom FC win 4-5 on penalties | | SK Tongeren.............3 | Witgoor Sp'rt Dessel..0 |
| FC Duffel................0 | Antwerp FC..............8 | SK Torhout..............1 | Germinal Ekeren.......7 |
| FC Eeklo................2 | AEC Mons...............1 | FC Roeselare...........3 | SK St.Niklaas..........1 |
| FC Namur...............1 | Racing Mechelen.......2 | SV Waregem............0 | Hoogstraten VV........1 |
| SC Menen..............1 | Racing Jette Wavre ...1 (aet.) | Patro Eisden...........1 | RC Tournai.............0 |
| Racing Jette Wavre win 2-3 on penalties | | SC Lokeren.............3 | KV Oostende...........1 |
| SV Bornem.............2 | SV Cercle Brugge.......1 | VK Tienen..............1 | FC Brugge..............1 |
| FC Liège...............5 | US Binchoise...........0 | Aubel FC...............0 | Beerschot VAV.........1 (aet.) |
| SC Eendracht Aalst...3 | AS Hemptinne..........0 | FC Verb'dering Geel....5 | Denderleeuw...........2 |
| Standard CL...........7 | SV Mol.................1 | RSC Anderlecht........4 | FC Poederlee..........2 |
| Lierse SK..............3 | Union St.Gilloise......2 (aet.) | AS Eupen...............1 | Racing Genk...........3 |
| TH Diest...............4 | FC Eendracht Zele.....1 | KV Kortrijk.............3 | FC Strombeek.........0 |
| FC Zwarte Leeuw.....2 | SFC Andrimont.........0 | FC Lommel Sk..........2 | VC Westerlo...........1 |
| FC Tilleur.............1 | AA Gent.................3 | Lyra TSV...............3 | RWD Molenbeek.......1 (aet.) |
| SC Hasselt............2 | SK Beveren.............2 | Lyra TSV win 3-1 on penalties | |
| KVO Aarschot........1 | St.Truiden VV...........1 | | |

## 1/16 FINALS

| | | | |
|---|---|---|---|
| Standard CL............4 | | Hoogstraten VV .......1 | Boom FC ...............0 |
| FC Liégeois............3 | | FC Roeselare..........2 | FC Lommel SK........4 |
| TH Diest...............0 | | Lyra TSV...............1 | SK Tongeren..........0 |
| FC Brugge.............2 | | SC Lokeren............1 | Stade Leuven.........1 (aet.) |
| Patro Eisden..........0 | | SC Lokeren win 11-10 on penalties | |
| AA Gent...............0 (aet.) | | SV Bornem.............5 | RSC Anderlecht......6 |
| Lierse SK..............2 | | Antwerp FC............5 | Beerschot VAV.......5 |
| Racing Mechelen win 4-5 on penalties | | SK Beveren............2 | FC Eeklo.............1 (aet.) |
| Charleroi SC...........2 (aet.) | | SK Beveren win 4-1 on penalties | |
| Racing Genk...........2 | | | |
| Racing Jette Wavre ...3 | | | |

## 1/8 FINALS

SC Charleroi...........5  Racing Jette Wavre ...0
FC Liégeois..........3  Racing Genk............1 (aet.)
FC Lommel SK ......0  Racing Mechelen.......0 (aet.)
FC Lommel SK win 8-7 on penalties
RSC Anderlecht.....0  FC Brugge ...............2

Antwerp FC ...........2  Hoogstraten VV .......0
FC Zwarte Leeuw ....0  SC Lokeren............3
SK Beveren ...........1  Standard CL............0
SK Tongeren...........1  KV Mechelen ..........2 (aet.)

## 1/4 FINALS

| | 1ST LEG | 2ND LEG | AGG. |
|---|---|---|---|
| FC Liégeois v SC Lokeren | 1-0 | 1-5 | 2-5 |
| Charleroi SC v FC Lommel SK | 0-2 | 1-3 | 1-5 |
| Royal Antwerp FC v KV Mechelen | 0-1 | 0-1 | 0-2 |
| FC Brugge v SK Beveren | 1-0 | 1-1 | 2-1 |

## SEMI-FINALS

| | 1ST LEG | 2ND LEG | AGG. |
|---|---|---|---|
| SC Lokeren v KV Mechelen | 1-3 | 1-1 | 2-4 |
| FC Brugge v FC Lommel SK | 1-0 | 1-0 | 2-0 |

## FINAL   15/6/91 (at Heysel Stadium, Brussels)

FC Brugge............3  KV Mechelen............1

FC Brugge : Verlinden, Staelers, Plovie, Janevski, Cossey, Creve, Van der Elst, Ceulemans, Borkelmans, Booy, Farina.

KVM : Preud'homme, Sanders, Clijsters, Albert, Bogers, P.Versavel, Emmers, Ingesson, B.Versavel, Wilmots, Severeyns.

| | | | |
|---|---|---|---|
| 1-0 | Farina | 28 | Referee : Van den Wijngaert |
| 2-0 | Booy | 76 | Attendance : 25,000 |
| 2-1 | B.Versavel | 80 | |
| 3-1 | Ceulemans pen. | 90 | |

# BELGIUM INTERNATIONAL REVIEW 1990

## INTERNATIONAL LINE-UPS 1990

| Match | Venue / Ref / Type (scorers) | Michel Preud'homme | Georges Grün | Leo Clijsters | Michel De Wolf | Patrick Vervoort | Marc Emmers | Marc Degryse | Bruno Versavel | Franky Van der Elst | Jan Ceulemans | Marc Van der Linden | Luc Nilis | Koenraad Sanders | Nico Claesen | Stefan Demol | Eric Gerets | Filip De Wilde | Lorenzo Staelens | Enzo Scifo | Marc Wilmots | Pascal Plovie | Philippe Albert | Geert Broeckaert | Erwin Vandenbergh | Danny Boffin |
|---|---|---|---|---|---|---|---|---|---|---|---|---|---|---|---|---|---|---|---|---|---|---|---|---|---|---|
| 17/1/90 GREECE 2 BELGIUM 0 | Athens — Ref: D'Elia (Italy) — Friendly | 1 | 2 | 3 | 4 | | | 7 | | 6 | 10 | 11 | | | (11) | 5 | | | | 8 | | | | | 9 | |
| 21/2/90 BELGIUM 0 SWEDEN 0 | Brussels — Ref: Kaupe (Austria) — Friendly | 1 | 3 | 2 | 5 | | | 9 | 7 | 6 | 10 | 11 | | | | 4 | | | | | (11) | | | | | |
| 26/5/90 BELGIUM 2 RUMANIA 2 | Brussels — Ref: Delmer (France) — Friendly (Scifo, Clijsters) | 1 | 2 | 3 | 5 | (7) | 9 | | 7 | | 10 | 8 | (11) | | | 5 | 4 | | | 6 | | | 2 | | (11) | |
| 2/6/90 BELGIUM 3 MEXICO 0 | Brussels — Ref: Damgaard (Denmark) — Friendly (Degryse 2, Versavel) | 1 | 4 | 5 | | (8) | 6 | 10 | 9 | 7 | | | (6) | | 11 | 5 | 4 | | 2 | 8 | | (6) | 3 | | | |
| 6/6/90 BELGIUM 1 POLAND 1 | Brussels — Ref: Philippi (Luxembourg) — Friendly (Emmers) | 1 | 3 | 5 | 5 | (9) | 10 | 10 | 8 | 6 | 10 | | (5) | (7) | (11) | 5 | 4 | | 3 | 8 | | | 2 | | | |
| 12/6/90 SOUTH KOREA 0 BELGIUM 2 | Verona — Ref: Mauro (USA) — World Cup (Degryse, De Wolf) | 1 | 2 | 6 | 5 | | 8 | 10 | 7 | 9 | 10 | 11 | 11 | | | 3 | 4 | | | 8 | | | 3 | | | |
| 17/6/90 URUGUAY 1 BELGIUM 3 | Verona — Ref: Kirschen (DDR) — World Cup (Clijsters, Scifo, Ceulemans) | 1 | 2 | 6 | 5 | (9) | (6) | 11 | 9 | 7 | 9 | (11) | 11 | | | 5 | 8 | | 3 | 8 | (8) | | | | | |
| 21/6/90 SPAIN 2 BELGIUM 1 | Verona — Ref: Lousteau (Argentina) — World Cup (Vervoort) | 1 | 2 | 5 | 5 | 10 | 9 | 7 | 9 | 7 | 10 | 11 | | | | 2 | 4 | | 8 | 8 | | | | | | |
| 26/6/90 ENGLAND 1 BELGIUM 0 (aet.) | Bologna — Ref: Mikkelsen (Denmark) — World Cup | 1 | | | | (11) | 11 | 11 | 11 | | | (3) | | | | 4 | 3 | | | 6 | | (6) | | | | |
| 12/9/90 BELGIUM 0 DDR 2 | Brussels — Ref: Blankenstein (Holland) — Friendly | | (4) | 5 | 5 | | 10 | 10 | 9 | 7 | 10 | 11 | | (7) | | 2 | 2 | (1) | 3 | 10 | (8) | (4) | 4 | 6 | 10 | (9) |
| 17/10/90 WALES 3 BELGIUM 1 | Cardiff — Ref: Röthlisberger (Switzerland) — EuroCh.Q. (Versavel) | 1 | 4 | | | 5 | 6 | | 9 | 6 | 10 | 11 | | (11) | | 4 | 5 | | 6 | 8 | 11 | | 4 | | (9) | 3 |
| **CAPS AT 31/12/90** | | 29 | 50 | 39 | 33 | 30 | 20 | 29 | 19 | 43 | 94 | 19 | 12 | 4 | 36 | 35 | 84 | 2 | 3 | 45 | 4 | 4 | 4 | 1 | 45 | 3 |
| **GOALS AT 31/12/90** | | | 4 | 3 | 1 | 3 | 1 | 10 | 3 | 3 | 22 | 8 | | | 12 | | 3 | | | 7 | | | | | 19 | |

---

## BELGIUM : All Time Records as at 31/12/90 - CAPS

1. Jan Ceulemans (Lierse SK/FC Brugge) — 94
2. Eric Gerets (Standard CL/Milan AC/PSV) — 84
3. Paul Van Himst (RSC Anderlecht) — 81
4. Vic Mees (Antwerp FC) — 68
5. George Heylens (RSC Anderlecht) — 67
6. Jef Jurion (RSC Anderlecht) — 64
6. Jean-Marie Pfaff (SK Beveren/FC Bayern München) — 64
8. Frankie Vercauteren (RSC Anderlecht/FC Nantes) — 63
9. Bernard Voorhoof (Lierse SK) — 61
10. Wilfried Van Moer (Antwerp FC/Standard CL/Beringen FC/SK Beveren) — 57

## BELGIUM : All Time Records as at 31/12/90 - GOALS

1. Bernard Voorhoof (Lierse SK) — (61) 30
1. Paul Van Himst (RSC Anderlecht) — (81) 30
3. Jef Mermans (RSC Anderlecht) — (56) 27
4. Robert De Veen (FC Brugge) — (23) 26
4. Raymond Braine (Beerschot AC/Sparta Praha) — (54) 26
6. Jan Ceulemans (Lierse SK/FC Brugge) — (94) 22
7. Rik Coppens (Beerschot FC) — (47) 21
8. Pol Anoul (FC Liégeois) — (48) 20
9. Jean Capelle (Standard CL) — (34) 19
9. Erwin Vandenbergh (Lierse SK/RSC Anderlecht/Lille OSC/AA Gent) — (45) 19

# BULGARIA Correspondent : DIMTCHO DIMITROV

## BULGARIA 1st Division — Season 1990/91

| | CSKA | SLAVIA | ETAR | LEVSKI | LOK S | PIRIN | BOTEV | LOK GO | SLIVEN | BEROE | CH'RETS | DUNAV | LOK PL | YANTRA | MINYOR | HASKOVO |
|---|---|---|---|---|---|---|---|---|---|---|---|---|---|---|---|---|
| CSKA SOFIA | | 0-0 | 1-0 | 1-1 | 0-2 | 1-1 | 7-1 | 2-1 | 3-1 | 3-0 | 2-3 | 5-0 | 2-0 | 2-0 | 3-0 | 3-1 |
| SLAVIA SOFIA | 0-0 | | 1-0 | 0-0 | 1-2 | 5-2 | 1-2 | 3-1 | 3-3 | 1-2 | 1-0 | 1-0 | 4-1 | 1-0 | 3-0 | 5-1 |
| ETAR VELIKO T'NOVO | 1-1 | 1-0 | | 4-2 | 1-0 | 0-0 | 4-0 | 2-1 | 2-0 | 2-0 | 3-2 | 2-0 | 2-0 | 3-1 | 2-0 | 3-0 |
| LEVSKI SOFIA | 0-1 | 3-4 | 0-1 | | 1-2 | 2-1 | 2-3 | 2-1 | 4-0 | 1-1 | 5-1 | 2-0 | 4-0 | 1-0 | 2-0 | 1-0 |
| LOKOMOTIV SOFIA | 0-3 | 0-1 | 1-1 | 2-2 | | 3-1 | 1-1 | 1-1 | 3-0 | 3-0 | 2-0 | 1-0 | 3-0 | 4-0 | 5-2 | 3-1 |
| PIRIN BLAGOEVGRAD | 2-2 | 1-1 | 2-0 | 0-3 | 4-0 | | 0-1 | 1-2 | 2-0 | 1-0 | 1-2 | 1-0 | 3-0 | 1-0 | 4-0 | 6-0 |
| BOTEV PLOVDIV | 3-2 | 1-1 | 0-1 | 4-1 | 1-1 | 2-0 | | 0-1 | 3-2 | 0-0 | 5-0 | 2-0 | 2-2 | 4-0 | 0-0 | 4-3 |
| LOK. GORNA ORY'HOV | 2-0 | 0-2 | 0-4 | 2-0 | 1-1 | 2-1 | 2-0 | | 1-0 | 2-3 | 3-1 | 3-1 | 2-0 | 3-1 | 3-0 | 1-0 |
| FK SLIVEN | 2-1 | 0-2 | 2-2 | 1-1 | 2-2 | 2-0 | 2-2 | 0-0 | | 1-0 | 1-0 | 2-1 | 2-1 | 5-1 | 0-0 | 5-1 |
| BEROE STARA Z'GORA | 1-0 | 1-3 | 0-0 | 1-1 | 1-3 | 5-0 | 1-2 | 3-2 | 0-1 | | 3-2 | 3-0 | 1-1 | 1-1 | 2-1 | 4-0 |
| CH'MORETS B'RGAS | 1-1 | 2-1 | 1-1 | 3-3 | 3-1 | 2-1 | 1-1 | 2-1 | 2-0 | 2-1 | | 5-1 | 0-0 | 0-0 | 2-0 | 1-0 |
| DUNAV RUSE | 1-2 | 0-0 | 0-1 | 1-0 | 1-1 | 0-1 | 0-0 | 2-1 | 2-1 | 1-0 | 2-2 | | 3-0 | 1-1 | 1-0 | 1-0 |
| LOKOMOTIV PLOVDIV | 0-1 | 1-1 | 1-1 | 1-1 | 1-1 | 2-0 | 1-1 | 3-2 | 2-0 | 2-0 | 5-0 | 1-0 | | 2-0 | 1-0 | 4-0 |
| YANTRA GABROVO | 1-1 | 3-1 | 1-2 | 1-1 | 3-1 | 2-0 | 0-2 | 2-1 | 1-1 | 1-1 | 1-0 | 3-1 | 0-0 | | 4-1 | 1-0 |
| MINYOR PERNIK | 1-1 | 1-1 | 1-1 | 0-1 | 2-0 | 1-0 | 3-2 | 1-0 | 5-2 | 3-1 | 3-0 | 1-1 | 3-1 | 3-0 | | 3-0 |
| FK HASKOVO | 2-0 | 1-0 | 3-2 | 2-4 | 1-1 | 0-1 | 2-0 | 1-0 | 2-1 | 1-2 | 1-1 | 0-2 | 3-1 | 0-2 | 1-1 | |

## BULGARIA 2nd Division — Season 1990/91

| | HEBAR | CH. MORE | BOTEV | SPARTAK V. | BDIN | SV VITSA | OSAM | SEPT. SLAVA | AKAD.SV | R. DOLINA | VELBAZHD | SPARTAK P. | DOBRUDZHA | CH. ZNAME | CHUMERNA | DOROSTOL | PIRIN | AKAD. SF | SL. BRYAG |
|---|---|---|---|---|---|---|---|---|---|---|---|---|---|---|---|---|---|---|---|
| HEBAR PAZARDZHIK | | 3-0 | 4-1 | 4-1 | 2-0 | 3-0 | 5-0 | 0-0 | 4-0 | 2-1 | 3-0 | 1-1 | 3-0 | 3-0 | 1-0 | 3-0 | 5-0 | 3-0 | 3-0 |
| CHERNO MORE VARNA | 1-3 | | 3-0 | 2-2 | 3-1 | 2-1 | 2-1 | 2-0 | 3-0 | 3-1 | 1-0 | 2-1 | 1-0 | 1-0 | 2-0 | 2-0 | 4-1 | 2-0 | 3-2 |
| BOTEV VRATSA | 0-2 | 4-1 | | 5-2 | 1-0 | 1-1 | 4-0 | 2-0 | 2-5 | 3-1 | 1-2 | 1-0 | 1-2 | 2-0 | 3-0 | 1-0 | 2-0 | 2-0 | 1-0 |
| SPARTAK VARNA | 0-0 | 1-1 | 2-0 | | 2-1 | 1-0 | 3-0 | 3-1 | 2-0 | 3-0 | 2-0 | 1-1 | 2-1 | 3-0 | 3-1 | 0-0 | 4-0 | 2-0 | 1-2 |
| BDIN VIDIN | 1-1 | 2-0 | 1-0 | 1-1 | | 0-0 | 3-0 | 1-2 | 0-0 | 2-2 | 1-0 | 1-0 | 1-0 | 1-1 | 0-1 | 0-1 | 2-0 | 1-0 | 2-0 |
| SVETKAVISTA TARGOV. | 1-0 | 2-0 | 2-1 | 2-0 | 2-0 | | 1-0 | 1-0 | 3-1 | 1-2 | 2-0 | 2-1 | 2-3 | 3-1 | 2-0 | 3-0 | 5-1 | 3-2 | 0-0 |
| OSAM LOVECH | 2-2 | 0-0 | 2-0 | 1-0 | 0-0 | 1-0 | | 0-1 | 3-0 | 2-0 | 1-1 | 2-0 | 1-0 | 3-0 | 3-0 | 0-1 | 3-1 | 3-0 | 1-0 |
| SEPT. SLAVA MIHAILOVGR. | 0-1 | 6-0 | 4-0 | 2-0 | 2-2 | 2-0 | 4-0 | | 2-1 | 2-0 | 5-1 | 3-0 | 0-1 | 2-0 | 2-0 | 1-3 | 3-1 | 3-2 | 1-2 |
| AKADEMIK SVISHTOV | 2-0 | 0-0 | 3-0 | 3-1 | 4-2 | 2-0 | 1-0 | 5-0 | | 2-1 | 2-1 | 1-0 | 2-0 | 1-1 | 3-0 | 1-0 | 2-0 | 2-0 | 1-0 |
| ROSOVA DOLINA K'ZANLUK | 1-1 | 1-0 | 2-1 | 1-0 | 4-1 | 0-1 | 2-0 | 1-1 | 1-0 | | 1-0 | 1-1 | 0-3 | 2-0 | 3-0 | 0-0 | 12-1 | 4-0 | 3-0 |
| VELBAZHD KYUSTENDIL | 1-1 | 1-0 | 3-0 | 1-0 | 2-1 | 2-0 | 0-0 | 2-2 | 1-2 | 1-1 | | 2-0 | 1-1 | 2-0 | 2-1 | 2-0 | 2-0 | 5-2 | 4-0 |
| SPARTAK PLEVEN | 0-2 | 1-0 | 2-1 | 0-1 | 3-0 | 2-1 | 1-0 | 2-0 | 1-2 | 2-0 | 4-1 | | 3-1 | 2-2 | 4-2 | 1-1 | 0-0 | 3-0 | 3-1 |
| DOBRUDZHA TOLBUHIN | 1-0 | 4-1 | 4-1 | 1-0 | 0-0 | 1-0 | 6-0 | 4-3 | 0-0 | 1-0 | 4-0 | 1-0 | | 2-1 | 0-0 | 0-0 | 2-0 | 2-0 | 4-0 |
| CH. ZNAME PAVLIKENI | 1-3 | 2-2 | 3-3 | 1-0 | 1-0 | 1-2 | 2-0 | 2-3 | 2-1 | 3-1 | 1-0 | 2-0 | 1-1 | | 1-0 | 1-0 | 1-0 | 2-0 | 1-0 |
| CHUMERNA ELENA | 1-2 | 0-0 | 1-1 | 1-0 | 3-0 | 2-0 | 5-2 | 1-1 | 2-1 | 1-0 | 1-0 | 3-2 | 0-1 | 6-1 | | 0-0 | 2-0 | 2-1 | 2-1 |
| DOROSTOL SILISTRA | 2-1 | 2-3 | 1-1 | 2-1 | 2-1 | 4-0 | 4-0 | 1-0 | 1-0 | 3-1 | 1-0 | 0-0 | 2-1 | 4-0 | | | 3-1 | 5-0 | 4-1 |
| PIRIN RAZLOG | 1-1 | 0-3 | 2-0 | 0-0 | 1-0 | 1-6 | 1-1 | 1-2 | 1-1 | 1-0 | 1-1 | 1-1 | 1-1 | 1-0 | 1-1 | 0-1 | | 1-7 | 1-0 |
| AKADEMIK SOFIA | 2-2 | 2-0 | 1-0 | 1-1 | 1-0 | 0-1 | 2-2 | 2-0 | 1-2 | 2-2 | 2-1 | 1-0 | 0-0 | 1-0 | 2-1 | 0-2 | 2-1 | | 2-1 |
| SLANCHEV BRYAG N'BAR | 2-2 | 1-2 | 0-0 | 0-1 | 2-1 | 2-0 | 2-1 | 1-0 | 1-1 | 3-0 | 4-0 | 1-2 | 3-2 | 3-0 | 3-1 | 0-1 | 2-1 | 2-0 | |

# BULGARIA 1ST DIVISION 1990/91
## LEAGUE TABLE FINAL

| | P | W | D | L | F | A | Pts |
|---|---|---|---|---|---|---|---|
| Etar Veliko Tirnovo | 30 | 18 | 8 | 4 | 49 | 21 | 44 |
| CSKA Sofia | 30 | 14 | 9 | 7 | 51 | 28 | 37 |
| Slavia Sofia | 30 | 14 | 9 | 7 | 48 | 29 | 37 |
| Lokomotiv Sofia | 30 | 13 | 10 | 7 | 50 | 36 | 36 |
| Botev Plovdiv | 30 | 13 | 10 | 7 | 49 | 41 | 36 |
| Levski Sofia | 30 | 12 | 9 | 9 | 51 | 38 | 33 |
| Chernomorets Bourgas | 30 | 11 | 8 | 11 | 41 | 50 | 30 |
| Lok. Gorna Oryahovitsa | 30 | 13 | 3 | 14 | 42 | 39 | 29 |
| Beroe Stara Zagora | 30 | 10 | 7 | 13 | 38 | 41 | 27 |
| Minyor Pernik | 30 | 10 | 7 | 13 | 36 | 44 | 27 |
| Lokomotiv Plovdiv | 30 | 9 | 9 | 12 | 34 | 42 | 27 |
| Pirin Blagoevgrad | 30 | 11 | 4 | 15 | 38 | 40 | 26 |
| FK Sliven | 30 | 9 | 8 | 13 | 39 | 49 | 26 |
| Yantra Gabrovo | 30 | 9 | 8 | 13 | 31 | 44 | 26 |
| Dunav Ruse | 30 | 8 | 6 | 16 | 23 | 42 | 22 |
| FK Haskovo | 30 | 7 | 3 | 20 | 27 | 63 | 17 |

Champions : - Etar Veliko Tirnovo
Relegated : - Dunav Ruse and FK Haskovo

## TOP SCORERS

| | | |
|---|---|---|
| 1. | Ivailo Yordanov (Lokomotiv GO) | 21 |
| 2. | Yordan Lechkov (FK Sliven) | 18 |
| | Petar Mihtarski (Levski) | 18 |
| 4. | Vladimir Stoyanov (Chernomorets) | 17 |
| 5. | Boncho Genchev (Etar) | 15 |
| 6. | Stefan Draganov (Lokomotive Pl) | 14 |
| | Todor Pramatarov (Lokomotiv Sf) | 14 |
| 8. | Vercho Mitov (Minyor) | 13 |
| 9. | Yasen Petrov (Botev) | 11 |
| | Stanimir Stoilov (Levski) | 11 |
| 11. | Boris Hvoinev (Botev) | 10 |
| | Georgi Kumanov (Haskovo) | 10 |
| | Hristo Marashliev (CSKA) | 10 |
| | Todor Zaitsev (Botev) | 10 |

# BULGARIA 2ND DIVISION 1990/91
## LEAGUE TABLE FINAL

| | P | W | D | L | F | A | Pts |
|---|---|---|---|---|---|---|---|
| Hebar Pazardzhik | 36 | 22 | 10 | 4 | 76 | 23 | 54 |
| Dobrudzha Dobritch | 36 | 19 | 8 | 9 | 53 | 28 | 46 |
| Dorostol Silistra | 36 | 19 | 8 | 9 | 50 | 26 | 46 |
| Akademik Svishtov | 36 | 20 | 6 | 10 | 54 | 36 | 46 |
| Cherno More Varna | 36 | 19 | 6 | 11 | 52 | 45 | 44 |
| Montana Mihailovgrad | 36 | 18 | 5 | 13 | 61 | 43 | 41 |
| Svetkavitsa Targovishte | 36 | 19 | 3 | 14 | 50 | 39 | 41 |
| Spartak Varna | 36 | 15 | 8 | 13 | 46 | 36 | 38 |
| Rosova Dolina Kazanluk | 36 | 13 | 7 | 16 | 52 | 47 | 33 |
| Spartak Pleven | 36 | 13 | 7 | 16 | 44 | 42 | 33 |
| Velbazhd Kyustendil | 36 | 13 | 7 | 16 | 42 | 49 | 33 |
| Osam Lovech | 36 | 12 | 8 | 16 | 35 | 53 | 32 |
| Botev Vratsa | 36 | 13 | 5 | 18 | 46 | 56 | 31 |
| Chumerna Elena | 36 | 13 | 5 | 18 | 41 | 54 | 31 |
| FK Pavlikeni | 36 | 12 | 7 | 17 | 36 | 56 | 31 |
| Slanchev Briag Nesebar | 36 | 13 | 4 | 19 | 42 | 52 | 30 |
| Bdin Vidin | 36 | 9 | 18 | 30 | 44 | 27 | |
| Akademik Sofia | 36 | 11 | 5 | 20 | 38 | 63 | 27 |
| Pirin Razlog | 36 | 6 | 8 | 22 | 25 | 81 | 20 |

Promoted : - Hebar Pazardzhik and Dobrudzha Dobritch
Relegated : - Bdin Vidin, Akademik Sofia and Pirin Razlog.

League increased to 20 clubs for Season 1991/92

## NAME CHANGES DURING SEASON

Dobrudzha Tolbuhin to Dobrudzha Dobritch
Septemvriiska Slava Mihailovgrad to Montana Mihailovgrad
Cherveno Zname Pavlikeni to FK Pavlikeni

# BULGARIA 3RD DIV. NORTH-WEST 1990/91
## LEAGUE TABLE FINAL

| | P | W | D | L | F | A | Pts |
|---|---|---|---|---|---|---|---|
| Chavdar Byala Slatina | 30 | 17 | 8 | 5 | 51 | 30 | 42 |
| Kom Berkovitsa | 30 | 13 | 8 | 9 | 38 | 27 | 34 |
| Lokomotiv Levski | 30 | 15 | 4 | 11 | 44 | 34 | 34 |
| Lokomotiv Drianovo | 30 | 14 | 4 | 12 | 42 | 33 | 32 |
| FK Tryavna | 30 | 14 | 3 | 13 | 53 | 32 | 31 |
| Storgozya Pleven | 30 | 10 | 10 | 10 | 32 | 30 | 30 |
| Levski Lom | 30 | 11 | 7 | 12 | 42 | 31 | 29 |
| FK Teteven | 30 | 11 | 7 | 12 | 37 | 43 | 29 |
| Lokomotiv Mezdra | 30 | 12 | 5 | 13 | 31 | 38 | 29 |
| Rakovski Sevlievo | 30 | 12 | 5 | 13 | 31 | 38 | 29 |
| Iskar Roman | 30 | 10 | 9 | 11 | 27 | 41 | 29 |
| Metalik Lyaskovets | 30 | 12 | 4 | 14 | 34 | 43 | 28 |
| Mizya Knezha | 30 | 12 | 3 | 15 | 42 | 51 | 27 |
| Yantra Poli Trambesh | 30 | 11 | 4 | 15 | 50 | 55 | 26 |
| Osam II Lovech | 30 | 11 | 4 | 15 | 43 | 50 | 26 |
| Chavdar Troyan | 30 | 9 | 7 | 14 | 25 | 46 | 25 |

Name Change : - Dunav Lom to Levski Lom
Promoted : - Chavdar Byala Slatina

# BULGARIA 3RD DIVISION NORTH-EAST 1990/91
## LEAGUE TABLE FINAL

| | P | W | D | L | F | A | Pts |
|---|---|---|---|---|---|---|---|
| FK Shumen | 30 | 25 | 1 | 4 | 84 | 14 | 51 |
| Lokomotiv Ruse | 30 | 24 | 3 | 3 | 80 | 17 | 51 |
| Ludogorets Razgrad | 30 | 13 | 6 | 11 | 35 | 28 | 32 |
| Polikhim Devnya | 30 | 13 | 4 | 13 | 38 | 32 | 30 |
| Zarya Krushari | 30 | 14 | 1 | 15 | 42 | 50 | 29 |
| Druzhba Ishirkovo | 30 | 12 | 5 | 13 | 29 | 42 | 29 |
| Chernolomets Popovo | 30 | 12 | 4 | 14 | 30 | 27 | 28 |
| Ovech Provadia | 30 | 11 | 6 | 13 | 32 | 37 | 28 |
| Sportist Gen. Toshevo | 30 | 12 | 3 | 15 | 37 | 34 | 27 |
| FK Kubrat | 30 | 10 | 7 | 13 | 38 | 42 | 27 |
| Kaliakra Kavarna | 30 | 9 | 9 | 12 | 24 | 34 | 27 |
| Septemvri Tervel | 30 | 11 | 4 | 15 | 33 | 51 | 26 |
| Chernomorets Balchik | 30 | 11 | 4 | 15 | 19 | 38 | 26 |
| FK Isperikh | 30 | 12 | 2 | 16 | 40 | 66 | 26 |
| FK Dulovo | 30 | 10 | 3 | 17 | 32 | 47 | 23 |
| FK Preslav | 30 | 8 | 4 | 18 | 23 | 57 | 20 |

Name Change : - Chervena Zvezda Dulovo to FK Dulovo
Promoted : - FK Shumen

# BULGARIA 3RD DIV. SOUTH WEST 1990/91
## LEAGUE TABLE FINAL

| | P | W | D | L | F | A | Pts |
|---|---|---|---|---|---|---|---|
| Belasitsa Petrich | 28 | 15 | 7 | 6 | 43 | 36 | 37 |
| Vihren Sandanski | 28 | 13 | 10 | 5 | 37 | 21 | 36 |
| Pirin Goche Delchev | 28 | 14 | 5 | 9 | 48 | 35 | 33 |
| Strumska Sl.Radomir | 28 | 13 | 6 | 9 | 31 | 24 | 32 |
| Rilski Sp. Samokov | 28 | 14 | 2 | 12 | 67 | 61 | 30 |
| FK Bankya | 28 | 13 | 4 | 11 | 42 | 40 | 30 |
| Chepinets Velingrad | 28 | 13 | 3 | 12 | 51 | 42 | 29 |
| NSA Sofia | 28 | 9 | 9 | 10 | 44 | 34 | 27 |
| Marek Stanke Dimitr. | 28 | 10 | 7 | 11 | 29 | 31 | 27 |
| Minyor Rudozem | 28 | 11 | 4 | 13 | 38 | 33 | 26 |
| Svoboda Peshtera | 28 | 11 | 4 | 13 | 39 | 38 | 26 |
| Rodopa Smolyan | 28 | 9 | 7 | 12 | 30 | 40 | 25 |
| Minyor Bobov Dol | 28 | 9 | 7 | 12 | 26 | 37 | 25 |
| Minyor Eleshnitsa | 28 | 9 | 6 | 13 | 42 | 52 | 24 |

Septemvri Sofia expelled, all Matches awarded 0-3

Name Change : - VIF Sofia to NSA Sofia
Promoted : - Belasitsa Petrich

# BULGARIA 3RD DIVISION SOUTH EAST 1990/91
## LEAGUE TABLE FINAL

| | P | W | D | L | F | A | Pts |
|---|---|---|---|---|---|---|---|
| Neftokhimik Bourgas | 30 | 21 | 5 | 4 | 77 | 25 | 47 |
| Spartak Plovdiv | 30 | 17 | 6 | 7 | 50 | 21 | 40 |
| Maritsa Plovdiv | 30 | 15 | 7 | 8 | 49 | 29 | 37 |
| Metalik Sopot | 30 | 13 | 10 | 7 | 35 | 30 | 36 |
| FK Dimitrovgrad | 30 | 14 | 7 | 9 | 63 | 36 | 35 |
| Maritsa Istok Radnevo | 30 | 12 | 9 | 9 | 45 | 34 | 33 |
| Granichar Svilengrad | 30 | 12 | 8 | 10 | 45 | 34 | 32 |
| Yavorov Chirpan | 30 | 13 | 6 | 11 | 41 | 30 | 32 |
| Rodopi Momchilgrad | 30 | 14 | 3 | 13 | 44 | 58 | 31 |
| Cherno More Pomorie | 30 | 8 | 12 | 10 | 33 | 38 | 28 |
| FK Karlovo | 30 | 11 | 5 | 14 | 38 | 45 | 27 |
| Laskov Yambol | 30 | 9 | 7 | 14 | 40 | 47 | 25 |
| Energetik Galabovo | 30 | 10 | 5 | 15 | 31 | 61 | 25 |
| Arda Kardjali | 30 | 8 | 7 | 15 | 24 | 35 | 23 |
| Hebros Harmanli | 30 | 8 | 7 | 15 | 30 | 50 | 23 |
| Lokomotiv St.Zagora | 30 | 1 | 4 | 25 | 14 | 86 | 6 |

Promoted : - Neftokhimik Bourgas

# CUP BULGARIAN FUTBOL SOIUZ 1990/91*

*\* Previously Cup of the Soviet Army*

## 1/8 FINALS

```
Svoboda Peshtera......1    Lok.Gorna Oryahov.....
Dunav Ruse............0    Botev Plovdiv.........4    Spartak Varna.........0
Slavia Sofia win 2-4 on penalties                    Spartak Pleven........2
                          Minyor Pernik.........0    Beroe Stara Zagora....0 (aet.)
Ludogorets Razgrad....1    Neftokhimik Bourgas..2
Etar Veliko Tirnovo...6    Velbazhd Kyustendil..1    Beroe Stara Zagora win 3-4 on penalties
Rodopa Smolyan........2    Levski Sofia..........3
```

## 1/4 FINALS

```
Etar Veliko Tirnovo...2    Slavia Sofia..........0
Beroe Stara Zagora....0    Lok.Gorna Oryahov.....2
Neftokhimik Bourgas...2    Botev Plovdiv.........0
Svoboda Peshtera......0    Levski Sofia..........9
```

## SEMI-FINALS

```
Neftokhimik Bourgas...2    Levski Sofia..........1
Etar Veliko Tirnovo...1    Lok.Gorna Oryahov.....0
```

## FINAL   5/6/91 (at Sliven)

Etar Veliko Tirnovo....2    Neftokhimik Bourgas....1

Etar : Donev, Prodanov, Parvanov, Gaidarski, Chervenkov, Dimov, Raschev (Popivanov 78), Georgiev, Genchev (Christov 70), Kiriakov, Kislov.

Neftokhimik : Kiuchukov, Mindov, Tikhomirov, Rakov, Matushev, Mikhov, Tsonev, Gotskov (Stoianov 72), Dobrevski, Stoichev (Vasilev 61), Banev.

```
0-1  Dobrevski   26        Referee : Hristo Tsonchev
1-1  Rashev      41        Attendance : 6,000
2-1  Gaidarski   66
```

---

# BULGARIA CUP OF THE REPUBLIC 1990/91

## 1/16 FINALS

| | 1ST LEG | 2ND LEG | AGG. |
|---|---|---|---|
| FK Dimitrovgrad v Sparta Varna | 2-1 | 1-3 | 3-4 |
| Dorostol Silistra v Lokomotiv Sofia | 0-0 | 1-3 | 1-3 |
| Dobrudzha Dobritch v Botev Plovdiv | 1-1 | 1-5 | 2-6 |
| Svetkavitsa Targovishta v Hebar Pazardzhik | 2-1 | 0-3 | 2-4 |
| Akademik Sofia v Chumerna Elena | 1-1 | 1-3 | 2-4 |
| Lokomotiv Gorna Oryahovitsa v Levski Sofia | 0-1 | 0-5 | 0-6 |
| Strumska Slava Radomir v Lokomotiv Plovdiv (Loko.Pl. win on pens.) | 2-0 | 0-2 | 2-2 |
| Bdin Vidin v Yantra Gabrovo | 2-0 | 0-5 | 2-5 |
| Beroe Stara Zagora v Minyor Pernik | 3-3 | 3-0 | 6-3 |
| Chernomorets Bourgas v Spartak Pleven | 4-0 | 0-0 | 4-0 |
| Pirin Blagoevgrad v Lokomotiv Ruse | 2-0 | 1-2 | 3-2 |
| Slavia Sofia v NSA Sofia | 2-0 | 2-1 | 4-1 |
| FK Sliven v Akademik Svishtov | 3-1 | 3-6 | 6-7 |
| Dunav Ruse v Etar Veliko Tirnovo | 1-0 | 1-3 | 2-3 |
| Pirin Goche Delchev v FK Haskovo | 2-0 | 1-2 | 3-2 |
| CSKA Sofia v Armeets Plovdiv | 3-2 | 3-1 | 6-3 |

## 1/4 FINALS   Played in Groups

### GROUP A

```
Botev Plovdiv.........2    Chernomorets B'gas...1
Pirin Blagoevgrad....2    Akademik Svishtov....1
Botev Plovdiv........1    Pirin Blagoevgrad....0
Chernomorets B'gas...1    Akademik Svishtov....0
Botev Plovdiv........0    Akademik Svishtov....0
Chernomorets B'gas...1    Pirin Blagoevgrad....1
```

#### LEAGUE TABLE FINAL

| | | | | | | | |
|---|---|---|---|---|---|---|---|
| Botev Plovdiv | 3 | 2 | 1 | 0 | 3 | 1 | 5 |
| Chernomorets Bourgas | 3 | 1 | 1 | 1 | 3 | 3 | 3 |
| Pirin Blagoevgrad | 3 | 1 | 1 | 1 | 3 | 3 | 3 |
| Akademik Svishtov | 3 | 0 | 1 | 2 | 1 | 3 | 1 |

### GROUP B

```
Slavia Sofia.........4    Pirin Goche Delchev..0
Lokomotiv Sofia......1    Lokomotiv Plovdiv....0
Pirin Goche Delchev..3    Lokomotiv Plovdiv....0
Lokomotiv Sofia......2    Slavia Sofia.........0
Lokomotiv Sofia......2    Pirin Goche Delchev..0
Slavia Sofia.........1    Lokomotiv Plovdiv....1
```

#### LEAGUE TABLE FINAL

| | | | | | | | |
|---|---|---|---|---|---|---|---|
| Lokomotiv Sofia | 3 | 3 | 0 | 0 | 5 | 0 | 6 |
| Slavia Sofia | 3 | 1 | 1 | 1 | 5 | 3 | 3 |
| Pirin Goche Delchev | 3 | 1 | 0 | 2 | 3 | 6 | 2 |
| Lokomotiv Plovdiv | 3 | 0 | 1 | 2 | 1 | 5 | 1 |

### GROUP C

```
Etar Veliko Tirnovo...3    Spartak Varna........0
Beroe Stara Zagora....2    Yantra Gabrovo.......1
Yantra Gabrovo........4    Spartak Varna........0
Etar Veliko Tirnovo...3    Beroe Stara Zagora...0
Etar Veliko Tirnovo...3    Yantra Gabrovo.......2
Beroe Stara Zagora....2    Spartak Varna........1
```

#### LEAGUE TABLE FINAL

| | | | | | | | |
|---|---|---|---|---|---|---|---|
| Etar Veliko Tirnovo | 3 | 3 | 0 | 0 | 9 | 2 | 6 |
| Beroe Stara Zagora | 3 | 2 | 0 | 1 | 4 | 5 | 4 |
| Yantra Gabrovo | 3 | 1 | 0 | 2 | 7 | 5 | 2 |
| Spartak Varna | 3 | 0 | 0 | 3 | 1 | 9 | 0 |

### GROUP D

```
CSKA Sofia...........1    Chumerna Elena.......0
Levski Sofia.........1    Hebar Pazardzhik.....0
Levski Sofia.........2    CSKA Sofia...........0
Hebar Pazardzhik.....3    Chumerna Elena.......0
Levski Sofia.........3    Chumerna Elena.......1
CSKA Sofia...........2    Hebar Pazardzhik.....0
```

#### LEAGUE TABLE FINAL

| | | | | | | | |
|---|---|---|---|---|---|---|---|
| Levski Sofia | 3 | 3 | 0 | 0 | 6 | 1 | 6 |
| CSKA Sofia | 3 | 2 | 0 | 1 | 3 | 2 | 4 |
| Hebar Pazardzhik | 3 | 1 | 0 | 2 | 3 | 3 | 2 |
| Chumerna Elena | 3 | 0 | 0 | 3 | 1 | 7 | 0 |

## SEMI-FINALS

| | 1ST LEG | 2ND LEG | AGG. |
|---|---|---|---|
| Botev Plovdiv v Etar Veliko Tirnovo | 3-0 | 1-1 | 4-1 |
| Lokomotiv Sofia v Levski Sofia | 2-3 | 1-2 | 3-5 |

## FINAL   29/5/91 (at Veliko Tirnovo)

Levski Sofia..........2    Botev Plovdiv.........1

Levski : Popov, Pl.Nikolov, Khubchev, Borimirov, Vangelov, Slavchev, Donkov, Stoilov (Gruev 86), Mihtarski, Shalamanov, Yotov (Panchev 89).

Botev : Tenev, Pachev, Khrozov, Kochev, I. Dobrevski, Y. Petrov, Kostadinov, Zaitsev (Yosifov 66), Hvoinev, Zehtinski (A.Pashev 84), G.Dobrevski.

```
1-0  Donkov      57        Referee : S.Chakirov
1-1  Yosifov     69        Attendance : 10,000
2-1  Borimirov   80
```

# BULGARIA INTERNATIONAL REVIEW 1990

## INTERNATIONAL LINE-UPS 1990

| Match | Result / Venue / Competition (Scorers) — Referee | Valov | E. Dimitrov | T. Ivanov | Vasev | Bankov | Yanchev | Kostadinov | Stoichkov | Balakov | Yordanov | Todorov | Dochev | Lechkov | Mihtarski | I. Panchev | Georgiev | Zhelev | N. Iliev | Markov | Z. Yankov | Genchev | Valkov | P. Petkov | G. Dimitrov | B. Mihailov | Sirakov | Mladenov | Penev |
|---|---|---|---|---|---|---|---|---|---|---|---|---|---|---|---|---|---|---|---|---|---|---|---|---|---|---|---|---|---|
| 5/5/90 | BRAZIL 2 BULGARIA 1 — Campinas — Friendly (Kostadinov) — Ref: Tavares da Silva (Brazil) | 1 | | 3 | 4 | (4) | 10 | 7 | 8 | 11 | 9 | (11) | | | | | | | | | | | | | | | | | |
| 12/9/90 | SWITZERLAND 2 BULGARIA 0 — Geneve — EuroCh.Q. — Ref: Goethals (Belgium) | | | 3 | 4 | 10 | 8 | 7 | 8 | 11 | 11 | 10 | 6 | | | | (11) | | | | | | | | | | | | |
| 26/9/90 | SWEDEN 2 BULGARIA 0 — Solna — Friendly — Ref: Damgaard (Denmark) | | | 5 | | | | | 8 | 9 | | 11 | 3 | 9 | | | | 2 | 5 | | 6 | | | | | | | | |
| 17/10/90 | RUMANIA 0 BULGARIA 3 — Bucuresti — EuroCh.Q. (Sirakov, Todorov 2) — Ref: Santos (Portugal) | | | 3 | 4 | 5 | 7 | (10) | 8 | 11 | 7 | (6) | | (4) | | | | 2 | 5 | 4 | 6 | 7 | | | | 1 | 10 | | |
| 14/11/90 | BULGARIA 1 SCOTLAND 1 — Sofia — EuroCh.Q. (Todorov) — Ref: Kaupe (Austria) | | | | | 7 | 6 | (11) | | 11 | | | (2) | | (7) | (8) | | | | | 4 | | (7) | (9) | (10) | 1 | | 9 | |
| CAPS AT 31/12/90 | | 33 | 6 | 20 | 16 | 7 | 21 | 12 | 27 | 14 | 30 | 8 | 20 | | | 1 | | 2 | 40 | 21 | 6 | 1 | 1 | | 1 | 50 | 34 | 10 | 21 |
| GOALS AT 31/12/90 | | | | 2 | | 1 | 3 | 5 | 3 | 3 | 3 | 3 | 3 | 3 | 3 | | 3 | | 4 | | 3 | | | 3 | | 1 | 11 | 3 | 5 |

# CYPRUS Correspondent : JAN ALSSEMA

## CYPRUS 1ST DIVISION 1990/91

### LEAGUE TABLE FINAL

| | | | | | | | |
|---|---|---|---|---|---|---|---|
| Apollon Limassol | 26 | 19 | 6 | 1 | 60 | 20 | 44 |
| Anorthosis | 26 | 18 | 5 | 3 | 42 | 14 | 41 |
| APOEL Nicosia | 26 | 13 | 9 | 4 | 48 | 23 | 35 |
| Omonia Nicosia | 26 | 12 | 7 | 7 | 41 | 22 | 31 |
| AE Limassol | 26 | 10 | 8 | 8 | 36 | 36 | 28 |
| NEA Salamina | 26 | 9 | 9 | 8 | 38 | 31 | 27 |
| Pezoporikos | 26 | 8 | 11 | 7 | 35 | 28 | 27 |
| Aris Limassol | 26 | 9 | 6 | 11 | 33 | 40 | 24 |
| Alki Larnaca | 26 | 8 | 8 | 10 | 32 | 40 | 24 |
| EPA Larnaca | 26 | 7 | 10 | 9 | 29 | 37 | 24 |
| Olympiakos | 26 | 7 | 9 | 10 | 36 | 37 | 23 |
| EN Paralimni | 26 | 7 | 7 | 12 | 33 | 45 | 21 |
| APOP Paphos | 26 | 1 | 4 | 21 | 20 | 63 | 6 |
| APEP Limassol | 26 | 3 | 3 | 20 | 18 | 65 | 5 |

APEP Limassol 4 points deducted

Champions : - Apollon Limassol

Relegated : - APOP Paphos and APEP Limassol

### TOP SCORERS

1. Pecirovic (Apollon Limassol) — 19
   Xiouroupas (Omonia Nicosia) — 19
3. Cocic (APOEL Nicosia) — 18
4. Baceta (Olympiakos Nicosia) — 16
5. T.Zouvanis (Paralimni Famagusta) — 14
   Kouzil (AE Limassol) — 14

### PROMOTION/RELEGATION PLAY-OFF

| | 1ST LEG | 2ND LEG | AGG. |
|---|---|---|---|
| EN Paralimniou Famagusta v Ethnikos Akhnas | 4-0 | 3-1 | 7-1 |

### CYPRUS 1st Division Season 1990/91

| | APOEL | OMONIA | P'RIKOS | ARIS | APOLLON | AEL | ANORTHOSI | PARALIMNI | OLYMPIAKOS | SALAMINA | APOP | ALKI | EPA | APEP |
|---|---|---|---|---|---|---|---|---|---|---|---|---|---|---|
| APOEL NICOSIA | | 1-1 | 1-0 | 2-0 | 1-1 | 4-1 | 1-2 | 0-0 | 1-0 | 1-1 | 4-0 | 4-0 | 3-0 | 3-0 |
| OMONIA NICOSIA | 1-2 | | 1-1 | 0-2 | 0-2 | 1-0 | 4-1 | 2-0 | 2-0 | 0-1 | 6-0 | 0-0 | 3-2 | 3-0 |
| PEZOPORIKOS LARNACA | 1-1 | 1-1 | | 3-1 | 1-2 | 3-0 | 1-1 | 1-1 | 1-4 | 0-0 | 2-1 | 1-0 | 2-0 | 5-0 |
| ARIS LIMASSOL | 4-1 | 0-2 | 1-1 | | 0-5 | 4-3 | 1-0 | 1-1 | 4-1 | 1-1 | 2-0 | 1-1 | 1-1 | 1-0 |
| APOLLON LIMASSOL | 2-2 | 1-1 | 3-1 | 5-1 | | 1-0 | 3-1 | 3-0 | 2-0 | 5-2 | 2-0 | 0-0 | 5-2 | 3-0 |
| AE LIMASSOL | 2-2 | 1-1 | 2-2 | 4-0 | 0-2 | | 1-2 | 2-2 | 2-2 | 2-1 | 1-0 | 4-0 | 1-0 | 1-0 |
| ANORTHOSI FAMAGUSTA | 2-0 | 0-0 | 1-0 | 2-0 | 3-0 | 1-1 | | 3-1 | 0-0 | 0-0 | 5-0 | 1-0 | 4-0 | 2-0 |
| EN PARALIMNIOU FAMAGUSTA | 1-4 | 0-2 | 1-1 | 2-1 | 0-2 | 1-1 | 0-1 | | 2-1 | 1-1 | 2-1 | 2-1 | 0-1 | 6-1 |
| OLYMPIAKOS NICOSIA | 0-2 | 1-0 | 2-2 | 0-0 | 1-2 | 1-2 | 0-2 | 3-1 | | 3-1 | 4-2 | 2-3 | 2-2 | 2-1 |
| NEA SALAMINA | 1-0 | 2-1 | 1-2 | 3-0 | 1-3 | 5-1 | 0 | 4-0 | 1-1 | | 1-1 | 1-3 | 1-1 | 4-0 |
| APOP PAPHOS | 2-4 | 2-4 | 1-0 | 0-4 | 1-2 | 0-1 | 0-2 | 2-3 | 0-0 | 0-1 | | 3-3 | 1-1 | 0-1 |
| ALKI LARNACA | 0-0 | 0-3 | 1-3 | 1-0 | 1-1 | 0-1 | 0-1 | 3-2 | 1-1 | 2-1 | 2-1 | | 1-1 | 3-1 |
| EPA LARNACA | 1-1 | 1-0 | 0-0 | 1-0 | 0-2 | 0-1 | 0-2 | 3-2 | 1-1 | 0-0 | 4-1 | 2-1 | | 5-2 |
| APEP LIMASSOL | 0-3 | 1-2 | 1-0 | 0-3 | 1-1 | 1-1 | 1-2 | 0-2 | 0-4 | 2-3 | 2-1 | 3-5 | 0-0 | |

## CYPRUS 2ND DIVISION 1990/91

### LEAGUE TABLE FINAL

| | | | | | | | |
|---|---|---|---|---|---|---|---|
| Evagoras Paphos | 26 | 15 | 10 | 1 | 43 | 18 | 40 |
| Omonia Aradippou | 26 | 17 | 5 | 4 | 63 | 20 | 39 |
| Ethnikos Akhnas | 26 | 15 | 4 | 7 | 76 | 33 | 34 |
| Digenis Morphou | 26 | 10 | 9 | 7 | 37 | 30 | 29 |
| Akritas Chlorakas | 26 | 11 | 5 | 10 | 41 | 35 | 27 |
| Anagennisis Derinias | 26 | 10 | 6 | 10 | 51 | 39 | 26 |
| Onisilos Sotira | 26 | 10 | 6 | 10 | 44 | 45 | 26 |
| APEP Pelendria | 26 | 7 | 11 | 8 | 45 | 43 | 25 |
| Halkandras Dali | 26 | 11 | 3 | 12 | 51 | 52 | 25 |
| Doxa Katokopias | 26 | 9 | 6 | 11 | 49 | 46 | 24 |
| Orfeas Nicosia | 26 | 8 | 8 | 10 | 45 | 47 | 24 |
| Ermis Aradippou | 26 | 8 | 6 | 12 | 29 | 45 | 22 |
| Ethnikos Devteras | 26 | 5 | 7 | 14 | 39 | 75 | 17 |
| Elpida Xylofagou | 26 | 2 | 2 | 22 | 20 | 105 | 6 |

Promoted : - Evagoras and Omonia Aradippou

Relegated : - Ermis, Ethnikos Devteras and Elpida Xylofagou

## CYPRUS 3RD DIVISION 1990/91

### LEAGUE TABLE FINAL

| | | | | | | | |
|---|---|---|---|---|---|---|---|
| Othellos Athienou | 26 | 13 | 9 | 4 | 31 | 21 | 35 |
| Ethnikos Assia | 26 | 11 | 11 | 4 | 29 | 20 | 33 |
| Apollon Limpia | 26 | 10 | 9 | 7 | 34 | 28 | 29 |
| Keravnos Strovolos | 26 | 13 | 3 | 10 | 40 | 36 | 29 |
| PAEEK Kerineia | 26 | 7 | 13 | 6 | 32 | 30 | 27 |
| AE Katholiki | 26 | 7 | 11 | 8 | 37 | 28 | 25 |
| Tsaggaris Pelendria | 26 | 9 | 7 | 10 | 37 | 37 | 25 |
| Adonis Dali | 26 | 8 | 9 | 9 | 21 | 21 | 25 |
| Digenis Ipsonas | 26 | 7 | 11 | 8 | 32 | 33 | 25 |
| ThOI Lakatamia | 26 | 9 | 7 | 10 | 34 | 41 | 25 |
| APEAN Agia Napa | 26 | 9 | 6 | 11 | 43 | 35 | 24 |
| AE Zakaki | 26 | 8 | 7 | 11 | 31 | 27 | 23 |
| OKhEN Peristerona | 26 | 6 | 9 | 11 | 24 | 33 | 21 |
| AS Ormideia | 26 | 6 | 6 | 14 | 23 | 58 | 18 |

Promoted : - Othellos Athienou, Ethnikos Assia and Apollon Limpia.

## CYPRUS CUP 1990/91

### 1/16 FINALS

| | 1ST LEG | 2ND LEG | AGG. |
|---|---|---|---|
| Omonia Aradippou v Olympiakos Nicosia | 0-0 | 0-1 | 0-1 |
| Evagoras Paphos v Doxa Katokopias | 3-0 | 3-1 | 6-1 |
| Ethnikos Assia v APEP Limassol | 1-2 | 0-2 | 1-4 |
| EN Paralimni Famagusta v Anorthosi Famagusta | 1-2 | 0-2 | 1-4 |
| AE Limassol v APOP Paphos | 3-0 | 1-1 | 4-1 |
| Akritas Chlorakas v Alki Larnaca | 4-0 | 0-2 | 4-2 |
| Halkandras Dali v APEP Pelendria | 1-5 | 1-1 | 2-6 |
| Onisilos Sotira v AE Zakaki | 3-3 | 2-1 | 5-4 |
| Tsaggaris Pelendria v Orfeas Nicosia | 1-2 | 4-6 | 5-8 |
| APEI Ipsonas v EPA Larnaca | 0-6 | 0-8 | 0-14 |
| Pezoporikos Larnaca v Elpida Xylofagou | 5-1 | 8-2 | 13-3 |
| AE Katholiki v Ethnikos Akhnas | 1-3 | 1-1 | 2-4 |
| NEA Salamina v Anagennisis Derinias (Derinias win on the away goals rule) | 1-2 | 1-0 | 2-2 |
| Ermis Aradippou v Omonia Nicosia | 1-6 | 0-6 | 1-12 |
| Aris Limassol v Ethnikos Devteras | 7-0 | 2-3 | 9-3 |
| Apollon Limassol v APOEL Nicosia | 3-2 | 2-1 | 5-3 |

## INTERNATIONAL LINE-UPS 1990

| | 1. Marios Onisiforou | 2. John Kalotheou | 3. Kostas Miamiliotis | 4. George Christodoulou | 5. Avram Michael Socratous | 6. John Yiangoudakis | 7. Andreas Andreou (Kantilos) | 8. Pavlos Savva | 9. Spyros Kastanas | 10. Kostas Konstantiniou | 11. Panikos Xiourouppas | Panayotis Orphanides | Angelos Tsolakis | Andreas Charitou | Floros Nicolaou | Panikos Punnas | Nikodimos Papavassiliou | George Konstantiniou |
|---|---|---|---|---|---|---|---|---|---|---|---|---|---|---|---|---|---|---|
| **31/10/90** HUNGARY 4 CYPRUS 2 — Budapest — Ref: Kotherja (Albania) EuroCh.Q. (Xiourouppas, Tsolakis) | 1 | 2 | 3 | 4 | 5 | 6 | (2) | 8 | 4 | (9) | 11 | (5) | (6) | | | | | |
| **14/11/90** CYPRUS 0 NORWAY 3 — Nicosia — Ref: Petrovic (Yugoslavia) EuroCh.Q. | | 2 | 3 | | 5 | | | 8 | 9 | 10 | 11 | | 9 | | 10 | 7 | | |
| **22/12/90** CYPRUS 0 ITALY 4 — Limassol — Ref: Gregr (Czechoslovakia) EuroCh.Q. | | | 3 | 7 | 5 | 6 | | 8 | 4 | (9) | 11 | | 9 | 1 | 10 | | 1 | 11 |
| **CAPS AT 31/12/90** | 2 | 10 | 33 | 18 | 30 | 43 | 18 | 22 | 11 | 4 | 20 | 5 | 4 | 19 | 31 | 7 | 1 | 1 |
| **GOALS AT 31/12/90** | | | | 1 | | | | 2 | | | (8) | (5) | (6) | 1 | 10 | 1 | 1 | (8) |

---

### 1/8 FINALS

| | 1ST LEG | 2ND LEG | AGG. |
|---|---|---|---|
| EPA Larnaca v Apollon Limassol | 0-3 | 0-3 | 0-6 |
| Omonia Nicosia v APEP Pelendria | 1-0 | 2-0 | 3-0 |
| Olympiakos Nicosia v Evagoras Paphos | 2-1 | 1-1 | 3-2 |
| Akritas Chlorakas v Onisilos Sotira | 2-1 | 0-0 | 2-1 |
| Aris Limassol v Orfeas Nicosia | 4-1 | 1-1 | 5-2 |
| Pezoporikos Larnaca v Anagennisis Derinias | 4-0 | 9-1 | 13-1 |
| AE Limassol v APEP Limassol | 6-0 | 1-1 | 7-1 |
| Anorthosi Famagusta v Ethnikos Akhnas (Ethnikos win 3-1 on penalties) | 0-1 | 1-0 | 1-1 |

### 1/4 FINALS

| | 1ST LEG | 2ND LEG | AGG. |
|---|---|---|---|
| Pezoporikos Larnaca v Aris Limassol | 3-1 | 2-0 | 5-1 |
| AE Limassol v Apollon Limassol | 0-0 | 2-1 | 2-1 |
| Ethnikos Akhnas v Olympiakos Nicosia (Olympiakos win 1-3 on penalties) | 1-2 | 2-1 | 3-3 |
| Omonia Nicosia v Akritas Chlorakas | 2-0 | 3-0 | 5-0 |

### SEMI-FINALS

| | 1ST LEG | 2ND LEG | AGG. |
|---|---|---|---|
| AE Limassol v Olympiakos Nicosia | 0-0 | 1-2 | 1-2 |
| Pezoporikos Larnaca v Omonia Nicosia (Omonia win 4-2 on penalties) | 1-0 | 0-1 | 1-1 |

### FINAL  9/6/91 (at Nicosia)

Omonia Nicosia.......1  Olympiakos Nicosia....0

1-0  Panikos Xiourouppas  57  Referee: Louis Louzou

---

## CYPRUS : All Time Records as at 31/12/90 - CAPS

1. Nicos Pantziaras — 46
2. John Yiangoudakis — 43
3. Andreas Stylianou — 37
4. Stephanos Michael — 35
5. Kostas Miamiliotis — 35
6. Floros Nicolaou — 33
7. Klitos Erotocritou — 31
8. Pavlos Savva — 30
9. Avram Michael Socratous — 30
10. Andreas Elia (Andrelis) — 25
    Pambos Papadopoulos — 24

## CYPRUS : All Time Records as at 31/12/90 - GOALS

1. Phivos Vrahimis — (17) 8
2. Sotiris Kaifas — (17) 6
3. Pambos Papadopoulos — (24) 5
4. Gregory Savva — (17) 4
   Stephanos Michael — (35) 4

# CZECHOSLOVAKIA  Correspondent : FRANTISEK SYKORA

## CZECHOSLOVAKIA 1st Division — Season 1990/91

| | SPARTA | OSTRAVA | INTER | BOHEMIANS | SLOVAN | NITRA | DUKLA P | OLOMOUC | VITKOVICE | SLAVIA | CHEB | BRNO | B. BYSTRICA | D. STREDA | HRADEC | PRESOV |
|---|---|---|---|---|---|---|---|---|---|---|---|---|---|---|---|---|
| SPARTA PRAHA | | 0-0 | 3-0 | 5-0 | 0-0 | 3-1 | 5-1 | 1-0 | 3-0 | 3-1 | 3-1 | 3-3 | 3-0 | 1-1 | 4-1 | 2-2 |
| BANIK OSTRAVA | 2-1 | | 0-1 | 4-0 | 3-1 | 1-0 | 2-0 | 1-3 | 0-1 | 3-4 | 5-0 | 2-0 | 2-1 | 4-0 | 2-1 | 0-0 |
| INTER BRATISLAVA | 1-0 | 1-1 | | 1-0 | 0-0 | 3-3 | 4-0 | 3-2 | 2-0 | 4-1 | 1-1 | 1-0 | 2-1 | 1-1 | 0-1 | 1-1 |
| BOHEMIANS PRAHA | 0-0 | 3-2 | 2-2 | | 2-0 | 2-1 | 2-2 | 1-2 | 2-1 | 1-1 | 2-1 | 1-1 | 1-0 | 2-2 | 4-1 | 3-2 |
| SLOVAN BRATISLAVA | 0-3 | 2-1 | 4-0 | 4-0 | | 1-0 | 1-0 | 3-1 | 3-0 | 4-1 | 2-0 | 4-2 | 4-0 | 2-0 | 0-1 | 1-0 |
| FC NITRA | 1-0 | 0-0 | 3-0 | 0-0 | 0-1 | | 2-1 | 0-0 | 3-2 | 3-0 | 0-3 | 4-0 | 0-1 | 0-2 | 1-1 | 3-0 |
| DUKLA PRAHA | 1-3 | 1-0 | 4-2 | 0-4 | 1-0 | 1-0 | | 2-0 | 1-1 | 0-0 | 2-1 | 1-1 | 2-3 | 2-0 | 3-3 | 1-0 |
| SIGMA OLOMOUC | 1-0 | 1-0 | 3-2 | 3-0 | 1-1 | 3-0 | 4-0 | | 3-1 | 2-2 | 1-2 | 0-0 | 2-1 | 2-1 | 2-0 | 2-0 |
| TJ VITKOVICE | 5-4 | 4-3 | 3-2 | 2-1 | 3-3 | 2-0 | 3-1 | 4-1 | | 1-0 | 0-2 | 2-0 | 1-2 | 2-2 | 4-0 | 1-0 |
| SLAVIA PRAHA | 3-3 | 4-1 | 2-1 | 1-0 | 2-1 | 1-1 | 0-3 | 1-1 | 3-1 | | 2-1 | 3-0 | 1-1 | 0-1 | 4-1 | 2-2 |
| SKP UNION CHEB | 0-2 | 2-1 | 0-0 | 3-0 | 2-3 | 1-0 | 4-0 | 2-3 | 2-0 | 0-0 | | 2-1 | 3-0 | 0-0 | 2-0 | 3-0 |
| ZBROJOVKA BRNO | 0-1 | 0-1 | 0-0 | 1-2 | 1-2 | 0-1 | 0-2 | 0-4 | 0-0 | 3-0 | 0-2 | | 0-1 | 1-1 | 4-1 | 0-0 |
| DUKLA BANSKA BYSTRICA | 0-2 | 2-1 | 1-1 | 2-0 | 0-0 | 0-0 | 1-2 | 1-0 | 3-0 | 1-2 | 1-1 | 3-0 | | 1-1 | 4-1 | 3-2 |
| DAC DUNAJSKA STREDA | 0-0 | 1-5 | 1-3 | 1-0 | 2-0 | 0-1 | 2-1 | 2-1 | 1-0 | 0-0 | 4-2 | 4-0 | 2-0 | | 2-1 | 2-1 |
| SPART. HRADEC KRALOVE | 3-0 | 0-2 | 2-1 | 2-0 | 0-0 | 3-1 | 0-1 | 3-2 | 2-1 | 0-0 | 2-1 | 0-0 | 1-1 | | | 0-0 |
| TATRAN AGRO PRESOV | 0-0 | 0-1 | 2-1 | 3-0 | 1-0 | 3-1 | 4-2 | 1-3 | 2-1 | 3-2 | 3-1 | 2-0 | 1-1 | 2-2 | 5-0 | |

### TOP SCORERS
1. Roman Kukleta (Sparta Praha) — 17
2. Pavol Vytykac (Tatran Agro Presov) — 15
3. Jiri Bartl (TJ Vitkovice) — 14
4. Pavel Kuka (Slavia Praha) — 13
   Stefan Rusnak (Dukla Banska Bystrica) — 13
6. Radek Drulak (Sigma Olomouc) — 12
7. Pavel Cerny (Sparta Praha) — 11
   Radim Necas (Banik Ostrava) — 11
   Zbynek Ollender (Banik Ostrava) — 11
10. Pavol Dina (DAC Dunajska Streda) — 10
   Jiri Kabyl (SKP Union Cheb) — 10
   Marek Trval (TJ Vitkovice) — 10
13. Miroslav Bazik (Dukla Banska Bystrica) — 9
   Viktor Dvirnik (Inter Bratislava) — 9
   Pavel Hapal (Sigma Olomouc) — 9
   Miroslav Hirko (Slovan Bratislava) — 9
   Jan Marosi (Sigma Olomouc) — 9
18. Gabriel Bertalan (SKP Union Cheb) — 8
   Viliam Hyravy (Banik Ostrava) — 8
   Bartolomej Jurasko (Inter Bratislava) — 8
   Igor Klojch (ГC Nitra) — 8
   Frantisek Myslivecek (Bohemians Praha) — 8
   Jan Sanytrnik (Bohemians Praha) — 8
   Horst Siegl (Sparta Praha) — 8

## CZECHOSLOVAKIA 1ST DIV. 1990/91
### LEAGUE TABLE FINAL

| | P | W | D | L | F | A | Pts |
|---|---|---|---|---|---|---|---|
| Sparta Praha | 30 | 15 | 9 | 6 | 58 | 28 | 39 |
| Slovan Bratislava | 30 | 16 | 6 | 8 | 47 | 27 | 38 |
| Sigma Olomouc | 30 | 16 | 5 | 9 | 52 | 35 | 37 |
| DAC Dunajska Streda | 30 | 12 | 11 | 7 | 39 | 36 | 35 |
| Banik Ostrava | 30 | 14 | 4 | 12 | 50 | 34 | 32 |
| SKP Union Cheb | 30 | 13 | 6 | 11 | 44 | 36 | 32 |
| Inter Bratislava | 30 | 10 | 10 | 10 | 41 | 42 | 30 |
| Dukla Banska Bystrica | 30 | 11 | 8 | 11 | 35 | 37 | 30 |
| Slavia Praha | 30 | 10 | 10 | 10 | 44 | 48 | 30 |
| Tatran Agro Presov | 30 | 10 | 9 | 11 | 42 | 39 | 29 |
| Dukla Praha | 30 | 12 | 5 | 13 | 38 | 52 | 29 |
| TJ Vitkovice | 30 | 12 | 4 | 14 | 47 | 52 | 28 |
| Bohemians Praha | 30 | 10 | 7 | 13 | 35 | 50 | 27 |
| Sp'tak Hradec Kralove | 30 | 10 | 7 | 13 | 33 | 52 | 27 |
| FC Nitra | 30 | 9 | 7 | 14 | 30 | 35 | 25 |
| Zbrojovka Brno | 30 | 2 | 8 | 20 | 19 | 52 | 12 |

Champions : - Sparta Praha
Relegated : - FC Nitra and Zbrojovka Brno

### NAME CHANGE DURING SEASON
TJ Sigma ZTS Olomouc to SK Olomouc Sigma MZ

## CZECHOSLOVAKIA 2ND DIVISION (CZECH) 1990/91
### LEAGUE TABLE FINAL

| | P | W | D | L | F | A | Pts |
|---|---|---|---|---|---|---|---|
| Dynamo Ceske Budejovice | 30 | 18 | 4 | 8 | 57 | 36 | 40 |
| Skoda Plzen | 30 | 14 | 10 | 6 | 40 | 22 | 38 |
| FC Svit Zlin | 30 | 15 | 8 | 7 | 45 | 28 | 38 |
| Ostroj Opava | 30 | 14 | 8 | 8 | 38 | 24 | 36 |
| BSS Brandys nad Labem | 30 | 15 | 4 | 11 | 49 | 47 | 34 |
| Mova Slusovice | 30 | 12 | 8 | 10 | 45 | 32 | 32 |
| Banik Havirov | 30 | 11 | 9 | 10 | 41 | 35 | 31 |
| AS Mlada Boleslav | 30 | 12 | 6 | 12 | 41 | 34 | 30 |
| SK Xaverov Praha | 30 | 13 | 3 | 14 | 51 | 52 | 29 |
| Poldi SONP Kladno | 30 | 9 | 10 | 11 | 43 | 41 | 28 |
| VTZ Chomutov | 30 | 12 | 4 | 14 | 38 | 51 | 28 |
| Slovan Liberec | 30 | 11 | 5 | 14 | 34 | 44 | 27 |
| Synthesia Pardubice | 30 | 10 | 6 | 14 | 40 | 47 | 26 |
| Agro Drnovice | 30 | 10 | 6 | 14 | 28 | 38 | 26 |
| Sklo Union Teplice | 30 | 9 | 7 | 14 | 36 | 54 | 25 |
| Spolana Neratovice | 30 | 5 | 2 | 23 | 23 | 64 | 12 |

Promoted : - Dynamo Ceske Budejovice
Relegated : - Sklo Union Teplice and Spolana Neratovice

### NAME CHANGES
SK Zlin to FC Svit Zlin
JZD Slusovice to FK DAK Slusovice to Mova Slusovice
DP Xaverov-HP Praha to SK Xaverov Praha
VCHZ Pardubice to Synthesia Pardubice
Sokol Drnovice to Agro Drnovice

## CZECHOSLOVAKIA 2ND DIVISION (SLOVAK) 1990/91
### LEAGUE TABLE FINAL

| | P | W | D | L | F | A | Pts |
|---|---|---|---|---|---|---|---|
| Spartak Trnava | 30 | 17 | 7 | 6 | 65 | 25 | 41 |
| Jednota VSS Kosice | 30 | 16 | 3 | 11 | 38 | 37 | 35 |
| Slovan Agro Levice | 30 | 14 | 6 | 10 | 46 | 32 | 34 |
| FK Senec | 30 | 14 | 6 | 10 | 40 | 36 | 34 |
| SH Senica | 30 | 13 | 5 | 12 | 41 | 30 | 31 |
| Sparta Povazska Bystrica | 30 | 12 | 7 | 11 | 44 | 34 | 31 |
| Agro Hurbanovo | 30 | 11 | 9 | 10 | 32 | 31 | 31 |
| SK Zilina | 30 | 12 | 6 | 12 | 61 | 46 | 30 |
| Duslo Sala | 30 | 12 | 6 | 12 | 36 | 39 | 30 |
| Lokomotiva Kosice | 30 | 14 | 2 | 14 | 40 | 45 | 30 |
| SKP Bratislava | 30 | 10 | 9 | 11 | 35 | 34 | 29 |
| Magnezit SM Jelsava | 30 | 12 | 5 | 13 | 25 | 40 | 29 |
| Chemlon Humenné | 30 | 9 | 10 | 11 | 33 | 34 | 28 |
| Tesla Stropkov | 30 | 10 | 8 | 12 | 24 | 38 | 28 |
| SK Zemplin Michalovce | 30 | 9 | 6 | 15 | 33 | 54 | 24 |
| Spoje Bratislava | 30 | 6 | 3 | 21 | 23 | 61 | 15 |

Promoted : - Spartak TAZ Trnava
Relegated : - SK Zemplin Michalovce and Spoje Bratislava

### NAME CHANGES
ZTS Kosice to Jednota VSS Kosice
PZN Senec to FK Senec
ZVL Povazska Bystrica to Sparta Povazska Bystrica
ZVL Zilina to SK Zilina
CH Bratislava to SKP Bratislava

# CZECHOSLOVAKIA 3RD DIVISION (CZECH) 1990/91

## GROUP A
### LEAGUE TABLE FINAL

| | P | W | D | L | F | A | Pts |
|---|---|---|---|---|---|---|---|
| Svarc Benesov | 30 | 19 | 6 | 5 | 61 | 25 | 44 |
| TJ Nachod | 30 | 20 | 2 | 8 | 56 | 30 | 42 |
| UD Pribram | 30 | 17 | 2 | 11 | 65 | 48 | 36 |
| VTJ Karlovy Vary | 30 | 16 | 4 | 10 | 63 | 48 | 36 |
| Banik Most | 30 | 15 | 6 | 9 | 47 | 35 | 36 |
| TJ Rakovnik | 30 | 13 | 8 | 9 | 56 | 44 | 34 |
| LIAZ Jablonec | 30 | 15 | 3 | 12 | 44 | 42 | 33 |
| VS Tabor | 30 | 13 | 6 | 11 | 44 | 37 | 32 |
| FK Chmel Blsany | 30 | 12 | 8 | 10 | 43 | 39 | 32 |
| Vagonka Ceska Lipa | 30 | 13 | 5 | 12 | 49 | 47 | 31 |
| Agro Turnov | 30 | 15 | 0 | 15 | 45 | 46 | 30 |
| SKPP Susice | 30 | 11 | 7 | 12 | 47 | 43 | 29 |
| TJ Montaze Praha | 30 | 8 | 7 | 15 | 31 | 56 | 23 |
| Sokol Sveradice | 30 | 5 | 8 | 17 | 44 | 65 | 18 |
| Kovostroj Decin | 30 | 6 | 3 | 21 | 38 | 72 | 15 |
| SKP Union Cheb 'B' | 30 | 1 | 8 | 21 | 27 | 83 | 10 |

**NAME CHANGES**
CSAD Benesov to Svarc Benesov
Ruda Hvezda Susice to SKPP Susice

Promoted :- Svarc Benesov

## GROUP B
### LEAGUE TABLE FINAL

| | P | W | D | L | F | A | Pts |
|---|---|---|---|---|---|---|---|
| TZ Trinec | 30 | 21 | 6 | 3 | 60 | 19 | 48 |
| SKP Znojmo Prace | 30 | 20 | 6 | 4 | 65 | 27 | 46 |
| ZD Bohumin | 30 | 13 | 11 | 6 | 41 | 27 | 37 |
| Dukla Praha 'B' | 30 | 14 | 6 | 10 | 57 | 44 | 34 |
| Selce | 30 | 14 | 6 | 10 | 44 | 34 | 34 |
| SS Uherske Hradiste | 30 | 14 | 5 | 11 | 47 | 30 | 33 |
| Banik Ostrava 'B' | 30 | 13 | 7 | 10 | 53 | 39 | 33 |
| Banik CSA Karvina | 30 | 12 | 9 | 9 | 34 | 34 | 33 |
| Jiskra Stare Mesto | 30 | 12 | 7 | 11 | 37 | 31 | 31 |
| KPS Brno | 30 | 13 | 5 | 12 | 54 | 37 | 31 |
| Unex Unicov | 30 | 11 | 9 | 10 | 34 | 44 | 31 |
| Slavia Praha 'B' | 30 | 11 | 7 | 12 | 43 | 43 | 29 |
| Sigma Dolni Benesov | 30 | 9 | 8 | 13 | 35 | 40 | 26 |
| Zdas Zdar nad Sazavou | 30 | 9 | 8 | 13 | 31 | 39 | 26 |
| VP Frydek-Mistek | 30 | 7 | 6 | 17 | 27 | 56 | 20 |
| Bohemians Praha 'B' | 30 | 6 | 4 | 20 | 19 | 30 | 16 |
| VTJ Sigma Hodonin | 30 | 3 | 1 | 26 | 24 | 95 | 7 |

**NAME CHANGES**
Ruda Hvezda Znojmo to SKP Znojmo Prace
KS Brno to KPS Brno
Stojirny Unicov to Unex Unicov

Promoted :- TZ Trinec

# CZECHOSLOVAKIA 3RD DIVISION (SLOVAK) 1990/91

## GROUP A
### LEAGUE TABLE FINAL

| | P | W | D | L | F | A | Pts |
|---|---|---|---|---|---|---|---|
| Banik Prievidza | 30 | 18 | 5 | 7 | 59 | 23 | 41 |
| Spartak ZTS Dubnica | 30 | 15 | 6 | 9 | 54 | 35 | 36 |
| Gumarne Puchov | 30 | 11 | 12 | 7 | 45 | 19 | 34 |
| Elektrosvit N.Zamky | 30 | 12 | 10 | 8 | 36 | 32 | 34 |
| Spartak Tatra Banovce | 30 | 13 | 7 | 10 | 49 | 41 | 33 |
| Tempo Partizanske | 30 | 11 | 11 | 8 | 47 | 41 | 33 |
| SSK Hutnik Sered | 30 | 12 | 8 | 10 | 37 | 27 | 32 |
| Doprastav Bratislava | 30 | 13 | 6 | 11 | 39 | 38 | 32 |
| Tesla Vrable | 30 | 11 | 9 | 10 | 36 | 37 | 31 |
| BAZ Dubravka | 30 | 10 | 11 | 9 | 41 | 42 | 31 |
| VTJ Trencin | 30 | 11 | 7 | 12 | 45 | 52 | 29 |
| Slovan Bratislava 'B' | 30 | 10 | 9 | 11 | 36 | 40 | 29 |
| TTS Trencin | 30 | 9 | 11 | 10 | 38 | 48 | 29 |
| TS Topolcany | 30 | 10 | 6 | 14 | 53 | 53 | 26 |
| Iskra Matador Bratislava | 30 | 10 | 6 | 14 | 27 | 38 | 26 |
| Agroprogres Zlate Klasy | 30 | 2 | 8 | 20 | 16 | 78 | 12 |

Promoted :- Banik Prievidza

## GROUP B
### LEAGUE TABLE FINAL

| | P | W | D | L | F | A | Pts |
|---|---|---|---|---|---|---|---|
| VSZ Kosice | 30 | 20 | 6 | 4 | 72 | 33 | 46 |
| LB Spisska Nova Ves | 30 | 17 | 10 | 3 | 60 | 32 | 44 |
| BZ Ruzomberok | 30 | 17 | 1 | 12 | 60 | 34 | 35 |
| Partizan Bardejov | 30 | 15 | 5 | 10 | 50 | 34 | 35 |
| ZVL Bytca | 30 | 13 | 7 | 10 | 40 | 35 | 33 |
| Slavoj Trebisov | 30 | 13 | 4 | 13 | 51 | 49 | 30 |
| Bardejovska Nova Ves | 30 | 11 | 7 | 12 | 46 | 43 | 29 |
| Bukoza Vranov | 30 | 13 | 3 | 14 | 47 | 51 | 29 |
| Agrokombinat Budkovce | 30 | 14 | 1 | 15 | 36 | 40 | 29 |
| Slovan ZZ Giraltovce | 30 | 10 | 9 | 11 | 34 | 42 | 29 |
| FK Cadca | 30 | 11 | 5 | 14 | 52 | 45 | 27 |
| Slovan Rimavska Sobota | 30 | 10 | 7 | 13 | 39 | 45 | 27 |
| Kysucke Nove Mesto | 30 | 12 | 3 | 15 | 40 | 54 | 27 |
| Banik Handlova | 30 | 9 | 8 | 13 | 54 | 58 | 26 |
| PPS Detva | 30 | 6 | 8 | 16 | 27 | 59 | 20 |
| ZTS Martin | 30 | 6 | 6 | 18 | 36 | 58 | 18 |

**NAME CHANGES**
ZZO Cadca to FK Cadca
ZTS Detva to PPS Detva

Promoted :- VSZ Kosice

# CZECHOSLOVAKIA : SLOVAK CUP 1990/91

## 1ST ROUND
| | | | |
|---|---|---|---|
| BZ Ruzomberok | 2 | SK Zemplin Michal. | 0 |
| Partizan Bardejov | 3 | FK Cadca | 0 |
| TTS Trencin | 0 | SK Zilina | 6 |
| SKP Bratislava | 1 | Slovan Duslo Sala | 1 |
| | | Selce | ... |
| Silvan Rimav. Sobota | 1 | Tesla Vrable | 4 |
| | | Magnezit Jelsava | 1 |
| Gumarne Puchov | 0 | Slovan Levice | 0 |
| | | Druzst. pri Hornade | 1 |
| Devin | 0 | Banik Prievidza | 1 |
| Strojar Nitra | 1 | Chemlon Humenné | 1 |
| | | FK SH Senica | 0 |
| | | Spoje Bratislava | 3 |

SKP Bratislava win 3-2 on penalties
Magnezit Jelsava win 6-7 on penalties
Gumarne Puchov win 4-2 on penalties
Banik Prievidza win 4-5 on penalties

## 2ND ROUND
| | | | |
|---|---|---|---|
| Magnezit Jelsava | 1 | SKP Bratislava | 0 |
| Spisska Nova Ves | 3 | Agrok'mb. Budkovce | 0 |
| Jednota VSS Kosice | 3 | Tesla Stropkov | 4 |
| Spoje Bratislava | 1 | Banik Prievidza | 0 |
| Elektro. Nové Zámky | 0 | PZN Senec | ... |

PZN Senec win 3-4 on penalties
Lokomotiva Kosice win 4-2 on penalties

## 3RD ROUND
| | | | |
|---|---|---|---|
| SK Zilina | 0 | FC Nitra | 0 |
| Spoje Bratislava | 1 | Banik Prievidza | 1 |

FC Nitra win 2-3 on penalties
Spoje Bratislava win 5-4 on penalties

## 1/4 FINALS
| | | | |
|---|---|---|---|
| Sparta Pov. Bystrica | 0 | Slovan Bratislava | 1 |
| Spartak TAZ Trnava | 2 | Tatran Agro Presov | 1 |

## SEMI-FINALS
Spartak Trnava v Dukla Banska Bystrica
Spartak Trnava win 4-1 on penalties
Slovan Bratislava v FC Nitra
FC Nitra win 3-4 on penalties

| | 1ST LEG | 2ND LEG | AGG. |
|---|---|---|---|
| Dukla B'ska Bystrica v Spartak Trnava | 1-1 | 1-1 | 2-2 |
| Slovan Bratislava v FC Nitra | 2-2 | 1-3 | 3-5 |

## FINAL    8/5/91 (at Ruzomberok)
Spartak Trnava .....1    FC Nitra .....0

Trnava : Simurka, Frcala, Ovad (Zemanik 85), Michalicka, Klinovsky (Tibensky 63), Mokros, Gabriel, Duchon, Sadlon, Solar.
Nitra : Paluch, Mihok, Hipp, Kostolani, Hucko, Dekys, Sovic, Blaho, Belak, Klejch, Majoros.

1-0    Gabriel 25

Referee : Krchnak
Attendance : 2,630

# CZECHOSLOVAKIA : CZECH CUP 1990/91

## 1ST ROUND

| | | | |
|---|---|---|---|
| Hradisko | 4 | Avia Cakovice | 1 |
| Duchcov | 2 | Jirkov | 1 |
| Slavia Karlovy Vary | 4 | ChZ CSSP Litvinov | 0 |
| Protivin | 1 | Fezko Strakonice | 4 |

## 2ND ROUND

| | | | |
|---|---|---|---|
| Slavia Karlovy Vary | 1 | Roudnice | 0 |
| VTJ Slany | 3 | Brnany | 1 |
| Rudna | 2 | Sp'tk BBS Br'dys n.L. | 1 |
| Lokomotiva Trutnov | 0 | TJ Benesov Svarc | 0 |
| *Lokomotiva Trutnov win 5-4 on penalties* | | | |
| Novy Jicin | 6 | TZ Trinec | 1 |
| Sigma Hranice | 2 | FC Svit Zlin | 0 |
| Cesky Krumlov | 7 | SK UD Pribram | 1 |
| CZ Strakonice | 4 | Milevsko | 2 |
| Jiskra Kyjov | 0 | SS Uherske Hradiste | 0 |
| *Jiskra Kyjov win 3-1 on penalties* | | | |
| Jiskra Holice | 3 | Spartak Chocen | 1 |
| Svitavy | 1 | Tesla Pardubice | 0 |
| Spartak Radotin | 1 | LIAZ Jablonec | 1 |
| *LIAZ Jablonec win 2-3 on penalties* | | | |
| JZD Olesnik | 0 | VS Tabor | 3 |
| Spartak Jihlava | 3 | KS Brno | 1 |
| Agrostroj Prostejov | 2 | Hulin | 1 |
| Spartak Pelhrimov | 3 | Agro Drnovice | 6 |
| Tatran Prachatice | 2 | VTJ Tachov | 0 |
| Hradisko | 1 | TJ Montaze Praha | 2 |
| *Hradisko win 12-11 on penalties* | | | |
| Sp'tk Uhersky Brod | 1 | Jiskra Stare Mesto | 3 |
| Tatran Postorna | 2 | Banik CSA Karvina | 0 |
| Nova huf Ostrava | 1 | ZD Bohumin | 2 |
| Kablo Krocehlavy | 5 | SK Plzen | 4 |
| Fezko Strakonice | 1 | VTJ Pisek | 0 |
| *VTJ Pisek win 4-1 on penalties* | | | |
| Sig. Dolni Benesov | 1 | VTZ Chomutov | 2 |
| Viktoria Zizkov | | *win 4-1 on penalties* | |
| Sepap Steti | 0 | VTJ Karlovy Vary | 5 |
| Slavoj Litomerice | 1 | TJ Rakovnik | 1 |
| *Slavoj Litomerice win 4-3 on penalties* | | | |
| Okula Nyrsko | 0 | SKPP Susice | 7 |
| Spartak Prerov | 1 | SKP Znojmo | 2 |
| Slavoj Bruntal | 0 | Strojirny Unicov | 1 |
| *Strojirny Unicov win 2-4 on penalties* | | | |
| Duchcov | 1 | Vagonka Ceska Lipa | 3 |
| TJ Prestice | 1 | JZD Blsany | 3 |

## 3RD ROUND

| | | | |
|---|---|---|---|
| Kovo Decin | 0 | SONP Poldi Kladno | 2 |
| Motorlet Praha | 1 | TJ Rudna | 1 |
| *Motorlet Praha win 7-6 on penalties* | | | |
| TJ Agro Kolin | 1 | VCHZ Pardubice | 2 |
| VTJ Hodonin | 0 | Sigma Olomouc | 2 |
| VS Tabor | 0 | Dyn. Ceske Budejov | 1 |
| Agrozet Prostejov | 1 | Zbrojovka Brno | 6 |
| Svitavy | 0 | Spartak Hr. Kralove | 6 |
| Tatran Prachatice | 1 | LIAZ Jablonec | 1 |
| *Tatran Prachatice win 5-3 on penalties* | | | |
| Sp'tk Uhersky Brod | 2 | Jiskra Stare Mesto | 2 |
| *Jiskra Stare Mesto win 3-5 on penalties* | | | |
| ZD Bohumin | 1 | TJ Vitkovice | 3 |
| VTJ Pisek | 2 | Skoda Plzen | 1 |
| Kompresory Praha | 1 | VTJ Karlovy Vary | 1 |
| VTJ Zatec | 3 | SKPP Susice | 0 |
| SKP Znojmo Prace | 0 | Ostroj Opava | 1 |
| FC Agro Turnov | 2 | Sklo Union Teplice | 2 |
| AS Mlada Boleslav | 4 | VTJ Slany | 1 |
| US Praha | 1 | Dukla Praha | 6 |
| Lokomotiva Trutnov | 0 | Sparta Kutna Hora | 0 |
| Sigma Hranice | 0 | TZ Trinec | 1 |
| CZ Strakonice | 0 | SK UD Pribram | 8 |
| Spartak Jihlava | 1 | Jiskra Kyjov | 0 |
| Jiskra Holice | 0 | Agro Drnovice | 0 |
| Hradisko | 1 | Slavia Praha | 8 |
| Tatran Postorna | 2 | FK DAK Slusovice | 2 |
| *Tatran Postorna win 1-0 on penalties* | | | |
| Orlova Dul D'brava | 1 | Banik Havirov | 4 |
| Kablo Krocehlavy | 1 | Viktoria Zizkov | 1 |
| *Kablo Krocehlavy win 5-3 on penalties* | | | |
| Slavoj Litomerice | 2 | Sparta Praha | 10 |
| EME Melnik | 2 | SK Xaverov Praha | 5 |
| Strojirny Unicov | 2 | Banik Ostrava | 2 |
| *Banik Ostrava win 2-3 on penalties* | | | |

## 4TH ROUND

| | | | |
|---|---|---|---|
| SONP Poldi Kladno | 5 | Motorlet Praha | 1 |
| Lokomotiva Trutnov | 4 | TZ Trinec | 1 |
| SK UD Pribram | 4 | Spartak Jihlava | 1 |
| *Spartak Jihlava win 7-6 on penalties* | | | |
| Jiskra Holice | 1 | Spartak Hr. Kralove | 3 |
| Tatran Prachatice | 2 | Tatran Postorna | 1 |
| Banik Havirov | 2 | Kablo Krocehlavy | 1 |
| VTJ Karlovy Vary | 2 | VTJ Vitkovice | 1 |
| Ostroj Opava | 6 | Sparta Praha | 4 |
| Banik Ostrava | 0 | Sparta Praha | 4 |
| *Banik Ostrava win 3-4 on penalties* | | | |
| AS Mlada Boleslav | 1 | Dukla Praha | 2 |
| TJ Agro Kolin | 1 | Sigma Olomouc | 4 |
| Dyn. Ceske Budejov | 6 | Zbrojovka Brno | 1 |
| Jiskra Holice | 1 | Jiskra Stare Mesto | 3 |
| Tatran Prachatice | 2 | VTJ Pisek | 2 |
| Banik Havirov | 2 | SK Xaverov Praha | 4 |
| FC Agro Turnov | | Bohemians Praha | 2 |
| *FC Agro Turnov win 7-6 on penalties* | | | |
| Vagonka Ceska Lipa | 0 | Bohemians Praha | 2 |
| JZD Blsany | 1 | SKP Union Cheb | 1 |
| Sokol Sveradice | 2 | Banik Most | 1 |

## 5TH ROUND

| | | | |
|---|---|---|---|
| SK Xaverov Praha | 1 | Banik Ostrava | 2 |
| Jiskra Stare Mesto | 0 | Banik Havirov | 2 |
| Spartak Jihlava | 1 | Dyn. Ceske Budejov | 2 |
| Sokol Sveradice | 1 | Bohemians Praha | 0 |
| Spartak Hr. Kralove | 1 | Slavia Praha | 3 |
| SONP Poldi Kladno | 2 | Dukla Praha | 2 |
| *Dukla Praha win 4-5 on penalties* | | | |
| Lokomotiva Trutnov | 1 | Sigma Olomouc | 0 |
| Sparta Praha | 3 | VTJ Pisek | 0 |

## 1/4 FINALS

| | | | |
|---|---|---|---|
| Dyn. Ceske Budejov | 0 | Slavia Praha | 0 |
| *Dynamo Ceske Budejovice win 8-7 on penalties* | | | |
| Sokol Sveradice | 1 | Banik Ostrava | 4 |
| Lokomotiva Trutnov | 0 | Dukla Praha | 1 |
| Banik Havirov | 0 | Sparta Praha | 2 |

## SEMI-FINALS

| | | | |
|---|---|---|---|
| Dyn. Ceske Budejov | 3 | Dukla Praha | 0 |
| Sparta Praha | 0 | Banik Ostrava | 1 |

## FINAL 8/5/91 (at Teplice)

Banik Ostrava ......4   Dynamo Ceske Budejovice......2

Ostrava : Schmucker, Zalesky, Sialni, Vrto, Remes (Ollender 46), Skarabela, Necas, Hyravy, Casko, Kula, Chylek.

C.Budejovice : Hejnicek, Koller, Drahokoupil, Konvalina, Wohlgemuth (Tomasek 73), Fujdiar, Poborsky, Korinek, Jindracek, Urban, Vacha (Lerch 15)

| | | |
|---|---|---|
| 0-1 | Urban | 10 |
| 0-2 | Fujdiar | 50 |
| 1-2 | Casko | 57 |
| 2-2 | Sialini | 66 |
| 3-2 | Kula | 71 |
| 4-2 | Skarabela | 76 |

Referee : Pelisek
Attendance : 1,821

## CZECHOSLOVAKIA CUP FINAL 1990/91

Played annually between the winners of the Czech and Slovak Cups

Banik Ostrava ......6   Spartak Trnava......1   (at Frydek-Mistek 22/5/91)

Ostrava : Schmucker, Zalesky, Sia ini, Vrto, Kula (Sloncik 77), Remes, Hyravy, Skarabela, Necas, Casko, Chylek (Ollender 46)

Trnava : Simurka, Frcala, Hutta, Mokros, Michalicka, Klinovsky, Ovad, Gabriel (Balic 77), Duchon (Zemanik 77), Sadlon, Solar.

| | | |
|---|---|---|
| 1-0 | Hyravy | 2 |
| 2-0 | Chylek | 5 |
| 3-0 | Kula | 28 |
| 4-0 | Hyravy | 67 |
| 4-1 | Vrto o.g. | 76 |
| 5-1 | Casko | 80 |
| 6-1 | Skarabela | 88 |

Referee : Christov
Attendance : 7,000

# INTERNATIONAL LINE-UPS 1990

| Date | Match | Venue | Referee | Competition | Scorers |
|---|---|---|---|---|---|
| 21/2/90 | SPAIN 1 CZECHOSLOVAKIA 0 | Alicante | Phillipoz (Switzerland) | Friendly | |
| 4/4/90 | CZECHOSLOVAKIA 0 EGYPT 1 | Brno | Kappel (Austria) | Friendly | |
| 25/4/90 | ENGLAND 4 CZECHOSLOVAKIA 2 | London | Girard (France) | Friendly | (Skuhravy, Kubík) |
| 26/5/90 | WESTERN GERMANY 1 CZECHOSLOVAKIA 0 | Düsseldorf | Galler (Switzerland) | Friendly | |
| 10/6/90 | USA 1 CZECHOSLOVAKIA 5 | Firenze | Röthlisberger (Switzerland) | World Cup | (Skuhravy 2, Bílek, Hasek, M.Luhovy) |
| 15/6/90 | AUSTRIA 0 CZECHOSLOVAKIA 1 | Firenze | Smith (Scotland) | World Cup | (Bílek) |
| 19/6/90 | ITALY 2 CZECHOSLOVAKIA 0 | Roma | Quiniou (France) | World Cup | |
| 23/6/90 | COSTA RICA 1 CZECHOSLOVAKIA 4 | Bari | Kirschen (DDR) | World Cup | (Skuhravy 3, Kubík) |
| 1/7/90 | WESTERN GERMANY 1 CZECHOSLOVAKIA 0 | Milano | Kohl (Austria) | World Cup | |
| 29/8/90 | FINLAND 1 CZECHOSLOVAKIA 1 | Kuusankoski | Mikkelsen (Denmark) | Friendly | (Kuka) |
| 26/9/90 | CZECHOSLOVAKIA 1 ICELAND 0 | Kosice | Kolev (Bulgaria) | EuroCh.Q. | (Danek) |
| 13/10/90 | FRANCE 2 CZECHOSLOVAKIA 1 | Paris | Courtney (England) | EuroCh.Q. | (Skuhravy) |
| 14/11/90 | CZECHOSLOVAKIA 3 SPAIN 2 | Praha | Tritschler (Germany) | EuroCh.Q. | (Danek 2, Moravcík) |

## Players — Caps and Goals at 31/12/90

| Player | CAPS at 31/12/90 | GOALS at 31/12/90 |
|---|---|---|
| Jan Stejskal | 24 | |
| Miroslav Kadlec | 28 | |
| Július Bielik | 18 | |
| Vladimír Kinier | 10 | |
| Václav Nemecek | 20 | |
| Michal Bílek | 29 | 10 |
| Ivan Hasek | 50 | 3 |
| Jozef Chovanec | 48 | 2 |
| L'ubomír Moravcik | 24 | 6 |
| Milan Luhovy | 29 | 11 |
| Tomás Skuhravy | 31 | 11 |
| Vladimír Weiss | 19 | 1 |
| Pavel Cerny | 3 | |
| Ján Kocian | 20 | 3 |
| Jiri Nemec | 2 | |
| Viliam Hyravy | | |
| Václav Danek | 18 | |
| Lubos Luhovy | 1 | |
| Ludek Miklosko | 33 | |
| Frantisek Straka | 35 | |
| Lubos Kubík | 27 | 9 |
| Ivo Knoflícek | 34 | 7 |
| Stanislav Griga | 34 | 8 |
| Michal Hipp | 4 | |
| Ivo Stas | 1 | |
| Dusan Tittel | 3 | |
| Karel Kula | 28 | |
| Roman Sedlácek | 1 | |
| Pavel Kuka | 2 | 1 |
| Milos Belák | 2 | |
| Jaroslav Silhavy | 1 | |
| Ladislav Pecko | 1 | |

## CZECHOSLOVAKIA : All Time Records as at 31/12/90 - CAPS

1. Zdenek Nehoda (Dukla Praha/SC Amaliendorf) — 90
2. Ladislav Novák (ATK/ÚDA/Dukla Praha) — 75
3. Marián Masny (Slovan Bratislava) — 75
4. Frantisek Plánicka (Slavia Praha) — 73
5. Karol Dobias (Spartak Trnava/Bohemians Praha) — 67
6. Josef Masopust (Uda/Dukla Praha) — 63
7. Ivo Viktor (Dukla Praha) — 63

## CZECHOSLOVAKIA : All Time Records as at 31/12/90 - GOALS

1. Antonin Puc (Slavia Praha) — (59) 34
2. Zdenek Nehoda (Dukla Praha/SC Amaliendorf) — (90) 31
3. Oldrich Nejedly (Sparta Praha) — (43) 28
4. Josef Silny (Slavia Praha/Sparta Praha) — (50) 28
5. Adolf Scherer (CH Bratislava/Slovnaft Bratislava) — (36) 22
6. Frantisek Svoboda (Slavia Praha) — (42) 21
7. Marián Masny (Slovan Bratislava) — (75) 18

# DENMARK Correspondent : FRANK JÜRGENSEN

| DENMARK 1st Division Season 1990 | OB | BRØNDBY | LYNGBY | VEJLE | AGF | B 1903 | SILKEBORG | FREM | NAESTVED | IKAST | AAB | HERFØLGE | KB | VIBORG |
|---|---|---|---|---|---|---|---|---|---|---|---|---|---|---|
| OB ODENSE | | 0-3 | 2-2 | 0-0 | 0-0 | 0-0 | 1-0 | 0-2 | 3-1 | 1-1 | 1-1 | 7-1 | 4-0 | 3-1 |
| BRØNDBYERNES IF | 3-0 | | 2-0 | 4-2 | 1-1 | 2-2 | 2-0 | 1-0 | 0-0 | 2-0 | 2-2 | 4-0 | 1-0 | 4-1 |
| LYNGBY BK | 2-0 | 2-3 | | 0-1 | 0-1 | 0-0 | 1-2 | 3-0 | 2-2 | 2-3 | 2-2 | 1-0 | 2-0 | 5-1 |
| VEJLE BK | 1-1 | 0-0 | 1-1 | | 2-1 | 2-2 | 1-4 | 1-1 | 2-1 | 3-0 | 2-1 | 2-1 | 2-0 | 2-0 |
| AGF AARHUS | 0-0 | 1-2 | 1-3 | 1-0 | | 1-4 | 3-1 | 1-1 | 0-0 | 1-1 | 0-2 | 4-0 | 1-0 | 2-0 |
| B 1903 GENTOFTE | 2-0 | 1-3 | 2-0 | 0-0 | 1-1 | | 2-0 | 1-1 | 2-0 | 2-2 | 1-0 | 2-1 | 3-3 | 7-0 |
| SILKEBORG IF | 0-1 | 1-1 | 2-2 | 2-2 | 2-2 | 2-1 | | 1-2 | 3-0 | 2-0 | 1-0 | 1-0 | 4-0 | 1-0 |
| BK FREM KØBENHAVN | 1-1 | 1-0 | 0-0 | 2-2 | 0-0 | 1-1 | 1-2 | | 1-1 | 1-0 | 2-2 | 3-3 | 1-1 | 3-1 |
| NAESTVED IF | 2-0 | 1-4 | 0-6 | 2-0 | 3-2 | 0-0 | 0-0 | 0-0 | | 1-1 | 0-2 | 0-0 | 0-1 | 0-0 |
| IKAST FS | 1-0 | 0-0 | 1-2 | 1-0 | 0-1 | 3-1 | 1-0 | 1-1 | 3-1 | | 4-0 | 4-1 | 0-0 | 5-1 |
| AAB AALBORG | 1-2 | 1-3 | 0 1 | 1-1 | 2-1 | 2-1 | 1-1 | 1-0 | 1-0 | 2-2 | | 1-1 | 2-1 | 0-0 |
| HERFØLGE BK | 1-0 | 0-0 | 0-2 | 2-1 | 0-0 | 1-2 | 1-1 | 1-1 | 0-1 | 1-0 | 3-3 | | 2-6 | 1-0 |
| KB FREDERIKSBERG | 1-2 | 0-1 | 2-2 | 2-1 | 0-4 | 0-3 | 1-2 | 0-5 | 0-2 | 1-2 | 2-1 | 0-0 | | 2-2 |
| VIBORG FF | 1-3 | 0-2 | 2-1 | 2-1 | 0-1 | 2-1 | 0-0 | 0-2 | 1-2 | 0-2 | 0-1 | 1-0 | 3-1 | |

## DENMARK 1ST DIVISION 1990
### LEAGUE TABLE FINAL

| | | | | | | | |
|---|---|---|---|---|---|---|---|
| Brøndbyernes IF | 26 | 17 | 8 | 1 | 50 | 16 | 42 |
| B 1903 Gentofte | 26 | 10 | 11 | 5 | 44 | 27 | 31 |
| Ikast FS | 26 | 11 | 8 | 7 | 38 | 27 | 30 |
| Silkeborg IF | 26 | 11 | 8 | 7 | 35 | 26 | 30 |
| BK Frem København | 26 | 7 | 15 | 4 | 33 | 25 | 29 |
| Lyngby BK | 26 | 10 | 8 | 8 | 44 | 30 | 28 |
| AGF Aarhus | 26 | 9 | 10 | 7 | 31 | 25 | 28 |
| OB Odense | 26 | 9 | 9 | 8 | 32 | 28 | 27 |
| Vejle BK | 26 | 8 | 10 | 8 | 32 | 32 | 26 |
| AaB Aalborg | 26 | 8 | 10 | 8 | 32 | 34 | 26 |
| Naestved IF | 26 | 6 | 10 | 10 | 20 | 34 | 22 |
| Herfølge BK | 26 | 4 | 9 | 13 | 21 | 47 | 17 |
| KB Frederiksberg | 26 | 4 | 6 | 16 | 24 | 52 | 14 |
| Viborg FF | 26 | 5 | 4 | 17 | 19 | 52 | 14 |

Champions : - Brøndbyernes IF

Note : Summer Season to be made Autumn/Spring Season commencing 1991/92. A shortened championship version will therefore be played during Spring Season 1991. At the same time leagues are to be restructured, consisting of 1 Premier Division, 1 1st Division and 2 2nd Divisions, all of 10 clubs each, and 4 3rd Divisions of 16 clubs.

### TOP SCORERS
1. Bent Christensen (Brøndbyernes IF) — 17
2. Michael Pedersen (Ikast FS) — 16
3. Per Frandsen (B 1903) — 15
4. Peter Nielsen (Lyngby BK) — 14
5. Flemming Christensen (Lyngby BK) — 13
   Jørgen Juul Jensen (B 1903) — 13
   Søren Lyng (BK Frem) — 13
8. Søren Andersen (AGF) — 10
   Torben Frank (Brøndbyernes IF) — 10
10. Peter Møller (AaB) — 9

| PLAY-OFFS FOR 2 PREMIER DIVISION PLACES | 1ST LEG | 2ND LEG | AGG. |
|---|---|---|---|
| B 1913 v Vejle BK (Vejle BK win 3-4 on penalties) | 0-1 | 1-0 (aet.) | 1-1 |
| AaB v B 1909 | 4-0 | 6-5 | 10-5 |

| DENMARK 2nd Division Season 1990 | B 1913 | BRØNSHØJ | B 1909 | OKS | HELSINGØR | ESBJERG | FREMAD A | AVARTA | ROSKILDE | VANLØSE | N' SUNDBY | B 93 | SVENDBORG | GREVE |
|---|---|---|---|---|---|---|---|---|---|---|---|---|---|---|
| B 1913 ODENSE | | 3-0 | 1-1 | 3-1 | 2-1 | 3-2 | 1-1 | 1-1 | 1-0 | 2-2 | 2-2 | 6-1 | 2-0 | 4-0 |
| BRØNSHØJ BK | 1-1 | | 1-0 | 0-5 | 2-0 | 1-6 | 1-1 | 1-0 | 3-1 | 1-2 | 2-5 | 3-0 | 3-1 | 1-1 |
| B 1909 ODENSE | 1-1 | 2-1 | | 4-4 | 3-1 | 2-0 | 4-2 | 3-3 | 3-2 | 5-1 | 3-0 | 2-2 | 3-2 | 2-1 |
| OKS ODENSE | 0-1 | 0-5 | 0-0 | | 0-0 | 1-0 | 0-1 | 3-0 | 1-1 | 1-1 | 1-1 | 1-1 | 3-0 | 0-0 |
| HELSINGØR IF | 0-1 | 1-0 | 3-1 | 2-1 | | 2-1 | 1-1 | 1-1 | 3-0 | 0-0 | 1-0 | 5-3 | 0-0 | 1-0 |
| ESBJERG FB | 0-0 | 1-2 | 1-2 | 2-0 | 2-0 | | 1-2 | 3-1 | 2-0 | 1-2 | 2-0 | 1-0 | 1-1 | 0-0 |
| BK FREMAD AMAGER | 2-1 | 0-1 | 1-1 | 1-3 | 1-1 | 3-4 | | 3-2 | 3-1 | 0-1 | 0-1 | 2-1 | 1-1 | 3-2 |
| BK AVARTA RØDOVRE | 0-2 | 1-3 | 1-1 | 2-2 | 0-1 | 1-2 | 1-1 | | 4-0 | 0-2 | 1-1 | 2-2 | 1-2 | 2-0 |
| ROSKILDE B 1906 | 0-1 | 2-1 | 1-1 | 0-0 | 1-2 | 1-3 | 1-2 | 2-0 | | 0-1 | 1-0 | 3-0 | 1-1 | 1-1 |
| VANLØSE IF | 2-2 | 1-3 | 0-0 | 3-0 | 2-2 | 0-2 | 0-0 | 2-0 | 2-2 | | 2-1 | 1-0 | 1-2 | 1-1 |
| NØRRESUNDBY BK | 3-0 | 0-1 | 0-4 | 0-2 | 0-0 | 4-0 | 1-1 | 2-1 | 2-0 | 3-0 | | 0-1 | 0-2 | 1-1 |
| B 93 KØBENHAVN | 2-2 | 3-3 | 1-1 | 1-0 | 0-2 | 2-4 | 3-2 | 0-3 | 0-0 | 2-2 | 1-0 | | 1-2 | 0-0 |
| SVENDBORG FB | 1-1 | 0-0 | 2-1 | 1-1 | 3-0 | 1-1 | 2-0 | 4-0 | 3-3 | 0-1 | 1-1 | 1-0 | | 2-2 |
| GREVE IF | 4-2 | 2-4 | 2-4 | 1-3 | 2-4 | 1-2 | 3-1 | 3-0 | 3-4 | 0-0 | 2-2 | 4-0 | 2-5 | |

## DENMARK 2ND DIVISION 1990
### LEAGUE TABLE FINAL

| | | | | | | | |
|---|---|---|---|---|---|---|---|
| B 1909 Odense | 26 | 12 | 11 | 3 | 54 | 34 | 35 |
| B 1913 Odense | 26 | 12 | 11 | 3 | 46 | 28 | 35 |
| Helsingør IF | 26 | 12 | 8 | 6 | 34 | 27 | 32 |
| Svendborg fB | 26 | 10 | 11 | 5 | 40 | 30 | 31 |
| Brønshøj BK | 26 | 13 | 5 | 8 | 44 | 39 | 31 |
| Vanløse IF | 26 | 10 | 11 | 5 | 32 | 30 | 31 |
| Esbjerg fB | 26 | 13 | 4 | 9 | 44 | 32 | 30 |
| BK Fremad Amager | 26 | 9 | 9 | 8 | 36 | 38 | 27 |
| OKS Odense | 26 | 7 | 11 | 8 | 33 | 31 | 25 |
| Nørresundby BK | 26 | 6 | 8 | 12 | 29 | 33 | 20 |
| Greve IF | 26 | 4 | 10 | 12 | 38 | 49 | 18 |
| Roskilde B 1906 | 26 | 5 | 8 | 13 | 28 | 43 | 18 |
| B 93 København | 26 | 4 | 9 | 13 | 27 | 52 | 17 |
| BK Avarta Rødovre | 26 | 3 | 8 | 15 | 28 | 47 | 14 |

| PLAY-OFFS FOR 2 1ST DIVISION PLACES | 1ST LEG | 2ND LEG | AGG. |
|---|---|---|---|
| Brønshøj BK v IF Skjold Birkerød | 2-1 | 2-2 | 4-3 |
| Vanløse IF v Horsens fS (Vanløse IF win on the away goals rule) | 0-0 | 1-1 | 1-1 |

## DENMARK 3RD DIVISION EAST 1990
### LEAGUE TABLE FINAL

| | P | W | D | L | F | A | Pts |
|---|---|---|---|---|---|---|---|
| IF Skjold Birkerod | 26 | 15 | 4 | 7 | 45 | 25 | 34 |
| AB Bagsvaerd | 26 | 12 | 9 | 5 | 47 | 30 | 33 |
| Skovshoved IF | 26 | 14 | 4 | 8 | 42 | 32 | 32 |
| Koge BK | 26 | 10 | 10 | 6 | 45 | 36 | 30 |
| Ringsted IF | 26 | 13 | 4 | 9 | 44 | 40 | 30 |
| Ballerup IF | 26 | 12 | 6 | 8 | 49 | 42 | 30 |
| Taarnby BK | 26 | 9 | 7 | 10 | 36 | 31 | 25 |
| Slagelse B & I | 26 | 8 | 7 | 11 | 34 | 34 | 23 |
| Glostrup IC | 26 | 8 | 6 | 12 | 27 | 34 | 22 |
| Hvidovre IF | 26 | 6 | 10 | 10 | 33 | 36 | 22 |
| Holbaek B & I | 26 | 7 | 7 | 12 | 32 | 49 | 21 |
| Dragor BK | 26 | 5 | 9 | 12 | 32 | 49 | 19 |
| B 1901 Nykobing Fal. | 26 | 7 | 2 | 17 | 32 | 57 | 16 |

**PLAY-OFFS FOR 2 2ND DIVISION PLACES**
HIK Hellerup v Olstykke FC
Herning Fremad v Norre Aaby IK

## DENMARK 3RD DIVISION WEST 1990
### LEAGUE TABLE FINAL

| | P | W | D | L | F | A | Pts |
|---|---|---|---|---|---|---|---|
| Horsens fS | 26 | 16 | 5 | 5 | 59 | 26 | 37 |
| Varde IF | 26 | 15 | 6 | 5 | 48 | 30 | 36 |
| Holstebro BK | 26 | 14 | 6 | 6 | 55 | 39 | 34 |
| Kastrup BK | 26 | 12 | 6 | 8 | 48 | 31 | 30 |
| Randers Freja FC | 26 | 11 | 8 | 7 | 44 | 28 | 30 |
| Olstykke BK | 26 | 10 | 10 | 6 | 44 | 34 | 30 |
| IK Skovbakken Aarhus | 26 | 10 | 9 | 7 | 49 | 42 | 29 |
| Stubbekobing BK | 26 | 10 | 8 | 8 | 33 | 32 | 28 |
| Glamsbjerg | 26 | 10 | 8 | 8 | 44 | 38 | 28 |
| Norre Aaby IK | 26 | 8 | 9 | 9 | 33 | 24 | 25 |
| Kolding IF | 26 | 8 | 6 | 12 | 34 | 42 | 22 |
| Lumby/Sohus | 26 | 7 | 6 | 13 | 32 | 34 | 20 |
| Frem Nraby | 26 | 6 | 5 | 15 | 27 | 43 | 17 |
| Ullerslev BK | 26 | 7 | 0 | 19 | 15 | 59 | 8 |

## DENMARK 4TH DIVISION GROUP 1 1990
### LEAGUE TABLE FINAL

| | P | W | D | L | F | A | Pts |
|---|---|---|---|---|---|---|---|
| HIK Hellerup | 26 | 20 | 4 | 2 | 60 | 18 | 44 |
| Horsholm/Usserod IK | 26 | 17 | 6 | 3 | 66 | 24 | 40 |
| Roskilde KFUM | 26 | 16 | 5 | 5 | 65 | 39 | 37 |
| Vanlose IF II | 26 | 13 | 6 | 7 | 65 | 43 | 32 |
| FK Viking Ronne | 26 | 13 | 4 | 9 | 53 | 35 | 30 |
| BK Fremad Amager II | 26 | 13 | 4 | 9 | 66 | 40 | 30 |
| Lyngby BK II | 26 | 11 | 7 | 8 | 49 | 36 | 29 |
| OB Kobenhavn | 26 | 10 | 3 | 13 | 45 | 52 | 23 |
| Gladsaxe/Hero BK | 26 | 7 | 8 | 11 | 33 | 40 | 22 |
| Roskilde B 1906 II | 26 | 8 | 5 | 13 | 40 | 40 | 21 |
| Hvidovre IF II | 26 | 8 | 5 | 13 | 35 | 55 | 21 |
| Hellas Kobenhavn | 26 | 6 | 4 | 16 | 34 | 64 | 16 |
| Taarnby BK II | 26 | 6 | 3 | 17 | 16 | 34 | 15 |
| Nyker IF | 26 | 1 | 5 | 20 | 20 | 97 | 7 |

| | 1ST LEG | 2ND LEG | AGG. |
|---|---|---|---|
| Albertslund IF | 2-2 | 2-1 | 4-3 |
| B 1903 II | 1-4 | 1-1 | 2-5 |

## DENMARK 4TH DIVISION GROUP 2 1990
### LEAGUE TABLE FINAL

| | P | W | D | L | F | A | Pts |
|---|---|---|---|---|---|---|---|
| BK Frem II | 26 | 20 | 3 | 3 | 78 | 18 | 43 |
| Albertslund IF | 26 | 18 | 4 | 4 | 72 | 25 | 40 |
| Jyderup SG & I | 26 | 13 | 9 | 4 | 45 | 30 | 35 |
| B 1903 II | 26 | 14 | 7 | 5 | 68 | 42 | 35 |
| Herlev IF | 26 | 12 | 6 | 8 | 51 | 44 | 32 |
| Humlebaek BK | 26 | 11 | 6 | 9 | 57 | 56 | 28 |
| AB | 26 | 8 | 11 | 7 | 47 | 47 | 22 |
| Bronshoj BK | 26 | 8 | 6 | 12 | 44 | 62 | 22 |
| IF Skjold Birkerod | 26 | 4 | 15 | 44 | 62 | 17 | |
| Aabenraa BK | 26 | 4 | 18 | 35 | 86 | 12 | |
| Nakskov BK | 26 | 9 | 17 | 37 | 51 | | |
| Viborg FF | 26 | 18 | 30 | 89 | 8 | | |
| IK Skovbakken | 26 | 3 | 21 | | | | |
| Frederikshavn fl. | 26 | 3 | | | | | |

### 1ST ROUND
| | 1ST LEG | 2ND LEG | AGG. |
|---|---|---|---|
| Frederikssund IK | 2-0 | 0-0 | 2-0 |

## DENMARK 4TH DIVISION GROUP 3 1990
### LEAGUE TABLE FINAL

| | P | W | D | L | F | A | Pts |
|---|---|---|---|---|---|---|---|
| Vejle BK II | 26 | 19 | 4 | 3 | 85 | 29 | 37 |
| Norre Aaby IK | 26 | 17 | 3 | 6 | 62 | 34 | 37 |
| Vordingborg IF | 26 | 15 | 4 | 7 | 57 | 40 | 34 |
| Dalum IF | 26 | 9 | 10 | 7 | 45 | 37 | 28 |
| Ullerslev BK | 26 | 9 | 9 | 8 | 37 | 41 | 27 |
| Bramming BK | 26 | 10 | 9 | 9 | 42 | 50 | 27 |
| Haderslev FK | 26 | 11 | 3 | 12 | 49 | 45 | 25 |
| Nakskov BK | 26 | 11 | 3 | 12 | 49 | 53 | 25 |
| OB II | 26 | 10 | 5 | 11 | 40 | 51 | 25 |
| B 1909 II | 26 | 8 | 8 | 10 | 39 | 24 | |
| B 1913 II | 26 | 6 | 11 | 9 | 35 | 38 | 23 |
| Nyborg G & I | 26 | 7 | 6 | 13 | 43 | 68 | 20 |
| UIU Sonderborg | 26 | 7 | 2 | 17 | 31 | 58 | 16 |
| OKS II | 26 | 3 | 5 | 18 | 31 | 58 | 11 |

## DENMARK 4TH DIVISION GROUP 4 1990
### LEAGUE TABLE FINAL

| | P | W | D | L | F | A | Pts |
|---|---|---|---|---|---|---|---|
| Silkeborg IF II | 26 | 15 | 7 | 4 | 50 | 29 | 37 |
| Aalborg Chang | 26 | 14 | 4 | 8 | 47 | 34 | 32 |
| Vildbjerg Sf | 26 | 12 | 7 | 7 | 47 | 27 | 31 |
| Skive IK | 26 | 13 | 5 | 8 | 41 | 27 | 31 |
| AaB | 26 | 12 | 6 | 8 | 42 | 27 | 30 |
| Ikast FS II | 26 | 10 | 10 | 6 | 43 | 34 | 30 |
| Olstykke FC | 26 | 14 | 2 | 10 | 57 | 42 | 30 |
| FK Viking Ronne | 26 | 10 | 8 | 8 | 43 | 42 | 28 |
| Bronshoj BK | 26 | 4 | 8 | 14 | 18 | 35 | |
| AGF II | 26 | 10 | 6 | 10 | 51 | 42 | 26 |
| AaB II | 26 | 10 | 8 | 8 | 54 | 37 | 28 |
| Lindholm IF | 26 | 10 | 8 | 8 | 50 | 46 | 28 |
| Esbjerg fB II | 26 | 9 | 10 | 7 | 32 | 35 | 28 |
| Hobro | 26 | 7 | 9 | 10 | 35 | 42 | 23 |
| Brande IF | 26 | 6 | 3 | 17 | 29 | 58 | 15 |
| IHF Aarhus | 26 | 5 | 3 | 18 | 19 | 75 | 13 |
| Aalborg Freja | 26 | 4 | 2 | 20 | 32 | 61 | 10 |

## DENMARK CUP 1989/90

### 1ST ROUND
HIK Hellerup 2 — Roskilde B 1906 4
B 93 — Koge BK
Dragor BK — SB 50 Ishoj
Kastrup BK — Humlebaek BK
Herlufsholm — Albertslund IF
Olstykke FC — Kolding BK
Aabyhoj — Hjorring IF
Koge BK — Espergaerde IF
Espergaerde IF — Herning Fremad
Ronne IK — Tarup-Paarup IF
Olstykke BK — Bramming BK
Holstebro BK — Horsens fS

### 2ND ROUND
BK Fremad Valby 2 — FK Viking Ronne 2 (aet)
FK Viking Ronne win 2-3 on penalties
Albertslund IF 2 — B 93
B 1901 6 — BK Fremad Amager 1
Skovshoved IF — Helsingor IF
Helsingor IF win 3-4 on penalties
Herfolge BK 8 — Bronshoj BK
AB 3 — Roskilde B 1906
BK Frem — Fredericia KFUM
Bronshoj BK 4 — Odense KFUM
IF Skjold Birkerod 2 — Brondbyernes IF
Nakskov BK — Bramming BK
OB 2 — B 1909

### 3RD ROUND
Esbjerg fB 1 — AB 0 (aet)
Ikast fS — Vejle BK
B 1901 — Silkeborg IF
Holstebro BK — Aabenraa BK
AaB 3 — B 93
Olstykke FC 2 — BK Frem
FK Viking Ronne — Bronshoj BK
Naestved IF 3 — B 1909
IK Skovbakken — Odense KFUM

### 4TH ROUND
Naestved IF 1 — KB
Olstykke FC 0 — Vejle BK
Helsingor IF 2 — Silkeborg IF
Helsingor IF 6 — Randers Freja FC
AaB

### 2ND ROUND
B 93 — Esbjerg fB
Dragor BK — Ikast fS
Albertslund IF — B 1901
Skovshoved IF — Helsingor IF
BK Fremad Amager — Herfolge BK
Espergaerde IF — BK Frem
Frederica KFUM — Bramming BK
Odense KFUM — Brandbyernes IF
Randers Freja FC — B 1913

### 3RD ROUND
Esbjerg fB — AB
Helsingor IF win 3-4 on penalties
B 1901 — Silkeborg IF
Hobro — Aabenraa BK
Hobro — Holstebro BK
Frederikshavn fl. — AaB
Hobro — Frem Hjorring
Hobro — B 1913

### 4TH ROUND
Naestved IF 1 — Lyngby BK 2
Esbjerg fB 4 — B 1913
Helsingor IF 0 — AGF
Silkeborg IF 4 — Bronshoj BK
IK Skovbakken — AaB

### 1ST ROUND (SECOND COLUMN)
Taarnby BK 0 — Holbaek B & I 3
Vanlose IF 2 — IF Skjold Birkerod 4
Koge BK 7 — ØB 1
Olstykke FC — ØB
Herlufsholm — B 1909
Frederica KFUM — Aabyhoj
Norre Aaby IK — Kolding IF
Brande IF — Nakskov BK
Odense KFUM — Lumby/Sohus
Hobro — Frem Broby
Spjald — OKS
Hellas — SB 50 Ishoj
B 1901 — Jaegersborg
Helsingor IF — Holeby
Ronne IK — Skovlunde IF
FK Viking Ronne — Frihedеn
Holstebro BK — Radovre
Holstebro Valby — Greve IF
BK Freja Aalborg — Korsor
Viborg FF — Esbjerg fB
Randers Freja FC — IHF Aarhus
— Veigaard

### Cup far right column (DENMARK CUP 1989/90)
Roskilde B 1906 4 — Koge BK
Dragsholm 2 — Kastrup BK 2
Humlebaek BK — Herlufsholm
Albertslund IF 5 — Kolding BK 0
Kolding IF 3 — Nakskov BK
Frederica KFUM 1 — Frem Hjorring
Frem Hjorring 3 — Struer
Grenaa — Giostrup IC 5
Frederikshavn fl. 3 — BK Fremad Amager 7
Svendborg fB 3 — Norresundby BK
AB 2 — Hvidovre IF 3
Ringsted IF 2 — SB 50 Ishoj 0
Slagelse B & I 1 — Dragor BK
Skovshoved IF 2 — BK Avarta 1
Norresundby BK 3 — B 1909
Brammen BK 3 — Aabenraa BK 3

Koge BK 2 — Dragor BK 2
SB 50 Ishoj 1 — Viborg FF 3
Frihedеn — KB
Espergaerde IF 6 — Odense KFUM 3
Holbaek B & I 3 — Randers Freja FC 4
B 93 — Herning Fremad
OB — Norresundby BK
B 1913 — Ullerslev BK

Randers Freja FC 4 — Roskilde B 1906 4
Ikast fS 0 — AGF
B 1901 — Viborg FF 7
Vejle BK 3 — Lyngby BK
Aabenraa BK 0 — B 1913
Holstebro BK 1 — Lyngby BK
B 1913 — AGF
Svendborg fB 1 — Bronshoj BK

## 1/4 FINALS

| | | |
|---|---|---|
| Helsingor IF | 0 | |
| Silkeborg IF | 1 | |
| AGF Aarhus | 1 | |
| Svendborg IB | 2 | |
| Lyngby BK | 1 | Brondbyernes IF ... 0 |
| | | Vejle BK ... 3 |

## SEMI-FINALS

| | 1ST LEG | 2ND LEG | AGG. |
|---|---|---|---|
| Vejle BK v Lyngby BK | 1-2 | 0-3 | 1-5 |
| AGF v Ølstykke FC | 1-0 | 1-0 | 2-0 |

## FINAL  24/5/90 at Københavns Idraetspark

Lyngby BK ... 0    AGF Aarhus ... 0 (aet.)

Lyngby BK : J.Rindom, H.Larsen, V.Andersen (E.Larsen), M.Gothenborg, C.Christiansen, M.Wieghorst, J.Helt, M.Schäfer (F.Nielsen), F.Christensen, P.Nielsen, A.Kuhn.

AGF : T.Rasmussen, L.Skov, M.Rieper, C.Thomsen, L.Frisch, T.Christensen, U.Jacobsen (E.Madsen), L.Lundkvist, S.Andersen, H.Jespersen (J.Stampe), S.Tofting.

Referee : Jan Damgaard    Attendance : 2,000

## FINAL REPLAY  31/5/90 at Københavns Idraetspark

Lyngby BK ... 6    AGF Aarhus ... 1

Lyngby BK : J.Rindom, H.Larsen, M.Gothenborg, C.Christiansen, E.Larsen, M.Wieghorst (K.Clem), J.Helt (M.Schäfer), D-F Nielsen, P.Nielsen, F.Christensen, A.Kuhn.

AGF : T.Rasmussen, L.Skov, M.Rieper, J.Stampe (H.Jespersen), C.Thomsen, L.Frisch, S.Tofting, U.Jacobsen, T.Christensen, L.Lundkvist (S.Andersen), E.Madsen.

| | | |
|---|---|---|
| 1-0 | H.Larsen | 23 |
| 2-0 | P.Nielsen | 40 |
| 3-0 | K.Clem | 61 |
| 4-0 | F.Christensen | 64 |
| 4-1 | T.Christensen | 71 |
| 5-1 | M.Schäfer | 78 |
| 6-1 | F.Christensen | 86 |

Referee : Kim Milton Nielsen    Attendance : 8,600

# DENMARK CUP 1990/91

## 1ST ROUND

| | | | |
|---|---|---|---|
| Aabyhoj IF | 4 | Thisted IK | 2 |
| Kolding IF | 1 | Fredericia KFUM | 2 |
| Horsens fS | 5 | Spjald | 2 |
| Holstebro BK | 5 | Dalum IF | 1 |
| Haarby BK | 1 | Aabenraa BK | 4 |
| Randers Freja FC | 2 | Egebjerg | 4 |
| Hobro | 0 | Svendborg IB | 3 |
| Hjorring IF | 0 | B 1913 | 2 |
| Asaa BK | 3 | IK Skovbakken | 1 |
| Assens | 0 | Norresundby BK | 3 |
| Skovshoved IF | 0 | Skamby BK | 4 |
| Dragor BK | 1 | IF 32 Glostrup | 3 |
| B 1901 | 0 | Bronshoj BK | 2 |
| FK Viking Ronne | 5 | ØB | 1 |
| Hvidovre IF | 5 | FB Frederiksberg | 0 |
| Albertslund IF | 3 | BK Fremad Valby | 2 |
| IF Skjold Birkerod | 3 | Vordingborg IF | 9 |
| HIK Hellerup | 5 | Rodby BK | 0 |
| Stubbekobing BK | 1 | Valby BK | 0 |
| Glostrup IC | 1 | Ballerup IF | 3 |
| | | Frederikssund IK | 4 |

| | | | |
|---|---|---|---|
| Herning Fremad | 3 | Struer | 2 |
| Bramming BK | 2 | Hammel GF | 5 |
| Esbjerg fB | 4 | Varde IF | 2 |
| Ulbjerg IF | 2 | Odense KFUM | 6 |
| UIU Sonderborg | 3 | B 1909 | 5 |
| Lindholm IF | 1 | B 52 Aalborg | 3 |
| Norre Aaby IK | 3 | Korsor BK | 1 |
| Skamby BK | 2 | OKS | 6 |
| Ølstykke FC | 4 | Slagelse B & I | 2 |
| Ringsted IF | 2 | Brande IF | 4 |
| Roskilde B 1906 | 3 | Soro | 1 |
| FB Frederiksberg | 0 | Lillerod | 2 |
| BK Fremad Valby | 2 | Holbaek B & I | 1 |
| Vordingborg IF | 9 | BK Avarta | 2 |
| Vanlose IF | 4 | Hillerod GI | 3 |
| Rodby BK | 0 | Ryvang Kobenhavn | 3 |
| Ballerup IF | 3 | Koge BK | 0 |
| Frederikssund IK | 4 | BK Fremad Amager | 9 |
| | | Lundtofte | 0 |
| | | Greve IF | 2 |

## 2ND ROUND

| | | | |
|---|---|---|---|
| Brande IF | 0 | OKS | 5 |
| Varde IF | 1 | Asaa BK | 1 |
| Varde IF win on penalties | | B 1913 win on penalties | |
| Egebjerg | 0 | Egebjerg | 0 |
| B 1909 | 1 | B 1909 | 1 |

| | | |
|---|---|---|
| Herning Fremad | 3 | Hobro ... 0 |
| Viborg FF | 3 | Norresundby BK ... 2 |
| Holstebro BK | 3 | Fredericia KFUM ... 3 (aet.) |
| Holstebro BK win on penalties | | |
| Hillerod GI | 1 | Aalborg Chang ... 2 |
| Bronshoj BK | 0 | Aabyhoj IF ... 5 |
| IF Skjold Birkerod | 1 | UIU Sonderborg ... 1 |
| KB | | Esbjerg fB ... 3 |
| AB | | ØB ... 0 |
| Ballerup IF | 3 | Kastrup BK ... 3 |
| | | IF 32 Glostrup ... 4 |
| | | Helsingor IF ... 2 |
| | | Ringsted IF ... 2 |

| | |
|---|---|
| Norre Aaby IK | 1 |
| Aabenraa BK | 0 |
| Bramming BK | 2 |
| Hadersley FK | 2 |
| Roskilde B 1906 | 1 |
| Vordingborg IF | 1 |
| BK Avarta | 1 (aet.) |
| Helsingor IF | 3 (aet.) |
| Greve IF | 3 |
| Vanlose IF | 1 |

## 3RD ROUND

| | | | |
|---|---|---|---|
| B 1913 | 2 | Naestved IF | 1 (aet.) |
| OKS | 1 | Brondbyernes IF | 3 |
| AB | 2 | Bramming BK | 2 |
| Varde IF | 0 | AaB | 2 |
| Kastrup BK | 2 | IF 32 Glostrup | 0 |
| Ølstykke FC | 2 | AGF | 2 |
| | | Hillerod GI win on penalties | |
| Esbjerg fB | 2 | Bronshoj BK | 3 |
| Vejle BK | 4 | Roskilde B 1906 | 1 |
| OB | 5 | Ringsted IF | 2 |

| | |
|---|---|
| BK Frem | 3 |
| Herfolge BK | 5 (aet.) |
| B 1903 | 1 |
| Hvidovre IF | 1 |
| Hillerod GI | 2 (aet.) |
| Silkeborg IF | 0 |
| Viborg FF | 2 |

## 4TH ROUND

| | | | |
|---|---|---|---|
| OB | 3 | Viborg FF | |
| Brondbyernes IF | 5 | Hillerod GI | 1 |
| Herfolge BK | 1 | B 19 '3 Odense | 1 (aet.) |
| Herfolge BK win on penalties | | | |
| B 1903 Gentofte | 0 | Vejle BK | |

| | | | |
|---|---|---|---|
| Kastrup BK | 1 | Ikast FS | 1 |
| AB Bagsvaerd | | Bronshoj BK | 2 |
| Hvidovre IF | 1 | AaB Aalborg | 2 (aet.) |
| | | AaB Aalborg win on penalties | |

## 1/4 FINALS

| | | | |
|---|---|---|---|
| AaB Aalborg | 5 | Herfolge BK | 1 |
| Brondbyernes IF | 1 | Vejle 3K | 0 |
| AB Bagsvaerd | 2 | OB Odense | 5 (aet.) |
| Ølstykke FC | | Ikast FS | 1 (aet.) |
| Ølstykke FC win 3-2 on penalties | | | |

## SEMI-FINALS

| | 1ST LEG | 2ND LEG | AGG. |
|---|---|---|---|
| AaB Aalborg v Brondbyernes IF | 2-2 | 1-0 | 3-2 |
| OB Odense v Ølstykke FC | 3-0 | 2-0 | 5-0 |

## FINAL  9/5/91 (at Odense)

OB ... 0    AaB ... 0 (aet.)

OB : L.Hogh, S.Nedergaard, J.Hensen, T.Helveg, L.Hansen, G.T.Gray, U.Moseby, L.Jakobsen (K.Ziegler) (B.Christensen), D.Petersen, K.Bordinggaard, M.Donnerup.

AaB : N.C.Jorgensen, H.V.Kristersen, S.Larsen, S.Thorst, C.Facius (H.Hansen), I.Simonsen, P.Moller, H.Rasmussen, P.Rasmussen, T.Boye, J.Jessen (S.Dissing).

Referee : Svend Erik Christensen    Attendance : 13,700

## FINAL REPLAY  14/6/91 'at Odense'

OB ... 0    AaB ... 0 (aet.)

OB : L.Hogh, G.T.Gray, J.Hansen, T.Helveg, S.Nedergaard, P.Hjorth (J.Thorup), U.Moseby, L.Jakobsen, K.Bordinggaard, M.Donnerup, D.Petersen (J.Harder).

AaB : N.C.Jorgensen, H.V.Kristersen, I.Simonsen, S.Thorst, T.Boye, C.Facius (K.Sand), H.Rasmussen, P.Rasmussen, H.Hansen, P.Moller, S.Dissing (C.Steinlein).

Referee : John P.Nielsen    Attendance : 4,554

OB WIN 4-3 ON PENALTIES.

| DENMARK Premier Division Spring 1991 | BRØNDBY | B 1903 | IKAST | SILKEBORG | FREM | LYNGBY | AGF | OB | VEJLE | AaB |
|---|---|---|---|---|---|---|---|---|---|---|
| BRØNDBYERNES IF | | 1-0 | 2-1 | 2-1 | 4-1 | 0-3 | 0-0 | 0-0 | 3-1 | 2-2 |
| B1903 Gentofte | 0-1 | | 0-0 | 1-1 | 0-1 | 2-0 | 3-0 | 0-0 | 3-0 | 4-1 |
| IKAST FS | 0-1 | 1-0 | | 1-2 | 2-1 | 1-0 | 1-1 | 0-0 | 0-2 | 0-0 |
| SILKEBORG IF | 1-0 | 0-1 | 1-0 | | 1-1 | 4-3 | 3-3 | 2-2 | 0-0 | 1-1 |
| BK FREM København | 1-1 | 1-2 | 1-0 | 2-2 | | 2-1 | 2-2 | 3-0 | 1-1 | 1-2 |
| LYNGBY BK | 1-1 | 4-1 | 5-0 | 5-2 | 1-1 | | 2-1 | 1-0 | 1-0 | 2-0 |
| AGF Aarhus | 1-2 | 2-1 | 3-2 | 2-1 | 2-1 | 1-1 | | 3-1 | 0-0 | 6-1 |
| OB Odense | 1-1 | 0-0 | 3-0 | 6-0 | 1-1 | 1-1 | 0-0 | | 4-2 | 1-1 |
| VEJLE BK | 1-3 | 1-0 | 3-0 | 1-0 | 1-2 | 0-2 | 1-1 | 0-0 | | 5-1 |
| AaB Aalborg | 0-2 | 4-1 | 2-0 | 2-1 | 1-2 | 1-2 | 4-1 | 5-1 | 1-1 | |

## DENMARK PREMIER DIVISION SPRING 1991

### LEAGUE TABLE FINAL

| | | | | | | | |
|---|---|---|---|---|---|---|---|
| Brøndbyernes IF | 18 | 10 | 6 | 2 | 26 | 15 | 26 |
| Lyngby BK | 18 | 10 | 4 | 4 | 35 | 18 | 24 |
| AGF Aarhus | 18 | 6 | 8 | 4 | 29 | 26 | 20 |
| BK Frem København | 18 | 6 | 7 | 5 | 25 | 24 | 19 |
| OB Odense | 18 | 3 | 11 | 4 | 21 | 20 | 17 |
| AaB Aalborg | 18 | 6 | 5 | 7 | 29 | 33 | 17 |
| B 1903 Gentofte | 18 | 6 | 4 | 8 | 19 | 18 | 16 |
| Velje BK | 18 | 5 | 6 | 7 | 20 | 22 | 16 |
| Silkeborg IF | 18 | 4 | 7 | 7 | 23 | 33 | 15 |
| Ikast FS | 18 | 3 | 4 | 11 | 9 | 27 | 10 |

Champions : - Brøndbyernes IF
Relegated : - Ikast FS

| PROMOTION/RELEGATION PLAY-OFF | 1ST LEG | 2ND LEG | AGG. |
|---|---|---|---|
| Silkeborg IF v B 1909 Odense | 3-4 | 2-0 | 5-4 |

### TOP SCORERS

1. Bent Christensen (Brøndbyernes IF) — 11
2. Peter Møller (AaB) — 9
   Per Pedersen (Lyngby BK) — 9
4. Søren Andersen (AGF) — 8
   Flemming Christensen (Lyngby BK) — 8
6. Heine Fernandez (Silkeborg IF) — 7
7. Jan Bartram (AGF) — 6
   Torben Christensen (AGF) — 6
   Torben Frank (Lyngby BK) — 6
   Peter Nielsen (Lyngby BK) — 6
   Thomas Thorninger (Vejle BK) — 6

| DENMARK 1st Division Spring 1991 | NAESTVED | HERFØLGE | KB | VIBORG | B 1909 | B 1913 | HELSINGØR | SVENDBORG | BRØNSHØJ | VANLØSE |
|---|---|---|---|---|---|---|---|---|---|---|
| NAESTVED IF | | 2-1 | 4-0 | 0-0 | 2-2 | 2-1 | 2-0 | 2-5 | 1-1 | 3-2 |
| HERFØLGE BK | 2-2 | | 5-1 | 1-0 | 1-2 | 0-2 | 2-2 | 2-2 | 1-0 | 0-0 |
| KB Frederiksberg | 0-3 | 1-1 | | 2-2 | 2-0 | 1-0 | 4-0 | 2-1 | 1-2 | 0-3 |
| VIBORG FF | 4-2 | 1-2 | 2-1 | | 3-1 | 2-2 | 8-3 | 2-1 | 1-1 | 1-1 |
| B 1909 Odense | 2-0 | 2-2 | 3-0 | 2-0 | | 1-0 | 4-3 | 1-0 | 0-1 | 2-1 |
| B 1913 Odense | 0-1 | 3-1 | 2-0 | 1-1 | 1-2 | | 1-1 | 1-1 | 0-2 | 0-2 |
| HELSINGØR IF | 0-0 | 1-1 | 2-4 | 0-1 | 0-1 | 2-1 | | 2-1 | 1-1 | 1-1 |
| SVENDBORG fB | 1-4 | 0-1 | 1-7 | 2-0 | 1-1 | 1-1 | 1-1 | | 4-1 | 1-4 |
| BRØNSHØJ BK | 1-2 | 3-1 | 1-1 | 3-0 | 2-1 | 2-3 | 4-1 | 1-1 | | 0-3 |
| VANLØSE IF | 4-3 | 2-1 | 1-1 | 1-0 | 2-1 | 0-1 | 0-2 | 0-0 | 1-1 | |

## DENMARK 1ST DIVISION SPRING 1991

### LEAGUE TABLE FINAL

| | | | | | | | |
|---|---|---|---|---|---|---|---|
| Naestved IF | 18 | 9 | 5 | 4 | 35 | 26 | 23 |
| B1909 Odense | 18 | 10 | 3 | 5 | 28 | 21 | 23 |
| Vanløse IF | 18 | 8 | 6 | 4 | 28 | 18 | 22 |
| Brønshøj BK | 18 | 7 | 6 | 5 | 27 | 23 | 20 |
| Viborg FF | 18 | 6 | 6 | 6 | 28 | 26 | 18 |
| Herfølge BK | 18 | 5 | 7 | 6 | 25 | 26 | 17 |
| KB Frederiksberg | 18 | 6 | 4 | 8 | 28 | 33 | 16 |
| B 1913 Odense | 18 | 5 | 5 | 8 | 20 | 22 | 15 |
| Svendborg fB | 18 | 3 | 7 | 8 | 24 | 33 | 13 |
| Helsingør IF | 18 | 3 | 7 | 8 | 22 | 37 | 13 |

Promoted : - Naestved IF
Relegated : - Svendborg fB and Helsingør IF

## DENMARK 2ND DIV.EAST SPRING 1991

### LEAGUE TABLE FINAL

| | | | | | | | |
|---|---|---|---|---|---|---|---|
| HIK Hellerup | 18 | 9 | 5 | 4 | 28 | 16 | 23 |
| BK Fremad Amager | 18 | 10 | 2 | 6 | 30 | 16 | 22 |
| AB Bagsvaerd | 18 | 7 | 6 | 5 | 29 | 27 | 20 |
| Greve IF | 18 | 6 | 7 | 5 | 29 | 26 | 19 |
| IF Skjold Birkerød | 18 | 7 | 5 | 6 | 30 | 28 | 19 |
| B 93 København | 18 | 5 | 7 | 6 | 26 | 27 | 17 |
| Skovshoved IF | 18 | 6 | 5 | 7 | 25 | 34 | 17 |
| Roskilde B 1906 | 18 | 5 | 6 | 7 | 20 | 25 | 16 |
| Køge BK | 18 | 3 | 8 | 7 | 18 | 30 | 14 |
| Kastrup BK | 18 | 4 | 5 | 9 | 23 | 29 | 13 |

Promoted : - HIK Hellerup

## DENMARK 2ND DIV.WEST SPRING 1991

### LEAGUE TABLE FINAL

| | | | | | | | |
|---|---|---|---|---|---|---|---|
| Nørresundby BK | 18 | 11 | 5 | 2 | 36 | 16 | 27 |
| Randers Freja FC | 18 | 9 | 7 | 2 | 30 | 17 | 25 |
| Esbjerg fB | 18 | 8 | 6 | 4 | 27 | 14 | 22 |
| Horsens fS | 18 | 6 | 8 | 4 | 30 | 25 | 20 |
| Holstebro BK | 18 | 9 | 2 | 7 | 43 | 30 | 20 |
| OKS Odense | 18 | 7 | 5 | 6 | 32 | 27 | 19 |
| Ringsted IF | 18 | 7 | 3 | 8 | 19 | 25 | 17 |
| Nørre Aaby IK | 18 | 5 | 5 | 8 | 20 | 31 | 15 |
| Varde IF | 18 | 3 | 5 | 10 | 24 | 44 | 11 |
| BK Avarta Rødovre | 18 | 0 | 4 | 14 | 11 | 43 | 4 |

Promoted : - Nørresundby BK

No relegation, matches played in 3rd Division Spring 1991 belong to Season 1991/92.

## INTERNATIONAL LINE-UPS 1990

| Date | Match | Venue | Referee | Type | Scorers |
|---|---|---|---|---|---|
| 5/2/90 | UAE 1 DENMARK 1 | Dubai | Ref: Salem Saed (UAE) | Friendly | (J.Larsen) |
| 14/2/90 | EGYPT 0 DENMARK 0 | Cairo | Ref: Hill (England) | Friendly | |
| 11/4/90 | DENMARK 1 TURKEY 0 | Kobenhavn | Ref: Van Langenhove (Belgium) | Friendly | (L.Jakobsen) |
| 15/5/90 | ENGLAND 1 DENMARK 0 | London | Ref: McCluskey (Scotland) | Friendly | |
| 30/5/90 | WESTERN GERMANY 1 DENMARK 0 | Gelsenkirchen | Ref: Midgley (England) | Friendly | |
| 6/6/90 | NORWAY 1 DENMARK 2 | Trondheim | Ref: Larsson (Sweden) | Friendly | (F.Povlsen, M.Laudrup) |
| 5/9/90 | SWEDEN 0 DENMARK 1 | Västeras | Ref: Hope (Scotland) | Friendly | (B.Christensen) |
| 11/9/90 | DENMARK 1 WALES 0 | Kobenhavn | Ref: Palsi (Finland) | Friendly | (B.Laudrup) |
| 10/10/90 | DENMARK 4 FAROER IS. 1 | Kobenhavn | Ref: Haraldsson (Iceland) | EuroCh.Q. | (M.Laudrup 2, L.Eistrup, F.Povlsen) |
| 17/10/90 | NORTHERN IRELAND 1 DENMARK 1 | Belfast | Ref: Philipp (Luxembourg) | EuroCh.Q. | (J.Bartram) |
| 14/11/90 | DENMARK 0 YUGOSLAVIA 2 | Kobenhavn | Ref: Midgley (England) | EuroCh.Q. | |

### Appearances (part 1)

| Date | P.Schmeichel | H.Risom | J.Hansen | L.Olsen | J.Larsen | H.Larsen | J.Helt | J.Molby | M.Bruun | B.Christensen | L.Jakobsen | J.Svinggaard | B.Rasmussen | K.Vilfort | B.Steen Nielsen | H.Andersen | J.Jensen | C.Nielsen | M.Laudrup |
|---|---|---|---|---|---|---|---|---|---|---|---|---|---|---|---|---|---|---|---|
| 5/2/90 | 1 | 2 | 3 | 4 | 5 | 6 | 7 | 8 | 9 | 10 | 11 | (9) | (10) | | | | | | |
| 14/2/90 | 1 | 2 | 3 | 4 | 5 | 6 | 7 | 8 | 9 | 10 | 11 | | (10) | | (6) | | | | |
| 11/4/90 | 1 | | 3 | 4 | 5 | 6 | 7 | (8) | 6 | 11 | 11 | | | (7) | | | | | 10 |
| 15/5/90 | 1 | | | 4 | | | | | (10) | | (9) | | | 8 | | 2 | 8 | 9 | 10 |
| 30/5/90 | 1 | (11) | | 4 | | | | | 10 | 11 | | | | 8 | | 5 | 7 | | |
| 6/6/90 | | 2 | 4 | 4 | (2) | | | | 6 | 11 | | | | 8 | | 5 | 7 | | 10 |
| 5/9/90 | 1 | | | 4 | 6 | | | 5 | | 11 | | | | 8 | | 5 | 7 | | |
| 11/9/90 | 1 | | | 4 | | | | | | 10 | | | | 8 | | 5 | | | |
| 10/10/90 | 1 | | | 4 | 7 | | | | | | | | | 7 | | | | | |
| 17/10/90 | 1 | | | 4 | | | (10) | | | | | | | 8 | | | | | |
| 14/11/90 | 1 | | | 4 | | | | | | | | | | 8 | | | (9) | | 10 |
| **CAPS AT 31/12/90** | 38 | 8 | 0 | 47 | 19 | 9 | 39 | 5 | 6 | 8 | 4 | 1 | 3 | 34 | 1 | 23 | 34 | 13 | 64 |
| **GOALS AT 31/12/90** | | 8 | 0 | 3 | 1 | 1 | 1 | | 6 | 1 | 1 | 1 | | 5 | | 2 | 1 | 7 | 26 |

### Appearances (part 2)

| Date | J.Sivebaek | Kent Nielsen | J.Bartram | F.Povlsen | B.Laudrup | P.Frandsen | B.Skaarup | T.Rasmussen | J.Juul Jensen | M.Rieper | J.Heintze | J.Olsen | J.Friis-Hansen | M.Molnar | K.Bordinggaard | S.Lyng | J.Molby | L.Eistrup | E.Rasmussen |
|---|---|---|---|---|---|---|---|---|---|---|---|---|---|---|---|---|---|---|---|
| 5/2/90 | | | | | | | | | | | | | | | | | | | |
| 14/2/90 | | | | | | | | | | | | | | | | | | | |
| 11/4/90 | | | | | | | | | | | | | | | | | | | |
| 15/5/90 | | | | | | | | | | | | | | | | | | | |
| 30/5/90 | 2 | 3 | 6 | 9 | 11 | | | | | | | 7 | | 10 | | | | | |
| 6/6/90 | 2 | 3 | 6 | 9 | 11 | (6) | | | | | 5 | (7) | | | | | | | |
| 5/9/90 | 3 | 3 | 7 | 9 | 11 | | | | (9) | | 6 | | | (9) | (9) | | (10) | | |
| 11/9/90 | | 3 | 7 | 9 | 11 | | (10) | 1 | | | 7 | | | | (10) | (10) | 7 | (8) | |
| 10/10/90 | 2 | 3 | 6 | 9 | | (11) | | 1 | | 1 | 5 | | 9 | | | | | (11) | |
| 17/10/90 | 2 | 3 | 6 | 9 | | | | 1 | | | 5 | | | | | | | (7) | |
| 14/11/90 | 2 | 3 | 6 | 9 | | | | | | | 5 | | | (10) | | | 7 | | 1 |
| **CAPS AT 31/12/90** | 69 | 39 | 30 | 37 | 22 | 2 | 2 | 33 | 1 | 1 | 23 | 43 | 1 | 4 | | | 33 | 17 | 1 |
| **GOALS AT 31/12/90** | 1 | 3 | 5 | 14 | 5 | | | | | | 5 | 5 | | | | | 2 | 9 | |

## DENMARK : All Time Records as at 31/12/90 - CAPS

1. Morten Olsen (B1901/Cercle Brugge/RWDM/RSC Anderlecht/1FC Köln) — 102
2. Per Rontved (Bronshoj BK/SV Werder Bremen/Randers Freja FC) — 75
3. Jens Jorn Bertelsen (Esbjerg fB/FC Seraing/FC Rouen/FC Aarau) — 69
   Preben Elkjaer (1FC Köln/SC Lokeren/Hellas Verona) — 69
   John Sivebaek (Vejle BK/Manchester United/AS St.Etienne) — 69
6. Soren Lerby (Ajax/FC Bayern München/AS Monaco/PSV) — 67
7. Michael Laudrup (Brondbyernes IF/Lazio/Juventus/FC Barcelona) — 64
8. Henning Munk Jensen (AaB/PSV) — 62
9. Soren Busk (Westfalia Herne/MVV/AA Gent/AS Monaco/Wiener SK) — 61
10. Bent Hansen (B1903) — 59

## DENMARK : All Time Records as at 31/12/90 - GOALS

1. Poul 'Tist' Nielsen (KB) — 52 (39)
2. Pauli Jorgensen (BK Frem) — 44 (47)
3. Ole Madsen (HIK Hellerup) — 43 (51)
4. Preben Elkjaer (1FC Köln/SC Lokeren/Hellas Verona) — 38 (69)
5. Henning Enoksen (Vejle BK/AGF) — 29 (54)
6. Michael Laudrup (Brondbyernes IF/Lazio/Juventus/FC Barcelona) — 26 (64)
7. Michael Rohde (B93) — 22 (40)
8. Allan Simonsen (Vejle BK/Borussia Mönchengladbach/FC Barcelona) — 21 (56)
9. Jens Peder Hansen (Esbjerg fB) — 18 (38)
10. Karl Aage Hansen (AB) — 17 (22)
    Carl Aage Praest (ØB) — 17 (24)
    Poul Pedersen (AIA) — 17 (50)

# ENGLAND Correspondent : JAN BUITENGA

**ENGLAND 1st Division Season 1990/91**

| | LIVERPOOL | ASTON VILLA | TOTT. HOTSPUR | ARSENAL | CHELSEA | EVERTON | SOUTHAMPTON | WIMBLEDON | NOTTS. FOREST | NORWICH CITY | Q.PK. RANGERS | COVENTRY CITY | MAN. UNITED | MAN. CITY | CRYST. PALACE | DERBY COUNTY | LUTON TOWN | LEEDS UTD. | SHEFF. UTD. | SUNDERLAND |
|---|---|---|---|---|---|---|---|---|---|---|---|---|---|---|---|---|---|---|---|---|
| LIVERPOOL | ■ | 2-1 | 2-0 | 0-1 | 2-0 | 3-1 | 3-2 | 1-1 | 2-0 | 3-0 | 1-3 | 1-1 | 4-0 | 2-2 | 3-0 | 2-0 | 4-0 | 3-0 | 2-0 | 2-1 |
| ASTON VILLA | 0-0 | ■ | 3-2 | 0-0 | 2-2 | 2-2 | 1-1 | 1-2 | 1-1 | 2-1 | 2-2 | 2-1 | 1-1 | 1-5 | 2-0 | 3-2 | 1-2 | 0-0 | 2-1 | 3-0 |
| TOTT. HOTSPUR | 1-3 | 2-1 | ■ | 0-0 | 1-1 | 3-3 | 2-0 | 4-2 | 1-1 | 2-1 | 0-0 | 2-2 | 1-2 | 3-1 | 1-1 | 3-0 | 2-1 | 0-0 | 4-0 | 3-3 |
| ARSENAL | 3-0 | 5-0 | 0-0 | ■ | 4-1 | 1-0 | 4-0 | 2-2 | 1-1 | 2-0 | 2-0 | 6-1 | 3-1 | 2-2 | 4-0 | 3-0 | 2-1 | 2-0 | 4-1 | 1-0 |
| CHELSEA | 4-2 | 1-0 | 3-2 | 2-1 | ■ | 1-2 | 0-2 | 0-0 | 0-0 | 1-1 | 2-0 | 2-1 | 3-2 | 1-1 | 2-1 | 2-1 | 3-3 | 1-2 | 2-2 | 3-2 |
| EVERTON | 2-3 | 1-0 | 1-1 | 1-1 | 2-2 | ■ | 3-0 | 1-2 | 0-0 | 1-0 | 3-0 | 1-0 | 0-1 | 2-0 | 0-0 | 2-0 | 1-0 | 2-3 | 1-2 | 2-0 |
| SOUTHAMPTON | 1-0 | 1-1 | 3-0 | 1-1 | 3-3 | 3-4 | ■ | 1-1 | 1-1 | 1-0 | 3-1 | 2-1 | 1-1 | 2-1 | 2-3 | 0-1 | 1-2 | 2-0 | 2-0 | 3-1 |
| WIMBLEDON | 1-2 | 0-0 | 5-1 | 0-3 | 2-1 | 2-1 | 1-1 | ■ | 3-1 | 0-0 | 3-0 | 1-0 | 1-3 | 1-1 | 0-3 | 3-1 | 2-0 | 0-1 | 1-1 | 2-2 |
| NOTTS. FOREST | 2-1 | 2-2 | 1-2 | 0-2 | 7-0 | 3-1 | 3-1 | 2-1 | ■ | 5-0 | 1-1 | 3-0 | 1-1 | 1-3 | 0-1 | 1-0 | 2-2 | 4-3 | 2-0 | 2-0 |
| NORWICH CITY | 1-1 | 2-0 | 2-1 | 0-0 | 1-3 | 1-0 | 3-1 | 0-4 | 2-6 | ■ | 1-0 | 2-2 | 0-3 | 1-2 | 0-3 | 2-1 | 1-3 | 2-0 | 3-0 | 3-2 |
| Q. PK. RANGERS | 1-1 | 2-1 | 0-0 | 1-3 | 1-0 | 1-1 | 2-1 | 0-1 | 1-2 | 1-3 | ■ | 1-0 | 1-1 | 1-0 | 1-2 | 1-1 | 6-1 | 2-0 | 1-2 | 3-2 |
| COVENTRY CITY | 0-1 | 2-1 | 2-0 | 0-2 | 1-0 | 3-1 | 1-2 | 0-0 | 2-2 | 2-0 | 3-1 | ■ | 2-2 | 3-1 | 3-1 | 3-0 | 2-1 | 1-1 | 0-0 | 0-0 |
| MAN. UNITED | 1-1 | 1-1 | 1-1 | 0-1 | 2-3 | 0-2 | 3-2 | 2-1 | 0-1 | 3-0 | 3-1 | 2-0 | ■ | 1-0 | 2-0 | 3-1 | 4-1 | 1-1 | 2-0 | 3-0 |
| MAN. CITY | 0-3 | 2-1 | 2-1 | 0-1 | 2-1 | 1-0 | 3-3 | 1-1 | 3-1 | 2-1 | 2-1 | 2-0 | 3-3 | ■ | 0-2 | 2-1 | 3-0 | 2-3 | 2-0 | 3-2 |
| CRYST. PALACE | 1-0 | 0-0 | 1-0 | 0-0 | 2-1 | 0-0 | 2-1 | 4-3 | 2-2 | 1-3 | 0-0 | 2-1 | 3-0 | 1-3 | ■ | 2-1 | 1-0 | 1-1 | 1-0 | 2-1 |
| DERBY COUNTY | 1-7 | 0-2 | 0-1 | 0-2 | 4-6 | 2-3 | 6-2 | 1-1 | 2-1 | 0-0 | 1-1 | 1-1 | 0-0 | 1-1 | 0-2 | ■ | 2-1 | 0-1 | 1-1 | 3-3 |
| LUTON TOWN | 3-1 | 2-0 | 0-0 | 1-1 | 2-0 | 1-1 | 3-4 | 0-1 | 1-0 | 0-1 | 1-2 | 1-0 | 0-1 | 2-2 | 1-1 | 2-0 | ■ | 1-0 | 0-1 | 1-2 |
| LEEDS UTD. | 4-5 | 5-2 | 0-2 | 2-2 | 4-1 | 2-0 | 2-1 | 3-0 | 3-1 | 3-0 | 2-3 | 2-0 | 0-0 | 1-2 | 3-0 | 2-1 | | ■ | 2-1 | 5-0 |
| SHEFF. UTD. | 1-3 | 2-1 | 2-2 | 0-2 | 1-0 | 0-0 | 4-1 | 1-2 | 3-2 | 2-1 | 1-0 | 0-1 | 2-1 | 1-1 | 0-1 | 1-0 | 2-1 | 0-2 | ■ | 0-2 |
| SUNDERLAND | 0-1 | 1-3 | 0-0 | 0-0 | 1-0 | 2-2 | 1-0 | 0-0 | 1-0 | 1-2 | 0-1 | 0-0 | 2-1 | 1-1 | 2-1 | 1-2 | 2-0 | 0-1 | 0-1 | ■ |

## ENGLAND 1ST DIVISION 1990/91

### LEAGUE TABLE FINAL

| | | | | | | | |
|---|---|---|---|---|---|---|---|
| Arsenal | 38 | 24 | 13 | 1 | 74 | 18 | 83 |
| Liverpool | 38 | 23 | 7 | 8 | 77 | 40 | 76 |
| Crystal Palace | 38 | 20 | 9 | 9 | 50 | 41 | 69 |
| Leeds United | 38 | 19 | 7 | 12 | 65 | 47 | 64 |
| Manchester City | 38 | 17 | 11 | 10 | 64 | 53 | 62 |
| Manchester United | 38 | 16 | 12 | 12 | 58 | 45 | 59 |
| Wimbledon | 38 | 14 | 14 | 10 | 53 | 46 | 56 |
| Nottingham Forest | 38 | 14 | 12 | 12 | 65 | 50 | 54 |
| Everton | 38 | 13 | 12 | 13 | 50 | 46 | 51 |
| Tottenham Hotspur | 38 | 11 | 16 | 11 | 51 | 50 | 49 |
| Chelsea | 38 | 13 | 10 | 15 | 58 | 69 | 49 |
| Queen's Park Rangers | 38 | 12 | 10 | 16 | 44 | 53 | 46 |
| Sheffield United | 38 | 13 | 7 | 18 | 36 | 55 | 46 |
| Southampton | 38 | 12 | 9 | 17 | 58 | 69 | 45 |
| Norwich City | 38 | 13 | 6 | 19 | 41 | 64 | 45 |
| Coventry City | 38 | 11 | 11 | 16 | 42 | 49 | 44 |
| Aston Villa | 38 | 9 | 14 | 15 | 46 | 58 | 41 |
| Luton Town | 38 | 10 | 7 | 21 | 42 | 61 | 37 |
| Sunderland | 38 | 8 | 10 | 20 | 38 | 60 | 34 |
| Derby County | 38 | 5 | 9 | 24 | 37 | 75 | 24 |

Arsenal 2 points deducted
Manchester United 1 point deducted

Champions : - Arsenal
Relegated : - Sunderland and Derby County
League to be increased to 22 clubs for Season 1991/92

### TOP SCORERS

| | | |
|---|---|---|
| 1. | Alan Smith (Arsenal) | 22 |
| 2. | Lee Chapman (Leeds United) | 21 |
| 3. | John Fashanu (Wimbledon) | 20 |
| | Niall Quinn (Manchester City) | 20 |
| 5. | Matthew Le Tissier (Southampton) | 19 |
| | David Platt (Aston Villa) | 19 |
| 7. | Roy Wegerle (Queen's Park Rangers) | 18 |
| 8. | Dean Saunders (Derby County) | 17 |
| 9. | John Barnes (Liverpool) | 16 |
| | Lars Elstrup (Luton Town) | 16 |
| | Ian Rush (Liverpool) | 16 |
| | David White (Manchester City) | 16 |
| 13. | Gary Lineker (Tottenham Hotspur) | 15 |
| 14. | Nigel Clough (Nottingham Forest) | 14 |
| | Rodney Wallace (Southampton) | 14 |
| | Ian Wright (Crystal Palace) | 14 |
| 17. | Steve Bruce (Manchester United) | 13 |
| | Brian Deane (Sheffield United) | 13 |
| | Brian McClair (Manchester United) | 13 |
| | Paul Merson (Arsenal) | 13 |

Arsenal's Manager George Graham with the Football League Championship Trophy.

| ENGLAND 2nd Division 1990/91 | SHEFF. WED. | CHARL. ATH. | MILLWALL | NEWC. UTD. | SWIN. TOWN | BLACK.RVRS | W.HAM UTD. | OLDHM.ATH. | IPSWICH TN. | WOLVES | PORT VALE | PORTSMTH. | LEICS. CITY | HULL CITY | WATFORD | PLYM. ARG. | OXFD. UTD. | B. & H. ALB. | BARNSLEY | WEST BROM | MIDDLESBR. | BRIST.RVRS | BRISTL.CITY | NOTTS CO. |
|---|---|---|---|---|---|---|---|---|---|---|---|---|---|---|---|---|---|---|---|---|---|---|---|---|
| SHEFF. WED. | | 0-0 | 2-1 | 2-2 | 2-1 | 3-1 | 1-1 | 2-2 | 2-2 | 2-2 | 1-1 | 2-1 | 0-0 | 5-1 | 2-0 | 3-0 | 0-2 | 1-1 | 3-1 | 1-0 | 2-0 | 2-1 | 3-1 | 2-2 |
| CHARL. ATH. | 0-1 | | 0-0 | 1-0 | 1-2 | 0-0 | 1-1 | 1-1 | 1-1 | 1-0 | 0-1 | 2-1 | 1-2 | 2-1 | 1-2 | 0-1 | 3-3 | 1-2 | 2-1 | 2-0 | 0-1 | 2-2 | 2-1 | 3-1 |
| MILLWALL | 4-2 | 3-1 | | 0-1 | 1-0 | 2-1 | 1-1 | 0-0 | 1-1 | 2-1 | 1-2 | 2-0 | 2-1 | 3-3 | 0-2 | 4-1 | 1-2 | 3-0 | 4-1 | 4-1 | 2-2 | 1-1 | 1-2 | 1-2 |
| NEWC. UTD. | 1-0 | 1-3 | 1-2 | | 1-1 | 1-0 | 1-1 | 3-2 | 2-2 | 0-0 | 2-0 | 2-1 | 2-1 | 1-2 | 1-0 | 2-0 | 2-2 | 0-0 | 0-0 | 1-1 | 0-0 | 0-2 | 0-0 | 0-2 |
| SWIN. TOWN | 2-1 | 1-1 | 0-0 | 3-2 | | 1-1 | 0-1 | 2-2 | 1-0 | 1-0 | 1-2 | 3-0 | 5-2 | 3-1 | 1-2 | 1-1 | 0-0 | 1-3 | 1-2 | 2-1 | 1-3 | 0-2 | 0-1 | 1-2 |
| BLACK.RVRS | 1-0 | 2-2 | 1-0 | 0-1 | 2-1 | | 3-1 | 2-0 | 0-1 | 1-1 | 1-1 | 1-1 | 4-1 | 2-1 | 0-2 | 0-0 | 1-3 | 1-2 | 1-2 | 0-3 | 1-0 | 2-2 | 0-1 | 0-1 |
| W.HAM UTD. | 1-3 | 2-1 | 3-1 | 1-1 | 2-0 | 1-0 | | 2-0 | 3-1 | 1-1 | 0-0 | 1-1 | 1-0 | 7-1 | 1-0 | 2-2 | 2-0 | 2-1 | 3-2 | 3-1 | 0-0 | 1-0 | 1-0 | 1-2 |
| OLDHM.ATH. | 3-2 | 1-1 | 1-1 | 1-1 | 3-2 | 1-1 | 1-1 | | 2-0 | 4-1 | 2-0 | 3-1 | 2-0 | 1-2 | 4-1 | 5-3 | 3-0 | 6-1 | 2-0 | 2-1 | 2-0 | 2-0 | 2-1 | 2-1 |
| IPSWICH TN. | 0-2 | 4-4 | 0-3 | 2-1 | 1-1 | 2-1 | 0-1 | 1-2 | | 0-0 | 3-0 | 2-2 | 3-2 | 2-0 | 1-1 | 3-1 | 1-1 | 1-3 | 2-0 | 1-0 | 0-1 | 2-1 | 1-1 | 0-0 |
| WOLVES | 3-2 | 3-0 | 4-1 | 2-1 | 1-2 | 2-3 | 2-1 | 2-3 | 2-2 | | 3-1 | 3-1 | 2-1 | 0-0 | 0-0 | 3-3 | 2-3 | 0-5 | 2-2 | 1-0 | 1-1 | 4-0 | | 0-2 |
| PORT VALE | 1-1 | 1-1 | 0-2 | 0-1 | 3-1 | 3-0 | 0-1 | 1-0 | 1-2 | 1-2 | | 3-2 | 2-0 | 0-0 | 0-0 | 5-1 | 1-0 | 0-1 | 0-1 | 1-2 | 3-1 | 3-2 | 3-2 | 0-1 |
| PORTSMTH. | 2-0 | 0-1 | 0-0 | 0-1 | 2-1 | 3-2 | 0-1 | 1-4 | 1-1 | 0-0 | 2-4 | | 3-1 | 5-1 | 0-1 | 3-1 | 1-1 | 1-0 | 0-0 | 1-1 | 0-3 | 3-1 | 4-1 | 2-1 |
| LEICS. CITY | 2-4 | 1-2 | 1-2 | 5-4 | 2-2 | 1-3 | 1-2 | 0-0 | 1-2 | 1-0 | 1-1 | 2-1 | | 0-1 | 1-1 | 3-0 | 2-1 | 2-1 | 4-3 | 3-2 | 3-0 | 2-1 | | |
| HULL CITY | 0-1 | 2-2 | 1-1 | 2-1 | 1-1 | 3-1 | 0-0 | 2-2 | 3-3 | 1-2 | 3-2 | 0-2 | 5-2 | | 1-1 | 2-0 | 3-3 | 0-1 | 1-2 | 1-1 | 0-0 | 2-0 | 1-2 | 1-2 |
| WATFORD | 2-2 | 2-1 | 1-2 | 1-2 | 2-2 | 0-3 | 0-1 | 1-1 | 1-1 | 3-1 | 2-1 | 0-1 | 1-0 | 0-1 | | 2-0 | 1-1 | 0-1 | 0-0 | 1-1 | 0-3 | 1-1 | 2-3 | 1-3 |
| PLYM. ARG. | 1-1 | 2-0 | 3-2 | 0-1 | 3-3 | 4-1 | 0-1 | 1-2 | 0-0 | 1-0 | 2-0 | 1-1 | 2-0 | 4-1 | 1-1 | | 2-2 | 2-0 | 1-1 | 2-0 | 1-1 | 1-2 | 1-0 | 0-0 |
| OXFD. UTD. | 2-2 | 1-1 | 0-0 | 0-0 | 2-4 | 0-0 | 2-1 | 5-1 | 2-1 | 1-1 | 5-2 | 1-0 | 2-2 | 1-0 | 0-1 | 0-0 | | 3-0 | 2-0 | 1-3 | 2-5 | 3-1 | 3-1 | 3-3 |
| B. & H. ALB. | 0-4 | 3-2 | 0-0 | 4-2 | 3-3 | 1-0 | 1-0 | 1-2 | 1-1 | 1-2 | 3-2 | 3-0 | 3-1 | 3-0 | 3-2 | 0-3 | 1-0 | | 2-0 | 2-4 | 0-1 | 0-1 | 0-0 | |
| BARNSLEY | 1-1 | 1-1 | 1-2 | 1-1 | 5-1 | 0-1 | 1-0 | 0-1 | 5-1 | 1-1 | 1-1 | 4-0 | 1-1 | 3-1 | 2-1 | 1-0 | 3-0 | 2-1 | | 1-1 | 1-0 | 1-0 | 2-0 | 1-0 |
| WEST BROM | 1-2 | 1-0 | 0-1 | 1-1 | 2-1 | 2-0 | 0-0 | 0-0 | 1-2 | 1-1 | 1-1 | 0-0 | 2-1 | 1-1 | 1-1 | 1-3 | 2-0 | 1-1 | 1-1 | | 0-1 | 3-1 | 1-0 | 2-2 |
| MIDDLESBR. | 0-2 | 1-2 | 2-1 | 3-0 | 2-0 | 0-1 | 0-0 | 0-1 | 1-1 | 2-0 | 4-0 | 1-2 | 6-0 | 3-0 | 1-2 | 0-0 | 0-0 | 2-0 | 1-0 | 3-2 | | 1-2 | 2-1 | 1-0 |
| BRIST.RVRS | 0-1 | 2-1 | 1-0 | 1-1 | 2-1 | 1-2 | 0-1 | 2-0 | 1-0 | 1-1 | 2-0 | 1-2 | 0-0 | 1-1 | 3-1 | 0-0 | 1-0 | 1-3 | 2-1 | 1-1 | 2-0 | | 3-2 | 1-1 |
| BRISTL.CITY | 1-1 | 0-1 | 1-4 | 1-0 | 0-4 | 4-2 | 1-1 | 1-2 | 4-2 | 1-1 | 1-1 | 4-1 | 1-0 | 4-1 | 3-2 | 1-1 | 3-1 | 3-1 | 1-0 | 2-0 | 3-0 | 1-0 | | 3-2 |
| NOTTS CO. | 0-2 | 2-2 | 0-1 | 3-0 | 0-0 | 4-1 | 0-1 | 2-0 | 3-1 | 1-1 | 1-1 | 2-1 | 0-2 | 2-1 | 1-0 | 4-0 | 3-1 | 2-1 | 2-3 | 4-3 | 3-2 | 3-2 | 3-2 | |

## ENGLAND 2ND DIVISION 1990/91

### LEAGUE TABLE FINAL

| | | | | | | | |
|---|---|---|---|---|---|---|---|
| Oldham Athletic | 46 | 25 | 13 | 8 | 83 | 53 | 88 |
| West Ham United | 46 | 24 | 15 | 7 | 60 | 34 | 87 |
| Sheffield Wednesday | 46 | 22 | 16 | 8 | 80 | 51 | 82 |
| Notts County | 46 | 23 | 11 | 12 | 76 | 55 | 80 |
| Millwall | 46 | 20 | 13 | 13 | 70 | 51 | 73 |
| Brighton & Hove Albion | 46 | 21 | 7 | 18 | 63 | 69 | 70 |
| Middlesbrough | 46 | 20 | 9 | 17 | 66 | 47 | 69 |
| Barnsley | 46 | 19 | 12 | 15 | 63 | 48 | 69 |
| Bristol City | 46 | 20 | 7 | 19 | 68 | 71 | 67 |
| Oxford United | 46 | 14 | 19 | 13 | 69 | 66 | 61 |
| Newcastle United | 46 | 14 | 17 | 15 | 49 | 56 | 59 |
| Wolverhampton Wanderers | 46 | 13 | 19 | 14 | 63 | 63 | 58 |
| Bristol Rovers | 46 | 15 | 13 | 18 | 56 | 59 | 58 |
| Ipswich Town | 46 | 13 | 18 | 15 | 60 | 68 | 57 |
| Port Vale | 46 | 15 | 12 | 19 | 56 | 64 | 57 |
| Charlton Athletic | 46 | 13 | 17 | 16 | 57 | 61 | 56 |
| Portsmouth | 46 | 14 | 11 | 21 | 58 | 70 | 53 |
| Plymouth Argyle | 46 | 12 | 17 | 17 | 54 | 68 | 53 |
| Blackburn Rovers | 46 | 14 | 10 | 22 | 51 | 66 | 52 |
| Watford | 46 | 12 | 15 | 19 | 45 | 59 | 51 |
| Swindon Town | 46 | 12 | 14 | 20 | 65 | 73 | 50 |
| Leicester City | 46 | 14 | 8 | 24 | 60 | 83 | 50 |
| West Bromwich Albion | 46 | 10 | 18 | 18 | 52 | 61 | 48 |
| Hull City | 46 | 10 | 15 | 21 | 57 | 85 | 45 |

### PROMOTION PLAY-OFFS

| | 1ST LEG | 2ND LEG | AGG. |
|---|---|---|---|
| Brighton & Hove Albion v Millwall | 4-1 | 2-1 | 6-2 |
| Middlesbrough v Notts County | 1-1 | 0-1 | 1-2 |

**PLAY-OFF FINAL**

Notts County..............3     Brighton & Hove Alb. ..1

Promoted : - Oldham Athletic, West Ham United, Sheffield
Wednesday and Notts County

Relegated : - West Bromwich Albion and Hull City

## ENGLAND 3RD DIVISION 1990/91

### LEAGUE TABLE FINAL

| | | | | | | | |
|---|---|---|---|---|---|---|---|
| Cambridge United | 46 | 25 | 11 | 10 | 75 | 45 | 86 |
| Southend United | 46 | 26 | 7 | 13 | 77 | 51 | 85 |
| Grimsby Town | 46 | 24 | 11 | 11 | 66 | 44 | 83 |
| Bolton Wanderers | 46 | 24 | 11 | 11 | 64 | 50 | 83 |
| Tranmere Rovers | 46 | 23 | 9 | 14 | 64 | 46 | 78 |
| Brentford | 46 | 21 | 13 | 12 | 59 | 47 | 76 |
| Bury | 46 | 20 | 13 | 13 | 67 | 56 | 73 |
| Bradford City | 46 | 20 | 10 | 16 | 62 | 54 | 70 |
| AFC Bournemouth | 46 | 19 | 13 | 14 | 58 | 58 | 70 |
| Wigan Athletic | 46 | 20 | 9 | 17 | 71 | 54 | 69 |
| Huddersfield Town | 46 | 18 | 13 | 15 | 57 | 51 | 67 |
| Birmingham City | 46 | 16 | 17 | 13 | 45 | 49 | 65 |
| Leyton Orient | 46 | 18 | 10 | 18 | 55 | 58 | 64 |
| Stoke City | 46 | 16 | 12 | 18 | 55 | 59 | 60 |
| Reading | 46 | 17 | 8 | 21 | 53 | 66 | 59 |
| Exeter City | 46 | 16 | 9 | 21 | 58 | 52 | 57 |
| Preston North End | 46 | 15 | 11 | 20 | 54 | 67 | 56 |
| Shrewsbury Town | 46 | 14 | 10 | 22 | 61 | 68 | 52 |
| Chester City | 46 | 14 | 9 | 23 | 46 | 58 | 51 |
| Swansea City | 46 | 13 | 9 | 24 | 49 | 72 | 48 |
| Fulham | 46 | 10 | 16 | 20 | 41 | 56 | 46 |
| Crewe Alexandra | 46 | 11 | 11 | 24 | 62 | 80 | 44 |
| Rotherham United | 46 | 10 | 12 | 24 | 50 | 87 | 42 |
| Mansfield Town | 46 | 8 | 14 | 24 | 42 | 63 | 38 |

Promoted : - Cambridge United, Southend United, Grimsby Town, Tranmere Rovers

Relegated : - Crewe Alexandra, Rotherham United and Mansfield Town

### PROMOTION PLAY-OFFS

| | 1ST LEG | 2ND LEG | AGG. |
|---|---|---|---|
| Brentford v Tranmere Rovers | 2-2 | 0-1 | 2-3 |
| Bury v Bolton Wanderers | 1-1 | 0-1 | 1-2 |

### PLAY-OFF FINAL

Tranmere Rovers ...... 1    Bolton Wanderers......0  (aet.)

## ENGLAND 4TH DIVISION 1990/91

### LEAGUE TABLE FINAL

| | | | | | | | |
|---|---|---|---|---|---|---|---|
| Darlington | 46 | 22 | 17 | 7 | 68 | 38 | 83 |
| Stockport County | 46 | 23 | 13 | 10 | 84 | 47 | 82 |
| Hartlepool United | 46 | 24 | 10 | 12 | 67 | 48 | 82 |
| Peterborough United | 46 | 21 | 17 | 8 | 67 | 45 | 80 |
| Blackpool | 46 | 23 | 10 | 13 | 78 | 47 | 79 |
| Burnley | 46 | 23 | 10 | 13 | 70 | 51 | 79 |
| Torquay United | 46 | 18 | 18 | 10 | 64 | 47 | 72 |
| Scunthorpe United | 46 | 20 | 11 | 15 | 71 | 62 | 71 |
| Scarborough | 46 | 19 | 12 | 15 | 59 | 56 | 69 |
| Northampton Town | 46 | 18 | 13 | 15 | 57 | 58 | 67 |
| Doncaster Rovers | 46 | 17 | 14 | 15 | 56 | 46 | 65 |
| Rochdale | 46 | 15 | 17 | 14 | 50 | 53 | 62 |
| Cardiff City | 46 | 15 | 15 | 16 | 43 | 54 | 60 |
| Lincoln City | 46 | 14 | 17 | 15 | 50 | 61 | 59 |
| Gillingham | 46 | 12 | 18 | 16 | 67 | 60 | 54 |
| Walsall | 46 | 12 | 17 | 17 | 48 | 51 | 53 |
| Hereford United | 46 | 13 | 14 | 19 | 53 | 58 | 53 |
| Chesterfield | 46 | 13 | 14 | 19 | 47 | 62 | 53 |
| Maidstone United | 46 | 13 | 12 | 21 | 66 | 71 | 51 |
| Carlisle United | 46 | 13 | 9 | 24 | 47 | 89 | 48 |
| York City | 46 | 11 | 13 | 22 | 45 | 57 | 46 |
| Halifax Town | 46 | 12 | 10 | 24 | 59 | 79 | 46 |
| Aldershot | 46 | 10 | 11 | 25 | 61 | 101 | 41 |
| Wrexham | 46 | 10 | 10 | 26 | 48 | 74 | 40 |

Promoted : - Darlington, Stockport County, Hartlepool United, Peterborough United and Torquay United

League temporarily reduced to 23 clubs for Season 1991/92

### PROMOTION PLAY-OFFS

| | 1ST LEG | 2ND LEG | AGG. |
|---|---|---|---|
| Scunthorpe United v Blackpool | 1-1 | 1-2 | 2-3 |
| Torquay United v Burnley | 2-0 | 0-1 | 2-1 |

### PLAY-OFF FINAL

Torquay United ..........2    Blackpool ..................2  (aet.)
Torquay United win 5-4 on penalties

## GM VAUXHALL CONFERENCE 1990/91

### LEAGUE TABLE FINAL

| | | | | | | | |
|---|---|---|---|---|---|---|---|
| Barnet | 42 | 26 | 9 | 7 | 103 | 52 | 87 |
| Colchester United | 42 | 25 | 10 | 7 | 68 | 35 | 85 |
| Altrincham | 42 | 23 | 13 | 6 | 87 | 46 | 82 |
| Kettering Town | 42 | 23 | 11 | 8 | 67 | 45 | 80 |
| Wycombe Wanderers | 42 | 21 | 11 | 10 | 75 | 46 | 74 |
| Telford United | 42 | 20 | 7 | 15 | 62 | 52 | 67 |
| Macclesfield Town | 42 | 17 | 12 | 13 | 63 | 52 | 63 |
| Runcorn | 42 | 16 | 10 | 16 | 69 | 67 | 58 |
| Merthyr Tydfil | 42 | 16 | 9 | 17 | 62 | 61 | 57 |
| Barrow | 42 | 15 | 12 | 15 | 59 | 65 | 57 |
| Welling United | 42 | 13 | 15 | 14 | 55 | 57 | 54 |
| Northwich Victoria | 42 | 13 | 13 | 16 | 65 | 75 | 52 |
| Kidderminster Harriers | 42 | 14 | 10 | 18 | 56 | 67 | 52 |
| Yeovil Town | 42 | 13 | 11 | 18 | 58 | 58 | 50 |
| Stafford Rangers | 42 | 12 | 14 | 16 | 48 | 51 | 50 |
| Cheltenham Town | 42 | 12 | 12 | 18 | 54 | 72 | 48 |
| Gateshead | 42 | 14 | 6 | 22 | 52 | 92 | 48 |
| Boston United | 42 | 12 | 11 | 19 | 55 | 69 | 47 |
| Slough Town | 42 | 13 | 6 | 23 | 51 | 80 | 45 |
| Bath City | 42 | 10 | 12 | 20 | 55 | 61 | 42 |
| Sutton United | 42 | 10 | 9 | 23 | 62 | 82 | 39 |
| Fisher Athletic | 42 | 5 | 15 | 22 | 38 | 79 | 30 |

Promoted to 4th Division : - Barnet

Relegated : - Sutton United and Fisher Athletic

## VAUXHALL FOOTBALL LGE. 1990/91

### LEAGUE TABLE FINAL

| | |
|---|---|
| Redbridge Forest | 42-93 |
| Enfield | 42-89 |
| Aylesbury United | 42-83 |
| Woking | 42-82 |
| Kingstonian | 42-75 |
| Grays Athletic | 42-68 |
| Marlow | 42-67 |
| Hayes | 42-65 |
| Carshalton Athletic | 42-64 |
| Wivenhoe Town | 42-59 |
| Wokingham | 42-58 |
| Windsor & Eton | 42-55 |
| Bishop's Stortford | 42-54 |
| Dagenham | 42-50 |
| Hendon | 42-46 |
| St.Albans City | 42-45 |
| Bognor Regis Town | 42-44 |
| Basingstoke Town | 42-43 |
| Staines Athletic | 42-39 |
| Harrow Borough | 42-38 |
| Barking | 42-34 |
| Leyton-Wingate | 42-28 |

Staines 1 point deducted

## HFS LOANS LEAGUE 1990/91

### LEAGUE TABLE FINAL

| | |
|---|---|
| Witton Albion | 40-93 |
| Stalybridge Celtic | 40-77 |
| Morecambe | 40-71 |
| Fleetwood Town | 40-69 |
| Southport | 40-68 |
| Marine | 40-65 |
| Bishop Auckland | 40-61 |
| Buxton | 40-59 |
| Leek Town | 40-56 |
| Frickley Athletic | 40-54 |
| Hyde United | 40-53 |
| Goole Town | 40-52 |
| Chorley | 40-47 |
| Droylsden | 40-47 |
| Mossley | 40-45 |
| Horwich RMI | 40-45 |
| Matlock Town | 40-43 |
| Bangor City | 40-39 |
| South Liverpool | 40-39 |
| Gainsborough Trinity | 40-38 |
| Shepshed Charterhouse | 40-25 |

Buxton 3 points deducted
Mossley 4 points deducted

## BEAZER HOMES PREMIER LEAGUE 1990/91

### LEAGUE TABLE FINAL

| | |
|---|---|
| Farnborough Town | 42-85 |
| Gloucester City | 42-83 |
| Cambridge City | 42-77 |
| Dover Athletic | 42-74 |
| Bromsgrove Rovers | 42-71 |
| Worcester City | 42-66 |
| Burton Albion | 42-60 |
| Halesowen Town | 42-60 |
| VS Rugby | 42-59 |
| Bashley | 42-57 |
| Dorchester Town | 42-57 |
| Wealdstone | 42-56 |
| Dartford | 42-54 |
| Rushden Town | 42-53 |
| Atherstone United | 42-52 |
| Moor Green | 42-51 |
| Poole Town | 42-49 |
| Chelmsford City | 42-48 |
| Crawley Town | 42-48 |
| Waterlooville | 42-46 |
| Gravesend & Northfleet | 42-34 |
| Weymouth | 42-24 |

Staines 1 point deducted

# ENGLAND LEAGUE CUP 1990/91

| 1ST ROUND | 1ST LEG | 2ND LEG | | AGG. |
|---|---|---|---|---|
| Stockport County v Burnley | 0-2 | 1-0 | | 1-2 |
| Birmingham City v AFC Bournemouth | 0-1 | 1-1 | | 1-2 |
| Brentford v Hereford United | 2-0 | 0-1 | | 2-1 |
| Carlisle United v Scunthorpe United | 1-0 | 1-1 | | 2-1 |
| Chesterfield v Hartlepool United | 1-2 | 2-2 | | 3-4 |
| Darlington v Blackpool (Darlington win on the away goals rule) | 0-0 | 1-1 | (aet.) | 1-1 |
| Doncaster Rovers v Rotherham United | 2-6 | 1-2 | | 3-8 |
| Fulham v Peterborough United | 1-2 | 0-2 | | 1-4 |
| Gillingham v Shrewsbury Town | 1-0 | 0-2 | | 1-2 |
| Grimsby Town v Crewe Alexandra (Crewe win on the away goals rule) | 2-1 | 0-1 | (aet.) | 2-2 |
| Halifax Town v Lincoln City | 2-0 | 0-1 | | 2-1 |
| Mansfield Town v Cardiff City | 1-1 | 0-3 | | 1-4 |
| Middlesbrough v Tranmere Rovers | 1-1 | 2-1 | | 3-2 |
| Preston North End v Chester City | 2-0 | 1-5 | (aet.) | 3-5 |
| Reading v Oxford United | 0-1 | 1-2 | | 1-3 |
| Rochdale v Scarborough | 4-0 | 3-3 | | 7-3 |
| Southend United v Aldershot | 2-1 | 2-2 | | 4-3 |
| Walsall v Cambridge United | 4-2 | 1-2 | | 5-4 |
| Wigan Athletic v Barnsley (Barnsley win 4-3 on penalties) | 0-1 | 1-0 | (aet.) | 1-1 |
| York City v Wrexham | 0-1 | 0-2 | | 0-3 |
| Bradford City v Bury | 2-0 | 2-3 | (aet.) | 4-3 |
| Brighton & Hove Albion v Northampton Town | 0-2 | 1-1 | | 1-3 |
| Bristol Rovers v Torquay United | 1-2 | 1-1 | | 2-3 |
| Exeter City v Notts County | 1-1 | 0-1 | | 1-2 |
| Huddersfield Town v Bolton Wanderers | 0-3 | 1-2 | | 1-5 |
| Maidstone United v Leyton Orient | 2-2 | 1-4 | | 3-6 |
| Stoke City v Swansea City | 0-0 | 1-0 | | 1-0 |
| West Bromwich Albion v Bristol City | 2-2 | 0-1 | (aet.) | 2-3 |

| 2ND ROUND | 1ST LEG | 2ND LEG | | AGG. |
|---|---|---|---|---|
| Port Vale v Oxford United | 0-2 | 0-0 | | 0-2 |
| AFC Bournemouth v Millwall | 0-0 | 1-2 | | 1-2 |
| Cardiff City v Portsmouth | 1-1 | 1-3 | (aet.) | 2-4 |
| Carlisle United v Derby County | 1-1 | 0-1 | | 1-2 |
| Chester City v Arsenal | 0-1 | 0-5 | | 0-6 |
| Crystal Palace v Southend United | 8-0 | 2-1 | | 10-1 |
| Darlington v Swindon Town | 3-0 | 0-4 | | 3-4 |

**England's 1990 World Cup Squad**

# ENGLAND F.A. CUP 1990/91

## 3RD ROUND

| Match | | |
|---|---|---|
| Hull City v Wolverhampton Wanderers (Hull City win on the away goals rule) | 0-0 | 1-1 |
| Liverpool v Crewe Alexandra | 5-1 | 9-2 |
| Luton Town v Bradford City (Bradford City win 5-4 on penalties) | 1-1 (aet) | 2-2 |
| Middlesbrough v Newcastle United | 1-1 (aet) | 1-2 |
| Northampton Town v Sheffield United | 2-0 | 1-3 |
| Notts County v Oldham Athletic | 0-1 | |
| Plymouth Argyle v Wimbledon | 1-2 | |
| Rochdale v Southampton | 1-0 | 2-5 (aet) |
| Rotherham United v Blackburn Rovers | 1-1 | 3-5 |
| Shrewsbury Town v Ipswich Town | 0-5 | |
| Sunderland v Bristol City | 1-1 | |
| Wrexham v Everton | 0-5 | |
| Aston Villa v Barnsley | 1-0 | |
| Charlton Athletic v Leyton Orient | 0-1 | |
| Coventry City v Bolton Wanderers | 2-2 | 2-3 |
| Halifax Town v Manchester United | 1-3 | |
| Leicester City v Leeds United | 1-0 | |
| Norwich City v Watford | 2-0 | |
| Nottingham Forest v Burnley | 4-1 | |
| Queen's Park Rangers v Peterborough United | 3-1 | |
| Sheffield Wednesday v Brentford | 2-1 | |
| Torquay United v Manchester City | 0-4 | |
| Tottenham Hotspur v Hartlepool United | 5-0 | |
| Walsall v Chelsea | 0-4 | |
| West Ham United v Stoke City | 3-0 | |

### (stacked results)

| | | | |
|---|---|---|---|
| Ipswich Town | 0 | Southampton | 2 |
| Middlesbrough | 2 | Norwich City | 1-3 |
| Tottenham Hotspur | 2 | Bradford City | 3-0 |
| Chelsea | 1 | Portsmouth | 0 |
| Derby County | 0 | Sunderland | 1-1 |
| Manchester United | 6 | Liverpool | 4-2 |
| Oldham Athletic | 3 | Nottingham Forest | 0-4 |
| Plymouth Argyle | 2 | Nottingham Forest | 2 |
| Sheffid Wednesday | 0 | Swindon Town | 1-9 |

## REPLAYS

| | | | |
|---|---|---|---|
| Portsmouth | 2 | Chelsea | 3 |
| Leyton Orient | 0 | Crystal Palace | 1 |
| Swindon Town | 0 | Sheffield Wednesday | 1 |

## 4TH ROUND

| | | | |
|---|---|---|---|
| Queen's Pk Rangers | 0 | Leeds United | 3 |
| Southampton | 2 | Crystal Palace | 2 |
| Aston Villa | 3 | Middlesbrough | 2 |
| Oxford United | 1 | Chelsea | 2 |

## REPLAY

| | | | |
|---|---|---|---|
| Derby County | 1 | Sheffield Wednesday | 2 |

## 5TH ROUND

| | | | |
|---|---|---|---|
| Crystal Palace | 1 | Sheffield Wednesday | 2 |
| Chelsea | 3 | Tottenham Hotspur | |
| Southampton | 1 | Manchester United | 1 |
| Coventry City | 0 | Sheffield Wednesday | 1 |

## REPLAYS

| | | | |
|---|---|---|---|
| Manchester United | 3 | Southampton | 2 |

## SEMI-FINALS

| | 1ST LEG | 2ND LEG | AGG. |
|---|---|---|---|
| Manchester United v Leeds United | 2-1 | 1-0 | 3-1 |
| Chelsea v Sheffield Wednesday | 0-2 | 1-3 | 1-5 |

## FINAL

21/4/91 at Wembley Stadium, London

**Sheffield Wednesday .... 1    Manchester United .... 0**

Sheffield W : Turner, Nilsson, King, Harkes (Madden 87), Shirtliff, Pearson, Wilson, Sheridan, Hirst, Williams, Worthington.

Manchester U : Sealey, Irwin, Blackmore, Bruce, Webb (Phelan 56), Pallister, Robson, Ince, McClair, Hughes, Sharpe.

1-0  Sheridan  37

Referee : R.Lewis
Attendance : 77,612

---

## 1ST ROUND

| | | | |
|---|---|---|---|
| Aldershot | 6 | Atherstone United | 3 |
| Aylesbury United | 0 | Barnet | 2 |
| Birmingham City | 1 | Bishop Auckland | 2 |
| Blackpool | 2 | Boston United | 1 |
| AFC Bournemouth | 2 | Scarborough | 0 |
| Brentford | 5 | Preston North End | 1 |
| Chester City | 0 | Rotherham United | 1 |
| Cardiff City | 0 | Lincoln City | 1 |
| Darlington | 1 | Hereford United | 2 |
| Chorley | 2 | Doncaster Rovers | 1 |
| Bury | 1 | Scunthorpe United | 2 |
| York City | 1 | Hayes | 1 |
| Exeter City | 2 | Maidstone United | 4 |
| Colchester United | 3 | Preston North End | 1 |
| Reading | 2 | Rotherham United | 0 |
| Cambridge United | 2 | Leek Town | 2 |
| Tranmere Rovers | 2 | Torquay United | 4 |
| Halesowen Town | 1 | Crewe Alexandra | 4 |
| Wrexham | 1 | Cambridge United | 2 |
| Peterborough United | 1 | Tranmere Rovers | 2 |
| Halifax Town | 2 | Huddersfield Town | 2 |
| Woking | 0 | | |

## REPLAYS

| | | | |
|---|---|---|---|
| York City | 1 | Maidstone United | 1 |
| Peterborough United | 2 | Scunthorpe United | 2 |
| Chelmsford City | 0 | Hayes | 1 |
| Kidderminst. Harriers | 1 | Woking | 1 (aet) |
| Stoke City | 0 | Telford United | 0 |
| Wycombe Wand'ers | 4 | Sutton United | 0 |
| Kidderminst. Harriers | 1 | Woking | 0 |

## 2ND ROUND

| | | | |
|---|---|---|---|
| Fulham | 0 | Cambridge United | 0 |
| Barnet | 0 | AFC Bournemouth | 2 |
| Scunthorpe United | 3 | Northampton Town | 0 |
| Wigan Athletic | 2 | Tranmere Rovers | 2 |
| Huddersfield Town | 1 | Hartlepool United | 0 |
| Rotherham United | 1 | Blackpool | 2 |
| Birmingham City | 1 | Brentford | 3 |
| Colchester United | 0 | Leyton Orient | 1 |
| Leek Town | 0 | Chester City | 1 |
| Whitley Bay | 0 | Barrow | 0 |

## 2ND REPLAY

| | | | |
|---|---|---|---|
| Kidderminst. Harriers | 1 | Woking | 0 |

1-0  Sheridan  37

## REPLAYS

Cambridge United....2 — Fulham....1
Chester City....4 — Leek Town....0
Leyton Orient....4 — Colchester United....1
Northampton Town....0 — Barnet....1
Halifax Town....1 — Rotherham United....2
Peterborough United....2 — Wycombe Wanders....0

## 3RD ROUND

Arsenal....2 — Sunderland....1
Barnet....0 — Portsmouth....5
Blackpool....0 — Bolton Wanderers....1
Brighton & Hove Alb.....3 — Scunthorpe United....2
Charlton Athletic....1 — Everton....2
Chester City....2 — Coventry City....1
Hull City....2 — Leyton Orient....1
Mansfield Town....0 — Sheffield Wednesday....2
Millwall....1 — Leicester City....1
Norwich City....2 — Bristol City....1
Port Vale....2 — Peterborough United....1
Shrewsbury Town....4 — Watford....1
Swansea City....0 — Rotherham United....1
Aldershot....0 — West Ham United....0 (at Upton Pk)
Barnsley....1 — Wolverhampton Wn.....0
Crystal Palace....0 — Nottingham Forest....0
Leeds United....6

## REPLAYS

Liverpool....3 — Blackburn Rovers....0
Wigan Athletic....1 — Coventry City....1
Plymouth Argyle....1 — Middlesbrough....2
Nottingham Forest....2 — Crystal Palace....2 (aet.)
Swindon Town....1 — Leyton Orient....0

## 2ND REPLAY

Nottingham Forest....3 — Crystal Palace....0

## 4TH ROUND

Cambridge United....2 — Middlesbrough....0
Crewe Alexandra....4 — Rotherham United....1
Luton Town....1 — West Ham United....1
Millwall....4 — Sheffield Wednesday....4
Notts County....1 — Oldham Athletic....2
Port Vale....4 — Manchester City....1
Tottenham Hotspur....4 — Oxford United....2
Woking....0 — Everton....1 (at Goodison Park)
Newcastle United....2 — Nottingham Forest....2

## REPLAY

Southampton....2 — Coventry City....0
Leeds United....1 — Arsenal....1 (aet.)
West Ham United....5 — Luton Town....0

## 2ND REPLAY

Arsenal....0 — Leeds United....0 (aet.)

## 3RD REPLAY

Leeds United....1 — Arsenal....2

## 5TH ROUND

Cambridge United....4 — Sheffield Wednesday....0
Portsmouth....0 — Tottenham Hotspur....2
Liverpool....0 — Everton....0
Southampton....1 — Nottingham Forest....1

## REPLAYS

Coventry City....2 — Brighton & Hove Alb.....2
Leeds United....1 — Sheff'ld Wednesday....1 (aet.)
West Ham United....5 — Nottingham Forest....3

## 2ND REPLAY

Everton....1 — Liverpool....0

## 6TH ROUND

Arsenal....2 — Cambridge United....1
Norwich City....0 — West Ham United....2
Tottenham Hotspur....2 — Notts County....1
Nottingham Forest....3

## SEMI-FINALS

Tottenham Hotspur....3 — Arsenal....1
Nottingham Forest....4 — West Ham United....0

## FINAL

**18/5/91 (at Wembley Stadium, London)**

Tottenham Hotspur....2   Nottingham Forest....1 (aet.)

Tottenham H: Thorstvedt, Edinburgh, Van den Hauwe, Sedgley, Howells, Mabbutt, Stewart, Gascoigne (Nayim 17), Samways (Walsh 81), Lineker, Allen.

Nottingham F: Crossley, Charles, Pearce, Walker, Chettle, Keane, Crosby, Parker, Clough, Glover (Laws 107), Woan (Hodge 61).

| | | |
|---|---|---|
| 0-1 | Pearce | 15 |
| 1-1 | Stewart | 54 |
| 2-1 | Walker o.g. | 93 |

Referee : R.Milford
Attendance : 80,000

## ENGLAND : All Time Records as at 31/12/90 - CAPS

| | | |
|---|---|---|
| 1. | Peter Shilton (Leicester City/Stoke City/Nottingham Forest/Southampton/Derby County) | 125 |
| 2. | Bobby Moore (West Ham United) | 108 |
| 3. | Bobby Charlton (Manchester United) | 106 |
| 4. | Billy Wright (Wolverhampton Wanderers) | 105 |
| 5. | Bryan Robson (West Bromwich Albion/Manchester United) | 87 |
| 6. | Kenny Sansom (Crystal Palace/Arsenal) | 86 |
| 7. | Ray Wilkins (Chelsea/Manchester United/Milan AC) | 84 |
| 8. | Terry Butcher (Ipswich Town/Rangers) | 77 |
| 9. | Tom Finney (Preston North End) | 76 |
| 10. | Gordon Banks (Leicester City/Stoke City) | 73 |

## ENGLAND : All Time Records as at 31/12/90 - GOALS

| | | | |
|---|---|---|---|
| 1. | Bobby Charlton (Manchester United) | (106) | 49 |
| 2. | Jimmy Greaves (Chelsea/Tottenham Hotspur) | (57) | 44 |
| 3. | Gary Lineker (Leicester City/Everton/FC Barcelona/Tottenham Hotspur) | (61) | 37 |
| 4. | Nat Lofthouse (Bolton Wanderers) | (33) | 30 |
| | Tom Finney (Preston North End) | (76) | 30 |
| 6. | Vivian Woodward (Tottenham Hotspur/Chelsea) | (23) | 29 |
| 7. | Steve Bloomer (Derby County/Middlesbrough) | (23) | 28 |
| 8. | Bryan Robson (West Bromwich Albion/Manchester United) | (87) | 26 |
| 9. | Stan Mortensen (Blackpool) | (25) | 24 |
| | Geoff Hurst (West Ham United) | (49) | 24 |

# INTERNATIONAL LINE-UPS 1990

| Date | Match | Venue | Referee | Competition (Scorers) |
|---|---|---|---|---|
| 28/3/90 | ENGLAND 1 BRAZIL 0 | London | Ref: Peschel (DDR) | Friendly (Lineker) |
| 25/4/90 | ENGLAND 4 CZECHOSLOVAKIA 2 | London | Ref: Girard (France) | Friendly (Bull 2, Pearce, Gascoigne) |
| 15/5/90 | ENGLAND 1 DENMARK 0 | London | Ref: McCluskey (Scotland) | Friendly (Lineker) |
| 22/5/90 | ENGLAND 1 URUGUAY 2 | London | Ref: D'Elia (Italy) | Friendly (Barnes) |
| 2/6/90 | TUNISIA 1 ENGLAND 1 | Tunis | Ref: Medjiba (Tunisia) | Friendly (Bull) |
| 11/6/90 | REPUBLIC OF IRELAND 1 ENGLAND 1 | Cagliari | Ref: Schmidhuber (Germany) | World Cup (Lineker) |
| 16/6/90 | HOLLAND 0 ENGLAND 0 | Cagliari | Ref: Petrovic (Yugoslavia) | World Cup |
| 21/6/90 | EGYPT 0 ENGLAND 1 | Cagliari | Ref: Rothlisberger (Switzerland) | World Cup (Wright) |
| 26/6/90 | BELGIUM 0 ENGLAND 1 (aet.) | Bologna | Ref: Mikkelsen (Denmark) | World Cup (Platt) |
| 1/7/90 | CAMEROON 2 ENGLAND 3 (aet.) | Napoli | Ref: Codesal (Mexico) | World Cup (Platt, Lineker 2) |
| 4/7/90 | WESTERN GERMANY 1 ENGLAND 1 (aet.) | Torino | Ref: Wright (Brazil) | World Cup (Lineker) — WESTERN GERMANY WIN 4-3 ON PENALTIES |
| 7/7/90 | ITALY 2 ENGLAND 1 | Bari | Ref: Quiniou (France) | World Cup (Platt) |
| 12/9/90 | ENGLAND 1 HUNGARY 0 | London | Ref: Fredriksson (Sweden) | Friendly (Lineker) |
| 17/10/90 | ENGLAND 2 POLAND 0 | London | Ref: Lanese (Italy) | EuroCh.Q. (Lineker, Beardsley) |
| 14/11/90 | REPUBLIC OF IRELAND 1 ENGLAND 1 | Dublin | Ref: D'Elia (Italy) | EuroCh.Q. (Platt) |

| Date | Shilton | Stevens | Pearce | McMahon | Walker | Butcher | Platt | Waddle | Beardsley | Lineker | Barnes | Woods | Gascoigne | Dixon | Steven | Robson | Bull | Hodge | Seaman | Dorigo | Wright | Rocastle | Parker | Webb | Adams | Cowans |
|---|---|---|---|---|---|---|---|---|---|---|---|---|---|---|---|---|---|---|---|---|---|---|---|---|---|---|
| 28/3/90 | 1 | 2 | 3 | 4 | 5 | 6 | (4) | 8 | (9) | 10 | 11 | (1) | | | | 7 | 9 | | | (3) | (6) | | | | | |
| 25/4/90 | 1 | 2 | 3 | 4 | 5 | 6 | (4) | | (10) | 10 | | | 8 | 2 | (7) | 7 | 9 | 11 | (1) | | | | | | | |
| 15/5/90 | 1 | | 3 | | 5 | 6 | | 8 | 9 | 10 | 11 | (1) | (4) | | | 7 | (9) | | | | | | | | | |
| 22/5/90 | 1 | 2 | 3 | 4 | 5 | 6 | | 8 | 9 | 10 | 11 | (1) | (4) | | | 7 | (9) | | | (3) | (6) | | | | | |
| 2/6/90 | | | 3 | (7) | 5 | 6 | (9) | 8 | (10) | 11 | 10 | 1 | | | | 7 | (10) | | | | 6 | | | (9) | | |
| 11/6/90 | 1 | | 3 | 4 | 5 | 6 | | 8 | 9 | 10 | 11 | | 8 | | | 7 | (9) | | | | | | | | | |
| 16/6/90 | 1 | | 3 | (7) | 5 | 6 | (7) | 7 | (10) | 10 | 11 | | 8 | | (3) | 7 | | | | | 4 | | 2 | | | |
| 21/6/90 | 1 | | 3 | | 5 | 5 | (6) | 7 | (11) | 10 | 10 | | 8 | | (3) | | | | | | 4 | | 2 | | | |
| 26/6/90 | 1 | | 3 | | 5 | 5 | 8 | 7 | (10) | 11 | 9 | | 8 | | | | | | | | 4 | | 2 | | | |
| 1/7/90 | 1 | | 3 | | 5 | 3 | 7 | 7 | (9) | 10 | 11 | | 8 | | | | | | | | 4 | | 2 | | | |
| 4/7/90 | 1 | | 3 | | 5 | 3 | 7 | 8 | 7 | 11 | 10 | | 8 | | (3) | | | | | | 4 | | 2 | | | |
| 7/7/90 | 1 | 2 | 3 | | 5 | 3 | 7 | 8 | 7 | 11 | 11 | | 8 | | 7 | | | 4 | | | | | | | | |
| 12/9/90 | | | 3 | 9 | 5 | | | | 10 | 11 | 9 | 1 | 8 | 2 | | 7 | | | | (6) | | (9) | | | | |
| 17/10/90 | | | 6 | | 4 | | 6 | (10) | (9) | 11 | 11 | 1 | 8 | 2 | | 9 | 10 | | (1) | | | | | (9) | | |
| 14/11/90 | | | | 9 | 4 | | 7 | 6 | 10 | 11 | 11 | 1 | 8 | 2 | | | | | | | 6 | | | | 3 | |
| CAPS AT 31/12/90 | 125 | 41 | 33 | 16 | 28 | 77 | 14 | 61 | 47 | 61 | 60 | 19 | 19 | 4 | 23 | 87 | 13 | 22 | 3 | 5 | 33 | 11 | 13 | 20 | 18 | 10 |
| GOALS AT 31/12/90 | | 1 | 1 | | | 3 | 4 | 6 | 8 | 37 | 10 | | 2 | | 3 | 26 | 4 | | | | 1 | | | 3 | 4 | 2 |

# FAROER ISLANDS Correspondent : UTLAGI

## FAROER ISLANDS 1ST DIVISION 1990

### 1st Division results table

| FAROER ISLANDS 1st Division Season 1990 | B 71 | HB | B 68 | VB | KI | B 36 | GI | SIF | MB | TB |
|---|---|---|---|---|---|---|---|---|---|---|
| B 71 (Sandur) | | 2-1 | 1-0 | 1-2 | 2-2 | 2-3 | 0-2 | 0-1 | 0-2 | 1-0 |
| HB (Torshavn) | 2-0 | | 1-1 | 4-2 | 2-2 | 2-1 | 2-1 | 3-1 | 3-0 | 1-1 |
| B 68 (Toftir) | 2-1 | 0-0 | | 4-1 | 0-2 | 1-0 | 0-2 | 1-1 | 1-1 | 1-0 |
| VB (Vagur) | 1-1 | 3-1 | 1-1 | | 0-1 | 3-1 | 2-0 | 2-1 | 2-3 | 0-0 |
| KI (Klakksvik) | 1-1 | 0-3 | 2-1 | 0-2 | | 0-1 | 2-2 | 3-0 | 6-5 | 5-2 |
| B 36 (Torshavn) | 2-2 | 2-1 | 3-1 | 2-1 | 2-0 | | 1-0 | 3-0 | 1-1 | 1-2 |
| GI (Gøtu) | 1-2 | 3-3 | 0-1 | 1-1 | 7-1 | 2-1 | | 1-2 | 1-0 | 2-0 |
| SIF (Sandavagur) | 0-0 | 1-3 | 2-0 | 3-1 | 3-2 | 2-4 | 0-2 | | 0-1 | 2-0 |
| MB (Midvag) | 1-1 | 2-2 | 2-2 | 2-1 | 1-1 | 4-0 | 0-0 | 0-1 | | 1-2 |
| TB (Tvøroyri) | 2-0 | 0-3 | 0-2 | 1-2 | 2-0 | 3-2 | 2-1 | 3-0 | 1-2 | |

### LEAGUE TABLE FINAL

| | | | | | | | |
|---|---|---|---|---|---|---|---|
| HB (Torshavn) | 18 | 9 | 6 | 3 | 37 | 22 | 24 |
| B 36 (Torshavn) | 18 | 9 | 2 | 7 | 30 | 27 | 20 |
| MB (Midvagur) | 18 | 6 | 7 | 5 | 28 | 25 | 19 |
| GI (Gøtu) | 18 | 7 | 4 | 7 | 28 | 20 | 18 |
| VB (Vagur) | 18 | 7 | 4 | 7 | 27 | 27 | 18 |
| B 68 (Toftir) | 18 | 6 | 6 | 6 | 19 | 20 | 18 |
| KI (Klakksvik) | 18 | 6 | 5 | 7 | 30 | 36 | 17 |
| TB (Tvøroyri) | 18 | 7 | 2 | 9 | 21 | 26 | 16 |
| SIF (Sandvagur) | 18 | 7 | 2 | 9 | 20 | 29 | 16 |
| B 71 (Sandur) | 18 | 4 | 6 | 8 | 17 | 25 | 14 |

Champions : - HB (Torshavn)
Relegated : - SIF (Sandvagur) & B 71 (Sandur)

### TOP SCORERS

| | |
|---|---|
| 1.Gunnar Mohr (HB) | 10 |
| Jens-Erik Rasmussen (MB) | 10 |
| 3.Per Dalheim (GI) | 9 |
| Torkil Nielsen (SIF) | 9 |

## FAROER ISLANDS 2ND DIVISION 1990

### 2nd Division results table

| FAROER ISLANDS 2nd Division Season 1990 | IF | LIF | NSI | SI | GI Res. | SUMBA | SKALA | B 36 Res. | ROYN | FRAM |
|---|---|---|---|---|---|---|---|---|---|---|
| IF (Fuglafjørdur) | | 0-2 | 1-3 | 2-4 | 0-0 | 3-2 | 2-0 | 9-0 | 0-1 | 4-1 |
| LIF (Lorvik) | 2-3 | | 0-2 | 0-0 | 1-1 | 0-2 | 2-1 | 3-0 | 0-0 | 3-1 |
| NSI (Runavik) | 3-1 | 3-3 | | 2-0 | 5-1 | 0-1 | 2-0 | 1-1 | 9-1 | 9-0 |
| SI (Sørvag) | 2-4 | 1-1 | 0-1 | | 4-2 | 1-2 | 1-2 | 0-0 | 2-0 | 4-0 |
| GI Reserves | 4-0 | 1-0 | 0-3 | 2-3 | | 2-3 | 1-1 | 3-0 | 7-1 | 5-2 |
| SUMBA (Sumba) | 2-2 | 3-0 | 0-1 | 1-1 | 4-0 | | 5-2 | 1-0 | 1-0 | 7-0 |
| SKALA (Skala) | 2-2 | 2-3 | 0-1 | 2-0 | 1-1 | 3-2 | | 1-0 | 4-1 | 2-1 |
| B 36 Reserves | 1-5 | 1-1 | 0-2 | 0-2 | 4-0 | 0-0 | 0-2 | | 2-2 | 1-3 |
| ROYN (Hvalba) | 0-4 | 1-1 | 1-3 | 4-1 | 2-1 | 2-3 | 1-0 | 6-1 | | 0-0 |
| FRAM (Torshavn) | 2-2 | 2-8 | 0-3 | 2-1 | 0-0 | 5-5 | 2-6 | 3-1 | 1-1 | |

### LEAGUE TABLE FINAL

| | | | | | | | |
|---|---|---|---|---|---|---|---|
| NSI (Runavik) | 18 | 15 | 2 | 1 | 53 | 10 | 32 |
| Sumba (Sumba) | 18 | 11 | 4 | 3 | 44 | 22 | 26 |
| IF (Fuglafjørdur) | 18 | 8 | 4 | 6 | 44 | 31 | 20 |
| LIF (Lørvik) | 18 | 6 | 7 | 5 | 30 | 24 | 19 |
| Skala (Skala) | 18 | 8 | 3 | 7 | 31 | 27 | 19 |
| SI (Sørvag) | 18 | 6 | 4 | 8 | 27 | 27 | 16 |
| GI Reserves | 18 | 5 | 5 | 8 | 31 | 34 | 15 |
| Royn (Hvalba) | 18 | 5 | 5 | 8 | 24 | 40 | 15 |
| Fram (Torshavn) | 18 | 3 | 5 | 10 | 25 | 62 | 11 |
| B 36 Reserves | 18 | 1 | 5 | 12 | 12 | 44 | 7 |

Promoted : - NSI (Runavik) & Sumba
Relegated : - Fram (Torshavn) & B 36 Res.

## FAROER ISLANDS 3RD DIVISION 1990

### LEAGUE TABLE FINAL

| | | | | | | | |
|---|---|---|---|---|---|---|---|
| KI Reserves | 18 | 11 | 6 | 1 | 45 | 24 | 28 |
| Streymur (Hvalvik) | 18 | 9 | 7 | 2 | 42 | 22 | 25 |
| TB Reserves | 18 | 10 | 2 | 6 | 54 | 39 | 22 |
| B 68 Reserves | 18 | 7 | 7 | 4 | 35 | 26 | 21 |
| EB (Eidi) | 18 | 6 | 7 | 5 | 28 | 21 | 19 |
| HB Reserves | 18 | 7 | 4 | 7 | 49 | 40 | 18 |
| IF Reserves | 18 | 6 | 4 | 8 | 30 | 37 | 16 |
| NSI Reserves | 18 | 5 | 5 | 8 | 34 | 33 | 15 |
| VB Reserves | 18 | 3 | 5 | 10 | 24 | 37 | 11 |
| LIF Reserves | 18 | 1 | 3 | 14 | 12 | 74 | 5 |

Promoted : - KI Reserves & Streymur (Hvalvik)

## FAROER ISLANDS CUP 1990

### 1ST ROUND

| | | | |
|---|---|---|---|
| IF (Fuglafjørdur) ........4 | SI (Sorvagur) .............2 | EB (Eidi).....................1 | B 36 (Torshavn).........2 |
| Royn (Hvalba) ............1 | SIF (Sandvagur) ........4 | VB (Vagur) ................2 | Sumba (Sumba)........0 |
| Fram (Torshavn).........1 | Skala (Skala).............2 (aet.) | | |

### 2ND ROUND

| | | | |
|---|---|---|---|
| SIF (Sandvagur).........1 | MB (Midvagur)...........3 | KI (Klakksvik) .............2 | HB (Torshavn) ...........1 |
| TB (Tvøroyri).............9 | Streymur (Hvalvik).....1 | LIF (Lorvik) .................5 | IF (Fuglafjørdur) ........0 |
| B71 (Sandur).............5 | Skala (Skala).............1 | B 36 (Torshavn) .........3 | NSI (Runavik)............0 |
| AB (Argir) .................1 | GI (Gøtu) ..................9 | VB (Vagur) ................6 | B 68 (Toftir) ..............0 |

### 1/4 FINALS

| | | | |
|---|---|---|---|
| B 71 (Sandur).............2 | MB (Midvagur)...........3 | VB (Vagur) ................1 | KI (Klakksvik) ............1 (aet.) |
| GI (Gøtu)...................6 | LIF (Lorvik) ................1 | KI win 5-6 on penalties | |
| TB (Tvøroyri).............4 | B 36 (Torshavn).........0 | | |

### SEMI FINALS

| | 1ST LEG | 2ND LEG | AGG. |
|---|---|---|---|
| TB (Tvøroyri) v GI (Gøtu) | 3-1 | 1-4 | 4-5 |
| MB (Midvagur) v KI (Klakksvik) | 0-3 | 3-2 | 3-5 |

### FINAL

KI (Klakksvik) .............6    GI (Gøtu) ...................1

# FAROER ISLANDS INTERNATIONAL REVIEW 1990

## INTERNATIONAL LINE-UPS 1990

| | Jens-Martin Knudsen | Joannes Jakobsen | Tummas-Eli Hansen | Mikkjal Danielsen | Julian Hansen | Allan Mørkøre | Torkil Nielsen | Jan Dam | Abraham Hansen | Kari Reynheim | Kurt Mørkøre | Magni Jarnskor | Gunnar Mohr |
|---|---|---|---|---|---|---|---|---|---|---|---|---|---|
| 12/6/90 SHETLAND ISLANDS 0 FAROER ISLANDS 2 Lerwick Friendly | | | | | | | | | | | | | |
| 8/8/90 FAROER ISLANDS 2 ICELAND 3 Torshavn Friendly (K.Mørkøre, Ö.Hansen) Ref: Mikkelsen (Denmark) | | | | | | | | | | | | | |
| 12/9/90 FAROER ISLANDS 1 AUSTRIA 0 Landskrona EuroCh.Q. (T.Nielsen) Ref: Nervik (Norway) | 1 | 2 | 3 | 4 | 5 | 6 | 7 | 8 | 9 | 10 | 11 | (6) | (11) |
| 10/10/90 DENMARK 4 FAROER ISLANDS 1 København EuroCh.Q. (A.Mørkøre) Ref: Haraldsson (Iceland) | 1 | 2 | 3 | 4 | 5 | 6 | 7 | 8 | 9 | 10 | 11 | | |
| CAPS AT 31/12/90 | 11 | 28 | 6 | 24 | 19 | 3 | 19 | 6 | 20 | 19 | 9 | 8 | 4 |

We regret that line-up details for matches against Shetland Islands and Iceland are not available. Caps totals are as made available by the F.A. of the Faroer Islands. In our opinion, however, it is considered likely that they contain appearances for the Faroer Islands in friendly matches not recognised as full internationals.

## FINLAND FUTISLIGA 1990

### LEAGUE TABLE FINAL

| | | | | | | | |
|---|---|---|---|---|---|---|---|
| FC Kuusysi | 22 | 14 | 5 | 3 | 34 | 12 | 33 |
| RoPS | 22 | 12 | 5 | 5 | 29 | 17 | 29 |
| HJK | 22 | 11 | 6 | 5 | 40 | 29 | 28 |
| KuPS | 22 | 8 | 8 | 6 | 24 | 22 | 24 |
| Reipas | 22 | 7 | 9 | 6 | 35 | 21 | 23 |
| TPS | 22 | 7 | 9 | 6 | 27 | 20 | 23 |
| MP | 22 | 6 | 11 | 5 | 20 | 22 | 23 |
| Haka | 22 | 8 | 6 | 8 | 27 | 34 | 22 |
| Ilves | 22 | 6 | 8 | 8 | 37 | 33 | 20 |
| OTP | 22 | 4 | 7 | 11 | 16 | 32 | 15 |
| KPV | 22 | 6 | 3 | 13 | 15 | 32 | 15 |
| Kumu | 22 | 1 | 7 | 14 | 13 | 43 | 9 |

Relegated : - KPV & Kumu

### TOP SCORERS (excluding play-offs)

| | |
|---|---|
| 1.Marek Czakon (Ilves) | 16 |
| 2.Jari Litmanen (Reipas) | 14 |
| 3.Marko Rajamäki (TPS) | 13 |
| 4.Kimmo Tarkkio (HJK) | 12 |
| 5.Marcus Gayle (KuPS) | 9 |
| Ari Tegelberg (RoPS) | 9 |
| 7.Michael Belfield (Reipas) | 8 |
| Seppo Nikkilä (Ilves) | 8 |
| 9.Petri Järvinen (Kuusysi) | 7 |
| Steve Polack (RoPS) | 7 |

### PLAY OFFS

KPV 1 OTP 2 (at Ylivieska)
KPV to play test matches against 1st Division Runners Up.

New Championship play-off system introduced for Season 1990. Top 8 clubs to play off on knock out basis, drawn matches to be followed by penalty shoot-out, and 2 victories needed for club to progress to the following stage.

| 1/4 FINALS | 1ST MATCH | 2ND MATCH | 3RD MATCH |
|---|---|---|---|
| FC Kuusysi v Haka | 3-1 | 2-2 (6-5) | |
| RoPS v MP | 1-1 (4-5) | 2-1 | 0-1 |
| TPS v HJK | 0-0 (3-2) | 1-2 | 1-3 |
| KuPS v Reipas | 1-1 (4-5) | 0-2 | |

| SEMI-FINALS | 1ST MATCH | 2ND MATCH |
|---|---|---|
| HJK v Reipas | 3-2 | 3-2 |
| FC Kuusysi v MP | 3-1 | 1-0 |

**3RD/4TH PLACE MATCH**
Reipas 1 MP 6

Results of Penalty Shoot-Outs shown in brackets.

| FINAL | 1ST MATCH | 2ND MATCH |
|---|---|---|
| FC Kuusysi v HJK | 1-1 (4-5) | 0-1 |

Champions : - HJK

Note : Championship Play-Offs abandoned for Season 1991. Futisliga clubs to play one another 3 times.

## FINLAND 1ST DIVISION 1990

### LEAGUE TABLE FINAL

| | | | | | | | |
|---|---|---|---|---|---|---|---|
| PPT | 22 | 12 | 8 | 2 | 52 | 19 | 32 |
| Jaro | 22 | 12 | 6 | 4 | 43 | 19 | 30 |
| PK-37 | 22 | 10 | 7 | 5 | 37 | 27 | 27 |
| Elo | 22 | 8 | 7 | 7 | 36 | 32 | 23 |
| MyPa | 22 | 9 | 5 | 8 | 36 | 32 | 23 |
| TP-55 | 22 | 8 | 7 | 7 | 30 | 27 | 23 |
| KontU | 22 | 8 | 7 | 7 | 30 | 33 | 23 |
| KePS | 22 | 7 | 7 | 8 | 20 | 31 | 21 |
| JoKu | 22 | 7 | 5 | 10 | 28 | 32 | 19 |
| VanPa | 22 | 4 | 8 | 10 | 21 | 44 | 16 |
| Koparit | 22 | 5 | 5 | 12 | 29 | 41 | 15 |
| GrIFK | 22 | 5 | 2 | 15 | 26 | 51 | 12 |

Promoted : - PPT & Jaro
Relegated : - VanPa, Koparit & GrIFK
League is to consist of 11 clubs for Season 1991.
Elo have been declared bankrupt.

**PROMOT./RELEG. TEST MATCHES**

| | 1ST LEG | 2ND LEG | AGG. |
|---|---|---|---|
| KPV v Jaro | 0-1 | 2-4 | 2-5 |

### FINLAND 1st Division Season 1990

| FINLAND 1st Division Season 1990 | KEPS | JARO | KOPARIT | PPT | MYPA | PK-37 | ELO | VANPA | KONTU | JOKU | GRIFK | TP-55 |
|---|---|---|---|---|---|---|---|---|---|---|---|---|
| KEPS (Kemi) | | 0-2 | 0-4 | 0-1 | 0-1 | 2-0 | 2-1 | 1-1 | 0-0 | 3-2 | 0-3 | 1-1 |
| JARO (Jakobstad) | 2-0 | | 2-2 | 0-3 | 1-0 | 2-1 | 2-2 | 6-0 | 6-0 | 0-0 | 0-0 | 1-0 |
| KOPARIT (Kuopio) | 1-2 | 1-2 | | 4-2 | 1-2 | 0-2 | 1-2 | 0-0 | 4-0 | 3-2 | 0-1 | 2-0 |
| PPT (Pori) | 3-0 | 1-1 | 7-0 | | 2-2 | 1-1 | 4-0 | 6-1 | 2-0 | 4-1 | 2-1 | 1-1 |
| MYPA (Myllykoski) | 0-2 | 1-3 | 4-1 | 1-3 | | 1-0 | 2-0 | 3-0 | 2-2 | 0-3 | 2-3 | 1-1 |
| PK-37 (Iisalmi) | 1-1 | 3-5 | 1-0 | 1-1 | 2-0 | | 1-0 | 2-0 | 4-1 | 1-1 | 4-2 | 1-1 |
| ELO (Kuopio) | 0-0 | 1-3 | 1-1 | 2-2 | 1-1 | 4-2 | | 2-0 | 2-2 | 2-0 | 3-2 | 2-0 |
| VANPA (Vantaa) | 1-2 | 0-0 | 2-2 | 0-1 | 1-5 | 1-1 | 3-3 | | 0-0 | 1-0 | 3-2 | 1-1 |
| KONTU (Helsinki) | 1-1 | 1-0 | 2-1 | 1-1 | 4-1 | 0-1 | 1-0 | 3-0 | | 5-0 | 3-1 | 1-3 |
| JOKU (Joutseno) | 0-0 | 1-0 | 3-0 | 1-1 | 1-1 | 2-3 | 1-2 | 1-2 | 2-0 | | 1-0 | 1-0 |
| GRIFK (Kauniainen) | 1-3 | 0-4 | 0-0 | 0-4 | 0-4 | 1-4 | 0-5 | 3-1 | 0-1 | 4-3 | | 0-1 |
| TP-55 (Seinäjoki) | 5-0 | 2-1 | 4-1 | 1-0 | 1-2 | 1-1 | 2-1 | 0-3 | 2-2 | 0-2 | 3-2 | |

## FINLAND 2ND DIVISION WEST 1990

### LEAGUE TABLE FINAL

| | | | | | | | |
|---|---|---|---|---|---|---|---|
| P-Iirot (Rauma) | 22 | 15 | 3 | 4 | 51 | 20 | 33 |
| HIK (Hangö) | 22 | 12 | 8 | 2 | 56 | 22 | 32 |
| R-Pallo (Rauma) | 22 | 11 | 5 | 6 | 40 | 19 | 27 |
| TuTo (Turku) | 22 | 9 | 8 | 5 | 25 | 22 | 26 |
| TPV (Tampere) | 22 | 9 | 6 | 7 | 27 | 23 | 24 |
| TuPa (Turku) | 22 | 7 | 5 | 10 | 39 | 47 | 19 |
| ToiP-49 (Toijala) | 22 | 6 | 7 | 9 | 34 | 43 | 19 |
| VaKP (Valkeakoski) | 22 | 7 | 5 | 10 | 32 | 45 | 19 |
| PIF (Pargas) | 22 | 7 | 4 | 11 | 31 | 38 | 18 |
| MIFK (Mariehamn) | 22 | 6 | 5 | 11 | 31 | 43 | 17 |
| SalPa (Salo) | 22 | 6 | 5 | 11 | 31 | 48 | 17 |
| HPK (Hämeenlinna) | 22 | 1 | 11 | 10 | 23 | 50 | 13 |

Promoted : - P-Iirot
Relegated : - MIFK, SalPa &HPK

## FINLAND 2ND DIVISION NORTH 1990

### LEAGUE TABLE FINAL

| | | | | | | | |
|---|---|---|---|---|---|---|---|
| OLS (Oulu) | 22 | 16 | 4 | 2 | 54 | 15 | 36 |
| Kraft (Närpes) | 22 | 11 | 10 | 1 | 40 | 17 | 32 |
| JyP-77 (Jyväskylä) | 22 | 14 | 1 | 7 | 43 | 28 | 29 |
| VPS (Vaasa) | 22 | 11 | 5 | 6 | 51 | 29 | 27 |
| KajHa (Kajaani) | 22 | 10 | 6 | 6 | 51 | 31 | 26 |
| NIK (Nykarleby) | 22 | 7 | 8 | 7 | 32 | 32 | 22 |
| GBK (Karleby) | 22 | 6 | 7 | 9 | 24 | 45 | 19 |
| KPT-85 (Kemi) | 22 | 7 | 3 | 12 | 43 | 40 | 17 |
| BK-IFK (Vaasa) | 22 | 6 | 5 | 11 | 25 | 43 | 17 |
| KaPa (Kajaani) | 22 | 4 | 8 | 10 | 22 | 37 | 16 |
| J-Ilves (Haavisto) | 22 | 4 | 6 | 12 | 28 | 70 | 14 |
| OPS (Oulu) | 22 | 3 | 3 | 16 | 28 | 54 | 9 |

Promoted : - OLS
Relegated : - KaPa, J-Ilves & OPS

Promoted from 3rd Division for Season 1991 : - TiPS (Vantaa), EIF (Ekenäs), AIFK (Turku), EuPa (Kauttua), RRR (Tampere), STPS (Savonlinna), Kings SC (Kuopio), Sepsi-78 (Seinäjoki) & RoRe (Rovaniemi).

## FINLAND 2ND DIVISION EAST 1990

### LEAGUE TABLE FINAL

| | | | | | | | |
|---|---|---|---|---|---|---|---|
| FinnPa (Helsinki) | 22 | 16 | 3 | 3 | 61 | 20 | 35 |
| HIFK (Helsinki) | 22 | 16 | 2 | 4 | 66 | 29 | 34 |
| PU-62 (Mikkeli) | 22 | 16 | 2 | 4 | 38 | 27 | 34 |
| Ponnistus (Helsinki) | 22 | 13 | 3 | 6 | 54 | 26 | 29 |
| LauTP (Lappeenranta) | 22 | 13 | 2 | 7 | 60 | 29 | 28 |
| KTP (Kotka) | 22 | 12 | 1 | 9 | 37 | 41 | 25 |
| PeKa (Kotka) | 22 | 6 | 5 | 11 | 21 | 43 | 17 |
| LaPa (Lappeenranta) | 22 | 7 | 2 | 13 | 29 | 42 | 16 |
| EBK (Espoo) | 22 | 5 | 5 | 12 | 36 | 51 | 15 |
| Gnistan (Helsinki) | 22 | 5 | 4 | 13 | 20 | 42 | 14 |
| Kiffen (Helsinki) | 22 | 3 | 3 | 16 | 17 | 40 | 9 |
| Sudet (Kouvola) | 22 | 2 | 4 | 16 | 14 | 63 | 8 |

Promoted : - FinnPa
Relegated : - Gnistan, Kiffen & Sudet
League to consist of 11 clubs for Season 1991, LauTP and LaPa combining and continuing as LaPa.

# FINLAND SUOMEN CUP 1990

## 6TH ROUND

| | | | | | | | |
|---|---|---|---|---|---|---|---|
| Jaro | 0 | MyPa | 1 | RRR | 3 | FC Espoo | 0 |
| RoLa | 1 | FinnPa | 2 | Haka | 3 | KePS | 1 (aet.) |
| GrIFK | 2 | PP-70 | 1 | HIFK | 0 | Ilves | 4 |
| KontU | 3 | TuTo | 0 | KPV | 1 | Reipas | 2 |
| Kumu | 2 | KTP | 1 (aet.) | Kuusysi | 6 | Kings SC | 0 |
| MP | 0 | HJK | 6 | OTP | 3 | Koparit | 1 |
| RoPS | 2 | TPS | 1 (aet.) | PPT | 4 | TP-55 | 1 |
| Elo | 0 | KuPS | 2 | PK-37 | 2 | VaKP | 1 |

## 7TH ROUND

| | | | | | | | |
|---|---|---|---|---|---|---|---|
| PPT | 2 | HJK | 4 | PK-37 | 2 | KontU | 2 (aet.) |
| RoPS | 5 | FinnPa | 0 | KontU win 4-5 on penalties | | | |
| Reipas | 3 | GrIFK | 0 | MyPa | 1 | Ilves | 5 |
| RRR | 0 | Kumu | 2 | KuPS | 2 | Kuusysi | 0 (aet.) |
| Haka | 0 | OTP | 1 | | | | |

## 1/4 FINALS

| | | | | | | | |
|---|---|---|---|---|---|---|---|
| KuPS | 4 | KontU | 0 | Reipas | 1 | HJK | 3 |
| Kumu | 4 | OTP | 2 | Ilves | 1 | RoPS | 0 |

## SEMI FINALS

| | | | | | | | |
|---|---|---|---|---|---|---|---|
| HJK | 3 | KuPS | 1 | Kumu | 1 | Ilves | 3 |

## FINAL    13/10/1990 (at Olympic Stadium, Helsinki)

| | | | |
|---|---|---|---|
| Ilves | 2 | HJK | 1 |

Ilves : T.Koivistoinen, A.Uimonen, J.Mäkëla, M.Juntunen, P.Ojala, M.Aaltonen, J.Aaltonen (P.Mattila 70), M.Dziadulewicz, **A.Hjelm**, S.Nikkilä, M.Czakon.

HJK : J.Karjalainen, J.Europaeus, J.Vuorela, M.Kanerva, P.Onttonen, P.Tiainen (E.Valla 71), P.Tauriainen, P.Rautiainen, J.Suokonautio, K.Granlund (A.Hyrylainen 71), K.Tarkkio.

0-1   J.Suokonautio 11
1-1   A.Hjelm 27
2-1   M.Czakon 50

## FINLAND : All Time Records as at 31/12/90 - CAPS

| | | |
|---|---|---|
| 1. | Arto Tolsa (KTP/Beerschot AC) | 76 |
| 2. | Esko Ranta (I-Kissat/TPV/TaPa/Haka) | 69 |
| 3. | Juhani Peltonen (Haka/Hamburger SV) | 68 |
| 4. | Hannu Turunen (KTP/KuPS) | 66 |
| 5. | Miika Toivola (PiTU/TPS/HJK) | 63 |
| 6. | Stig-Goran Myntii (VIFK) | 61 |
| 7. | Ari Hjelm (Ilves/Stuttgarter Kickers) | 60 |
| 8. | Frans Karjagin (HIFK) | 58 |
| | Esa Pekonen (FC Kuusysi/AIK) | 58 |
| | Jukka Ikäläinen (Örgryte IS/KePS/Kiruna FF) | 58 |

## FINLAND : All Time Records as at 31/12/90 - GOALS

| | | | |
|---|---|---|---|
| 1. | Verner Eklöf (HIFK/HJK) | (32) | 17 |
| 2. | Aulis Koponen (HPS) | (39) | 16 |
| | Gunnar Aström (HIFK) | (44) | 16 |
| 4. | Jorma Vaihela (TuTo/PoPa/RU-38) | (33) | 13 |
| | William Kanerva (HJK/HPS) | (51) | 13 |
| 6. | Kalevi Lehtovirta (TuWE/TuPy/TPS) | (44) | 12 |
| | Kai Pahlman (HPS/HJK) | (56) | 12 |
| 8. | Ernst Grönlund (HIFK) | (38) | 11 |
| | Mika Lipponen (TPS/FC Twente/FC Aarau) | (45) | 11 |
| | Tommy Lindholm (PIF/TuTo/TPS/HIFK/Reipas) | (47) | 11 |
| | Matti Paatelainen (HPS/HIFK/Haka) | (48) | 11 |
| | Ari Hjelm (Ilves/Stuttgarter Kickers) | (60) | 11 |
| | Juhani Peltonen (Haka/Hamburger SV) | (68) | 11 |

# FINLAND INTERNATIONAL REVIEW 1990

## INTERNATIONAL LINE-UPS 1990

| Date | Match | Venue | Referee | Type | Scorers |
|---|---|---|---|---|---|
| 12/2/90 | UAE 1 FINLAND 1 | Sharjah | Ref: Al Amash (UAE) | Friendly | (P.Tiainen) |
| 15/2/90 | KUWAIT 0 FINLAND 1 | Cairo | Ref: Al Hamamsi (Egypt) | Friendly | (Aaltonen) |
| 7/3/90 | SWEDEN OLYMPIC XI 3 FINLAND 1 | Tyringe | Ref: Nielsen (Denmark) | Friendly | (Ruhanen) |
| 10/3/90 | USA 2 FINLAND 1 | Tampa | Ref: Saras (Costa Rica) | Friendly | (Tarkkio) |
| 15/5/90 | GREECE OLYMPIC XI 2 FINLAND 2 | Athens | Ref: Karamanis | Friendly | (Helin, J.Mäkelä) |
| 16/5/90 | REPUBLIC OF IRELAND 1 FINLAND 1 | Dublin | Ref: Gifford (Wales) | Friendly | (Tauriainen) |
| 27/5/90 | SWEDEN 6 FINLAND 0 | Solna | Ref: Presberg (Norway) | Friendly | |
| 28/5/90 | JAPAN OLYMPIC XI 0 FINLAND ... | Jämsänkoski | Ref: Sandell (Sweden) | Friendly | |
| 29/8/90 | FINLAND 1 CZECHOSLOVAKIA 1 | Kuusankoski | Ref: Mikkelsen (Denmark) | Friendly | (Järvinen) |
| 11/9/90 | FINLAND 0 PORTUGAL OLYMPIC XI 1 | Lahti | Ref: Ulrich (Czechoslovakia) | Olympic Q. | |
| 12/9/90 | FINLAND 0 PORTUGAL 0 | Helsinki | Ref: Marko (Czechoslovakia) | EuroCh.Q. | |
| 11/11/90 | TUNISIA 1 FINLAND 2 | Tunis | Ref: Hansal (Algeria) | Friendly | (Paatelainen, Tegelberg) |
| 25/11/90 | MALTA 1 FINLAND 1 | Ta'Qali | Ref: Sadik Deda (Turkey) | EuroCh.Q. | (Holmgren) |

### Line-ups (first-half of squad)

| Date | O.Huttunen | J.Vuorela | J.Europaeus | E.Holmgren | M.Aaltonen | J.Saastamoinen | P.Tiainen | P.Tauriainen | J.Huhtamaki | H.Olila | J.Turunen | I.Mäkelä | N.Grönholm | J.Rinne | P.Jakonen | M.Lipponen | A.Heim | T.Koivistoinen | K.Nieminen | J.Kangaskorpi | S.Ylä-Jussila | M.Walden | R.Rissanen | P.Helin | Y.Happonen | T.Tajpale |
|---|---|---|---|---|---|---|---|---|---|---|---|---|---|---|---|---|---|---|---|---|---|---|---|---|---|---|
| 12/2/90 | 1 | 2 | 3 | 4 | 5 | 6 | 7 | 8 | 9 | 10 | 11 | (7) | (9) | (11) | | | | | | | | | | | | |
| 15/2/90 | | 2 | 4 | 5 | 6 | 7 | 8 | (3) | (6) | 3 | | 9 | (8) | (7) | 1 | 10 | 11 | | | | | | | | | |
| 7/3/90 | | | | | | | | | | | | | | | | | | | 2 | 3 | 4 | 5 | 6 | 7 | 8 | 9 |
| 10/3/90 | | | | | | | | | | | | | | | | | | | | | | | | | | |
| 15/5/90 | | | | | (8) | | | | | | | | | | | | | | 2 | 3 | 4 | 5 | 6 | 7 | 9 | (10) |
| 16/5/90 | 1 | 2 | 4 | 9 | | 7 | 8 | 6 | (3) | 5 | | | | | | | 11 | | | | | | | | | |
| 27/5/90 | 1 | 2 | 4 | 9 | | 7 | 8 | 6 | (3) | 5 | | | | | | | | | | | | | | | | |
| 28/5/90 | | | | | | | | | | | | | | | | | | 1 | 2 | 3 | 4 | 5 | 6 | 7 | 9 | |
| 29/8/90 | 1 | 3 | 2 | 4 | | | | 7 | | | (6) | | | 10 | | (9) | 10 | | | | | | | | | |
| 11/9/90 | | | 2 | 4 | | | | | | | (2) | | (2) | | | (9) | | | | | | | | | | |
| 12/9/90 | 1 | | 2 | 5 | 3 | | | 9 | 7 | | 5 | 11 | | 6 | 1 | 10 | 8 | | | | | | | | | |
| 11/11/90 | 1 | | 2 | | | | | 9 | | 3 | | | 3 | 6 | 2 | 10 | 8 | | | | | | | | | 2 |
| 25/11/90 | 1 | 2 | 2 | | | | 11 | 9 | | 3 | | | 3 | | | | | | | | | | | 1 | | |
| CAPS AT 31/12/90 | 49 | 11 | 53 | 35 | 3 | 6 | 11 | 20 | 7 | 3 | 5 | 11 | 3 | 18 | 2 | 45 | 60 | 1 | 4 | 4 | 5 | 4 | 4 | 4 | 3 | 2 |
| GOALS AT 31/12/90 | | 1 | 1 | 1 | 1 | 1 | 2 | | | | | | | | | 11 | 11 | | | | | | | 1 | | |

### Line-ups (second-half of squad)

| Date | J.Ruhanen | K.Suominen | M.Holm | V.Rantanen | T.Tiainen | A.Heikkinen | J.Littmanen | K.Tarkkio | I.Lius | A.Niemi | J.Mäkelä | S.Arajärvi | K.Kankkunen | H.Jäntti | P.Sulonen | M.Kanerva | M.Myyry | P.Järvinen | M-M.Paatelainen | V.Tauriainen | K.Laukkanen | E.Petäjä | A.Roth | T.Paavola | I.Remes | A.Tegelberg |
|---|---|---|---|---|---|---|---|---|---|---|---|---|---|---|---|---|---|---|---|---|---|---|---|---|---|---|
| 7/3/90 | 10 | 11 | (1) | (2) | (8) | 3 | 8 | | 11 | 1 | 8 | 9 | (11) | | | | | | | | | | | | | |
| 10/3/90 | 11 | | (1) | | | | 8 | 10 | 11 | | | | | 2 | | | 8 | | | | | | | | | |
| 15/5/90 | 10 | 11 | | | (7) | | (2) | 7 | 9 | 1 | 8 | 9 | | 3 | | | (2) | | 11 | | | 6 | 8 | | | |
| 16/5/90 | | | | | | 4 | 8 | 9 | | | | 11 | | | 5 | 5 | | 10 | 11 | | 1 | | 8 | | | |
| 27/5/90 | | | | | | | | | | | | | | | | | | 7 | | | | | | | | |
| 28/5/90 | 10 | | | | | 5 | 8 | | | 1 | 8 | 11 | | | 5 | | | | | | | 6 | | | | |
| 29/8/90 | | | | | | 6 | | | | | | | | | | 4 | (7) | 9 | 11 | | 1 | | | (3) | 3 | |
| 11/9/90 | 10 | | | | | | | | | 1 | | | | | | | | | | (9) | | | | 3 | | |
| 12/9/90 | | | | | | 3 | 8 | | | | | | 11 | | | 4 | (9) | 9 | 11 | | 1 | 4 | | (6) | | (9) |
| 11/11/90 | | | | | | 5 | 7 | | | | | | | | | | 6 | | 11 | | | | | | | (10) |
| 25/11/90 | | | | | | 4 | 7 | | | | | | | | | | | | | | | | | | | |
| CAPS AT 31/12/90 | 4 | 3 | 1 | 1 | 4 | 20 | 9 | 22 | 35 | 3 | 3 | 3 | 2 | 2 | 7 | 23 | 32 | 23 | 23 | - | 30 | 54 | 7 | 14 | 29 | 6 |
| GOALS AT 31/12/90 | 1 | 1 | | 1 | 1 | | | 3 | 4 | | 1 | | | | | | 2 | 4 | 4 | 1 | | | | | 1 | 1 |

# FRANCE  Correspondent : JEAN SORTI

| FRANCE 1st Division Season 1990/91 | MARSEILLE | BORDEAUX | MONACO | SOCHAUX | PARIS SG | AUXERRE | NANTES | LYON | TOULOUSE | BREST | CANNES | TOULON | M'PELLIER | METZ | ST.ETIENNE | CAEN | LILLE | NICE | NANCY | RENNES |
|---|---|---|---|---|---|---|---|---|---|---|---|---|---|---|---|---|---|---|---|---|
| OLYMP. MARSEILLE | | 2-0 | 1-0 | 0-0 | 2-1 | 1-0 | 6-0 | 7-0 | 1-0 | 3-1 | 0-1 | 3-3 | 2-0 | 3-0 | 3-1 | 2-1 | 2-0 | 1-0 | 6-2 | 4-1 |
| GIROND. BORDEAUX | 1-1 | | 0-0 | 1-0 | 3-0 | 1-1 | 2-0 | 0-0 | 2-1 | 1-4 | 1-1 | 0-1 | 1-0 | 1-1 | 2-1 | 1-1 | 1-1 | 3-0 | 5-0 | 1-0 |
| AS MONACO | 1-3 | 2-0 | | 1-0 | 2-0 | 0-0 | 2-1 | 0-0 | 2-1 | 5-0 | 0-0 | 2-1 | 3-1 | 2-0 | 2-0 | 2-0 | 1-1 | 2-1 | 2-2 | 2-1 |
| FC SOCHAUX | 2-1 | 1-0 | 0-2 | | 0-0 | 0-1 | 1-1 | 1-2 | 0-1 | 1-1 | 0-0 | 0-0 | 0-0 | 1-1 | 2-0 | 1-0 | 0-0 | 0-0 | 1-0 | 4-0 |
| PARIS-ST.GERMAIN FC | 0-1 | 1-0 | 0-2 | 0-2 | | 1-1 | 1-1 | 3-0 | 3-0 | 1-1 | 0-0 | 4-0 | 2-0 | 2-1 | 4-2 | 3-2 | 2-0 | 0-2 | 2-1 | 1-1 |
| AJ AUXERRE | 4-0 | 0-0 | 0-1 | 4-1 | 0-1 | | 0-2 | 1-0 | 2-1 | 2-2 | 0-3 | 3-0 | 3-2 | 3-1 | 2-0 | 3-0 | 3-2 | 5-1 | 1-1 | 4-0 |
| FC NANTES | 1-1 | 0-0 | 3-1 | 0-0 | 2-0 | 2-3 | | 0-0 | 0-0 | 1-0 | 1-0 | 0-0 | 1-1 | 1-1 | 2-1 | 0-0 | 0-0 | 2-2 | 1-0 | 2-0 |
| OLYMP. LYONNAIS | 2-2 | 1-0 | 1-0 | 1-0 | 0-0 | 1-0 | 2-0 | | 4-1 | 2-0 | 1-0 | 1-1 | 3-3 | 3-1 | 1-1 | 3-2 | 2-1 | 1-0 | 0-1 | 0-0 |
| TOULOUSE FC | 0-2 | 0-0 | 1-2 | 0-0 | 2-1 | 0-0 | 2-0 | 3-1 | | 0-0 | 2-2 | 1-1 | 0-0 | 2-1 | 0-0 | 3-2 | 2-2 | 1-2 | 0-0 | 2-0 |
| FC BREST ARMOR. | 1-1 | 4-0 | 1-0 | 0-0 | 0-0 | 1-3 | 1-0 | 3-0 | 0-0 | | 3-2 | 2-2 | 1-1 | 1-0 | 0-1 | 5-0 | 1-0 | 4-0 | 3-3 | 0-0 |
| AS CANNES | 0-0 | 1-1 | 1-2 | 1-1 | 2-0 | 0-3 | 2-1 | 3-2 | 0-0 | 0-0 | | 0-0 | 2-1 | 0-1 | 0-1 | 1-1 | 2-1 | 2-1 | 1-0 | 1-0 |
| SC TOULON | 0-1 | 0-2 | 1-1 | 1-0 | ⊗ | 2-3 | 3-1 | 1-0 | 1-0 | 1-2 | 0-0 | | 1-1 | 2-1 | 3-0 | 0-0 | 0-0 | 1-2 | 2-0 | 1-0 |
| MONTPELLIER HSC | 0-0 | 2-1 | 2-1 | 2-0 | 4-0 | 1-2 | 1-1 | 1-0 | 2-0 | 1-0 | 0-0 | 0-0 | | 5-2 | 0-0 | 0-0 | 1-2 | 3-0 | 5-0 | 1-0 |
| FC METZ | 0-2 | 1-0 | 1-1 | 2-2 | 2-2 | 1-0 | 2-0 | 1-2 | 2-1 | 0-0 | 0-0 | 0-0 | 0-0 | | 3-1 | 1-1 | 2-2 | 1-0 | 4-0 | 2-0 |
| AS ST.ETIENNE | 1-1 | 0-0 | 1-0 | 2-1 | 1-1 | 2-1 | 1-3 | 0-1 | 1-4 | 6-1 | 1-0 | 3-0 | 1-0 | 2-1 | | 0-0 | 0-0 | 1-0 | 4-1 | 0-0 |
| STADE MALH. CAEN | 0-0 | 2-0 | 0-2 | 2-0 | 2-0 | 0-1 | 1-0 | 1-0 | 2-0 | 1-2 | 0-1 | 2-0 | 1-0 | 4-1 | 1-0 | | 0-0 | 2-1 | 4-1 | 2-0 |
| LILLE OSC | 1-0 | 0-0 | 0-0 | 0-1 | 0-0 | 1-0 | 1-1 | 1-1 | 3-0 | 1-0 | 0-2 | 4-1 | 0-0 | 4-1 | 3-2 | 1-0 | | 0-0 | 0-2 | 1-1 |
| OGC NICE | 0-1 | 0-0 | 0-0 | 3-0 | 1-1 | 1-1 | 1-1 | 1-1 | 1-1 | 2-0 | 0-0 | 0-0 | 2-0 | 1-2 | 2-0 | 0-0 | 4-1 | | 3-0 | 2-2 |
| AS NANCY-LORRAINE | 2-0 | 0-2 | 4-0 | 2-0 | 0-2 | 1-1 | 3-2 | 2-0 | 1-1 | 0-0 | 2-0 | 2-1 | 1-1 | 0-1 | 1-0 | 0-0 | 1-1 | 2-1 | | 0-0 |
| STADE RENNAIS FC | 1-1 | 2-1 | 1-1 | 1-1 | 2-1 | 2-2 | 2-0 | 2-0 | 2-0 | 3-0 | 1-1 | 0-0 | 1-2 | 0-2 | 0-2 | 1-1 | 1-3 | 0-3 | 1-0 | |

⊗ The match SC Toulon v Paris-St.Germain FC was abandoned after 43 minutes after a linesman was hit by an object thrown from the crowd. The score at the time was Toulon 0 Paris SG 0, and although the match was later awarded to Paris SG the 0-0 score is shown in goals for and against columns of league table.

## FRANCE 1ST DIVISION 1990/91

### LEAGUE TABLE FINAL

| | | | | | | | |
|---|---|---|---|---|---|---|---|
| Olympique Marseille | 38 | 22 | 11 | 5 | 67 | 28 | 55 |
| AS Monaco | 38 | 20 | 11 | 7 | 51 | 30 | 51 |
| AJ Auxerre | 38 | 19 | 10 | 9 | 63 | 36 | 48 |
| AS Cannes | 38 | 12 | 17 | 9 | 32 | 28 | 41 |
| Olympique Lyon | 38 | 15 | 11 | 12 | 39 | 44 | 41 |
| Lille OSC | 38 | 11 | 17 | 10 | 39 | 37 | 39 |
| Montpellier HSC | 38 | 12 | 14 | 12 | 44 | 35 | 38 |
| SM Caen | 38 | 13 | 12 | 13 | 38 | 36 | 38 |
| Paris-St.Germain FC | 38 | 13 | 12 | 13 | 40 | 42 | 38 |
| Girondins Bordeaux | 38 | 11 | 15 | 12 | 34 | 32 | 37 |
| FCA Brest | 38 | 11 | 15 | 12 | 45 | 46 | 37 |
| FC Metz | 38 | 12 | 12 | 14 | 44 | 51 | 36 |
| AS St.Etienne | 38 | 13 | 9 | 16 | 40 | 46 | 35 |
| OGC Nice | 38 | 10 | 14 | 14 | 40 | 42 | 34 |
| FC Nantes | 38 | 9 | 16 | 13 | 34 | 44 | 34 |
| SC Toulon | 38 | 9 | 16 | 13 | 31 | 41 | 34 |
| AS Nancy-Lorraine | 38 | 11 | 11 | 16 | 38 | 58 | 33 |
| FC Sochaux | 38 | 8 | 16 | 14 | 24 | 33 | 32 |
| Toulouse FC | 38 | 8 | 15 | 15 | 33 | 45 | 31 |
| Stade Rennes | 38 | 7 | 14 | 17 | 29 | 51 | 28 |

Champions : - Olympique Marseille
Relegated : - Girondins Bordeaux, FCA Brest and OGC Nice all expelled for financial reasons.

### NAME CHANGE FOR SEASON 1991/92

Girondins de Bordeaux to AN des Girondins Bordeaux

### TOP SCORERS

| | | |
|---|---|---|
| 1. | Jean-Pierre Papin (Olympique Marseille) | 23 |
| 2. | Kalman Kovacs (AJ Auxerre) | 16 |
| 3. | Laurent Blanc (Montpellier HSC) | 14 |
| | Francois Omam-Biyik (Stade Rennes) | 14 |
| | Enzo Scifo (AJ Auxerre) | 14 |
| 6. | Aliocha Asanovic (FC Metz) | 13 |
| 7. | Bernard Ferrer (FCA Brest) | 12 |
| | Daniel Xuereb (Montpellier HSC) | 12 |
| 9. | Fabrice Divert (SM Caen) | 11 |
| 10. | Jules Bocandé (OGC Nice) | 10 |
| | Francois Brisson (Lille OSC) | 10 |
| | Francois Calderaro (FC Metz) | 10 |
| | Christophe Cocard (AJ Auxerre) | 10 |
| | Fabrice Mège (OGC Nice) | 10 |
| | Amara Simba (AS Cannes) | 10 |
| | Safet Susic (Paris-St.Germain FC) | 10 |
| | Ryszard Tarasiewicz (AS Nancy-Lorraine) | 10 |
| | Zlatko Vujovic (Paris-St.Germain FC) | 10 |
| | George Weah (AS Monaco) | 10 |
| 20. | Roberto Cabanas (Olympique Lyon) | 9 |
| | Ramon Diaz (AS Monaco) | 9 |
| | Christophe Robert (FC Nantes) | 9 |

| FRANCE 2nd Division A Season 1990/91 | MULHOUSE | STRASBOURG | NIMES | ALÈS | MARTIGUES | BASTIA | AVIGNON | ISTRES | DIJON | GUEUGNON | LOUHANS-C | ANNECY | CHAUMONT | V'CIENNES | DUNKERQUE | RODEZ | ÉPINAL | AJACCIO |
|---|---|---|---|---|---|---|---|---|---|---|---|---|---|---|---|---|---|---|
| FC MULHOUSE | | 1-0 | 1-2 | 4-2 | 0-3 | 0-2 | 0-1 | 0-1 | 1-0 | 2-2 | 2-1 | 2-1 | 3-0 | 0-0 | 5-0 | 5-0 | 1-0 | 2-0 |
| RC STRASBOURG | 0-3 | | 3-1 | 5-1 | 2-0 | 2-1 | 1-1 | 3-1 | 6-0 | 4-1 | 0-0 | 1-1 | 6-0 | 2-1 | 3-0 | 3-1 | 2-1 | 2-0 |
| NIMES OLYMPIQUE | 1-0 | 3-2 | | 0-1 | 1-0 | 2-1 | 2-1 | 1-1 | 1-2 | 1-0 | 2-0 | 1-0 | 3-0 | 1-0 | 3-0 | 1-0 | 0-0 | 0-0 |
| OLYMPIQUE ALÈS | 2-0 | 2-1 | 0-0 | | 1-1 | 1-0 | 2-2 | 4-0 | 0-0 | 1-0 | 1-0 | 1-0 | 1-0 | 1-0 | 1-0 | 0-0 | 2-1 | 1-0 |
| FC MARTIGUES | 2-1 | 1-2 | 1-1 | 1-2 | | 1-1 | 0-0 | 3-0 | 4-2 | 0-1 | 0-0 | 1-0 | 2-1 | 1-2 | 1-0 | 1-1 | 1-1 | 4-1 |
| SC BASTIA | 1-1 | 0-2 | 4-2 | 3-0 | 3-0 | | 0-0 | 2-1 | 1-0 | 1-0 | 2-0 | 2-2 | 4-0 | 2-2 | 2-2 | 1-2 | 0-1 | 1-0 |
| OLYMPIQUE AVIGNONNAIS | 2-1 | 1-0 | 3-0 | 1-1 | 1-0 | 2-2 | | 1-2 | 1-0 | 3-0 | 1-2 | 1-0 | 4-1 | 0-0 | 0-0 | 2-2 | 3-1 | 1-1 |
| ISTRES SF | 0-0 | 2-4 | 0-1 | 2-2 | 2-0 | 0-3 | 4-3 | | 4-0 | 2-0 | 1-0 | 1-0 | 1-0 | 0-0 | 2-0 | 1-0 | 1-2 | 3-0 |
| CERCLE DIJON FOOTBALL | 0-0 | 2-0 | 0-2 | 1-1 | 2-2 | 1-2 | 1-1 | 4-2 | | 0-0 | 2-0 | 3-1 | 0-0 | 1-1 | 0-0 | 1-3 | 1-2 | 1-1 |
| FC GUEUGNON | 1-0 | 2-2 | 1-0 | 0-1 | 1-4 | 1-1 | 2-0 | 1-1 | 6-0 | | 0-0 | 1-0 | 1-0 | 0-0 | 0-0 | 1-1 | 2-0 | 1-0 |
| CS LOUHANS-CUISEAUX 71 | 3-0 | 1-4 | 1-1 | 0-1 | 0-2 | 1-0 | 1-1 | 1-1 | 1-1 | | | 0-0 | 2-2 | 0-0 | 1-0 | 2-0 | 4-1 | 0-0 |
| FC ANNECY | 0-0 | 1-0 | 1-1 | 3-0 | 1-0 | 1-0 | 0-0 | 0-1 | 2-1 | 0-0 | 3-1 | | 0-0 | 0-0 | 2-0 | 2-0 | 1-0 | 1-1 |
| EACF CHAUMONT | 3-2 | 3-1 | 0-0 | 1-0 | 0-1 | 3-3 | 2-1 | 1-1 | 0-1 | 1-0 | 1-1 | 0-1 | | 1-2 | 1-0 | 1-1 | 1-4 | 4-2 |
| US VALENCIENNES | 2-1 | 2-1 | 1-1 | 1-1 | 0-0 | 1-0 | 4-1 | 2-0 | 1-0 | 0-0 | 0-0 | 0-0 | 1-0 | | 2-0 | 0-0 | 2-1 | 1-0 |
| US DUNKERQUE | 1-1 | 0-0 | 1-0 | 1-0 | 2-3 | 1-0 | 1-1 | 0-0 | 2-0 | 0-0 | 2-1 | 0-0 | 0-2 | 0-0 | | 1-1 | 0-0 | 2-0 |
| STADE RODEZ FOOTBALL | 1-1 | 0-3 | 1-3 | 2-1 | 2-0 | 0-0 | 2-0 | 0-0 | 2-0 | 1-0 | 2-1 | 1-1 | 1-1 | 1-0 | 1-1 | | 1-1 | 2-1 |
| ÉPINAL FC | 1-1 | 0-1 | 1-1 | 0-1 | 3-1 | 2-0 | 1-1 | 2-3 | 0-1 | 0-4 | 0-1 | 2-1 | 1-0 | 0-0 | 1-0 | 1-0 | | 2-1 |
| GAZÉLEC FC AJACCIO | 0-0 | 3-2 | 0-1 | 2-1 | 1-1 | 1-1 | 1-1 | 1-0 | 2-1 | 1-0 | 2-1 | 3-0 | 0-1 | 1-2 | 2-0 | 1-0 | 1-0 | |

The match Ajaccio 1 Avignon 1 was later awarded Ajaccio 1 Avignon 0. The match Chaumont 0 Martigues 1 was later awarded to Chaumont with a score of 0-0 applying for goals for and against in the League table.

## FRANCE 2ND DIVISION A 1990/91
### LEAGUE TABLE FINAL

| | | | | | | | |
|---|---|---|---|---|---|---|---|
| Nimes Olympique | 34 | 17 | 10 | 7 | 40 | 27 | 44 |
| RC Strasbourg | 34 | 19 | 5 | 10 | 70 | 37 | 43 |
| US Valenciennes | 34 | 13 | 17 | 4 | 30 | 17 | 43 |
| Olympique Alès | 34 | 17 | 9 | 8 | 37 | 32 | 43 |
| Istres SF | 34 | 14 | 9 | 11 | 41 | 41 | 37 |
| SEC Bastia | 34 | 12 | 11 | 11 | 46 | 35 | 35 |
| Olympique Avignon | 34 | 10 | 15 | 9 | 41 | 37 | 35 |
| SR Rodez | 34 | 10 | 14 | 10 | 32 | 38 | 34 |
| FC Annecy | 34 | 10 | 13 | 11 | 26 | 25 | 33 |
| FC Mulhouse | 34 | 11 | 10 | 13 | 41 | 35 | 32 |
| FC Martigues | 34 | 11 | 10 | 13 | 41 | 38 | 32 |
| FC Gueugnon | 34 | 9 | 14 | 11 | 30 | 29 | 32 |
| Epinal FC | 34 | 11 | 8 | 15 | 33 | 40 | 30 |
| GFC Ajaccio | 34 | 11 | 8 | 15 | 30 | 39 | 30 |
| EACF Chaumont | 34 | 10 | 10 | 14 | 32 | 50 | 30 |
| CS Louhans-Cuiseaux | 34 | 7 | 14 | 13 | 28 | 36 | 28 |
| US Dunkerque | 34 | 6 | 14 | 14 | 17 | 36 | 26 |
| CF Dijon | 34 | 7 | 11 | 16 | 29 | 52 | 25 |

Promoted : - Nimes Olympique
Relegated : - Olympique Avignon (to 3rd Div.), CF Dijon (to 4th Div.), & EACF Chaumont (to 5th Div.) all for financial reasons.

## FRANCE 2ND DIVISION B 1990/91
### LEAGUE TABLE FINAL

| | | | | | | | |
|---|---|---|---|---|---|---|---|
| Le Havre AC | 34 | 18 | 11 | 5 | 52 | 17 | 47 |
| RC Lens | 34 | 14 | 14 | 6 | 49 | 26 | 42 |
| Stade Laval | 34 | 16 | 9 | 9 | 49 | 29 | 41 |
| SCO Angers | 34 | 16 | 8 | 10 | 52 | 32 | 40 |
| FC Rouen | 34 | 15 | 10 | 9 | 46 | 26 | 40 |
| Stade Reims | 34 | 13 | 11 | 10 | 38 | 29 | 37 |
| En-Avant Guingamp | 34 | 12 | 11 | 11 | 35 | 37 | 35 |
| AS St.Seurin | 34 | 10 | 14 | 10 | 33 | 37 | 34 |
| FC Tours | 34 | 9 | 15 | 10 | 26 | 32 | 33 |
| AS Red Star 93 | 34 | 9 | 14 | 11 | 36 | 43 | 32 |
| AS Beauvais | 34 | 9 | 13 | 12 | 21 | 25 | 31 |
| La Roche-sur-Yon VF | 34 | 10 | 11 | 13 | 35 | 46 | 31 |
| FC Bourges | 34 | 10 | 11 | 13 | 35 | 51 | 31 |
| Le Mans UC 72 | 34 | 8 | 14 | 12 | 28 | 33 | 30 |
| Chamois Niort | 34 | 9 | 11 | 14 | 26 | 33 | 29 |
| US Orléans | 34 | 7 | 14 | 13 | 29 | 41 | 28 |
| US Créteil | 34 | 7 | 12 | 15 | 28 | 52 | 26 |
| Olympique St.Quentin | 34 | 7 | 11 | 16 | 24 | 53 | 25 |

Promoted : - Le Havre AC and RC Lens
Relegated : - Stade Reims, Chamois Niort and US Creteil all for financial reasons.

### 2ND DIVISION CHAMPIONSHIP PLAY-OFFS

| | 1ST LEG | 2ND LEG | AGG. |
|---|---|---|---|
| Le Havre AC v Nimes Olympique | 3-0 | 0-0 | 3-0 |

## 1ST/2ND DIVISION PROMOTION/RELEGATION PLAY-OFFS
### 1ST STAGE

RC Strasbourg..........3  Stade Laval................1      RC Lens ....................1   US Valenciennes .......0

### 2ND STAGE

| | 1ST LEG | 2ND LEG | AGG. |
|---|---|---|---|
| RC Strasbourg v RC Lens | 1-1 | 1-3 | 2-4 |

### 3RD STAGE

| | 1ST LEG | 2ND LEG | AGG. |
|---|---|---|---|
| Toulouse FC v RC Lens | 4-0 | 0-1 | 4-1 |

Note : Later FCA Brest and OGC Nice were both expelled from the 1st Division and RC Lens were awarded a 1st Division place.

| FRANCE 2nd Division B Season 1990/91 | ROUEN | LAVAL | LE HAVRE | BEAUVAIS | NIORT | LENS | CRÉTEIL | ANGERS | ST.SEURIN | GUINGAMP | TOURS | LA ROCHE/Y | REIMS | ORLÉANS | RED STAR | BOURGES | ST.QUENTIN | LE MANS |
|---|---|---|---|---|---|---|---|---|---|---|---|---|---|---|---|---|---|---|
| FC ROUEN | ■ | 2-4 | 1-0 | 2-0 | 0-0 | 0-0 | 4-0 | 3-1 | 5-1 | 0-0 | 3-2 | 4-1 | 0-2 | 3-0 | 1-0 | 6-1 | 1-0 | 2-0 |
| STADE LAVALLOIS | 1-2 | ■ | 1-0 | 2-1 | 1-1 | 0-1 | 3-0 | 3-1 | 0-0 | 2-1 | 1-0 | 3-0 | 2-0 | 2-1 | 0-1 | 1-3 | 8-0 | 0-1 |
| LE HAVRE AC | 1-0 | 1-1 | ■ | 2-0 | 2-1 | 3-2 | 3-0 | 1-0 | 2-0 | 4-2 | 2-1 | 2-0 | 1-1 | 5-1 | 2-0 | 0-0 | 3-0 | 3-0 |
| AS BEAUVAIS-OISE | 1-0 | 1-1 | 1-1 | ■ | 1-0 | 0-0 | 0-0 | 1-0 | 2-0 | 1-0 | 0-0 | 0-1 | 0-1 | 1-1 | 1-1 | 1-0 | 4-1 | 0-0 |
| CHAMOIS NIORTAIS | 0-0 | 0-0 | 2-1 | 2-0 | ■ | 0-2 | 2-1 | 2-0 | 2-1 | 0-1 | 1-0 | 0-1 | 1-2 | 1-1 | 0-0 | 0-1 | 0-1 | 1-0 |
| RC LENS | 1-1 | 2-0 | 1-0 | 0-0 | 0-0 | ■ | 3-0 | 0-1 | 3-0 | 6-2 | 2-1 | 3-1 | 1-1 | 0-0 | 4-0 | 2-2 | 2-2 | 2-0 |
| US CRÉTEIL | 1-0 | 1-2 | 0-0 | 1-0 | 1-0 | 2-2 | ■ | 1-2 | 1-1 | 1-3 | 2-2 | 1-1 | 0-0 | 1-0 | 0-2 | 2-0 | 0-0 | 2-1 |
| SCO ANGERS | 0-1 | 2-2 | 0-0 | 0-1 | 4-2 | 1-1 | 2-0 | ■ | 1-0 | 1-0 | 3-0 | 2-0 | 4-1 | 3-0 | 1-1 | 3-0 | 5-0 | 2-2 |
| AS ST.SEURIN-SUR-L'ISLE | 1-1 | 2-1 | 0-0 | 2-0 | 0-0 | 1-0 | 3-3 | 1-1 | ■ | 0-0 | 1-0 | 0-0 | 1-1 | 3-1 | 2-2 | 2-0 | 2-0 | 1-0 |
| EN-AVANT DE GUINGAMP | 0-0 | 0-1 | 0-0 | 0-0 | 0-0 | 1-0 | 1-2 | 3-1 | 2-1 | ■ | 2-0 | 2-0 | 2-1 | 1-0 | 2-2 | 1-2 | 0-0 | 2-1 |
| FC TOURS | 1-0 | 1-0 | 0-0 | 2-1 | 2-0 | 1-0 | 2-2 | 0-3 | 0-0 | 2-2 | ■ | 2-2 | 0-0 | 0-0 | 1-0 | 0-0 | 1-0 | 0-0 |
| LA ROCHE-SUR-YON VF | 2-2 | 0-1 | 0-2 | 1-0 | 2-3 | 0-2 | 2-0 | 0-2 | 1-0 | 0-0 | 1-1 | ■ | 1-0 | 1-1 | 2-1 | 3-1 | 2-2 | 1-1 |
| STADE DE REIMS | 1-0 | 1-0 | 0-2 | 1-0 | 1-0 | 2-0 | 2-0 | 2-0 | 1-2 | 4-0 | 0-1 | 1-1 | ■ | 3-0 | 1-1 | 1-1 | 0-0 | 0-0 |
| US ORLÉANS | 1-1 | 0-0 | 0-0 | 0-1 | 3-0 | 1-1 | 1-1 | 0-1 | 1-0 | 0-2 | 1-1 | 1-1 | 2-0 | ■ | 4-1 | 1-2 | 1-2 | 2-1 |
| AS RED STAR 93 | 2-0 | 1-1 | 0-6 | 1-1 | 1-1 | 1-1 | 0-0 | 0-2 | 1-2 | 3-0 | 2-0 | 1-0 | 3-2 | 1-2 | ■ | 2-2 | 3-0 | 0-0 |
| FC BOURGES | 0-1 | 1-3 | 0-2 | 1-1 | 2-2 | 2-2 | 4-1 | 2-1 | 2-2 | 2-1 | 1-1 | 2-0 | 1-1 | 0-0 | 0-0 | ■ | 1-0 | 0-5 |
| OLYMP. ST.QUENTINOIS | 1-0 | 0-0 | 1-1 | 0-0 | 1-0 | 1-2 | 1-0 | 0-0 | 3-1 | 0-2 | 1-1 | 3-4 | 1-4 | 0-1 | 1-2 | 0-1 | ■ | 1-1 |
| LE MANS UC 72 | 0-0 | 1-2 | 1-0 | 1-0 | 0-2 | 1-1 | 3-1 | 2-2 | 0-0 | 0-0 | 0-0 | 2-3 | 1-0 | 1-1 | 1-0 | 3-1 | 0-1 | ■ |

The match Le Mans 2 La Roche 3 was later awarded Le Mans 0 La Roche 3. The match Bourges 2 Lens 2 was later awarded Bourges 0 Lens 2. The match Bourges 1 Tours 1 was later awarded Bourges 0 Tours 1.

## FRANCE 3RD DIVISION CENTRE 1990/91
### LEAGUE TABLE FINAL

| | | | | | | | | |
|---|---|---|---|---|---|---|---|---|
| AJ Auxerre A | 30 | 18 | 8 | 4 | 50 | 13 | 44 |
| LB Châteauroux | 30 | 14 | 11 | 5 | 43 | 28 | 39 |
| Olympique Lyon A | 30 | 15 | 5 | 10 | 41 | 32 | 35 |
| AAC Troyes | 30 | 11 | 12 | 7 | 35 | 26 | 34 |
| JGA Nevers | 30 | 11 | 12 | 7 | 34 | 29 | 34 |
| CO Le Puy | 30 | 13 | 7 | 10 | 39 | 24 | 33 |
| EDS Montlucon | 30 | 12 | 8 | 10 | 35 | 31 | 32 |
| FC Gueugnon A | 30 | 10 | 9 | 11 | 32 | 33 | 29 |
| AS St.Etienne A | 30 | 8 | 13 | 9 | 32 | 38 | 29 |
| FC Montceau | 30 | 8 | 12 | 10 | 40 | 36 | 28 |
| Melun Dammarie 77 | 30 | 9 | 9 | 12 | 33 | 47 | 27 |
| AS Lyon La Duchère | 30 | 8 | 10 | 12 | 25 | 35 | 26 |
| AS Evry | 30 | 6 | 13 | 11 | 25 | 35 | 25 |
| OC Châteaudun | 30 | 8 | 8 | 14 | 27 | 43 | 24 |
| US Joué-les-Tours | 30 | 5 | 13 | 12 | 31 | 45 | 23 |
| SCO Angers A | 30 | 5 | 8 | 17 | 25 | 52 | 18 |

Promoted : - LB Châteauroux
Relegated : - CO Le Puy (to 5th Div.) and FC Montceau both for financial reasons, US Joué-les-Tours and SCO Angers A.

## FRANCE 3RD DIVISION CENTRE-WEST 1990/91
### LEAGUE TABLE FINAL

| | | | | | | | | |
|---|---|---|---|---|---|---|---|---|
| FC Perpignan | 30 | 21 | 4 | 5 | 44 | 15 | 46 |
| SO Châtellerault | 30 | 17 | 10 | 3 | 45 | 20 | 44 |
| FC Blagnac | 30 | 12 | 13 | 5 | 42 | 29 | 37 |
| Stade Mont-de-Marsan | 30 | 15 | 6 | 9 | 45 | 22 | 36 |
| AS Muret | 30 | 12 | 11 | 7 | 34 | 24 | 35 |
| ES Brive | 30 | 14 | 7 | 9 | 38 | 34 | 35 |
| Villenave-D'Ornon | 30 | 10 | 11 | 9 | 27 | 36 | 31 |
| FC Sète | 30 | 8 | 13 | 9 | 26 | 34 | 29 |
| Girondins Bordeaux A | 30 | 7 | 14 | 9 | 29 | 29 | 28 |
| ASC Angoulême | 30 | 11 | 6 | 13 | 32 | 42 | 28 |
| ES La Rochelle | 30 | 8 | 11 | 11 | 31 | 29 | 27 |
| Toulouse FC A | 30 | 9 | 6 | 15 | 24 | 27 | 24 |
| AS Libourne | 30 | 5 | 14 | 11 | 26 | 39 | 24 |
| FC Pau | 30 | 5 | 13 | 12 | 23 | 42 | 23 |
| Chamois Niort A | 30 | 6 | 10 | 14 | 22 | 36 | 22 |
| CA Castets-en-Dorthe | 30 | 1 | 9 | 20 | 20 | 50 | 11 |

Promoted : - FC Perpignan
Relegated : - Chamois Niort A and CA Castets-en-Dorthe

# FRANCE 3RD DIVISION EAST 1990/91

### LEAGUE TABLE FINAL

| Team | P | W | D | L | F | A | Pts |
|---|---|---|---|---|---|---|---|
| CS Sedan-Ardennes | 30 | 12 | 15 | 3 | 33 | 17 | 39 |
| AS Nancy-Lorraine A | 30 | 14 | 7 | 9 | 58 | 36 | 35 |
| OCM Charleville | 30 | 11 | 13 | 6 | 40 | 33 | 35 |
| FC Sochaux A | 30 | 13 | 8 | 9 | 56 | 38 | 34 |
| Paris FC | 30 | 11 | 12 | 7 | 33 | 22 | 34 |
| FC Mulhouse A | 30 | 10 | 14 | 6 | 35 | 26 | 34 |
| Racing Paris Un | 30 | 13 | 6 | 11 | 36 | 29 | 32 |
| RC Besancon | 30 | 10 | 11 | 9 | 37 | 32 | 31 |
| FC Metz A | 30 | 11 | 6 | 13 | 38 | 40 | 28 |
| ASP Vauban Strasbourg | 30 | 8 | 12 | 10 | 27 | 31 | 28 |
| AS Baumes-L'Isle | 30 | 8 | 11 | 11 | 33 | 42 | 27 |
| Stade Reims A | 30 | 8 | 10 | 12 | 27 | 35 | 26 |
| RC Lons-le-Saunier | 30 | 6 | 13 | 11 | 32 | 40 | 25 |
| SR St.Die | 30 | 7 | 11 | 12 | 32 | 52 | 25 |
| RC Strasbourg A | 30 | 8 | 9 | 13 | 34 | 47 | 25 |
| AS Sarreguemines | 30 | 5 | 12 | 13 | 22 | 44 | 22 |

Promoted :- CS Sedan-Ardennes
Relegated :- ASP Vauban Strasbourg (to 5th Div. for financial reasons), Stade Reims A, RC Lons-le-Saunier and AS Sarreguemines.

### NAME CHANGE FOR SEASON 1991/92
Racing Paris Un to Racing 92

# FRANCE 3RD DIVISION WEST 1990/91

### LEAGUE TABLE FINAL

| Team | P | W | D | L | F | A | Pts |
|---|---|---|---|---|---|---|---|
| RC Ancenis | 32 | 14 | 15 | 3 | 36 | 19 | 43 |
| FC Nantes A | 32 | 13 | 16 | 3 | 43 | 23 | 42 |
| Stade Laval A | 32 | 14 | 13 | 5 | 35 | 23 | 41 |
| CSFC Lorient | 32 | 14 | 9 | 9 | 39 | 23 | 37 |
| Quimper CFC | 32 | 12 | 13 | 7 | 32 | 45 | 37 |
| FCA Brest A | 32 | 13 | 11 | 8 | 43 | 29 | 37 |
| AS Cherbourg | 32 | 9 | 15 | 8 | 33 | 24 | 33 |
| US Avranches | 32 | 11 | 11 | 10 | 40 | 35 | 33 |
| SLK St.Pol-de-Léon | 32 | 11 | 11 | 10 | 33 | 39 | 33 |
| Stade Lucon | 32 | 10 | 11 | 11 | 33 | 31 | 31 |
| Stade Rennes A | 32 | 10 | 11 | 11 | 25 | 31 | 31 |
| US Montagnarde | 32 | 12 | 7 | 13 | 32 | 45 | 31 |
| En Avant Guingamp A | 32 | 10 | 9 | 13 | 34 | 36 | 29 |
| FC St. Lo | 32 | 7 | 15 | 10 | 29 | 33 | 29 |
| US Concarneau | 32 | 10 | 9 | 13 | 36 | 43 | 29 |
| FC Vannes | 32 | 7 | 9 | 16 | 31 | 46 | 23 |
| Véloce US Vannes | 32 | 2 | 6 | 24 | 16 | 67 | 10 |

Promoted :- RC Ancenis
Relegated :- Véloce US Vannes.

# FRANCE 3RD DIVISION NORTH 1990/91

### LEAGUE TABLE FINAL

| Team | P | W | D | L | F | A | Pts |
|---|---|---|---|---|---|---|---|
| SCP Amiens | 30 | 17 | 9 | 4 | 57 | 35 | 43 |
| St.Leu VO 95 | 30 | 16 | 8 | 6 | 45 | 24 | 40 |
| RUFC Calais | 30 | 15 | 8 | 7 | 50 | 28 | 38 |
| US Fécamp | 30 | 14 | 9 | 7 | 51 | 34 | 37 |
| Paris-St.Germain FC A | 30 | 15 | 6 | 9 | 60 | 44 | 36 |
| Le Havre AC A | 30 | 13 | 9 | 8 | 41 | 37 | 35 |
| AC Le Touquet | 30 | 10 | 11 | 9 | 49 | 36 | 31 |
| RC Lens A | 30 | 12 | 6 | 12 | 36 | 37 | 30 |
| US Villecresnes 94 | 30 | 8 | 14 | 8 | 36 | 37 | 30 |
| ES Wasquehal | 30 | 9 | 10 | 11 | 34 | 25 | 28 |
| Lille OSC A | 30 | 8 | 10 | 12 | 32 | 38 | 26 |
| US St.Omer | 30 | 6 | 13 | 11 | 37 | 51 | 25 |
| US Mauberge | 30 | 8 | 8 | 14 | 26 | 40 | 24 |
| FC Rouen A | 30 | 8 | 8 | 14 | 39 | 56 | 24 |
| ES Arques | 30 | 5 | 7 | 18 | 27 | 58 | 17 |
| US Valenciennes A | 30 | 4 | 8 | 18 | 21 | 61 | 16 |

Promoted :- SCP Amiens
Relegated :- ES Arques and US Valenciennes A

# FRANCE 3RD DIVISION SOUTH 1990/91

### LEAGUE TABLE FINAL

| Team | P | W | D | L | F | A | Pts |
|---|---|---|---|---|---|---|---|
| Montpellier HSC A | 30 | 16 | 9 | 5 | 38 | 22 | 41 |
| FC Grenoble | 30 | 17 | 6 | 7 | 59 | 31 | 40 |
| US Endoume Marseille | 30 | 16 | 7 | 7 | 53 | 32 | 39 |
| USJOA Valence | 30 | 11 | 12 | 7 | 25 | 21 | 34 |
| AS Cannes A | 30 | 12 | 8 | 10 | 40 | 33 | 32 |
| AS St.Priest | 30 | 12 | 8 | 10 | 34 | 28 | 32 |
| Stade Vallauris | 30 | 11 | 9 | 10 | 34 | 28 | 31 |
| FC Valence | 30 | 10 | 10 | 10 | 35 | 32 | 30 |
| Stade St.Raphael | 30 | 9 | 12 | 9 | 32 | 36 | 30 |
| AS Monaco A | 30 | 8 | 11 | 11 | 32 | 39 | 27 |
| Olympique Marseille A | 30 | 9 | 9 | 12 | 28 | 37 | 27 |
| SC Toulon A | 30 | 9 | 9 | 12 | 44 | 48 | 27 |
| SEC Bastia A | 30 | 10 | 6 | 14 | 44 | 48 | 26 |
| OGC Nice A | 30 | 9 | 8 | 13 | 36 | 38 | 26 |
| US Canet-en-Roussillon | 30 | 6 | 10 | 14 | 32 | 55 | 22 |
| US Cluses-Scionzier | 30 | 4 | 8 | 18 | 18 | 52 | 16 |

Promoted :- FC Grenoble
Relegated :- US Canet-en-Roussillon & US Cluses-Scionzier

Montpellier HSC A.....2    FC Perpignan...........0
Montpellier were later disqualified for fielding a 1st team player

# 3RD DIVISION CHAMPIONSHIP PLAY-OFFS

### 1ST ROUND
CS Sedan-Ardennes.. 5    RC Ancenis............0

### SEMI-FINALS
AJ Auxerre A......... 4    SCP Amiens...........1

### FINAL
CS Sedan-Ardennes...1    AJ Auxerre A..........1 (aet)
Sedan win 4-1 on penalties.

# RELEGATION PLAY-OFFS

### GROUP A

| Team | P | W | D | L | F | A | Pts |
|---|---|---|---|---|---|---|---|
| SR St.Die | 2 | 1 | 1 | 0 | 6 | 3 | 3 |
| US Concarneau | 2 | 1 | 0 | 1 | 5 | 8 | 2 |
| FC Rouen A | 2 | 0 | 1 | 1 | 5 | 6 | 1 |

FC Pau ...........0    US Concarneau .......2

### GROUP B

| Team | P | W | D | L | F | A | Pts |
|---|---|---|---|---|---|---|---|
| OGC Nice A | 2 | 2 | 0 | 0 | 6 | 0 | 4 |
| FC Pau | 2 | 1 | 0 | 1 | 4 | 2 | 2 |
| OC Châteaudun | 2 | 0 | 0 | 2 | 0 | 8 | 0 |

OC Châteaudun.........5    FC Rouen .......1

Note :- Winners of each group automatically gain 3rd Division places for Season 1991/92, numbers 2 and 3 in each group play-off further to decide the order of preference should any further places become vacant.

# FRANCE 4TH DIVISION GROUP A 1990/91

### LEAGUE TABLE FINAL

| Team | P | W | D | L | F | A | Pts |
|---|---|---|---|---|---|---|---|
| Gravelines | 26 | 15 | 8 | 3 | 50 | 20 | 38 |
| FC Compiègne | 26 | 12 | 11 | 3 | 46 | 27 | 35 |
| USGB Boulogne | 26 | 13 | 8 | 5 | 42 | 27 | 34 |
| RC Epernay | 26 | 11 | 11 | 4 | 39 | 26 | 33 |
| AS Beauvais A | 26 | 12 | 9 | 5 | 24 | 17 | 33 |
| Stade Béthune | 26 | 9 | 9 | 8 | 39 | 36 | 27 |
| Football Roubaix | 26 | 10 | 7 | 9 | 34 | 31 | 27 |
| FC Versailles 78 | 26 | 7 | 11 | 8 | 28 | 31 | 25 |
| US Chantilly | 26 | 6 | 9 | 11 | 26 | 34 | 21 |
| Friville | 26 | 5 | 10 | 11 | 22 | 33 | 20 |
| US Dunkerque A | 26 | 8 | 4 | 14 | 26 | 38 | 20 |
| CS Meaux | 26 | 4 | 11 | 11 | 18 | 35 | 19 |
| US Tourcoing | 26 | 6 | 6 | 14 | 23 | 43 | 18 |
| FC Chalon-sur-Saône | 26 | 4 | 6 | 16 | 28 | 48 | 14 |

Promoted :- Gravelines and USGB Boulogne

# FRANCE 4TH DIVISION GROUP B 1990/91

### LEAGUE TABLE FINAL

| Team | P | W | D | L | F | A | Pts |
|---|---|---|---|---|---|---|---|
| SM Caen A | 26 | 18 | 6 | 2 | 56 | 15 | 42 |
| Aubervilliers | 26 | 15 | 10 | 1 | 41 | 13 | 40 |
| Olympique Noisy-le-Sec | 26 | 14 | 7 | 5 | 37 | 19 | 35 |
| Condé Sports | 26 | 12 | 8 | 6 | 35 | 22 | 32 |
| AS Poissy | 26 | 12 | 7 | 7 | 37 | 19 | 31 |
| CAL Lisieux | 26 | 9 | 9 | 8 | 31 | 31 | 27 |
| AS Corbeil-Essonnes | 26 | 8 | 7 | 11 | 31 | 31 | 23 |
| Granville | 26 | 8 | 7 | 11 | 26 | 32 | 23 |
| AS Bayeux | 26 | 7 | 9 | 10 | 26 | 38 | 23 |
| US Fécamp A | 26 | 8 | 6 | 12 | 29 | 36 | 22 |
| Evreux AC | 26 | 6 | 10 | 10 | 25 | 39 | 22 |
| Pavilly | 26 | 6 | 9 | 11 | 19 | 38 | 21 |
| USM Malakoff | 26 | 5 | 7 | 14 | 23 | 43 | 17 |
| US Normande | 26 | 2 | 5 | 19 | 17 | 48 | 9 |

Promoted :- SM Caen A and Aubervilliers

# FRANCE 4TH DIVISION GROUP C 1990/91

### LEAGUE TABLE FINAL

| Team | P | W | D | L | F | A | Pts |
|---|---|---|---|---|---|---|---|
| ESCB Yutz | 26 | 18 | 6 | 2 | 59 | 17 | 42 |
| FC Thionville | 26 | 15 | 9 | 2 | 48 | 15 | 39 |
| US Forbach | 26 | 16 | 6 | 4 | 50 | 25 | 38 |
| CS Blénod | 26 | 14 | 8 | 4 | 47 | 14 | 36 |
| Haguenau | 26 | 10 | 7 | 9 | 34 | 41 | 27 |
| ASPTT Metz | 26 | 11 | 4 | 11 | 28 | 30 | 26 |
| ASM Belfort | 26 | 9 | 5 | 12 | 42 | 49 | 23 |
| Red Star St.Avold | 26 | 8 | 7 | 11 | 28 | 41 | 23 |
| ES Florange-Ebange | 26 | 7 | 7 | 12 | 27 | 42 | 21 |
| CO St.Dizier | 26 | 5 | 10 | 11 | 22 | 31 | 20 |
| Vandoeuvre | 26 | 8 | 3 | 15 | 31 | 55 | 19 |
| FC Red Star Mulhouse | 26 | 5 | 7 | 14 | 29 | 37 | 17 |
| AS Mulhouse | 26 | 7 | 3 | 16 | 21 | 47 | 17 |
| FC Wissembourg | 26 | 5 | 6 | 15 | 28 | 51 | 16 |

Promoted :- ESCB Yutz and FC Thionville

# FRANCE 4TH DIVISION GROUP D 1990/91

### LEAGUE TABLE FINAL

| Team | P | W | D | L | F | A | Pts |
|---|---|---|---|---|---|---|---|
| CS St.Brieuc | 26 | 14 | 8 | 4 | 38 | 22 | 36 |
| La-Roche-sur-Yon VF A | 26 | 11 | 12 | 3 | 33 | 18 | 34 |
| FC Tours A | 26 | 11 | 10 | 5 | 36 | 23 | 32 |
| FC Nantes B | 26 | 12 | 7 | 7 | 47 | 31 | 31 |
| US St.Malo | 26 | 11 | 9 | 6 | 43 | 31 | 31 |
| US La Flèche | 26 | 10 | 8 | 8 | 39 | 27 | 28 |
| Sablé | 26 | 10 | 8 | 8 | 39 | 25 | 28 |
| SO Cholet | 26 | 10 | 6 | 10 | 44 | 29 | 26 |
| USSC Redon | 26 | 8 | 8 | 10 | 29 | 38 | 24 |
| UC Le Mans 72 A | 26 | 7 | 9 | 10 | 24 | 25 | 23 |
| ES Segré | 26 | 8 | 6 | 12 | 26 | 36 | 22 |
| US Pont-L'Abbe | 26 | 5 | 8 | 13 | 24 | 48 | 18 |
| Stade Quimper A | 26 | 4 | 10 | 12 | 25 | 40 | 18 |
| DC Carhaix | 26 | 2 | 8 | 16 | 22 | 52 | 12 |

Promoted :- CS St. Brieuc and La-Roche-sur-Yon VF A

## FRANCE 4TH DIVISION GROUP E 1990/91
### LEAGUE TABLE FINAL

| Team | P | W | D | L | F | A | Pts |
|---|---|---|---|---|---|---|---|
| US Annemasse | 26 | 15 | 7 | 4 | 37 | 17 | 37 |
| AS Beaune | 26 | 14 | 6 | 6 | 37 | 25 | 34 |
| Grenoble Norcap | 26 | 14 | 6 | 6 | 32 | 16 | 34 |
| FCSA Rumilly | 26 | 14 | 6 | 6 | 42 | 27 | 34 |
| FA Cournon-D'Auvergne | 26 | 13 | 7 | 6 | 55 | 31 | 33 |
| Grenoble-Isère | 26 | 11 | 9 | 6 | 34 | 15 | 31 |
| CS Thonon | 26 | 8 | 11 | 7 | 21 | 22 | 27 |
| CS Louhans-Cuiseaux A | 26 | 8 | 10 | 8 | 41 | 35 | 26 |
| FC Jojo Grenoble | 26 | 9 | 6 | 11 | 29 | 34 | 24 |
| CF Dijon A | 26 | 10 | 4 | 12 | 34 | 24 | 24 |
| AS Roanne | 26 | 8 | 8 | 12 | 33 | 42 | 24 |
| Vermondans | 26 | 8 | 6 | 12 | 31 | 33 | 22 |
| Ambert | 26 | 3 | 5 | 18 | 21 | 51 | 11 |
| FC Monceau A | 26 | 2 | 4 | 20 | 14 | 81 | 8 |

Promoted :- US Annemasse and FCSA Rumilly

## FRANCE 4TH DIVISION GROUP G 1990/91
### LEAGUE TABLE FINAL

| Team | P | W | D | L | F | A | Pts |
|---|---|---|---|---|---|---|---|
| CSC Thouars | 26 | 14 | 9 | 3 | 39 | 17 | 37 |
| Toulouse Fontaines | 26 | 13 | 8 | 5 | 34 | 19 | 34 |
| AFC Aurillac | 26 | 13 | 7 | 6 | 34 | 20 | 33 |
| FC Trélissac | 26 | 14 | 5 | 7 | 41 | 29 | 33 |
| Stade Rodez A | 26 | 10 | 8 | 8 | 38 | 36 | 28 |
| La Pallice AM | 26 | 8 | 12 | 6 | 25 | 24 | 28 |
| Stadoeste Tarbes | 26 | 9 | 7 | 10 | 44 | 36 | 25 |
| Cugnaux | 26 | 9 | 7 | 10 | 28 | 23 | 25 |
| CCUS Saintes | 26 | 9 | 6 | 11 | 41 | 38 | 24 |
| St.Jean-de-Luz | 26 | 5 | 13 | 8 | 23 | 29 | 23 |
| Olympique Niort St.Liguaire | 26 | 7 | 9 | 10 | 33 | 42 | 23 |
| CS Arpajon | 26 | 7 | 6 | 13 | 18 | 41 | 20 |
| EB Orthez | 26 | 4 | 15 | 7 | 23 | 49 | 18 |
| FC Montauban | 26 | 7 | 2 | 17 | 24 | 46 | 16 |

Promoted :- CSC Thouars and Toulouse Fontaines

## FRANCE 4TH DIVISION GROUP F 1990/91
### LEAGUE TABLE FINAL

| Team | P | W | D | L | F | A | Pts |
|---|---|---|---|---|---|---|---|
| ES Viry-Châtillon | 26 | 12 | 9 | 5 | 35 | 26 | 33 |
| Amicale Lucé | 26 | 11 | 10 | 5 | 32 | 18 | 32 |
| AAJ Blois | 26 | 12 | 8 | 6 | 29 | 18 | 32 |
| RC Fontainebleau | 26 | 9 | 10 | 7 | 33 | 30 | 28 |
| INF Clairefontaine | 26 | 9 | 8 | 9 | 31 | 23 | 27 |
| AJ Auxerre B | 26 | 9 | 9 | 8 | 27 | 26 | 27 |
| Stade PEPP Poitiers | 26 | 11 | 4 | 11 | 28 | 26 | 26 |
| ES Wasquehal | 26 | 8 | 10 | 8 | 28 | 26 | 26 |
| Olymp. Marseille A | 26 | 8 | 10 | 8 | 36 | 33 | 26 |
| AS Decize | 26 | 8 | 10 | 8 | 32 | 38 | 26 |
| USL Châteauroux | 26 | 9 | 7 | 10 | 43 | 37 | 25 |
| Stade Auxerre | 26 | 9 | 4 | 13 | 28 | 41 | 22 |
| Montmorillon | 26 | 9 | 4 | 13 | 28 | 46 | 22 |
| US Orléans A | 26 | 7 | 7 | 12 | 33 | 40 | 21 |
| AS Moulins | 26 | 5 | 7 | 14 | 19 | 38 | 17 |

Promoted :- ES Viry-Châtillon and Amicale Lucé

## FRANCE 4TH DIVISION GROUP H 1990/91
### LEAGUE TABLE FINAL

| Team | P | W | D | L | F | A | Pts |
|---|---|---|---|---|---|---|---|
| ES Fréjus | 26 | 12 | 10 | 4 | 35 | 20 | 34 |
| AS Aix-en-Provence | 26 | 10 | 12 | 4 | 33 | 19 | 32 |
| FC Hyères | 26 | 12 | 6 | 8 | 29 | 22 | 30 |
| Indépend.Pont-St.Esprit | 26 | 9 | 10 | 7 | 29 | 27 | 28 |
| Istres SF A | 26 | 10 | 7 | 9 | 40 | 35 | 27 |
| Arles AC | 26 | 9 | 8 | 9 | 35 | 32 | 26 |
| Montélimar | 26 | 9 | 8 | 9 | 28 | 22 | 26 |
| CABG Lucciana | 26 | 8 | 10 | 8 | 38 | 40 | 26 |
| FC Martigues A | 26 | 8 | 9 | 9 | 28 | 30 | 25 |
| Nimes Olympique A | 26 | 7 | 10 | 9 | 32 | 36 | 24 |
| FA L'Ile-Rousse | 26 | 8 | 8 | 10 | 29 | 35 | 24 |
| ASB Béziers | 26 | 7 | 10 | 9 | 31 | 48 | 24 |
| Olympique Alès A | 26 | 7 | 7 | 13 | 25 | 35 | 19 |
| US Cagnes | 26 | 5 | 8 | 13 | 24 | 39 | 18 |

Promoted :- ES Fréjus and AS Aix-en-Provence

## 4TH DIVISION CHAMPIONSHIP PLAY-OFFS

### 1/4 FINALS
| | | | | |
|---|---|---|---|---|
| SM Caen A | 4 | Graveleines | 0 | |
| ES Viry-Châtillon | 3 | ES Fréjus | 5 | |
| CS St.Brieuc | 0 | ESCB Yutz | 2 | |
| US Annemasse | 2 | CSC Thouars | 5 | |

### SEMI-FINALS
| | | | | |
|---|---|---|---|---|
| CSC Thouars | 1 | SM Caen A | 0 | |
| ES Fréjus | 4 | ESCB Yutz | 1 | (aet.) |

### FINAL
ES Fréjus 1 — CSC Thouars 0

## FRANCE CUP 1990/91

### 1/32 FINALS
| | | | |
|---|---|---|---|
| SCO Angers | 2 | Olympique Lyon | 0 |
| Chamois Niort | 1 | SM Caen | 0 |
| FC Mulhouse | 0 | AS Monaco | 1 |
| Olymp.St.Quentin | 0 | AJ Auxerre | 2 |
| Toulouse FC | 3 | Lille OSC | 4 |
| AS Nancy-Lorraine | 3 | AS Cannes | 2 |
| ES Dunkerque | 2 | Olympique Avignon | 0 |
| FC Bourges | 1 | Paris-St-Germain FC | 1 |
| FC Rouen | 1 | Stade Rennes | 0 |
| CF Dijon | 3 | OGC Nice | 1 |
| AS St.Seurin | 1 | Epinal FC | 2 |
| US Orléans | 2 | SC Toulon | 4 (aet.) |
| Girondins Bordeaux | 4 | FC Metz | 3 |
| Montpellier HSC | 2 | FCA Brest | 3 |
| Red Star 93 | 1 | Ajaccio GFC | 3 |
| US Valenciennes | 3 | Olympique Alès | 3 |
| UC Le Mans 72 | 2 | Stade Rodez | 1 |
| AS St.Priest | 2 | FC Tours | 2 |
| ECAC Chaumont | 1 | AS Beauvais | 2 |
| Melun Dammarie 77 | 1 | FC Annecy | 2 |
| AAC Troyes | 1 | US Fécamp | 1 |
| SCP Amiens | 1 | | |

US Fécamp win 5-3 on penalties

### 1/16 FINALS
| | | | |
|---|---|---|---|
| AJ Auxerre | 1 | AS St.Etienne | 0 |
| Montpellier HSC | 0 | Chamois Niort | 1 |
| Stade Rodez | 1 | FC Metz | 1 (aet.) |
| CF Dijon | 0 | Olymp.Marseille | 3 |
| AS Cannes | 3 | US Valenciennes | 0 |
| US Fécamp | 0 | FC Nantes | 1 (aet.) |
| FC Gueugnon | 1 | FC Nantes | |
| St.Christ.Chât'roux | 3 | AS St.Priest | 4 |
| ECAC Chaumont | 1 | UC Le Mans 72 | 2 (aet.) |
| Melun Dammarie 77 | 1 | ES Brive | |
| AAC Troyes | 1 | FC Rouen | 0 |
| US Fécamp | 1 | | |

Stade Rodez win 4-3 on penalties
FC Gueugnon win 7-6 on penalties

### 1/8 FINALS
| | | | |
|---|---|---|---|
| Lille OSC | 1 | AS Monaco | 3 |
| FC Annecy | 1 | AS Nancy-Lorraine | 0 (aet.) |
| FC Tours | 0 | Toulouse FC | 0 |
| Paris-St-Germain FC | 1 | FC Bourges | 0 |
| FC Sochaux | 0 | SCO Angers | 3 |
| St.Christ.Chât'roux | 2 | SC Toulon | 1 |
| Olympique Alès | 0 | FC Gueugnon | 1 |
| FC Tours | 2 | Stade Laval | 1 |

FC Gueugnon win 1-4 on penalties

### 1/4 FINALS
| | | | |
|---|---|---|---|
| FC Nantes | 1 | Olymp. Marseille | 2 (aet.) |
| FC Gueugnon | 1 | AS Cannes | 1 (aet.) |
| FC Sochaux | | AS Monaco | 3 |
| FC Tours | | Stade Rodez | 2 |
| | | Stade Laval | 1 |

FC Gueugnon win 3-4 on penalties

### SEMI-FINALS
| | | | |
|---|---|---|---|
| Olymp. Marseille | 4 | Stade Rodez | 1 |
| AS Monaco | 5 | FC Gueugnon | 0 |

### FINAL
AS Monaco 1 — Olympique Marseille 0

8/6/91 (at Parc des Princes, Paris)

1-0 Passi 90

Marseille : Olmeta, Amoros, Mozer, Boli, Casoni, Germain, Fournier (Stojkovic 46), Waddle, Vercruysse, Pelé, Papin

Monaco : Ettori, Puel, Mendy, Petit, Sonor, Dib, Sauzée, Djorkaeff (Passi 59), Rui Barros, Fofana (Diaz 75), Weah.

Referee : Quiniou
Attendance : 44,123

# FRANCE INTERNATIONAL REVIEW 1990

## INTERNATIONAL LINE-UPS 1990

| Match | Gilles Rousset | Franck Silvestre | Basile Boli | Franck Sauzée | Manuel Amoros | Laurent Blanc | Marcel Dib | Rémy Garde | Bernard Pardo | Eric Cantona | Pascal Vahirua | Didier Deschamps | Jean-Pierre Papin | Eric Di Meco | Jean-Marc Ferreri | Bruno Martini | Bernard Casoni | Luis Fernandez | Christian Perez | Philippe Tibeut | Jean-Philippe Durand | Fabrice Divert | Emmanuel Petit | Jocelyn Angloma | David Ginola |
|---|---|---|---|---|---|---|---|---|---|---|---|---|---|---|---|---|---|---|---|---|---|---|---|---|---|
| 21/1/90 KUWAIT 0 FRANCE 1 — Al Kuwait — Ref: Al Kandi (Kuwait) — Friendly (Blanc) | 1 | 2 | 3 | 4 | 5 | 6 | 7 | 8 | 9 | 10 | 11 | (9) | (10) | (10) | (11) | | | | | | | | | | |
| 24/1/90 DDR 0 FRANCE 3 — Al Kuwait — Ref: Al Moussa (Kuwait) — Friendly (Cantona 2, Deschamps) | | (4) | | 4 | 2 | 6 | (6) | (9) | 7 | 10 | 11 | 8 | (10) | 5 | 9 | 1 | 3 | | | | | | | | |
| 28/2/90 FRANCE 2 WESTERN GERMANY 1 — Montpellier — Ref: Ramos Marcos (Spain) — Friendly (Papin, Cantona) | | | | | 2 | (3) | | 9 | 8 | 11 | (7) | 6 | 10 | 5 | | 1 | 4 | 7 | | | | | | | |
| 28/3/90 HUNGARY 1 FRANCE 3 — Budapest — Ref: Diakonowicz (Poland) — Friendly (Cantona 2, Sauzée) | | 2 | (7) | 4 | 5 | (4) | | | 6 | 10 | | | | | | 1 | 3 | 7 | 9 | 11 | (5) | (11) | | | |
| 15/8/90 FRANCE 0 POLAND 0 — Paris — Ref: Midgley (England) — Friendly | | | (6) | 4 | 2 | | | | | 10 | (7) | | 11 | | 7 | 1 | 5 | 6 | 9 | | (2) | | 3 | | |
| 5/9/90 ICELAND 1 FRANCE 2 — Reykjavik — Ref: Syme (Scotland) — EuroCh.Q. (Papin, Cantona) | | (9) | 3 | 4 | 2 | 6 | | | 7 | 10 | | 8 | 11 | | | 1 | 5 | (11) | 9 | | (6) | | | | |
| 13/10/90 FRANCE 2 CZECHOSLOVAKIA 1 — Paris — Ref: Courtney (England) — EuroCh.Q. (Papin 2) | | (9) | 2 | 7 | | 3 | | | 7 | 10 | | 6 | 11 | | | 1 | 4 | (5) | | | 8 | 1 | | 5 | |
| 17/11/90 ALBANIA 0 FRANCE 1 — Tiranë — Ref: Galler (Switzerland) — EuroCh.Q. (Boli) | | | 2 | 5 | | 3 | | | 7 | 10 | | 6 | | | | 1 | 4 | | 9 | 10 | | 1 | 1 | (11) | (10) |
| CAPS AT 31/12/90 | 1 | 9 | 25 | 18 | 70 | 13 | 6 | 3 | 12 | 16 | 6 | 11 | 27 | 6 | 37 | 13 | 15 | 48 | 11 | 2 | 10 | 1 | 1 | 2 | 1 |
| GOALS AT 31/12/90 | | | 1 | 2 | 1 | 2 | | | | 10 | | | 10 | | 3 | | | 5 | 1 | | 1 | | 1 | 1 | |

## FRANCE : All Time Records as at 31/12/90 - CAPS

1. Maxime Bossis (FC Nantes/Racing Club de Paris) — 76
2. Michel Platini (AS Nancy-Lorraine/AS St.Etienne/Juventus FC) — 72
3. Manuel Amoros (AS Monaco/Olympique Marseille) — 70
4. Marius Tresor (Olympique Marseille/Girondins Bordeaux) — 65
5. Roger Marche (Stade de Reims/Racing Club de Paris) — 63
6. Robert Jonquet (Stade de Reims) — 58
   Henri Michel (FC Nantes) — 58
8. Patrick Battiston (FC Metz/AS St.Etienne/Girondins Bordeaux/AS Monaco) — 56
9. Didier Six (US Valenciennes/RC Lens/Olympique Marseille/SV Cercle Brugge/RC Strasbourg/VfB Stuttgart/FC Mulhouse 93) — 52
   Jean Tigana (Olympique Lyon/Girondins Bordeaux) — 52

## FRANCE : All Time Records as at 31/12/90 - GOALS

1. Michel Platini (AS Nancy-Lorraine/AS St.Etienne/Juventus FC) — (72) 41
2. Just Fontaine (OGC Nice/Stade de Reims) — (20) 27
3. Jean Nicolas (FC Rouen) — (25) 20
   Paul Nicolas (Red Star) — (35) 20
5. Jean Vincent (Lille OSC/Stade de Reims) — (45) 20
6. Jean Baratte (Lille OSC) — (32) 19
7. Roger Piantoni (AS Nancy-Lorraine/Stade de Reims) — (38) 18
   Raymond Kopa (Stade de Reims/Real Madrid CF) — (45) 18
9. Emile Veinante (FC Metz/Racing Club de Paris) — (23) 17
10. Herve Revelli (AS St.Etienne) — (29) 15
    Dominique Rocheteau (AS St.Etienne/Paris-St.Germain FC) — (49) 15

# THE UNIFICATION OF GERMANY

The reunification of Germany became politically a fact on the 1st of July 1990. Although a mood of optimism was prevalent at the time, events during the past 12 months have shown that many problems will take years to solve.

As far as football is concerned, reunification brings important changes to the structure of the game as well as again raising questions brought about by the dual existence of the Federal Republic of Germany and the German Democratic Republic. We therefore consider explanations necessary regarding the documentation to be found in 'FOOTBALL IN EUROPE'.

## INTERNATIONAL REVIEWS

It has of course been our policy to compile separate annual reviews for DDR (German Democratic Republic/East Germany) and West Germany (Federal Republic of Germany). Due to their dual existence we have ignored matches played by Germany between 1908 and 1942 when calculating All Time Records of caps and goals. It should be pointed out however that the DFB (the football federation of the Federal Republic of Germany) has always recognised these matches as they were played under their control. We have always felt that following this example would have brought into question the existence of the DDR and have therefore restricted West German International Reviews to matches played by West Germany since 1950. Reunification has caused us to rethink this policy as the new International Review for Germany would be quite meaningless if only matches played between 1908 and 1942 were used for calculating all time records. It has therefore been decided to calculate these records from the matches played by Germany between 1908 and 1942 together with those played by West Germany between 1950 and 1990. In other words, all matches played under the control of the DFB. Another major problem has arisen in determining the final match played by West Germany, as of course the DFB has no reason to make any definition. To simplify matters 'FOOTBALL IN EUROPE' has considered the World Cup Final of 1990 to be the final match played by West Germany although we must stress that this is purely a question of individual interpretation. Consequently, all matches played under control of the DFB during Season 1990/91 are found in the new International Review for Germany.

There are strong arguments for deeming the matches played in August and October against Portugal and Sweden as played by West Germany, however, this would also bring about complications. A match was planned during November 1990 between the teams of East and West Germany to celebrate the unification of the two football federations. As it happened however, the match did not take place due to the fear of crowd violence. By considering all matches played up to this date as West German matches however would seem at cross purposes as Germany played a qualification match for the European Championships against Luxembourg in October. At the same time it should be stated that the final match of the DDR was played in September against Belgium. Incidentally, we have received queries concerning the match played by the DDR on 28/7/90 against the USA. This match was not recognized as a full International by the football federation of the DDR, their team being made up of 2nd Division Players and referred to as an Olympic XI.

We hope now to have made the position clear regarding the calculation of caps and goals in the International Reviews of Western Germany and Germany to be found in this publication. To sum up, that of West Germany includes matches played between 1950 and 1990, and that of Germany between 1908 and 1990, inclusive of those played by Western Germany but exclusive of those played by the DDR.

## STRUCTURE OF LEAGUES AND CUPS

The reunification of Germany has brought about the need to create a single structure for the leagues and cup competitions of the DDR and Western Germany. In reality this has meant the old DDR competitions being swallowed up by the West German structure under control of the DFB.

The question will probably remain whether Season 1990/91 was the last for the DDR or the first for the new Germany. The old DDR league and cup structure in fact remained intact, being referred to as region Nordost by the DFB, a reference that was not accepted in the region itself. In fact, UEFA has accepted European Cup entrants for Season 1991/92 from the old DDR competitions despite the non-existence of the country since July 1990.

In order to accommodate clubs from the DDR, the 1 Bundesliga has been increased to 20 clubs and the 2 Bundesliga to 24 clubs for season 1991/92. It must surely be claimed that the DDR clubs have been poorly treated as they provide no more than 8 of the 44 Bundesliga clubs. In fact Season 1991/92 will be the first of 3 transitional seasons as the 1 Bundesliga will be reduced to 16 clubs for season 1993/94. For this reason, the 2 Bundesliga is split into 2 groups of 12 clubs, to form promotion and relegation sections for the 2nd half of the season.

In fact, clubs from West Germany have hardly been affected at all by the restructuring of the leagues. The only disadvantage felt was that 2 clubs were promoted from the Amateur Oberliga instead of the usual four. For Season 1991/92 the Amateur Oberliga will consist of 10 sections, 3 being created for DDR clubs, also requiring to include clubs from the old Amateur-Oberliga Berlin. Promotion play offs at the end of Season 1991/92 will also include clubs finishing in 4th place in the 2 2 Bundesliga relegation sections.

One single cup competition (DFB Pokal) will exist for Season 1991/92, 88 clubs competing in order to accommodate the DDR clubs. This will, of course, mean that an extra round of 24 matches is necessary in order to arrive at 64 clubs.

Due to the uncertainty concerning the exact date of football reunification, we consider it permissible to still refer to the DDR and West Germany in the 1990/91 edition of 'FOOTBALL IN EUROPE', particularly when bearing in mind that the original league structures still existed. Of course, the reunification of the country has led to numerous name changes to the DDR clubs, a process that may continue for some time.

The old DDR clubs would appear to face a very uncertain future, particularly as the region as a whole now faces economic problems of astronomical proportions. The DFB pursues a strict policy in the granting of professional licences, dependant on the financial position of the clubs. At the end of Season 1990/91 Rot-Weiss Essen have had their licence revoked and Hertha

BSC and Mainz 05 only retained theirs' following an appeal. In order to survive at Bundesliga level it will therefore probably be necessary for the DDR clubs to attract considerable Western sponsorship over the coming years.

At the end of season 1990/91 Bundesliga places were granted to DDR clubs as follows : -

1 Bundesliga - 2 places for champions and runners up of Oberliga

2 Bundesliga - 4 places for 3rd, 4th, 5th and 6th clubs of Oberliga

2 places for Winners of 2 play-off sections comprising 7th, 8th, 9th, 10th, 11th and 12th placed clubs of Oberliga plus 2 2Liga Champions

## COMPOSITION OF BUNDESLIGAS FOR SEASON 1991/92

**1 BUNDESLIGA**

| | |
|---|---|
| 1FC Kaiserslautern | SG Wattenscheid 09 |
| FC Bayern München | Fortuna Düsseldorf |
| SV Werder Bremen | Karlsruher SC |
| nheim | |
| Eintracht Frankfurt | VfL Bochum |
| Hamburger SV | 1FC Nürnberg |
| VfB Stuttgart | FC Schalke 04 |
| 1FC Köln | MSV Duisburg |
| Bayer Leverkusen | Stuttgarter Kickers |
| Borussia M'gladbach | FC Hansa Rostock |
| Borussia Dortmund | Dynamo Dresden |

**2 BUNDESLIGA NORD**

FC St.Pauli
Bayer Uerdingen
 Hertha BSC

Blau-Weiss 90
Hannover 96
SC Fortuna Köln
VfB Oldenburg
Eintr. Braunschweig
VfL Osnabrück
SV Meppen
FC Remscheid
Stahl Brandenburg

**2 BUNDESLIGA SÜD**

FC Homburg
1FC Saarbrücken
SV Waldhof Man-

FSV Mainz 05
SC Freiburg
SV Darmstadt 98
TSV 1860 München
Rot-Weiss Erfurt
Hallescher FC
Chemnitzer FC
Carl Zeiss Jena
VfB Leipzig

Name Changes : -  Hallescher FC Chemie to Hallescher FC
1FC Lokomotive Leipzig to VfB Leipzig

West Germany's 1990 World Cup Squad with the FIFA World Cup Trophy.

# DDR Correspondent : JAN BUITENGA

| DDR Oberliga Season 1990/91 | DRESDEN | CHEMNITZ | MAGDEBURG | FC BERLIN | JENA | ROSTOCK | COTTBUS | LOK L'ZIG | HFC CHEMIE | BR'BURG | ERFURT | E'STADT | FRANKFURT | SACHSEN |
|---|---|---|---|---|---|---|---|---|---|---|---|---|---|---|
| 1FC DYNAMO DRESDEN | ■ | 1-1 | 1-0 | 4-1 | 2-0 | 0-0 | 1-1 | 2-0 | 3-1 | 1-0 | 3-0 | 3-3 | 5-0 | 7-0 |
| CHEMNITZER FC | 0-0 | ■ | 0-2 | 1-0 | 1-1 | 0-2 | 1-1 | 2-1 | 1-1 | 1-0 | 2-0 | 3-0 | 2-0 | 0-0 |
| 1FC MAGDEBURG | 3-1 | 4-0 | ■ | 3-3 | 4-3 | 2-1 | 5-1 | 1-1 | 2-0 | 1-0 | 1-2 | 0-4 | 1-0 | 0-0 |
| FC BERLIN | 1-4 | 2-1 | 0-0 | ■ | 0-1 | 0-3 | 1-2 | 1-0 | 0-0 | 1-0 | 0-0 | 1-1 | 2-1 | 1-1 |
| FC CARL ZEISS JENA | 3-2 | 1-2 | 2-0 | 4-0 | ■ | 0-3 | 2-0 | 3-1 | 0-2 | 1-1 | 0-0 | 2-1 | 4-1 | 1-0 |
| FC HANSA ROSTOCK | 3-1 | 1-1 | 2-0 | 3-2 | 3-1 | ■ | 2-0 | 1-4 | 1-1 | 2-0 | 0-1 | 1-1 | 2-0 | 2-1 |
| FC ENERGIE COTTBUS | 1-1 | 0-2 | 0-0 | 0-1 | 0-2 | 1-1 | ■ | 1-1 | 1-0 | 1-1 | 0-1 | 0-0 | 0-1 | 4-1 |
| 1FC LOKOMOTIVE LEIPZIG | 1-2 | 3-0 | 2-0 | 2-2 | 2-0 | 3-2 | 3-1 | ■ | 0-3 | 2-0 | 2-0 | 0-0 | 4-3 | 1-0 |
| HALLESCHER FC CHEMIE | 3-1 | 0-0 | 2-0 | 1-0 | 3-1 | 1-1 | 1-1 | 2-2 | ■ | 0-2 | 1-2 | 2-0 | 1-1 | 2-1 |
| BSV STAHL BRANDENBURG | 4-1 | 1-1 | 2-2 | 1-0 | 3-2 | 2-3 | 2-1 | 1-1 | 2-1 | ■ | 2-1 | 2-1 | 4-2 | 0-0 |
| FC ROT-WEISS ERFURT | 0-0 | 0-0 | 1-0 | 4-0 | 1-1 | 1-1 | 3-1 | 1-1 | 3-2 | 2-1 | ■ | 2-0 | 2-1 | 0-1 |
| EISENHÜTTENSTADTER FC S | 0-0 | 2-1 | 0-0 | 0-0 | 3-2 | 0-0 | 2-1 | 3-0 | 2-4 | 0-0 | 0-0 | ■ | 3-0 | 3-0 |
| FC VORWÄRTS FRANKFURT/O | 1-2 | 0-1 | 3-2 | 1-2 | 1-2 | 1-3 | 2-2 | 2-0 | 3-3 | 0-0 | 4-1 | 0-0 | ■ | 1-3 |
| FC SACHSEN LEIPZIG | 1-0 | 0-0 | 1-1 | 1-4 | ⊗ | 1-1 | 1-0 | 0-0 | 1-3 | 3-3 | 2-2 | 1-0 | 3-0 | ■ |

⊗ The match Sachsen Leipzig v Carl Zeiss Jena was abandoned after 83 minutes due to a crowd disturbance. The score at the time was Sachsen Leipzig 0 Carl Zeiss Jena 1. The match was later awarded Sachsen Leipzig 0 Carl Zeiss Jena 2. Sachsen Leipzig were obliged to play their following home game against Stahl Brandenburg on a neutral ground.

## DDR OBERLIGA 1990/91
### LEAGUE TABLE FINAL

| | | | | | | | |
|---|---|---|---|---|---|---|---|
| FC Hansa Rostock | 26 | 13 | 9 | 4 | 44 | 25 | 35 |
| 1FC Dynamo Dresden | 26 | 12 | 8 | 6 | 48 | 28 | 32 |
| FC Rot-Weiss Erfurt | 26 | 11 | 9 | 6 | 30 | 26 | 31 |
| Hallescher FC Chemie | 26 | 10 | 9 | 7 | 40 | 31 | 29 |
| Chemnitzer FC | 26 | 9 | 11 | 6 | 24 | 23 | 29 |
| FC Carl Zeiss Jena | 26 | 12 | 4 | 10 | 41 | 36 | 28 |
| 1FC Lokomotive Leipzig | 26 | 10 | 8 | 8 | 37 | 33 | 28 |
| BSV Stahl Brandenburg | 26 | 9 | 9 | 8 | 34 | 31 | 27 |
| Eisenhüttenstadt. FC Stahl | 26 | 7 | 12 | 7 | 29 | 25 | 26 |
| 1FC Magdeburg | 26 | 9 | 8 | 9 | 34 | 32 | 26 |
| FC Berlin | 26 | 7 | 8 | 11 | 25 | 39 | 22 |
| FC Sachsen Leipzig | 26 | 6 | 10 | 10 | 23 | 38 | 22 |
| FC Energie Cottbus | 26 | 3 | 10 | 13 | 21 | 38 | 16 |
| FC Vict. 91 Frankfurt/Oder | 26 | 4 | 5 | 17 | 29 | 54 | 13 |

Champions : - FC Hansa Rostock

Name Change during Winter Break : -
FC Vorwärts Frankfurt/Oder to FC Victoria 91 Frankfurt/Oder

Leagues disbanded for Season 1991/92. Clubs become part of German League system.

### TOP SCORERS
1. Torsten Gütschow (Dynamo Dresden) — 20
2. Lutz Schülbe (HFC Chemie) — 13
3. Henri Fuchs (Hansa Rostock) — 11
4. Heiko Laessig (1FC Magdeburg) — 10
5. Carsten Klee (Carl Zeiss Jena) — 9
   Armin Romstedt (Rot-Weiss Erfurt) — 9
7. Timo Löhnert (Eisenhüttenstadt) — 8
   Jürgen Rische (Lokomotive Leipzig) — 8
   Uwe Rösler (Dynamo Dresden) — 8
10. Jörg Nowotny (HFC Chemie) — 7
    Heiko Peschke (Carl Zeiss Jena) — 7
    Jürgen Raab (Carl Zeiss Jena) — 7
    Florian Weichert (Hansa Rostock) — 7

## DDR 2 LIGA A 1990/91
### LEAGUE TABLE FINAL

| | | | | | | | |
|---|---|---|---|---|---|---|---|
| 1FC Union Berlin | 30 | 16 | 10 | 4 | 68 | 30 | 42 |
| SV Chemie Guben | 30 | 15 | 11 | 4 | 53 | 36 | 41 |
| BSV Rotation Berlin | 30 | 17 | 5 | 8 | 64 | 38 | 39 |
| FV Fortschritt Bischofswer. | 30 | 16 | 7 | 7 | 45 | 27 | 39 |
| PFV Bergmann-Bors. Berlin | 30 | 14 | 10 | 6 | 60 | 36 | 38 |
| MSV Post Neubrandenburg | 30 | 13 | 9 | 8 | 47 | 37 | 35 |
| Aktivist Schwarze Pumpe | 30 | 12 | 10 | 8 | 45 | 35 | 34 |
| FSV Lok. Altmark Stendal | 30 | 10 | 12 | 8 | 36 | 31 | 32 |
| FC Stahl Hennigsdorf | 30 | 12 | 8 | 10 | 48 | 47 | 32 |
| FSV Glück.Brieske-Senften | 30 | 8 | 15 | 7 | 34 | 35 | 31 |
| Greifswalder SC | 30 | 10 | 9 | 11 | 37 | 42 | 29 |
| SV Hafen Rostock | 30 | 6 | 11 | 13 | 21 | 38 | 23 |
| FSV Rot-Weiss Prenzlau | 30 | 5 | 11 | 14 | 36 | 54 | 21 |
| SV Motor Eberswalde | 30 | 6 | 9 | 15 | 31 | 51 | 21 |
| PSV Schwerin | 30 | 8 | 4 | 18 | 43 | 75 | 20 |

TSV 1860 Stralsund withdrew during the Winter break.

## DDR 2 LIGA B 1990/91
### LEAGUE TABLE FINAL

| | | | | | | | |
|---|---|---|---|---|---|---|---|
| FSV Zwickau | 30 | 20 | 6 | 4 | 77 | 27 | 46 |
| FC Wismut Aue | 30 | 18 | 10 | 2 | 73 | 24 | 46 |
| SV Stahl Thale | 30 | 12 | 15 | 3 | 44 | 23 | 39 |
| Chemnitzer SV 51 | 30 | 16 | 7 | 7 | 54 | 40 | 39 |
| FSV Soem.Sömmerda | 30 | 12 | 11 | 7 | 50 | 35 | 35 |
| FSV Wismut Gera | 30 | 10 | 13 | 7 | 54 | 35 | 33 |
| 1FC Markkleeberg | 30 | 13 | 7 | 10 | 36 | 28 | 33 |
| TSG Meissen | 30 | 13 | 6 | 11 | 37 | 35 | 32 |
| BSV Borna | 30 | 11 | 9 | 10 | 45 | 44 | 31 |
| SV Motor Weimar | 30 | 9 | 9 | 12 | 45 | 44 | 27 |
| FC Stahl Riesa | 30 | 9 | 9 | 12 | 32 | 40 | 27 |
| 1 Suhler SV 06 | 30 | 8 | 10 | 12 | 26 | 39 | 26 |
| Wacker 90 Nordhaus. | 30 | 6 | 11 | 13 | 29 | 42 | 23 |
| FC Anhalt Dessau | 30 | 8 | 5 | 17 | 39 | 50 | 21 |
| FSV Kali Wer.Tiefen. | 30 | 7 | 5 | 18 | 30 | 59 | 19 |
| SV German.Ilmenau | 30 | 0 | 3 | 27 | 16 | 99 | 3 |

Name Changes during the Season : -
SC Chemie Guben 1990 to SV Chemie Guben
ASG Motor Stralsund to TSV 1860 Stralsund

Note : The penultimate match between Zwickau and Aue was abandoned due to crowd trouble with the score Zwickau 1 Aue 4. The following day, the score was allowed to stand as the result, the decision being qualified as irreversible. In their final match Zwickau won 9-0 away to Kali Werra Tiefenort to take the championship on Goal difference. Protests from Wismut Aue were to no avail, FSV Zwickau taking their place in the Bundesliga Play-Offs.

## PLAY-OFFS FOR TWO 2 BUNDESLIGA PLACES FOR SEASON 1991/92

### GROUP 1
| | | | |
|---|---|---|---|
| 1FC Magdeburg.........1 | 1FC Union Berlin .......1 |
| FC Berlin...................3 | Stahl Brandenburg.....1 |
| Union Berlin ..............1 | FC Berlin...................0 |
| Stahl Brandenburg.....1 | 1FC Magdeburg.........0 |
| FC Berlin...................0 | 1FC Magdeburg.........0 |
| Stahl Brandenburg.....2 | Union Berlin ..............1 |
| Union Berlin ..............2 | 1FC Magdeburg.........0 |
| Stahl Brandenburg.....0 | FC Berlin...................2 |
| FC Berlin...................2 | Union Berlin ..............0 |
| 1FC Magdeburg.........2 | Stahl Brandenburg....3 |
| 1FC Magdeburg.........3 | FC Berlin...................5 |
| Union Berlin ..............0 | Stahl Brandenburg....2 |

#### LEAGUE TABLE FINAL
| | | | | | | | |
|---|---|---|---|---|---|---|---|
| Stahl Brandenburg | 6 | 4 | 1 | 1 | 9 | 6 | 9 |
| FC Berlin | 6 | 3 | 2 | 1 | 10 | 5 | 8 |
| 1FC Union Berlin | 6 | 2 | 1 | 3 | 5 | 7 | 5 |
| 1FC Magdeburg | 6 | 0 | 2 | 4 | 6 | 12 | 2 |

### GROUP 2
| | |
|---|---|
| FC Sachsen Leipzig ...0 | 1FC Lok.Leipzig.........1 |
| FSV Zwickau ..............0 | Eisenhüttenstadt........1 |
| Lokomotive Leipzig.....0 | FSV Zwickau ..............0 |
| Eisenhüttenstadt.........3 | Sachsen Leipzig ........0 |
| FSV Zwickau ..............1 | Sachsen Leipzig ........2 |
| Eisenhüttenstadt.........0 | Lokomotive Leipzig....0 |
| Lokomotive Leipzig....4 | Sachsen Leipzig ........0 |
| Eisenhüttenstadt.........2 | FSV Zwickau ............2 |
| FSV Zwickau ..............0 | Lokomotive Leipzig....3 |
| Sachsen Leipzig ........1 | Eisenhüttenstadt........2 |
| Sachsen Leipzig ........1 | FSV Zwickau ............2 |
| Lokomotive Leipzig....3 | Eisenhüttenstadt........0 |

#### LEAGUE TABLE FINAL
| | | | | | | | |
|---|---|---|---|---|---|---|---|
| Lokomotive Leipzig | 6 | 4 | 2 | 0 | 11 | 0 | 10 |
| Eisenhüttenstadt | 6 | 3 | 2 | 1 | 8 | 6 | 8 |
| FSV Zwickau | 6 | 1 | 2 | 3 | 5 | 9 | 4 |
| Sachsen Leipzig | 6 | 1 | 0 | 5 | 4 | 13 | 2 |

## DDR 2nd Division A — Season 1990/91

| | B'WERDA | 1FC UNION | ROTATION | SCHW.PUMPE | GREIFSWALD | ROSTOCK | BB BERLIN | NEUBR'BURG | STRALSUND | GUBEN | SCHWERIN | H'DORF | PRENZLAU | STENDAL | BR.-SENFT | EBERSWALDE |
|---|---|---|---|---|---|---|---|---|---|---|---|---|---|---|---|---|
| FV FORTSCHRITT B'WERDA | ■ | 1-2 | 2-1 | 2-0 | 2-1 | 4-0 | 1-4 | 2-0 | 3-2 | 1-2 | 0-0 | 2-0 | 2-1 | 0-0 | 1-1 | 3-1 |
| 1FC UNION BERLIN | 1-0 | ■ | 2-0 | 2-0 | 1-1 | 3-1 | 2-2 | 3-2 | ⊗ | 5-5 | 4-0 | 7-0 | 0-0 | 2-0 | 5-1 | 1-3 |
| BSV ROTATION BERLIN | 0-0 | 2-2 | ■ | 2-3 | 2-1 | 6-0 | 0-3 | 4-1 | 3-1 | 1-2 | 5-0 | 1-0 | 4-2 | 3-0 | 3-1 | 0-0 |
| AKTIVIST SCHWARZE PUMPE | 1-0 | 0-1 | 0-2 | ■ | 0-0 | 1-1 | 4-3 | 1-1 | ⊗ | 1-1 | 5-1 | 0-0 | 1-1 | 0-0 | 0-2 | 4-1 |
| GREIFSWALDER SC | 1-1 | 2-1 | 2-4 | 2-1 | ■ | 1-1 | 0-1 | 1-2 | ⊗ | 3-2 | 2-1 | 3-2 | 2-1 | 0-0 | 1-1 | 3-0 |
| SV HAFEN ROSTOCK | 1-2 | 1-1 | 0-0 | 2-1 | 1-1 | ■ | 0-0 | 0-0 | ⊗ | 0-0 | 2-1 | 3-0 | 0-1 | 1-0 | 0-1 | 1-0 |
| PFV BERGMANN-BORSIG | 3-1 | 1-1 | 5-1 | 2-1 | 4-0 | 1-1 | ■ | 2-2 | ⊗ | 3-0 | 4-1 | 5-4 | 2-1 | 0-3 | 1-2 | 2-0 |
| MSV POST NEUBRANDENBURG | 1-0 | 3-2 | 0-1 | 0-1 | 2-0 | 1-0 | 1-1 | ■ | 2-0 | 2-2 | 2-1 | 3-1 | 1-1 | 4-0 | 1-0 | 3-0 |
| ASG MOTOR STRALSUND | ⊗ | 0-6 | ⊗ | 1-2 | 0-3 | 3-1 | 0-3 | ⊗ | ■ | ⊗ | ⊗ | 0-3 | 2-2 | ⊗ | ⊗ | ⊗ |
| SC CHEMIE GUBEN 1990 | 0-2 | 1-1 | 1-5 | 1-1 | 2-0 | 1-0 | 2-0 | 1-1 | 2-1 | ■ | 6-0 | 1-0 | 3-2 | 1-0 | 0-0 | 3-1 |
| PSV SCHWERIN | 2-3 | 0-2 | 1-0 | 1-5 | 1-1 | 2-1 | 3-3 | 4-2 | 3-1 | 2-5 | ■ | 2-5 | 7-2 | 2-2 | 2-0 | 1-0 |
| FC STAHL HENNIGSDORF | 0-0 | 0-1 | 3-1 | 1-1 | 2-1 | 1-0 | 2-1 | 2-1 | ⊗ | 2-2 | 6-2 | ■ | 1-0 | 3-3 | 1-0 | 1-1 |
| FSV ROT-WEISS PRENZLAU | 0-2 | 1-1 | 1-4 | 1-1 | 1-2 | 1-0 | 1-1 | 2-2 | ⊗ | 0-1 | 2-0 | 2-2 | ■ | 0-0 | 0-0 | 4-2 |
| FSV LOK ALTMARK STENDAL | 0-2 | 1-0 | 2-3 | 1-3 | 4-1 | 4-0 | 0-0 | 1-0 | 2-1 | 0-0 | 2-0 | 1-0 | 5-2 | ■ | 0-0 | 1-1 |
| FSV GLUCKAUF BR.-SENFT | 2-2 | 1-1 | 2-3 | 2-3 | 0-0 | 1-1 | 1-0 | 2-2 | 2-1 | 0-0 | 2-1 | 2-2 | 4-2 | 1-1 | ■ | 1-1 |
| MOTOR EBERSWALDE | 0-2 | 1-6 | 1-1 | 1-2 | 2-0 | 0-0 | 1-1 | 2-3 | 3-1 | 2-4 | 1-0 | 1-2 | 2-0 | 1-1 | 0-0 | ■ |

⊗ Matches awarded 2-0 to the opponents of TSV 1860 Stralsund. Results of matches played during first half of season allowed to stand in final league table.

## DDR 2nd Division B — Season 1990/91

| | AUE | RIESA | ZWICKAU | DESSAU | THALE | MEISSEN | SÖMMERDA | SUHL | CHEMNITZ | GERA | WEIMAR | ILMENAU | M'BERG | TIEFENORT | BORNA | NORDHAUSEN |
|---|---|---|---|---|---|---|---|---|---|---|---|---|---|---|---|---|
| FC WISMUT AUE | ■ | 4-0 | 5-3 | 1-0 | 2-1 | 2-2 | 1-2 | 2-2 | 1-1 | 2-0 | 4-1 | 2-0 | 2-0 | 7-0 | 1-0 | 0-0 |
| STAHL RIESA | 1-1 | ■ | 1-2 | 2-0 | 0-0 | 1-4 | 1-1 | 2-0 | 2-2 | 1-2 | 1-1 | 4-3 | 0-0 | 1-0 | 1-1 | 1-0 |
| FSV ZWICKAU | ⊗ | 4-1 | ■ | 2-1 | 0-0 | 1-2 | 2-2 | ⊗ | 1-0 | 2-0 | 3-1 | 9-0 | 4-0 | 4-0 | 5-2 | 5-1 |
| FC ANHALT DESSAU | 1-1 | 2-0 | 1-2 | ■ | 0-2 | 1-1 | 1-0 | 1-0 | 4-1 | 1-1 | 0-3 | 10-0 | 2-3 | 1-2 | 0-2 | 2-2 |
| SV STAHL THALE | 2-2 | 1-3 | 0-0 | 3-0 | ■ | 1-0 | 1-1 | 4-0 | 3-1 | 1-1 | 1-1 | ⊗ | 3-3 | 2-0 | 2-1 | 2-0 |
| TSG MEISSEN | 0-1 | 1-0 | 0-4 | 1-0 | 0-0 | ■ | 0-2 | 1-3 | 0-1 | 4-2 | 0-0 | 3-0 | 1-2 | 1-0 | 0-3 | 0-0 |
| SOEMTRON SÖMMERDA | 0-1 | 1-2 | 1-1 | 2-0 | 0-0 | 3-2 | ■ | 0-0 | 1-1 | 2-1 | 1-1 | 6-1 | 2-0 | 5-2 | 1-1 | 1-1 |
| 1 SUHLER SV 06 | 0-0 | 0-0 | 0-2 | 3-1 | 1-4 | 0-1 | 2-1 | ■ | 2-1 | 0-0 | 0-0 | 1-1 | 1-0 | 2-1 | 2-3 | 1-0 |
| CHEMNITZER SV 51-HECK. | 4-3 | 3-1 | 0-1 | 2-1 | 2-1 | 3-1 | 3-1 | 4-1 | ■ | 1-0 | 2-2 | 2-0 | 3-2 | 2-1 | 0-0 | 5-2 |
| FSV WISMUT GERA | 1-1 | 2-0 | 3-1 | 7-1 | 2-2 | 1-1 | 3-1 | 1-1 | 1-1 | ■ | 4-2 | 6-1 | 0-0 | 8-0 | 1-1 | 1-0 |
| MOTOR WEIMAR | 0-3 | 0-1 | 1-1 | 0-2 | 0-1 | 0-1 | 1-2 | 1-1 | 0-2 | 2-0 | ■ | 4-0 | 2-1 | 5-3 | 3-2 | 1-1 |
| SV GERMANIA ILMENAU | 1-1 | 0-3 | 0-2 | 0-1 | 0-2 | 0-2 | 0-2 | 0-0 | 2-3 | 0-2 | 2-7 | ■ | 1-2 | 1-2 | 1-2 | 0-0 |
| 1FC MARKKLEEBERG | 0-0 | 1-0 | 0-0 | 3-0 | 0-0 | 0-1 | 1-0 | 2-0 | 0-1 | 3-1 | 1-0 | 3-0 | ■ | 3-0 | 3-0 | 0-0 |
| FSV KALI WERRA TIEF. | 1-5 | 2-1 | 0-9 | 2-2 | 2-2 | 1-4 | 3-3 | 3-2 | 3-1 | 1-1 | 3-1 | 2-1 | 0-2 | ■ | 1-5 | 1-2 |
| BSV BORNA | 0-2 | 1-0 | 0-2 | 2-1 | 0-0 | 0-2 | 1-3 | 1-0 | 2-2 | 2-2 | 1-3 | 2-0 | 3-1 | 2-2 | ■ | 4-2 |
| WACKER 90 NORDHAUSEN | 0-3 | 1-1 | 1-2 | 0-2 | 1-1 | 3-1 | 1-3 | 0-1 | 1-0 | 0-0 | 0-2 | 3-1 | 1-0 | 5-0 | 1-1 | ■ |

⊗ Stahl Thale v Germania Ilmenau, Ilmenau failed to appear, later awarded Stahl Thale 2 Germania Ilmenau 0.
FSV Zwickau v Suhler SV, Suhl failed to appear, later awarded FSV Zwickau 2 Suhler SV 0
FSV Zwickau v FC Wismut Aue, match abandoned after 66 minutes due to crowd disturbance, Score at the time FSV Zwickau 1 FC Wismut Aue 4 allowed to stand in final table.

# DDR INTERNATIONAL REVIEW 1990

## INTERNATIONAL LINE-UPS 1990

| Date | Match | Venue | Type | Referee | Scorers (DDR) |
|---|---|---|---|---|---|
| 24/1/90 | FRANCE 3 DDR 0 | Al Kuwait | Friendly | Ref: Al Moussa (Kuwait) | |
| 27/1/90 | KUWAIT 1 DDR 2 | Al Kuwait | Friendly | Ref: Al Haddad (Kuwait) | (Wuckel 2) |
| 28/3/90 | DDR 3 USA 2 | Berlin | Friendly | Ref: Wiesel (W.Germany) | (Kirsten 3) |
| 11/4/90 | DDR 2 EGYPT 0 | Karl-Marx-Stadt | Friendly | Ref: Nervik (Norway) | (Peschke, Sammer) |
| 25/4/90 | SCOTLAND 0 DDR 1 | Glasgow | Friendly | Ref: Midgley (England) | (Doll) |
| 13/5/90 | BRAZIL 3 DDR 3 | Rio de Janeiro | Friendly | Ref: Felix (Brazil) | (Doll, Ernst, Steinmann) |
| 12/9/90 | BELGIUM 0 DDR 2 | Brussels | Friendly | Ref: Blankenstein (Holland) | (Sammer 2) |

### Player appearances / Caps & Goals at 31/12/90

| Player | Caps | Goals |
|---|---|---|
| Dirk Heyne | 9 | |
| Andreas Wagenhaus | 3 | |
| Matthias Mauksch | 1 | |
| Burkhard Reich | 6 | |
| Hendryk Herzog | 7 | |
| Jörg Stübner | 47 | 1 |
| Matthias Sammer | 23 | 6 |
| Dariusz Wosz | 7 | |
| Rico Steinmann | 23 | |
| Ulf Kirsten | 49 | 14 |
| Thomas Doll | 29 | 7 |
| Uwe Weidemann | 10 | |
| Hilmar Weilandt | 2 | |
| Marcus Wuckel | 4 | |
| Ronny Teuber | 1 | |
| Matthias Lindner | 22 | |
| Uwe Rösler | 5 | |
| Heiko Peschke | 5 | |
| Dirk Schuster | 4 | |
| Steffen Büttner | 3 | |
| Rainer Ernst | 56 | 19 |
| Andreas Thom | 51 | 17 |
| Stefan Minkwitz | 2 | |
| Stefan Böger | 4 | |
| Steffen Heidrich | 1 | |
| Perry Bräutigam | 3 | |
| Ralf Hauptmann | 4 | |
| Jens Schmidt | 1 | |
| Detlef Schössler | 18 | |
| Jörg Schwanke | 1 | |
| Heiko Bonan | 2 | |
| Heiko Scholz | 7 | |
| Jens Adler | 1 | |
| Torsten Kracht | 2 | |

---

## DDR POKAL 1990/91

### 1ST ROUND

| Home | | Away | |
|---|---|---|---|
| Chemnitzer SV 51 | 2 | 1FC Lok Leipzig | 2 |
| SV Hafen Rostock | 0 | FC Berlin | 3 |
| Motor Eberswalde | 2 | BSV Stahl Branden | 6 |
| Stahl Riesa | 2 | Eisenhüttenstadt | 6 |
| Motor Görlitz | 1 | FC Energie Cottbus | 6 |
| Chemie Wolfen | 0 | FC Rot-Weiss Erfurt | 1 |
| Einheit Templin | 1 | FC Hansa Rostock | 5 |
| Wacker 90 Nordh. | 1 | Akt. Schwarze Pmp. | 5 |
| SC Guben 1990 | 3 | TSG Meissen | 1 |
| Buna Schkopau | 2 | Bergm.-Borsig Berlin | 1 |
| Wernigeröder FC | 2 | Germania Ilmenau | 2 (aet) |
| EK Veilsdorf | 0 | Motor Weimar | 6 |
| FSV Kitzscher | 0 | FC Wismut Aue | 11 |
| Hydraulik N.P'chim | 0 | Greifswalder SC | 2 |
| 1 Suhler SV 06 | 0 | Chemnitzer FC | 3 |
| TSV 1860 Stralsund | 0 | 1FC Magdeburg | 1 |
| Soentron Sömmerda | 0 | HFC Chemie | 5 |
| BG Berlin | 0 | FC Vorwärts Frank. | 5 |
| Motor Zeulenroda | 0 | 1FC Sachsen Leipzig | 2 |
| Union Mühlhausen | 0 | 1FC Dyn. Dresden | 9 |
| Glück.Brieske-Senft. | 1 | FSV Zwickau | 6 |
| Wismut Gera | 1 | SV Stahl Thale | 6 |
| SV Hennigsdorf | 0 | FSV Velten 90 | 6 |
| Fort. Bischofswerda | 3 | Motor Schönebeck | 0 |
| Stahl Hennigsdorf | 0 | MSV Eisleben | 0 |
| PSV Schwerin | 3 (aet) | Motor Ludwigsfelde | 1 |
| SV Optik Rathenow | 6 | Anhalt Dessau | 1 |
| 1FC Markkleeberg | 2 | Greifswalder SC II | 1 |
| Post Neubrand'burg | 2 | 1FC Union Berlin | 3 |

Wernigeröder FC win 4-1 on penalties.

Byes were awarded to Carl Zeiss Jena, BSV Rotation Berlin and FC Wismut Aue II

### 2ND ROUND

| Home | | Away | |
|---|---|---|---|
| FC Energie Cottbus | 0 | Chemnitzer FC | 2 |
| FC Hansa Rostock | 2 | HFC Chemie | 0 |
| FSV Zwickau | 1 | 1FC Dyn. Dresden | 2 (aet) |
| Eisenhüttenstadt | 1 | Chemie Guben | 0 |
| 1FC Sachsen Leipzig | 0 | FC Carl Zeiss Jena | 2 |
| Akt. Schwarze Pmp. | 0 | BSV Stahl B'burg | 8 |
| Greifswalder SC | 1 | 1FC Lok Leipzig | 1 |
| 1FC Rot-Weiss Erfurt | 2 | FC Berlin | 2 |

### 3RD ROUND

| Home | | Away | |
|---|---|---|---|
| FC Vorwärts Frank. | 4 | 1FC Magdeburg | 0 |
| Wismut Aue II | 0 | FC Carl Zeiss Jena | 2 |
| 1FC Markkleeberg | 4 | Greifswalder SC | 2 (aet) |
| Buna Schkopau | 2 | Rot-Weiss Prenzlau | 1 (aet) |
| Eisenhüttenstadt | 4 | Motor Weimar | 3 (aet) |
| 1FC Dyn. Dresden | 4 | FC Vorwärts Frank. | 4 |
| BSV Stahl B'burg | 3 | 1FC Magdeburg | 4 |
| Wernigeröder FC | 1 | Greifswalder SC | 2 (aet) |

### 1/4 FINALS

| Home | | Away | |
|---|---|---|---|
| FC Vorwärts Frank. | 4 | 1FC Magdeburg | 0 |
| FC Hansa Rostock | 1 | Rot-Weiss Erfurt | 0 |
| 1FC Markkleeberg | 2 | SV Stahl Thale | 1 |
| SV Optik Rathenow | 0 | FC Rot-Weiss Erfurt | 5 |
| 1FC Lok Leipzig | 2 | BSV Stahl B'burg | 0 |
| Eisenhüttenstadt | 1 | FC Carl Zeiss Jena | 0 |
| 1FC Union Berlin | 1 | Chemnitzer FC | 0 |

### SEMI-FINALS

| Home | | Away | |
|---|---|---|---|
| Eisenhüttenstadt | 2 | 1FC Union Berlin | 0 |
| 1FC Lok Leipzig | 1 | Hansa Rostock | 1 (aet) |

FC Hansa Rostock win 1-3 on penalties.

### FINAL

2/6/91 (at Friedrich Ludwig Jahn Sportpark, Berlin)

FC Hansa Rostock ......1 Eisenhüttenstädter FC Stahl ......0

Rostock: Hoffmann, Werner, Alms, März, Wahl, Caligiuri, Röhrich, Dowe, Weilandt (Rillich 75), Weichert, Fuchs (Schünz 85).

Hütte: Rudwaleit, Backasch, A.Wittke, Kluge, Bartz, Rambow, Schnürer, Menze, K.Schulz (Lann 65), Milanovic (Richert 60), Löhnert.

Referee: K.Scheurell
Attendance: 4,800

# WESTERN GERMANY Correspondent : JAN BUITENGA

**WESTERN GERMANY**
1 Bundesliga
Season 1990/91

| | MÜNCHEN | KÖLN | FRANKFURT | DORTMUND | LEVERKUSEN | STUTTGART | BREMEN | NÜRNBERG | DÜSSELDORF | KSC | HSV | K'LAUTERN | ST.PAULI | UERDINGEN | M'GLADBACH | BOCHUM | HERTHA | W'SCHEID |
|---|---|---|---|---|---|---|---|---|---|---|---|---|---|---|---|---|---|---|
| FC BAYERN MÜNCHEN | | 2-2 | 2-0 | 2-3 | 1-1 | 2-1 | 1-1 | 1-0 | 0-1 | 3-0 | 6-1 | 4-0 | 0-1 | 2-2 | 4-1 | 2-2 | 7-3 | 7-0 |
| 1FC KÖLN | 4-0 | | 2-1 | 0-1 | 1-1 | 1-6 | 1-0 | 3-1 | 1-1 | 0-0 | 1-0 | 2-6 | 2-0 | 3-1 | 1-3 | 0-0 | 2-1 | 1-1 |
| SG EINTRACHT FRANKFURT | 1-4 | 1-0 | | 3-1 | 3-1 | 4-0 | 0-0 | 0-1 | 5-1 | 3-0 | 0-6 | 4-3 | 1-1 | 4-0 | 5-1 | 1-1 | 5-1 | 4-0 |
| BV 09 BORUSSIA DORTMUND | 2-3 | 1-2 | 0-3 | | 1-1 | 0-3 | 1-1 | 0-2 | 1-1 | 2-2 | 1-1 | 0-2 | 5-2 | 1-0 | 1-1 | 1-0 | 3-1 | 2-2 |
| BAYER 04 LEVERKUSEN | 1-2 | 2-0 | 2-2 | 1-2 | | 0-0 | 0-0 | 2-2 | 1-1 | 1-0 | 2-2 | 2-2 | 3-1 | 1-0 | 2-5 | 4-2 | 3-1 | 2-1 |
| VFB STUTTGART | 0-3 | 3-2 | 2-1 | 7-0 | 0-2 | | 0-1 | 2-1 | 1-1 | 2-2 | 2-0 | 2-2 | 2-1 | 3-1 | 1-1 | 2-2 | 4-0 | 1-4 |
| SV WERDER BREMEN | 1-0 | 2-1 | 1-1 | 1-1 | 1-1 | 0-1 | | 0-0 | 3-1 | 2-0 | 3-1 | 1-2 | 1-0 | 4-3 | 3-0 | 2-1 | 6-0 | 1-1 |
| 1FC NÜRNBERG | 0-1 | 0-4 | 0-2 | 1-1 | 1-0 | 0-1 | 2-3 | | 3-0 | 0-0 | 3-1 | 1-4 | 5-2 | 1-1 | 2-2 | 3-2 | 1-4 | 4-2 |
| FORTUNA 95 DÜSSELDORF | 1-2 | 0-2 | 1-0 | 0-0 | 0-2 | 0-4 | 1-2 | 3-0 | | 5-2 | 2-1 | 0-0 | 0-0 | 0-2 | 4-1 | 3-4 | 4-2 | 2-1 |
| KARLSRUHER SC | 2-3 | 1-1 | 2-2 | 1-2 | 2-0 | 0-0 | 1-1 | 2-0 | 1-1 | | 2-2 | 4-2 | 1-1 | 2-0 | 3-2 | 3-2 | 3-0 | 1-3 |
| HAMBURGER SV | 2-3 | 1-1 | 0-1 | 4-0 | 3-1 | 2-0 | 3-2 | 4-0 | 1-0 | 2-2 | | 1-3 | 5-0 | 2-0 | 3-0 | 1-0 | 2-0 | 0-0 |
| 1FC KAISERSLAUTERN | 2-1 | 2-2 | 1-1 | 2-2 | 2-1 | 2-0 | 1-0 | 3-1 | 0-0 | 3-2 | 1-0 | | 1-0 | 2-0 | 2-3 | 4-1 | 4-3 | 1-1 |
| FC SANKT PAULI | 0-0 | 2-0 | 1-1 | 0-2 | 1-0 | 2-2 | 0-0 | 0-0 | 2-3 | 2-0 | 0-2 | 1-0 | | 1-1 | 1-1 | 3-3 | 2-2 | 1-1 |
| BAYER 05 UERDINGEN | 1-1 | 0-3 | 2-3 | 1-3 | 1-1 | 2-0 | 0-0 | 0-0 | 1-2 | 1-1 | 0-0 | 3-7 | 2-0 | | 1-1 | 4-1 | 1-2 | 0-2 |
| BORUSSIA MÖNCHENGLADB. | 1-1 | 2-2 | 1-1 | 2-1 | 1-1 | 2-0 | 1-1 | 2-0 | 2-0 | 2-1 | 1-1 | 2-2 | 1-1 | 1-1 | | 1-2 | 2-0 | 1-1 |
| VFL BOCHUM | 1-2 | 1-0 | 0-0 | 2-2 | 3-1 | 1-1 | 1-2 | 0-0 | 0-0 | 0-1 | 0-1 | 0-2 | 3-0 | 0-2 | 3-0 | | 4-2 | 0-0 |
| HERTHA BSC | 0-0 | 0-0 | 1-0 | 2-2 | 1-2 | 0-2 | 0-0 | 2-4 | 0-1 | 1-1 | 1-4 | 0-2 | 1-2 | 0-0 | 1-1 | 2-4 | | 2-3 |
| SG WATTENSCHEID 09 | 3-2 | 0-3 | 1-0 | 1-1 | 1-2 | 2-2 | 2-0 | 0-1 | 2-0 | 1-1 | 0-1 | 0-0 | 2-2 | 0-0 | 1-1 | 0-4 | 3-1 | |

## GERMANY 1 BUNDESLIGA 1990/91

### LEAGUE TABLE FINAL

| | | | | | | | |
|---|---|---|---|---|---|---|---|
| 1FC Kaiserslautern | 34 | 19 | 10 | 5 | 72 | 45 | 48 |
| FC Bayern München | 34 | 18 | 9 | 7 | 74 | 41 | 45 |
| SV Werder Bremen | 34 | 14 | 14 | 6 | 46 | 29 | 42 |
| SG Eintracht Frankfurt | 34 | 15 | 10 | 9 | 63 | 40 | 40 |
| Hamburger SV | 34 | 16 | 8 | 10 | 60 | 38 | 40 |
| VfB Stuttgart | 34 | 14 | 10 | 10 | 57 | 44 | 38 |
| 1FC Köln | 34 | 13 | 11 | 10 | 50 | 43 | 37 |
| Bayer 04 Leverkusen | 34 | 11 | 13 | 10 | 47 | 46 | 35 |
| Borussia Mönchengladbach | 34 | 9 | 17 | 8 | 49 | 54 | 35 |
| BV 09 Borussia Dortmund | 34 | 10 | 14 | 10 | 46 | 57 | 34 |
| SG Wattenscheid 09 | 34 | 9 | 15 | 10 | 42 | 51 | 33 |
| Fortuna 95 Düsseldorf | 34 | 11 | 10 | 13 | 40 | 49 | 32 |
| Karlsruher SC | 34 | 8 | 15 | 11 | 46 | 52 | 31 |
| VfL Bochum | 34 | 9 | 11 | 14 | 50 | 52 | 29 |
| 1FC Nürnberg | 34 | 10 | 9 | 15 | 40 | 54 | 29 |
| FC Sankt Pauli | 34 | 6 | 15 | 13 | 33 | 53 | 27 |
| Bayer 05 Uerdingen | 34 | 5 | 13 | 16 | 34 | 54 | 23 |
| Hertha BSC | 34 | 3 | 8 | 23 | 37 | 84 | 14 |

Champions : - 1FC Kaiserslautern
Relegated : - FC St.Pauli, Bayer 05 Uerdingen and Hertha BSC

1 Bundesliga to be increased to 20 clubs for Season 1991/92

### TOP SCORERS

1. Roland Wohlfarth (Bayern München) — 21
2. Jan Furtok (Hamburger SV) — 20
3. Andreas Möller (Eintracht Frankfurt) — 16
4. Thomas Allofs (Fortuna Düsseldorf) — 15
   Wynton Rufer (Werder Bremen) — 15
6. Maurice Banach (1FC Köln) — 14
7. Souleyman Sane (Wattenscheid 09) — 13
8. Hans-Jörg Criens (Bor. M'gladbach) — 12
   Fritz Walter (VfB Stuttgart) — 12
10. Ulf Kirsten (Bayer Leverkusen) — 11
    Stefan Kohn (VfL Bochum) — 11
    Stefan Kuntz (1FC Kaiserslautern) — 11
    Nando (Hamburger SV) — 11
    Matthias Sammer (VfB Stuttgart) — 11
    Rainer Schütterle (Karlsruher SC) — 11
16. Klaus Allofs (Werder Bremen) — 10
17. Stefan Effenberg (Bayern München) — 9
    Demir Hotic (1FC Kaiserslautern) — 9
    Thomas Kastenmeier (Bor. M'gladbach) — 9
    Bruno Labbadia (1FC Kaiserslautern) — 9
    Brian Laudrup (Bayern München) — 9
    Christian Schreier (Bayer Leverkusen) — 9
    Ralf Sturm (1FC Köln) — 9

| WESTERN GERMANY 2 Bundesliga Season 1990/91 | MANNHEIM | HOMBURG | S'BRÜCKEN | S'GART K | SCHALKE | ESSEN | B'SCHWEIG | HANNOVER | BW 90 | DUISBURG | MEPPEN | MÜNSTER | FREIBURG | F KÖLN | OSNABRÜCK | DARMSTADT | OLDENBURG | HAVELSE | MAINZ | SCHWFURT |
|---|---|---|---|---|---|---|---|---|---|---|---|---|---|---|---|---|---|---|---|---|
| SVW MANNHEIM | | 1-3 | 2-0 | 1-3 | 1-3 | 5-2 | 1-1 | 2-0 | 4-0 | 1-1 | 3-0 | 3-1 | 2-0 | 1-0 | 4-1 | 2-1 | 4-3 | 1-2 | 3-0 | |
| FC HOMBURG-SAAR | 1-1 | | 0-0 | 2-0 | 2-1 | 2-1 | 1-0 | 1-1 | 2-0 | 2-1 | 0-0 | 2-1 | 1-0 | 3-2 | 2-3 | 1-0 | 1-0 | 2-1 | 0-0 | 6-1 |
| 1FC SAARBRÜCKEN | 0-0 | 0-0 | | 0-0 | 1-1 | 2-0 | 4-1 | 1-0 | 0-0 | 0-1 | 2-0 | 4-1 | 2-3 | 1-1 | 2-1 | 1-0 | 4-1 | 0-0 | 0-0 | 5-2 |
| STUTTGARTER KICKS. | 3-0 | 4-1 | 2-0 | | 0-0 | 3-0 | 1-0 | 1-0 | 4-0 | 1-0 | 3-0 | 0-2 | 3-2 | 1-1 | 3-1 | 3-0 | 1-1 | 3-0 | 1-1 | 1-0 |
| FC SCHALKE 04 | 1-2 | 3-1 | 3-1 | 2-1 | | 3-1 | 2-1 | 2-0 | 1-1 | 1-0 | 2-0 | 3-1 | 3-1 | 2-1 | 1-0 | 1-0 | 4-1 | 3-0 | 3-0 | 2-0 |
| ROT-WEISS ESSEN | 1-1 | 0-0 | 1-1 | 0-2 | 0-0 | | 3-1 | 4-2 | 0-3 | 1-1 | 3-2 | 1-0 | 3-0 | 0-2 | 0-0 | 3-0 | 1-3 | 3-0 | 2-0 | 4-0 |
| EINTRACHT BRAUNS. | 1-1 | 1-0 | 0-1 | 2-1 | 0-1 | 0-0 | | 0-1 | 2-2 | 1-1 | 0-0 | 5-0 | 2-2 | 3-2 | 1-0 | 1-0 | 1-1 | 3-1 | 5-1 | 3-0 |
| HANNOVER 96 | 0-5 | 0-2 | 1-1 | 1-2 | 1-1 | 2-0 | 3-0 | | 3-1 | 2-0 | 2-0 | 3-1 | 0-2 | 3-3 | 0-1 | 2-2 | 0-0 | 2-1 | 3-1 | 1-1 |
| BLAU-WEISS 90 | 2-1 | 4-1 | 1-1 | 1-1 | 1-1 | 2-2 | 0-0 | 1-1 | | 2-2 | 2-0 | 1-1 | 2-1 | 0-0 | 0-0 | 2-0 | 1-1 | 3-1 | 2-1 | 6-1 |
| MSV DUISBURG | 1-1 | 4-0 | 1-0 | 2-0 | 1-1 | 4-2 | 3-3 | 4-2 | 1-0 | | 4-0 | 5-0 | 1-0 | 3-0 | 2-1 | 2-0 | 1-0 | 3-0 | 2-0 | 2-1 |
| SV MEPPEN | 0-0 | 3-0 | 0-0 | 1-2 | 2-0 | 1-0 | 1-0 | 1-1 | 0-0 | 0-1 | | 1-1 | 4-1 | 1-1 | 1-1 | 2-1 | 0-0 | 2-0 | 1-1 | 2-1 |
| PREUSSEN MÜNSTER | 0-0 | 0-0 | 1-0 | 0-0 | 0-3 | 0-0 | 1-1 | 0-1 | 0-2 | 2-0 | 0-1 | | 1-1 | 2-0 | 2-2 | 1-0 | 3-1 | 2-1 | 2-3 | 5-0 |
| SC FREIBURG | 0-2 | 0-0 | 0-0 | 1-0 | 3-0 | 4-0 | 3-2 | 1-1 | 0-0 | 0-2 | 2-1 | 3-2 | | 2-0 | 0-1 | 1-2 | 1-1 | 1-0 | 2-1 | 3-1 |
| SC FORTUNA KÖLN | 1-0 | 1-1 | 3-4 | 0-2 | 1-1 | 2-1 | 2-3 | 1-1 | 2-1 | 2-2 | 1-1 | 1-1 | 0-1 | | 2-2 | 1-1 | 1-1 | 3-1 | 3-1 | 2-0 |
| VFL OSNABRÜCK | 1-0 | 1-0 | 0-2 | 2-3 | 0-3 | 1-1 | 2-0 | 1-1 | 1-1 | 0-2 | 3-2 | 3-1 | 1-4 | 0-1 | | 1-4 | 3-3 | 3-2 | 0-0 | 2-0 |
| SV DARMSTADT 98 | 1-1 | 0-0 | 1-0 | 0-2 | 2-2 | 3-2 | 2-1 | 1-0 | 1-1 | 2-2 | 1-0 | 0-0 | 2-1 | 1-2 | 1-1 | | 0-0 | 5-2 | 0-1 | 3-3 |
| VFB OLDENBURG | 5-0 | 1-0 | 0-1 | 1-1 | 0-0 | 2-0 | 2-3 | 1-1 | 3-5 | 1-1 | 2-2 | 4-0 | 2-2 | 2-0 | 3-2 | 3-0 | | 2-2 | 1-2 | 3-0 |
| TSV HAVELSE | 1-1 | 1-1 | 0-2 | 2-1 | 1-2 | 1-4 | 1-0 | 1-2 | 1-2 | 1-1 | 1-0 | 4-1 | 0-3 | 0-2 | 1-5 | 3-3 | 3-2 | | 1-2 | 4-1 |
| FSV MAINZ 05 | 3-1 | 0-2 | 1-0 | 3-3 | 1-1 | 1-0 | 1-4 | 2-1 | 2-2 | 1-1 | 2-1 | 0-0 | 0-0 | 1-3 | 3-2 | 1-1 | 2-0 | 2-1 | | 2-0 |
| FC SCHWEINFURT 05 | 3-1 | 0-1 | 2-1 | 1-4 | 0-1 | 0-2 | 0-0 | 1-3 | 1-1 | 0-6 | 0-1 | 0-0 | 2-2 | 1-1 | 0-3 | 0-5 | 2-3 | 1-1 | 0-0 | |

## GERMANY 2 BUNDESLIGA 1990/91

### LEAGUE TABLE FINAL

| | | | | | | | |
|---|---|---|---|---|---|---|---|
| FC Schalke 04 | 38 | 23 | 11 | 4 | 64 | 29 | 57 |
| MSV Duisburg | 38 | 21 | 11 | 6 | 70 | 34 | 53 |
| Stuttgarter Kickers | 38 | 21 | 9 | 8 | 63 | 32 | 51 |
| FC 08 Homburg-Saar | 38 | 16 | 13 | 9 | 42 | 37 | 45 |
| 1FC Saarbrücken | 38 | 15 | 14 | 9 | 47 | 30 | 44 |
| Blau-Weiss 90 Berlin | 38 | 12 | 20 | 6 | 55 | 42 | 44 |
| SV Waldhof Mannheim | 38 | 15 | 12 | 11 | 60 | 47 | 42 |
| FSV Mainz 05 | 38 | 14 | 13 | 11 | 45 | 52 | 41 |
| SC Freiburg | 38 | 15 | 10 | 13 | 54 | 48 | 40 |
| Hannover 96 | 38 | 12 | 14 | 12 | 49 | 49 | 38 |
| SC Fortuna Köln | 38 | 11 | 15 | 12 | 51 | 53 | 37 |
| VfB Oldenburg | 38 | 10 | 16 | 12 | 58 | 53 | 36 |
| Eintracht Braunschweig | 38 | 12 | 11 | 15 | 53 | 52 | 35 |
| VfL Osnabrück | 38 | 12 | 11 | 15 | 51 | 55 | 35 |
| Rot-Weiss Essen | 38 | 12 | 10 | 16 | 49 | 52 | 34 |
| SV Meppen | 38 | 10 | 14 | 14 | 35 | 42 | 34 |
| SV Darmstadt 98 | 38 | 10 | 13 | 15 | 46 | 54 | 33 |
| Preussen Münster | 38 | 8 | 13 | 17 | 35 | 59 | 29 |
| TSV Havelse | 38 | 6 | 7 | 25 | 44 | 82 | 19 |
| FC Schweinfurt 05 | 38 | 2 | 9 | 27 | 26 | 95 | 13 |

Promoted : - FC Schalke 04, MSV Duisburg and Stuttgarter Kickers
Relegated : - Preussen Münster, TSV Havelse and FC Schweinfurt

Note : League to consist of 2 groups of 12 clubs each for Season

Due to financial problems Rot-Weiss Essen have forfeited their professional licence for Season 1991/92, taking their place in the Amateur Oberliga. SV Darmstadt 98 therefore retain their 2 Bundesliga place.

### PROMOTION/RELEGATION PLAY-OFF

| | 1ST LEG | 2ND LEG | AGG. |
|---|---|---|---|
| FC St.Pauli v Stuttgarter Kickers | 1-1 | 1-1 | 2-2 |

Stuttgarter Kickers ..... 3    FC St.Pauli ................ 1
(at Gelsenkirchen)

## PROMOTION PLAY OFFS

### GROUP NORTH LEAGUE TABLE FINAL

| | | | | | | | |
|---|---|---|---|---|---|---|---|
| FC Remscheid | 8 | 5 | 3 | 0 | 16 | 5 | 13 |
| VfL Wolfsburg | 8 | 4 | 1 | 3 | 15 | 14 | 9 |
| Göttingen 05 | 8 | 3 | 2 | 3 | 14 | 12 | 8 |
| SC Verl | 8 | 3 | 2 | 3 | 15 | 17 | 8 |
| Tennis-Borussia | 8 | 1 | 0 | 7 | 6 | 18 | 2 |

### GROUP SOUTH LEAGUE TABLE FINAL

| | | | | | | | |
|---|---|---|---|---|---|---|---|
| TSV München 1860 | 6 | 3 | 3 | 0 | 11 | 5 | 9 |
| Hessen Kassel | 6 | 2 | 3 | 1 | 8 | 6 | 7 |
| 1FC Pforzheim | 6 | 2 | 1 | 3 | 8 | 11 | 5 |
| Borussia Neunkirchen | 6 | 0 | 3 | 3 | 5 | 10 | 3 |

Promoted to 2 Bundesliga : - FC Remscheid and TSV München 1860

# GERMANY AMATEUR-OBERLIGA 1990/91

## NORD LEAGUE TABLE FINAL

| Team | P | W | D | L | F | A | Pts |
|---|---|---|---|---|---|---|---|
| Vfl Wolfsburg | 34 | 25 | 3 | 6 | 81 | 36 | 53 |
| SC Göttingen 05 | 34 | 18 | 8 | 8 | 60 | 30 | 44 |
| SV Werder Bremen Amat. | 34 | 17 | 9 | 8 | 90 | 57 | 43 |
| Holstein Kiel | 34 | 17 | 8 | 9 | 54 | 33 | 42 |
| Hamburger SV Amat. | 34 | 17 | 6 | 11 | 56 | 45 | 40 |
| SC Norderstedt | 34 | 15 | 10 | 9 | 49 | 39 | 40 |
| TuS Celle | 34 | 12 | 10 | 12 | 59 | 61 | 34 |
| Bremer SV | 34 | 13 | 8 | 13 | 63 | 70 | 34 |
| VfL Stade | 34 | 13 | 7 | 14 | 51 | 59 | 33 |
| VfL Herzlake | 34 | 12 | 7 | 15 | 48 | 54 | 31 |
| TuS Hoisdorf | 34 | 10 | 11 | 13 | 55 | 66 | 31 |
| FC Altona 93 | 34 | 14 | 2 | 18 | 54 | 49 | 30 |
| SpVgg 07 Göttingen | 34 | 12 | 6 | 16 | 54 | 52 | 30 |
| Eintracht Nordhorn | 34 | 8 | 13 | 13 | 37 | 43 | 29 |
| Concordia Hamburg | 34 | 11 | 7 | 16 | 46 | 57 | 29 |
| SV Wolfenbüttel | 34 | 7 | 12 | 15 | 33 | 65 | 26 |
| Eutin 08 | 34 | 6 | 10 | 18 | 38 | 65 | 22 |
| Arminia Hannover | 34 | 6 | 9 | 19 | 43 | 78 | 21 |

## BERLIN LEAGUE TABLE FINAL

| Team | P | W | D | L | F | A | Pts |
|---|---|---|---|---|---|---|---|
| Tennis Borussia | 30 | 19 | 7 | 4 | 68 | 35 | 45 |
| Türkiyemspor | 30 | 17 | 10 | 3 | 60 | 27 | 44 |
| Hertha 03 Zehlendorf | 30 | 15 | 8 | 7 | 56 | 21 | 38 |
| Spandauer SV | 30 | 14 | 8 | 8 | 54 | 36 | 36 |
| Reinickendorfer Füchse | 30 | 13 | 7 | 10 | 48 | 36 | 33 |
| Hertha BSC Amat. | 30 | 11 | 10 | 9 | 47 | 40 | 32 |
| Spandauer BC | 30 | 10 | 11 | 9 | 46 | 44 | 31 |
| Blau-Weiss 90 Amat. | 30 | 11 | 9 | 10 | 45 | 48 | 31 |
| Wacker 04 | 30 | 11 | 7 | 12 | 42 | 55 | 29 |
| BFC Preussen | 30 | 9 | 10 | 11 | 52 | 48 | 28 |
| SC Charlottenburg | 30 | 10 | 7 | 13 | 46 | 50 | 27 |
| SC Gatow | 30 | 7 | 12 | 11 | 42 | 48 | 26 |
| VfB Lichterfelde | 30 | 9 | 6 | 15 | 40 | 53 | 24 |
| Marathon 02 | 30 | 6 | 9 | 15 | 33 | 63 | 21 |
| Rapide Wedding | 30 | 5 | 8 | 17 | 19 | 56 | 18 |
| Tasmania 73 | 30 | 5 | 7 | 18 | 31 | 67 | 17 |

## BAYERN LEAGUE TABLE FINAL

| Team | P | W | D | L | F | A | Pts |
|---|---|---|---|---|---|---|---|
| TSV 1860 München | 32 | 22 | 10 | 0 | 62 | 21 | 54 |
| SpVgg Unterhaching | 32 | 20 | 7 | 5 | 76 | 33 | 47 |
| SpVgg Weiden | 32 | 18 | 7 | 7 | 63 | 38 | 43 |
| FC Bayern München Amat. | 32 | 16 | 7 | 9 | 58 | 39 | 39 |
| MTV Ingolstadt | 32 | 15 | 7 | 10 | 63 | 46 | 37 |
| TSV Eching | 32 | 14 | 8 | 10 | 69 | 59 | 36 |
| FC Memmingen | 32 | 13 | 9 | 10 | 48 | 43 | 35 |
| FC Augsburg | 32 | 13 | 6 | 13 | 51 | 47 | 32 |
| SV Lohhof | 32 | 11 | 10 | 11 | 45 | 43 | 32 |
| TSV Vestenbergsgreuth | 32 | 10 | 10 | 12 | 51 | 55 | 30 |
| Jahn Regensburg | 32 | 11 | 8 | 13 | 41 | 53 | 30 |
| SV Türk Gücü München | 32 | 10 | 9 | 13 | 45 | 51 | 29 |
| SpVgg Plattling | 32 | 10 | 7 | 15 | 45 | 60 | 27 |
| SpVgg Bayreuth | 32 | 10 | 6 | 16 | 41 | 52 | 26 |
| 1FC Amberg | 32 | 9 | 6 | 17 | 44 | 76 | 24 |
| VfB Helmbrechts | 32 | 5 | 4 | 23 | 32 | 83 | 14 |
| Würzburger Kickers | 32 | 2 | 5 | 25 | 25 | 83 | 9 |

## BADEN-WÜRTTEMBERG LEAGUE TABLE FINAL

| Team | P | W | D | L | F | A | Pts |
|---|---|---|---|---|---|---|---|
| 1FC Pforzheim | 34 | 19 | 11 | 4 | 64 | 34 | 49 |
| SpVgg Ludwigsburg | 34 | 17 | 11 | 6 | 53 | 28 | 45 |
| SSV Reutlingen | 34 | 15 | 12 | 7 | 53 | 34 | 42 |
| SV Schwetzingen | 34 | 16 | 8 | 10 | 52 | 39 | 40 |
| SV Sandhausen | 34 | 14 | 12 | 8 | 53 | 44 | 40 |
| VfB Stuttgart Amat. | 34 | 16 | 8 | 10 | 50 | 46 | 40 |
| SSV Ulm 46 | 34 | 13 | 13 | 8 | 40 | 33 | 39 |
| Karlsruher SC Amat. | 34 | 13 | 11 | 10 | 50 | 43 | 37 |
| VfR Mannheim | 34 | 11 | 12 | 11 | 30 | 29 | 34 |
| FV 09 Weinheim | 34 | 11 | 12 | 11 | 42 | 42 | 34 |
| SC Pfullendorf | 34 | 9 | 14 | 11 | 46 | 48 | 32 |
| VfL Sindelfingen | 34 | 11 | 10 | 13 | 43 | 45 | 32 |
| FC Marbach | 34 | 10 | 11 | 13 | 48 | 51 | 31 |
| VfB Gaggenau | 34 | 9 | 13 | 12 | 42 | 47 | 31 |
| VfL Kirchheim/Teck | 34 | 7 | 15 | 12 | 44 | 52 | 29 |
| SC Geislingen | 34 | 8 | 8 | 18 | 43 | 65 | 24 |
| Offenburger FV | 34 | 9 | 4 | 21 | 31 | 57 | 22 |
| VfB Eppingen | 34 | 1 | 11 | 22 | 30 | 77 | 13 |

## HESSEN LEAGUE TABLE FINAL

| Team | P | W | D | L | F | A | Pts |
|---|---|---|---|---|---|---|---|
| Hessen Kassel | 34 | 24 | 6 | 4 | 74 | 33 | 54 |
| Rot-Weiss Frankfurt | 34 | 20 | 10 | 4 | 79 | 38 | 50 |
| Kickers Offenbach | 34 | 20 | 7 | 7 | 59 | 31 | 47 |
| Viktoria Aschaffenburg | 34 | 13 | 15 | 6 | 48 | 31 | 41 |
| SV Wehen | 34 | 14 | 9 | 11 | 68 | 59 | 37 |
| FSV Frankfurt | 34 | 14 | 9 | 11 | 51 | 51 | 37 |
| SG Hoechst | 34 | 13 | 10 | 11 | 68 | 66 | 36 |
| Eintracht Frankfurt Amat. | 34 | 14 | 7 | 13 | 44 | 52 | 35 |
| SpVgg Bad Homburg | 34 | 13 | 8 | 13 | 53 | 39 | 34 |
| Borussia Fulda | 34 | 9 | 14 | 11 | 57 | 74 | 32 |
| Rot-Weiss Walldorf | 34 | 8 | 15 | 11 | 44 | 53 | 31 |
| Eintracht Haiger | 34 | 11 | 8 | 15 | 48 | 48 | 30 |
| VfR Bürstadt | 34 | 10 | 10 | 14 | 41 | 55 | 30 |
| SV Wiesbaden | 34 | 9 | 11 | 14 | 41 | 48 | 29 |
| Viktoria Sindlingen | 34 | 7 | 12 | 15 | 38 | 61 | 26 |
| KSV Baunatal | 34 | 6 | 13 | 15 | 44 | 60 | 25 |
| VfL Marburg | 34 | 4 | 13 | 17 | 45 | 79 | 21 |
| Viktoria Griesheim | 34 | 3 | 13 | 18 | 33 | 70 | 19 |

## NORDHEIN LEAGUE TABLE FINAL

| Team | P | W | D | L | F | A | Pts |
|---|---|---|---|---|---|---|---|
| FC Remscheid | 32 | 23 | 6 | 3 | 52 | 11 | 52 |
| Alemannia Aachen | 32 | 20 | 10 | 2 | 66 | 28 | 50 |
| Wuppertaler SV | 32 | 18 | 8 | 6 | 67 | 44 | 44 |
| Bayer Leverkusen Amat. | 32 | 18 | 7 | 7 | 67 | 37 | 43 |
| Rheydter SV | 32 | 15 | 12 | 5 | 51 | 31 | 42 |
| SC Jülich 1910 | 32 | 14 | 8 | 10 | 43 | 32 | 36 |
| FV Bad Honnef | 32 | 13 | 8 | 11 | 48 | 51 | 34 |
| Hambom 07 | 32 | 13 | 8 | 11 | 51 | 45 | 34 |
| ETB Schwarz-Weiss Essen | 32 | 11 | 7 | 14 | 45 | 43 | 29 |
| 1FC Bocholt | 32 | 11 | 7 | 14 | 39 | 42 | 29 |
| Viktoria Köln | 32 | 10 | 5 | 17 | 58 | 65 | 25 |
| VfB Homberg | 32 | 9 | 5 | 18 | 43 | 49 | 23 |
| 1FC Viersen | 32 | 8 | 7 | 17 | 29 | 56 | 21 |
| TuS Langerwehe | 32 | 8 | 4 | 20 | 41 | 60 | 20 |
| 1FC Köln Amat. | 32 | 6 | 5 | 21 | 44 | 57 | 17 |
| Bonner SC | 32 | 5 | 6 | 21 | 30 | 60 | 16 |
| Sportsfreunden Katernberg | 32 | 2 | 5 | 25 | 27 | 77 | 9 |

## WESTFALEN LEAGUE TABLE FINAL

| Team | P | W | D | L | F | A | Pts |
|---|---|---|---|---|---|---|---|
| SC Verl | 30 | 18 | 8 | 4 | 65 | 32 | 44 |
| ASC Schöppingen | 30 | 17 | 9 | 4 | 65 | 30 | 43 |
| VfR Sölde | 30 | 17 | 8 | 5 | 48 | 29 | 42 |
| Borussia Dortmund Amat. | 30 | 11 | 12 | 7 | 41 | 29 | 34 |
| Arminia Bielefeld | 30 | 15 | 3 | 12 | 55 | 39 | 33 |
| 1FC Recklinghausen | 30 | 9 | 15 | 6 | 38 | 37 | 33 |
| VfL Bochum Amat. | 30 | 10 | 12 | 8 | 46 | 41 | 32 |
| TuS Paderborn-Neuhaus | 30 | 11 | 9 | 10 | 47 | 40 | 31 |
| SpVgg Beckum | 30 | 10 | 11 | 9 | 33 | 34 | 31 |
| SpVgg Erkenschwick | 30 | 6 | 14 | 10 | 42 | 51 | 26 |
| Rot-Weiss Lüdenscheid | 30 | 9 | 7 | 14 | 31 | 51 | 25 |
| SpVgg Marl | 30 | 8 | 8 | 14 | 48 | 58 | 24 |
| DSC Wanne-Eickel | 30 | 6 | 12 | 12 | 36 | 46 | 24 |
| VfB Hüls | 30 | 9 | 4 | 17 | 34 | 48 | 22 |
| SC Hassel | 30 | 6 | 8 | 16 | 29 | 58 | 20 |
| VfB Rheine | 30 | 4 | 8 | 18 | 22 | 62 | 16 |

## SÜDWEST LEAGUE TABLE FINAL

| Team | P | W | D | L | F | A | Pts |
|---|---|---|---|---|---|---|---|
| Borussia Neunkirchen | 34 | 24 | 6 | 4 | 74 | 33 | 54 |
| Eintracht Trier | 34 | 22 | 8 | 4 | 71 | 27 | 52 |
| FSV Salmrohr | 34 | 23 | 5 | 6 | 82 | 36 | 51 |
| Südwest Ludwigshafen | 34 | 15 | 10 | 9 | 50 | 61 | 40 |
| SV Edenkoben | 34 | 15 | 9 | 10 | 50 | 52 | 39 |
| FSV Saarwellingen | 34 | 15 | 8 | 11 | 50 | 46 | 38 |
| 1FC Saarbrücken Amat. | 34 | 12 | 11 | 11 | 51 | 55 | 35 |
| 1FC Kaiserslautern Amat. | 34 | 14 | 7 | 13 | 54 | 49 | 35 |
| FK Pirmasens | 34 | 12 | 10 | 12 | 48 | 40 | 34 |
| Saar 05 Saarbrücken | 34 | 12 | 8 | 14 | 45 | 53 | 32 |
| SV Geinsheim | 34 | 9 | 13 | 12 | 45 | 59 | 31 |
| VfL Hamm | 34 | 10 | 10 | 14 | 38 | 50 | 30 |
| TuS Mayen | 34 | 8 | 13 | 13 | 42 | 51 | 29 |
| Wormatia Worms | 34 | 10 | 8 | 16 | 34 | 35 | 28 |
| Sportsfreunden Eisbachtal | 34 | 7 | 14 | 13 | 33 | 50 | 28 |
| Hassia Bingen | 34 | 9 | 10 | 15 | 37 | 52 | 28 |
| FSG Schiffweiler | 34 | 6 | 6 | 22 | 36 | 77 | 18 |
| SC Hauenstein | 34 | 1 | 8 | 25 | 26 | 81 | 10 |

# GERMANY INTERNATIONAL REVIEW 1990

## INTERNATIONAL LINE-UPS 1990

| | Bodo Illgner | Thomas Berthold | Stefan Reuter | Jürgen Kohler | Guido Buchwald | Andreas Brehme | Uwe Bein | Lothar Matthäus | Andreas Möller | Karl-Heinz Riedle | Rudi Völler | Knut Reinhardt | Manfred Binz | Jürgen Klinsmann | Raimond Aumann | Thomas Helmer | Thomas Strunz | Thomas Hässler | Matthias Sammer | Andreas Thom |
|---|---|---|---|---|---|---|---|---|---|---|---|---|---|---|---|---|---|---|---|---|
| 29/8/90 — PORTUGAL 1 GERMANY 1 — Lisboa — Ref: Lo Bello (Italy) — Friendly (Matthäus) | 1 | 2 | 3 | 4 | 5 | 6 | | 8 | 9 | 10 | 11 | | | (11) | | | | 7 | | |
| 10/10/90 — SWEDEN 1 GERMANY 3 — Solna — Ref: Worrall (England) — Friendly (Klinsmann, Völler, Brehme) | 1 | 3 | | 4 | 5 | 6 | | 8 | 9 | | 11 | (8) | | 11 | | | | | | |
| 31/10/90 — LUXEMBOURG 2 GERMANY 3 — Luxembourg — Ref: Nielsen (Denmark) — EuroCh.Q. (Klinsmann, Bein, Völler) | 1 | 3 | 4 | | 5 | 6 | 9 | 8 | | | 11 | (6) | 2 | 11 | | | | | | |
| 19/12/90 — GERMANY 4 SWITZERLAND 0 — Stuttgart — Ref: Longhi (Italy) — Friendly (Völler, Riedle, Thom, Matthäus) | 1 | | 4 | | 4 | 6 | 7 | 8 | 10 | (11) | 11 | 2 | | 10 | | | | | | (9) |
| CAPS AT 31/12/90 | 25 | 46 | 24 | 34 | 41 | 60 | 12 | 85 | 14 | 13 | 73 | 4 | 3 | 29 | 4 | 2 | 2 | 20 | 1 | 1 |
| GOALS AT 31/12/90 | | 1 | | | | 8 | 3 | 16 | 3 | 3 | 40 | | | 9 | | | | 1 | | 1 |

## WESTERN GERMANY DFB POKAL 1990/91

### 1ST ROUND
| Waldhof Mannheim | 3 | VfL Bochum | 2 |
|---|---|---|---|
| Killa Kiel | 1 | FC St.Pauli | 4 |
| Eintracht Trier | 0 | VfB Stuttgart | 6 |
| Alemannia Aachen | 0 | FV 09 Weinheim | 1 (aet.) |
| FC Miltach | 1 | Bayer Uerdingen | 3 |
| DSC Wanne Eickel | 1 | Hertha BSC | 3 |
| Wattenscheid 09. | 3 | SSV Reutlingen | 1 |
| Werder Bremen Am. | 1 | SpVgg Fürth | 3 |
| SpVgg Weiden | 1 | Bor. Neunkirchen | 2 |
| S.W. Ludwigshafen | 1 | 1FC Kaiserslautern | 7 |
| Stuttgarter Kickers | 4 | Hessen Kassel | 1 |
| FC Wangen | 1 | Rot-Weiss Essen | 2 |
| Teutonia Waltrop | 1 | Eint. Braunschweig | 1 (aet.) |
| SC Pfullendorf | 0 | MSV Duisburg | 2 |
| Viktoria Köln | 2 | VfL Osnabrück | 4 |
| SV Hilden-Nord. | 2 | SC Freiburg | 1 (aet.) |
| SV Ludweiler. | 0 | SV Meppen | 3 |

### 2ND ROUND
| Werder Bremen. | 2 | Bayer Leverkusen | 1 |
|---|---|---|---|
| Eintracht Frankfurt. | 0 | Karlsruher SC | 0 (aet.) |
| 1FC Kaiserslautern. | 1 | VfB Stuttgart | 2 |
| Hertha BSC | 1 | Hamburger SV | 2 (aet.) |
| MSV Duisburg | 1 | Fortuna Düsseldorf | 0 |
| Schalke 04 | 4 | Hannover 96 | 0 (aet.) |
| VfL Osnabrück | 0 | Bor. M'gladbach | 0 (aet.) |

### REPLAYS
| Schalke 04 | 0 | Preussen Münster | 4 |
|---|---|---|---|
| SpVgg Fürth | 0 | SV Hilden-Nord | 3 |
| FV 09 Weinheim | 1 | Stuttgarter Kickers | 2 |

### REPLAYS
| 1FC Nürnberg | 0 | Eintracht Frankfurt | 2 (aet.) |
|---|---|---|---|
| Hamburger SV | 2 | Hannover 96 | 1 |

### 3RD ROUND
| Preussen Münster | 0 | VfB Stuttgart | 1 |
|---|---|---|---|
| Bayer Uerdingen | 4 | Rot-Weiss Essen | 2 (aet.) |
| MSV Duisburg | 3 | Blau-Weiss 90 | 2 (aet.) |
| Hamburger SV | 1 | Wattenscheid 09 | 1 (aet.) |
| Eintracht Frankfurt | 3 | 1FC Saarbrücken | 2 (aet.) |

### REPLAY
| Wattenscheid 09 | 2 | Hamburger SV | 1 (aet.) |
|---|---|---|---|

### 1/4 FINALS
| Bayer Uerdingen | 1 | 1FC Köln | 1 |
|---|---|---|---|
| MSV Duisburg | 4 | VfB Stuttgart | 0 (aet.) |
| Eintracht Frankfurt | 3 | Hessen Kassel | 0 |
| Werder Bremen | 2 | Wattenscheid 09 | 2 (aet.) |

### REPLAYS
| MSV Duisburg | 0 | VfB Stuttgart | 0 (aet.) |
|---|---|---|---|
| 1FC Köln | 3 | Bayer Uerdingen | 0 |
| Werder Bremen | 2 | Wattenscheid 09 | 1 (aet.) |

### SEMI-FINALS
| MSV Duisburg | 0 | Werder Bremen | 6 |
|---|---|---|---|
| 1FC Köln | 3 | Eintracht Frankfurt | 2 |

### FINAL
22/6/91 (at Olympiastadion, Berlin)

SV Werder Bremen 1   1FC Köln 1 (aet.)

1-0 Eilts 48
1-1 Banach 62

SV WERDER BREMEN WIN 4-3 ON PENALTIES

Bremen : Reck, Bratseth, Votava, Borowka, Wolter, Eilts, Hermann (Sauer 75), Neubarth (Hartgen 70), Bode, Rufer, Allofs.

Köln : Illgner, Jensen, Baumann, Gielchen, Greiner, Littbarski, Higi, Andersen (Rudy 96), Götz, Sturm (Heldt 70), Banach.

Referee : Schmidhuber (Ottobrunn)
Attendance : 73,270

# WESTERN GERMANY INTERNATIONAL REVIEW 1990

## INTERNATIONAL LINE-UPS 1990

| Match | Bodo Illgner | Klaus Augenthaler | Thomas Berthold | Alois Reinhardt | Andreas Brehme | Thomas Häßler | Andreas Möller | Lothar Matthäus | Uwe Bein | Jürgen Klinsmann | Karl-Heinz Riedle | Pierre Littbarski | Jürgen Kohler | Guido Buchwald | Rudi Völler | Raimond Aumann | Olaf Thon | Frank Mill | Andreas Köpke | Paul Steiner | Stefan Reuter | Hans Pflügler | Günter Hermann |
|---|---|---|---|---|---|---|---|---|---|---|---|---|---|---|---|---|---|---|---|---|---|---|---|
| 28/2/90 FRANCE 2 WESTERN GERMANY 1 Montpellier — Ref: Ramos Marcos (Spain) — Friendly (Möller) | 1 | 2 | 3 | 4 | 5 | 6 | 7 | 8 | 9 | 10 | 11 | (11) | | | | | | | | | | | |
| 25/4/90 WESTERN GERMANY 3 URUGUAY 3 Stuttgart — Ref: Karlsson (Sweden) — Friendly (Matthäus, Völler, Klinsmann) | 1 | | 2 | | 5 | 6 | (7) | 8 | 9 | 10 | | 7 | 3 | 4 | 11 | (1) | (9) | (6) | | | | | |
| 26/5/90 WESTERN GERMANY 1 CZECHOSLOVAKIA 0 Düsseldorf — Ref: Galler (Switzerland) — Friendly (Bein) | 1 | 2 | (9) | | 5 | 6 | (7) | 3 | 9 | 10 | | 7 | 3 | 4 | 11 | | (10) | (6) | (1) | | | | |
| 30/5/90 WESTERN GERMANY 1 DENMARK 0 Gelsenkirchen — Ref: Midgley (England) — Friendly (Völler) | | | (7) | | 5 | 6 | (9) | 8 | 9 | 10 | (11) | 7 | 3 | 4 | 11 | 1 | (10) | (6) | | | | | |
| 10/6/90 YUGOSLAVIA 1 WESTERN GERMANY 4 Milano — Ref: Mikkelsen (Denmark) — World Cup (Matthäus 2, Klinsmann, Völler) | 1 | 2 | 3 | | 5 | 7 | (9) | 8 | 9 | 10 | (11) | (7) | | 4 | 11 | | (8) | (10) | (1) | (2) | (3) | (5) | (6) |
| 15/6/90 UAE 1 WESTERN GERMANY 5 Milano — Ref: Spirin (USSR) — World Cup (Völler 2, Klinsmann, Matthäus, Bein) | 1 | 2 | 3 | | 5 | 7 | | 8 | 9 | 10 | 10 | (7) | | 4 | 11 | | | | | | 6 | 5 | |
| 19/6/90 COLOMBIA 1 WESTERN GERMANY 1 Milano — Ref: Snoddy (N.Ireland) — World Cup (Littbarski) | 1 | 2 | 3 | | 6 | | | 8 | | 10 | (10) | (3) | 5 | 9 | 11 | | (7) | | | | 6 | | |
| 24/6/90 HOLLAND 1 WESTERN GERMANY 2 Milano — Ref: Loustau (Argentina) — World Cup (Klinsmann, Brehme) | 1 | 2 | 4 | | 6 | | | 8 | | 10 | (10) | 7 | 5 | 9 | 11 | | | | | | 3 | | |
| 1/7/90 CZECHOSLOVAKIA 0 WESTERN GERMANY 1 Milano — Ref: Kohl (Austria) — World Cup (Matthäus) | 1 | 2 | 3 | | 5 | 7 | (9) | 8 | 9 | 11 | 10 | 7 | 4 | 7 | 11 | | | | | | 3 | | |
| 4/7/90 ENGLAND 1 WESTERN GERMANY 1 (aet.) Torino — Ref: Wright (Brazil) — World Cup (Brehme) — WESTERN GERMANY WIN 4-3 ON PENALTIES | 1 | 2 | 3 | | 9 | 6 | | 7 | | 10 | (11) | | 5 | 4 | 11 | | 8 | | | | (6) | | |
| 8/7/90 ARGENTINA 0 WESTERN GERMANY 1 Roma — Ref: Mendez (Mexico) — World Cup (Brehme) | 1 | 2 | 6 | | 5 | 7 | | 8 | | 11 | | 9 | 4 | 3 | 10 | | | | | | (6) | | |
| **CAPS AT 31/12/90** | 22 | 27 | 42 | 4 | 57 | 17 | 12 | 81 | 10 | 25 | 10 | 73 | 31 | 39 | 69 | 3 | 35 | 17 | 1 | 1 | 22 | 11 | 2 |
| **GOALS AT 31/12/90** | | | 1 | | 7 | 1 | 3 | 14 | 2 | 7 | 2 | 18 | | | 37 | | 3 | | | | 1 | | |

## DDR : All Time Records as at 31/12/90 - CAPS

1. Joachim Streich (FC Hansa Rostock/1FC Magdeburg) — 102
2. Hans-Jürgen Dörner (SG Dynamo Dresden) — 100
3. Jürgen Croy (Motor/Sachsenring Zwickau) — 94
4. Konrad Weise (FC Carl Zeiss Jena) — 86
5. Eberhard Vogel (SC Motor/SC/FC Karl-Marx-Stadt/FC Carl Zeiss Jena) — 74
6. Bernd Bransch (Hallescher FC Chemie/FC Carl Zeiss Jena) — 72
7. Peter Ducke (SC Motor/FC Carl Zeiss Jena) — 68
8. Lothar Kurbjuweit (BSG Stahl Riesa/FC Carl Zeiss Jena) — 66
   Martin Hoffmann (1FC Magdeburg) — 66
10. Ronald Kreer (1FC Lokomotive Leipzig) — 65

## WESTERN GERMANY : All Time Records as at 31/12/90 - CAPS

1. Franz Beckenbauer (FC Bayern München) — 103
2. Hans-Hubert Vogts (VfL Borussia Mönchengladbach) — 96
3. Sepp Maier (FC Bayern München) — 95
4. Karl-Heinz Rummenigge (FC Bayern München) — 95
5. Wolfgang Overath (1FC Köln) — 81
   Karl-Heinz Förster (VfB Stuttgart) — 81
   Lothar Matthäus (VfL Borussia Mönchengladbach/FC Bayern München/Internazionale FC) — 81
8. Harald Schumacher (1FC Köln) — 76
9. Pierre Littbarski (1FC Köln/Racing Club de Paris) — 73
10. Uwe Seeler (Hamburger SV) — 72
    Hans-Peter Briegel (1FC Kaiserslautern/Hellas Verona) — 72

## GERMANY : All Time Records as at 31/12/90 - CAPS

1. Franz Beckenbauer (FC Bayern München) — 103
2. Hans-Hubert Vogts (VfL Borussia Mönchengladbach) — 96
3. Sepp Maier (FC Bayern München) — 95
4. Karl-Heinz Rummenigge (FC Bayern München/Internazionale FC) — 95
5. Lothar Matthäus (VfL Borussia Mönchengladbach/FC Bayern München/Internazionale FC) — 85
6. Wolfgang Overath (1FC Köln) — 81
   Karl-Heinz Förster (VfB Stuttgart) — 81
8. Harald Schumacher (1FC Köln) — 76
9. Pierre Littbarski (1FC Köln/Racing Club de Paris) — 73
   Rudi Völler (SV Werder Bremen/AS Roma) — 73

## DDR : All Time Records as at 31/12/90 - GOALS

1. Joachim Streich (FC Hansa Rostock/1FC Magdeburg) — (102) 55
2. Hans-Jürgen Kreische (SG Dynamo Dresden) — (50) 25
3. Eberhard Vogel (SC Motor/SC/FC Karl-Marx-Stadt/FC Carl Zeiss Jena) — (74) 25
4. Henning Frenzel (SC Lokomotive/SC/1FC Lokomotive Leipzig) — (56) 19
5. Rainer Ernst (Berliner FC Dynamo/FC Berlin) — (45) 17
6. Andreas Thom (Berliner FC Dynamo/Bayer Leverkusen) — (51) 17
7. Jürgen Nöldner (ASK/FC Vorwärts Berlin) — (30) 16
   Martin Hoffmann (1FC Magdeburg) — (66) 16
9. Jürgen Sparwasser (1FC Magdeburg) — (53) 15
   Peter Ducke (SC Motor/FC Carl Zeiss Jena) — (68) 15

## WESTERN GERMANY : All Time Records as at 31/12/90 - GOALS

1. Gerd Müller (FC Bayern München) — (62) 68
2. Karl-Heinz Rummenigge (FC Bayern München/InternazionaleFC) — (95) 45
3. Uwe Seeler (Hamburger SV) — (72) 43
4. Rudi Völler (SV Werder Bremen/AS Roma) — (69) 37
5. Klaus Fischer (FC Schalke 04/1FC Köln) — (45) 32
6. Max Morlock (1FC Nürnberg) — (26) 21
7. Helmut Rahn (Rot-Weiss Essen/1FC Köln) — (40) 21
8. Pierre Littbarski (1FC Köln/Racing Club de Paris) — (73) 18
9. Klaus Allofs (Fortuna 95 Düsseldorf/1FC Köln/Olympique Marseille) — (56) 17
   Wolfgang Overath (1FC Köln) — (81) 17

## GERMANY : All Time Records as at 31/12/90 - GOALS

1. Gerd Müller (FC Bayern München) — (62) 68
2. Karl-Heinz Rummenigge (FC Bayern München/InternazionaleFC) — (95) 45
3. Uwe Seeler (Hamburger SV) — (72) 43
4. Rudi Völler (SV Werder Bremen/AS Roma) — (73) 40
5. Fritz Walter (1FC Kaiserslautern) — (61) 33
6. Klaus Fischer (FC Schalke 04/1FC Köln) — (45) 32
7. Ernst Lehner (Schwaben Augsburg/Blau-Weiss 90) — (65) 30
8. Edmund Conen (FV Saarbrücken/Stuttgarter Kickers) — (28) 27
9. Richard Hofmann (Meerane 07/Dresdner SC) — (25) 24
10. Max Morlock (1FC Nürnberg) — (26) 21
    Helmut Rahn (Rot-Weiss Essen/1FC Köln) — (40) 21

# GREECE Correspondent : GEORGE KUSUNELOS

**GREECE 1st Division Season 1990/91**

| | PAO | AEK | PAOK | OLYMPIAKOS | IRAKLIS | OFI | ARIS | LARISA | PANIONIOS | DOXA | XANTHI | SERRES | LEVADIAKOS | IONIKOS | APOLLON | ATHINAIKOS | PANAHAIKI | YANINA |
|---|---|---|---|---|---|---|---|---|---|---|---|---|---|---|---|---|---|---|
| PANATHINAIKOS | ■ | 4-0 | ⊗ | 0-1 | 1-0 | 3-0 | 3-0 | 3-3 | 6-1 | 3-0 | 6-2 | 2-0 | 4-0 | 2-0 | 5-0 | 2-1 | 0-0 | 3-0 |
| AEK | 1-2 | ■ | 0-0 | 1-0 | 4-0 | 3-1 | 4-1 | 5-2 | 1-0 | 3-0 | 6-0 | 1-0 | 3-1 | 2-0 | 1-1 | 0-0 | 3-2 | 0-1 |
| PAOK | 1-1 | 1-1 | ■ | 3-2 | 2-1 | 0-0 | 2-1 | 2-1 | 1-0 | 1-1 | 2-0 | 1-0 | 2-3 | 4-1 | 3-0 | 1-0 | 4-1 | 4-1 |
| OLYMPIAKOS | 0-0 | 3-1 | 3-2 | ■ | 0-0 | 1-1 | 5-1 | 2-0 | 4-1 | 4-0 | 8-1 | 3-1 | 3-0 | 2-1 | 7-1 | ⊗ | 6-0 | 3-0 |
| IRAKLIS | 0-2 | 0-1 | 0-0 | 0-2 | ■ | 2-0 | 1-0 | 2-1 | 4-3 | 2-2 | 0-0 | 1-1 | 3-2 | 1-0 | 5-2 | 2-0 | 1-0 | 4-0 |
| OFI | 1-3 | 1-0 | 0-0 | 0-0 | 4-1 | ■ | 1-0 | 2-0 | 1-0 | 0-2 | 1-0 | 0-0 | 2-1 | 5-3 | 3-0 | 0-1 | 1-1 | 1-1 |
| ARIS | 1-0 | 2-1 | 0-1 | 1-1 | 0-0 | 1-1 | ■ | 1-0 | 2-0 | 1-0 | 0-0 | 0-1 | 1-1 | 2-1 | 3-1 | 1-2 | 2-0 | 3-0 |
| LARISA | 1-2 | 1-2 | 1-1 | 1-1 | 0-1 | 2-0 | 0-1 | ■ | 1-1 | 2-1 | 1-0 | 4-2 | 2-1 | 0-0 | 0-1 | 2-0 | 1-0 | 3-0 |
| PANIONIOS | 1-1 | 0-3 | 2-0 | 1-6 | 1-3 | 2-2 | 0-0 | 0-0 | ■ | 2-1 | 1-1 | 2-1 | 2-1 | 3-? | 1-0 | 2-0 | 1-1 | 4-1 |
| DOXA | 0-1 | 2-0 | 1-0 | 3-2 | 1-1 | 1-1 | 1-3 | 2-0 | 2-0 | ■ | 1-0 | 2-0 | 3-1 | 4-1 | 3-0 | 1-1 | 0-0 | 3-0 |
| XANTHI | 1-3 | 2-0 | 1-2 | 1-0 | 0-0 | 2-1 | 1-1 | 6-2 | 1-1 | 2-0 | ■ | 0-0 | 2-0 | 2-0 | 1-1 | 0-2 | 2-0 | 3-0 |
| PANSERAIKOS | 1-3 | 1-0 | 2-1 | 2-2 | 0-0 | 2-3 | 1-0 | 0-0 | 1-2 | 4-0 | 2-1 | ■ | 1-0 | 2-2 | 0-0 | 0-2 | 0-0 | 1-0 |
| LEVADIAKOS | 0-0 | 0-3 | 2-2 | 0-1 | 1-0 | 1-1 | 4-1 | 0-2 | 2-1 | 1-1 | 2-0 | 2-1 | ■ | 2-2 | 1-0 | 1-0 | 2-0 | 1-0 |
| IONIKOS | 1-1 | 1-1 | 3-2 | 2-2 | 1-2 | 0-2 | 0-0 | 3-0 | 2-0 | 1-0 | 1-0 | 2-0 | 1-0 | ■ | 1-1 | 2-1 | 1-0 | 2-0 |
| APOLLON | 1-4 | 2-5 | 4-2 | 1-1 | 0-1 | 3-1 | 1-1 | 1-1 | 2-2 | 1-0 | 2-1 | 0-1 | 3-0 | 1-0 | ■ | 2-1 | 1-0 | 1-1 |
| ATHINAIKOS | 0-0 | 1-0 | 0-5 | 0-1 | 1-0 | 1-0 | 2-1 | 1-1 | 0-0 | 6-2 | 2-0 | 2-2 | 1-0 | 2-0 | 3-2 | ■ | 2-0 | 1-2 |
| PANAHAIKI | 3-2 | 0-2 | 3-2 | 0-1 | 3-2 | 0-0 | 2-2 | 2-0 | 0-0 | 2-1 | 5-1 | 3-0 | 1-1 | 2-0 | 1-3 | 0-3 | ■ | 4-1 |
| YANINA | 1-2 | 1-1 | 0-2 | 0-0 | 1-0 | 1-0 | 0-0 | 0-3 | 1-1 | 0-1 | 0-0 | 1-0 | 2-1 | 1-0 | 2-2 | 1-0 | 0-0 | ■ |

⊗ The match Panathinaikos v PAOK was abandoned after 76 minutes with the score Panathinaikos 3 PAOK 0. The score was allowed to stand and PAOK received a 3 point penalty. The match AEK 1 Olympiakos 2 was ordered to be replayed on a neutral ground, Result AEK 1 Olympiakos 0 (at Rodos). The match Olympiakos 2 Athinaikos 2 was later awarded Olympiakos 0 Athinaikos 2 and Olympiakos received a 2 point penalty. Ionikos received a 5 point penalty due to alleged match fixing, however this decision was rescinded after the allegations could not be proven.

## GREECE 1ST DIVISION 1990/91

### LEAGUE TABLE FINAL

| | | | | | | | |
|---|---|---|---|---|---|---|---|
| Panathinaikos | 34 | 23 | 8 | 3 | 77 | 22 | 54 |
| Olympiakos | 34 | 19 | 10 | 5 | 77 | 28 | 46 |
| AEK | 34 | 18 | 6 | 10 | 59 | 33 | 42 |
| PAOK | 34 | 16 | 9 | 9 | 56 | 39 | 38 |
| Iraklis | 34 | 14 | 9 | 11 | 40 | 36 | 37 |
| Athinaikos | 34 | 16 | 5 | 13 | 40 | 33 | 37 |
| Doxa | 34 | 14 | 6 | 14 | 42 | 45 | 34 |
| OFI | 34 | 11 | 12 | 11 | 37 | 38 | 34 |
| Aris | 34 | 11 | 11 | 12 | 34 | 38 | 33 |
| Panionios | 34 | 9 | 12 | 13 | 38 | 54 | 30 |
| Apollonas | 34 | 10 | 10 | 14 | 41 | 62 | 30 |
| Larisa | 34 | 10 | 9 | 15 | 38 | 46 | 29 |
| Panahaiki | 34 | 9 | 10 | 15 | 36 | 48 | 28 |
| Panseraikos | 34 | 9 | 10 | 15 | 30 | 42 | 28 |
| Xanthi | 34 | 9 | 10 | 15 | 35 | 53 | 28 |
| Ionikos | 34 | 9 | 9 | 16 | 37 | 50 | 27 |
| Levadiakos | 34 | 10 | 7 | 17 | 35 | 51 | 27 |
| Yanina | 34 | 8 | 9 | 17 | 20 | 54 | 25 |

Olympiakos 2 points deducted
PAOK 3 points deducted

Champions : - Panathinaikos
Relegated : - Ionikos, Levadiakos and Yanina

Note : Clubs finishing level on points are separated by results of matches played against one another.

### TOP SCORERS

| | | |
|---|---|---|
| 1. | Saravakos (Panathinaikos) | 23 |
| 2. | Warzycha (Panathinaikos) | 18 |
| 3. | Anastopoulos (Olympiakos) | 16 |
| 4. | Vaitsis (Panahaiki) | 15 |
| 5. | Batista (AEK) | 13 |
| 6. | Skartados (PAOK) | 12 |
| 7. | A.Karasavvidis (Apollon) | 11 |
| | Protasov (Olympiakos) | 11 |
| | Savichev (Olympiakos) | 11 |
| 10. | Kalogeropoulos (Ionikos) | 10 |
| | Petrounov (Panseraikos) | 10 |
| 12. | Antoniou (Panathinaikos) | 8 |
| | Demetriadis (Aris) | 8 |
| | Lemonis (Levadiakos) | 8 |
| | Tsalouhidis (Olympiakos) | 8 |

| GREECE 2nd Division Season 1990/91 | KALAMARIA | VOLOS | ETHNIKOS | KASTORIA | EDESAIKOS | H' GIAKOS | M' DONIKOS | ATROMITOS | KORINTHOS | EORDAIKOS | VERIA | EAR | DIAGORAS | PIERIKOS | YANITSA | KAVALA | P' GIAKOS | PR' TIKI |
|---|---|---|---|---|---|---|---|---|---|---|---|---|---|---|---|---|---|---|
| APOLLON THESALONIKI | ■ | 3-2 | 2-1 | 3-2 | 3-2 | 2-1 | 2-1 | 3-2 | 0-0 | 2-0 | 3-0 | 2-1 | 1-1 | 1-1 | 2-0 | 3-1 | 2-0 | 3-2 |
| OLYMPIAKOS VOLOS | 0-0 | ■ | 0-0 | 0-0 | 0-2 | 1-1 | 3-1 | 2-1 | 1-1 | 0-0 | 1-2 | 4-3 | 0-0 | 0-1 | 2-0 | 1-0 | 2-1 | 0-0 |
| ETHNIKOS | 2-0 | 3-0 | ■ | 2-1 | 2-0 | 2-0 | 5-1 | 2-0 | 2-1 | 1-0 | 0-0 | 2-0 | 4-1 | 0-0 | 0-0 | 1-0 | 3-1 | 2-0 |
| KASTORIA | 3-2 | 1-1 | 0-0 | ■ | 2-0 | 0-0 | 4-1 | 4-1 | 1-0 | 3-0 | 0-0 | 1-1 | 2-0 | 1-1 | 2-1 | 2-1 | 1-0 | 1-1 |
| EDESAIKOS | 0-3 | 1-0 | 1-2 | 3-0 | ■ | 3-0 | 1-0 | 0-0 | 1-0 | 0-0 | 2-1 | 0-0 | 1-0 | 5-2 | 0-0 | 2-1 | 2-1 | 4-0 |
| HARAVGIAKOS | 3-1 | 1-0 | 0-0 | 2-1 | 0-0 | ■ | 2-1 | 2-0 | 1-1 | 2-0 | 0-0 | 1-0 | 2-0 | 0-0 | 2-0 | 1-0 | 5-2 | 1-1 |
| MAKEDONIKOS | 1-4 | 0-2 | 2-1 | 2-2 | 1-0 | 1-0 | ■ | 0-2 | 2-0 | 1-1 | 2-1 | 3-2 | 1-1 | 1-0 | 0-0 | 1-1 | 2-0 | 1-0 |
| ATROMITOS | 1-1 | 1-0 | 0-1 | 4-1 | 1-0 | 2-0 | 1-2 | ■ | 0-1 | 1-0 | 1-0 | 3-1 | 2-1 | 0-2 | 1-1 | 2-2 | 1-1 | 4-0 |
| KORINTHOS | 3-1 | 6-0 | 1-0 | 2-0 | 4-0 | 1-0 | 3-0 | 1-0 | ■ | 3-2 | 2-0 | 2-0 | 2-0 | 2-1 | 0-0 | 0-0 | 0-0 | 2-0 |
| EORDAIKOS | 2-1 | 0-2 | 1-2 | 0-1 | 1-0 | 1-0 | 2-1 | 2-0 | 1-0 | ■ | 2-1 | 1-1 | 2-0 | 2-1 | 2-0 | 1-1 | 1-0 | 4-1 |
| VERIA | 4-1 | 0-1 | 2-2 | 4-1 | 1-0 | 2-1 | 0-1 | 0-2 | 0-1 | 2-1 | ■ | 4-1 | 0-0 | 1-2 | 1-0 | 1-1 | 2-1 | 3-0 |
| EAR | 1-1 | 1-3 | 0-0 | 3-1 | 1-0 | 2-1 | 2-0 | 1-0 | 0-0 | 1-1 | 2-0 | ■ | 1-0 | 2-0 | 2-0 | 4-1 | 0-0 | 2-0 |
| DIAGORAS | 3-0 | 2-0 | 3-0 | 2-0 | 1-0 | 1-0 | 1-0 | 2-1 | 2-1 | 2-0 | 2-2 | 2-0 | ■ | 0-0 | 1-0 | 1-2 | 1-0 | 1-0 |
| PIERIKOS | 1-0 | 1-2 | 1-1 | 3-0 | 2-2 | 3-0 | 2-0 | 3-1 | 2-1 | 4-1 | 3-2 | 1-0 | 2-1 | ■ | 0-1 | 8-0 | 1-1 | 3-0 |
| ANAYENISI YANITSA | 1-0 | 1-0 | 0-0 | 1-1 | 0-0 | 2-0 | 2-1 | 1-0 | 2-1 | 2-0 | 2-0 | 1-0 | 1-0 | 2-1 | ■ | 1-1 | 0-1 | 2-0 |
| KAVALA | 2-1 | 3-3 | 0-0 | 2-1 | 1-0 | 0-0 | 1-1 | 0-2 | 1-1 | 2-1 | 2-0 | 0-1 | 3-0 | 0-0 | 1-0 | ■ | 3-1 | 1-0 |
| PANARGIAKOS | 2-2 | 1-0 | 2-0 | 1-0 | 1-1 | 2-0 | 0-0 | 1-0 | 1-1 | 2-1 | 1-1 | 2-2 | 0-0 | 0-0 | 4-1 | 3-0 | ■ | 3-0 |
| PROODEFTIKI | 2-1 | 2-1 | 2-2 | 1-0 | 3-1 | 1-1 | 3-1 | 1-1 | 0-0 | 2-0 | 1-1 | 0-0 | 0-0 | 1-0 | 1-0 | 2-1 | 1-0 | ■ |

## GREECE 2ND DIVISION 1990/91

### LEAGUE TABLE FINAL

| | | | | | | | |
|---|---|---|---|---|---|---|---|
| Ethnikos | 34 | 17 | 12 | 5 | 45 | 22 | 46 |
| Korinthos | 34 | 16 | 10 | 8 | 44 | 21 | 42 |
| Pierikos | 34 | 15 | 10 | 9 | 52 | 31 | 40 |
| Apollonas Thesaloniki | 34 | 16 | 7 | 11 | 56 | 48 | 39 |
| Anayenisi Yanitsa | 34 | 13 | 9 | 12 | 25 | 27 | 35 |
| EAR | 34 | 12 | 10 | 12 | 38 | 37 | 34 |
| Edesaikos | 34 | 12 | 8 | 14 | 34 | 34 | 32 |
| Haravgiakos | 34 | 11 | 10 | 13 | 30 | 33 | 32 |
| Panargiakos | 34 | 10 | 12 | 12 | 36 | 36 | 32 |
| Kastoria | 34 | 11 | 10 | 13 | 40 | 45 | 32 |
| Olympiakos Volos | 34 | 11 | 10 | 13 | 34 | 40 | 32 |
| Kavala | 34 | 10 | 12 | 12 | 35 | 46 | 32 |
| Atromitos | 34 | 12 | 6 | 16 | 38 | 39 | 30 |
| Diagoras | 34 | 14 | 8 | 12 | 32 | 30 | 30 |
| Eordaikos | 34 | 12 | 6 | 16 | 33 | 42 | 30 |
| Proofdeftiki | 34 | 10 | 10 | 14 | 28 | 47 | 30 |
| Makedonikos | 34 | 11 | 7 | 16 | 33 | 51 | 29 |
| Veria | 34 | 10 | 9 | 15 | 38 | 42 | 29 |

Diagoras 6 points deducted

Promoted : - Ethnikos, Korinthos and Pierikos
Relegated : - Eordaikos, Proofdeftiki, Makedonikos and Veria

## GREECE 3RD DIVISION 1990/91

### NORTH LEAGUE TABLE FINAL

| | | | | | | | |
|---|---|---|---|---|---|---|---|
| Nausa | 34 | 16 | 13 | 5 | 58 | 32 | 45 |
| Trikala | 34 | 16 | 10 | 8 | 40 | 27 | 42 |
| Anayenisi Kolindros | 34 | 14 | 11 | 9 | 41 | 28 | 39 |
| Kozani | 34 | 11 | 14 | 9 | 37 | 34 | 36 |
| Asteras Ambelokipi | 34 | 11 | 12 | 11 | 36 | 27 | 34 |
| Nigrita | 34 | 13 | 8 | 13 | 48 | 46 | 34 |
| Anayenisi Neapoli | 34 | 11 | 12 | 11 | 35 | 36 | 34 |
| PAO Nei Epivates | 34 | 11 | 12 | 11 | 27 | 28 | 34 |
| AE Pondii Veria | 34 | 13 | 8 | 13 | 32 | 35 | 34 |
| Preveza | 34 | 13 | 8 | 13 | 41 | 45 | 34 |
| Anayenisi Halkidona | 34 | 11 | 12 | 11 | 37 | 42 | 34 |
| Kiriaki | 34 | 12 | 10 | 12 | 37 | 46 | 34 |
| Niki Volos | 34 | 12 | 9 | 13 | 49 | 41 | 33 |
| Lamia | 34 | 13 | 7 | 14 | 36 | 42 | 33 |
| Odiseas Kordelio | 34 | 11 | 10 | 13 | 42 | 39 | 32 |
| Anayenisi Karditsa | 34 | 10 | 10 | 14 | 26 | 36 | 30 |
| Aspida Xanthi | 34 | 9 | 9 | 16 | 39 | 53 | 27 |
| Kilkisiakos | 34 | 7 | 9 | 18 | 26 | 54 | 23 |

Promoted : - Nausa and Trikala
Relegated : - Lamia, Odiseas Kordelio, Anayenisi Karditsa, Aspida Xanthi and Kilisiakos

### SOUTH LEAGUE TABLE FINAL

| | | | | | | | |
|---|---|---|---|---|---|---|---|
| Doxa Vironas | 34 | 19 | 9 | 6 | 54 | 28 | 47 |
| Egaleo | 34 | 15 | 15 | 4 | 40 | 24 | 45 |
| Kalamata | 34 | 19 | 4 | 11 | 46 | 27 | 42 |
| Ilisiakos | 34 | 16 | 8 | 10 | 38 | 32 | 40 |
| Sparti | 34 | 14 | 9 | 11 | 34 | 28 | 37 |
| Panetolikos | 34 | 13 | 11 | 10 | 33 | 28 | 37 |
| Kalithea | 34 | 14 | 8 | 12 | 30 | 31 | 36 |
| Panelefsiniakos | 34 | 12 | 11 | 11 | 39 | 30 | 35 |
| Paniliakos | 34 | 11 | 12 | 11 | 37 | 31 | 34 |
| Haidari | 34 | 13 | 7 | 14 | 32 | 31 | 33 |
| Thriamvos | 34 | 11 | 11 | 12 | 37 | 40 | 33 |
| Aris Nikea | 34 | 11 | 10 | 13 | 34 | 36 | 32 |
| Mesolongi | 34 | 10 | 12 | 12 | 28 | 33 | 32 |
| Olympi. Lutraki | 34 | 12 | 8 | 14 | 27 | 37 | 32 |
| Irodotos | 34 | 10 | 8 | 16 | 27 | 32 | 28 |
| Ethnikos Asteras | 34 | 11 | 6 | 17 | 27 | 35 | 28 |
| Aharnaikos | 34 | 7 | 10 | 17 | 24 | 51 | 24 |
| Panarkadikos | 34 | 6 | 5 | 23 | 21 | 54 | 17 |

Promoted : - Doxa Vironas and Egaleo
Relegated : - Olympiakos Lutraki, Irodotos, Ethnikos Asteras, Aharnaikos and Panarkadikos.
Expelled : - Aris Nikea

Promoted from 4th Division for Season 1991/92 : - Panafpliakos, Fostiras, Posidonas Iraklio, Patra, Rodos, Apollonas Larisa, Anayenisi Arta, Posidonas Mihaniona, Pandramaikos and Panargiakos Orestiko.

# GREECE CUP 1990/91

## 1ST ROUND
Winners and Runners Up of each group qualify for 1/16 finals

### GROUP 1
| Team | P | W | D | L | F | A | Pts |
|---|---|---|---|---|---|---|---|
| Panathinaikos | 4 | 3 | 1 | 0 | 12 | 3 | 7 |
| Apollon Thesaloniki | 4 | 2 | 1 | 1 | 12 | 4 | 5 |
| Diagoras | 4 | 1 | 3 | 0 | 5 | 4 | 5 |
| Aris Nikea | 4 | 0 | 2 | 2 | 3 | 8 | 2 |
| Panilejakos | 4 | 0 | 1 | 3 | 1 | 14 | 1 |

### GROUP 2
| Team | P | W | D | L | F | A | Pts |
|---|---|---|---|---|---|---|---|
| Panionios | 4 | 4 | 0 | 0 | 12 | 2 | 8 |
| Ethnikos Asteras | 4 | 1 | 2 | 1 | 5 | 7 | 4 |
| Anayenisi Kolindros | 4 | 1 | 1 | 2 | 5 | 7 | 3 |
| Lamia | 4 | 1 | 1 | 2 | 5 | 5 | 3 |
| Odiseas Kordelio | 4 | 1 | 0 | 3 | 3 | 9 | 2 |

### GROUP 3
| Team | P | W | D | L | F | A | Pts |
|---|---|---|---|---|---|---|---|
| Haravgiakos | 4 | 2 | 2 | 0 | 6 | 3 | 6 |
| Proodeftiki | 4 | 1 | 3 | 0 | 4 | 3 | 5 |
| Pierikos | 4 | 0 | 4 | 0 | 3 | 3 | 4 |
| Ethnikos | 4 | 1 | 2 | 1 | 3 | 4 | 4 |
| PAS Yanina | 4 | 0 | 1 | 3 | 1 | 4 | 1 |

### GROUP 4
| Team | P | W | D | L | F | A | Pts |
|---|---|---|---|---|---|---|---|
| Doxa Virona | 4 | 3 | 0 | 1 | 10 | 3 | 6 |
| Aris Thesaloniki | 4 | 3 | 0 | 1 | 11 | 2 | 6 |
| Olympiakos Volos | 4 | 2 | 1 | 1 | 11 | 9 | 5 |
| Korinthos | 4 | 1 | 1 | 2 | 5 | 6 | 3 |
| Aspida Xanthi | 4 | 0 | 0 | 4 | 3 | 13 | 0 |

### GROUP 5
| Team | P | W | D | L | F | A | Pts |
|---|---|---|---|---|---|---|---|
| Athinaikos | 4 | 4 | 0 | 0 | 7 | 1 | 8 |
| Panargiakos | 4 | 3 | 0 | 1 | 6 | 3 | 6 |
| Kastoria | 4 | 1 | 1 | 2 | 2 | 3 | 3 |
| Anayenisi Yanitsa | 4 | 0 | 2 | 2 | 3 | 7 | 2 |
| Atromitos | 4 | 0 | 1 | 3 | 3 | 7 | 1 |

### GROUP 6
| Team | P | W | D | L | F | A | Pts |
|---|---|---|---|---|---|---|---|
| Nausa | 4 | 3 | 1 | 0 | 9 | 6 | 7 |
| Iraklis | 4 | 3 | 0 | 1 | 9 | 3 | 6 |
| Trikala | 4 | 0 | 3 | 1 | 3 | 4 | 3 |
| Aharnaikos | 4 | 0 | 2 | 2 | 2 | 4 | 2 |
| Niki Volos | 4 | 0 | 2 | 2 | 3 | 9 | 2 |

### GROUP 7
| Team | P | W | D | L | F | A | Pts |
|---|---|---|---|---|---|---|---|
| Anayenisi Karditsa | 4 | 2 | 1 | 1 | 7 | 5 | 5 |
| Ionikos | 4 | 2 | 1 | 1 | 5 | 5 | 5 |
| Veria | 4 | 2 | 1 | 1 | 5 | 4 | 5 |
| Panetolikos | 4 | 0 | 3 | 1 | 5 | 6 | 3 |
| Kalithea | 4 | 0 | 2 | 2 | 2 | 6 | 2 |

### GROUP 8
| Team | P | W | D | L | F | A | Pts |
|---|---|---|---|---|---|---|---|
| Olympiakos Piraeus | 4 | 4 | 0 | 0 | 17 | 1 | 8 |
| Panelefsiniakos | 4 | 2 | 0 | 2 | 6 | 8 | 4 |
| Kozani | 4 | 2 | 0 | 2 | 4 | 5 | 4 |
| Haidari | 4 | 1 | 1 | 2 | 4 | 11 | 3 |
| PAO Kiriaki | 4 | 0 | 1 | 3 | 2 | 8 | 1 |

### GROUP 9
| Team | P | W | D | L | F | A | Pts |
|---|---|---|---|---|---|---|---|
| AEK | 3 | 3 | 0 | 0 | 10 | 1 | 6 |
| Panarkadikos | 3 | 1 | 1 | 1 | 3 | 2 | 3 |
| Mesolongi | 3 | 1 | 0 | 2 | 2 | 7 | 2 |
| Preveza | 3 | 0 | 1 | 2 | 1 | 6 | 1 |

### GROUP 10
| Team | P | W | D | L | F | A | Pts |
|---|---|---|---|---|---|---|---|
| Larisa | 3 | 2 | 1 | 0 | 5 | 1 | 5 |
| Eordaikos | 3 | 1 | 2 | 0 | 3 | 1 | 4 |
| Agrotikos Asteras | 3 | 0 | 2 | 1 | 2 | 4 | 2 |
| AE Pondii Veria | 3 | 0 | 1 | 2 | 1 | 4 | 1 |

### GROUP 11
| Team | P | W | D | L | F | A | Pts |
|---|---|---|---|---|---|---|---|
| PAOK | 3 | 3 | 0 | 0 | 8 | 3 | 6 |
| OFI | 3 | 2 | 0 | 1 | 9 | 3 | 4 |
| Makedonios | 3 | 0 | 2 | 1 | 6 | 6 | 2 |
| Kalamata | 3 | 0 | 0 | 3 | 2 | 13 | 0 |

### GROUP 12
| Team | P | W | D | L | F | A | Pts |
|---|---|---|---|---|---|---|---|
| Panseraikos | 3 | 2 | 1 | 0 | 7 | 5 | 5 |
| Edesaikos | 3 | 1 | 1 | 1 | 6 | 5 | 3 |
| Panahaiki | 3 | 1 | 0 | 2 | 7 | 6 | 2 |
| Sparti | 3 | 1 | 0 | 2 | 4 | 8 | 2 |

### GROUP 13
| Team | P | W | D | L | F | A | Pts |
|---|---|---|---|---|---|---|---|
| Apollon Athens | 3 | 3 | 0 | 0 | 9 | 1 | 6 |
| Ilisiakos | 3 | 2 | 0 | 1 | 5 | 8 | 4 |
| PAONE | 3 | 1 | 0 | 2 | 2 | 4 | 2 |
| Thriamvos | 3 | 0 | 0 | 3 | 1 | 4 | 0 |

### GROUP 14
| Team | P | W | D | L | F | A | Pts |
|---|---|---|---|---|---|---|---|
| Xanthi | 3 | 2 | 1 | 0 | 7 | 1 | 5 |
| Kilkisiakos | 3 | 1 | 1 | 1 | 4 | 3 | 3 |
| Egaleo | 3 | 1 | 0 | 2 | 2 | 2 | 2 |
| Nigrita | 3 | 0 | 0 | 3 | 1 | 7 | 0 |

### GROUP 15
| Team | P | W | D | L | F | A | Pts |
|---|---|---|---|---|---|---|---|
| EAR | 3 | 2 | 0 | 1 | 3 | 1 | 4 |
| Doxa Drama | 3 | 1 | 1 | 1 | 3 | 3 | 3 |
| Kavala | 3 | 1 | 1 | 1 | 4 | 5 | 3 |
| Halkidona | 3 | 1 | 0 | 2 | 4 | 5 | 2 |

### GROUP 16
| Team | P | W | D | L | F | A | Pts |
|---|---|---|---|---|---|---|---|
| Levadiakos | 3 | 2 | 0 | 1 | 4 | 1 | 4 |
| Olympiakos Lutraki | 3 | 1 | 1 | 1 | 5 | 3 | 3 |
| Irodotos | 3 | 1 | 1 | 1 | 4 | 5 | 3 |
| Anayenisi Neapoli | 3 | 1 | 0 | 2 | 2 | 7 | 2 |

## 1/16 FINALS
| Tie | 1ST LEG | 2ND LEG | AGG. |
|---|---|---|---|
| Olympiakos Lutraki v Anayenisi Karditsa | 2-0 | 0-3 | 2-3 |
| Larisa v Apollonas Athens (Larisa win on the away goals rule) | 0-0 | 1-1 | 1-1 |
| Athinaikos v Aris | 2-1 | 3-1 | 5-2 |
| Edesaikos v Apollonas Thesaloniki | 1-0 | 1-0 | 2-0 |
| Nausa v Doxa Drama | 2-4 | 1-0 | 3-4 |
| Ionikos v Ethnikos Asteras | 3-0 | 1-0 | 4-0 |
| Doxa Virona v Eordaikos | 0-0 | 0-2 | 0-2 |
| Panarkadikos v Kilkisiakos | 4-1 | 0-5 | 4-6 |
| Iraklis v Xanthi | 0-0 | 0-1 | 0-1 |
| Panseraikos v OFI (OFI win on the away goals rule) | 3-1 | 0-2 | 3-3 |
| EAR v Panargiakos (EAR win on the away goals rule) | 2-3 | 1-3 | 3-3 |
| Panelefsiniakos v Panionios | 2-3 | 0-5 | 2-8 |
| Olympiakos Piraeus v PAOK | 2-0 | 0-3 | 2-3 |
| Proodeftiki v Panathinaikos | 1-2 | 0-5 | 1-7 |
| Haravgiakos v AEK | 0-3 | 0-2 | 0-5 |
| Ilisiakos v Levadiakos | 1-1 | 2-4 | 3-5 |

## 1/8 FINALS
| Tie | 1ST LEG | 2ND LEG | AGG. |
|---|---|---|---|
| OFI v AEK | 3-0 | 1-3 | 4-3 |
| Panathinaikos v Levadiakos | 2-1 | 0-0 | 2-1 |
| Xanthi v PAOK | 2-1 | 0-2 | 2-3 |
| Doxa Drama v Eordaikos | 3-0 | 1-1 | 4-1 |
| Ionikos v Edesaikos (Ionikos win 5-4 on penalties) | 4-0 | 0-4 | 4-4 |
| Athinaikos v Anayenisi Karditsa | 3-0 | 2-1 | 5-1 |
| EAR v Panionios | 1-3 | 0-3 | 1-6 |
| Kilkisiakos v Larisa | 3-2 | 2-4 | 5-6 |

## 1/4 FINALS
| Tie | 1ST LEG | 2ND LEG | AGG. |
|---|---|---|---|
| Ionikos v Panathinaikos | 0-3 | 1-3 | 1-6 |
| PAOK v Larisa | 3-0 | 0-2 | 3-2 |
| Panionios v OFI (Panionios win 3-2 on penalties) | 2-0 | 0-2 | 2-2 |
| Athinaikos v Doxa | 2-0 | 1-0 | 3-0 |

## SEMI-FINALS
| Tie | 1ST LEG | 2ND LEG | AGG. |
|---|---|---|---|
| Panathinaikos v PAOK | 2-0 | 0-1 | 2-1 |
| Athinaikos v Panionios | 3-0 | 1-3 | 4-3 |

## FINAL

1st Leg    15/5/91

Athinaikos...............0    Panathinaikos.........3

Athinaikos : Sarganis, Butzukas Basayanis, Hatziangelis, Spiliotis, Theodorakos, Hatziraptis (Bong 73), Zotalis, Tsalakostas, Colev (Anastasiou 55), Tsavalias.

PAO : Wandzik, Apostolakis, Kalantzis, Kurbanas, Kalintzakis, Hristodoulou, Andoniou, Marangos, Yeorgakopoulos (Kalpakis 90), Frantzeskos (Vlahos 80), Warzycha.

0-1 Kurbanas 70          Referee : Dimitriadis
0-2 Warzycha pen. 84     Attendance : 20,000
0-3 Vlahos 90

2nd Leg    22/5/91

Panathinaikos..........2    Athinaikos.............1

PAO : Wandzik, Apostolakis, Kalantzis, Kurbanas, Kalintzakis, Yeorgamlis, Andoniou. Marangos (Saravakos 60). Hristodoulou, Vlahos (Frantzeskos 46), Warzycha.

Athinaikos : Kandas, Basayanis, Taprantzis (Bong 46), Hatziangelis, Spiliotis, Vrinios, Theodorakos, Hatziraptis, H.Dimopoulos, Zotalis (Anastasiou 71), Tsavalias.

0-1 Zotalis    pen.   45    Referee : Vasilakis
1-1 Saravakos         71    Attendance : 30,000
2-1 Kurbanas          84

PANATHINAIKOS WIN 5-1 ON AGGREGATE

# GREECE INTERNATIONAL REVIEW 1990

## INTERNATIONAL LINE-UPS 1990

**17/1/90** GREECE 2 BELGIUM 0 — Athens — Friendly — Ref: D'Elia (Italy) — (Tsaluhidis, Apostolakis)

**28/3/90** GREECE 2 ISRAEL 1 — Athens — Friendly — Ref: Nikakis (Greece) — (Manolas 2)

**30/5/90** ITALY 0 GREECE 0 — Perugia — Friendly — Ref: Dos Santos (Portugal)

**5/9/90** GREECE 1 ALBANIA 0 — Patra — Friendly — Ref: Vutsaras (Greece) — (Dimitriadis)

**10/10/90** GREECE 6 EGYPT 1 — Athens — Friendly — Ref: Spasov (Bulgaria) — (Tsaluhidis, Saravakos 5)

**31/10/90** GREECE 4 MALTA 0 — Athens — EuroCh.Q. — Ref: Craciunescu (Rumania) — (Tsiandakis, Karapialis, Saravakos, Borbokis)

**21/11/90** HOLLAND 2 GREECE 0 — Rotterdam — EuroCh.Q. — Ref: Nemeth (Hungary)

**19/12/90** GREECE 1 POLAND 2 — Athens — Friendly — Ref: Kefalas (Greece) — (Tsaluhidis)

| Player | 17/1 | 28/3 | 30/5 | 5/9 | 10/10 | 31/10 | 21/11 | 19/12 | CAPS 31/12/90 | GOALS 31/12/90 |
|---|---|---|---|---|---|---|---|---|---|---|
| Nikos Sarganis | 1 | | | | | | | 1 | 50 | — |
| Stratos Apostolakis | 2 | 2 | 2 | 2 | 2 | 2 | | | 37 | 1 |
| Mihalis Leondiadis | 3 | | | | | | | | 1 | — |
| Stelios Manolas | 4 | 4 | | 4 | 4 | 4 | 4 | | 49 | 5 |
| Yanis Kalintzakis | 5 | 5 | 5 | 5 | 5 | | | 4 | 15 | — |
| Panayotis Tsaluhidis | 6 | 6 | 7 | 7 | 8 | 6 | | 6 | 31 | 6 |
| Dimitris Saravakos | 7 | 7 | 9 | 10 | 7 | 7 | 10 | 7 | 61 | 18 |
| Stavros Stamatis | 8 | | | | | | | | 5 | — |
| Stefanos Borbokis | 9 | 9 | | (9) | | 11 | 6 | (11) | 18 | 3 |
| Spiros Marangos | 10 | 10 | 11 | 8 | 6 | | (9) | 11 | 11 | — |
| Nikos Tsiandakis | 11 | 11 | 6 | | 6 | | 11 | | 20 | 2 |
| Yorgos Kutulas | (2) | | (11) | (10) | | 11 | | (5) | 11 | — |
| Yorgos Tsifutis | (8) | | | | | | | | 2 | — |
| Theodoros Zakas | (9) | (7) | | | | | | | 3 | — |
| Kiriakos Karataidis | (10) | 3 | | | | | | | 4 | — |
| Yorgos Plitsis | | | | (1) | | | 1 | | 19 | — |
| Nikos Nioplias | | | 10 | | | 10 | (10) | 8 | 16 | 1 |
| Nikos Karayeorgiou | | (3) | | (9) | | | | | 8 | — |
| Zisis Tsekos | | (8) | | | | | | | 1 | — |
| Yanis Samaras | | (9) | (9) | | | | | | 16 | — |
| Nikos Kurbanas | | (5) | (10) | | | 5 | | | 6 | — |
| Theologos Papadopoulos | | 1 | 3 | 1 | 3 | 1 | 1 | | 17 | — |
| Yorgos Papadopoulos | | 3 | 3 | | 3 | | 1 | | 9 | — |
| Yorgos Tursunidis | | 8 | | | | | | | 1 | — |
| Savas Kofidis | | (11) | 11 | 9 | | 9 | 8 | | 52 | 1 |
| Pagonis Vakalopoulos | | | | | | | | | 9 | 1 |
| Vasilis Dimitriadis | | (3) | (6) | 10 | 11 | | | | 10 | 1 |
| Daniil Papadopoulos | | (9) | (11) | (3) | | | | | 5 | — |
| Yorgos Agoroyanis | | (11) | (3) | | | | | | 4 | — |
| Vasilis Karapialis | | 8 | | 7 | | | | | 8 | 1 |
| Aris Karasavidis | | | | 9 | | | | | 3 | — |
| Yorgos Athanasiadis | | | | | | | | 9 10 | 10 | — |

| HOLLAND Eredivisie Season 1990/91 | AJAX | PSV | TWENTE | VITESSE | RODA JC | VOLENDAM | FORTUNA S | RKC | GRONINGEN | DEN HAAG | FEYENOORD | SPARTA | WILLEM II | UTRECHT | MVV | NEC | SVV | HEERENVEEN |
|---|---|---|---|---|---|---|---|---|---|---|---|---|---|---|---|---|---|---|
| AJAX | | 3-1 | 1-1 | 3-0 | 4-1 | 3-1 | 2-0 | 0-0 | 1-1 | 5-0 | 2-0 | 1-0 | 3-1 | 1-1 | 1-0 | 7-0 | 2-0 | 4-0 |
| PSV | 4-1 | | 3-1 | 1-1 | 3-0 | 3-0 | 5-1 | 3-1 | 1-1 | 4-0 | 6-0 | 6-1 | 3-0 | 5-0 | 3-0 | 1-0 | 3-2 | 2-0 |
| FC TWENTE | 0-1 | 0-2 | | 0-2 | 4-1 | 0-0 | 1-0 | 1-1 | 4-2 | 2-1 | 1-1 | 0-1 | 2-0 | 1-1 | 4-1 | 5-0 | 2-1 | 3-3 |
| VITESSE | 1-3 | 1-1 | 1-0 | | 1-3 | 0-0 | 2-3 | 1-1 | 1-2 | 2-0 | 0-0 | 0-0 | 2-0 | 1-0 | 1-1 | 0-0 | 3-0 | 2-0 |
| RODA JC | 0-0 | 1-3 | 1-2 | 1-2 | | 2-1 | 1-1 | 1-0 | 0-0 | 5-1 | 0-0 | 2-2 | 1-0 | 1-2 | 1-0 | 2-2 | 1-0 | 1-0 |
| VOLENDAM | 0-3 | 0-2 | 3-1 | 2-1 | 2-0 | | 2-1 | 2-0 | 2-2 | 0-2 | 2-2 | 2-2 | 0-0 | 0-1 | 2-2 | 0-0 | 2-1 | 1-1 |
| FORT. SITTARD | 1-1 | 0-3 | 0-0 | 0-4 | 0-1 | 0-0 | | 0-2 | 0-0 | 3-1 | 3-2 | 1-1 | 2-0 | 0-2 | 1-1 | 3-1 | 1-0 | 1-0 |
| RKC | 1-1 | 0-3 | 6-6 | 1-1 | 4-1 | 1-1 | 1-1 | | 1-1 | 1-2 | 1-0 | 4-2 | 2-0 | 1-0 | 3-2 | 3-0 | 4-1 | 5-2 |
| FC GRONINGEN | 1-2 | 4-1 | 4-0 | 2-0 | 3-1 | 1-0 | 3-1 | 2-1 | | 2-0 | 1-1 | 4-0 | 4-1 | 2-2 | 2-1 | 2-1 | 2-2 | 3-0 |
| FC DEN HAAG | 0-1 | 3-0 | 1-5 | 1-1 | 3-1 | 1-3 | 0-0 | 2-2 | 1-2 | | 0-2 | 3-0 | 1-0 | 3-1 | 5-1 | 1-1 | 1-1 | 3-2 |
| FFYENOORD | 0-4 | 1-1 | 2-2 | 0-0 | 2-1 | 3-0 | 0-0 | 3-0 | 2-0 | 0-2 | | 4-3 | 0-1 | 0-0 | 6-0 | 0-0 | 1-1 | 1-1 |
| SPARTA | 0-0 | 1-0 | 1-3 | 1-1 | 1-1 | 1-2 | 2-2 | 0-0 | 1-1 | 0-0 | 1-1 | | 2-0 | 4-1 | 0-0 | 3-1 | 5-3 | 2-1 |
| WILLEM II | 3-2 | 0-2 | 2-1 | 0-0 | 2-0 | 4-1 | 3-2 | 4-2 | 1-2 | 5-0 | 3-2 | 6-1 | | 0-2 | 0-1 | 2-2 | 6-0 | 5-2 |
| FC UTRECHT | 0-0 | 1-1 | 1-0 | 1-1 | 2-1 | 1-0 | 2-0 | 2-0 | 4-0 | 0-0 | 2-0 | 2-0 | 1-0 | | 4-1 | 2-0 | 1-0 | 1-2 |
| MVV | 1-4 | 3-3 | 2-1 | 2-0 | 1-2 | 1-1 | 1-1 | 0-1 | 1-0 | 1-0 | 1-0 | 0-2 | 0-0 | 3-1 | | 1-2 | 2-0 | 2-0 |
| NEC | 0-5 | 1-1 | 1-3 | 0-2 | 1-2 | 1-2 | 0-2 | 0-0 | 0-3 | 0-0 | 2-1 | 3-1 | 0-2 | 1-1 | 2-1 | | 2-1 | 2-1 |
| SVV | 1-0 | 0-1 | 1-1 | 1-2 | 3-1 | 1-0 | 2-0 | 0-0 | 4-2 | 0-0 | 0-0 | 0-0 | 1-0 | 1-4 | 1-0 | 1-0 | | 1-2 |
| SC HEERENVEEN | 1-4 | 0-3 | 0-1 | 2-2 | 1-2 | 1-3 | 1-2 | 4-1 | 4-2 | 3-0 | 0-0 | 2-1 | 2-1 | 1-0 | 1-0 | 1-1 | 0-1 | |

## HOLLAND EREDIVISIE 1990/91
### LEAGUE TABLE FINAL

| | | | | | | | |
|---|---|---|---|---|---|---|---|
| PSV (Eindhoven) | 34 | 23 | 7 | 4 | 84 | 28 | 53 |
| Ajax (Amsterdam) | 34 | 22 | 9 | 3 | 75 | 21 | 53 |
| FC Groningen | 34 | 18 | 10 | 6 | 62 | 38 | 46 |
| FC Utrecht | 34 | 16 | 10 | 8 | 42 | 29 | 42 |
| Vitesse (Arnhem) | 34 | 11 | 15 | 8 | 39 | 32 | 37 |
| FC Twente (Enschede) | 34 | 13 | 10 | 11 | 58 | 48 | 36 |
| RKC (Waalwijk) | 34 | 11 | 13 | 10 | 51 | 49 | 35 |
| Feyenoord (Rott'dam) | 34 | 8 | 16 | 10 | 39 | 40 | 32 |
| Volendam | 34 | 10 | 12 | 12 | 37 | 45 | 32 |
| Roda JC (Kerkrade) | 34 | 12 | 7 | 15 | 40 | 53 | 31 |
| Willem II (Tilburg) | 34 | 13 | 4 | 17 | 53 | 50 | 30 |
| Fortuna Sittard | 34 | 9 | 12 | 13 | 33 | 47 | 30 |
| Sparta (Rotterdam) | 34 | 7 | 15 | 12 | 40 | 57 | 29 |
| FC Den Haag | 34 | 10 | 8 | 16 | 40 | 60 | 28 |
| MVV (Maastricht) | 34 | 9 | 9 | 16 | 38 | 56 | 27 |
| SVV (Schiedam) | 34 | 8 | 8 | 18 | 31 | 52 | 24 |
| SC Heerenveen | 34 | 9 | 6 | 19 | 41 | 63 | 24 |
| NEC (Nijmegen) | 34 | 6 | 11 | 17 | 27 | 62 | 23 |

Champions : - PSV

Relegated : - SC Heerenveen & NEC

## HOLLAND EERSTE DIVISIE 1990/91
### LEAGUE TABLE FINAL

| | | | | | | | |
|---|---|---|---|---|---|---|---|
| De Graafschap | 38 | 25 | 11 | 2 | 84 | 34 | 61 |
| NAC (Breda) | 38 | 21 | 14 | 3 | 94 | 50 | 56 |
| VVV (Venlo) | 38 | 21 | 7 | 10 | 73 | 46 | 49 |
| AZ (Alkmaar) | 38 | 15 | 15 | 8 | 56 | 38 | 45 |
| Helmond Sport | 38 | 14 | 16 | 8 | 57 | 43 | 44 |
| SC Heracles (Almelo) | 38 | 13 | 18 | 7 | 50 | 36 | 44 |
| Go Ahead Eagles | 38 | 14 | 15 | 9 | 57 | 43 | 43 |
| Dordrecht 90 | 38 | 15 | 13 | 10 | 63 | 51 | 43 |
| Eindhoven | 38 | 17 | 8 | 13 | 54 | 52 | 42 |
| RBC (Roosendaal) | 38 | 12 | 15 | 11 | 65 | 56 | 39 |
| Cambuur/Leeuwarden | 38 | 12 | 13 | 13 | 41 | 47 | 37 |
| Emmen | 38 | 10 | 16 | 12 | 54 | 67 | 36 |
| Telstar (Velsen) | 38 | 9 | 15 | 14 | 51 | 58 | 33 |
| Haarlem | 38 | 11 | 10 | 17 | 52 | 78 | 32 |
| Wageningen | 38 | 10 | 10 | 18 | 71 | 82 | 30 |
| FC Zwolle | 38 | 8 | 14 | 16 | 40 | 60 | 30 |
| BVV Den Bosch | 38 | 9 | 11 | 18 | 54 | 60 | 29 |
| SC Veendam | 38 | 5 | 15 | 18 | 47 | 78 | 25 |
| Excelsior (Rotterdam) | 38 | 8 | 7 | 23 | 50 | 82 | 23 |
| VC Vlissingen | 38 | 6 | 7 | 25 | 35 | 87 | 19 |

Period Champions : - De Graafschap, Eindhoven, VVV, NAC, Dordrecht 90 and FC Zwolle.

VC Vlissingen are renamed to VCV Zeeland for the Season 1991/92

### TOP SCORERS

| | |
|---|---|
| 1. Romario (PSV) | 25 |
| Dennis Bergkamp (Ajax) | 25 |
| 3. Earnest Stewart (Willem II) | 17 |
| 4. Juul Ellerman (PSV) | 16 |
| Claus Nielsen (FC Twente) | 16 |
| 6. Martin van Geel (Willem II) | 15 |
| 7. Marco Boogers (RKC) | 14 |
| Milko Djurovski (FC Groningen) | 14 |
| 9. Peter Houtman (Sparta) | 13 |
| Stefan Pettersson (Ajax) | 13 |
| 11. Hennie Meijer (FC Groningen) | 12 |
| Wlodimierz Smolarek (FC Utrecht) | 12 |
| 13. Johnny Bosman (PSV) | 11 |
| Gerald Vanenburg (PSV) | 11 |
| 15. Frank Berghuis (RKC) | 10 |
| Jos Roossien (FC Groningen) | 10 |
| 17. Harry van der Laan (Feyenoord) | 9 |
| 18. Graham Arnold (Roda JC) | 8 |
| John van den Brom (Vitesse) | 8 |
| John Clayton (Volendam) | 8 |
| Harris Huizingh (FC Groningen) | 8 |
| Mitar Mrkela (FC Twente) | 8 |
| Hans Vincent (MVV) | 8 |

SVV and Dordrecht 90 have combined to form SVV Dordrecht 90 for Season 1991/92

**PROMOTION/RELEGATION PLAY-OFF**

| | 1ST LEG | 2ND LEG | AGG. |
|---|---|---|---|
| NAC (Breda) v SVV (Schiedam) | 1-4 | 1-1 | 2-5 |

| HOLLAND Eerste Divisie Season 1990/91 | DEN BOSCH | HAARLEM | NAC | HERACLES | VVV | EINDHOVEN | EMMEN | GRAAFSCHAP | VEENDAM | GA EAGLES | WAGENINGEN | CAMBUUR/L | AZ | HELMOND SP | EXCELSIOR | ZWOLLE | RBC | TELSTAR | DORDRECHT | VLISSINGEN |
|---|---|---|---|---|---|---|---|---|---|---|---|---|---|---|---|---|---|---|---|---|
| BVV DEN BOSCH | | 1-1 | 2-1 | 1-1 | 1-2 | 0-1 | 1-2 | 0-2 | 5-1 | 3-1 | 1-2 | 0-2 | 0-1 | 1-3 | 2-0 | 4-1 | 3-0 | 0-0 | 1-1 | 1-1 |
| HAARLEM | 3-2 | | 0-0 | 0-0 | 0-3 | 0-3 | 1-1 | 1-4 | 1-1 | 1-1 | 4-3 | 2-0 | 0-4 | 1-1 | 2-1 | 1-2 | 3-2 | 1-0 | 1-2 | 2-0 |
| NAC | 3-1 | 6-4 | | 2-0 | 3-2 | 3-0 | 7-1 | 2-2 | 1-1 | 0-0 | 4-3 | 5-2 | 4-3 | 2-0 | 5-0 | 4-0 | 2-1 | 5-3 | 2-1 | 2-2 |
| SC HERACLES | 1-1 | 3-1 | 0-3 | | 1-1 | 4-0 | 2-0 | 0-1 | 2-0 | 2-2 | 1-1 | 0-0 | 1-1 | 0-2 | 1-3 | 1-1 | 1-1 | 0-0 | 1-0 | 1-0 |
| VVV | 4-6 | 3-0 | 0-0 | 0-0 | | 1-0 | 4-2 | 0-1 | 6-1 | 1-2 | 3-1 | 3-1 | 0-0 | 4-0 | 3-1 | 5-0 | 2-3 | 2-0 | 2-1 | 2-1 |
| EINDHOVEN | 2-1 | 3-1 | 3-0 | 2-1 | 0-3 | | 3-0 | 1-0 | 2-0 | 0-1 | 2-3 | 1-3 | 1-0 | 0-0 | 2-0 | 1-1 | 0-1 | 2-3 | 0-0 | 3-1 |
| EMMEN | 2-1 | 3-3 | 2-2 | 1-1 | 2-3 | 2-2 | | 3-3 | 1-0 | 2-2 | 3-1 | 1-0 | 2-2 | 1-1 | 3-2 | 2-2 | 0-1 | 2-2 | 1-2 | 1-0 |
| DE GRAAFSCHAP | 5-0 | 2-1 | 0-0 | 0-1 | 1-1 | 3-1 | 2-1 | | 4-2 | 2-1 | 4-4 | 1-1 | 3-2 | 3-1 | 4-2 | 3-1 | 3-0 | 2-1 | 3-0 | 3-0 |
| SC VEENDAM | 2-2 | 1-1 | 1-3 | 1-3 | 0-2 | 2-3 | 1-1 | 0-4 | | 0-0 | 3-1 | 2-3 | 1-1 | 1-1 | 1-2 | 0-0 | 0-3 | 1-1 | 4-2 | 5-1 |
| GO AHEAD EAGLES | 2-1 | 1-1 | 0-0 | 1-2 | 4-1 | 2-0 | 1-0 | 1-1 | 2-2 | | 3-1 | 2-0 | 2-0 | 0-0 | 5-1 | 4-2 | 1-1 | 1-1 | 0-1 | 1-0 |
| FC WAGENINGEN | 0-1 | 3-0 | 4-4 | 0-2 | 0-1 | 0-0 | 2-3 | 1-3 | 1-1 | 4-1 | | 6-1 | 3-3 | 3-0 | 4-2 | 2-1 | 0-0 | 0-1 | 0-3 | 6-2 |
| CAMBUUR/LEEUW'DN. | 3-1 | 3-0 | 1-2 | 2-0 | 0-0 | 1-1 | 1-0 | 0-0 | 0-0 | 1-0 | 1-1 | | 0-1 | 3-1 | 1-0 | 1-0 | 1-1 | 1-1 | 2-2 | 3-3 |
| AZ | 0-0 | 0-3 | 4-1 | 1-1 | 1-0 | 1-1 | 2-1 | 0-0 | 3-1 | 2-4 | 3-1 | 2-1 | | 0-0 | 3-0 | 4-1 | 2-2 | 0-1 | 1-0 | 6-1 |
| HELMOND SPORT | 2-1 | 5-1 | 2-2 | 0-0 | 1-2 | 2-0 | 0-0 | 0-0 | 2-3 | 3-3 | 3-1 | 2-0 | 1-0 | | 0-0 | 4-2 | 1-1 | 2-2 | 3-0 | 3-1 |
| EXCELSIOR | 2-2 | 2-4 | 0-4 | 1-4 | 3-0 | 1-4 | 1-1 | 0-2 | 5-1 | 0-0 | 2-2 | 0-2 | 0-1 | 0-1 | | 0-0 | 5-1 | 2-2 | 0-2 | 4-2 |
| FC ZWOLLE | 1-1 | 2-0 | 1-1 | 0-4 | 1-2 | 0-1 | 5-0 | 0-1 | 1-2 | 2-1 | 1-1 | 1-0 | 0-0 | 1-1 | 0-2 | | 2-1 | 1-0 | 2-2 | 0-0 |
| RBC | 2-1 | 2-3 | 1-1 | 2-2 | 0-0 | 6-1 | 1-2 | 2-3 | 2-2 | 1-0 | 5-1 | 4-0 | 0-1 | 1-1 | 3-1 | 2-2 | | 4-4 | 2-2 | 2-0 |
| TELSTAR | 0-3 | 4-1 | 1-2 | 3-3 | 2-0 | 0-1 | 2-2 | 1-3 | 2-0 | 0-2 | 2-3 | 0-0 | 1-1 | 0-4 | 3-1 | 0-0 | 1-1 | | 4-1 | 2-0 |
| DORDRECHT 90 | 2-2 | 2-3 | 2-2 | 1-1 | 6-2 | 3-3 | 1-1 | 2-2 | 1-1 | 2-1 | 3-0 | 1-0 | 0-0 | 2-0 | 5-1 | 2-0 | 0-3 | 2-0 | | 1-0 |
| VC VLISSINGEN | 1-0 | 2-0 | 0-4 | 0-2 | 0-3 | 2-4 | 0-2 | 0-4 | 3-2 | 2-2 | 5-2 | 0-0 | 0-0 | 1-4 | 0-3 | 0-3 | 2-0 | 2-1 | 0-3 | |

## PROMOTION PLAY-OFFS

### GROUP A

| NAC | 2 | FC Zwolle | 0 |
|---|---|---|---|
| AZ | 1 | NAC | 1 |
| FC Zwolle | 2 | AZ | 2 |
| AZ | 1 | FC Zwolle | 2 |
| FC Zwolle | 1 | NAC | 1 |
| NAC | 4 | AZ | 1 |

**LEAGUE TABLE FINAL**

| NAC | 4 | 2 | 2 | 0 | 8 | 3 | 6 |
|---|---|---|---|---|---|---|---|
| FC Zwolle | 4 | 1 | 2 | 1 | 5 | 6 | 4 |
| AZ | 4 | 0 | 2 | 2 | 5 | 9 | 2 |

### GROUP B

| VVV | 1 | Eindhoven | 1 |
|---|---|---|---|
| Eindhoven | 2 | Dordrecht 90 | 0 |
| Dordrecht 90 | 1 | VVV | 1 |
| VVV | 2 | Dordrecht 90 | 0 |
| Eindhoven | 1 | VVV | 2 |
| Dordrecht 90 | 3 | Eindhoven | 1 |

**LEAGUE TABLE FINAL**

| VVV | 4 | 2 | 2 | 0 | 6 | 3 | 6 |
|---|---|---|---|---|---|---|---|
| Eindhoven | 4 | 1 | 1 | 2 | 5 | 6 | 3 |
| Dordrecht 90 | 4 | 1 | 1 | 2 | 4 | 6 | 3 |

### PLAY-OFF FINAL

VVV (Venlo) v NAC (Breda)
VVV win on the away goals rule

| 1ST LEG | 2ND LEG | AGG. |
|---|---|---|
| 1-0 | 1-2 | 2-2 |

Promoted : - De Graafschap and VVV

# HOLLAND SATURDAY AMAT. 1990/91

## EERSTE KLASSE A
### LEAGUE TABLE FINAL

| Team | P | W | D | L | F | A | Pts |
|---|---|---|---|---|---|---|---|
| Quick Boys (Kat. aan Zee) | 26 | 20 | 4 | 2 | 68 | 22 | 44 |
| Katwijk (Katwijk aan Zee) | 26 | 12 | 11 | 3 | 41 | 22 | 35 |
| IJsselmeervogels (Sp'burg) | 26 | 12 | 9 | 5 | 49 | 32 | 33 |
| Noordwijk (Noordwijk) | 26 | 12 | 7 | 7 | 41 | 28 | 31 |
| DOSK (Kampen) | 26 | 9 | 9 | 8 | 40 | 38 | 27 |
| Rijnsburgse Boys (Rijnsb.) | 26 | 9 | 6 | 11 | 45 | 53 | 24 |
| VVOG (Harderwijk) | 26 | 9 | 6 | 11 | 39 | 50 | 24 |
| ARC (Alphen a/d Rijn) | 26 | 8 | 6 | 12 | 51 | 45 | 22 |
| FC Lisse (Lisse) | 26 | 8 | 6 | 12 | 41 | 45 | 22 |
| Urk (Urk) | 26 | 6 | 10 | 10 | 33 | 48 | 22 |
| Flevo Boys (Emmeloord) | 26 | 7 | 7 | 12 | 31 | 45 | 21 |
| Go Ahead K (Kampen) | 26 | 8 | 5 | 13 | 32 | 53 | 21 |
| Sparta N (Nijkerk) | 26 | 5 | 10 | 11 | 38 | 52 | 20 |
| Bennekom (Bennekom) | 26 | 4 | 10 | 12 | 35 | 51 | 18 |

### PLAY-OFF
Flevo Boys ...........5    Go Ahead K............1

## EERSTE KLASSE B
### LEAGUE TABLE FINAL

| Team | P | W | D | L | F | A | Pts |
|---|---|---|---|---|---|---|---|
| Excelsior M (Maassluis) | 26 | 18 | 6 | 2 | 62 | 27 | 42 |
| Rozenburg (Rozenburg) | 26 | 11 | 11 | 4 | 47 | 28 | 33 |
| Spijkenisse (Spijkenisse) | 26 | 11 | 9 | 6 | 45 | 33 | 31 |
| Vitesse D (Delft) | 26 | 10 | 9 | 7 | 44 | 36 | 29 |
| Huizen (Huizen) | 26 | 10 | 9 | 7 | 40 | 34 | 29 |
| Heerjandsam (Heerjands.) | 26 | 11 | 6 | 9 | 52 | 45 | 28 |
| Marken (Marken) | 26 | 11 | 5 | 10 | 38 | 32 | 27 |
| Barendrecht (Barendrecht) | 26 | 10 | 7 | 9 | 53 | 38 | 27 |
| NSVV (Numansdorp) | 26 | 7 | 12 | 7 | 42 | 39 | 26 |
| Altena (Nieuwendijk) | 26 | 7 | 9 | 10 | 35 | 35 | 23 |
| Serooskerke (Serooskerke) | 26 | 7 | 8 | 11 | 29 | 36 | 22 |
| ASWH (Hend. Ido Am'cht) | 26 | 7 | 6 | 13 | 35 | 42 | 20 |
| Excelsior P (Pernis) | 26 | 4 | 9 | 13 | 27 | 51 | 17 |
| DSVP (Pijnacker) | 26 | 3 | 4 | 19 | 21 | 67 | 10 |

# HOLLAND SUNDAY AMAT. 1990/91

## HOOFDKLASSE A
### LEAGUE TABLE FINAL

| Team | P | W | D | L | F | A | Pts |
|---|---|---|---|---|---|---|---|
| Elinkwijk (Utrecht) | 26 | 16 | 3 | 7 | 52 | 30 | 35 |
| Aalsmeer (Aalsmeer) | 26 | 11 | 9 | 6 | 36 | 22 | 31 |
| ADO 20 (Heemskerk) | 26 | 11 | 8 | 7 | 47 | 33 | 30 |
| Hollandia (Hoorn) | 26 | 11 | 7 | 8 | 39 | 25 | 29 |
| RCH (Heemstede) | 26 | 10 | 7 | 9 | 44 | 39 | 27 |
| Wilhelmus (Voorburg) | 26 | 8 | 10 | 8 | 32 | 36 | 26 |
| DWV (Amsterdam) | 26 | 9 | 8 | 9 | 28 | 32 | 26 |
| DHC (Delft) | 26 | 8 | 10 | 8 | 32 | 42 | 26 |
| AFC (Amsterdam) | 26 | 8 | 9 | 9 | 41 | 36 | 25 |
| DCV (Krimpen a/d IJssel) | 26 | 9 | 7 | 10 | 31 | 37 | 25 |
| Papendrecht (Papendr.) | 26 | 6 | 12 | 8 | 23 | 31 | 24 |
| UVS (Leiden) | 26 | 6 | 10 | 10 | 30 | 33 | 22 |
| Blauw Wit (Amsterdam) | 26 | 6 | 8 | 12 | 33 | 53 | 20 |
| WFC (Wormerveer) | 26 | 5 | 8 | 13 | 38 | 57 | 18 |

Relegated :- UVS, Blauw Wit and WFC.

Promoted :- Stormvogels (IJmuiden), EDO (Haarlem) and Alphense Boys (Alphen a/d Rijn).

## HOOFDKLASSE B
### LEAGUE TABLE FINAL

| Team | P | W | D | L | F | A | Pts |
|---|---|---|---|---|---|---|---|
| De Treffers (Groesbeek) | 26 | 19 | 2 | 5 | 61 | 32 | 40 |
| Babberich (Babberich) | 26 | 16 | 5 | 5 | 44 | 21 | 37 |
| Rheden (Rheden) | 26 | 12 | 6 | 8 | 36 | 27 | 30 |
| Quick 20 (Oldenzaal) | 26 | 10 | 10 | 6 | 35 | 27 | 30 |
| AGOVV (Apeldoorn) | 26 | 9 | 8 | 9 | 41 | 37 | 26 |
| Stevo (Geesteren) | 26 | 10 | 6 | 10 | 38 | 41 | 26 |
| Achilles 94 (Assen) | 26 | 8 | 9 | 9 | 40 | 38 | 25 |
| Achilles 29 (Groesbeek) | 26 | 8 | 9 | 9 | 33 | 36 | 25 |
| SC Enschede (Enschede) | 26 | 10 | 5 | 11 | 32 | 43 | 25 |
| SVBO (Barger Oosterveld) | 26 | 9 | 6 | 11 | 32 | 30 | 24 |
| FVC (Huizum) | 26 | 8 | 8 | 10 | 42 | 45 | 24 |
| Hoogeveen (Hoogeveen) | 26 | 7 | 8 | 11 | 26 | 32 | 22 |
| De Zweef (Nijverdal) | 26 | 6 | 5 | 15 | 25 | 46 | 17 |
| Germanicus (Coevorden) | 26 | 3 | 7 | 16 | 24 | 52 | 13 |

Relegated :- Hoogeveen, De Zweef and Germanicus.

Promoted :- WKE (Emmen), Sneek/Hovis (Sneek) & HSC 21 (Haaksbergen).

## EERSTE KLASSE C
### LEAGUE TABLE FINAL

| Team | P | W | D | L | F | A | Pts |
|---|---|---|---|---|---|---|---|
| DOVO (Veenendaal) | 26 | 16 | 4 | 6 | 59 | 28 | 36 |
| GVVV (Veenendaal) | 26 | 15 | 6 | 5 | 50 | 24 | 36 |
| Spakenburg (Spakenburg) | 26 | 13 | 9 | 4 | 57 | 33 | 35 |
| ACV (Assen) | 26 | 13 | 6 | 7 | 53 | 28 | 32 |
| WHC (Wezep) | 26 | 11 | 7 | 8 | 48 | 34 | 29 |
| SC Genemuiden (G'muiden) | 26 | 11 | 7 | 8 | 58 | 46 | 29 |
| Drachtster Boys (Drachten) | 26 | 10 | 8 | 8 | 50 | 42 | 28 |
| De Vallevogels (Scherpen.) | 26 | 12 | 3 | 11 | 43 | 35 | 27 |
| Oranje Nassau (Groningen) | 26 | 8 | 9 | 9 | 35 | 34 | 25 |
| Lunteren (Lunteren) | 26 | 10 | 5 | 11 | 42 | 56 | 25 |
| DETO (Vriezenveen) | 26 | 7 | 8 | 11 | 36 | 50 | 22 |
| Be Quick 28 (Zwolle) | 26 | 6 | 9 | 11 | 26 | 47 | 21 |
| WVF (Zwolle) | 26 | 2 | 6 | 18 | 17 | 70 | 10 |
| SC Elim (Elim) | 26 | 2 | 5 | 19 | 17 | 64 | 9 |

### CHAMPIONSHIP PLAY-OFF
GVVV v DOVO

| | RESULT | REPLAY |
|---|---|---|
| | 1-1 (aet) | 1-2 |

## HOOFDKLASSE C
### LEAGUE TABLE FINAL

| Team | P | W | D | L | F | A | Pts |
|---|---|---|---|---|---|---|---|
| TOP (Oss) | 26 | 16 | 9 | 1 | 54 | 16 | 41 |
| SV Meerssen (Meerssen) | 26 | 12 | 11 | 3 | 41 | 24 | 35 |
| Venray (Venray) | 26 | 12 | 8 | 6 | 48 | 34 | 32 |
| Geldrop (Geldrop) | 26 | 12 | 7 | 7 | 46 | 36 | 31 |
| EHC (Hoensbroek) | 26 | 8 | 14 | 4 | 49 | 31 | 30 |
| TSC (Oosterhout) | 26 | 11 | 6 | 9 | 43 | 28 | 28 |
| De Baronie (Breda) | 26 | 9 | 9 | 8 | 28 | 32 | 27 |
| Panningen (Panningen) | 26 | 9 | 8 | 9 | 33 | 38 | 26 |
| DESK (Kaatsheuvel) | 26 | 8 | 8 | 10 | 44 | 36 | 24 |
| LONGA (Tilburg) | 26 | 7 | 10 | 9 | 43 | 48 | 24 |
| BVV (Den Bosch) | 26 | 8 | 8 | 10 | 31 | 37 | 24 |
| Volharding (Vierlingsbeek) | 26 | 5 | 9 | 12 | 43 | 63 | 19 |
| Wilhelmina (Den Bosch) | 26 | 1 | 5 | 20 | 13 | 69 | 7 |

## CHAMPIONSHIP PLAY-OFF FINALS

| | | | | |
|---|---|---|---|---|
| Quick Boys | ...2 | Excelsior M | ...2 | |
| DOVO | ...3 | Excelsior M | ...3 | |
| DOVO | ...2 | Quick Boys | ...3 | |
| Excelsior M | ...1 | DOVO | ...2 | |
| Excelsior M | ...3 | Quick Boys | ...2 | |
| Quick Boys | ...2 | DOVO | ...0 | |

### LEAGUE TABLE FINAL

| Team | P | W | D | L | F | A | Pts |
|---|---|---|---|---|---|---|---|
| Quick Boys | 4 | 2 | 1 | 1 | 9 | 7 | 5 |
| Excelsior M | 4 | 1 | 2 | 1 | 9 | 9 | 4 |
| DOVO | 4 | 1 | 1 | 2 | 7 | 9 | 3 |

Relegated :- Go Ahead K, Sparta N, Bennekom, Excelsior P, DSVP, WVF and SC Elim.

Promoted :- Zwart Wit 28 (Rotterdam), Kozakken Boys (Werkendam), Scheveningen (Scheveningen), SDVB (Barneveld), DVS 33 (Ermelo), IJVV (IJsselmuiden) and Broekster Boys (Damwoude).

## CHAMPIONSHIP PLAY-OFFS

| | | | | |
|---|---|---|---|---|
| Elinkwijk | ...1 | TOP | ...0 | |
| De Treffers | ...3 | Elinkwijk | ...1 | |
| TOP | ...3 | De Treffers | ...1 | |
| TOP | ...0 | Elinkwijk | ...0 | |
| Elinkwijk | ...3 | De Treffers | ...2 | |
| De Treffers | ...3 | TOP | ...1 | |

### LEAGUE TABLE FINAL

| Team | P | W | D | L | F | A | Pts |
|---|---|---|---|---|---|---|---|
| De Treffers | 4 | 2 | 1 | 1 | 8 | 7 | 5 |
| Elinkwijk | 4 | 1 | 2 | 1 | 4 | 4 | 4 |
| TOP | 4 | 1 | 1 | 2 | 4 | 5 | 3 |

TOP admitted to Eerste Divisie.

Relegated :- BVV, Volharding and Wilhelmina.

Promoted :- UDI 19 (Uden), Magriet (Oss), SVN (Nieuwenhagen) and Wilhelmina 08 (Weert).

## AMATEUR CHAMPIONSHIP OF HOLLAND

De Treffers v Quick Boys

| | 1ST LEG | 2ND LEG | AGG. |
|---|---|---|---|
| | 5-1 | 4-3 | 9-4 |

# HOLLAND KNVB BEKER 1990/91

## 1ST ROUND

| | | | |
|---|---|---|---|
| De Treffers | 2 | Willem II | 3 |
| ACV | 0 | Sparta | 4 |
| SC Enschede | 0 | NEC | 2 |
| LONGA | 0 | FC Utrecht | 2 |
| VVOG | 0 | Wageningen | 3 |
| NSVV | 2 | SC Heracles | 2 (aet) |
| SC Heracles win 2-4 on penalties | | | |
| SC Genemuiden | 2 | De Graatschap | 3 (aet) |
| Quick Boys | 5 | Helmond Sport | 2 |
| De Valleivogels | 3 | Vlissingen | 5 (aet) |
| Achilles 94 | 2 | RBC | 1 |
| DWV | 1 | Telstar | 2 |
| AFC | 0 | Cambuur/Leeuw | 1 |
| Halsteren | 2 | Go Ahead Eagles | 2 |
| Spartaan 20 | 0 | Eindhoven | 4 |

| | | | |
|---|---|---|---|
| Bennekom | 0 | MVV | 6 |
| Geldrop | 3 | SC Heerenveen | 2 |
| Concordia SVD | 0 | SVV | 4 |
| Rijnsburgse Boys | 3 | Ajax | 3 |
| Spijkenisse | 1 | SC Veendam | 4 |
| Vitesse Delft | 0 | VVV | 4 |
| Dordrecht 90 | 4 | PSV | 8 |
| NAC | 5 | Roda JC | |
| Noordwijk | 1 | FC Zwolle | 1 (aet) |
| Oranje Nassau | 0 | Excelsior | 3 |
| Babberich | 2 | BVV Den Bosch | 4 (aet) |
| Elinkwijk | 4 | AZ | 3 |
| DCV | 1 | Haarlem | 3 |
| TSC | 0 | SV Meersen | 2 |
| Hoogeveen | 1 | Emmen | 3 |
| Vitesse (Reserves) | 1 | BVV Den Bosch | 2 (aet) |

## SUPPLEMENTARY ROUND

| | | | |
|---|---|---|---|
| Quick Boys | 1 | NEC | 2 |
| Cambuur/Leeuw | 1 | Go Ahead Eagles | 2 |
| Rijnsburgse Boys | 0 | Dordrecht 90 | 2 |
| Eindhoven | 1 | Wageningen | 3 (aet) |

## 2ND ROUND

| | | | |
|---|---|---|---|
| SC Heracles | 0 | Feyenoord | 1 |
| Dordrecht 90 | 1 | FC Twente | 0 |
| NAC | 1 | RKC | 0 |
| VVV | 0 | FC Utrecht | 1 |
| Vlissingen | 1 | FC Groningen | 3 |
| Go Ahead Eagles | 2 | Vitesse | 3 |
| Sparta | 1 | Volendam | 0 |

| | | | |
|---|---|---|---|
| Emmen | 0 | Roda JC | 4 |
| PSV | 2 | FC Zwolle | 1 |
| SVV | 2 | Fortuna Sittard | 1 |
| NEC | 1 | Wageningen | 2 |
| Excelsior | 0 | Ajax | 5 |
| FC Den Haag | 5 | Haarlem | 3 |
| Elinkwijk | 1 | Willem II | 3 (aet) |

| | | | |
|---|---|---|---|
| SV Meersen | 2 | De Graafschap | 2 (aet) |
| De Graafschap win 4-5 on penalties. | | | |
| Geldrop | 1 | BVV Den Bosch | 4 |

## 3RD ROUND

| | | | |
|---|---|---|---|
| Roda JC | 2 | FC Utrecht | 1 |
| Ajax | 3 | FC Groningen | 1 |
| SC Veendam | 2 | Feyenoord | 2 |
| BVV Den Bosch | 4 | Sparta | 0 |
| PSV | 8 | Wageningen | 1 |
| De Graafschap | 1 | Dordrecht 90 | 1 (aet) |
| Dordrecht 90 win 3-4 on penalties. | | | |
| Vitesse | 3 | FC Den Haag | 1 |
| Willem II | 5 | SVV | 0 |

## 1/4 FINALS

| | | | |
|---|---|---|---|
| Roda JC | 1 | Ajax | 0 |
| BVV Den Bosch | 2 | Vitesse | 0 (aet) |
| Willem II | 1 | Feyenoord | 2 |
| Dordrecht 90 | 1 | PSV | 3 (aet) |

## SEMI-FINALS

| | | | |
|---|---|---|---|
| BVV Den Bosch | 2 | Roda JC | 2 (aet) |
| BVV Den Bosch win 4-2 on penalties. | | | |
| PSV | 0 | Feyenoord | 1 |

## FINAL   2/6/91 (At Feyenoord Stadium, Rotterdam)

| | | | |
|---|---|---|---|
| Feyenoord | 1 | BVV Den Bosch | 0 |

1-0 Witschge 8    Referee : J.Blankenstein    Attendance : 52000

Blinker.

Den Bosch : Van Grinsven, Bults, Meulendijk, Van Eck, Laponder, Brocken, Jan Gösgens (Derksen 78), Van Der Borgt, Nijhuis (Netten 46).

Feyenoord : De Goeij, Van Gobbel, Metgod, De Wolf, Fräser, Scholten, Sabau, Rob Witschge, Taument, Kiprich (Griga 74), Van Schijndel, De Gier.

The final stages of the match were marred by the encroachment of spectators on the field of play. BVV Den Bosch took the Dutch FA to court after they had declared themselves responsible for the lack of organisation around the match. The court ruled that the second half of the match should be replayed behind closed doors, however, this decision was reversed on appeal and the result allowed to stand.

Holland's 1990 World Cup team

# HOLLAND INTERNATIONAL REVIEW 1990

## INTERNATIONAL LINE-UPS 1990

| Date | Match | Venue / Comp | Hans van Breukelen | Frank Rijkaard | Ronald Koeman | Adri van Tiggelen | Berry van Aerle | Gerald Vanenburg | Jan Wouters | Erwin Koeman | Richard Witschge | Johnny Bosman | Marco van Basten | Edward Sturing | Wim Kieft | Graeme Rutjes | Henk Fraser | Johnny van 't Schip | Marcel Peeper | Martin Laamers | René Eykelkamp | John van Loen | Ruud Gullit | Brian Roy | Danny Blind | Hans Gillhaus | Aron Winter | Stan Valckx | Frank de Boer | Dennis Bergkamp | Jerry de Jong | John van den Brom |
|---|---|---|---|---|---|---|---|---|---|---|---|---|---|---|---|---|---|---|---|---|---|---|---|---|---|---|---|---|---|---|---|---|
| 21/2/90 | HOLLAND 0 ITALY 0 — Ref: Biguet (France) | Rotterdam — Friendly | 1 | 2 | 3 | 4 | 5 | 6 | 7 | 8 | 9 | 10 | 11 | (2) | (11) | | | | | | | | | | | | | | | | | |
| 28/3/90 | USSR 2 HOLLAND 1 (R.Koeman) — Ref: Puhl (Hungary) | Kiev — Friendly | 1 | | 3 | | | | 7 | | 8 | 10 | | 2 | 11 | 4 | 5 | 6 | 9 | (6) | (9) | (10) | | | | | | | | | | |
| 30/5/90 | AUSTRIA 3 HOLLAND 2 (R.Koeman, van Basten) — Ref: Rössner (DDR) | Wien — Friendly | 1 | 4 | 3 | 5 | 2 | 6 | 7 | 8 | 9 | | 10 | | (11) | | | | | | | | 11 | (8) | | | | | | | | |
| 3/6/90 | YUGOSLAVIA 0 HOLLAND 2 (Rijkaard, van Basten) — Ref: Kaupe (Austria) | Zagreb — Friendly | 1 | 6 | 2 | 4 | 5 | | 7 | 9 | (9) | | 10 | | 11 | | | | | | | | 8 | | (5) | | | | | | | |
| 12/6/90 | EGYPT 1 HOLLAND 1 (Kieft) — Ref: Aladren (Spain) | Palermo — World Cup | 1 | 4 | 3 | 5 | 2 | | 6 | 9 | 8 | | 10 | | (6) | | | | | | | | 11 | | | | | | | | | |
| 16/6/90 | ENGLAND 0 HOLLAND 0 — Ref: Petrovic (Yugoslavia) | Cagliari — World Cup | 1 | 4 | 3 | 5 | 2 | | 7 | 9 | 8 | | 10 | | (9) | | (8) | | | | | | 6 | | | 11 | | | | | | |
| 21/6/90 | REPUBLIC OF IRELAND 1 HOLLAND 1 (Gullit) — Ref: Vautrot (France) | Palermo — World Cup | 1 | 4 | 3 | 5 | 2 | | 7 | | 8 | | 9 | | 10 | | | | | | | (10) | 6 | | | 11 | | | | | | |
| 24/6/90 | WESTERN GERMANY 2 HOLLAND 1 (R.Koeman) — Ref: Loustau (Argentina) | Milano — World Cup | 1 | 4 | 3 | | | (11) | 7 | | 8 | | 11 | | (2) | | | 5 | | | | | 10 | | | (8) | 6 | | | | | |
| 26/9/90 | ITALY 1 HOLLAND 0 — Ref: Petrovic (Yugoslavia) | Palermo — Friendly | 1 | | 3 | | | | 6 | | 8 | | 10 | | | (3) | | | | | | | 7 | | 5 | 11 | (9) | | | | | |
| 17/10/90 | PORTUGAL 1 HOLLAND 0 — Ref: Kirschen (DDR) | Porto — EuroCh.Q. | 1 | | | 3 | | 7 | 6 | | 7 | | 9 | | | 5 | | (3) | | | | | 10 | 11 | 5 | | (6) | 4 | | | | |
| 21/11/90 | HOLLAND 2 GREECE 0 (Bergkamp, van Basten) — Ref: Nemeth (Hungary) | Rotterdam — EuroCh.Q. | 1 | | 3 | 3 | | 5 | 4 | 4 | | | 9 | | | 2 | | 8 | | | | | | 11 | 2 | | (6) | 2 | 5 | 9 | 4 | |
| 19/12/90 | MALTA 0 HOLLAND 8 (van Basten 5, Winter, Bergkamp 2) — Ref: Blattmann (Switzerland) | Ta'Qali — EuroCh.Q. | 1 | | | | | | 4 | 6 | 7 | | 9 | | | | | 7 | | | | | 10 | 4 | | 9 | (9) | | | 8 | 3 | (10) |
| **CAPS AT 31/12/90** | | | 60 | 46 | 48 | 45 | 26 | 40 | 37 | 25 | 11 | 22 | 43 | 3 | 31 | 11 | 4 | 26 | 1 | 2 | 4 | 7 | 51 | 4 | 9 | 7 | 15 | 2 | 3 | 4 | 2 | 1 |
| **GOALS AT 31/12/90** | | | | 3 | 10 | | | 1 | 3 | | | 13 | 21 | | 10 | | | | | | | | 14 | | | 2 | 1 | | | 3 | 2 | |

## HOLLAND : All Time Records as at 31/12/90 - CAPS

1. Ruud Krol (Ajax/Vancouver Whitecaps/SSC Napoli) — 83
2. Wim Jansen (Feyenoord) — 65
3. Puck van Heel (Feyenoord) — 64
4. Willy van de Kerkhof (PSV) — 63
5. Wim Suurbier (Ajax/FC Metz/FC Schalke 04) — 60
   Hans van Breukelen (FC Utrecht/Nottingham Forest/PSV) — 60
7. Jan Klaassens (VVV/Feijenoord) — 57
8. Harry Denis (HBS) — 56
9. Gejus van der Meulen (HFC) — 54
10. Roel Wiersma (Donar/PSV) — 53

## HOLLAND : All Time Records as at 31/12/90 - GOALS

1. Faas Wilkes (Xerxes/Valencia CF/VVV/Fortuna 54) — (38) 35
2. Abe Lenstra (Heerenveen/SC Enschede) — (47) 33
   Johan Cruijff (Ajax/CF Barcelona) — (48) 33
4. Bep Bakhuys (ZAC/HBS) — (23) 28
5. Kick Smit (Haarlem) — (29) 26
6. Marco van Basten (Ajax/Milan AC) — (43) 21
7. Leen Vente (Neptunus/Feijenoord) — (21) 19
8. Mannes Francken (HFC) — (22) 17
   Tonny van der Linden (DOS) — (24) 17
   Wim Tap (ADO) — (33) 17
   Johan Neeskens (Ajax/CF Barcelona/New York Cosmos) — (49) 17

# HUNGARY Correspondent : PETER TÖRÖK

| HUNGARY 1st Division Season 1990/91 | U DÓZSA | MTK-VM | FTC | PÉCS | TATABÁNYA | VESZPRÉM | SIÓFOK | VASAS | VIDEOTON | BÉKÉSCSABA | VÁC | RÁBA ETO | HONVÉD | DEBRECEN | SZEGED | VOLÁN |
|---|---|---|---|---|---|---|---|---|---|---|---|---|---|---|---|---|
| UJPESTI DÓZSA SC | ■ | 3-2 | 0-5 | 2-1 | 0-1 | 1-0 | 1-1 | 1-0 | 2-0 | 1-0 | 0-2 | 2-2 | 1-2 | 1-0 | 1-0 | 3-1 |
| MTK-VM SK | 2-1 | ■ | 1-0 | 1-2 | 0-1 | 0-1 | 2-0 | 1-2 | 1-0 | 1-1 | 1-2 | 2-1 | 2-4 | 1-0 | 2-0 | 3-0 |
| FERENCVÁROSI TC | 1-0 | 4-0 | ■ | 1-0 | 1-2 | 2-2 | 1-0 | 1-0 | 4-0 | 4-0 | 0-0 | 1-2 | 1-1 | 3-2 | 3-1 | 1-0 |
| PÉCSI MSC | 1-0 | 2-2 | 1-1 | ■ | 1-0 | 0-0 | 2-1 | 1-0 | 2-0 | 0-2 | 0-0 | 3-0 | 2-1 | 1-0 | 1-0 | 1-0 |
| TATABÁNYA BÁNYÁSZ SC | 3-1 | 1-1 | 0-0 | 2-1 | ■ | 3-3 | 0-2 | 2-4 | 0-0 | 2-1 | 2-0 | 4-0 | 0-0 | 3-1 | 1-0 | 2-1 |
| VESZPRÉMI SE | 2-2 | 1-0 | 2-1 | 1-0 | 1-1 | ■ | 4-0 | 0-1 | 2-2 | 3-0 | 1-0 | 0-1 | 0-0 | 0-1 | 0-0 | 4-3 |
| SIÓFOKI BÁNYÁSZ SE | 3-0 | 0-0 | 0-0 | 1-0 | 1-1 | 0-0 | ■ | 1-2 | 3-2 | 0-0 | 1-0 | 2-1 | 1-0 | 2-1 | 0-0 | 0-0 |
| VASAS SC | 2-5 | 0-2 | 2-3 | 1-1 | 1-2 | 0-1 | 3-0 | ■ | 1-1 | 1-0 | 1-2 | 2-1 | 1-1 | 0-0 | 1-1 | 2-4 |
| VIDEOTON-WALTHAM SC | 3-0 | 3-0 | 1-1 | 0-0 | 2-1 | 1-0 | 3-1 | 1-1 | ■ | 3-0 | 0-2 | 1-1 | 1-3 | 3-2 | 1-0 | 4-1 |
| BÉKÉSCSABAI ESSC | 3-1 | 0-0 | 1-1 | 0-1 | 1-0 | 2-0 | 2-1 | 0-1 | 2-4 | ■ | 0-1 | 1-1 | 0-2 | 3-0 | 1-2 | 0-1 |
| VÁCI IZZÓ MTE | 0-2 | 3-2 | 1-1 | 1-4 | 1-0 | 0-0 | 0-0 | 2-0 | 2-2 | 0-0 | ■ | 2-1 | 2-3 | 2-1 | 1-0 | 3-1 |
| RÁBA ETO | 0-1 | 3-1 | 0-1 | 2-1 | 1-1 | 0-1 | 0-0 | 4-0 | 3-0 | 0-0 | 1-1 | ■ | 1-1 | 1-1 | 2-1 | 1-1 |
| BUDAPESTI HONVÉD SE | 1-0 | 2-1 | 2-1 | 1-0 | 1-0 | 1-1 | 0-1 | 1-1 | 2-0 | 3-0 | 3-0 | 1-2 | ■ | 1-0 | 1-0 | 4-0 |
| DEBRECENI VSC | 0-0 | 1-7 | 0-2 | 0-0 | 0-0 | 2-2 | 1-1 | 1-0 | 3-0 | 2-1 | 1-2 | 2-0 | 0-1 | ■ | 3-1 | 2-0 |
| SZEGED SC | 0-4 | 0-0 | 0-1 | 0-2 | 4-2 | 0-2 | 2-0 | 2-1 | 1-0 | 2-1 | 1-0 | 4-1 | 1-3 | 0-0 | ■ | 1-0 |
| BUDAPEST VOLÁN SC | 1-0 | 1-0 | 1-1 | 0-1 | 2-0 | 1-0 | 0-2 | 1-1 | 0-1 | 1-2 | 0-3 | 3-2 | 0-4 | 2-0 | 2-2 | ■ |

**TOP SCORERS**
1. József Gregor (Honvéd) — 15
2. Pál Fischer (Ferencváros) — 12
3. Dénes Váczi (Tatabánya) — 11
4. Attila Belansky (Pecs) — 10
5. Antal Füle (Vác) — 9
   Péter Galaschek (Vasas) — 9
   István Sallói (Videoton) — 9
   Ferenc Simon (Tatabánya) — 9
9. Tibor Csehi (Honvéd) — 8
   László Répási (Vác) — 8
   Zoltán Takács (Szeged) — 8

**NAME CHANGES DURING SEASON**
Veszprémi SE to Veszprémi FC (Sep)
Békéscsabai Elore Spartacus SC to Békéscsabai Elore FC (Nov.)
Raba Vasas Eto Gyór to Gyóri Raba ETO (Nov.)
Ujpesti Dózsa SC to Ujpesti TE (Feb)
Budapesti Volán SC to Volán FC (Feb)

**CHANGES FOR SEASON 1991/92**
Budapesti Honvéd SE to Kispesti Honvéd FC
Volán FC taken over by Gánz Danubius SE.
Debreceni MTE taken over by Budafok MTE-Törley
Paksi SE declined promotion from 3rd Division for financial reasons, similarly, Komló chose relegation to 3rd Division allowing Szolnoki MÁV-MTE to retain 2nd Division status. Metripond SE no longer exist.

## HUNGARY 1ST DIVISION 1990/91

**LEAGUE TABLE FINAL**

| | | | | | | | |
|---|---|---|---|---|---|---|---|
| Budapesti Honvéd SE | 30 | 19 | 7 | 4 | 50 | 20 | 45 |
| Ferencvárosi TC | 30 | 15 | 10 | 5 | 47 | 22 | 40 |
| Pécsi MSC | 30 | 15 | 7 | 8 | 32 | 20 | 37 |
| Váci Izzó MTE | 30 | 14 | 8 | 8 | 35 | 29 | 36 |
| Veszprémi FC | 30 | 11 | 12 | 7 | 34 | 25 | 34 |
| Tatabányai Bányász SC | 30 | 12 | 9 | 9 | 37 | 32 | 33 |
| Siófoki Bányász SE | 30 | 10 | 11 | 9 | 25 | 28 | 31 |
| Videoton-Waltham SC | 30 | 11 | 8 | 11 | 39 | 41 | 30 |
| Ujpesti TE | 30 | 13 | 4 | 13 | 36 | 39 | 30 |
| MTK-VM SK | 30 | 10 | 6 | 14 | 38 | 39 | 26 |
| Gyóri Raba ETO | 30 | 8 | 10 | 12 | 35 | 41 | 26 |
| Vasas SC | 30 | 8 | 8 | 14 | 32 | 43 | 24 |
| Szeged SC | 30 | 9 | 6 | 15 | 26 | 37 | 24 |
| Debreceni VSC | 30 | 7 | 8 | 15 | 27 | 40 | 22 |
| Békéscsabai Elore FC | 30 | 7 | 7 | 16 | 24 | 39 | 21 |
| Volán FC | 30 | 8 | 5 | 17 | 28 | 50 | 21 |

Champions : - Budapesti Honvéd SE
Relegated : - Szeged SC, Debreceni VSC, Békéscsabai EFC and Volán FC

**PROMOTION/RELEGATION PLAY-OFFS**

| | 1ST LEG | 2ND LEG | AGG. |
|---|---|---|---|
| Szeged SC v Diósgyóri VTK | 1-2 | 1-1 | 2-3 |
| Zalaegerszegi TE v Debreceni VSC | 2-1 | 1-1 | 3-2 |

## HUNGARY 2ND DIV. WEST 1990/91

**LEAGUE TABLE FINAL**

| | | | | | | | |
|---|---|---|---|---|---|---|---|
| Haladás VSE | 30 | 18 | 7 | 5 | 58 | 26 | 43 |
| Zalaegerszegi TE | 30 | 17 | 8 | 5 | 53 | 26 | 42 |
| Dunaferr SE | 30 | 16 | 9 | 5 | 48 | 27 | 41 |
| III Kérület TTVE | 30 | 14 | 12 | 4 | 23 | 13 | 40 |
| Nagykanizsai Olaj.SE | 30 | 11 | 10 | 9 | 42 | 35 | 32 |
| Oroszlányi BSK | 30 | 10 | 10 | 10 | 21 | 27 | 30 |
| Dorogi Bányász SC | 30 | 11 | 6 | 13 | 38 | 32 | 28 |
| Paksi Atomerómu SE | 30 | 10 | 8 | 12 | 35 | 34 | 28 |
| Mohácsi Uj Barazda | 30 | 8 | 11 | 11 | 20 | 26 | 27 |
| Sabaria-Tipo SE | 30 | 8 | 10 | 12 | 29 | 33 | 26 |
| BKV Elóre SC | 30 | 9 | 8 | 13 | 30 | 39 | 26 |
| Soproni SE | 30 | 8 | 10 | 12 | 33 | 43 | 26 |
| Szekszárdi Dózsa SE | 30 | 7 | 11 | 12 | 33 | 42 | 25 |
| Komlói Bányász SK | 30 | 9 | 5 | 16 | 30 | 45 | 23 |
| Budafok MTE-Törley | 30 | 8 | 6 | 16 | 32 | 59 | 22 |
| Ajka Hungalu SK | 30 | 6 | 9 | 15 | 20 | 38 | 21 |

Promoted : - Haladás VSE and Zalaegerszegi TE
Relegated : - Komlói Bányász SK, Budafok MTE-Törley and Ajka Hungalu SK

## HUNGARY 2ND DIVISION EAST 1990/91

**LEAGUE TABLE FINAL**

| | | | | | | | |
|---|---|---|---|---|---|---|---|
| BVSC-Mavtranssped | 30 | 18 | 9 | 3 | 45 | 24 | 45 |
| Diósgyóri VTK | 30 | 17 | 10 | 3 | 56 | 27 | 44 |
| Csepel SC | 30 | 18 | 5 | 7 | 43 | 29 | 41 |
| Nyiregyházi VSC | 30 | 14 | 9 | 7 | 42 | 21 | 37 |
| Kazincbarcikai VSE | 30 | 16 | 3 | 11 | 59 | 42 | 35 |
| Kabai ESE | 30 | 12 | 9 | 9 | 41 | 26 | 33 |
| Bajai SK | 30 | 12 | 9 | 9 | 29 | 24 | 33 |
| Eger SE | 30 | 11 | 7 | 12 | 38 | 36 | 29 |
| Salgótarjani Sik. SE | 30 | 8 | 10 | 12 | 39 | 38 | 26 |
| Kecskeméti SC | 30 | 6 | 13 | 11 | 32 | 43 | 25 |
| Debreceni MTE | 30 | 7 | 11 | 12 | 24 | 37 | 25 |
| Szarvasi VSSE | 30 | 8 | 8 | 14 | 34 | 48 | 24 |
| Hatvan-DEKO KVSC | 30 | 9 | 5 | 16 | 33 | 40 | 23 |
| Szolnoki MÁV-MTE | 30 | 8 | 7 | 15 | 29 | 49 | 23 |
| Kecskeméti TE | 30 | 8 | 6 | 16 | 27 | 57 | 22 |
| Metripond SE | 30 | 5 | 5 | 20 | 22 | 52 | 15 |

Promoted : - BVSC-Mavtranssped and Diósgyóri VTK
Relegated : - Szolnoki MÁV-MTE, Kecskeméti TE and Metripond SE

**NAME CHANGE DURING SEASON**
Budapesti VSC to Budapesti VSC-Mavtranssped

## HUNGARY 3RD DIV. EAKONY 1990/91

**LEAGUE TABLE FINAL**

| | P | W | D | L | F | A | Pts |
|---|---|---|---|---|---|---|---|
| Ajkai Bányász SK | 30 | 19 | 5 | 6 | 53 | 27 | 43 |
| Keszthelyi Haladás SE | 30 | 17 | 8 | 5 | 63 | 22 | 42 |
| Betka-MAV DAC | 30 | 16 | 6 | 8 | 51 | 21 | 38 |
| Motim TE | 30 | 15 | 6 | 9 | 50 | 38 | 36 |
| Répceelaki Bányász SK | 30 | 13 | 10 | 7 | 43 | 33 | 36 |
| Győri Dózsa SE | 30 | 10 | 13 | 7 | 31 | 24 | 33 |
| Nike-Füzfői AK | 30 | 13 | 6 | 11 | 39 | 35 | 32 |
| Herendi Porcelán SK | 30 | 11 | 10 | 9 | 35 | 34 | 32 |
| Tapolcai Bauxitbán. SE | 30 | 13 | 5 | 12 | 48 | 41 | 31 |
| Körmendi Dózsa SE | 30 | 11 | 8 | 11 | 37 | 40 | 30 |
| Zala Volán MTE | 30 | 9 | 5 | 16 | 38 | 45 | 23 |
| Hegyeshalom VSE | 30 | 7 | 9 | 14 | 25 | 34 | 23 |
| Celldömölki VMSE | 30 | 7 | 7 | 16 | 20 | 49 | 21 |
| Petőháza | 30 | 7 | 6 | 16 | 26 | 48 | 21 |
| Kemenesalja | 30 | 7 | 7 | 16 | 34 | 58 | 21 |
| Papai SE | 30 | 6 | 6 | 18 | 21 | 65 | 18 |

Promoted :- Ajkai Bányász SK

## HUNGARY 3RD DIV. MATRA 1990/91

**LEAGUE TABLE FINAL**

| | P | W | D | L | F | A | Pts |
|---|---|---|---|---|---|---|---|
| Bagi SE | 30 | 17 | 11 | 2 | 60 | 24 | 45 |
| Salgótarjani Kohász | 30 | 18 | 7 | 5 | 48 | 25 | 43 |
| Gyöngyösi SE | 30 | 13 | 12 | 5 | 38 | 20 | 38 |
| Volán Rakóczi | 30 | 15 | 4 | 11 | 59 | 45 | 34 |
| Salgótarjani BTC | 30 | 12 | 10 | 8 | 33 | 27 | 34 |
| Törökszentmiklos | 30 | 14 | 5 | 11 | 57 | 35 | 33 |
| Szolnoki Cukor | 30 | 11 | 11 | 8 | 41 | 33 | 33 |
| Balassagyarmat | 30 | 12 | 6 | 12 | 46 | 46 | 30 |
| Bélapatfalvai Épitok | 30 | 12 | 6 | 12 | 52 | 55 | 30 |
| Jászberény | 30 | 13 | 6 | 11 | 54 | 40 | 28 |
| Dány | 30 | 9 | 7 | 13 | 37 | 44 | 25 |
| Apci Vasas | 30 | 7 | 10 | 13 | 30 | 43 | 24 |
| Nagyrede | 30 | 8 | 8 | 14 | 29 | 48 | 24 |
| Borsodnádazd | 30 | 8 | 5 | 17 | 27 | 50 | 21 |
| Pászló | 30 | 7 | 7 | 16 | 31 | 62 | 19 |
| Salgo Óblós | 30 | 6 | 1 | 23 | 27 | 72 | 11 |

Jászberény 4 points ceducted
Pászló 2 points deducted
Salgo Óblós 2 points deducted
Promoted :- Bagi SE

## HUNGARY 3RD DIVISION DRÁVA 1990/91

**LEAGUE TABLE FINAL**

| | P | W | D | L | F | A | Pts |
|---|---|---|---|---|---|---|---|
| Paksi SE | 28 | 19 | 4 | 5 | 63 | 23 | 42 |
| Kaposvári Rákóczi FC | 28 | 17 | 5 | 6 | 42 | 23 | 39 |
| Pécsi VSK | 28 | 15 | 8 | 5 | 51 | 15 | 38 |
| Kaposvári Honvéd | 28 | 11 | 10 | 7 | 35 | 33 | 32 |
| Marcali | 28 | 12 | 6 | 10 | 33 | 27 | 30 |
| Siklósi TSE | 28 | 12 | 6 | 10 | 33 | 29 | 30 |
| Bölyi Medosz SE | 28 | 11 | 8 | 9 | 47 | 35 | 29 |
| Barcs | 28 | 8 | 13 | 7 | 29 | 34 | 29 |
| MAV Nagykanizsai TE | 28 | 9 | 8 | 11 | 35 | 39 | 26 |
| Kisdorog | 28 | 10 | 6 | 12 | 42 | 47 | 26 |
| Kaposvári Épitők | 28 | 8 | 12 | 8 | 25 | 38 | 24 |
| Boglárfalle | 28 | 9 | 5 | 14 | 27 | 34 | 23 |
| Somberek | 28 | 8 | 7 | 13 | 35 | 45 | 23 |
| Csurgó | 28 | 5 | 7 | 16 | 23 | 53 | 17 |
| Mázaszaszvari Bányasz | 28 | 5 | 2 | 21 | 22 | 68 | 12 |
| Dombóvári Vasas withdrew | | | | | | | |

Promoted :- Paksi SE

## HUNGARY 3RD DIVISION TISZA 1990/91

**LEAGUE TABLE FINAL**

| | P | W | D | L | F | A | Pts |
|---|---|---|---|---|---|---|---|
| Hajdunánási Bocskai SE | 30 | 18 | 6 | 6 | 53 | 30 | 42 |
| Mátészalka | 30 | 16 | 8 | 6 | 53 | 34 | 40 |
| Ozdi Kohász SE | 30 | 14 | 12 | 4 | 42 | 26 | 40 |
| Tiszavasvári | 30 | 15 | 9 | 6 | 48 | 37 | 39 |
| Rakamaz | 30 | 14 | 8 | 8 | 49 | 35 | 36 |
| Kisvárda | 30 | 12 | 11 | 7 | 33 | 27 | 35 |
| Balmazujváros | 30 | 14 | 7 | 9 | 45 | 44 | 35 |
| Debreceni Kinizsi | 30 | 13 | 8 | 9 | 41 | 33 | 34 |
| Borsodi Epitok Volán | 30 | 13 | 6 | 11 | 35 | 32 | 32 |
| Edelényi Bányász | 30 | 9 | 9 | 12 | 24 | 29 | 27 |
| Olefin SC | 30 | 10 | 6 | 14 | 33 | 35 | 26 |
| Szerencs Honvéd | 30 | 9 | 7 | 14 | 40 | 42 | 25 |
| Levelek | 30 | 6 | 9 | 15 | 31 | 53 | 21 |
| Sajóbábony | 30 | 5 | 11 | 14 | 29 | 48 | 21 |
| Hajdúböszörmény | 30 | 4 | 6 | 20 | 26 | 52 | 14 |
| Püspökladány | 30 | 4 | 5 | 21 | 20 | 52 | 13 |

Promoted :- Hajdunánási Bocskai SE

## HUNGARY 3RD DIVISION DUNA 1990/91

**LEAGUE TABLE FINAL**

| | P | W | D | L | F | A | Pts |
|---|---|---|---|---|---|---|---|
| Erzsébeti SMTK | 30 | 19 | 7 | 4 | 77 | 20 | 45 |
| Pénzügyőri SE | 30 | 16 | 10 | 4 | 52 | 23 | 42 |
| Esztergomi Vasas | 30 | 15 | 11 | 4 | 45 | 31 | 41 |
| Péti MTE | 30 | 15 | 8 | 7 | 40 | 33 | 38 |
| Dunai Kőolaj | 30 | 15 | 8 | 7 | 54 | 42 | 38 |
| Rákosmenti TK | 30 | 15 | 6 | 9 | 50 | 39 | 36 |
| Gödöllo | 30 | 12 | 9 | 9 | 43 | 40 | 33 |
| Fok-Gyem. | 30 | 10 | 8 | 12 | 42 | 50 | 28 |
| Honvéd Hargita | 30 | 11 | 5 | 14 | 44 | 38 | 27 |
| Várpalotai Bányász | 30 | 7 | 13 | 10 | 42 | 49 | 27 |
| Diadem Dunakeszi VSE | 30 | 12 | 3 | 15 | 39 | 52 | 27 |
| Érdi VSE | 30 | 6 | 14 | 10 | 33 | 37 | 26 |
| H.Szondi SE | 30 | 10 | 5 | 15 | 34 | 42 | 25 |
| Peremarton | 30 | 8 | 4 | 18 | 35 | 38 | 20 |
| Malév | 30 | 5 | 8 | 17 | 48 | 71 | 18 |
| Tatai HAC | 30 | 2 | 5 | 23 | 15 | 88 | 9 |

Promoted :- Erzsebeti SMTK

## HUNGARY 3RD DIVISION ALFÖDI 1990/91

**LEAGUE TABLE FINAL**

| | P | W | D | L | F | A | Pts |
|---|---|---|---|---|---|---|---|
| Miskei TSZ SK | 30 | 19 | 11 | 0 | 71 | 10 | 49 |
| Kiskörös | 30 | 18 | 7 | 5 | 52 | 23 | 43 |
| Szegedi Dózsa | 30 | 12 | 13 | 5 | 40 | 29 | 37 |
| Cegledi Honvéd | 30 | 15 | 5 | 10 | 47 | 33 | 35 |
| Csongrád | 30 | 12 | 11 | 7 | 44 | 31 | 35 |
| Gyulai SE | 30 | 13 | 9 | 8 | 30 | 32 | 35 |
| Dömsöd | 30 | 12 | 10 | 8 | 47 | 35 | 34 |
| Mezőtúri Honvéd | 30 | 12 | 9 | 9 | 32 | 31 | 30 |
| Dabas | 30 | 11 | 8 | 11 | 43 | 43 | 30 |
| Oroszházai MTK | 30 | 8 | 13 | 9 | 37 | 40 | 29 |
| Kiskundorozsma | 30 | 10 | 8 | 12 | 33 | 38 | 28 |
| Nagyszenas | 30 | 8 | 10 | 12 | 20 | 38 | 20 |
| Kiskunfélegyházai H. | 30 | 6 | 8 | 16 | 30 | 38 | 20 |
| Mezőkovácshaza | 30 | 6 | 7 | 17 | 32 | 48 | 19 |
| Határör Dózsa | 30 | 3 | 9 | 18 | 23 | 50 | 15 |
| Mezőhegyes | 30 | 5 | 5 | 20 | 20 | 85 | 15 |

Promoted :- Miskei TSZ SK

## HUNGARY CUP 1990/91

### 1/16 FINALS

| | | | |
|---|---|---|---|
| Haladás VSE | 0 | Vid'ton-Waltham SC | 3 |
| Dorog Bányász SC | 2 | Győri Rába ETO | 0 |
| Olefin SC | 0 | Budapesti Honvéd SE | 7 |
| Komlói Bányász SK | 1 | MTK-VM SK | 0 |
| Várpolatai Bányász | 1 | Ujpesti Dózsa SC | 3 |
| Salgótar.Siküveg SE | 0 | Budapesti Volán SC | 0 |
| Kazincbarcikai VSE | 1 | Debreceni VSC | 0 |
| Budafok MTE-Torley | 0 | Szeged SC | 0 |

Budapesti Volán SC win 3-5 on penalties
Budafok MTE win 4-3 on penalties

| | |
|---|---|
| Siófoki Bányász SE | 1 |
| Váci Izzó MTE | 3 |
| Veszprémi FC | 3 |
| Békéscsabai EFC | 3 |
| Vasas SC | 8 |
| Pécsi MSC | 5 |
| Tatabán.Bányá. SC | 5 |
| Ferencvárosi TC | 2 |

### 1/8 FINALS

| | 1ST LEG | 2ND LEG | AGG. |
|---|---|---|---|
| Diósgyóri VTK v Budapesti Honvéd SE | 0-0 | 3-2 | 3-2 |
| Ujpesti TE v Paksi Atomerómu SE (Paksi win on the away goals rule) | 1-1 | 1-1 | 1-1 |
| Váci Izzó MTE v Videoton-Waltham SC | 1-0 | 2-0 | 3-0 |
| Budafok MTE-Törley v Kazincbarcikai VSE | 0-3 | 1-4 | 1-7 |
| Tatabányai Bányász SC v MTK-VM SK | 1-0 | 1-1 | 2-1 |
| Veszprémi FC v Dorogi Bányász SC | 0-0 | 0-1 | 0-1 |
| Pécsi MSC v Ferencvárosi TC | 0-3 | 0-2 | 0-5 |
| Volán FC v Vasas SC | 2-1 | 0-0 | 2-1 |

### 1/4 FINALS

| | 1ST LEG | 2ND LEG | AGG. |
|---|---|---|---|
| Diósgyóri VTK v Paksi Atomerómu SE | 0-1 | 0-0 | 0-1 |
| Ferencvárosi TC v Volán FC | 3-0 | 1-2 | 4-2 |
| Kazincbarcikai VSE v Tatabányai Bányász SC | 2-1 | 2-1 | 4-2 |
| Dorogi Bányász SC v Váci Izzó MTE (Vác win on the away goals rule) | 2-2 | 1-1 | 3-3 |

### SEMI-FINALS

| | 1ST LEG | 2ND LEG | AGG. |
|---|---|---|---|
| Ferencvárosi TC v Paksi Atomerómu SE | 4-0 | 1-2 | 5-2 |
| Váci Izzó MTE v Kazincbarcikai VSE | 1-0 | 0-0 | 1-0 |

Promoted :- Miskei TSZ SK

## FINAL  18/6/91 (at Diósgyór)

Ferencvárosi TC.......1    Váci Izzó MTE.........0

FTC : Balogh, Limperger, Pintér, Telek, Páling, Topor (Fischer 85), Vanicsek, Patkós (Szekere 23), Nasser, Dzurják, Kereszturi.
Vác : Koszta, Bánföldi, Kosztolnik, Sándor (Kerekes 63), Zirko, Gyimesi, Vig, Romanek, Szalai, Füle, Répási.

1-0 Nasser Bouiche    27    Referee : Vágner    Attendance : 8,000

# INTERNATIONAL LINE-UPS 1990

| Date | Result | Venue | Referee | Competition | Scorers |
|---|---|---|---|---|---|
| 20/3/90 | HUNGARY 2 USA 0 | Budapest | Ref : Holzmann (Austria) | Friendly | (Petres, Limperger) |
| 28/3/90 | HUNGARY 1 FRANCE 3 | Budapest | Ref : Diakonowicz (Poland) | Friendly | (Pinter) |
| 11/4/90 | AUSTRIA 3 HUNGARY 0 | Salzburg | Ref : Hackett (England) | Friendly | |
| 28/5/90 | UAE 0 HUNGARY 3 | Nimes | Ref : Benchabane (France) | Friendly | |
| 2/6/90 | HUNGARY 3 COLOMBIA 1 | Budapest | Ref : Zvi (Israel) | Friendly | (G.Bognár, K.Kovács 2) |
| 5/9/90 | HUNGARY 4 TURKEY 1 | Budapest | Ref : Listkiewicz (Poland) | EuroCh.Q. | (K.Kovács, Kozma, Kiprich 2) |
| 12/9/90 | ENGLAND 1 HUNGARY 0 | London | Ref : Fredriksson (Sweden) | Friendly | |
| 10/10/90 | NORWAY 0 HUNGARY 0 | Bergen | Ref : Spillane (Rep.Ireland) | EuroCh.Q. | (L.Diszl) |
| 17/10/90 | HUNGARY 1 ITALY 1 | Budapest | Ref : Karlsson (Sweden) | EuroCh.Q. | |
| 31/10/90 | HUNGARY 4 CYPRUS 2 | Budapest | Ref : Kotherja (Albania) | EuroCh.Q. | (Kiprich 2, o.g., Lórincz) |

## Line-up table 1 — caps and goals at 31/12/90

| Player | CAPS AT 31/12/90 | GOALS AT 31/12/90 |
|---|---|---|
| István Brockhauser | 1 | – |
| Tamás Mónos | 10 | – |
| Attila Pinter | 18 | 3 |
| János Palaczky | 3 | – |
| Géza Mészöly | 7 | – |
| Zsolt Limperger | 10 | 1 |
| Zsolt Máriási | 5 | – |
| György Bognár | 39 | 6 |
| Róbert Jován | 3 | – |
| József Duró | 4 | – |
| Tamás Petres | 4 | 1 |
| Zoltán Csucsánszky | | – |
| Ferenc Lakatos | 1 | – |
| Tibor Balog (MTK) | 7 | – |
| Pal Fischer | 12 | – |
| Tibor Simon | 3 | – |
| Kálmán Kovács | 33 | 11 |
| Lajos Detari | 41 | 10 |
| Emil Lórincz | 4 | 1 |
| Gábor Márton | 1 | – |
| Károly Gelei | 1 | – |

## Line-up table 2 — caps and goals at 31/12/90

| Player | CAPS AT 31/12/90 | GOALS AT 31/12/90 |
|---|---|---|
| László Disztl | 17 | 1 |
| Imre Garaba | 79 | 3 |
| István Varga | 8 | – |
| Ferenc Mészáros | 20 | 4 |
| József Szalma | 8 | – |
| József Kiprich | 44 | 15 |
| József Gáspár | 4 | – |
| László Bodnár | 1 | – |
| Ferenc Csik | 1 | – |
| Zsolt Petry | 6 | – |
| Zoltán Aczel | 2 | – |
| Zsolt Bücs | 2 | – |
| István Kozma | 24 | 1 |
| János Marozsán | 1 | – |
| József Keller | 18 | – |
| Dénes Eszenyi | 1 | – |
| István Urbányi | 2 | – |
| József Gregor | 2 | – |
| Balázs Bérczy | 2 | – |
| Ervin Kovács | 16 | 1 |
| Imre Fodor | 4 | – |
| Vendel Rugovics | 1 | – |
| Csaba Horváth | 1 | – |
| György Katona | 2 | – |
| Tibor Simon | 2 | – |

---

## HUNGARY : All Time Records as at 31/12/90 - CAPS

1. József Bozsik (Honvéd) — (84) 83
2. László Fazekas (Ujpesti Dózsa/Antwerp FC) — (68) 75
3. Gyula Grosics (Mateosz/Honvéd/Tatabánya) — (68) 58
4. Ferenc Puskás (Honvéd) — (71) 49
5. Sándor Mátrai (Ferencváros) — (61) 42
6. Imre Garaba (Honvéd/Stade Rennes/Charleroi SC) — (68) 39
7. Ferenc Sipos (MTK/Honvéd) — (76) 36
8. Máté Fenyvesi (Ferencváros) — (39) 32
   Ferenc Bene (Ujpesti Dózsa) — (70) 32
   László Bálint (Ferencváros/FC Brugge/Toulouse FC) — (75) 31

## HUNGARY : All Time Records as at 31/12/90 - GOALS

1. Ferenc Puskás (Honvéd) — 100
2. Sándor Kocsis (Ferencváros/Honvéd) — 92
3. Imre Schlosser (Ferencváros/MTK/Wiener AC) — 86
4. Lajos Tichy (Honvéd) — 84
5. György Sárosi (Ferencváros) — 80
6. Nándor Hidegkuti (MTK) — 79
7. Ferenc Bene (Ujpesti Dózsa) — 77
8. Gyula Zsengellér (Ujpesti Dózsa) — 76
   Tibor Nyilasi (Ferencváros/FK Austria Wien) — 76
10. Flórián Albert (Ferencváros) — 76

# ICELAND Correspondent : UTLAGI

| ICELAND 1st Division Season 1990 | KA | FH | FRAM | KR | VALUR | IA | THOR | VIKINGUR | STJARNAN | IBV |
|---|---|---|---|---|---|---|---|---|---|---|
| KA (Akureyri) | ■ | 4-0 | 0-1 | 0-1 | 0-1 | 2-1 | 1-2 | 2-0 | 0-3 | 1-1 |
| FH (Hafnarfjordur) | 1-0 | ■ | 2-1 | 1-3 | 0-1 | 2-1 | 0-1 | 1-1 | 5-1 | 1-2 |
| FRAM (Reykjavik) | 4-0 | 2-2 | ■ | 3-0 | 3-2 | 4-0 | 1-0 | 0-1 | 1-3 | 3-4 |
| KR (Reykjavik) | 2-0 | 3-2 | 0-1 | ■ | 3-0 | 2-0 | 2-0 | 2-1 | 1-0 | 0-1 |
| VALUR (Reykjavik) | 2-0 | 2-0 | 1-2 | 2-1 | ■ | 1-0 | 0-0 | 1-1 | 0-1 | 4-1 |
| IA (Akranes) | 2-1 | 2-3 | 0-2 | 1-3 | 2-3 | ■ | 3-1 | 0-2 | 0-0 | 3-4 |
| THOR (Akureyri) | 2-1 | 1-2 | 0-0 | 1-2 | 1-2 | 0-1 | ■ | 4-1 | 0-2 | 0-1 |
| VIKINGUR (Reykjavik) | 0-1 | 2-0 | 0-1 | 1-1 | 2-2 | 2-2 | 0-0 | ■ | 1-0 | 0-4 |
| STJARNAN (Gardabaer) | 1-3 | 0-1 | 1-6 | 1-3 | 2-1 | 2-0 | 3-0 | 1-0 | ■ | 1-1 |
| IBV (Vestmannaeyjar) | 4-2 | 2-1 | 0-4 | 2-2 | 2-4 | 2-1 | 2-0 | 2-2 | 4-3 | ■ |

| ICELAND 2nd Division Season 1990 | FYLKIR | IBK | VIDIR | SELFOSS | UBK | TINDASTOLL | LEIFTUR | IR | UMFG | KS |
|---|---|---|---|---|---|---|---|---|---|---|
| FYLKIR (Reykjavik) | ■ | 0-2 | 1-4 | 5-2 | 1-2 | 1-2 | 3-0 | 0-1 | 6-0 | 6-1 |
| IBK (Keflavik) | 1-2 | ■ | 0-2 | 0-0 | 0-1 | 3-2 | 1-3 | 1-2 | 2-1 | 1-0 |
| VIDIR (Gardur) | 0-0 | 3-3 | ■ | 0-3 | 2-2 | 3-1 | 5-0 | 2-0 | 4-1 | 1-0 |
| SELFOSS (Selfoss) | 1-2 | 1-2 | 3-4 | ■ | 3-2 | 1-1 | 3-2 | 1-0 | 1-0 | 5-1 |
| UBK (Kopavogur) | 0-0 | 0-1 | 0-0 | 3-1 | ■ | 1-1 | 3-1 | 0-0 | 2-1 | 1-0 |
| TINDASTOLL (Saudarkrokur) | 1-1 | 1-0 | 1-2 | 0-5 | 0-1 | ■ | 2-0 | 3-1 | 1-1 | 2-1 |
| LEIFTUR (Olafsfjördur) | 1-3 | 0-0 | 0-0 | 1-1 | 1-0 | 1-0 | ■ | 0-1 | 1-2 | 4-1 |
| IR (Reykjavik) | 1-2 | 0-0 | 2-3 | 5-1 | 1-5 | 3-1 | 2-1 | ■ | 0-1 | 2-1 |
| UMFG (Grindavik) | 2-0 | 1-2 | 2-3 | 2-1 | 1-0 | 1-1 | 0-2 | 0-1 | ■ | 2-1 |
| KS (Siglufjördur) | 0-1 | 2-0 | 1-2 | 3-1 | 1-2 | 2-0 | 1-1 | 2-1 | 3-2 | ■ |

## ICELAND 1ST DIVISION 1990
### LEAGUE TABLE FINAL

| | | | | | | | |
|---|---|---|---|---|---|---|---|
| Fram (Reykjavik) | 18 | 12 | 2 | 4 | 39 | 16 | 38 |
| KR (Reykjavik) | 18 | 12 | 2 | 4 | 31 | 17 | 38 |
| IBV (Vestmannaeyjar) | 18 | 11 | 4 | 3 | 39 | 32 | 37 |
| Valur (Reykjavik) | 18 | 10 | 3 | 5 | 29 | 21 | 33 |
| Stjarnan (Gardabaer) | 18 | 8 | 2 | 8 | 25 | 27 | 26 |
| FH (Hafnarfjordur) | 18 | 7 | 2 | 9 | 24 | 29 | 23 |
| Vikingur (Reykjavik) | 18 | 4 | 7 | 7 | 17 | 24 | 19 |
| KA (Akureyri) | 18 | 5 | 1 | 12 | 18 | 28 | 16 |
| Thor (Akureyri) | 18 | 4 | 3 | 11 | 13 | 24 | 15 |
| IA (Akranes) | 18 | 3 | 2 | 13 | 19 | 36 | 11 |

Champions : - Fram
Relegated : - Thor and IA

### TOP SCORERS

| | |
|---|---|
| 1. Hördur Magnússon (FH) | 13 |
| 2. Gudmundur Steinsson (Fram) | 10 |
| Ragnar Margeirsson (KR) | 10 |
| 4. Hlynur Stefánsson (IBV) | 9 |
| 5. Antony Karl Gregory (Valur) | 8 |
| Jón Erling Ragnarsson | 8 |
| Tómas Ingi Tómasson (IBV) | 8 |

## ICELAND 2ND DIVISION 1990
### LEAGUE TABLE FINAL

| | | | | | | | |
|---|---|---|---|---|---|---|---|
| Vidir (Gardur) | 18 | 12 | 5 | 1 | 40 | 20 | 41 |
| UBK (Kopavogur) | 18 | 9 | 5 | 4 | 25 | 15 | 32 |
| Fylkir (Reykjavik) | 18 | 9 | 3 | 6 | 34 | 21 | 30 |
| IR (Reykjavik) | 18 | 8 | 2 | 8 | 23 | 24 | 26 |
| IBK (Keflavik) | 18 | 7 | 4 | 7 | 19 | 21 | 25 |
| Selfoss (Selfoss) | 18 | 7 | 3 | 8 | 34 | 33 | 24 |
| Tindastoll (Saudarkrökur) | 18 | 5 | 5 | 8 | 20 | 28 | 20 |
| UMFG (Grindavik) | 18 | 6 | 2 | 10 | 20 | 31 | 20 |
| Leiftur (Olafsfjördur) | 18 | 5 | 4 | 9 | 19 | 28 | 19 |
| KS (Siglufjördur) | 18 | 5 | 1 | 12 | 21 | 34 | 16 |

Promoted : - Vidir and UBK
Relegated : - Leiftur and KS

## ICELAND 3RD DIVISION 1990
### LEAGUE TABLE FINAL

| | | | | | | | |
|---|---|---|---|---|---|---|---|
| Thróttur (Reykjavik) | 18 | 16 | 1 | 1 | 64 | 13 | 49 |
| Haukar (Hafnafjördur) | 18 | 14 | 1 | 3 | 48 | 18 | 43 |
| IK (Kopavogur) | 18 | 13 | 1 | 4 | 51 | 25 | 40 |
| Thróttur (Neskaupstadur) | 18 | 8 | 3 | 7 | 49 | 34 | 27 |
| Dalvík (Dalvík) | 18 | 8 | 2 | 8 | 41 | 29 | 26 |
| Völsungur (Husavik) | 18 | 6 | 6 | 6 | 28 | 29 | 24 |
| Reynir (Arskogsstrond) | 18 | 6 | 2 | 10 | 29 | 41 | 20 |
| BI (Isafjördur) | 18 | 5 | 2 | 11 | 29 | 45 | 17 |
| Einherji (Vopnafjördur) | 18 | 2 | 4 | 12 | 27 | 48 | 10 |
| TBA (Akureyri) | 18 | 1 | 0 | 17 | 11 | 95 | 3 |

Promoted : - Thróttur R and Haukar
Relegated : - Einherji and TBA

## ICELAND 4TH DIVISION GROUP A 1990
### LEAGUE TABLE FINAL

| | P | W | D | L | F | A | Pts |
|---|---|---|---|---|---|---|---|
| Grotta (Seltjarnarnes) | 12 | 10 | 2 | 0 | 37 | 7 | 32 |
| Reynir (Sangerdi) | 12 | 9 | 0 | 3 | 30 | 16 | 27 |
| Snaefell (Stykkiskolmur) | 12 | 6 | 1 | 5 | 28 | 23 | 19 |
| Njardvik (Njardvik) | 12 | 4 | 3 | 5 | 17 | 20 | 15 |
| Armann (Reykjavik) | 12 | 4 | 1 | 7 | 15 | 22 | 13 |
| Fjolnir (Reykjavik) | 12 | 3 | 1 | 8 | 13 | 28 | 10 |
| Ernir (Selfoss) | 12 | 1 | 2 | 9 | 13 | 37 | 5 |

## ICELAND 4TH DIVISION GROUP B 1990
### LEAGUE TABLE FINAL

| | P | W | D | L | F | A | Pts |
|---|---|---|---|---|---|---|---|
| Vikverji (Reykjavik) | 12 | 9 | 0 | 3 | 45 | 17 | 27 |
| Aegir (Thorlakshofn) | 12 | 8 | 2 | 2 | 19 | 16 | 26 |
| Vikingur (Olafsvik) | 12 | 6 | 1 | 5 | 25 | 18 | 19 |
| Stokkseyri. | 12 | 4 | 4 | 4 | 26 | 26 | 16 |
| Fylkir | 12 | 4 | 3 | 5 | 30 | 28 | 15 |
| Leiknir F. | 12 | 2 | 4 | 6 | 22 | 38 | 10 |
| Sindri. | 12 | 2 | 0 | 10 | 9 | 33 | 6 |

## ICELAND 4TH DIVISION GROUP C 1990
### LEAGUE TABLE FINAL

| | P | W | D | L | F | A | Pts |
|---|---|---|---|---|---|---|---|
| Skallagrimur (Borganes) | 10 | 8 | 2 | 0 | 35 | 10 | 26 |
| Leiknir (Reykjavik) | 10 | 7 | 2 | 1 | 34 | 8 | 23 |
| Arvakur (Reykjavik) | 10 | 4 | 3 | 3 | 27 | 21 | 15 |
| Hveragerdi (Hveragerdi) | 10 | 2 | 3 | 5 | 24 | 22 | 9 |
| Stokkseyri (Stokkseyri) | 10 | 1 | 4 | 5 | 15 | 42 | 7 |
| Lettir (Reykjavik) | 10 | 0 | 2 | 8 | 8 | 40 | 2 |

## ICELAND 4TH DIVISION GROUP D 1990
### LEAGUE TABLE FINAL

| | P | W | D | L | F | A | Pts |
|---|---|---|---|---|---|---|---|
| Hvöt (Blonduos) | 8 | 6 | 1 | 1 | 18 | 7 | 19 |
| Kormakur (Hvammstangi) | 8 | 5 | 0 | 3 | 21 | 8 | 15 |
| Neisti (Hofsos) | 8 | 4 | 2 | 2 | 13 | 5 | 14 |
| Geislinn (Holmavik) | 8 | 1 | 2 | 5 | 5 | 26 | 5 |
| Thrymur (Saudarkrokur) | 8 | 1 | 1 | 6 | 8 | 19 | 4 |

## ICELAND 4TH DIVISION GROUP E 1990
### LEAGUE TABLE FINAL

| | P | W | D | L | F | A | Pts |
|---|---|---|---|---|---|---|---|
| Magni (Grenivik) | 10 | 8 | 2 | 0 | 53 | 11 | 26 |
| HSTh.b (Myvatnssveit) | 10 | 8 | 1 | 1 | 50 | 10 | 25 |
| UMSE.b (Eyjafjordur) | 10 | 4 | 2 | 4 | 34 | 15 | 14 |
| SM (Eyjafjordur) | 10 | 4 | 1 | 5 | 23 | 26 | 13 |
| Austri (Raufarhofn) | 10 | 2 | 0 | 8 | 15 | 58 | 6 |
| Umf Narfi (Hirsey) | 10 | 1 | 0 | 9 | 6 | 61 | 3 |

## ICELAND 4TH DIVISION GROUP F 1990
### LEAGUE TABLE FINAL

| | P | W | D | L | F | A | Pts |
|---|---|---|---|---|---|---|---|
| Sindri (Hornafjordur) | 16 | 13 | 2 | 1 | 78 | 15 | 41 |
| Huginn (Seydisfjordur) | 16 | 10 | 3 | 3 | 39 | 18 | 33 |
| Hottur (Egilsstadir) | 16 | 10 | 1 | 5 | 46 | 15 | 31 |
| KSH (Stodfj./Breiddal.) | 16 | 8 | 0 | 8 | 42 | 31 | 24 |
| Austri (Eskifjordur) | 16 | 7 | 3 | 6 | 35 | 25 | 24 |
| Leiknir (Faskrudsfjordur) | 16 | 7 | 3 | 6 | 34 | 22 | 24 |
| Valur (Reydarfjordur) | 16 | 5 | 4 | 7 | 42 | 36 | 19 |
| Neisti (Djupivogur) | 16 | 2 | 2 | 12 | 17 | 72 | 8 |
| UMF Sjarnan (Berufjord.) | 16 | 1 | 2 | 13 | 8 | 108 | 5 |

## ICELAND 4TH DIVISION CHAMPIONSHIP PLAY-OFFS 1990

Promoted :- Magni and Skallagrimur

---

## ICELAND CUP 1990

### 1ST ROUND
| | | | |
|---|---|---|---|
| Fylkir | 2 | UMFG | 1 |
| Ernir | 2 | IBK | 3 |
| Hafnir | 0 | Vidir | 4 |
| Hottur | 0 | Einherji | 1 |
| Leiftur | 3 | Volsungur | 1 |
| UMFN | 1 | Armann | 0 |
| Selfoss | 6 | TBR. | 0 |
| TBA | 0 | Magni. | 2 |
| Vikingur O. | 0 | Aegir | 1 |
| Huginn | 4 | Sindri | 4 (aet) |

Sindri win 3-4 on penalties

Byes :- IK, Grotta, Stokkseyri, Tindastoll, Hvöt, HSth.b, Neisti H.

### 2ND ROUND
| | | | |
|---|---|---|---|
| Neisti H. | 0 | Grotta | 4 |
| BÍ. | 1 | KS | 6 |
| IBK | 2 | Magni | 0 |
| Leiftur | 5 | Reynir S | 1 |
| Stokkseyri. | 1 | Skallagrimur | 1 |
| Reynir A | 2 | (aet) | |
| Selfoss | 6 | (aet) | |

### 3RD ROUND
| | | | |
|---|---|---|---|
| Grotta | 0 | UBK | 3 |
| HSth.b | 2 | KS | 5 |
| Sindri. | 2 | Tindastoll | 2 |
| Throttur R. | 0 | Einherji | 3 |

### 4TH ROUND
| | | | |
|---|---|---|---|
| IA. | 2 | KA | 0 |
| IBK | 1 | Selfoss | 3 |
| Sindri. | 0 | KR | 2 |
| Afturelding | 1 | Leiftur | 3 |

IBK win 4-2 on penalties

### EXTRA ROUND (Northern Iceland)
| | | | |
|---|---|---|---|
| KS | 5 | Tindastoll | 4 |

### 1/4 FINALS
| | | | |
|---|---|---|---|
| IA. | 2 | Thor. | 0 |
| IBK | 3 | IR | 3 (aet) |
| FH | 1 | KS | 1 |
| Sindri. | 0 | Valur | 3 |
| Stjarnan | | | |

IBK win 4-2 on penalties

Valur win 4-2 on penalties

### SEMI-FINALS
| | | | |
|---|---|---|---|
| Valur | 2 | Vikingur | 0 |
| Selfoss | 3 | IA | 3 |
| IBK | 2 | KR | 4 |

Selfoss win 5-4 on penalties

### FINAL  26/8/90 at Laugardalsvöllur
KR ...... 1   Valur ...... 1 (aet)

1-0  R.Kristiansson  29
1-1  T.Bogason  74

KR : O.Gotskálksson, S.Björgvinsson, T.Egilsson (A.Arnarson 103), G.Oddsson, R.Kristinsson, H.Björnsson, T.Haldórsson, (B.Rafnsson 95), G.Skúlason, R.Magerisson, A.Edvaldsson, P.Pétursson.

Valur : B.Sigurdsson, T.Thráinsson, S.Hreinsson, M-B.Pétursson, E-P.Tómasson, A.Loftsson (G-M.Másson 61), A.Gylfason, S.Adolfsson (S.Kristjánsson 104), A-K.Gregory, T.Bogason, B.Bragason.

### FINAL REPLAY  29/8/90 at Laugardalsvöllur
KR ...... 0   Valur ...... 0 (aet)

KR : O.Gotskálksson, S.Björgvinsson, T.Egilsson, G.Oddsson, R.Kristinsson, R.Magerisson, A.Edvaldsson, P.Pétursson, G.Skúlason, T.Haldórsson, (S.Jónsson, E-P.Tómasson, A.Gylfason 85).

Valur : B.Sigurdsson, T.Thráinsson, S.Hreinsson, M-B.Pétursson, E-P.Tómasson, A.Loftsson (G-M.Másson 61), A.Gylfason, S.Adolfsson, A-K.Gregory, T.Bogason, B.Bragason (S.Kristjánsson 108).

VALUR WIN 4-5 ON PENALTIES.

Haukar w.o. Fjolnir (Withdrew)

# ICELAND INTERNATIONAL REVIEW 1990

## INTERNATIONAL LINE-UPS 1990

| Date | Match | Venue | Referee | Type | Scorers |
|---|---|---|---|---|---|
| 28/3/90 | LUXEMBOURG 1 ICELAND 2 | Esch-sur-Alzette | Ref: Crucke (Belgium) | Friendly | (P.Pétursson, O.Thórdarson) |
| 4/4/90 | BERMUDA 0 ICELAND 4 | Hamilton | | Friendly | (P.Pétursson 2, P.Ormslev, K.Einarsson) |
| 8/4/90 | USA 4 ICELAND 1 | St.Louis | Ref: Navarrete (Spain) | Friendly | (P.Pétursson) |
| 30/5/90 | ICELAND 2 ALBANIA 0 | Reykjavik | Ref: McKnight (N.Ireland) | EuroCh.Q. | (A.Gudjohnsen, A.Edvaldsson) |
| 8/8/90 | FAROER ISLANDS 2 ICELAND 3 | Torshavn | Ref: Mikkelsen (Denmark) | Friendly | (A-K.Gregory 2, A.Gudjohnsen) |
| 5/9/90 | ICELAND 1 FRANCE 2 | Reykjavik | Ref: Syme (Scotland) | EuroCh.Q. | (A.Edvaldsson) |
| 26/9/90 | CZECHOSLOVAKIA 1 ICELAND 0 | Kosice | Ref: Kolev (Bulgaria) | EuroCh.Q. | |
| 10/10/90 | SPAIN 2 ICELAND 1 | Sevilla | Ref: Mintoff (Malta) | EuroCh.Q. | (Si.Jónsson) |

### Line-ups – part 1

| Date | Bjarni Sigurdsson | Atli Edvaldsson | Gudni Bergsson | Gunnar Gislason | Ommar Orygsson | Petur Arnthorsson | Olafur Thordarson | Thorvaldur Orygsson | Sigurdur Gretarsson | Eyjolfur Sverrisson | Petur Petursson | Runar Kristinsson | Petur Ormslev | Birkir Kristinsson | Ingvar Gudmundsson | Alexander Hognason | Saevar Jonsson | Vidar Thorkelsson | Bjarni Jonsson |
|---|---|---|---|---|---|---|---|---|---|---|---|---|---|---|---|---|---|---|---|
| 28/3/90 | 1 | 2 | 3 | 4 | 5 | 6 | 7 | 8 | 9 | 10 | 11 | (4) | (10) | | | | | | |
| 4/4/90 | | | | | | 7 | | | | | 10 | | 6 | | | | 4 | 3 | 6 |
| 8/4/90 | | | | | | 7 | | | | | 10 | | 9 | 1 | | | 5 | | |
| 30/5/90 | | 3 | 4 | | (11) | | 2 | 6 | 8 | | 10 | | | | | | 5 | | |
| 8/8/90 | | | | | 5 | | | | | | | 7 | 8 | (1) | | | | | |
| 5/9/90 | 1 | 4 | 2 | | | | 9 | 8 | 6 | | 11 | (7) | 7 | | 2 | 3 | 3 | | |
| 26/9/90 | 1 | 4 | 2 | | | | 9 | 7 | 7 | | | | 6 | | 2 | 5 | 3 | | |
| 10/10/90 | 1 | 4 | 2 | | | | 9 | | 7 | | | | (8) | | | | 3 | | |
| **CAPS AT 31/12/90** | 37 | 64 | 35 | 46 | 8 | 28 | 38 | 12 | 33 | 1 | 41 | 15 | 39 | 5 | 10 | 2 | 58 | 26 | 2 |
| **GOALS AT 31/12/90** | | 8 | 3 | 3 | | | 2 | 6 | 5 | | 11 | | 5 | | | 2 | 1 | | |

### Line-ups – part 2

| Date | Kjartan Einarsson | Olafur Kristjansson | Thormodur Egilsson | Kristinn R.Jonsson | Hördur Magnusson | Haraldur Ingolfsson | Arnor Gudjohnsen | Gudmundur Torfason | Kristjan Jonsson | Thorgrimur Thrainsson | Einar Páll Tómasson | Steingrimur Birgisson | Andri Martensson | Anthony Karl Gregory | Adalsteinn Adalsteinsson | Atli Einarsson | Tómas Ingi Tómasson | Ragnar Margeirsson | Sigurdur Jónsson |
|---|---|---|---|---|---|---|---|---|---|---|---|---|---|---|---|---|---|---|---|
| 4/4/90 | 11 | (2) | (8) | (9) | (11) | | | | | | | | | | | | | | |
| 8/4/90 | 10 | | | (9) | | (7) | | | | | | | | | | | | | |
| 30/5/90 | | | | | | | | 11 | (6) | | | | | | | | | | |
| 8/8/90 | | | (6) | | | | 9 | 11 | 6 | | | | 4 | 10 | (9) | (10) | (11) | | |
| 5/9/90 | | | | | | | 10 | 10 | 5 | 5 | | 4 | 3 | | | | | | |
| 26/9/90 | | | | | | | 9 | 11 | (6) | 5 | 6 | 3 | 3 | | | | | (6) | |
| 10/10/90 | | | | | | | 10 | 10 | 6 | 5 | | | | | | | | 2 | 1 |
| **CAPS AT 31/12/90** | 2 | 1 | 2 | 4 | 1 | | 35 | 25 | 14 | 17 | 1 | 3 | 3 | 2 | 4 | 1 | 1 | 43 | 21 |
| **GOALS AT 31/12/90** | 1 | | | | | | 5 | 4 | | | | 1 | | 2 | | | 1 | | 1 |

## ICELAND : All Time Records as at 31/12/90 - CAPS

1. Marteinn Geirsson (Fram/Union St.Gilloise) — 67
2. Atli Edvaldsson (Valur/Borussia Dortmund/Fortuna Düsseldorf/Bayer Uerdingen/Genclerbirligi/KR) — 64
3. Saevar Jónsson (Valur/SV Cercle Brugge/SK Brann/Solothurn) — 58
4. Arni Sveinsson (IA) — 50
5. Gunnar Gislason (KA/KR/Moss FK/BK Häcken) — 46
6. Matthias Hallgrimsson (IA/IS Halmia) — 45
7. Asgeir Sigurvinsson (IBV.Standard CL/FC Bayern München/VfB Stuttgar') — 45
8. Ragnar Margeirsson (IBK/SV Cercle Brugge/Waterschei Thor/Fram/KR) — 43
9. Pétur Pétursson (IA/Feyenoord/RSC Anderlecht/Antwerp FC/Hercules Alcante/KR) — 41
10. Gudgeir Leifsson (Vikingur/Fram/Charleroi SC/IBV/FC Bulle/Edmonton Drillers) — 39
    Teitur Thórdarson (IA/Jönköping Södra IF/Osters IF/RC Lens/Yverdon-Sports) — 39

## ICELAND : All Time Records as at 31/12/90 - GOALS

1. Rikhardur Jónsson (Fram/IA) — (33) 17
2. Pétur Pétursson (IA/Feyenoord/RSC Anderlecht/Antwerp FC/Hercules Alicante/KR) — (41) 11
3. Matthias Hallgrimsson (IA/IS Halmia) — (45) 11
4. Thórdur Thórdarson (IA) — (18) 9
5. Teitur Thórdarson (IA/Jönköping Södra IF/Osters IF/RC Lens/Yverdon-Sports) — (39) 9
6. Gudmundur Steinsson (Fram/Kickers Offe'nbach) — (19) 8
   Atli Edvaldsson (Valur/Borussia Dortmund/Fortuna Düsseldorf/Bayer Uerdingen/Genclerbirligi/KR) — (64) 8
   Marteinn Geirsson (Fram/Union St.Gilloise) — (67) 8
9. Gudmundur Thorbjörnsson (Valur/FC Baden) — (37) 7
10. Hermann Gunnarsson (Valur/IBA) — (20) 6
    Ellert Schram (KR) — (23) 6

# IRELAND Correspondent : JOHN MOORE

| LEAGUE OF IRELAND<br>Premier Division<br>Season 1990/91 | ST.PATS. ATH. | DERRY C. | DUNDALK | SHAMROCK R. | CORK C. | BOHEMIANS | SHELBOURNE | GALWAY U. | LIMERICK C. | ATHLONE T. | WATERFORD | SLIGO R. |
|---|---|---|---|---|---|---|---|---|---|---|---|---|
| **ST. PATRICK'S ATHLETIC** | | 1-0 | 0-0 | 2-1 | 1-1 | 2-0 | 1-1 | 4-0 | 3-0 | 3-0 | 2-0 | 2-0 |
|  | | | | | 0-3 | | 1-0 | 0-0 | 1-1 | | | 1-0 |
| **DERRY CITY** | 0-1 | | 0-1 | 0-0 | 0-0 | 1-1 | 2-0 | 6-1 | 1-0 | 5-0 | 6-2 | 1-1 |
|  | 1-0 | | 0-1 | | 1-3 | 2-1 | | | | 0-1 | | |
| **DUNDALK** | 3-0 | 1-0 | | 0-0 | 0-0 | 4-1 | 1-5 | 2-0 | 3-0 | 3-0 | 0-0 | 0-2 |
|  | 0-0 | | | | | 3-0 | 2-0 | 2-0 | | | 1-0 | |
| **SHAMROCK ROVERS** | 0-0 | 1-1 | 0-0 | | 4-0 | 0-2 | 2-3 | 2-0 | 4-1 | 0-0 | 3-1 | 2-1 |
|  | 2-4 | 2-5 | 1-2 | | | | | | | 3-1 | | 0-0 |
| **CORK CITY** | 0-0 | 1-1 | 1-1 | 1-1 | | 1-0 | 0-0 | 1-0 | 1-0 | 2-0 | 1-0 | 1-0 |
|  | | 0-1 | 0-0 | | | | | 1-0 | 2-2 | 2-1 | 2-0 | |
| **BOHEMIANS** | 0-1 | 0-0 | 0-2 | 2-3 | 0-1 | | 1-0 | 3-0 | 2-0 | 0-1 | 1-1 | 0-2 |
|  | 2-1 | | | 1-2 | 1-1 | | 0-1 | 0-0 | | | | 1-1 |
| **SHELBOURNE** | 1-2 | 1-0 | 1-2 | 3-0 | 0-2 | 1-1 | | 3-1 | 5-0 | 0-0 | 4-0 | 2-1 |
|  | | 1-0 | | 1-0 | 0-2 | | | | 3-1 | | 3-0 | 1-1 |
| **GALWAY UNITED** | 0-4 | 3-1 | 2-3 | 2-4 | 1-3 | 1-0 | 2-1 | | 1-2 | 0-2 | 2-1 | 0-2 |
|  | | 2-1 | | 0-1 | | | 3-5 | | 4-1 | | 1-1 | |
| **LIMERICK CITY** | 2-1 | 0-4 | 0-4 | 2-1 | 1-6 | 0-2 | 0-4 | 0-3 | | 0-0 | 1-2 | 1-1 |
|  | | 0-2 | 0-3 | 0-3 | | 2-3 | | | | 1-0 | 0-2 | |
| **ATHLONE TOWN** | 1-1 | 1-4 | 0-1 | 0-2 | 1-1 | 3-0 | 0-5 | 0-1 | 0-1 | | 1-1 | 0-2 |
|  | 2-1 | | 1-3 | | | 1-0 | 0-1 | 2-2 | | | | 1-2 |
| **WATERFORD UNITED** | 0-5 | 0-2 | 1-3 | 0-3 | 0-2 | 1-1 | 0-1 | 0-1 | 1-0 | 3-1 | | 0-1 |
|  | 0-1 | 1-4 | | 0-3 | | 2-1 | | | | 2-1 | | |
| **SLIGO ROVERS** | 0-0 | 0-0 | 2-0 | 2-1 | 0-1 | 1-0 | 2-2 | 3-1 | 1-1 | 1-0 | 1-0 | |
|  | | 0-0 | 0-0 | | 1-2 | | | | 0-0 | 0-1 | 3-0 | |

## LEAGUE OF IRELAND PREMIER DIV. 1990/91

### LEAGUE TABLE FINAL

| | | | | | | | |
|---|---|---|---|---|---|---|---|
| Dundalk | 33 | 22 | 8 | 3 | 52 | 17 | 52 |
| Cork City | 33 | 19 | 12 | 2 | 45 | 18 | 50 |
| St.Patrick's Athletic | 33 | 17 | 10 | 6 | 46 | 21 | 44 |
| Shelbourne | 33 | 18 | 6 | 9 | 59 | 30 | 42 |
| Sligo Rovers | 33 | 13 | 12 | 8 | 34 | 22 | 38 |
| Shamrock Rovers | 33 | 14 | 9 | 10 | 51 | 37 | 37 |
| Derry City | 33 | 13 | 9 | 11 | 51 | 28 | 35 |
| Galway United | 33 | 9 | 5 | 19 | 34 | 61 | 23 |
| Bohemians | 33 | 7 | 8 | 18 | 27 | 42 | 22 |
| Athlone Town | 33 | 6 | 7 | 20 | 22 | 53 | 19 |
| Waterford United | 33 | 6 | 5 | 22 | 22 | 62 | 17 |
| Limerick City | 33 | 6 | 5 | 22 | 21 | 73 | 17 |

Champions : - Dundalk
Relegated : - Waterford United and Limerick City

### TOP SCORERS

| | | |
|---|---|---|
| 1. | Hanrahan (Dundalk) | 18 |
| 2. | Morley (Cork City) | 15 |
| 3. | Newe (Shelbourne) | 14 |
| 4. | Ennis (St.Patrick's Athletic) | 12 |

## LEAGUE OF IRELAND 1ST DIV.1990/91

### LEAGUE TABLE FINAL

| | | | | | | | |
|---|---|---|---|---|---|---|---|
| Drogheda United | 27 | 15 | 11 | 1 | 38 | 14 | 41 |
| Bray Wanderers | 27 | 16 | 6 | 5 | 40 | 17 | 38 |
| Cobh Ramblers | 27 | 12 | 8 | 7 | 31 | 20 | 32 |
| Finn Harps | 27 | 14 | 4 | 9 | 40 | 30 | 32 |
| St.James' Gate | 27 | 13 | 3 | 11 | 37 | 38 | 29 |
| UCD | 27 | 11 | 5 | 11 | 32 | 25 | 27 |
| Kilkenny City | 27 | 7 | 11 | 9 | 29 | 32 | 25 |
| Home Farm | 27 | 5 | 7 | 15 | 26 | 46 | 17 |
| Longford Town | 27 | 5 | 7 | 15 | 20 | 44 | 17 |
| Monaghan United | 27 | 4 | 4 | 19 | 27 | 54 | 12 |

Promoted : - Drogheda United and Bray Wanderers

Note : Newcastle West resigned from the League prior to commencement of Season 1990/91, their place being taken over by St.James'Gate.

## LEAGUE OF IRELAND 1st Division — Season 1990/91

| | DROGHEDA UTD. | UCD | BRAY WANDS. | KILKENNY CITY | HOME FARM | FINN HARPS | COBH RAMBLERS | LONGFORD UTD. | MONAGHAN UTD. | ST.JAMES GATE |
|---|---|---|---|---|---|---|---|---|---|---|
| **DROGHEDA UNITED** | | 2-0 | 2-0 | 1-1 | 2-1 | 2-0 | 2-0 | 3-1 | 3-2 | 2-1 |
| | | | | | | | 3-1 | 2-0 | 1-1 | 2-2 |
| **UCD** | 1-1 | | 1-2 | 0-1 | 3-0 | 1-0 | 0-0 | 3-1 | 2-0 | 0-1 |
| | 0-0 | | | | | | 0-1 | 0-0 | 1-0 | |
| **BRAY WANDERERS** | 0-0 | 1-0 | | 1-1 | 2-0 | 1-1 | 1-2 | 3-0 | 2-0 | 0-2 |
| | 0-0 | 2-0 | | | | | 0-2 | | 3-1 | 3-0 |
| **KILKENNY CITY** | 1-1 | 1-1 | 0-2 | | 1-3 | 1-2 | 0-0 | 0-0 | 2-0 | 3-0 |
| | 1-4 | 3-0 | 0-1 | | 1-1 | | | | 2-0 | |
| **HOME FARM** | 0-1 | 1-2 | 0-2 | 1-1 | | 4-2 | 2-2 | 3-0 | 3-3 | 0-3 |
| | 0-1 | 1-2 | 0-3 | | | 0-0 | | | | |
| **FINN HARPS** | 0-0 | 2-1 | 2-2 | 3-1 | 2-2 | | 1-0 | 5-0 | 2-1 | 0-3 |
| | 1-0 | | 0-1 | 3-0 | 2-0 | | | 0-1 | | 0-2 |
| **COBH RAMBLERS** | 0-2 | 1-0 | 0-0 | 0-0 | 1-0 | 2-1 | | 1-1 | 3-0 | 0-1 |
| | | | | 0-1 | 5-0 | 1-0 | | | 3-0 | |
| **LONGFORD TOWN** | 0-0 | 0-2 | 0-1 | 3-3 | 0-0 | 1-3 | 1-1 | | 1-3 | 0-1 |
| | | 0-1 | 2-1 | | | | 3-1 | | | 0-2 |
| **MONAGHAN UNITED** | 0-1 | 0-4 | 0-3 | 1-1 | 0-1 | 2-3 | 1-2 | 2-1 | | 1-2 |
| | | | 2-1 | 1-2 | 0-1 | | | 0-2 | | 2-2 |
| **ST. JAMES GATE** | 0-0 | 1-5 | 1-3 | 1-2 | 2-1 | 1-3 | 0-2 | 1-2 | 2-4 | |
| | | 3-2 | | 1-0 | 2-0 | | | 0-1 | | |

Note : Newcastle West resigned from the League prior to commencement of Season 1990/91, their place being taken over by St. James' Gate.

## F.A. OF IRELAND CUP 1990/91

### 1ST ROUND

| | | | |
|---|---|---|---|
| Cardonagh | 0 | Limerick City | 0 |
| Drogheda United | 4 | Parkvilla | 1 |
| Edenmore | 1 | Sligo Rovers | 2 |
| Longford Town | 0 | Shelbourne | 3 |
| Midleton | 2 | Bray Wanderers | 0 |
| Portlaoise | 3 | Home Farm | 1 |
| Shamrock Rovers | 4 | Finn Harps | 3 |
| Waterford United | 2 | St.Joseph's Boys | 1 |
| Cork City | 2 | Bohemians | 3 |
| Dundalk | 0 | Ashtown Villa | 1 |
| Galway United | 3 | Cobh Ramblers | 1 |
| Mallow United | 0 | Athlone Town | 1 |
| Monaghan United | 1 | Elm Rovers | 2 |
| St.Patrick's Athletic | 0 | Derry City | 0 |
| UCD | 1 | Kilkenny City | 1 |
| Wayside Celtic | 0 | St.James' Gate | 2 |

**REPLAYS**

| | | | |
|---|---|---|---|
| Derry City | 1 | St.Patrick's Athletic | 0 |
| Kilkenny City | 2 | UCD | 0 |
| Limerick City | 3 | Cardonagh | 0 |

### 2ND ROUND

| | | | |
|---|---|---|---|
| Athlone Town | 2 | Bohemians | 0 |
| Drogheda United | 0 | Waterford United | 2 |
| Limerick City | 1 | Elm Rovers | 0 |
| Portlaoise | 2 | Kilkenny City | 3 |
| Derry City | 1 | Ashtown Villa | 2 |
| Galway United | 2 | Shelbourne | 0 |
| Midleton | 0 | St.James' Gate | 1 |
| Sligo Rovers | 2 | Shamrock Rovers | 2 |

**REPLAY**

| | | | |
|---|---|---|---|
| Shamrock Rovers | 0 | Sligo Rovers | 0 (aet.) |

Shamrock Rovers win 4-2 on penalties

### 1/4 FINALS

| | | | |
|---|---|---|---|
| Athlone Town | 0 | Shamrocks Rovers | 0 |
| Limerick City | 1 | Galway United | 2 |
| Kilkenny City | 1 | Ashtown Villa | 0 |
| Waterford United | 0 | St.James' Gate | 1 |

**REPLAY**

| | | | |
|---|---|---|---|
| Shamrock Rovers | 1 | Athlone Town | 0 |

### SEMI-FINALS

| | | | |
|---|---|---|---|
| Kilkenny City | 0 | Shamrock Rovers | 1 |
| St.James' Gate | 1 | Galway United | 3 |

### FINAL  12/5/91 at Lansdowne Road, Dublin

Galway United ........... 1    Shamrock Rovers ...... 0

Galway U : McIntyre, Rodgers, Cleary, Nolan, Morris-Burke (Lally 65), P.Campbell, Wyse (Cassidy 86), Carpenter, Mernagh, Keane, Glynn.

Shamrock R : Kavanagh, Connell, Murphy, Eccles, Cooney, Devine (Power 86), D.Campbell, Poutch (O'Connor 86), Treacy, Larkins, Swan.

1-0  Glynn      85        Referee : Purcell
Attendance : 15,257

# LEAGUE OF IRELAND LEAGUE CUP 1990/91

## 1ST ROUND

### GROUP A

| Cobh Ramblers..........1 | Kilkenny City .............2 |
| Waterford United........0 | Cork City ...................3 |
| Cobh Ramblers..........0 | Waterford United........0 |
| Kilkenny City .............1 | Cork City ...................1 |
| Cork City ...................3 | Cobh Ramblers..........0 |
| Waterford United........0 | Kilkenny City .............0 |

**LEAGUE TABLE FINAL**

| | | | | | | | |
|---|---|---|---|---|---|---|---|
| Cork City | 3 | 2 | 1 | 0 | 7 | 1 | 5 |
| Kilkenny City | 3 | 1 | 2 | 0 | 3 | 2 | 4 |
| Waterford United | 3 | 0 | 2 | 1 | 0 | 3 | 2 |
| Cobh Ramblers | 3 | 0 | 1 | 2 | 1 | 5 | 1 |

### GROUP B

| Limerick City ............. 5 | Longford Town ...........1 |
| Longford Town .......... 2 | Connacht Snr.Lge.XI..1 |
| Galway United ........... 5 | Limerick City .............0 |
| Connacht Snr.Lge.XI . 1 | Limerick City .............3 |
| Longford Town .......... 0 | Galway United ...........3 |
| Galway United ........... 5 | Connacht Snr.Lge.XI..0 |

**LEAGUE TABLE FINAL**

| | | | | | | | |
|---|---|---|---|---|---|---|---|
| Galway United | 3 | 3 | 0 | 0 | 13 | 0 | 6 |
| Limerick City | 3 | 2 | 0 | 1 | 8 | 7 | 4 |
| Longford Town | 3 | 1 | 0 | 2 | 3 | 9 | 2 |
| Connacht Senior Lge. XI | 3 | 0 | 0 | 3 | 2 | 10 | 0 |

### GROUP C

| Drogheda United........2 | Athlone Town .............1 |
| Dundalk.....................2 | Monaghan United.......1 |
| Athlone Town .............4 | Monaghan United.......2 |
| Drogheda United........0 | Dundalk....................0 |
| Dundalk.....................1 | Athlone Town .............1 |
| Monaghan United ......0 | Drogheda United........4 |

**LEAGUE TABLE FINAL**

| | | | | | | | |
|---|---|---|---|---|---|---|---|
| Drogheda United | 3 | 2 | 1 | 0 | 6 | 1 | 5 |
| Dundalk | 3 | 1 | 2 | 0 | 3 | 2 | 4 |
| Athlone Town | 3 | 1 | 1 | 1 | 6 | 5 | 3 |
| Monaghan United | 3 | 0 | 0 | 3 | 3 | 10 | 0 |

### GROUP D

| Fanad United ............. 1 | Finn Harps .................1 |
| Derry City.................. 0 | Sligo Rovers .............0 |
| Fanad United ............. 1 | Sligo Rovers .............0 |
| Finn Harps ................. 3 | Derry City.................3 |
| Sligo Rovers ............... 4 | Finn Harps .................1 |
| Derry City.................. 8 | Fanad United .............0 |

**LEAGUE TABLE FINAL**

| | | | | | | | |
|---|---|---|---|---|---|---|---|
| Derry City | 3 | 1 | 2 | 0 | 11 | 3 | 4 |
| Sligo Rovers | 3 | 1 | 1 | 1 | 4 | 2 | 3 |
| Fanad United | 3 | 1 | 1 | 1 | 2 | 9 | 3 |
| Finn Harps | 3 | 0 | 2 | 1 | 5 | 8 | 2 . |

### GROUP E

| St.James' Gate ..........0 | Shelbourne.................5 |
| Shamrock Rovers .....0 | Home Farm ................0 |
| Home Farm.................2 | St.James' Gate ..........2 |
| Shelbourne ................1 | Shamrock Rovers .....1 |
| Home Farm.................0 | Shelbourne.................3 |
| Shamrock Rovers .....4 | St.James' Gate ..........1 |

**LEAGUE TABLE FINAL**

| | | | | | | | |
|---|---|---|---|---|---|---|---|
| Shelbourne | 3 | 2 | 1 | 0 | 9 | 1 | 5 |
| Shamrock Rovers | 3 | 1 | 2 | 0 | 5 | 2 | 4 |
| Home Farm | 3 | 0 | 2 | 1 | 2 | 5 | 2 |
| St.James' Gate | 3 | 0 | 1 | 2 | 3 | 11 | 1 |

### GROUP F

| Bray Wanderers......... 1 | Bohemians.................2 |
| UCD ........................... 1 | St.Patrick's Athletic ....0 |
| Bohemians................. 0 | UCD ...........................0 |
| St.Patrick's Athletic .... 0 | Bray Wanderers .........0 |
| St.Patrick's Athletic .... 3 | Bohemians.................1 |
| UCD ........................... 0 | Bray Wanderers .........1 |

**LEAGUE TABLE FINAL**

| | | | | | | | |
|---|---|---|---|---|---|---|---|
| St.Patrick's Athletic | 3 | 1 | 1 | 1 | 3 | 2 | 3 |
| Bray Wanderers | 3 | 1 | 1 | 1 | 2 | 2 | 3 |
| UCD | 3 | 1 | 1 | 1 | 1 | 1 | 3 |
| Bohemians | 3 | 1 | 1 | 1 | 3 | 4 | 3 |

## 1/4 FINALS

| Galway United ..........0 | Derry City..................1 |
| St.Patrick's Athletic ....3 | Shelbourne................1 (aet.) |
| Limerick City ............. 2 | Cork City ...................0 (aet.) |
| Shamrock Rovers ...... 2 | Drogheda United........0 |

## SEMI-FINALS

| Limerick City .............1 | Shamrock Rovers ......0 |
| Derry City.................. 1 | St.Patrick's Athletic ....0 |

## FINAL   27/2/91 at The Brandywell, Derry

Derry City...................2     Limerick City .............0

Derry C : Dalton, Vaudequin, Curran, Gauld, McCarthy (Gorman 46), Brady (McCann 82), Carlyle, Healy, Hegarty, Hanrahan, Speak.

Limerick C : Grace, J.Lyons, Power, O'Halloran, Kerley (Finnan 48), Hartnett (D.Lyons 82), Hogan, Shanahan, Walsh , Fitzgerald, Ryan.

1-0  Hanrahan           Attendance : 6,800
2-0  Healy

# REPUBLIC OF IRELAND INTERNATIONAL REVIEW 1990

## INTERNATIONAL LINE-UPS 1990

| Match | Pat Bonner | Chris Morris | Steve Staunton | Mick McCarthy | Kevin Moran | Ronnie Whelan | Andy Townsend | John Byrne | Bernie Slaven | Tony Cascarino | John Sheridan | Chris Hughton | David O'Leary | Kevin Sheedy | Gerry Peyton | Gary Waddock | Paul McGrath | Niall Quinn | David Kelly | Liam Brady | Ray Houghton | John Aldridge | Alan McLoughlin | Frank Stapleton | Denis Irwin | Mark Kelly |
|---|---|---|---|---|---|---|---|---|---|---|---|---|---|---|---|---|---|---|---|---|---|---|---|---|---|---|
| 28/3/90 REPUBLIC OF IRELAND 1 WALES 0 — Dublin — Friendly — (Slaven) — Ref: Gunn (England) | 1 | 2 | 3 | 4 | 5 | 6 | 7 | 8 | 9 | 10 | 11 | (3) | (5) | (6) | | | | | | | | | | | | |
| 25/4/90 REPUBLIC OF IRELAND 1 USSR 0 — Dublin — Friendly — (Staunton) — Ref: Kleinaitis (USA) | | 2 | 5 | 3 | (4) | | 8 | | | | | (2) | 4 | 9 | 1 | 6 | 7 | 10 | 11 | | | | | | | |
| 16/5/90 REPUBLIC OF IRELAND 1 FINLAND 1 — Dublin — Friendly — (Sheedy) — Ref: Gifford (Wales) | 1 | (3) | 3 | 4 | | | (6) | 11 | 9 | 10 | | 2 | 5 | (11) | | | 7 | | | 6 | 8 | (9) | | | | |
| 27/5/90 TURKEY 0 REPUBLIC OF IRELAND 0 — Izmir — Friendly — Ref: Kirkov (USSR) | 1 | 2 | 5 | | 4 | | 9 | (7) | | 11 | (9) | (5) | 3 | 8 | | 7 | | | | | 7 | 10 | | | | |
| 2/6/90 MALTA 0 REPUBLIC OF IRELAND 3 — Ta'Qali — Friendly — (Quinn, Townsend, Stapleton) — Ref: Azzopardi (Malta) | | | 5 | | 4 | | (9) | 6 | 9 | | 8 | 2 | 3 | | 1 | | | 10 | 11 | | | | 7 | (11) | | |
| 11/6/90 ENGLAND 1 REPUBLIC OF IRELAND 1 — Cagliari — World Cup — (Sheedy) — Ref: Schmidhuber (W.Germany) | 1 | 2 | 5 | 3 | 4 | | 10 | | | 11 | | | | 8 | | | 6 | (11) | | | 7 | 9 | (9) | | | |
| 17/6/90 EGYPT 0 REPUBLIC OF IRELAND 0 — Palermo — World Cup — Ref: Van Langenhove (Belgium) | 1 | 2 | 5 | 3 | 4 | | 8 | | | 11 | | | | 9 | | | 6 | | | | 7 | 10 | (10) | | | |
| 21/6/90 HOLLAND 1 REPUBLIC OF IRELAND 1 — Palermo — World Cup — (Quinn) — Ref: Vautrot (France) | 1 | 2 | 5 | 3 | 4 | (9) | 8 | | | (10) | | | | 9 | | | 6 | 11 | | | 7 | 10 | | | | |
| 25/6/90 RUMANIA 0 REPUBLIC OF IRELAND 0 (aet.) — Genova — World Cup — Ref: Wright (Brazil) — REPUBLIC OF IRELAND WIN 4-5 ON PENALTIES | 1 | 2 | 5 | 3 | 4 | | 8 | | | (11) | | | (5) | 9 | | | 7 | 10 | | | 6 | 11 | | | | |
| 30/6/90 ITALY 1 REPUBLIC OF IRELAND 0 — Roma — World Cup — Ref: Valente (Portugal) | 1 | 2 | 5 | 3 | 4 | | 8 | | | (10) | (11) | | 4 | 9 | | | | | | | 7 | 11 | | | | |
| 12/9/90 REPUBLIC OF IRELAND 1 MOROCCO 0 — Dublin — Friendly — (D.Kelly) — Ref: McKnight (N.Ireland) | 1 | | 5 | 3 | 4 | 7 | 8 | | | | (8) | | | | | | | 11 | 10 | | | | | | | 9 |
| 17/10/90 REPUBLIC OF IRELAND 5 TURKEY 0 — Dublin — EuroCh.Q. — (Aldridge 3, O'Leary, Quinn) — Ref: Fredriksson (Sweden) | 1 | 2 | 3 | 4 | (7) | | 7 | | | (9) | | | 4 | | | | | 9 | | | 8 | 10 | (9) | | 2 | |
| 14/11/90 REPUBLIC OF IRELAND 1 ENGLAND 1 — Dublin — EuroCh.Q. — (Cascarino) — Ref: D'Elia (Italy) | 1 | 2 | 5 | 3 | 4 | 6 | 9 | | | (10) | | | 4 | | | | 7 | 10 | | | 8 | 11 | (6) | | 2 | 4 |
| **CAPS AT 31/12/90** | 46 | 27 | 21 | 50 | 56 | 41 | 20 | 16 | 4 | 29 | 11 | 51 | 54 | 33 | 28 | 20 | 42 | 22 | 7 | 72 | 37 | 37 | 5 | 70 | 2 | 4 |
| **GOALS AT 31/12/90** | | | 1 | | 6 | 3 | 1 | | 1 | 6 | 1 | | | 6 | | | 3 | 6 | 5 | 9 | 6 | 13 | | 20 | | |

## REPUBLIC OF IRELAND : All Time Records as at 31/12/90 - CAPS

1. Liam Brady (Arsenal/Juventus/Sampdoria/Internazionale/Ascoli/West Ham United) — 72
2. Frank Stapleton (Arsenal/Manchester United/Ajax/Derby County/Le Havre AC/Blackburn Rovers) — 70
3. Johnny Giles (Manchester United/Leeds United/West Bromwich Albion/Shamrock Rovers) — 59
4. Don Givens (Manchester United/Luton Town/Queen's Park Rangers/Birmingham City/Xamax FC) — 56
5. Kevin Moran (Manchester United/Sporting Gijon/Blackburn Rovers) — 56
6. David O'Leary (Arsenal) — 54
7. Mick Martin (Bohemians/Manchester United/West Bromwich Albion/Newcastle United) — 51
   Chris Hughton (Tottenham Hotspur) — 51
9. Paddy Mulligan (Shamrock Rovers/Chelsea/Crystal Palace/West Bromwich Albion) — 50
   Mick McCarthy (Manchester City/Celtic/Olympique Lyon/Millwall) — 50

## REPUBLIC OF IRELAND : All Time Records as at 31/12/90 - GOALS

1. Frank Stapleton (Arsenal/Manchester United/Ajax/Derby County/Le Havre AC/Blackburn Rovers) — (70) 20
2. Don Givens (Manchester United/Luton Town/Queen's Park Rangers/Birmingham City/Xamax FC) — (56) 19
3. Jimmy Dunne (Sheffield United/Arsenal/Southampton/Shamrock Rovers) — (15) 14
   Noel Cantwell (West Ham United/Manchester United) — (36) 14
5. Gerry Daly (Manchester United/Derby County/Coventry City/Birmingham City/Shrewsbury Town) — (47) 13
6. Liam Brady (Arsenal/Juventus/Sampdoria/Internazionale/Ascoli/West Ham United) — (72) 9
7. Patrick Curtis (Shelbourne/Bristol City/Ipswich Town/Exeter City) — (17) 8
   Tony Grealish (Orient/Luton Town/Brighton & Hove Albion/West Bromwich Albion) — (43) 8
9. Patrick Moore (Shamrock Rovers/Aberdeen) — (9) 7
   Alf Ringstead (Sheffield United) — (20) 7

# ITALY Correspondent : FRANCESCO MASCALCHI

| ITALY Serie A Season 1990/91 | NAPOLI | MILAN | INTER | JUVENTUS | SAMPDORIA | ROMA | ATALANTA | BOLOGNA | LAZIO | BARI | GENOA | FIORENTINA | LECCE | CESENA | TORINO | PISA | CAGLIARI | PARMA |
|---|---|---|---|---|---|---|---|---|---|---|---|---|---|---|---|---|---|---|
| NAPOLI | ■ | 1-1 | 1-1 | 1-1 | 1-4 | 1-1 | 2-0 | 3-2 | 2-1 | 1-0 | 1-0 | 1-0 | 2-2 | 1-0 | 2-1 | 2-1 | 1-2 | 4-2 |
| MILAN | 4-1 | ■ | 0-1 | 2-0 | 0-1 | 1-1 | 0-1 | 6-0 | 3-1 | 2-0 | 1-0 | 2-1 | 1-0 | 2-0 | 1-0 | 1-0 | 2-0 | 0-0 |
| INTERNAZIONALE | 2-1 | 0-1 | ■ | 2-0 | 0-2 | 2-1 | 3-1 | 1-0 | 2-0 | 5-1 | 2-1 | 1-1 | 5-0 | 2-0 | 1-0 | 6-3 | 1-1 | 2-1 |
| JUVENTUS | 1-0 | 0-3 | 4-2 | ■ | 0-0 | 5-0 | 1-1 | 1-1 | 0-0 | 3-1 | 0-1 | 2-1 | 0-0 | 3-0 | 1-2 | 4-2 | 2-2 | 5-0 |
| SAMPDORIA | 4-1 | 2-0 | 3-1 | 1-0 | ■ | 2-1 | 4-1 | 2-1 | 1-1 | 3-2 | 1-2 | 1-0 | 3-0 | 1-0 | 1-2 | 4-2 | 2-2 | 1-0 |
| ROMA | 1-1 | 0-0 | 1-1 | 0-1 | 0-1 | ■ | 2-1 | 4-1 | 1-1 | 1-0 | 3-1 | 4-0 | 3-0 | 4-1 | 2-0 | 0-2 | 0-0 | 1-1 |
| ATALANTA | 0-0 | 0-2 | 1-1 | 0-0 | 1-1 | 2-2 | ■ | 4-0 | 4-1 | 2-0 | 0-0 | 2-1 | 2-1 | 3-0 | 0-1 | 1-0 | 2-1 | 0-0 |
| BOLOGNA | 1-0 | 1-1 | 0-0 | 0-1 | 0-3 | 2-3 | 1-1 | ■ | 1-2 | 3-0 | 0-3 | 1-1 | 1-1 | 0-1 | 1-0 | 0-1 | 1-2 | 1-3 |
| LAZIO | 0-2 | 1-1 | 0-0 | 1-0 | 3-3 | 1-1 | 2-2 | 3-1 | ■ | 1-1 | 1-1 | 2-1 | 2-0 | 1-1 | 2-1 | 0-0 | 1-1 | 0-0 |
| BARI | 0-0 | 2-1 | 1-1 | 2-0 | 1-1 | 0-1 | 4-1 | 4-0 | 0-0 | ■ | 4-0 | 0-0 | 1-1 | 1-0 | 2-1 | 2-0 | 4-1 | 2-2 |
| GENOA | 1-1 | 1-1 | 3-0 | 2-0 | 0-0 | 3-0 | 2-0 | 0-0 | 3-1 | 3-1 | ■ | 3-2 | 0-0 | 4-1 | 0-0 | 4-2 | 2-2 | 2-1 |
| FIORENTINA | 0-0 | 0-0 | 0-0 | 1-0 | 0-0 | 1-1 | 3-1 | 1-0 | 1-1 | 1-1 | 2-2 | ■ | 0-0 | 2-0 | 0-0 | 4-0 | 4-1 | 2-3 |
| LECCE | 0-0 | 0-3 | 0-2 | 0-1 | 1-0 | 1-1 | 0-0 | 1-3 | 1-0 | 1-1 | 0-3 | 2-0 | ■ | 2-0 | 1-1 | 1-1 | 2-0 | 1-0 |
| CESENA | 0-0 | 0-1 | 1-5 | 1-1 | 0-1 | 1-1 | 0-1 | 3-2 | 1-1 | 4-2 | 1-1 | 0-4 | 3-1 | ■ | 2-2 | 1-1 | 3-0 | 0-1 |
| TORINO | 1-1 | 1-1 | 2-0 | 1-1 | 1-1 | 1-0 | 0-0 | 4-1 | 0-0 | 4-0 | 5-2 | 1-1 | 2-0 | 2-1 | ■ | 1-0 | 1-1 | 0-0 |
| PISA | 1-1 | 0-1 | 0-1 | 1-5 | 0-3 | 0-1 | 0-2 | 2-2 | 0-1 | 1-0 | 0-0 | 0-4 | 4-0 | 3-2 | 2-0 | ■ | 1-0 | 0-2 |
| CAGLIARI | 1-1 | 1-1 | 0-3 | 0-0 | 0-0 | 0-0 | 1-1 | 0-0 | 0-1 | 1-1 | 1-0 | 1-1 | 2-0 | 0-0 | 1-2 | 2-1 | ■ | 2-1 |
| PARMA | 1-0 | 2-0 | 0-0 | 1-2 | 0-0 | 2-1 | 1-0 | 1-1 | 0-0 | 1-0 | 2-1 | 1-0 | 0-0 | 2-0 | 0-0 | 2-3 | 2-0 | ■ |

## TOP SCORERS

| | | |
|---|---|---|
| 1. | Gianluca Vialli (Sampdoria) | 19 |
| 2. | Lothar Matthäus (Internazionale) | 16 |
| 3. | Carlos Aguilera (Genoa) | 15 |
| | Tomas Skuhravy (Genoa) | 15 |
| 5. | Roberto Baggio (Juventus) | 14 |
| | Massimo Ciocci (Cesena) | 14 |
| | Jürgen Klinsmann (Internazionale) | 14 |
| 8. | Giorgio Bresciani (Torino) | 13 |
| | Alessandro Melli (Parma) | 13 |
| 10. | Luis Joao Paulo (Bari) | 12 |
| | Roberto Mancini (Sampdoria) | 12 |
| 12. | Michele Padovano (Pisa) | 11 |
| | Ruben Evair (Atalanta) | 11 |
| | Marco van Basten (Milan) | 11 |
| | Rudi Völler (Roma) | 11 |
| 16. | Claudio Caniggia (Atalanta) | 10 |
| | Paulino Evair (Atalanta) | 10 |
| 18. | Antonio Careca (Napoli) | 9 |
| | Karl-Heinz Riedle (Lazio) | 9 |
| | Kubilay Türkyilmaz (Bologna) | 9 |

## ITALY SERIE A 1990/91

### LEAGUE TABLE FINAL

| | | | | | | | |
|---|---|---|---|---|---|---|---|
| UC Sampdoria | 34 | 20 | 11 | 3 | 57 | 24 | 51 |
| Milan AC | 34 | 18 | 10 | 6 | 46 | 19 | 46 |
| Internazionale FC | 34 | 18 | 10 | 6 | 56 | 31 | 46 |
| Genoa FC 1893 | 34 | 14 | 12 | 8 | 51 | 36 | 40 |
| Torino Calcio | 34 | 12 | 14 | 8 | 40 | 29 | 38 |
| Parma AC | 34 | 13 | 12 | 9 | 35 | 31 | 38 |
| Juventus FC | 34 | 13 | 11 | 10 | 45 | 32 | 37 |
| Napoli SSC | 34 | 11 | 15 | 8 | 37 | 37 | 37 |
| AS Roma | 34 | 11 | 14 | 9 | 43 | 37 | 36 |
| Atalanta BC | 34 | 11 | 13 | 10 | 38 | 37 | 35 |
| Lazio SS | 34 | 8 | 19 | 7 | 33 | 36 | 35 |
| AC Fiorentina | 34 | 8 | 15 | 11 | 40 | 34 | 31 |
| AS Bari | 34 | 9 | 11 | 14 | 41 | 47 | 29 |
| Cagliari Calcio | 34 | 6 | 17 | 11 | 29 | 44 | 29 |
| US Lecce | 34 | 6 | 13 | 15 | 20 | 47 | 25 |
| SC Pisa | 34 | 8 | 6 | 20 | 34 | 60 | 22 |
| AC Cesena | 34 | 5 | 9 | 20 | 28 | 58 | 19 |
| Bologna FC | 34 | 4 | 10 | 20 | 29 | 63 | 18 |

Champions : - UC Sampdoria

Relegated : - US Lecce, SC Pisa, AC Cesena and Bologna FC

**Sampdoria's Pagiluca & Lombardo pictured with the Italian League trophy.**

## ITALY Serie B — Season 1990/91

| | UDINESE | VERONA | CREMONESE | ASCOLI | ANCONA | REGGINA | REGGIANA | FOGGIA | PESCARA | BRESCIA | PADOVA | AVELLINO | TRIESTINA | COSENZA | BARLETTA | MESSINA | MODENA | LUCCHESE | TARANTO | S'TANA |
|---|---|---|---|---|---|---|---|---|---|---|---|---|---|---|---|---|---|---|---|---|
| UDINESE | ■ | 2-0 | 1-1 | 1-0 | 0-0 | 2-1 | 3-1 | 1-1 | 2-1 | 2-2 | 2-2 | 0-0 | 1-1 | 4-0 | 1-0 | 3-3 | 1-1 | 2-1 | 4-0 | 2-0 |
| VERONA | 2-0 | ■ | 2-0 | 4-0 | 2-0 | 1-0 | 1-1 | 2-1 | 1-0 | 1-1 | 0-0 | 1-0 | 1-1 | 1-0 | 0-0 | 3-0 | 1-0 | 0-1 | 2-1 | 0-0 |
| CREMONESE | 0-1 | 1-1 | ■ | 1-0 | 1-0 | 3-2 | 1-1 | 2-0 | 1-1 | 1-0 | 1-1 | 0-0 | 0-0 | 2-1 | 2-2 | 0-0 | 2-0 | 1-0 | 0-0 | 2-1 |
| ASCOLI | 2-1 | 1-1 | 0-0 | ■ | 1-1 | 0-0 | 2-0 | 5-2 | 0-0 | 4-1 | 1-2 | 2-0 | 1-0 | 2-0 | 2-0 | 5-1 | 3-0 | 2-0 | 2-1 | 0-0 |
| ANCONA | 0-2 | 1-1 | 0-2 | 2-0 | ■ | 0-0 | 1-1 | 1-0 | 3-2 | 1-1 | 1-1 | 0-1 | 2-0 | 3-3 | 1-0 | 1-1 | 3-1 | 2-2 | 1-0 | 3-0 |
| REGGINA | 2-1 | 0-1 | 1-1 | 0-0 | 1-1 | ■ | 1-0 | 2-4 | 2-0 | 3-0 | 0-1 | 2-0 | 1-2 | 0-0 | 2-0 | 1-0 | 0-1 | 1-1 | 0-0 | 1-1 |
| REGGIANA | 1-1 | 4-0 | 0-0 | 3-3 | 1-2 | 2-0 | ■ | 1-2 | 1-1 | 1-1 | 2-0 | 0-0 | 1-0 | 7-4 | 2-1 | 4-1 | 1-0 | 2-2 | 1-1 | 0-0 |
| FOGGIA | 2-2 | 1-0 | 1-0 | 2-1 | 2-0 | 1-1 | 2-1 | ■ | 3-3 | 1-0 | 1-1 | 5-0 | 5-1 | 5-0 | 2-0 | 2-3 | 1-0 | 3-0 | 1-0 | 4-0 |
| PESCARA | 2-2 | 0-1 | 1-0 | 0-0 | 1-2 | 1-0 | 2-0 | 2-0 | ■ | 2-0 | 2-2 | 0-0 | 2-0 | 2-0 | 3-0 | 0-1 | 0-2 | 0-0 | 1-3 | 1-1 |
| BRESCIA | 3-0 | 1-1 | 0 0 | 2-1 | 2-0 | 0-0 | 1-2 | 0-0 | 1-1 | ■ | 0-0 | 1-0 | 1-0 | 1-1 | 2-0 | 1-0 | 0-0 | 2-1 | 0-0 | 1-2 |
| PADOVA | 2-1 | 0-0 | 0-1 | 1-0 | 1-2 | 3-1 | 3-1 | 0-0 | 1-0 | 0-1 | ■ | 1-0 | 1-0 | 3-0 | 4-3 | 5-1 | 1-1 | 0-0 | 0-0 | 1-1 |
| AVELLINO | 2-0 | 1-0 | 1-0 | 1-1 | 1-0 | 1-1 | 1-2 | 1-2 | 0-0 | 1-0 | 2-1 | ■ | 0-0 | 0-0 | 3-1 | 2-0 | 1-0 | 1-1 | 1-3 | 0-0 |
| TRIESTINA | 1-1 | 1-1 | 0-0 | 0-0 | 5-0 | 0-0 | 2-3 | 0-2 | 1-1 | 1-1 | 2-0 | 2-1 | ■ | 2-2 | 2-0 | 1-1 | 1-1 | 0-0 | 1-1 | 2-1 |
| COSENZA | 3-1 | 0-0 | 1-0 | 1-1 | 2-1 | 0-0 | 2-1 | 1-1 | 1-1 | 0-0 | 2-0 | 0-0 | 1-2 | ■ | 1-1 | 1-0 | 2-0 | 1-0 | 2-0 | 1-0 |
| BARLETTA | 0-1 | 1-5 | 0-1 | 0-0 | 1-0 | 2-1 | 0-0 | 1-0 | 0-0 | 1-1 | 1-1 | 3-0 | 1-0 | ⊗ | ■ | 4-0 | 0-1 | 2-0 | 1-0 | 0-0 |
| MESSINA | 2-2 | 3-1 | 0-0 | 1-1 | 1-1 | 2-0 | 1-0 | 5-2 | 1-0 | 0-0 | 2-0 | 1-1 | 1-0 | 2-2 | 3-0 | ■ | 0-0 | 0-0 | 0-0 | 1-1 |
| MODENA | 1-1 | 2-2 | 0-0 | 1-2 | 0-0 | 0-0 | 0-2 | 1-3 | 0-0 | 1-1 | 2-0 | 3-1 | 3-0 | 2-0 | 1-0 | 1-1 | ■ | 0-1 | 2-0 | 3-0 |
| LUCCHESE | 1-0 | 1-0 | 1-1 | 0-0 | 1-1 | 2-2 | 1-1 | 2-0 | 0-0 | 0-0 | 2-1 | 1-2 | 2-1 | 1-0 | 0-0 | 0-0 | 1-1 | ■ | 1-1 | 1-0 |
| TARANTO | 1-1 | 1-0 | 1-0 | 2-2 | 1-1 | 1-0 | 0-0 | 0-2 | 0-0 | 1-0 | 0-1 | 1-0 | 2-1 | 1-1 | 0-0 | 2-2 | 0-1 | 1-1 | ■ | 1-1 |
| SALERNITANA | 1-1 | 2-2 | 0-0 | 2-1 | 1-0 | 2-0 | 1-1 | 1-1 | 0-3 | 2-0 | 0-0 | 1-1 | 2-1 | 2-0 | 2-2 | 0-0 | 1-1 | 0-0 | 0-0 | ■ |

⊗ The match between Barletta and Cosenza was abandoned after 47 minutes, with the score Barletta 1 Cosenza 1. The match was later awarded Barletta 0 Cosenza 2.

---

## ITALY SERIE B 1990/91
### LEAGUE TABLE FINAL

| | | | | | | | | |
|---|---|---|---|---|---|---|---|---|
| Foggia | 38 | 21 | 9 | 8 | 67 | 36 | 51 |
| Verona | 38 | 15 | 15 | 8 | 42 | 29 | 45 |
| Cremonese | 38 | 12 | 19 | 7 | 28 | 21 | 43 |
| Ascoli | 38 | 13 | 16 | 9 | 48 | 34 | 42 |
| Padova | 38 | 13 | 15 | 10 | 41 | 36 | 41 |
| Lucchese | 38 | 10 | 20 | 8 | 29 | 30 | 40 |
| Reggiana | 38 | 12 | 15 | 11 | 52 | 45 | 39 |
| Udinese | 38 | 13 | 17 | 8 | 53 | 43 | 38 |
| Brescia | 38 | 9 | 19 | 10 | 29 | 32 | 37 |
| Ancona | 38 | 11 | 15 | 12 | 38 | 43 | 37 |
| Taranto | 38 | 10 | 17 | 11 | 28 | 33 | 37 |
| Messina | 38 | 9 | 19 | 10 | 34 | 45 | 37 |
| Pescara | 38 | 9 | 18 | 11 | 36 | 32 | 36 |
| Modena | 38 | 10 | 16 | 12 | 35 | 35 | 36 |
| Salernitana | 38 | 7 | 22 | 9 | 29 | 38 | 36 |
| Avellino | 38 | 11 | 14 | 13 | 27 | 36 | 36 |
| Cosenza | 38 | 11 | 14 | 13 | 38 | 50 | 36 |
| Reggina | 38 | 7 | 16 | 15 | 29 | 37 | 30 |
| Triestina | 38 | 7 | 16 | 15 | 33 | 43 | 30 |
| Barletta | 38 | 8 | 12 | 18 | 29 | 47 | 28 |

Udinese 5 points deducted

**RELEGATION PLAY OFF : -**
Cosenza .................... 1   Salernitana ................ 0 (aet.)

Promoted : - Foggia, Verona, Cremonese and Ascoli
Relegated : - Salernitana, Reggina, Triestina and Barletta

---

## ITALY SERIE C1 A 1990/91
### LEAGUE TABLE FINAL

| | | | | | | | | |
|---|---|---|---|---|---|---|---|---|
| Piacenza | 34 | 15 | 15 | 4 | 42 | 22 | 45 |
| Como | 34 | 15 | 14 | 5 | 33 | 17 | 44 |
| Venezia | 34 | 15 | 14 | 5 | 37 | 21 | 44 |
| Empoli | 34 | 14 | 10 | 10 | 34 | 32 | 38 |
| Fano | 34 | 11 | 14 | 9 | 33 | 29 | 36 |
| Spezia | 34 | 11 | 14 | 9 | 23 | 23 | 36 |
| Monza | 34 | 10 | 15 | 9 | 37 | 31 | 35 |
| Pro Sesto | 34 | 9 | 17 | 8 | 29 | 26 | 35 |
| Pavia | 34 | 11 | 12 | 11 | 37 | 35 | 34 |
| Vicenza | 34 | 10 | 14 | 10 | 26 | 27 | 34 |
| Baracca Lugo | 34 | 9 | 14 | 11 | 25 | 28 | 32 |
| Casale | 34 | 10 | 12 | 12 | 34 | 39 | 32 |
| Carpi | 34 | 6 | 19 | 9 | 21 | 26 | 31 |
| Chievo | 34 | 8 | 15 | 11 | 23 | 29 | 31 |
| Varese | 34 | 8 | 14 | 12 | 29 | 32 | 30 |
| Carrarese | 34 | 8 | 14 | 12 | 20 | 25 | 30 |
| Trento | 34 | 4 | 18 | 12 | 29 | 42 | 26 |
| Mantova | 34 | 3 | 13 | 18 | 21 | 49 | 19 |

**PROMOTION PLAY-OFF : -**
Venezia .................... 2   Como ........................ 1
Promoted : - Piacenza and Venezia
Relegated : - Varese, Carrarese, Trento and Mantova

---

## ITALY SERIE C1 B 1990/91
### LEAGUE TABLE FINAL

| | | | | | | | | |
|---|---|---|---|---|---|---|---|---|
| Casertana | 34 | 15 | 15 | 4 | 41 | 16 | 45 |
| Palermo | 34 | 15 | 13 | 6 | 40 | 24 | 43 |
| Casarano | 34 | 13 | 14 | 7 | 34 | 23 | 40 |
| Perugia | 34 | 13 | 13 | 8 | 37 | 26 | 39 |
| Fidelis Andria | 34 | 13 | 13 | 8 | 30 | 25 | 39 |
| Siena | 34 | 10 | 18 | 6 | 31 | 30 | 38 |
| Licata | 34 | 10 | 16 | 8 | 33 | 32 | 36 |
| Ternana | 34 | 12 | 12 | 10 | 35 | 43 | 36 |
| Arezzo | 34 | 9 | 17 | 8 | 27 | 23 | 35 |
| Siracusa | 34 | 9 | 15 | 10 | 38 | 35 | 33 |
| Catania | 34 | 12 | 9 | 13 | 39 | 38 | 33 |
| Monopoli | 34 | 8 | 17 | 9 | 32 | 32 | 33 |
| Giarre | 34 | 12 | 8 | 14 | 28 | 30 | 32 |
| Catanzaro | 34 | 8 | 16 | 10 | 28 | 28 | 32 |
| Nola | 34 | 9 | 14 | 11 | 31 | 33 | 32 |
| Torres | 34 | 10 | 10 | 14 | 36 | 42 | 30 |
| Battipagliese | 34 | 5 | 12 | 17 | 15 | 40 | 22 |
| Puteolana | 34 | 3 | 8 | 23 | 24 | 59 | 14 |

**RELEGATION PLAY-OFF : -**
Catanzaro .................. 2   Nola ........................ 1
Promoted : - Casertana and Palermo
Relegated : - Nola, Torres, Battipagliese & Puteolana.
Catanzaro later had 3 points deducted and were relegated in place of Nola.

## ITALY SERIE C2 A 1990/91
### LEAGUE TABLE FINAL

| Team | P | W | D | L | F | A | Pts |
|---|---|---|---|---|---|---|---|
| Alessandria | 34 | 15 | 15 | 4 | 31 | 14 | 45 |
| Massese | 34 | 12 | 20 | 2 | 31 | 18 | 44 |
| Viareggio | 34 | 13 | 17 | 4 | 40 | 19 | 43 |
| Livorno | 34 | 10 | 18 | 6 | 23 | 18 | 38 |
| Gubbio | 34 | 12 | 12 | 10 | 27 | 25 | 36 |
| Novara | 34 | 12 | 11 | 11 | 29 | 26 | 35 |
| Cuneo | 34 | 11 | 13 | 10 | 33 | 30 | 35 |
| Poggibonsi | 34 | 13 | 9 | 12 | 26 | 35 | 35 |
| Olbia | 34 | 4 | 25 | 5 | 22 | 25 | 33 |
| Pontedera | 34 | 9 | 14 | 11 | 24 | 27 | 32 |
| Prato | 34 | 11 | 10 | 13 | 33 | 33 | 32 |
| Ponsacco | 34 | 7 | 18 | 9 | 21 | 30 | 32 |
| Montevarchi | 34 | 7 | 17 | 10 | 20 | 21 | 31 |
| Tempio | 34 | 6 | 19 | 9 | 17 | 26 | 31 |
| Cecina | 34 | 8 | 15 | 11 | 32 | 33 | 31 |
| Derthona | 34 | 8 | 14 | 12 | 24 | 35 | 30 |
| Sarzanese | 34 | 7 | 15 | 12 | 26 | 36 | 29 |
| Oltrepo | 34 | 4 | 12 | 18 | 20 | 43 | 20 |

Promoted :- Alessandria and Massese

## ITALY SERIE C2 B 1990/91
### LEAGUE TABLE FINAL

| Team | P | W | D | L | F | A | Pts |
|---|---|---|---|---|---|---|---|
| Palazzolo | 34 | 16 | 13 | 5 | 51 | 32 | 45 |
| Solbiatese | 34 | 17 | 10 | 7 | 44 | 28 | 44 |
| Spal | 34 | 15 | 12 | 7 | 39 | 29 | 42 |
| Ravenna | 34 | 12 | 14 | 8 | 40 | 36 | 37 |
| Pergocrema | 34 | 11 | 15 | 8 | 37 | 31 | 37 |
| Valdagno | 34 | 13 | 10 | 11 | 33 | 31 | 36 |
| Legnano | 34 | 12 | 11 | 11 | 30 | 27 | 35 |
| Fiorenzuola | 34 | 7 | 20 | 7 | 27 | 35 | 34 |
| Centese | 34 | 9 | 16 | 9 | 18 | 19 | 34 |
| Leffe | 34 | 11 | 11 | 12 | 24 | 27 | 33 |
| Virescit | 34 | 8 | 16 | 10 | 22 | 27 | 32 |
| Suzzara | 34 | 7 | 18 | 9 | 28 | 32 | 32 |
| Lecco | 34 | 8 | 15 | 11 | 33 | 37 | 31 |
| Ospitaletto | 34 | 8 | 15 | 11 | 26 | 32 | 31 |
| Pievigina | 34 | 5 | 19 | 10 | 14 | 28 | 29 |
| Cittadella | 34 | 7 | 12 | 15 | 24 | 40 | 26 |
| Saronno | 34 | 5 | 13 | 16 | 21 | 37 | 24 |
| Treviso | 34 | 5 | 13 | 16 | 16 | 23 | 23 |

### PROMOTION PLAY-OFF :-
Solbiatese..............1     Spal..............1     0

Promoted :- Palazzolo and Spal

## ITALY SERIE C2 C 1990/91
### LEAGUE TABLE FINAL

| Team | P | W | D | L | F | A | Pts |
|---|---|---|---|---|---|---|---|
| Chieti | 34 | 18 | 14 | 2 | 40 | 14 | 50 |
| Sambenedettese | 34 | 14 | 18 | 2 | 33 | 16 | 46 |
| Teramo | 34 | 14 | 13 | 7 | 32 | 17 | 41 |
| Vastese | 34 | 12 | 15 | 7 | 25 | 20 | 39 |
| Vis Pesaro | 34 | 13 | 11 | 10 | 38 | 19 | 37 |
| Francavilla | 34 | 11 | 13 | 10 | 34 | 31 | 35 |
| Bisceglie | 34 | 10 | 13 | 11 | 27 | 21 | 33 |
| Rimini | 34 | 10 | 13 | 11 | 23 | 23 | 33 |
| Trani | 34 | 11 | 9 | 14 | 26 | 27 | 33 |
| Giulianova | 34 | 9 | 15 | 10 | 28 | 21 | 33 |
| Molfetta | 34 | 11 | 8 | 15 | 25 | 26 | 31 |
| Civitanovese | 34 | 10 | 11 | 13 | 26 | 30 | 31 |
| Lanciano | 34 | 10 | 11 | 13 | 27 | 34 | 31 |
| Jesi | 34 | 9 | 14 | 11 | 14 | 29 | 32 |
| Altamura | 34 | 10 | 9 | 15 | 28 | 42 | 29 |
| Fasano | 34 | 7 | 15 | 12 | 22 | 42 | 29 |
| Riccione | 34 | 5 | 17 | 12 | 24 | 30 | 27 |
| Martina | 34 | 8 | 10 | 16 | 21 | 40 | 26 |

Promoted :- Chieti and Sambenedettese

## ITALY SERIE C2 D 1990/91
### LEAGUE TABLE FINAL

| Team | P | W | D | L | F | A | Pts |
|---|---|---|---|---|---|---|---|
| Ischia | 34 | 16 | 14 | 4 | 32 | 15 | 46 |
| Acireale | 34 | 15 | 15 | 4 | 41 | 27 | 45 |
| Sangiuseppese | 34 | 12 | 15 | 7 | 31 | 20 | 39 |
| Lodigiani | 34 | 11 | 16 | 7 | 32 | 25 | 38 |
| Vigor Lamezia | 34 | 11 | 16 | 7 | 38 | 28 | 38 |
| Atletico Leonzio | 34 | 8 | 20 | 6 | 35 | 22 | 36 |
| Pro Cavese | 34 | 9 | 18 | 7 | 30 | 28 | 36 |
| Latina | 34 | 10 | 15 | 9 | 28 | 28 | 35 |
| Astrea | 34 | 10 | 14 | 10 | 36 | 37 | 34 |
| Potenza | 34 | 9 | 16 | 9 | 22 | 26 | 34 |
| Savoia | 34 | 11 | 11 | 12 | 38 | 30 | 33 |
| Formia | 34 | 9 | 15 | 10 | 24 | 29 | 33 |
| Turris | 34 | 8 | 20 | 6 | 28 | 28 | 32 |
| Castel di Sangro | 34 | 8 | 14 | 12 | 31 | 32 | 30 |
| Kroton | 34 | 7 | 15 | 12 | 22 | 38 | 29 |
| Enna | 34 | 7 | 13 | 14 | 27 | 40 | 27 |
| Celano | 34 | 3 | 19 | 12 | 21 | 35 | 25 |
| Ostiamare | 34 | 4 | 14 | 16 | 16 | 44 | 22 |

Promoted :- Ischia and Acireale

## ITALY CUP 1990/91

### 1ST ROUND

| | 1ST LEG | 2ND LEG | AGG. |
|---|---|---|---|
| Cosenza v Barletta | 0-1 | 3-0 | 3-1 |
| Fiorentina v Venezia | 4-1 | 0-0 | 4-1 |
| Reggiana v Como (Reggiana win on the away goals rule) | 0-1 | 2-1 | 2-2 |
| Reggiana v Modena | 1-3 | 1-1 | 2-4 |
| Cremonese v Mantova | 2-0 | 0-0 | 2-0 |
| Brescia v Salernitana | 0-0 | 3-1 | 3-1 |
| Verona v Palermo | 2-1 | 0-1 | 2-1 |
| Padova v Monza (Monza win on the away goals rule) | 3-1 | 0-2 | 3-3 |
| Avellino v Taranto | 1-1 | 0-2 | 1-3 |
| Udinese v Casertana | 4-1 | 0-1 | 4-2 |
| Foggia v Lucchese | 4-1 | 1-3 | 5-4 |
| Ascoli v Giarre | 0-2 | 1-2 | 1-2 |
| Ancona v Messina (Messina win on the away goals rule) | 2-2 | 1-1 | 3-3 |
| Pescara v Catanzaro | 1-0 | 2-0 | 3-0 |
| Lecce v Empoli (Lecce win 5-4 on penalties) | 0-0 | 0-0 | 0-0 |
| Triestina v Licata | 1-0 | 1-0 | 2-0 |

### 2ND ROUND

| | 1ST LEG | 2ND LEG | AGG. |
|---|---|---|---|
| Napoli v Cosenza | 3-0 | 2-0 | 5-0 |
| Fiorentina v Parma | 1-0 | 1-0 | 2-0 |
| Bologna v Reggiana | 4-1 | 0-1 | 4-2 |
| Modena v Lazio | 0-0 | 3-1 | 3-1 |
| Cesena v Cremonese | 4-3 | 0-2 | 4-5 |
| Sampdoria v Brescia | 1-1 | 4-0 | 5-1 |
| Verona v Torino | 1-1 | 0-3 | 1-4 |
| Monza v Internazionale | 0-4 | 1-1 | 1-5 |
| Juventus v Taranto | 2-0 | 1-2 | 3-2 |
| Udinese v Pisa | 0-1 | 0-1 | 0-2 |
| Roma v Foggia | 1-0 | 3-1 | 4-1 |
| Giarre v Genoa | 0-0 | 0-3 | 0-3 |
| Bari v Messina (Bari win 5-3 on penalties) | 2-0 | 0-2 | 2-2 |
| Atalanta v Pescara | 2-0 | 1-0 | 3-0 |
| Lecce v Cagliari | 4-0 | 1-0 | 5-0 |
| Milan v Triestina | 1-0 | 1-1 | 2-1 |

### 3RD ROUND

| | 1ST LEG | 2ND LEG | AGG. |
|---|---|---|---|
| Napoli v Fiorentina | 2-1 | 0-0 | 2-1 |
| Sampdoria v Cremonese | 1-1 | 3-2 | 4-3 |
| Juventus v Pisa | 3-2 | 2-1 | 5-3 |
| Roma v Genoa | 2-0 | 1-1 | 3-1 |
| Atalanta v Bari | 1-0 | 0-3 | 1-3 |
| Milan v Lecce | 3-0 | 2-2 | 5-2 |
| Internazionale v Torino (Torino win on the away goals rule) | 2-1 | 0-1 | 2-2 |
| Bologna v Modena | 1-0 | 2-1 | 3-1 |

### 1/4 FINALS

| | 1ST LEG | 2ND LEG | AGG. |
|---|---|---|---|
| Napoli v Bologna | 0-1 | 3-1 | 3-2 |
| Roma v Bologna | 1-1 | 2-0 | 3-1 |
| Torino v Sampdoria (Sampdoria win 3-2 on penalties) | 1-0 | 1-1 | 1-1 |
| Bari v Milan | 0-1 | 0-0 | 0-1 |

| SEMI-FINALS | 1ST LEG | 2ND LEG | AGG. |
|---|---|---|---|
| Napoli v Sampdoria | 1-0 | 0-2 | 1-2 |
| Milan v Roma | 0-0 | 0-1 | 0-1 |

## FINAL    1st Leg 30/5/91 (at Stadio Olimpico, Roma)

AS Roma ................... 3    UC Sampdoria ........... 1

Roma : Cervone, S.Pèllegrini, Carboni, Berthold, Aldair, Nela, Desideri, Di Mauro, Völler, Giannini (Gerolin 84), Rizzitelli (Muzzi 76).

Sampdoria : Pagliuca, Mannini, Katanec (Bonetti 84), Pari, Vierchowod, L.Pellegrini, Lombardo (Invernizzi 84), Cerezo,Vialli, Mancini, Dossena.

| 1-0 | L.Pellegrini o.g. | 13 | Referee : Pairetto |
|---|---|---|---|
| 1-1 | Katanec | 29 | Attendance : 55,067 |
| 2-1 | Berthold | 35 | |
| 3-1 | Völler pen. | 41 | |

2nd Leg 9/6/91 (at Stadio Luigi Ferraris, Genova)

UC Sampdoria ........... 1    AS Roma ................... 1

Sampdoria : Pagliuca, Mannini, Katanec, Pari, Vierchowod, Lanna (Branca 62), Lombardo, Cerezo, Vialli, Mancini, Invernizzi (Mikhailichenko 56).

Roma : Cervone, S.Pellegrini, Carboni, Gerolin, Aldair, Nela, Desideri, Di Mauro, Völler (Salsano 84), Giannini (Tempestilli 67), Rizzitelli.

| 0-1 | Völler pen. | 56 | Referee : Pezzella |
|---|---|---|---|
| 1-1 | Aldair o.g. | 79 | Attendance · 36,577 |

**AS ROMA WIN 4-2 ON AGGREGATE.**

## ITALY : All Time Records as at 31/12/90 - CAPS

| | | |
|---|---|---|
| 1. | Dino Zoff (Napoli/Juventus) | 112 |
| 2. | Giacinto Facchetti (Internazionale) | 94 |
| 3. | Marco Tardelli (Juventus/Internazionale) | 81 |
| 4. | Gaetano Scirea (Juventus) | 78 |
| 5. | Giuseppe Bergomi (Internazionale) | 75 |
| 6. | Giancarlo Antognoni (Fiorentina) | 73 |
| | Antonio Cabrini (Juventus) | 73 |
| 8. | Claudio Gentile (Juventus) | 71 |
| 9. | Alessandro Mazzola (Internazionale) | 70 |
| 10. | Tarcisio Burgnich (Internazionale) | 66 |

## ITALY : All Time Records as at 31/12/90 - GOALS

| | | | |
|---|---|---|---|
| 1. | Luigi Riva (Cagliari) | (42) | 35 |
| 2. | Giuseppe Meazza (Ambrosiana-Inter) | (53) | 33 |
| 3. | Silvio Piola (Lazio/Juventus/Novara) | (34) | 30 |
| 4. | Adolfo Baloncieri (Alessandria/Torino) | (47) | 25 |
| | Alessandro Altobelli (Internazionale) | (61) | 25 |
| 6. | Francesco Graziani (Torino/Fiorentina) | (64) | 23 |
| 7. | Alessandro Mazzola (Internazionale) | (70) | 22 |
| 8. | Paolo Rossi (Vicenza/Perugia/Juventus/Milan AC) | (48) | 20 |
| 9. | Roberto Bettega (Juventus) | (42) | 19 |
| 10. | Julio Libonatti (Torino) | (17) | 15 |
| | Angelo Schiavio (Bologna) | (21) | 15 |
| | Gino Colaussi (Triestina) | (26) | 15 |

**Italy's 1990 World Cup Team.**

# INTERNATIONAL LINE-UPS 1990

| Date | Match | Venue / Comp. | Referee (scorers) | Zenga | Ferrara | Maldini | Bergomi | Vierchowod | Ancelotti | Marocchi | De Napoli | Carnevale | Giannini | Baggio | Serena | De Agostini | Baresi | Donadoni | Schillaci | Ferri | Vialli | Berti | Tacconi | Crippa | Mancini | Eranio | Lombardo |
|---|---|---|---|---|---|---|---|---|---|---|---|---|---|---|---|---|---|---|---|---|---|---|---|---|---|---|---|
| 21/2/90 | HOLLAND 0  ITALY 0 | Rotterdam, Friendly | Biguet (France) | 1 | 2 | 3 | 4 |  | 6 |  | 8 |  | 10 | 11 | (9) | (10) |  | 7 | (11) |  |  |  |  |  | (7) |  |  |
| 31/3/90 | SWITZERLAND 0  ITALY 1 | Basel, Friendly | Assenmacher (W.Germany) — (De Agostini) | 1 | (2) | 3 | 2 | 5 | 7 |  | 8 | 11 | 10 | 6 | 9 | 4 |  |  | (10) |  |  |  |  |  |  |  |  |
| 9/6/90 | ITALY 1  AUSTRIA 0 | Roma, World Cup | Wright (Brazil) — (Schillachi) | 1 |  | 5 | 3 |  |  |  | 8 | 9 | 10 | (11) |  | (7) | 2 | 7 | (9) | 4 | 9 |  |  |  |  |  |  |
| 14/6/90 | ITALY 1  USA 0 | Roma, World Cup | Mendez (Mexico) — (Giannini) | 1 |  | 5 | 3 | (5) |  |  | 8 | 9 | 10 |  |  | 6 | 7 | 6 | (11) | 4 |  | (10) |  |  |  |  |  |
| 19/6/90 | ITALY 2  CZECHOSLOVAKIA 0 | Roma, World Cup | Quiniou (France) — (Schillachi, Baggio) | 1 |  | 5 |  | (5) |  |  | 5 |  | 8 | (7) |  | (6) |  |  | 11 | 4 |  |  |  |  |  |  |  |
| 25/6/90 | ITALY 2  URUGUAY 0 | Roma, World Cup | Courtney (England) — (Schillachi, Serena) | 1 |  | 5 | 3 | (10) |  |  | 6 |  | 8 | 10 | (11) | 2 |  | 11 | 10 | 4 |  |  |  | (6) |  |  |  |
| 30/6/90 | ITALY 1  REPUBLIC OF IRELAND 0 | Roma, World Cup | Silva Valente (Portugal) — (Schillachi) | 1 |  | 4 | 5 |  | (7) |  | 6 |  | 7 | 10 |  | 2 | 8 | 6 | 10 | 5 |  |  |  |  |  |  |  |
| 3/7/90 | ITALY 1  ARGENTINA 1 (aet.) | Napoli, World Cup | Vautrot (France) — (Schillachi) | 1 |  | 3 | 3 | (3) |  |  | 5 |  | 7 | (7) | (11) | 8 | 2 | 10 | 7 | 4 | 11 |  |  |  |  |  |  |
| 7/7/90 | ITALY 2  ENGLAND 1 | Bari, World Cup | Quiniou (France) — (Baggio, Scillachi) | 1 | 3 | 9 | 5 | 4 | 6 | 10 | 8 | 9 |  | 10 | (9) | 8 | 2 | 11 | 11 | 3 |  | (8) |  |  |  |  |  |
| 26/9/90 | ITALY 1  HOLLAND 0 | Palermo, Friendly | Petrovic (Yugoslavia) — (Baggio) | 1 |  |  | 2 |  | 6 | 8 | 6 | 11 | 7 | 11 |  | 9 | 4 | 7 | 3 |  |  |  | (1) |  |  |  |  |
| 17/10/90 | HUNGARY 1  ITALY 1 | Budapest, EuroCh.Q. | Karlsson (Sweden) — (Baggio) | 1 |  | 5 | 3 | (3) |  | 6 | 8 |  | 10 | 11 | (9) | 3 | 4 | 9 | 9 | 4 |  | (10) |  | (6) |  |  |  |
| 3/11/90 | ITALY 0  USSR 0 | Roma, EuroCh.Q. | Van Langenhove (Belgium) | 1 | 2 |  |  | 5 |  | 10 | 8 |  |  |  | 11 | 6 | 4 |  | 8 | 5 |  | 8 |  |  | 7 | 10 |  |
| 22/12/90 | CYPRUS 0  ITALY 4 | Limassol, EuroCh.Q. | Gregg (Czech.) — (Vierchowod, Serena 2, Lombardo) | 1 | 3 | 3 |  |  |  |  |  |  |  |  | 11 |  |  |  |  |  |  |  |  |  | 10 |  | 7 |
| CAPS AT 31/12/90 | | | | 46 | 19 | 28 | 75 | 34 | 25 | 10 | 47 | 10 | 42 | 16 | 24 | 33 | 49 | 36 | 12 | 39 | 45 | 17 | 6 | 6 | 21 | 1 | 1 |
| GOALS AT 31/12/90 | | | | | 3 |  | 6 | 1 | 1 |  | 1 | 2 | 4 | 7 | 5 | 4 | 1 | 1 | 6 | 4 | 11 | 3 |  |  | 4 | 1 | 1 |

ARGENTINA WIN 3–4 ON PENALTIES

Note : The match Italy 0   Greece 0 played 30/5/90 at Perugia has not been recognized as a full International by the Italian FA. The FA have therefore adhered to a FIFA ruling prohibiting the playing of Official International Matches in a country hosting the World Cup Finals, 2 weeks prior to their commencement.

It should be noted however, that the Greek FA have chosen to recognize the match as a full International.

# LUXEMBOURG Correspondent : JEAN-PIERRE SCHUMMER

| LUXEMBOURG 1st Division 1st Stage Season 1990/91 | UNION | BEGGEN. | JEUNESSE | SPORA | FOLA | GR'MACHER | RED BOYS | HESPERANGE | ARIS | PROGRÈS |
|---|---|---|---|---|---|---|---|---|---|---|
| UNION LUXEMBOURG | | 3-2 | 1-1 | 5-1 | 6-0 | 5-0 | 2-0 | 1-1 | 1-0 | 2-1 |
| AVENIR BEGGEN | 1-2 | | 1-3 | 3-0 | 8-0 | 2-1 | 5-4 | 1-1 | 2-1 | 1-1 |
| AS JEUNESSE D'ESCH | 1-0 | 1-5 | | 0-3 | 2-0 | 3-0 | 2-1 | 1-1 | 1-1 | 4-2 |
| CA SPORA LUXEMBOURG | 2-4 | 2-2 | 0-5 | | 0-1 | 1-0 | 2-0 | 2-1 | 4-1 | 2-1 |
| CS FOLA ESCH | 0-1 | 0-0 | 0-1 | 0-3 | | 0-2 | 0-2 | 1-3 | 2-0 | 0-2 |
| CS GREVENMACHER | 1-3 | 2-1 | 3-0 | 0-4 | 6-1 | | 0-2 | 2-1 | 1-0 | 1-0 |
| FA RED BOYS DIFFERDANGE | 1-2 | 1-0 | 0-3 | 4-0 | 2-0 | 1-0 | | 2-4 | 1-0 | 0-2 |
| SWIFT HESPERANGE | 2-1 | 0-1 | 3-3 | 1-2 | 2-1 | 1-2 | 2-5 | | 4-0 | 6-2 |
| ARIS BONNEVOIE | 0-2 | 1-2 | 0-0 | 0-3 | 0-2 | 0-3 | 1-3 | 1-2 | | 0-1 |
| PROGRÈS NIEDERCORN | 0-8 | 1-0 | 1-1 | 2-3 | 0-2 | 2-0 | 0-1 | 1-1 | 4-1 | |

Note : The match CS Grevenmacher 0 Red Boys Differdange 2 was later awarded CS Grevenmacher 5 Red Boys Differdange 0.

| LUXEMBOURG 2nd Division 1 1st Stage Season 1990/91 | ROSPORT | ETZELLA | WILTZ | HOLLERICH | DIEKIRCH | MERTZIG | PFAFFENTHAL | WASSERBILLIG | RM 86 | GASPERICH |
|---|---|---|---|---|---|---|---|---|---|---|
| VICTORIA ROSPORT | | 0-0 | 5-0 | 0-2 | 2-0 | 0-0 | 1-0 | 1-0 | 1-1 | 0-0 |
| ETZELLA ETTELBRUCK | 1-0 | | 0-1 | 3-1 | 0-1 | 2-2 | 5-1 | 2-0 | 1-4 | 7-0 |
| FC WILTZ 71 | 1-1 | 0-0 | | 6-2 | 7-2 | 3-3 | 5-1 | 1-1 | 7-0 | 1-1 |
| CS HOLLERICH | 1-1 | 0-1 | 4-2 | | 4-2 | 1-2 | 0-0 | 2-2 | 2-1 | 2-2 |
| FCM YOUNG BOYS DIEKIRCH | 0-2 | 0-7 | 2-4 | 3-4 | | 1-2 | 2-2 | 1-2 | 2-1 | 0-3 |
| SPORTING MERTZIG | 3-4 | 1-1 | 2-2 | 4-2 | 2-4 | | 3-0 | 2-3 | 2-0 | 3-3 |
| RED BLACK PFAFFENTHAL | 0-3 | 2-0 | 2-1 | 3-2 | 1-2 | 2-0 | | 1-1 | 2-2 | 0-0 |
| JEUNESSE WASSERBILLIG | 2-2 | 0-0 | 1-2 | 4-0 | 0-1 | 0-0 | 1-0 | | 6-0 | 1-0 |
| RM 86 LUXEMBOURG | 0-5 | 1-4 | 0-2 | 4-4 | 0-3 | 1-3 | 0-1 | | | 2-3 |
| TRICOLORE GASPERICH | 2-0 | 0-3 | 3-1 | 3-0 | 1-0 | 0-0 | 4-1 | 0-1 | 4-1 | |

| LUXEMBOURG 2nd Division 2 1st Stage Season 1990/91 | EISCHEN | AS DIFFERD. | WORMELDANGE | ALLIANCE | PÉTANGE | HOBSCHEID | HAUTCHARAGE | RUMELANGE | CHIERS | SANEM |
|---|---|---|---|---|---|---|---|---|---|---|
| OLYMPIQUE EISCHEN | | 0-1 | 1-1 | 2-1 | 0-1 | 0-2 | 0-3 | 4-4 | 1-3 | 0-2 |
| AS DIFFERDANGE | 4-1 | | 0-3 | 0-0 | 4-0 | 5-0 | 5-3 | 0-0 | 2-1 | 1-1 |
| KOEPPCHEN WORMELDANGE | 3-1 | 3-4 | | 1-3 | 3-1 | 1-2 | 2-2 | 2-1 | 3-0 | 1-0 |
| CS ALLIANCE DUDELANGE | 3-3 | 1-1 | 2-2 | | 1-1 | 4-1 | 0-2 | 3-0 | 2-0 | 0-2 |
| CS PÉTANGE | 2-1 | 0-0 | 1-2 | 1-0 | | 2-1 | 1-1 | 0-2 | 2-0 | 1-1 |
| CS HOBSCHEID | 2-1 | 2-2 | 0-1 | 1-1 | 2-3 | | 2-6 | 2-1 | 2-1 | 1-0 |
| JEUNESSE HAUTCHARAGE | 0-1 | 6-0 | 2-2 | 1-2 | 0-3 | 4-3 | | 1-0 | 5-1 | 2-0 |
| US RUMELANGE | 5-1 | 3-4 | 0-2 | 1-1 | 0-1 | 0-2 | 2-0 | | 0-2 | 2-0 |
| CHIERS RODANGE | 5-1 | 0-3 | 0-2 | 1-1 | 0-2 | 0-2 | 1-1 | 2-4 | | 0-0 |
| CS SANEM | 5-1 | 1-1 | 1-1 | 2-1 | 1-0 | 3-1 | 3-1 | 0-1 | 3-0 | |

## LUXEMBOURG 1ST DIVISION 1990/91
### 1ST STAGE LEAGUE TABLE FINAL

| Union Luxembourg | 18 | 14 | 2 | 2 | 49 | 14 | 30 |
|---|---|---|---|---|---|---|---|
| AS Jeunesse d'Esch | 18 | 9 | 6 | 3 | 32 | 22 | 24 |
| CA Spora Luxembourg | 18 | 11 | 1 | 6 | 34 | 30 | 23 |
| Avenir Beggen | 18 | 8 | 4 | 6 | 37 | 24 | 20 |
| CG Grevenmacher | 18 | 10 | 0 | 8 | 29 | 25 | 20 |
| Swift Hesperange | 18 | 7 | 5 | 6 | 36 | 29 | 19 |
| FA Red Boys Differdange | 18 | 9 | 0 | 9 | 28 | 30 | 18 |
| Progrès Niedercorn | 18 | 6 | 3 | 9 | 23 | 33 | 15 |
| CS Fola Esch | 18 | 4 | 1 | 13 | 10 | 40 | 9 |
| Aris Bonnevoie | 18 | 0 | 2 | 16 | 7 | 38 | 2 |

Top 6 clubs qualify for championship play-offs, half ponits gained in 1st Stage being carried forward as follows : - Union Luxembourg 15, Jeunesse d'Esch 12, Spora Luxembourg 11.5, Avenir Beggen 10, CS Grevenmacher 10, Swift Hesperange 9.5. Bottom 4 clubs, Red Boys Differdange, Progrès Niedercorn, Fola Esch and Aris Bonnevoie, join the top 4 clubs of each 2nd Division section to form 2 groups of 6 clubs playing-off for 4 1st Division places for Season 1991/92. Top 2 clubs of each group qualify.

## LUXEMBOURG 1ST DIVISION 1990/91
### CHAMPIONSHIP PLAY-OFFS LEAGUE TABLE FINAL

| Union Luxembourg | 10 | 5 | 3 | 2 | 12 | 8 | 28 |
|---|---|---|---|---|---|---|---|
| AS Jeunesse d'Esch | 10 | 5 | 3 | 2 | 16 | 9 | 25 |
| CA Spora Luxembourg | 10 | 4 | 3 | 3 | 17 | 11 | 22.5 |
| Avenir Beggen | 10 | 6 | 0 | 4 | 19 | 14 | 22 |
| CS Grevenmacher | 10 | 2 | 2 | 6 | 13 | 24 | 16 |
| Swift Hesperange | 10 | 2 | 1 | 7 | 12 | 23 | 14.5 |

Champions : - Union Luxembourg

### TOP SCORERS
1. Morocutti (Union Luxembourg) — 23
2. Thomé (AS Jeunesse d'Esch) — 18
3. Reiter (CA Spora Luxembourg) — 15
4. Wagner (CS Grevenmacher) — 14
5. Horn (CS Grevenmacher) — 13

| LUXEMBOURG 1st Division Championship Play-offs Spring 1991 | UNION | JEUNESSE | SPORA | BEGGEN | GREVENMACHER | HESPERANGE |
|---|---|---|---|---|---|---|
| UNION LUXEMBOURG | | 1-0 | 0-0 | 1-0 | 3-1 | 2-4 |
| JEUNESSE D'ESCH | 0-0 | | 2-2 | 1-2 | 2-2 | 2-1 |
| SPORA LUXEMBOURG | 1-1 | 0-3 | | 4-1 | 4-0 | 3-0 |
| AVENIR BEGGEN | 2-1 | 1-3 | 3-1 | | 6-0 | 1-0 |
| CS GREVENMACHER | 0-1 | 0-1 | 1-0 | 1-2 | | 5-2 |
| SWIFT HESPERANGE | 0-2 | 0-2 | 0-2 | 2-1 | 3-3 | |

| LUXEMBOURG 2nd Division 2nd Stage Promotion Group A Season 1990/91 | RED BOYS | FOLA | ETZELLA | ROSPORT | WILTZ | WASSERBILLIG |
|---|---|---|---|---|---|---|
| FA RED BOYS DIFFERDANGE | | 0-1 | 0-0 | 3-0 | 1-2 | 1-0 |
| CS FOLA ESCH | 2-3 | | 0-3 | 2-3 | 2-1 | 2-1 |
| ETZELLA ETTELBRUCK | 1-3 | 1-2 | | 2-1 | 0-1 | 1-0 |
| VICTORIA ROSPORT | 0-1 | 1-2 | 2-0 | | 4-7 | 1-0 |
| FC WILTZ 71 | 2-1 | 3-2 | 1-0 | 4-1 | | 0-2 |
| JEUNESSE WASSERBILLIG | 1-0 | 1-0 | 4-1 | 2-1 | 2-2 | |

| LUXEMBOURG 2nd Division 2nd Stage Relegation Group A Season 1990/91 | GASPERICH | HOLLERICH | DIEKIRCH | ALLIANCE | RUMELANGE | EISCHEN |
|---|---|---|---|---|---|---|
| TRICOLORE GASPERICH | | 1-1 | 1-1 | 0-0 | 2-1 | 3-3 |
| CS HOLLERICH | 1-2 | | 1-3 | 2-1 | 2-2 | 5-2 |
| FCM YOUNG BOYS DIEKIRCH | 0-1 | 2-4 | | 0-2 | 2-3 | 0-1 |
| CS ALLIANCE DUDELANGE | 1-1 | 1-3 | 1-2 | | 4-0 | 3-0 |
| US RUMELANGE | 1-1 | 1-3 | 1-0 | 1-2 | | 2-2 |
| OLYMPIQUE EISCHEN | 1-1 | 5-2 | 1-3 | 0-0 | 0-2 | |

| LUXEMBOURG 2nd Division 2nd Stage Promotion Group B Season 1990/91 | PROGRÈS | ARIS | WORMELDANGE | AS DIFFERD. | PÉTANGE | SANEM |
|---|---|---|---|---|---|---|
| PROGRÈS NIEDERCORN | | 3-3 | 4-1 | 2-2 | 3-1 | 1-0 |
| ARIS BONNEVOIE | 2-0 | | 1-1 | 0-0 | 2-1 | 1-1 |
| KOEPPCHEN WORMELDANGE | 3-1 | 0-2 | | 3-0 | 2-0 | 2-0 |
| AS DIFFERDANGE | 1-1 | 0-0 | 1-3 | | 2-1 | 0-1 |
| CS PÉTANGE | 1-1 | 0-0 | 2-0 | 1-1 | | 2-2 |
| CS SANEM | 0-1 | 0-0 | 1-2 | 1-1 | 3-0 | |

| LUXEMBOURG 2nd Division 2nd Stage Relegation Group B Season 1990/91 | MERTZIG | PFAFFENTHAL | RM 86 | HAUTCHARAGE | HOBSCHEID | CHIERS |
|---|---|---|---|---|---|---|
| SPORTING MERTZIG | | 2-1 | 4-1 | 1-1 | 4-0 | 6-1 |
| RED BLACK PFAFFENTHAL | 1-2 | | 5-6 | 1-3 | 0-1 | 0-2 |
| RM 86 LUXEMBOURG | 0-1 | 5-2 | | 4-3 | 2-4 | 1-3 |
| JEUNESSE HAUTCHARAGE | 3-2 | 0-3 | 4-2 | | 1-1 | 1-1 |
| CS HOBSCHEID | 2-1 | 1-0 | 2-2 | 4-1 | | 1-1 |
| CHIERS RODANGE | 0-0 | 0-1 | 0-0 | 1-2 | 3-0 | |

## LUXEMBOURG 2ND DIVISION 1 1990/91
### 1ST STAGE LEAGUE TABLE FINAL
| | | | | | | | |
|---|---|---|---|---|---|---|---|
| Etzella Ettelbruck | 18 | 9 | 5 | 4 | 37 | 14 | 23 |
| Victoria Rosport | 18 | 8 | 7 | 3 | 28 | 13 | 23 |
| FC Wiltz 71 | 18 | 8 | 6 | 4 | 46 | 30 | 22 |
| Jeunesse Wasserbillig | 18 | 8 | 6 | 4 | 26 | 15 | 22 |
| Tricolore Gasperich | 18 | 8 | 6 | 4 | 29 | 23 | 22 |
| Sporting Mertzig | 18 | 6 | 8 | 4 | 34 | 28 | 20 |
| CS Hollerich | 18 | 5 | 5 | 8 | 33 | 43 | 15 |
| Red Black Pfaffenthal | 18 | 5 | 5 | 8 | 21 | 33 | 15 |
| FCM Young Boys Diekirch | 18 | 6 | 1 | 11 | 24 | 44 | 13 |
| RM 86 Luxembourg | 18 | 1 | 3 | 14 | 18 | 53 | 5 |

## LUXEMBOURG 2ND DIVISION 2 1990/91
### 1ST STAGE LEAGUE TABLE FINAL
| | | | | | | | |
|---|---|---|---|---|---|---|---|
| Koeppchen Wormeldange | 18 | 10 | 5 | 3 | 35 | 21 | 25 |
| AS Differdange | 18 | 9 | 7 | 2 | 37 | 25 | 25 |
| CS Pétange | 18 | 9 | 4 | 5 | 22 | 19 | 22 |
| CS Sanem | 18 | 8 | 5 | 5 | 25 | 15 | 21 |
| Jeunesse Hautcharage | 18 | 8 | 4 | 6 | 40 | 28 | 20 |
| CS Alliance Dudelange | 18 | 5 | 8 | 5 | 26 | 22 | 18 |
| CS Hobscheid | 18 | 8 | 2 | 8 | 28 | 35 | 18 |
| US Rumelange | 18 | 6 | 3 | 9 | 26 | 27 | 15 |
| Chiers Rodange | 18 | 3 | 3 | 12 | 17 | 36 | 9 |
| Olympique Eischen | 18 | 2 | 3 | 13 | 19 | 47 | 7 |

Top 4 clubs of each section, play-off together with the bottom 4 clubs of 1st Division to decide 4 1st Division places for season 1991/92. Bottom 6 clubs of each section play off against 4 relegation places. 1st Stage records not carried forward to 2nd stage in any way.

## LUXEMBOURG 2ND DIVISION 1990/91
### PROMOTION GROUP A LEAGUE TABLE FINAL
| | | | | | | | |
|---|---|---|---|---|---|---|---|
| FC Wiltz 71 | 10 | 7 | 1 | 2 | 23 | 15 | 15 |
| Red Boys Differdange | 10 | 5 | 1 | 4 | 13 | 9 | 11 |
| Jeunesse Wasserbillig | 10 | 5 | 1 | 4 | 13 | 9 | 11 |
| CS Fola Esch | 10 | 5 | 0 | 5 | 15 | 17 | 10 |
| Etzella Ettelbruck | 10 | 3 | 1 | 6 | 9 | 14 | 7 |
| Victoria Rosport | 10 | 3 | 0 | 7 | 14 | 23 | 6 |

Red Boys retain their 1st Division status
Promoted : - FC Wiltz 71

### PROMOTION PLAY-OFF
FA Red Boys Differdange........3    Jeunesse Wasserbillig........2   (aet.)

## LUXEMBOURG 2ND DIVISION 1990/91
### PROMOTION GROUP B LEAGUE TABLE FINAL
| | | | | | | | |
|---|---|---|---|---|---|---|---|
| Koeppchen Wormeldange | 10 | 6 | 1 | 3 | 17 | 12 | 13 |
| Aris Bonnevoie | 10 | 3 | 7 | 0 | 11 | 6 | 13 |
| Progrès Niedercorn | 10 | 4 | 4 | 2 | 17 | 14 | 12 |
| CS Sanem | 10 | 2 | 4 | 4 | 9 | 10 | 8 |
| AS Differdange | 10 | 1 | 6 | 3 | 8 | 13 | 8 |
| CS Pétange | 10 | 1 | 4 | 5 | 9 | 16 | 6 |

Aris Bonnevoie retain their 1st Division status
Promoted : - Koeppchen Wormeldange

## LUXEMBOURG 2ND DIVISION 1990/91
### RELEGATION GROUP A LEAGUE TABLE FINAL

| | P | W | D | L | F | A | Pts |
|---|---|---|---|---|---|---|---|
| Tricolore Gasperich | 10 | 3 | 7 | 0 | 13 | 10 | 13 |
| CS Hollerich | 10 | 5 | 2 | 3 | 24 | 20 | 12 |
| CS Alliance Dudelange | 10 | 4 | 3 | 3 | 15 | 15 | 11 |
| US Rumelange | 10 | 4 | 3 | 3 | 15 | 9 | 11 |
| Olympique Eischen | 10 | 3 | 3 | 4 | 14 | 18 | 9 |
| FCM Young Boys Diekirch | 10 | 3 | 1 | 6 | 13 | 16 | 7 |

Relegated :- Olympique Eischen and FCM Young Boys Diekirch

### AMALGAMATIONS FOR SEASON 1991/92

CS Alliance Dudelange, US Dudelange and Stade Dudelange merge to form FC 91 Dudelange.
Chiers Rodange and Racing Rodange merge to form FC Rodange 91.
FC 91 Dudelange and FC Rodange 91 take the places of CS Alliance Dudelange and Chiers Rodange in the 2nd Division.
Promotion play-offs have taken place in the 4th and 5th Divisions to fill vacant places resulting from mergers.

## LUXEMBOURG 3RD DIVISION 1 1990/91
### LEAGUE TABLE FINAL

| | P | W | D | L | F | A | Pts |
|---|---|---|---|---|---|---|---|
| Claravallis Clervaux | 22 | 16 | 2 | 4 | 59 | 21 | 34 |
| Racing Troisvierges | 22 | 15 | 3 | 4 | 65 | 18 | 33 |
| Atert Bissen | 22 | 13 | 4 | 5 | 43 | 27 | 30 |
| Daring-Club Echternach | 22 | 11 | 6 | 5 | 47 | 35 | 28 |
| Orania Vianden | 22 | 11 | 3 | 8 | 54 | 45 | 25 |
| Jeunesse Scheren | 22 | 8 | 6 | 8 | 35 | 43 | 22 |
| Minerva Lintgen | 22 | 8 | 4 | 10 | 34 | 48 | 20 |
| US Mertert | 22 | 6 | 5 | 11 | 38 | 40 | 17 |
| FC Brouch | 22 | 6 | 4 | 12 | 26 | 41 | 16 |
| Egalite Weimerskirch | 22 | 5 | 6 | 11 | 41 | 58 | 16 |
| SC Redange/Attert | 22 | 4 | 5 | 13 | 34 | 58 | 13 |
| Jeunesse Useldange | 22 | 2 | 6 | 14 | 29 | 71 | 10 |

Promoted :- Claravallis Clervaux and Racing Troisvierges
Relegated :- Egalite Weimerskirch, SC Redange/Attert and Jeunesse Useldange

## LUXEMBOURG 4TH DIVISION 1 1990/91
### LEAGUE TABLE FINAL

| | P | W | D | L | F | A | Pts |
|---|---|---|---|---|---|---|---|
| Marisca Mersch | 22 | 16 | 3 | 3 | 54 | 24 | 35 |
| AS Wincrange | 22 | 14 | 3 | 5 | 49 | 21 | 31 |
| FC Green Boys Harl-Tarch. | 22 | 13 | 5 | 4 | 51 | 33 | 31 |
| US Rambrouch | 22 | 12 | 5 | 5 | 51 | 29 | 29 |
| AS Hosingen | 22 | 10 | 6 | 6 | 42 | 33 | 26 |
| Jeunesse Gilsdorf | 22 | 8 | 8 | 6 | 28 | 22 | 24 |
| SC Beckerich | 22 | 9 | 6 | 7 | 45 | 43 | 24 |
| US Boevange/Attert | 22 | 8 | 3 | 11 | 36 | 43 | 19 |
| FC 72 Erpeldange | 22 | 4 | 8 | 10 | 34 | 51 | 16 |
| AS Pratzerthal | 22 | 6 | 2 | 14 | 46 | 67 | 14 |
| Les M'tagnards Weiswamp | 22 | 4 | 5 | 13 | 27 | 50 | 13 |
| US Reisdorf | 22 | 2 | 2 | 20 | 21 | 68 | 6 |

Promoted :- Marisca Mersch, AS Wincrange & FC Green Boys
Relegated :- Les Montagnards Weiswampach and US Reisdorf

## LUXEMBOURG 2ND DIVISION 1990/91
### RELEGATION GROUP B LEAGUE TABLE FINAL

| | P | W | D | L | F | A | Pts |
|---|---|---|---|---|---|---|---|
| Sporting Mertzig | 10 | 6 | 2 | 2 | 23 | 10 | 14 |
| CS Hobscheid | 10 | 5 | 3 | 2 | 16 | 15 | 13 |
| Jeunesse Hautcharage | 10 | 4 | 3 | 3 | 19 | 20 | 11 |
| Chiers Rodange | 10 | 3 | 4 | 3 | 12 | 12 | 10 |
| RM 86 Luxembourg | 10 | 3 | 2 | 5 | 23 | 28 | 8 |
| Red Black Pfaffenthal | 10 | 1 | 2 | 7 | 8 | 14 | 4 |

Relegated :- RM 86 Luxembourg and Red Black Pfaffenthal

## LUXEMBOURG 3RD DIVISION 2 1990/91
### LEAGUE TABLE FINAL

| | P | W | D | L | F | A | Pts |
|---|---|---|---|---|---|---|---|
| The Belval Belvaux | 22 | 13 | 4 | 5 | 32 | 23 | 30 |
| FC Mondercange | 22 | 12 | 4 | 6 | 38 | 21 | 28 |
| AS Remich | 22 | 11 | 6 | 5 | 56 | 35 | 28 |
| Stade Dudelange | 22 | 9 | 7 | 6 | 38 | 26 | 25 |
| US Dudelange | 22 | 9 | 6 | 7 | 36 | 32 | 24 |
| US Sandweiler | 22 | 10 | 3 | 9 | 40 | 38 | 23 |
| The National Schifflange | 22 | 8 | 7 | 7 | 25 | 26 | 23 |
| US Mondorf | 22 | 10 | 2 | 10 | 39 | 35 | 22 |
| US Hostert | 22 | 8 | 4 | 10 | 35 | 31 | 20 |
| SC Tétange | 22 | 7 | 1 | 14 | 28 | 42 | 15 |
| Sporting Steinfort | 22 | 6 | 3 | 13 | 22 | 36 | 15 |
| CS Obercorn | 22 | 3 | 3 | 16 | 27 | 59 | 9 |

Promoted :- The Belval Belvaux and FC Mondercange
Relegated :- SC Tétange, Sporting Steinfort & CS Obercorn

## LUXEMBOURG 4TH DIVISION 2 1990/91
### LEAGUE TABLE FINAL

| | P | W | D | L | F | A | Pts |
|---|---|---|---|---|---|---|---|
| Sporting Betrange | 22 | 16 | 3 | 3 | 55 | 25 | 35 |
| Jeunesse Junglinster | 22 | 14 | 3 | 5 | 56 | 23 | 31 |
| Jeunesse Canach | 22 | 13 | 3 | 6 | 48 | 32 | 29 |
| Jeunesse Biwer | 22 | 12 | 2 | 8 | 36 | 30 | 26 |
| Vinesca Ehnen | 22 | 9 | 7 | 6 | 36 | 30 | 25 |
| FC Mamer 32 | 22 | 8 | 8 | 6 | 31 | 29 | 24 |
| Una Strassen | 22 | 8 | 7 | 7 | 40 | 31 | 23 |
| FC Kehlen | 22 | 8 | 4 | 10 | 35 | 44 | 20 |
| Résidence Walferdange | 22 | 6 | 7 | 9 | 30 | 36 | 19 |
| Olymp.Christnach-Wald. | 22 | 7 | 4 | 11 | 38 | 38 | 18 |
| FC Munsbach | 22 | 4 | 2 | 16 | 27 | 56 | 10 |
| FC Beyren-Udinesina | 22 | 1 | 2 | 19 | 19 | 77 | 4 |

Promoted :- Sporting Betrange, Jeunesse Junglinster and Jeunesse Canach
Relegated :- FC Munsbach and FC Beyren-Udinesina

## LUXEMBOURG 4TH DIVISION 3 1990/91
### LEAGUE TABLE FINAL

| | P | W | D | L | F | A | Pts |
|---|---|---|---|---|---|---|---|
| AS Schifflange | 22 | 11 | 8 | 3 | 39 | 18 | 30 |
| Blo-Weiss Itzig | 22 | 11 | 7 | 4 | 44 | 27 | 29 |
| Les Aiglons Dalheim | 22 | 11 | 6 | 5 | 45 | 25 | 28 |
| US Esch | 22 | 10 | 8 | 4 | 33 | 22 | 28 |
| SC Bettembourg | 22 | 12 | 2 | 8 | 47 | 27 | 26 |
| FC Hamm | 22 | 9 | 6 | 7 | 36 | 35 | 24 |
| Red Boys Aspelt | 22 | 8 | 6 | 8 | 38 | 36 | 22 |
| Yellow Boys Weiler | 22 | 7 | 7 | 8 | 38 | 32 | 21 |
| Red Star Merl Belair | 22 | 7 | 5 | 10 | 36 | 36 | 19 |
| ES Clemency | 22 | 5 | 6 | 11 | 36 | 48 | 16 |
| Blue Boys Muhlenbach | 22 | 5 | 6 | 11 | 27 | 40 | 16 |
| Racing Rodange | 22 | 1 | 3 | 18 | 13 | 86 | 5 |

Promoted :- AS Schifflange and Blo-Weiss Itzig
Relegated :- Blue Boys Muhlenbach and Racing Rodange

## PROMOTION PLAY-OFFS

FC Green Boys H-T...3    Jeunesse Canach.....0
Les Aiglons Dalheim...4    FC Green Boys H-T...3
Jeunesse Canach......5    Les Aiglons Dalheim...1

### LEAGUE TABLE FINAL

| | P | W | D | L | F | A | Pts |
|---|---|---|---|---|---|---|---|
| FC Green Boys Harl-Tarch. | 2 | 1 | 0 | 1 | 3 | 1 | 2 |
| Jeunesse Canach | 2 | 1 | 0 | 1 | 5 | 4 | 2 |
| Les Aiglons Dalheim | 2 | 1 | 0 | 1 | 2 | 5 | 2 |

## LUXEMBOURG 5TH DIVISION 1 1990/91
### LEAGUE TABLE FINAL

| | P | W | D | L | F | A | Pts |
|---|---|---|---|---|---|---|---|
| AS Colmarberg | 22 | 20 | 2 | 0 | 69 | 9 | 42 |
| US Folschette | 22 | 16 | 4 | 2 | 51 | 22 | 36 |
| SC Ell | 22 | 14 | 4 | 4 | 31 | 36 | 32 |
| FC 47 Bastendorf | 22 | 11 | 6 | 5 | 56 | 35 | 28 |
| Iska Boys Simmern | 22 | 11 | 3 | 8 | 49 | 39 | 25 |
| Racing 76 Heiderscheid | 22 | 6 | 5 | 11 | 38 | 39 | 17 |
| CS Bourscheid | 22 | 6 | 4 | 12 | 43 | 52 | 16 |
| US Feulen | 22 | 6 | 4 | 12 | 30 | 52 | 16 |
| Blo-Giel Hupperdange | 22 | 7 | 2 | 13 | 31 | 31 | 16 |
| Excelsior Grevels | 22 | 2 | 9 | 11 | 17 | 30 | 13 |
| Les Ardoisiers Perlé | 22 | 4 | 5 | 13 | 36 | 85 | 13 |
| USK Wilwerwitz | 22 | 4 | 2 | 16 | 23 | 64 | 10 |

Promoted :- AS Colmarberg and US Folschette
Berbourg

## LUXEMBOURG 5TH DIVISION 2 1990/91
### LEAGUE TABLE FINAL

| | P | W | D | L | F | A | Pts |
|---|---|---|---|---|---|---|---|
| Alisontia Steinsel | 22 | 17 | 3 | 2 | 80 | 28 | 37 |
| Old Boys Consdorf | 22 | 18 | 0 | 4 | 80 | 19 | 36 |
| Berdenia Berbourg | 22 | 15 | 3 | 4 | 71 | 33 | 33 |
| FC Lorentzweiler | 22 | 14 | 4 | 4 | 59 | 32 | 32 |
| Arantia Berdorf | 22 | 10 | 5 | 7 | 53 | 39 | 25 |
| Blo-Weiss Medernach | 22 | 11 | 1 | 10 | 62 | 41 | 23 |
| Rupensia Larochette | 22 | 9 | 4 | 9 | 47 | 44 | 22 |
| Syra Mensdorf | 22 | 8 | 4 | 10 | 39 | 53 | 20 |
| AS Luxembourg | 22 | 5 | 4 | 13 | 27 | 45 | 14 |
| Les Amis' Moselle R'schn. | 22 | 4 | 2 | 16 | 25 | 63 | 10 |
| US Moutfort-Medingen | 22 | 4 | 2 | 16 | 29 | 89 | 10 |
| Avenir Flaxweiler | 22 | 1 | 0 | 21 | 18 | 104 | 2 |

Promoted :- Alisontia Steinsel,Old Boys Consdf & B'denia Berbourg

# LUXEMBOURG 5TH DIVISION 3 1990/91

## LEAGUE TABLE FINAL

| | P | W | D | L | F | A | Pts |
|---|---|---|---|---|---|---|---|
| Progrès Cessange | 22 | 16 | 6 | 0 | 77 | 16 | 38 |
| FC Ehlerange | 22 | 16 | 2 | 4 | 52 | 19 | 34 |
| ES Schouweiler | 22 | 13 | 4 | 5 | 67 | 38 | 30 |
| JS Koerich | 22 | 11 | 7 | 4 | 38 | 24 | 29 |
| Titus Lamadelaine | 22 | 12 | 3 | 7 | 41 | 24 | 27 |
| Jeunesse 07 Kayl | 22 | 8 | 8 | 6 | 29 | 32 | 22 |
| Minière Lasauvage | 22 | 8 | 6 | 8 | 36 | 36 | 22 |
| US Bascharage | 22 | 7 | 8 | 7 | 36 | 49 | 20 |
| FC 33 Kopstal | 22 | 7 | 2 | 13 | 30 | 47 | 16 |
| 1FC Noertzange HF | 22 | 4 | 5 | 13 | 36 | 61 | 13 |
| Luna Obercorn | 22 | 4 | 5 | 13 | 35 | 59 | 11 |
| US Bous | 22 | 1 | 3 | 18 | 23 | 77 | 5 |

Promoted :- Progrès Cessange, FC Ehlerange and ES Schouweiler

## PROMOTION PLAY-OFFS

| | | | |
|---|---|---|---|
| SC Ell | 2 | Berdenia Berbourg | 2 |
| ES Schouweiler | 3 | SC Ell | 2 |
| Berdenia Berbourg | 5 | ES Schouweiler | 2 |

## LEAGUE TABLE FINAL

| | P | W | D | L | F | A | Pts |
|---|---|---|---|---|---|---|---|
| Berdenia Berbourg | 2 | 1 | 1 | 0 | 7 | 4 | 3 |
| ES Schouweiler | 2 | 1 | 0 | 1 | 5 | 7 | 2 |
| SC Ell | 2 | 0 | 1 | 1 | 4 | 5 | 1 |

# LUXEMBOURG CUP 1990/91

## PRELIMINARY ROUND

| | | | |
|---|---|---|---|
| AS Colmarberg | 1 | Marisca Mersch | 7 |
| US Boevange/Attert | 5 | US Rambrouch | 4 (aet) |
| Iska Boys Simmern | 2 | Avenir Flaxweiler | 4 |
| SC Beckerich | 8 | Excelsior Grevels | 0 |
| FC 72 Erpeldange | 0 | FC Green Boys H.T. | 1 |
| Jeun. Junglinster | 9 | Old Boys Consdorf | 0 |
| Jeunesse Canach | 10 | CS Bourscheid | 0 |
| Minière Canach | 1 | Les Aiglons Dalheim | 6 |
| ES Schouweiler | 3 | Progrès Cessange | 1 |
| Jeunesse 07 Kayl | 3 | US Bous | 2 (aet) |
| FC Munsbach | 4 | Red Boys Aspelt | 2 |
| FC Ehlerange | 0 | Vinesca Ehnen | 2 |
| Racing Rodange | 2 | FC Lorentzweiler | 3 |

## 1ST ROUND

| | | | |
|---|---|---|---|
| US Folschette | 3 | FC Kehlen | 2 |
| Arantia Berdorf | 2 | Berdenia Berbourg | 0 |
| FC Green Boys H-L | 2 | Marisca Mersch | 1 |
| AS Pratzerthal | 1 | FC 47 Bastendorf | 1 |
| SC Ell | 2 | AS Hosingen | 1 |
| US Reisdorf | 1 | Bio-Weiss Medern. | 5 |
| AS Schifflange | 8 | Una Strassen | 0 |
| SC Bettembourg | 1 | FC Marner 32 | 0 |
| Résiden.Walferdan. | 1 | Jeunesse Canach | 3 |
| US Hamm. | 4 | FC Beyren-Udinesina | 4 |
| FC Hamm. | 1 | LAM Remerschen | 0 |
| US Esch | 3 | Jeunesse 07 Kayl | 0 (aet) |
| FC Lorentzweiler | 3 | Progrès Cessange | 4 (aet) |

## 2ND ROUND

| | | | |
|---|---|---|---|
| FC Hamm. | 2 | US Hostert | 1 |
| AS Schifflange | 5 | Les M'ntag.Weiswmp | 1 |
| Rupensia Larochette | 5 | Jeunesse Glisdorf | 4 (aet) |
| FC 47 Bastendorf | 3 | AS Wincrange | 2 |
| Berdenia Berbourg | 0 | Bio-Weiss Medern. | 2 |
| Racing 76 Heidersch | 0 | Tricolore Gasperich | 3 |
| Jeunesse Biwer | 0 | AS Schifflange | 2 |
| Bio-Weiss Medern. | 2 | Jeunesse Junglister | 4 |
| Old Boys Consdorf | 0 | SC Beckerich | 0 |
| Les Aiglons Dalheim | 1 | Olympia Christ-Wald. | 1 |
| US Moutfort-Meding. | 1 | Etoile Sportive Clem. | 1 |
| US Esch | 6 | 1FC Noertzange HF | 0 |
| Luna Obercorn | 2 | FC Munsbach | 2 |
| Bio-Weiss Itzig | 2 | Vinesca Ehnen | 2 (aet) |
| Red Boys Aspelt | 2 | Bio-Weiss Itzig | 4 (aet) |
| AS Luxembourg | 2 | Red Star Merl-Belair. | 2 |
| FC Hamm | 5 | Les Aiglons Dalheim. | 3 |

## 3RD ROUND

| | | | |
|---|---|---|---|
| US Mondorf | 2 | Orania Vianden | 3 |
| US Mertert | 1 | JS Koerich | 2 |
| Sporting Bertange | 1 | Sporting Steinfort | 0 |
| Atert Bissen | 4 | FC Green Boys H-T. | 1 |
| SC Redange/Attert | 1 | Les Ardoisiers Perlé | 0 |
| Bio-Weiss Medern. | 1 | DC Echternach | 4 (aet) |
| Les Aiglons Dalheim | 0 | Rupensia Larochette | 5 (aet) |
| Jeunesse Schieren | 0 | Racing Troisvierges | 1 |
| The Belval Belvaux | 0 | Jeunesse Biwer | 5 |
| Bio-Weiss Medern. | 3 | US Esch | 0 ⊗ |
| The Nat. Schifflange. | 1 | AS Remich | 2 |
| FC Brouch | 0 | Progrès Cessange | 3 |
| FC Mondercange | 1 | Jeun. Wasserbillig | 4 |
| Progrès Cessange | 1 | US Boevange/Attert | 2 (aet) |
| SC Ell | 2 | SC Bettembourg | 3 |
| Jeun. Useldange | 0 | US Bascharage | 2 |

## 1/16 FINALS

| | | | |
|---|---|---|---|
| Aris Bonnevoie | 5 | Egalite Weimersk. | 4 ⊗ |
| Alliance Dudelange | 1 | Red Boys Differdan. | 4 |
| Chiers Rodange | 1 | Progrès Niedercorn | 2 |
| Stade Rodange | 0 | Spora Luxembourg | 2 |
| Egalite Weimerskirch | 4 | AS Differdange | 0 |
| Daring-Club Echtern. | 6 | CS Hollerich | 0 |
| US Rumelange | 0 | AS Remich | 2 |
| Stade Dudelange | 4 | Alliance Dudelange | 5 |
| Young Boys Diekirch | 4 | SC Bettembourg | 0 |
| FC Hamm | 3 | Red Black Pfaffenthal | 2 |
| Racing Troisvierges | 2 | Chiers Rodange | 2 (aet) |
| Koeppch.Wormeldan. | 4 | Sporting Mertzig | 1 |
| Victoria Rosport | 1 | US Dudelange | 2 |
| Tricolore Gasperich | 3 | Jeun. Hautcharage | 1 |
| FC Wiltz 71 | 1 | Racing Troisvierges | 0 (aet) |
| Progrès Cessange | 9 | Jeun. Wasserbillig | 4 ⊗ |

## 1/8 FINALS

| | | | |
|---|---|---|---|
| SC Bettembourg | 0 | Jeunesse d'Esch | 3 |
| Egalite Weimersk. | 1 | Red Boys Differdange | 3 (aet) |
| AS Schifflange | 0 | Swift Hesperange | 0 |
| Avenir Beggen | 5 | Fola Esch | 2 (aet) |
| Spora Luxembourg | 2 | Progrès Niedercorn | 0 |
| Tricolore Gasperich | 2 | Union Luxembourg | 0 |
| Union Luxembourg | 3 | Daring-Club Echtern. | 2 |
| RM 86 Luxembourg | 5 | CS Grevenmacher | 0 |

## 1/4 FINALS

| | | | |
|---|---|---|---|
| Avenir Beggen | 2 | Tricolore Gasperich | 0 |
| Red Boys Differdange | 1 | Jeunesse d'Esch | 2 |
| Swift Hesperange | 2 | CS Grevenmacher | 0 |
| Union Luxembourg | 2 | Spora Luxembourg | 0 |

## SEMI-FINALS

| | | | |
|---|---|---|---|
| Avenir Beggen | 0 | Union Luxembourg | 4 |
| Swift Hesperange | 1 | Jeunesse d'Esch | 2 |

⊗ After extra time and penalties

## FINAL

8/6/91 (at Stade Municipal, Luxembourg)

Union Sportive Luxembourg ...3  Jeunesse d'Esch ...0

| | | |
|---|---|---|
| Muller o.g. | 1-0 | 44 |
| Jeitz | 2-0 | 57 |
| Morocutti | 3-0 | 87 |

Union : J.Van Rijswijck, C.Ganser, T.Wolf, D.Borbiconi (Y.Picard), M.Birsens, G.Jeitz, J.Groff, L.Feiereisen, P.Morocutti, D.Mogenot, F.Mellinger.

Jeunesse : C.Hoffmann, J.Muller, R.Schaak, M.Bossi, P.Petry, P.Meyers, D.Scuto, M.Thome, H.Selimovic (M.Lamborelli), S.Marinelli (P.Romitelli), D.Theis.

Referee : Ecker

Attendance : 3,000

# LUXEMBOURG INTERNATIONAL REVIEW 1990

## INTERNATIONAL LINE-UPS 1990

| | Paul Koch | Frank Goergen | Pierre Petry | Marc Birsens | Marcel Bossi | Jean-Paul Girres | Carlo Weis | Denis Scuto | Joël Groff | Patrick Morocutti | Theo Malget | Marc Thoome | Gerard Jeitz | Theo Scholten | John Van Rijswijck | Guy Hellers | Jef Saibene | Roby Langers | Armin Krings |
|---|---|---|---|---|---|---|---|---|---|---|---|---|---|---|---|---|---|---|---|
| 28/3/90 LUXEMBOURG 1 ICELAND 2 Esch-sur-Alzette Friendly — Ref: Crucke (Belgium) (Malget) | 1 | 2 | 3 | 4 | 5 | 6 | 7 | 8 | 9 | 10 | 1* | (2) | (8) | (9) | | | | | |
| 31/10/90 LUXEMBOURG 2 GERMANY 3 Luxembourg EuroCh.Q. — Ref: Nielsen (Denmark) (Girres, Langers) | | | 2 | 5 | 4 | 7 | 8 | | 6 | | 3 | | (10) | | 1 | 9 | 10 | 11 | |
| 14/11/90 LUXEMBOURG 0 WALES 1 Luxembourg EuroCh.Q. — Ref: Ulrich (Czechoslovakia) | | | 5 | 4 | 3 | 7 | 9 | 2 | | 10 | 2 | | | | 1 | 6 | 8 | 11 | (10) |
| CAPS AT 31/12/90 | 1 | 1 | 15 | 9 | 52 | 50 | 58 | 2 | 5 | 6 | 36 | 7 | 21 | 21 | 35 | 30 | 11 | 39 | 10 |
| GOALS AT 31/12/90 | | | | | | 1 | | | | | 3 | | | | | 1 | | 5 | 1 |

## LUXEMBOURG : All Time Records as at 31/12/90 - CAPS

1. Francois Konter (Chiers Rodange/RSC Anderlecht/AA Gent) — 72
2. Gilbert Dresch (Avenir Beggen) — 63
3. Ernest Brenner (Aris Bonnevoie/Stade Dudelange) — 60
4. Carlo Weis (Spora Luxembourg/FC Metz/FC Winterslag/Stare Reims/FC Thionville/Avenir Beggen) — 58
5. Jeannot Moes (Avenir Beggen) — 55
6. Paul Philipp (Avenir Beggen/Union St.Gilloise/Standard CL/Charleroi SC) — 54
   Hubert Meunier (Progrès Niedercorn/Jeunesse d'Esch/Avenir Beggen) — 54
8. Fernand Brosius (Spora Luxembourg) — 52
   Nicolas Kettel (Stade Dudelange/Young Boys Diekirch) — 52
   Marcel Bossi (Progrès Niedercorn/Jeunesse d'Esch) — 52

## LUXEMBOURG : All Time Records as at 31/12/90 - GOALS

1. Léon Mart (Fola Esch) — (28) 16
2. Gustave Kemp (Progrès Niedercorn) — (24) 15
3. Camille Libar (Stade Dudelange) — (24) 14
4. Nicolas Kettel (Stade Dudelange/Young Boys Diekirch) — (52) 13
5. Francois Muller (Red Star Merl) — (26) 12
6. Léon Letsch (Spora Luxembourg) — (48) 11
7. Robert Theissen (Spora Luxembourg) — (15) 9
8. Jules Gales (Spora Luxembourg) — (23) 9
9. Camille Dimmer (Red Boys Differdange/Crossing Molenbeek) — (19) 8
   Johnny Leonard (Union Luxembourg/FC Metz/AA Gent) — (30) 8
   Gilbert Dussier (Red Boys Differdange/Jeunesse d'Esch/Röchling Völklingen/AS Nancy-Lorraine) — (39) 8
   Nico Braun (Union Luxembourg/FC Schalke 04/FC Metz/Charleroi SC) — (40) 8

| MALTA Premier Division Season 1990/91 | VALLETTA | SLIEMA WANDS | HAMRUN SPTNS | HIBERNIANS | FLORIANA | NAXXAR LIONS | ZURRIEQ | RABAT AJAX | BIRKIRKARA |
|---|---|---|---|---|---|---|---|---|---|
| VALLETTA FC | | 2-3 | 1-1 | 2-1 | 0-1 | 6-0 | 3-1 | 4-2 | 3-1 |
| SLIEMA WANDERERS | 3-0 | | 3-4 | 1-1 | 0-0 | 0-2 | 1-1 | 1-1 | 1-2 |
| HAMRUN SPARTANS | 0-0 | 2-2 | | 3-1 | 3-1 | 2-0 | 3-2 | 1-0 | 1-2 |
| HIBERNIANS | 1-1 | 2-2 | 1-2 | | 2-1 | 1-1 | 0-0 | 1-0 | 0-0 |
| FLORIANA | 1-0 | 1-0 | 1-0 | 1-1 | | 0-0 | 0-0 | 1-1 | 0-0 |
| NAXXAR LIONS | 0-3 | 0-1 | 1-3 | 0-1 | 0-4 | | 2-0 | 2-5 | 0-0 |
| ZURRIEQ | 0-2 | 0-6 | 0-0 | 1-0 | 1-0 | ⊗ | | 2-2 | 0-0 |
| RABAT AJAX | 0-1 | 0-0 | 2-3 | 0-2 | 2-1 | 0-0 | 1-0 | | 0-0 |
| BIRKIRKARA | 1-3 | 1-1 | 1-3 | 0-3 | 1-2 | 1-3 | 2-1 | 1-1 | |

## MALTA PREMIER DIVISION 1990/91
### LEAGUE TABLE FINAL

| | | | | | | | |
|---|---|---|---|---|---|---|---|
| Hamrun Spartans | 16 | 10 | 4 | 2 | 31 | 18 | 24 |
| Valletta FC | 16 | 8 | 3 | 5 | 28 | 17 | 19 |
| Floriana | 16 | 6 | 6 | 4 | 15 | 11 | 18 |
| Hibernians | 16 | 5 | 7 | 4 | 18 | 15 | 17 |
| Sliema Wanderers | 16 | 4 | 7 | 5 | 24 | 20 | 15 |
| Rabat Ajax | 16 | 4 | 6 | 6 | 18 | 19 | 14 |
| Zurrieq | 16 | 4 | 6 | 6 | 12 | 19 | 14 |
| Birkirkara | 16 | 3 | 7 | 6 | 13 | 22 | 13 |
| Naxxar Lions | 16 | 3 | 4 | 9 | 11 | 29 | 10 |

Champions : - Hamrun Spartans
Relegated : - Naxxar Lions (to 2nd Division)

League to be incresed to 10 clubs for Season 1991/92.
Note : - Due to matches awarded to Rabat Ajax and Zurrieq, Birkirkara finished in a relegation position. In order to be fair to Birkirkara it was therefore decided to increase the size of the Premier Division to 10 clubs for Season 1991/92, thus allowing Birkirkara to retain their place.

⊗ Naxxar Lions failed to appear for their final game, which was later awarded Zurrieq 2 Naxxar Lions 0. As punishment it was decided to relegate Naxxar Lions to next Season's 2nd Division, where the club will commence with a 5 point penalty. Furthermore the club was suspended from the 1990/91 FA Trophy.

The match Sliema Wanderers 1 Rabat Ajax 1 was later awarded Sliema Wanderers 0 Rabat Ajax 2.

The match Valletta FC 3 Zurrieq 1 was awarded Valletta FC 0 Zurrieq 2.

| MALTA 1st Division Season 1990/91 | TARXIEN RBWS. | ZEBBUG RANG. | MOSTA | ST.GEORGE'S | QORMI | MQABBA HAJ. | SENGLEA ATH. | ST.ANDREWS | GZIRA UTD. |
|---|---|---|---|---|---|---|---|---|---|
| TARXIEN RAINBOWS | | 0-0 | 1-1 | 1-0 | 0-0 | 0-1 | 2-1 | 0-3 | 0-0 |
| ZEBBUG RANGERS | 0-1 | | 1-0 | 0-1 | 1-2 | 0-1 | 2-1 | 0-0 | 0-0 |
| MOSTA | 1-0 | 1-0 | | 2-0 | 2-1 | 0-2 | 2-0 | 0-0 | 3-1 |
| ST.GEORGE'S | 2-1 | 0-0 | 1-0 | | 2-1 | 0-0 | 0-0 | 1-1 | 4-0 |
| QORMI | 2-0 | 1-0 | 1-1 | 1-1 | | 2-0 | 1-1 | 0-4 | 0-0 |
| MQABBA HAJDUKS | 5-1 | 1-0 | 2-1 | 2-0 | 2-1 | | 3-1 | 1-0 | 2-0 |
| SENGLEA ATHLETIC | 1-0 | 1-1 | 0-1 | 0-0 | 4-1 | 0-1 | | 0-3 | 0-0 |
| LUXOL ST.ANDREW'S | 5-0 | 4-2 | 2-0 | 4-1 | 6-1 | 0-1 | 1-0 | | 2-1 |
| GZIRA UNITED | 1-1 | 2-2 | 3-4 | 2-1 | 1-3 | 3-2 | 1-1 | 0-1 | |

## MALTA 1ST DIVISION 1990/91
### LEAGUE TABLE FINAL

| | | | | | | | |
|---|---|---|---|---|---|---|---|
| Mqabba Hajduks | 16 | 13 | 1 | 2 | 26 | 9 | 27 |
| Luxol St.Andrews | 16 | 11 | 2 | 3 | 35 | 9 | 24 |
| Mosta | 16 | 8 | 3 | 5 | 19 | 15 | 19 |
| St.Georges | 16 | 6 | 5 | 5 | 15 | 14 | 17 |
| Qormi | 16 | 5 | 5 | 6 | 18 | 25 | 15 |
| Gzira United | 16 | 2 | 7 | 7 | 15 | 26 | 11 |
| Tarxien Rainbows | 16 | 3 | 5 | 8 | 8 | 23 | 11 |
| Zebbug Rangers | 16 | 2 | 6 | 8 | 9 | 16 | 10 |
| Senglea Athletic | 16 | 2 | 6 | 8 | 11 | 19 | 10 |

Promoted : - Mqabba Hajduks and St.Andrews
Relegated : - Zebbug Rangers

League to be increased to 10 clubs for Season 1991/92.

The match St.Georges 0 Zebbug Rangers 0 was ordered to be replayed following an upheld protest from Zebbug Rangers. The result of the replayed match was St.Georges 0 Zebbug Rangers 0.
The match St.Georges 1 St.Andrews 1 was later awarded St.Georges 2 St.Andrews 0.

### 1ST/2ND DIVISION PROMOTION/RELEGATION PLAY-OFFS
Pieta Hotspurs ..........3    Zebbug Rangers ........2 (aet.)
Senglea Athletic ........2    St.Patricks ................1 (aet.)
St.Patricks ................2    Zebbug Rangers ........1 (aet.)

## MALTA 2ND DIVISION A 1990/91
### LEAGUE TABLE FINAL

| | | | | | | | |
|---|---|---|---|---|---|---|---|
| Mellieha | 12 | 8 | 3 | 1 | 19 | 6 | 19 |
| St.Patrick's | 12 | 7 | 2 | 3 | 16 | 9 | 16 |
| Gudja United | 12 | 5 | 4 | 3 | 16 | 12 | 14 |
| Kirkop United | 12 | 5 | 2 | 5 | 15 | 10 | 12 |
| Sirens | 12 | 3 | 2 | 7 | 18 | 21 | 8 |
| Fgura United | 12 | 3 | 2 | 7 | 8 | 18 | 8 |
| Santa Lucia | 12 | 2 | 3 | 7 | 6 | 22 | 7 |

Promoted : - Mellieha and St.Patricks

## MALTA 2ND DIVISION B 1990/91
### LEAGUE TABLE FINAL

| | | | | | | | |
|---|---|---|---|---|---|---|---|
| Ghargur | 12 | 7 | 5 | 0 | 24 | 5 | 19 |
| Pieta Hotspurs | 12 | 5 | 4 | 3 | 17 | 11 | 14 |
| Marsa | 12 | 4 | 4 | 4 | 14 | 18 | 12 |
| Luqa St.Andrew's | 12 | 3 | 5 | 4 | 17 | 19 | 11 |
| Siggiewi | 12 | 3 | 5 | 4 | 17 | 23 | 11 |
| Msida St.Josephs | 12 | 3 | 3 | 6 | 9 | 17 | 9 |
| Lija Athletic | 12 | 1 | 6 | 5 | 8 | 13 | 8 |

Promoted : - Ghargur and Pieta Hotspurs
Relegated : - Lija Athletic

### 2ND/3RD DIVISION PROMOTION/RELEGATION PLAY-OFFS
Balzan Youths ............4    Melita ........................3 (aet.)
Santa Lucia ................1    Lija Athletic ...............1 (aet.)
Santa Lucia win 5-4 on penalties

### 2ND DIVISION CHAMPIONSHIP PLAY-OFF
Ghargur .....................2    Mellieha ....................1 (aet.)

## MALTA 3RD DIVISION A 1990/91

### LEAGUE TABLE FINAL

| | | | | | | | |
|---|---|---|---|---|---|---|---|
| Vittoriosa Stars | 14 | 12 | 2 | 0 | 46 | 9 | 26 |
| Balzan Youths | 14 | 11 | 2 | 1 | 39 | 10 | 24 |
| Marsaxlokk | 14 | 9 | 1 | 4 | 27 | 20 | 19 |
| Zejtun Corinthians | 14 | 4 | 4 | 6 | 22 | 26 | 12 |
| San Gwann | 14 | 5 | 0 | 9 | 11 | 33 | 10 |
| Gozo FC | 14 | 5 | 0 | 9 | 18 | 34 | 10 |
| Dingli Swallows | 14 | 3 | 3 | 8 | 21 | 30 | 9 |
| Ta'Xbiex | 14 | 0 | 2 | 12 | 10 | 42 | 2 |

Promoted :- Vittoriosa Stars and Balzan Youths

### 3RD DIVISION CHAMPIONSHIP PLAY-OFF

Vittoriosa Stars ......3    St.Venera Lightnings .0

## GOZO FA 1ST DIVISION 1990/91

### LEAGUE TABLE FINAL

| | | | | | | | |
|---|---|---|---|---|---|---|---|
| Xewkija Tigers | 14 | 11 | 2 | 1 | 28 | 8 | 24 |
| Victoria Hotspurs | 14 | 11 | 2 | 1 | 22 | 9 | 24 |
| Sannat Lions | 14 | 7 | 2 | 4 | 23 | 16 | 16 |
| Xaghra United | 14 | 4 | 4 | 6 | 16 | 12 | 12 |
| Nadur Youngsters | 14 | 4 | 4 | 6 | 13 | 15 | 12 |
| Kercem Ajax | 14 | 2 | 6 | 6 | 7 | 13 | 10 |
| Ghajnsielem | 14 | 3 | 3 | 8 | 8 | 18 | 9 |
| Oratory Youths | 14 | 0 | 1 | 13 | 5 | 30 | 1 |

Champions :- Victoria Hotspurs
Relegated :- Ghajnsielem and Oratory Youths

### CHAMPIONSHIP PLAY-OFF

Victoria Hotspurs ......2    Xewkija Tigers ..........1

### 4TH PLACE PLAY-OFF

Xaghra United ..........2    Nadur Youngsters ........1

## MALTA CUP (FA TROPHY) 1990/91

### PRELIMINARY ROUND

Gozo FA XI ......3    Zebbug Rangers......2

### 1ST ROUND

Floriana ......3    Gozo FA XI................1

### 2ND ROUND

Sliema Wanderers ......5    Mosta...........0
Rabat Ajax ......3    Mqabba Hajduks......2 (aet.)
Hamrun Spartans ......2    Gzira United............0
Floriana ......3    Tarxien Rainbows......0

### 1/4 FINALS

Sliema Wanderers3Hibernians1(aet.)Hamrun Spartans2Zurrieq1
Floriana2Rabat AjaxOValletta FC4St.George's0

### SEMI-FINALS

Sliema Wanderers4Floriana1(aet.)Valletta FC2Hamrun Spartans1(aet.)

## MALTA 3RD DIVISION B 1990/91

### LEAGUE TABLE FINAL

| | | | | | | | |
|---|---|---|---|---|---|---|---|
| St.Venera Lightnings | 14 | 10 | 4 | 0 | 31 | 7 | 24 |
| Melita | 14 | 8 | 4 | 2 | 28 | 15 | 20 |
| Attard | 14 | 5 | 5 | 4 | 17 | 15 | 15 |
| Kalkara United | 14 | 4 | 6 | 4 | 21 | 25 | 14 |
| Mgarr United | 14 | 4 | 3 | 6 | 16 | 25 | 11 |
| B.Buga St.Peters | 14 | 3 | 4 | 7 | 14 | 24 | 10 |
| Ghaxaq | 14 | 4 | 2 | 8 | 15 | 23 | 10 |
| Qrendi | 14 | 2 | 4 | 8 | 15 | 23 | 8 |

Promoted :- St.Venera Lightnings

## GOZO FA 2ND DIVISION 1990/91

### LEAGUE TABLE FINAL

| | | | | | | | |
|---|---|---|---|---|---|---|---|
| Munxar Falcons | 10 | 6 | 2 | 2 | 15 | 6 | 14 |
| Zebbug Rovers | 10 | 5 | 3 | 2 | 14 | 9 | 13 |
| Qala St.Josephs | 10 | 4 | 5 | 1 | 13 | 8 | 13 |
| St.Lawrence Spurs | 10 | 2 | 5 | 4 | 9 | 7 | 9 |
| Victoria United | 10 | 2 | 4 | 4 | 6 | 11 | 8 |
| Gharb Rangers | 10 | 0 | 3 | 7 | 4 | 17 | 3 |

Promoted :- Munxar Falcons and Qala St.Josephs

### 2ND PLACE PLAY-OFF

Qala St.Josephs ......3    Zebbug Rovers.........0

## MALTA 2ND AND 3RD DIVISION CHALLENGE CUP 1990/91

### 1/4 FINALS

Luqa St.Andrew's......2    Sirens....................1
St.Patrick's............2    Msida St.Joseph's........2 (aet.)
St.Patrick's win 4-3 on penalties
Kirkop United............1    Melieha..................2
Fgura United............0    Siggiewi.................2 (aet.)
Melieha win 5-4 on penalties

### SEMI-FINALS

Kirkop United ......2    Luqa St.Andrew's .....0
St.Patrick's............2    Melieha..................0

### FINAL

St.Patrick's ......2    Kirkop United............1 (aet.)
1st Round played in groups

## MALTA SUPER CUP (LEAGUE & CUP WINNERS) 1989/90

5/1/91    Valletta FC ......3    Sliema Wanderers........0

Valletta : R.Cini, W.MacKay, C.Magri, C.Laferla R.Scibberas, J.Camilleri, G.Agius, B.Giorev, N.Saliba, J.Zarb, J.Zerafa.
Sliema W : Ashbury, S.Theuma, E.Zammit, J.Caruana, J.Navarro, Magri Overend (R.Walker) (A.Scardino), M.Gregory, C.Cluett, H.Suda, M.Taliana, S.Grech.

| 1-0 | J.Zerafa | 44 | Referee : V.ctor Mintoff |
|---|---|---|---|
| 2-0 | J.Camilleri | 53 | |
| 3-0 | J.Camilleri | 74 | |

## MALTA SUPER CUP (LEAGUE AND CUP WINNERS) 1990/91

25/5/91    Hamrun Spartans ......1    Valletta FC ......1 (aet.)

Hamrun S : I.Leigh, B.Mundee, A.Azzopardi (Ferech 43), M.Grech (J.Cutajar 112), J.Brincat, R.Vella, I.Zammit, Micallef, E.Brincat, M.Degiorgio, S.Sultana.
Valletta : R.Cini, W.MacKay, C.Magri, C.Laferla, R.Scibberas, J.Camilleri, G.Agius, B.Giorev (A.Busuttil 105), R.Briffa, J.Zarb (S.Sultana 51), J.Zerafa.

| 1-0 | C.Laferla | 11 |
|---|---|---|
| 1-1 | J.Brincat | 54 |

HAMRUN SPARTANS WIN 5-4 ON PENALTIES.

## GOZO FA SUPER CUP 1990/91

Victoria Hotspurs ......2    Xaghra United............2 (aet.)
Victoria Hotspurs win 4-2 on penalties

## FINAL    11/5/91 (at National Stadium, Ta'Qali)

Valletta .........2    Sliema Wanderers ......1 (aet.)

Valletta : R.Cini, W.MacKay, C.Magri, C.Laferla R.Scibberas, J.Camilleri, A.Busuttil (S.Sultana), B.Giorev, N.Saliba (R.Briffa), J.Zarb, J.Zerafa.
Sliema W : E.Barry, C.Cluett, E.Zammit, J.Caruana, A.Scarino, M.Gregory, H.Suda, R.Walker, M.Taliana (S.Theuma), S.Grech.

| 0-1 | H.Suda | 103 | Referee : Charles Agius |
|---|---|---|---|
| 1-1 | J.Camilleri | 109 | |
| 2-1 | C.Laferla | 117 | |

# MALTA INTERNATIONAL REVIEW 1990

## INTERNATIONAL LINE-UPS 1990

| Date | Result | Competition (scorer) | Venue | Referee |
|---|---|---|---|---|
| 7/2/90 | MALTA 1 NORWAY 1 | Friendly T (Scerri) | Ta'Qali | Ref: Azzopardi (Malta) |
| 10/2/90 | MALTA 1 SOUTH KOREA 2 | Friendly T (Laferla) | Ta'Qali | Ref: Presburg (Norway) |
| 5/5/90 | USA 1 MALTA 0 | Friendly | Piscataway | Ref: Angeles (USA) |
| 28/5/90 | MALTA 1 SCOTLAND 2 | Friendly (Degiorgo) | Ta'Qali | Ref: Longhi (Italy) |
| 2/6/90 | MALTA 0 REPUBLIC OF IRELAND 3 | Friendly | Ta'Qali | Ref: Azzopardi (Malta) |
| 31/10/90 | GREECE 4 MALTA 0 | EuroCh.Q. | Athens | Ref: Craciunescu (Rumania) |
| 25/11/90 | MALTA 1 FINLAND 1 | EuroCh.Q. (Suda) | Ta'Qali | Ref: Sadik Deda (Turkey) |
| 19/12/90 | MALTA 0 HOLLAND 8 | EuroCh.Q. | | Ref: Blattman (Switzerland) |

| Player | 7/2 | 10/2 | 5/5 | 28/5 | 2/6 | 31/10 | 25/11 | 19/12 | CAPS | GOALS |
|---|---|---|---|---|---|---|---|---|---|---|
| Reggie Cini | 1 | 1 | | | | | | | 11 | |
| Edwin Camilleri | 2 | 2 | | | | | 2 | | 31 | |
| David Carabott | 3 | 3 | 4 | 2 | 4 | | 9 | 4 | 34 | 2 |
| Joseph Galea | 4 | 4 | 5 | 3 | 5 | | 4 | 5 | 26 | |
| Charles Scerri | 5 | 6 | 6 | (11) | 5 | | 5 | | 37 | 1 |
| Joseph Falzon | 6 | 7 | | | | | 7 | 6 | 2 | 1 |
| Hubert Suda | 7 | 11 | 10 | 9 | (11) | | 8 | (2) | 15 | |
| Raymond Vella | 8 | 8 | 7 | 8 | 8 | | | 8 | 44 | 1 |
| Joseph Zarb | 9 | (6) | 8 | 9 | (9) | | 11 | | 9 | 1 |
| Michael Degiorgo | 10 | 10 | 9 | 10 | 10 | | 10 | | 61 | 4 |
| Martin Gregory | 11 | | | 5 | 9 | | 5 | | 29 | 1 |
| Kristian Laferla | (6) | 4 | 3 | | | | 10 | | 17 | |
| David Cluett | | 1 | 1 | 1 | 1 | 1 | 1 | 1 | 25 | |
| Edmond Zammit | | (7) | (9) | | | | | | 1 | |
| Jesmond Zerafa | | (11) | 2 | 6 | (5) | | | (10) | 11 | |
| Silvio Vella | | 3 | 6 | 7 | 2 | | 3 | | 19 | |
| John Buttigieg | | | | 6 | 2 | | 6 | | 41 | |
| Joseph Brincat | | | | | | | | | 12 | |
| Bernard Licari | | | | 11 | 11 | | (2) | | 3 | |
| Jesmond Delia | | | | | | | | | 5 | |
| Carmel Busuttil | | | 7 | 7 | 7 | | 7 | | 44 | 16 |
| Joseph Camilleri | | | 11 | | | | | 5 | 5 | |

CAPS AT 31/12/90 / GOALS AT 31/12/90

## MALTA: All Time Records as at 31/12/90 - CAPS

1. Michael Degiorgio (Hamrun Spartans) — 61
2. John Holland (Floriana) — 59
3. Carmel Busuttil (Rabat Ajax/Verbania/Racing Genk) — 44
4. Raymond Vella (Marsa/Hamrun Spartans) — 44
5. Raymond Xuereb (Floriana/Hamrun Spartans) — 44
6. John Buttigieg (Sliema Wanderers/Brentford) — 41
7. Alex Azzopardi (Hamrun Spartans) — 40
8. Edwin Farrugia (Floriana/Hamrun Spartans) — 39
9. Charles Scerri (Sliema Wanderers/Hibernians) — 37
10. David Carabott (Hibernians) — 34

## MALTA: All Time Records as at 31/12/90 - GOALS

1. Carmel Busuttil (Rabat Ajax/Verbania/Racing Genk) — (44) 16
2. Raymond Xuereb (Floriana/Hamrun Spartans) — (43) 6
3. Michael Degiorgio (Hamrun Spartans) — (61) 4
4. Ernest Spiteri-Gonzi (Hibernians) — (20) 3
   Emanuele Fabri (Qormi) — (29) 3
   George Xuereb (Floriana/Hamrun Spartans) — 3
   Oliver Losco (Sliema Wanderers) — (30) 3
7. Dennis Mizzi (Floriana/Zurrieq) — ('5) 2
   Joseph Cini (Floriana) — (11) 2
   Sliema Wanderers/Hibernians — (14) 2
   Nardu Farrugia (Valletta FC) — (15) 2
   Eddie Theobald (Hibernians) — (16) 2
   Vincent Magro (Valletta FC) — (24) 2
   Willie Vassallo (Floriana) — (28) 2
   David Carabott (Hibernians) — (34) 2

## MALTA: GOZO FA KNOCK-OUT CUP 1990/91

### 1ST ROUND
Xewkija Tigers 2 — Oratory Youths 1
Xaghra United 1 — Victoria Hotspurs 0 (aet)
St.Lawrence Spurs 0 — Ghajnsielem 0 (aet)
St.Lawrence Spurs win 4-3 on penalties
Nadur Youngsters 2 — Munxar Falcons 0
Kercem Ajax 1 — Zebbug Rovers 0
Sannat Lions 2 — Victoria United 0
Byes - Gharb Rangers & Qala St.Josephs

### 1/4 FINALS
Xewkija Tigers 2 — Nadur Youngsters 1
Kercem Ajax 1 — St.Lawrence Spurs 1 (aet)
Kercem Ajax win 5-4 on penalties
Xaghra United 1 — Gharb Rangers 0
Sannat Lions 1 — Qala St.Josephs 0

### SEMI-FINALS
Xewkija Tigers 4 — Xaghra United 2 (aet)
Kercem Ajax 0 — Sannat Lions 0 (aet)
Kercem Ajax win 3-2 on penalties

### FINAL
Xewkija Tigers 2 — Kercem Ajax 0

## MALTA SUPER FIVE CUP 1990/91

Initial edition of a pre-season tournament to be played between the top 4 clubs from the previous season's Premier Division. Sponsored by Super Five Lottery.

### SEMI-FINALS
Sliema Wanderers 3 — Hibernians 1
Valletta FC 4 — Hamrun Spartans 0

### FINAL
Sliema Wanderers 3 — Valletta FC 0

### 3RD/4TH PLACE
Hibernians 3 — Hamrun Spartans 3 (aet)
Hibernians win 5-4 on penalties

## MALTA EURO CUP 1990/91

A pre-season tournament, played between Malta's European Cup entrants.

### LEAGUE TABLE FINAL

| | P | W | D | L | F | A | Pts |
|---|---|---|---|---|---|---|---|
| Sliema Wanderers | 2 | 2 | 0 | 0 | 5 | 1 | 4 |
| Hibernians | 2 | 1 | 0 | 1 | 2 | 3 | 2 |
| Valletta FC | 2 | 0 | 0 | 2 | 3 | 2 | 0 |

| IRISH LEAGUE Season 1990/91 | PORTADOWN | GLENAVON | GLENTORAN | LINFIELD | BALLYMENA | BANGOR | NEWRY TOWN | CLIFTONVILLE | LARNE | CARRICK R | COLERAINE | ARDS | CRUSADERS | DISTILLERY | BALLYCLARE | OMAGH TOWN |
|---|---|---|---|---|---|---|---|---|---|---|---|---|---|---|---|---|
| PORTADOWN | | 0-1 | 0-0 | 1-1 | 4-0 | 2-0 | 2-1 | 2-0 | 0-1 | 1-0 | 3-0 | 1-0 | 3-1 | 1-1 | 3-1 | 4-2 |
| GLENAVON | 2-1 | | 1-1 | 2-1 | 3-1 | 2-3 | 1-1 | 1-2 | 2-0 | 2-0 | 5-3 | 1-2 | 2-2 | 2-1 | 4-0 | 3-0 |
| GLENTORAN | 1-1 | 2-0 | | 1-0 | 2-0 | 0-1 | 2-2 | 3-2 | 1-0 | 2-1 | 4-0 | 1-1 | 2-0 | 3-1 | 2-1 | 4-1 |
| LINFIELD | 0-1 | 0-0 | 1-1 | | 3-0 | 2-1 | 1-2 | 0-4 | 4-2 | 1-0 | 2-1 | 1-0 | 2-0 | 2-2 | 3-1 | 0-0 |
| BALLYMENA UNITED | 0-2 | 4-3 | 2-3 | 2-2 | | 3-0 | 2-1 | 1-1 | 4-4 | 2-1 | 4-0 | 4-1 | 1-0 | 1-2 | 1-1 | 2-0 |
| BANGOR | 0-1 | 1-2 | 1-0 | 1-0 | 2-2 | | 2-0 | 4-2 | 2-0 | 2-1 | 3-1 | 1-1 | 2-1 | 2-1 | 3-0 | 3-0 |
| NEWRY TOWN | 1-3 | 1-0 | 2-0 | 3-1 | 3-0 | 1-1 | | 0-0 | 1-2 | 2-0 | 3-1 | 3-1 | 1-2 | 3-0 | 3-2 | 2-1 |
| CLIFTONVILLE | 1-2 | 0-2 | 2-1 | 2-2 | 1-3 | 2-0 | 6-0 | | 4-0 | 0-2 | 2-0 | 2-0 | 3-1 | 2-1 | 4-0 | 3-2 |
| LAHNE | 1-3 | 0-4 | 0-1 | 0-1 | 1-2 | 0-1 | 1-1 | 4-1 | | 1-0 | 2-0 | 0-2 | 2-2 | 0-4 | 1-1 | 3-3 |
| CARRICK RANGERS | 1-4 | 1-2 | 2-3 | 1-2 | 2-1 | 1-3 | 0-0 | 1-3 | 1-1 | | 1-0 | 2-5 | 2-2 | 0-2 | 1-2 | 0-3 |
| COLERAINE | 1-3 | 1-1 | 1-2 | 0-2 | 0-1 | 0-4 | 2-4 | 2-2 | 1-0 | 1-1 | | 0-1 | 1-1 | 3-4 | 2-1 | 1-4 |
| ARDS | 1-2 | 1-2 | 2-3 | 1-1 | 0-0 | 0-2 | 1-2 | 1-1 | 4-1 | 2-0 | 1-0 | | 0-0 | 2-1 | 4-3 | 5-1 |
| CRUSADERS | 2-3 | 1-3 | 2-0 | 2-2 | 0-0 | 3-2 | 2-1 | 1-1 | 5-0 | 3-3 | 4-1 | 0-2 | | 4-1 | 1-2 | 4-1 |
| DISTILLERY | 0-0 | 3-2 | 2-3 | 2-1 | 2-0 | 1-3 | 1-3 | 2-2 | 1-3 | 2-1 | 2-0 | 2-2 | 1-3 | | 4-1 | 0-1 |
| BALLYCLARE C'RADES | 0-3 | 3-3 | 0-1 | 1-1 | 1-5 | 0-2 | 0-2 | 1-3 | 3-3 | 1-0 | 1-1 | 1-0 | 2-3 | 2-0 | | 0-3 |
| OMAGH TOWN | 2-5 | 2-5 | 3-1 | 0-1 | 1-1 | 0-0 | 2-1 | 2-1 | 0-5 | 3-4 | 2-1 | 2-4 | 0-1 | 5-1 | 2-1 | |

## IRISH LEAGUE A SEASON 1990/91
### LEAGUE TABLE FINAL

| | | | | | | | |
|---|---|---|---|---|---|---|---|
| Portadown | 30 | 22 | 5 | 3 | 61 | 22 | 71 |
| Bangor | 30 | 19 | 4 | 7 | 52 | 29 | 61 |
| Glentoran | 30 | 18 | 6 | 6 | 50 | 32 | 60 |
| Glenavon | 30 | 17 | 6 | 7 | 63 | 38 | 57 |
| Newry Town | 30 | 15 | 5 | 10 | 50 | 42 | 50 |
| Cliftonville | 30 | 14 | 7 | 9 | 59 | 41 | 49 |
| Linfield | 30 | 12 | 10 | 8 | 40 | 34 | 46 |
| Ballymena United | 30 | 12 | 8 | 10 | 49 | 46 | 44 |
| Ards | 30 | 12 | 7 | 11 | 47 | 40 | 43 |
| Crusaders | 30 | 11 | 9 | 10 | 53 | 46 | 42 |
| Distillery | 30 | 10 | 5 | 15 | 47 | 57 | 35 |
| Omagh Town | 30 | 10 | 4 | 16 | 48 | 66 | 34 |
| Larne | 30 | 8 | 6 | 16 | 41 | 59 | 30 |
| Ballyclare Comr. | 30 | 5 | 6 | 19 | 33 | 68 | 21 |
| Carrick Rangers | 30 | 4 | 5 | 21 | 30 | 58 | 17 |
| Coleraine | 30 | 2 | 5 | 23 | 25 | 70 | 11 |

Champions :- Portadown

### TOP SCORERS
1. McBride (Glenavon) ... 22
2. Hamilton (Distillery) ... 19
3. Cowan (Portadown) ... 18
   McCartney (Glentoran) ... 18
5. Hunter (Crusaders) ... 17
6. Ralph (Newry Town) ... 16
7. Drake (Cliftonville) ... 14

# NORTHERN IRELAND ULSTER CUP 1990/91

## SECTION A
| Portadown | 2 | Larne | 1 |
| Crusaders | 2 | Ballymena United | 1 |
| Ballymena United | 0 | Portadown | 4 |
| Larne | 3 | Crusaders | 2 |
| Portadown | 2 | Crusaders | 1 |
| Ballymena United | 5 | Larne | 0 |

### LEAGUE TABLE FINAL
| Portadown | 3 | 3 | 0 | 0 | 8 | 2 | 9 |
| Ballymena United | 3 | 1 | 0 | 2 | 6 | 6 | 3 |
| Crusaders | 3 | 1 | 0 | 2 | 5 | 6 | 3 |
| Larne | 3 | 1 | 0 | 2 | 4 | 9 | 3 |

## SECTION B
| Glenavon | 5 | Carrick Rangers | 1 |
| Distillery | 0 | Bangor | 2 |
| Bangor | 1 | Glenavon | 2 |
| Carrick Rangers | 3 | Distillery | 3 |
| Bangor | 3 | Carrick Rangers | 0 |
| Glenavon | 5 | Distillery | 0 |

### LEAGUE TABLE FINAL
| Glenavon | 3 | 3 | 0 | 0 | 12 | 2 | 9 |
| Bangor | 3 | 2 | 0 | 1 | 6 | 2 | 6 |
| Carrick Rangers | 3 | 0 | 1 | 2 | 4 | 11 | 1 |
| Distillery | 3 | 0 | 1 | 2 | 3 | 10 | 1 |

## SECTION C
| Ballyclare C'rades | 0 | Newry Town | 3 |
| Glentoran | 1 | Coleraine | 0 |
| Newry Town | 1 | Glentoran | 1 |
| Coleraine | 3 | Ballyclare C'rades | 2 |
| Newry Town | 0 | Coleraine | 1 ⊗ |
| Glentoran | 4 | Ballyclare C'rades | 0 |

### LEAGUE TABLE FINAL
| Glentoran | 3 | 2 | 1 | 0 | 6 | 1 | 7 |
| Coleraine | 3 | 2 | 0 | 1 | 4 | 3 | 6 |
| Newry Town | 3 | 1 | 1 | 1 | 4 | 2 | 4 |
| Ballyclare C'rades | 3 | 0 | 0 | 3 | 2 | 10 | 0 |

⊗ Following Newry Town 1 Coleraine 2. Abandoned after 67 minutes due to floodlight failure.

## SECTION D
| Ards | 2 | Cliftonville | 2 |
| Linfield | 1 | Omagh Town | 1 |
| Linfield | 0 | Cliftonville | 0 |
| Ards | 1 | Omagh Town | 0 |
| Cliftonville | 1 | Omagh Town | 0 |
| Ards | 0 | Linfield | 1 |

### LEAGUE TABLE FINAL
| Cliftonville | 3 | 1 | 2 | 0 | 3 | 2 | 5 |
| Linfield | 3 | 1 | 2 | 0 | 2 | 1 | 5 |
| Ards | 3 | 1 | 1 | 1 | 3 | 3 | 4 |
| Omagh Town | 3 | 0 | 1 | 2 | 1 | 3 | 1 |

## 1/4 FINALS
| Cliftonville | 1 | Coleraine | 1 (aet.) |

Coleraine win 4-5 on penalties

| Portadown | 2 | Bangor | 1 |
| Glenavon | 4 | Ballymena United | 0 |
| Glentoran | 0 | Linfield | 1 |

## SEMI-FINALS
| Portadown | 4 | Linfield | 2 |
| Glenavon | 5 | Coleraine | 1 |

## FINAL
| Portadown | 1 | Glenavon | 1 (aet.) |

## FINAL REPLAY
| Portadown | 1 | Glenavon | 1 (aet.) |

Portadown win 3-2 on penalties

# NORTHERN IRELAND FLOODLIGHT CUP 1990/91

## 1ST ROUND
| | | | | |
|---|---|---|---|---|
| Ballymena United | 2 | | Distillery | 1 |
| Glenavon | 2 | | Coleraine | 0 |
| Linfield | 2 | | Ballyclare C'rades | 0 |
| Newry Town | 1 | | Carrick Rangers | 1 |
| Portadown | 4 | | Ards | 2 |

## 2ND ROUND
| | | | | |
|---|---|---|---|---|
| Ballymena United | 0 | (aet) | Bangor | 0 |
| Ballymena United win 5-4 on penalties | | | | |
| Newry Town | 0 | | Glenavon | 4 |

## SEMI-FINALS
| | | | | |
|---|---|---|---|---|
| Glenavon | 3 | | Omagh Town | 0 |

## FINAL
| | | | | |
|---|---|---|---|---|
| Portadown | 2 | | Glenavon | 0 |

---

# NORTHERN IRELAND IRISH LEAGUE CUP 1990/91

## 1ST ROUND
| | | | | |
|---|---|---|---|---|
| Ards | 4 | | Ballinamallard Utd | 1 |
| Bangor | 2 | | UU Jordanstown | 0 |
| Carrick Rangers | 1 | | Dundela | 2 |
| Crusaders | 5 | | Brantwood | 1 |
| Glentoran | 1 | | Banbridge Town | 0 |
| Omagh Town | 5 | | Limavady United | 0 ⊗ |
| Glenavon | 6 | | UU Coleraine | 0 |
| Larne | 4 | | Dungannon Swifts | 0 |
| Coleraine | 0 | | Queen's University | 1 |

## 2ND ROUND
| | | | | |
|---|---|---|---|---|
| Bangor | 3 | | Amagh City | 1 |
| Newry Town | 2 | | Ards | 3 |
| Larne | 2 | (aet) | Glenavon | 1 |
| Cliftonville | 1 | | RUC | 2 |

## 1/4 FINALS
| | | | | |
|---|---|---|---|---|
| Ards | 4 | | Larne | 0 |
| Bangor | 3 | | RUC | 0 |

## SEMI-FINALS
| | | | | |
|---|---|---|---|---|
| Ards | 4 | | Omagh Town | 1 |

## FINAL
| | | | | |
|---|---|---|---|---|
| Glentoran | 2 | | Ards | 0 |

Following Ballyclare Comrades 1 RUC 0, abandoned after 29 minutes
Following Omagh Town 2 Limavady United 0, abandoned after 38 minutes

Crusaders 1 Portadown 2
Linfield 0 Omagh Town 1
Crusaders win 2-3 on penalties
Omagh Town win 4-3 on penalties

Portadown 2 Ballymena United 2 (aet)
Portadown win 5-3 on penalties

---

# NORTHERN IRELAND GOLD CUP 1990/91

## SECTION A
| | | | | |
|---|---|---|---|---|
| Carrick Rangers | 0 | | Newry Town | 3 |
| Distillery | 1 | | Portadown | 1 |
| Carrick Rangers | 1 | | Portadown | 1 |

## SECTION B
| | | | | |
|---|---|---|---|---|
| Ards | 1 | | Coleraine | 1 |
| Cliftonville | 1 | | Ballymena United | 1 |
| Ballymena United | 3 | | Ards | 2 |

## FINAL
| | | | | |
|---|---|---|---|---|
| Glentoran | 2 | | Ards | 0 |

---

# IRISH CUP 1990/91

## 1/4 FINALS
| | | | | |
|---|---|---|---|---|
| Bangor | 1 | | Omagh Town | 0 |
| Glenavon | 1 | | Larne | 0 |

## SEMI-FINALS
| | | | | |
|---|---|---|---|---|
| Cliftonville | 1 | | Glenavon | 2 |

## FINAL
| | | | | |
|---|---|---|---|---|
| Portadown | 1 | | Bangor | 0 |

## 5TH ROUND
| | | | | |
|---|---|---|---|---|
| Portadown | 0 | | Newry Town | 0 |
| Distillery | 1 | | Crusaders | 1 |
| Omagh Town | 1 | | Ballymena United | 2 |
| Larne | 4 | | East Belfast | 1 |
| Tobermore United | 2 | | Loughgall | 4 |
| Ballinamallard | 0 | | Glentoran | 4 |
| Crewe United | 0 | | H'land & Wolff Wldrs | 1 |
| H'land & Wolff Wldrs | 1 | | Coagh United | 3 |

## REPLAYS
| | | | | |
|---|---|---|---|---|
| Crusaders | 3 | | Cliftonville | 2 |

## 6TH ROUND
| | | | | |
|---|---|---|---|---|
| Ards | 0 | | Donegal Celtic | 0 |
| Carrick Rangers | 1 | | Larne | 3 |
| Glenavon | 0 | | Bangor | 0 |
| Linfield | 2 | | Coleraine | 0 |

## REPLAYS
| | | | | |
|---|---|---|---|---|
| Crusaders | 3 | | Donegal Celtic | 0 |

## 1/4 FINALS
| | | | | |
|---|---|---|---|---|
| Ards | 3 | | Linfield | 2 |

# NORTHERN IRELAND INTERNATIONAL REVIEW 1990

## INTERNATIONAL LINE-UPS 1990

| | Paul Kee | Colin Hill | Mal Donaghy | John McClelland | Gerry Taggart | David McCreery | Danny Wilson | Jimmy Quinn | Colin Clarke | Kevin Wilson | Kingsley Black | Iain Dowie | Anton Rogan | Tommy Wright | Nigel Worthington | Alan McDonald | Robert Dennison | John Devine | Steve Morrow | Colin O'Neill | Stephen McBride |
|---|---|---|---|---|---|---|---|---|---|---|---|---|---|---|---|---|---|---|---|---|---|
| 27/3/90 NORTHERN IRELAND 2 NORWAY 3 Belfast — Friendly — Ref: King (Wales) — (Quinn, K.Wilson) | 1 | 2 | 3 | 4 | 5 | 6 | 7 | 8 | 9 | 10 | 11 | (4) | (6) | | | | | | | | |
| 18/5/90 NORTHERN IRELAND 1 URUGUAY 0 Belfast — Friendly — Ref: Cooper (Wales) — (K.Wilson) | | 2 | | | 4 | (7) | 8 | | | 10 | 11 | 9 | 6 | 1 | 3 | 5 | 7 | (2) | (6) | | |
| 12/9/90 NORTHERN IRELAND 0 YUGOSLAVIA 2 Belfast — EuroCh.Q. — Ref: Uilenberg (holland) | 1 | | 4 | | 2 | | 6 | | (8) | 10 | 9 | 11 | 7 | | 5 | 3 | 8 | | | | |
| 17/10/90 NORTHERN IRELAND 1 DENMARK 1 Belfast — EuroCh.Q. — Ref: Philippi (Luxembourg) — (Clarke) | 1 | | 2 | | 4 | | 7 | | 10 | | 11 | 9 | 6 | | 3 | 5 | | | | | (8) |
| 14/11/90 AUSTRIA 0 NORTHERN IRELAND 0 Wien — EuroCh.Q. — Ref: Biguet (France) | 1 | | 2 | | 3 | | 7 | | 10 | 11 | 9 | (10) | 8 | | 5 | 4 | 6 | | (9) | 8 | |
| CAPS AT 31/12/90 | 4 | 2 | 67 | 53 | 5 | 67 | 21 | 27 | 27 | 18 | 13 | 5 | 15 | 4 | 31 | 28 | 10 | 1 | 2 | 3 | 1 |
| GOALS AT 31/12/90 | | | | 1 | | | 1 | 6 | 8 | 2 | | | | | | 1 | | | | | |

## NORTHERN IRELAND : All Time Records as at 31/12/90 - CAPS

| | | |
|---|---|---|
| 1. | Pat Jennings (Watford/Tottenham Hotspur/Arsenal) | 119 |
| 2. | Sammy McIlroy (Manchester United/Stoke City/Manchester City/Örgryte IS) | 88 |
| 3. | Jimmy Nicholl (Manchester United/Toronto Blizzard/Sunderland/Rangers/West Bromwich Albion) | 73 |
| 4. | David McCreery (Manchester United/Queen's Park Rangers/Tulsa Roughnecks/Newcastle United/Heart of Midlothian) | 67 |
| | Mal Donaghy (Luton Town/Manchester United) | 67 |
| 6. | Martin O'Neill (Distillery/Nottingham Forest/Norwich City/Manchester City/Notts County) | 64 |
| 7. | Gerry Armstrong (Tottenham Hotspur/Watford/RCD Mallorca/West Bromwich Albion/Chesterfield) | 63 |
| 8. | Terry Neill (Arsenal/Hull City) | 59 |
| 9. | Billy Bingham (Sunderland/Luton Town/Everton/Port Vale) | 56 |
| | Danny Blanchflower (Barnsley/Aston Villa/Tottenham Hotspur) | 56 |

## NORTHERN IRELAND : All Time Records as at 31/12/90 - GOALS

| | | | |
|---|---|---|---|
| 1. | Joe Bambrick (Linfield/Chelsea) | (11) | 12 |
| | Billy Gillespie (Sheffield United) | (25) | 12 |
| | Gerry Armstrong (Tottenham Hotspur/Watford/RCD Mallorca/West Bromwich Albion/Chesterfield) | (63) | 12 |
| 4. | Johnny Crossan (Sparta/Sunderland/Manchester City/Middlesbrough) | (24) | 10 |
| | Peter McParland (Aston Villa/Wolverhampton Wanderers) | (34) | 10 |
| | Jimmy McIlroy (Burnley/Stoke City) | (55) | 10 |
| | Billy Bingham (Sunderland/Luton Town/Everton/Port Vale) | (56) | 10 |
| 8. | Olphie Stanfield (Distillery) | (30) | 9 |
| | George Best (Manchester United/Fulham) | (37) | 9 |
| | Norman Whiteside (Manchester United/Everton) | (38) | 9 |
| | Martin O'Neill (Distillery/Nottingham Forest/Norwich City/Manchester City/Notts County) | (64) | 9 |

Glenavon ........4   Ballyclare C'rades .....0   Larne........1   Glentoran........1

**REPLAY**
Glentoran ........4   Larne ........1

**SEMI-FINALS**
Ards........1   Portadown........2   Glenavon........3   Glentoran........3

**FINAL**   4/5/91 (at Windsor Park, Belfast)
Portadown........ 2   Glenavon........... 1

Portadown : Keenan, Major, Strain, Stewart, Curliss, Doolin, Rafferty, Cunningham, Davidson, Cowan, Fraser.
Glenavon : Beck, McKeown, McCullough, Byrne, Scappaticci, McDermott (Davies 69), Conville, Russell (McCann 80), McCoy, Ferguson, McBride.

Attendance : 15,000

1-0   Cowan 6
2-0   Cowan 44
2-1   Ferguson 46

# NORWAY  Correspondent : GEIR HØISTAD

NORWAY Correspondent : GEIR HØISTAD

| NORWAY 1st Division Season 1990 | LILLESTRØM | ROSENBORG | TROMSØ | MOLDE | K'VINGER | VIKING | BRANN | MOSS | START | VIF | FYLLINGEN | STR'GODSET |
|---|---|---|---|---|---|---|---|---|---|---|---|---|
| LILLESTRØM SK |  | 2-1 | 0-0 | 3-1 | 4-0 | 2-4 | 1-1 | 4-0 | 1-0 | 4-1 | 1-1 | 0-1 |
| ROSENBORG BK | 3-0 |  | 0-0 | 0-1 | 2-0 | 2-2 | 2-0 | 4-0 | 4-1 | 4-1 | 4-0 | 6-3 |
| TROMSØ IL | 2-1 | 1-3 |  | 0-0 | 3-1 | 3-1 | 0-1 | 3-1 | 1-1 | 3-1 | 3-0 | 3-0 |
| MOLDE FK | 3-2 | 1-7 | 1-0 |  | 1-0 | 2-3 | 6-2 | 1-1 | 1-0 | 4-1 | 2-0 | 0-2 |
| KONGSVINGER IL | 3-1 | 0-2 | 0-0 | 1-3 |  | 1-0 | 1-1 | 3-0 | 3-1 | 3-0 | 1-1 | 2-1 |
| VIKING FK | 1-0 | 1-1 | 1-1 | 2-0 | 1-1 |  | 1-2 | 5-2 | 2-0 | 1-2 | 1-0 | 4-0 |
| SK BRANN | 4-1 | 3-1 | 3-0 | 0-0 | 1-2 | 2-1 |  | 0-0 | 0-0 | 1-0 | 2-3 | 5-2 |
| MOSS FK | 1-3 | 2-2 | 1-2 | 0-1 | 3-0 | 1-2 | 0-2 |  | 3-2 | 5-1 | 1-2 | 2-4 |
| IK START | 1-0 | 2-4 | 1-3 | 2-0 | 4-0 | 3-2 | 3-1 | 3-0 |  | 6-2 | 1-1 | 1-1 |
| VAALERENGENS IF | 1-0 | 1-6 | 2-3 | 0-1 | 1-1 | 2-2 | 1-2 | 1-1 | 0-1 |  | 2-0 | 4-1 |
| FYLLINGEN IL | 0-0 | 1-1 | 0-2 | 2-2 | 2-1 | 1-3 | 0-0 | 1-0 | 4-1 | 2-0 |  | 2-0 |
| STRØMGODSET IF | 1-0 | 2-1 | 2-3 | 1-3 | 0-0 | 2-1 | 0-1 | 1-0 | 1-5 | 2-2 | 2-0 |  |

| NORWAY 2nd Division A Season 1990 | SOGNDAL | DJERV 1919 | BRYNE | STORD | AALESUND | HAM KAM | FRIGG | FAABERG | STRØMMEN | KRIST'SUND | OS | HØDD |
|---|---|---|---|---|---|---|---|---|---|---|---|---|
| SOGNDAL IL |  | 0-3 | 3-0 | 3-3 | 4-2 | 1-1 | 1-0 | 2-0 | 0-1 | 2-0 | 2-1 | 2-0 |
| SK DJERV 1919 | 0-1 |  | 1-0 | 0-0 | 1-0 | 2-1 | 2-0 | 1-0 | 0-1 | 1-1 | 1-0 | 1-3 |
| BRYNE IL | 2-1 | 1-1 |  | 2-0 | 1-0 | 1-2 | 2-1 | 2-1 | 1-0 | 6-0 | 0-2 | 2-1 |
| STORD TURN IL | 1-2 | 2-3 | 1-0 |  | 0-1 | 0-0 | 0-1 | 3-1 | 1-2 | 2-1 | 3-0 | 0-0 |
| AALESUND FK | 2-4 | 1-1 | 1-2 | 1-0 |  | 3-2 | 2-1 | 3-1 | 2-1 | 2-3 | 3-0 | 3-1 |
| HAMARKAMERATENE | 4-1 | 4-1 | 1-4 | 6-0 | 4-1 |  | 5-2 | 1-1 | 2-1 | 1-0 | 4-1 | 3-4 |
| FRIGG FK | 0-4 | 1-2 | 1-1 | 4-0 | 0-6 | 2-3 |  | 0-1 | 0-5 | 3-0 | 2-2 | 2-1 |
| FAABERG IL | 1-1 | 1-1 | 1-0 | 3-2 | 1-2 | 0-3 | 0-0 |  | 0-6 | 0-1 | 1-1 | 1-1 |
| STRØMMEN IL | 0-1 | 1-0 | 1-2 | 3-0 | 1-1 | 1-0 | 0-0 | 2-0 |  | 1-1 | 3-1 | 5-0 |
| KRISTIANSUND FK | 0-2 | 2-1 | 1-3 | 1-1 | 1-2 | 0-3 | 1-1 | 1-1 | 1-1 |  | 2-0 | 2-2 |
| OS TF | 2-3 | 1-0 | 0-1 | 2-1 | 1-1 | 1-1 | 0-1 | 0-0 | 0-4 | 2-1 |  | 0-0 |
| IL HØDD | 0-2 | 1-0 | 0-1 | 2-2 | 1-1 | 1-2 | 5-1 | 3-1 | 0-0 | 0-2 | 1-1 |  |

## NORWAY 1ST DIVISION 1990
### LEAGUE TABLE FINAL

| | | | | | | |
|---|---|---|---|---|---|---|
| Rosenborg BK (Trondheim) | 22 | 13 | 5 | 4 | 60 24 | 44 |
| Tromsø IL (Tromsø) | 22 | 12 | 6 | 4 | 36 21 | 42 |
| Molde FK (Molde) | 22 | 12 | 4 | 6 | 34 29 | 40 |
| SK Brann (Bergen) | 22 | 11 | 6 | 5 | 34 25 | 39 |
| Viking FK (Stavanger) | 22 | 10 | 5 | 7 | 41 30 | 35 |
| IK Start (Kristiansand) | 22 | 9 | 4 | 9 | 39 34 | 31 |
| Fyllingen IL (Fyllingdalen) | 22 | 7 | 7 | 8 | 23 30 | 28 |
| Kongsvinger IL (Kongsving) | 22 | 7 | 6 | 9 | 24 32 | 27 |
| Strømgodset IF (Drammen) | 22 | 8 | 3 | 11 | 29 45 | 27 |
| Lillestrøm SK (Lillestrøm) | 22 | 7 | 4 | 11 | 30 30 | 25 |
| Vaalerengens IF (Oslo) | 22 | 4 | 4 | 14 | 26 53 | 16 |
| Moss FK (Moss) | 22 | 3 | 4 | 15 | 24 47 | 13 |

Champions : - Rosenborg BK
Relegated : - Vaalerengens IF and Moss FK

## NORWAY : PROMOTION/RELEGATION PLAY-OFFS 1990

Bryne IL ..................... 5      Eik IF ......................... 1
Eik IF ......................... 1      Lillestrøm SK ............. 3
Lillestrøm SK ............. 2      Bryne IL ..................... 0

### LEAGUE TABLE FINAL

| | | | | | | | |
|---|---|---|---|---|---|---|---|
| Lillestrøm SK | 2 | 2 | 0 | 0 | 5 | 1 | 4 |
| Bryne IL | 2 | 1 | 0 | 1 | 5 | 3 | 2 |
| Eik IF | 2 | 0 | 0 | 2 | 2 | 8 | 0 |

Lillestrøm SK retain their 1st Division place.
### NAME CHANGE FOR SEASON 1991 : -
Vaalerengens IF to IL Vif Fotball

## TOP SCORERS

1. Tore André Dahlum (IK Start) — 20
2. Jahn-Ivar Jakobsen (Rosenborg BK) — 17
3. Mike McCabe (Tromsø IL) — 13
4. Petter Belsvik (Molde FK) — 12
   Halvor Storskogen (Strømgodset IF) — 12
6. Per Hilmar Nybø (SK Brann) — 11
7. Kjell Jonevret (Viking FK) — 9
8. Roger Nilsen (Viking FK) — 8
   Gøran Sørloth (Rosenborg BK) — 8
   Alf Kaare Tveit (Viking FK) — 8

## NORWAY 2ND DIVISION A 1990
### LEAGUE TABLE FINAL

| | | | | | | |
|---|---|---|---|---|---|---|
| Sogndal IL (Sogndal) | 22 | 15 | 3 | 4 | 42 23 | 48 |
| Bryne IL (Bryne) | 22 | 14 | 2 | 6 | 34 20 | 44 |
| Hamarkameratene (Hamar) | 22 | 13 | 4 | 5 | 53 28 | 43 |
| Strømmen IF (Strømmen) | 22 | 12 | 5 | 5 | 40 13 | 41 |
| Aalesunds FK (Aalesund) | 22 | 11 | 4 | 7 | 40 31 | 37 |
| SK Djerv 1919 (Haugesund) | 22 | 9 | 5 | 8 | 23 22 | 32 |
| IL Hødd (Ulsteinvik) | 22 | 5 | 8 | 9 | 27 34 | 23 |
| Kristiansund FK (Krist'sund) | 22 | 5 | 7 | 10 | 22 37 | 22 |
| Frigg FK (Oslo) | 22 | 5 | 5 | 12 | 23 43 | 20 |
| Os TF (Os) | 22 | 4 | 7 | 11 | 18 35 | 19 |
| Stord TIL (Stord) | 22 | 4 | 6 | 12 | 22 38 | 18 |
| Faaberg IL (Lillehammer) | 22 | 3 | 8 | 11 | 16 36 | 17 |

Promoted : - Sogndal IL
Relegated : - Os TF, Stord TIL and Faaberg IL

## NORWAY 2ND DIVISION B 1990
### LEAGUE TABLE FINAL

| | | | | | | |
|---|---|---|---|---|---|---|
| SFK Lyn (Oslo) | 22 | 14 | 3 | 5 | 50 23 | 45 |
| Eik IF (Tønsberg) | 22 | 14 | 3 | 5 | 45 22 | 45 |
| Mjøndalen IF (Mjøndalen) | 22 | 13 | 4 | 5 | 38 23 | 43 |
| FK Mjølner (Narvik) | 22 | 10 | 8 | 4 | 29 21 | 38 |
| Strindheim IL (Trondheim) | 22 | 11 | 2 | 9 | 30 26 | 35 |
| Sandefjord BK (Sandef'd) | 22 | 9 | 5 | 8 | 24 22 | 32 |
| Raade IL (Raade) | 22 | 6 | 5 | 11 | 24 31 | 23 |
| Fredrikstad FK (Fred'stad) | 22 | 5 | 8 | 9 | 18 33 | 23 |
| IF Pors (Porsgrunn) | 22 | 6 | 4 | 12 | 25 36 | 22 |
| IF Skarp (Haapet) | 22 | 5 | 7 | 10 | 19 34 | 22 |
| Namsos IL (Namsos) | 22 | 5 | 5 | 12 | 29 40 | 20 |
| SK Sprint/Jeløy (Moss) | 22 | 4 | 6 | 12 | 19 39 | 18 |

Promoted : - SFK Lyn
Relegated : - IF Skarp, Namsos IL and SK Sprint/Jeløy

| NORWAY 2nd Division B Season 1990 | MØLNER | NAMSOS | FRED'STAD | STRINDHEIM | RAADE | MJØNDALEN | LYN | PORS | EIK | SPRINT/J | SANDEFJORD | SKARP |
|---|---|---|---|---|---|---|---|---|---|---|---|---|
| FK MJØLNER | ■ | 2-2 | 0-0 | 0-1 | 1-1 | 3-0 | 1-0 | 1-1 | 2-1 | 2-0 | 2-0 | 1-2 |
| NAMSOS IL | 1-2 | ■ | 1-2 | 0-1 | 0-1 | 1-4 | 1-3 | 4-0 | 0-3 | 4-2 | 1-1 | 2-0 |
| FREDRIKSTAD FK | 2-2 | 0-0 | ■ | 2-0 | 1-4 | 2-4 | 1-1 | 1-1 | 0-0 | 1-0 | 0-3 | 1-1 |
| STRINDHEIM IL | 0-1 | 0-2 | 1-0 | ■ | 2-1 | 2-2 | 1-2 | 3-0 | 1-2 | 3-2 | 1-4 | 5-0 |
| RAADE IL | 1-1 | 0-3 | 3-0 | 0-1 | ■ | 1-0 | 0-1 | 3-1 | 0-1 | 1-1 | 0-0 | 3-1 |
| MJØNDALEN IF | 0-3 | 3-3 | 2-0 | 1-1 | 1-0 | ■ | 1-0 | 1-0 | 3-0 | 3-0 | 0-1 | 2-1 |
| SFK LYN | 3-1 | 5-0 | 4-1 | 2-1 | 4-1 | 2-4 | ■ | 3-0 | 1-1 | 1-1 | 0-1 | 3-1 |
| IF PORS | 1-1 | 2-1 | 0-1 | 0-1 | 6-2 | 2-0 | 2-0 | ■ | 1-3 | 2-3 | 1-2 | 1-0 |
| EIK IF | 5-0 | 3-1 | 3-0 | 2-1 | 2-1 | 1-2 | 2-4 | 1-2 | ■ | 0-0 | 2-1 | 1-0 |
| SK SPRINT/JELØY | 0-2 | 1-1 | 0-1 | 1-2 | 1-0 | 0-2 | 1-5 | 1-0 | 1-5 | ■ | 1-0 | 1-1 |
| SANDEFJORD BK | 0-1 | 2-0 | 2-2 | 2-1 | 2-0 | 0-3 | 0-3 | 1-1 | 1-2 | 1-0 | ■ | 0-1 |
| IF SKARP | 0-0 | 3-1 | 1-0 | 0-1 | 1-1 | 0-0 | 1-3 | 3-1 | 0-5 | 2-2 | 0-0 | ■ |

## NORWAY : All Time Records as at 31/12/90 - CAPS

1. Thorbjørn Svenssen (Sandefjord BK)                                                                104
2. Svein Grøndalen (Raufoss IL/Rosenborg BK/Moss FK)                                     77
3. Terje Kojedal (Hamarkameratene/FC Mulhouse 93/US Valenciennes)              66
4. Gunnar Thoresen (Larvik Turn IF)                                                                       64
   Erik Thorstvedt (Viking FK/Borussia Mönchengladbach/IFK Göteborg/Tottenham Hotspur)   64
6. Olav Nilsen (IL Viking)                                                                                        62
7. Roar Johansen (Fredrikstad FK)                                                                         61
8. Harry Boye Karlsen (Ørn FK/SFK Lyn/Larvik Turn IF)                                        58

## NORWAY : All Time Records as at 31/12/90 - GOALS

1. Jørgen Juve (SFK Lyn)                                                                                (45) 33
2. Einar Gundersen (Tønsberg Turn/Odd BK)                                                 (33) 26
3. Harald Hennum (Frigg FK/Skeid)                                                              (43) 25
4. Gunnar Thoresen (Larvik Turn IF)                                                            (64) 22
5. Odd Iversen (Rosenborg BK/RC Mechelen/Vaalerengens IF)                    (45) 19
   Olav Nilsen (IL Viking)                                                                            (62) 19

## NORWAY 3RD DIVISION A 1990

### LEAGUE TABLE FINAL

| | | | | | | | |
|---|---|---|---|---|---|---|---|
| Drøbak/Frogn IL (Drøbak) | 22 | 19 | 1 | 2 | 73 | 16 | 58 |
| IF Fram (Larvik) | 22 | 19 | 0 | 3 | 62 | 26 | 57 |
| Sarpsborg FK (Sarpsborg) | 22 | 16 | 1 | 5 | 65 | 27 | 49 |
| Odds BK (Skien) | 22 | 10 | 2 | 10 | 38 | 45 | 32 |
| Baerum SK (Sandvika) | 22 | 8 | 5 | 9 | 39 | 42 | 29 |
| Ullern IF (Oslo) | 22 | 8 | 4 | 10 | 38 | 36 | 28 |
| FK Ørn (Horten) | 22 | 9 | 1 | 12 | 28 | 37 | 28 |
| Asker SKK (Asker) | 22 | 7 | 7 | 8 | 29 | 45 | 28 |
| Selbak TIF (Sellebakk) | 22 | 7 | 2 | 13 | 27 | 44 | 23 |
| IL Runar (Sandefjord) | 22 | 6 | 3 | 13 | 32 | 57 | 21 |
| Askim FK (Askim) | 22 | 5 | 1 | 16 | 31 | 55 | 16 |
| Uraedds BK (Porsgrunn) | 22 | 3 | 3 | 16 | 26 | 58 | 12 |

Promoted : - Drøbak/Frogn IL
Relegated : - IL Runar, Askim FK and Uraedds BK

## NORWAY 3RD DIVISION B 1990

### LEAGUE TABLE FINAL

| | | | | | | | |
|---|---|---|---|---|---|---|---|
| Elverum IL (Elverum) | 22 | 16 | 4 | 2 | 60 | 21 | 52 |
| Kjelsaas IL (Oslo) | 22 | 12 | 5 | 5 | 40 | 21 | 41 |
| SF Grei (Oslo) | 22 | 11 | 4 | 7 | 43 | 38 | 37 |
| Bjørkelangen SF (Bjørkel.) | 22 | 10 | 4 | 8 | 35 | 33 | 34 |
| Eidsvold TF (Eidsvoll) | 22 | 11 | 1 | 10 | 35 | 36 | 34 |
| Skeid (Oslo) | 22 | 9 | 3 | 10 | 43 | 47 | 30 |
| Lørenskog IF (Skaarer) | 22 | 8 | 5 | 9 | 37 | 30 | 29 |
| Nybergsund IL (Nybergs'nd) | 22 | 8 | 5 | 9 | 30 | 34 | 29 |
| Aurskog/Finstadbru SK(Akg) | 22 | 7 | 5 | 10 | 32 | 38 | 26 |
| Raufoss IL (Raufoss) | 22 | 8 | 2 | 12 | 32 | 42 | 26 |
| Høland IL (Fosser i Høland) | 22 | 6 | 5 | 11 | 26 | 40 | 23 |
| Brumunddal IL (Brumundd.) | 22 | 3 | 3 | 16 | 26 | 59 | 12 |

Promoted : - Elverum IL
Relegated : - Raufoss IL, Høland IL and Brumunddal IL

## NORWAY 3RD DIVISION D 1990

### LEAGUE TABLE FINAL

| | | | | | | | |
|---|---|---|---|---|---|---|---|
| Fana IL (Nesttun) | 22 | 12 | 6 | 4 | 40 | 26 | 42 |
| Aasane IL (Ulset) | 22 | 13 | 2 | 7 | 50 | 26 | 41 |
| Volda TIL (Volda) | 22 | 10 | 9 | 3 | 39 | 20 | 39 |
| Lyngbø SK (Ytre L'vaag) | 22 | 9 | 8 | 5 | 28 | 19 | 35 |
| Stranda IL (Stranda) | 22 | 8 | 8 | 6 | 28 | 24 | 32 |
| Vadmyra IL (Loddefjord) | 22 | 7 | 9 | 6 | 21 | 13 | 30 |
| SFK Mercantile (Oslo) | 22 | 8 | 7 | 7 | 31 | 27 | 29 |
| Brattvaag IL (Brattvaag) | 22 | 6 | 8 | 8 | 21 | 32 | 26 |
| Førde IL (Førde) | 22 | 8 | 1 | 13 | 17 | 45 | 25 |
| Eid IL (Nordfjordeid) | 22 | 5 | 8 | 9 | 33 | 39 | 23 |
| Hareid IL (Hareid) | 22 | 4 | 7 | 11 | 25 | 44 | 19 |
| Stryn TIL (Stryn) | 22 | 4 | 4 | 14 | 24 | 42 | 16 |

Promoted : - Fana IL
Relegated : - Eid IL, Hareid IL and Stryn TIL

## NORWAY 3RD DIVISION E 1990

### LEAGUE TABLE FINAL

| | | | | | | | |
|---|---|---|---|---|---|---|---|
| Surnadal IL (Surnadal) | 22 | 16 | 2 | 4 | 57 | 26 | 50 |
| Aandalsnes IF (Aandalsn.) | 22 | 14 | 4 | 4 | 47 | 26 | 46 |
| IL Stjørdals/Blink (Stjørdal) | 22 | 12 | 4 | 6 | 47 | 35 | 40 |
| Steinkjer IL (Steinkjer) | 22 | 10 | 4 | 8 | 35 | 29 | 34 |
| Sunndal IL (Sunndalsøra) | 22 | 9 | 6 | 7 | 31 | 32 | 33 |
| KIL/Hemne FG (Kyrk'røra) | 22 | 9 | 4 | 9 | 32 | 39 | 31 |
| Melhus IL (Melhus) | 22 | 8 | 6 | 8 | 55 | 33 | 30 |
| SK Nessegutten (Levang) | 22 | 7 | 6 | 9 | 36 | 38 | 27 |
| Alvdal IL (Alvdal) | 22 | 7 | 5 | 10 | 30 | 38 | 26 |
| IL Sverre (Levanger) | 22 | 8 | 1 | 13 | 38 | 55 | 25 |
| Ready (Oslo) | 22 | 5 | 2 | 15 | 30 | 52 | 17 |
| Clausenengen FK (K'sund) | 22 | 3 | 4 | 15 | 26 | 61 | 13 |

Promoted : - Surnadal IL
Relegated : - IL Sverre, Ready and Clausenengen FK

# NORWAY 3RD DIVISION C 1990
## LEAGUE TABLE FINAL

| | P | W | D | L | F | A | Pts |
|---|---|---|---|---|---|---|---|
| SK Haugar (Haugesund) | 22 | 15 | 3 | 4 | 51 | 23 | 48 |
| SK Vard (Haugesund) | 22 | 14 | 4 | 4 | 56 | 23 | 46 |
| Randaberg IL (Randaberg) | 22 | 13 | 4 | 5 | 51 | 33 | 41 |
| IL Skade | 22 | 9 | 6 | 7 | 47 | 37 | 33 |
| FK Jerv (Grimstad) | 22 | 9 | 6 | 7 | 37 | 35 | 33 |
| Ulf-Sandnes (Sandnes) | 22 | 8 | 7 | 7 | 42 | 30 | 31 |
| Aalgaard FK (Aalgaard) | 22 | 8 | 5 | 9 | 31 | 39 | 29 |
| Skjold IL (Aksdal) | 22 | 8 | 4 | 10 | 40 | 44 | 28 |
| Figgjo IL (Figgjo) | 22 | 6 | 6 | 10 | 30 | 40 | 24 |
| Klepp IL (Kleppe) | 22 | 6 | 6 | 10 | 25 | 36 | 24 |
| FK Vidar (Stavanger) | 22 | 5 | 3 | 14 | 28 | 42 | 23 |
| IL Eiger (Egersund) | 22 | 5 | 2 | 15 | 25 | 63 | 17 |

Promoted: - SK Haugar
Relegated: - Klepp IL, FK Vidar and IL Eiger

# NORWAY 3RD DIVISION F 1990
## LEAGUE TABLE FINAL

| | P | W | D | L | F | A | Pts |
|---|---|---|---|---|---|---|---|
| Tromsdalen UIL (T'dalen) | 22 | 16 | 3 | 3 | 60 | 16 | 51 |
| FK Bodo/Glimt (Bodo) | 22 | 15 | 5 | 2 | 56 | 24 | 50 |
| FK Narvik/Nor (Narvik) | 22 | 14 | 3 | 5 | 42 | 24 | 45 |
| IL Stalkameratene (Mo) | 22 | 12 | 3 | 7 | 45 | 32 | 39 |
| FK Fauske/Sprint (F'ske) | 22 | 12 | 1 | 9 | 47 | 45 | 37 |
| Alta IF (Alta) | 22 | 10 | 5 | 7 | 32 | 31 | 35 |
| Harstad IL (Harstad) | 22 | 9 | 3 | 10 | 47 | 41 | 30 |
| Andenes IL (Andenes) | 22 | 9 | 3 | 10 | 40 | 34 | 30 |
| Sandnessjoen IL (S'sjoen) | 22 | 9 | 2 | 11 | 34 | 31 | 29 |
| Mosjoen IL (Mosjoen) | 22 | 6 | 5 | 11 | 30 | 42 | 23 |
| Nordkjosbotn IL (N'botn) | 22 | 6 | 3 | 13 | 25 | 57 | 21 |
| FK Luna (Straumsjoen) | 22 | 2 | 4 | 16 | 20 | 69 | 10 |

Promoted: - Tromsdalen UIL
Relegated: - Sandnessjoen IL, Mosjoen IL, Nordkjosbotn IL and FK Luna

Note: For Season 1991, 1st Division to become Premier Division, 2nd Division to become 1st Division, 3rd Division to become 2nd Division etc.

Promoted from 4th Division for Season 1991: - Sorumsand IF (Sorumsand), Tune IL (Sarpsborg), Lillestrom SK II (Lillestrom), Stabaek IF (Bekkestua), SK Falk (Horten), Strommen IF II (Drammen), IK Start II (Kristiansand), Viking FK II (Stavanger), SK Brann II (Bergen), Fyllingen IL II (Fyllingsdalen), Flora SK (Floro), Skarbovik IF (Aalesund), Molde FK II (Molde), Rosenborg BK II (Trondheim), Byaasen IL (Trondheim), FK Gevir/Vinkelen (Bodo), Grovfjord IL (Grovfjord), Skjervoy IK (Skjervoy) & Honningsvaag TIF (Honningsvaag).

# NORWAY CUP 1990

## 1ST ROUND
| Home | | Away | |
|---|---|---|---|
| Os TF | 1 | Lyngbo SK | 0 |
| Figgjo IL | 1 | Viking FK | 4 (aet.) |
| IF Pors | 1 | FK Jerv | 0 |
| IL Skade | 1 | Sandefjord BK | 4 |
| Eid IL | 1 | Volda TIL | 3 |
| Brattvaag IL | 1 | Skarbovik IF | 0 |
| Vadmyra IL | 2 | Aasane IL | 0 |
| SK Vard | 1 | Stord TIL | 2 |
| Aalgaard FK | 0 | Randaberg IL | 1 |
| IL Bjornar | 0 | SK Brann | 3 |
| SK Sprint/Jeloy | 0 | Selbak TIF | 2 |
| Aas IL | 0 | Moss FK | 3 |
| Andenes IL | 0 | FK Narvik/Nor | 1 |
| Brønnøysund IL | 3 | IL Stalkameratene | 4 (aet.) |
| Larvik TIF | 3 | Odds BK | 5 (aet.) |
| Gjerdrum IL | 0 | Ready | 5 |
| Nordkjosbotn IL | 0 | Tromsdalen UIL | 3 |
| IL Polarsjernen | 3 | Tromso IL | 4 |
| Frigg FK | 0 | Baerum SK | 1 |
| SBK Drafn | 1 | Raade IL | 4 |
| Nidelv IL | 0 | Nardo FK | 1 |
| Mosjoen IL | 3 | SK Nessegutten | 2 |
| Holand IL | 1 | Namsos IL | 6 (aet.) |
| Tynset IL | 1 | Steinkjer FK | 3 (aet.) |
| Elverum IL | 0 | Nybergsund IL | 3 |

## 2ND ROUND
| Home | | Away | |
|---|---|---|---|
| Os TF | 0 | Viking FK | 2 |
| SK Haugar | 2 | Aalesunds FK | 3 |
| IK Start | 5 | Ull-Sandnes | 3 |
| IL Hodd | 2 | SK Brann | 4 |
| Vadmyra IL | | SFK Lyn | 4 |
| Volda TIL | 2 | Moss FK | 5 |
| Nybergsund IL | 4 | IL Stalkameratene | 5 |
| Steinkjer IF | 3 | Raade IL | 2 |
| Strommen IF | 3 | Sarpsborg FK | 0 |
| Baerum SK | 1 | Rosenborg BK | 7 |
| Tromsdalen UIL | 2 | Kongsvinger IL | 6 |
| Mjondalen IF | 3 | Molde FK | 6 |
| IF Skarp | 3 | Aandalsnes IF | 4 |
| FK Mjolner | 6 | Strommdset IF | 4 |
| Clausenengen FK | 4 | Sogndal IL | 4 |
| Rauflass IL | 4 | Eik IF | 1 |
| Nybergsund IL | | IF Fram | 1 |
| Sandefjord BK | 4 | Askim IF | 0 |
| FK Donn | 2 | Surndal IL | 0 |
| Stranda IL | 3 | Alvdal IL | 4 (aet.) |
| Kopervik IL | 4 | Sogndal IL | 0 |
| FK Bodo/Glimt | 4 | Uraedds BK | 2 ⊗ |
| FK Orn | 4 | Aassiden IF | 1 |
| Klepp IL | 2 | Asker SKK | 0 |
| Sel IL | 1 | | |
| Stokke IL | 2 | | |
| Kjelsaas IL | 0 | | |
| Egersunds IK | 8 | | |
| Drobak/Frogn IL | 1 | | |
| Bjorkelangen SF | 2 | | |

## 3RD ROUND
| Home | | Away | |
|---|---|---|---|
| SK Haugar | 0 | Viking FK | 2 |
| Ull-Sandnes | 0 | SK Brann | 4 |
| IL Hodd | 3 | Aalesunds FK | 4 |
| SFK Lyn | 4 | FK Vidar | 0 |
| Bryne IL | 1 | SK Djerv 1919 | 1 |
| Lov-Ham IL | 1 | Styrn TIL | 0 |
| Fyllingen IL | 2 | Stranda IL | 1 |
| Kopervik IL | 3 | Skarbovik IF | 0 |
| Bjerkreim IK | | FK Donn | 5 |
| IK Start | 0 | IL Eiger | 5 |
| FK Mjolner | 6 | Harstad IL | 0 |
| Grovfjord IL | 2 | IL Runar | 0 |
| FK Bodo/Glimt | | IL Stjerdals/Blink | 0 |
| SK Nessegutten | 1 | Lorenskog IF | 0 |
| Raade IL | 4 | FK Fauske/Sprint | 3 |
| Skjold IL | 0 | IL Eiger | 5 |

## 4TH ROUND
| Home | | Away | |
|---|---|---|---|
| Viking FK | 0 | IK Start | 4 |
| SK Brann | 0 | SFK Lyn | 2 |
| Tromso IL | 5 | Raade IL | 0 |
| Kongsvinger IL | 1 | Molde FK | 0 |
| FK Fauske/Sprint | | Tistedalen TIF | 2 |
| Tromso IL | 0 | Rosenborg BK | 1 |

## 1/4 FINALS
| Home | | Away | |
|---|---|---|---|
| IK Start | 0 | Fyllingen IL | 1 |
| Tromso IL | 0 | Rosenborg BK | 1 |

## REPLAY
| Home | | Away | |
|---|---|---|---|
| Lillestrom SK | 4 | FK Mjolner | 0 |

## SEMI-FINALS
| Home | | Away | |
|---|---|---|---|
| Fyllingen IL | 2 | SK Brann | 0 |
| Rosenborg BK | 1 | Kongsvinger IL | 0 |

# NORWAY INTERNATIONAL REVIEW 1990

## INTERNATIONAL LINE-UPS 1990

| Player | 4/2/90 S.Korea | 7/2/90 Malta | 27/3/90 N.Ireland | 6/6/90 Denmark | 22/8/90 Sweden | 12/9/90 USSR | 10/10/90 Hungary | 31/10/90 Cameroon | 7/11/90 Tunisia | 14/11/90 Cyprus | CAPS | GOALS |
|---|---|---|---|---|---|---|---|---|---|---|---|---|
| Ola By Rise | 1 | | | 1 | | | | | | | 23 | |
| Hugo Hansen | 2 | | 2 | | | | | | | | 14 | |
| Rune Tangen | 3 | 4 | | | | | | | | | 3 | 1 |
| Jan-Halvor Halvorsen | 4 | | 4 | | 2 | | | (6) | | | 5 | |
| Gunnar Halle | 5 | 2 | 5 | 5 | 5 | 2 | 2 | 9 | | 9 | 27 | 1 |
| Karl-Petter Löken | 6 | 6 | 6 | 2 | | | | | | 5 | 22 | 1 |
| Lars Bohinen | 7 | 7 | | | | | | 7 | | 6 | 6 | 2 |
| Örjan Berg | 8 | (8) | | | (8) | 6 | | | | 2 | 14 | 1 |
| Jahn-Ivar Jakobsen | 9 | | (11) | (8) | | 9 | 9 | | | | 18 | |
| Jörn Andersen | 10 | (10) | 10 | 10 | 10 | 10 | (9) | | | | 27 | 5 |
| Jan-Aage Fjörtoft | 11 | 11 | 11 | 11 | 11 | 11 | 11 | (10) | (11) | (11) | 26 | 8 |
| Bent Skammelsrud | (9) | 9 | 9 | 9 | 8 | | | | | | 8 | 2 |
| Erik Thorstvedt | | 1 | 1 | 1 | 1 | 1 | 1 | 1 | | 1 | 64 | |
| Erland Johnsen | | 3 | 3 | 3 | 3 | | | | | | 18 | 2 |
| Stig-Inge Björnebye | | 5 | | | 9 | | (9) | (9) | 9 | | 10 | |
| Jan Berg | | 8 | | | | | | | | | 23 | |
| Goran Sörloth | | 10 | | | | | 10 | 11 | 11 | 10 | 31 | 9 |
| Per-Egil Ahlsen | | | 7 | | 7 | 7 | 8 | 8 | | | 45 | 3 |
| Tom Gulbrandsen | | | 8 | (7) | 6 | 8 | | 6 | | | 17 | |
| Rune Bratseth | | | | 4 | 4 | 4 | 4 | 3 | 3 | | 32 | 4 |
| Jan-Ove Pedersen | | | | 6 | | | 6 | | | | 2 | |
| Per-Ove Ludvigsen | | | | 7 | | | | | | | 1 | |
| Dag Riisnaes | | | | 8 | | | | | | | 2 | |
| Paal Lydersen | | | | | (9) | 5 | 5 | | | | 5 | |
| Tore Pedersen | | | | | | 3 | 3 | 2 | 3 | 2 | 5 | |
| Erik Pedersen | | | | | | (6) | 6 | 5 | 5 | (5) | 5 | 3 |
| Tore-André Dahlum | | | | | | (11) | (11) | 10 | 10 | 11 | 5 | 3 |
| Sverre Brandhaug | | | | | | | 7 | | | 7 | 2 | 2 |
| Roger Nilsen | | | | | | | | 4 | 4 | 4 | 2 | |
| Øivind Leonhardsen | | | | | | | | 6 | 8 | 8 | 3 | |
| Einar Rossbach | | | | | | | | 1 | 1 | 1 | 1 | |
| Kaare Ingebrigtsen | | | | | | | | | 6 | 6 | 1 | 1 |
| Claus Eftevaag | | | | | | | | | 7 | 7 | 1 | 1 |
| Tor-André Grenersen | | | | | | | | | (1) | | 1 | |
| Erik Mykland | | | | | | | | | | 1 | 1 | 1 |

**4/2/90** — SOUTH KOREA 2 NORWAY 3, Ta'Qali (Malta), Friendly. Ref: Agius (Malta). (Ø.Berg, Skammelsrud, Tangen)

**7/2/90** — MALTA 1 NORWAY 1, Ta'Qali (Malta), Friendly. Ref: Azzopardi (Malta). (Fjörtoft)

**27/3/90** — NORTHERN IRELAND 2 NORWAY 3, Belfast, Friendly. Ref: King (Wales). (Skammelsrud, Andersen, Johnsen)

**6/6/90** — NORWAY 1 DENMARK 2, Trondheim, Friendly. Ref: Persson (Sweden). (Andersen)

**22/8/90** — NORWAY 1 SWEDEN 2, Stavanger, Friendly. Ref: Nielsen (Denmark). (Ahlsen)

**12/9/90** — USSR 2 NORWAY 0, Moskva, EuroCh.Q. Ref: Forstinger (Austria).

**10/10/90** — NORWAY 0 HUNGARY 0, Bergen, EuroCh.Q. Ref: Spillane (Rep.Ireland).

**31/10/90** — NORWAY 6 CAMEROON 1, Oslo, Friendly. Ref: Sörensen (Denmark). (Bratseth, Bohinen, Dahlum, Fjörtoft 2, Sörloth)

**7/11/90** — TUNISIA 1 NORWAY 3, Tunis, Friendly. Ref: Madjiba (Algeria). (Dahlum 2, Ingebrigtsen)

**14/11/90** — CYPRUS 0 NORWAY 3, Nicosia, EuroCh.Q. Ref: Petrovic (Yugoslavia). (Sörloth, Bohinen, Brandhaug)

CAPS AT 31/12/90
GOALS AT 31/12/90

---

**FINAL** 20/10/90 at Bislett Stadion, Oslo

Rosenborg BK.......... 5    Fyllingen IL............. 1

RBK: By Rise, Husby, Sollied, Eggen, Henriksen, Ingebrigtsen, Brandhaug, Ø.Berg (R.Berg 80), Löken (Strand 75), Sörloth, Jakobsen.

Fyllingen: Bahus, Leiknes, I.Ludvigsen, P-O.Ludvigsen (Tengs 67), Ingebrigtsen (Pedersen 50), Brandthun, Bergset, Knutsen, Helgeland, Vikenes, Lyngvaer.

| | | |
|---|---|---|
| 1-0 | Löken | 13 |
| 2-0 | Sörloth | 20 |
| 3-0 | Jakobsen | 28 |
| 4-0 | Löken | 59 |
| 5-0 | Ingebrigtsen | 67 |
| 5-1 | Tengs | 89 |

⊗ after extra time and penalties.

Referee: Arild Haugstad (Lillehammer)
Attendance: 30,000

# POLAND Correspondent : DARIUSZ ROSTKOWSKI

## POLAND 1st Division — Season 1990/91

| POLAND 1st Division | LECH | ZAGLEBIE L | KATOWICE | ZAWISZA | OLIMPIA | GORNIK | LEGIA | LKS LODZ | WISLA | SLASK | STAL | RUCH | MOTOR | ZAGLEBIE S | HUTNIK | IGLOOPOL |
|---|---|---|---|---|---|---|---|---|---|---|---|---|---|---|---|---|
| KKS LECH POZNAN | ■ | 2-1 | 1-2 | 2-2 | 0-0 | 0-0 | 1-1 | 1-1 | 0-0 | 1-2 | 2-0 | 0-1 | 4-0 | 1-1 | 5-2 | 6-0 |
| MKS ZAGLEBIE LUBIN | 2-1 | ■ | 0-0 | 2-1 | 0-0 | 2-1 | 1-0 | 2-1 | 3-1 | 2-1 | 3-2 | 2-0 | 2-0 | 2-0 | 2-1 | 4-0 |
| GKS KATOWICE | 1-1 | 1-1 | ■ | 1-0 | 2-1 | 2-1 | 1-0 | 2-0 | 0-2 | 0-1 | 1-0 | 1-0 | 1-0 | 3-0 | 2-3 | 2-0 |
| WKS ZAWISZA BYDGOSZCZ | 0-2 | 2-1 | 0-1 | ■ | 2-2 | 0-3 | 0-0 | 2-0 | 0-0 | 0-1 | 2-0 | 1-0 | 3-2 | 3-0 | 1-0 | 1-1 |
| GKS OLIMPIA POZNAN | 3-2 | 1-1 | 3-0 | 1-0 | ■ | 1-2 | 0-0 | 1-0 | 1-3 | 0-0 | 1-0 | 0-0 | 0-2 | 4-3 | 1-2 | 2-2 |
| KS GORNIK ZABRZE | 0-1 | 2-2 | 2-0 | 3-1 | 6-1 | ■ | 3-1 | 2-0 | 2-2 | 0-0 | 3-0 | 3-0 | 2-2 | 3-0 | 1-1 | 0-0 |
| CWKS LEGIA WARSZAWA | 0-0 | 0-0 | 0-2 | 4-2 | 1-1 | 0-1 | ■ | 0-0 | 0-0 | 3-1 | 1-0 | 2-0 | 0-1 | 0-0 | 0-1 | 1-0 |
| LKS LODZ | 1-0 | 1-1 | 1-0 | 1-2 | 0-2 | 0-1 | 2-1 | ■ | 0-1 | 3-1 | 1-0 | 2-1 | 1-0 | 3-2 | 0-2 | 1-1 |
| GTS WISLA KRAKOW | 3-3 | 1-1 | 5-1 | 3-0 | 0-0 | 1-1 | 0-0 | 0-0 | ■ | 3-0 | 3-0 | 5-2 | 1-1 | 1-0 | 1-1 | 4-1 |
| WKS SLASK WROCLAW | 0-0 | 1-3 | 1-1 | 2-0 | 3-0 | 1-4 | 0-0 | 2-0 | 0-0 | ■ | 2-1 | 1-2 | 2-1 | 7-0 | 2-0 | 2-1 |
| FKS PZL-STAL MIELEC | 0-0 | 1-0 | 2-2 | 0-0 | 0-3 | 0-0 | 1-1 | 1-2 | 2-3 | 5-1 | ■ | 0-2 | 1-3 | 0-2 | 1-1 | 2-0 |
| KS RUCH CHORZOW | 2-1 | 0-1 | 1-1 | 0-0 | 1-1 | 0-0 | 0-1 | 0-1 | 3-2 | 1-1 | 5-1 | ■ | 0-0 | 2-0 | 1-1 | 1-1 |
| RKS MOTOR LUBLIN | 0-0 | 1-2 | 0-1 | 2-0 | 1-3 | 3-1 | 0-2 | 2-0 | 1-1 | 2-1 | 1-1 | 0-0 | ■ | 2-1 | 0-4 | 0-1 |
| GKS ZAGLEB. SOSNOWIEC | 1-6 | 1-4 | 0-1 | 1-0 | 2-2 | 1-3 | 1-3 | 0-2 | 2-4 | 1-2 | 1-1 | 0-0 | 1-2 | ■ | 0-2 | 0-1 |
| KS HUTNIK KRAKOW | 2-3 | 3-0 | 0-0 | 4-1 | 2-1 | 2-0 | 4-2 | 5-0 | 0-2 | 1-1 | 2-2 | 2-0 | 2-4 | 0-0 | ■ | 1-1 |
| LKS IGLOOPOL DEBICA | 0-2 | 0-0 | 0-1 | 2-1 | 2-2 | 0-5 | 1-0 | 1-1 | 1-0 | 2-2 | 1-1 | 4-0 | 0-0 | 5-0 | 0-2 | ■ |

The match Pegrotour Debica 0 Lech Poznan 2 was later awarded Pegrotour Debica 0 Lech Poznan 3
The match Olimpia Poznan 1 Zaglebie Lubin 1 was later awarded Olimpia Poznan 0 Zaglebie Lubin 3

## POLAND 1ST DIVISION 1990/91
### LEAGUE TABLE FINAL

| | | | | | | | |
|---|---|---|---|---|---|---|---|
| Zaglebie Lubin | 30 | 18 | 8 | 4 | 49 | 25 | 44 |
| Gornik Zabrze | 30 | 15 | 10 | 5 | 55 | 24 | 40 |
| Wisla Krakow | 30 | 13 | 14 | 3 | 52 | 26 | 40 |
| GKS Katowice | 30 | 16 | 7 | 7 | 33 | 26 | 39 |
| Hutnik Krakow | 30 | 14 | 9 | 7 | 53 | 34 | 37 |
| Lech Poznan | 30 | 10 | 13 | 7 | 49 | 28 | 33 |
| Slask Wroclaw | 30 | 12 | 9 | 9 | 41 | 37 | 33 |
| Olimpia Poznan | 30 | 9 | 12 | 9 | 37 | 41 | 30 |
| Legia Warszawa | 30 | 8 | 12 | 10 | 24 | 24 | 28 |
| Motor Lublin | 30 | 10 | 8 | 12 | 33 | 38 | 28 |
| LKS Lodz | 30 | 11 | 6 | 13 | 25 | 36 | 28 |
| Pegrotour Debica | 30 | 7 | 12 | 11 | 29 | 45 | 26 |
| Ruch Chorzow | 30 | 7 | 11 | 12 | 25 | 35 | 25 |
| Zawisza Bydgoszcz | 30 | 8 | 7 | 15 | 27 | 41 | 23 |
| Stal Mielec | 30 | 3 | 10 | 17 | 25 | 49 | 16 |
| Zaglebie Sosnowiec | 30 | 2 | 6 | 22 | 21 | 69 | 10 |

Champions : - Zaglebie Lubin

Note : Polish system of awarding an extra point for a victory by 3 goals or more no longer applied during Season 1990/91

League to be increased to 18 clubs for Season 1991/92

Name Change : - Igloopol Debica to Pegrotour Debica

## POLAND 2ND DIVISION 1990/91
### LEAGUE TABLE FINAL

| | | | | | | | |
|---|---|---|---|---|---|---|---|
| Stal Stalowa Wola | 38 | 18 | 13 | 7 | 45 | 24 | 49 |
| Widzew Lodz | 38 | 17 | 14 | 7 | 57 | 29 | 48 |
| Jagiellonia Bialystok | 38 | 17 | 14 | 7 | 46 | 29 | 48 |
| Miedz Legnica | 38 | 17 | 13 | 8 | 51 | 34 | 47 |
| Stilon Gorzow W | 38 | 17 | 13 | 8 | 46 | 29 | 47 |
| Rakow Czestochowa | 38 | 16 | 11 | 11 | 43 | 34 | 43 |
| Polonia Bytom | 38 | 15 | 11 | 12 | 51 | 38 | 41 |
| Siarka Tarnobrzeg | 38 | 12 | 15 | 11 | 47 | 46 | 39 |
| Szombierki Bytom | 38 | 14 | 11 | 13 | 40 | 41 | 39 |
| Gornik Walbrzych | 38 | 12 | 13 | 13 | 43 | 42 | 37 |
| Pogon Szczecin | 38 | 11 | 14 | 13 | 47 | 46 | 36 |
| Lechia Gdansk | 38 | 13 | 10 | 15 | 40 | 43 | 36 |
| Resovia Rzeszow | 38 | 11 | 14 | 13 | 38 | 42 | 36 |
| Odra Wodzislaw Sl. | 38 | 9 | 17 | 12 | 49 | 49 | 35 |
| Stal Rzeszow | 38 | 10 | 15 | 13 | 44 | 50 | 35 |
| Zaglebie Walbrzych | 38 | 9 | 17 | 12 | 27 | 33 | 35 |
| Korona Kielce | 38 | 11 | 12 | 15 | 32 | 43 | 34 |
| Gwardia Warszawa | 38 | 8 | 11 | 19 | 37 | 54 | 27 |
| Hutnik Warszawa | 38 | 9 | 8 | 21 | 35 | 63 | 26 |
| Ostrovia Ostrow | 38 | 4 | 14 | 20 | 28 | 77 | 22 |

Promoted : - Stal Stalowa Wola and Widzew Lodz
Relegated : - Hutnik Warszawa and Ostrovia Ostrow

### PLAY-OFFS FOR 2 2ND DIVISION PLACES

| | 1ST LEG | 2ND LEG | AGG. |
|---|---|---|---|
| Hutnik Warszawa v Gwardia Warszawa | 1-2 | 1-1 | 2-3 |
| Korona Kielce v Ostrovia Ostrow | 3-0 | 1-2 | 4-2 |

League to consist of 2 groups of 18 clubs each for Season 1991/92

### PLAY-OFFS FOR 2 1ST DIVISION PLACES

| | 1ST LEG | 2ND LEG | AGG. |
|---|---|---|---|
| Zaglebie Sosnowiec v Jagiellonia Bialystok | 0-2 | 2-0 | 2-2 |
| Zaglebie Sosnowiec win 3-1 on penalties | | | |
| Stal Mielec v Miedz Legnica | 3-0 | 1-3 | 4-3 |

### TOP SCORERS

1. Dziubinski (Wisla Krakow) — 21
2. Waligora (Hutnik Krakow) — 18
3. Kraus (Gornik Zabrze) — 16
4. Cyron (Gornik Zabrze) — 15
5. Mielcarski (Olimpia Poznan) — 14
6. Juskowiak (Lech Poznan) — 12
7. Gebura (Lech Poznan) — 11
8. Kujawa (Zaglebie Lubin) — 10
   Sermak (Hutnik Krakow) — 10
10. Grzesiak (Motor Lublin) — 9
    Sajdak (Stal Mielec) — 9
    Trzeciak (Lech Poznan) — 9
13. Kudyba (Zaglebie Lubin) — 8

| POLAND 2nd Division Season 1990/91 | WIDZEW | J'LONIA | STAL SW | POLONIA | ZAGLEBIE | GWARDIA | STAL R | GORNIK | STILON | ODRA | LECHIA | SIARKA | SZOMBIERKI | MIEDZ | POGON | RESOVIA | OSTROVIA | HUTNIK | RAKOW | KORONA |
|---|---|---|---|---|---|---|---|---|---|---|---|---|---|---|---|---|---|---|---|---|
| RTS WIDZEW LODZ | | 1-0 | 2-0 | 2-1 | 4-0 | 3-1 | 5-0 | 2-0 | 1-1 | 1-1 | 1-1 | 1-0 | 1-1 | 4-0 | 0-0 | 3-0 | 5-0 | 3-1 | 0-0 | 1-1 |
| MKSB JAGIELLON. B'STOK | 0-0 | | 1-0 | 2-1 | 0-0 | 2-2 | 1-0 | 1-0 | 4-0 | 0-0 | 2-0 | 2-2 | 2-0 | 1-1 | 2-1 | 3-1 | 3-1 | 2-1 | 2-0 | 1-0 |
| ZKS STAL STALOWA WOLA | 2-2 | 3-0 | | 1-0 | 0-0 | 1-0 | 3-1 | 1-0 | 3-0 | 1-0 | 1-0 | 2-0 | 2-1 | 0-0 | 4-0 | 1-0 | 5-1 | 0-1 | 1-0 | 1-0 |
| KS POLONIA BYTOM | 2-0 | 2-1 | 0-0 | | 0-1 | 3-1 | 4-2 | 3-2 | 1-2 | 0-0 | 1-0 | 4-1 | 2-0 | 0-0 | 2-0 | 1-3 | 1-1 | 5-1 | 3-1 | 2-0 |
| GKS ZAGLEB. WALBRZYCH | 1-2 | 1-1 | 0-0 | 0-0 | | 2-0 | 1-0 | 0-0 | 1-0 | 0-0 | 2-0 | 2-2 | 1-1 | 0-0 | 1-0 | 0-1 | 1-1 | 0-0 | 0-1 | 0-0 |
| WKS GWARDIA WARSZAWA | 0-0 | 0-0 | 2-0 | 1-3 | 1-2 | | 1-1 | 2-2 | 2-0 | 1-3 | 3-0 | 2-1 | 2-3 | 2-1 | 1-2 | 2-1 | 0-0 | 1-2 | 2-0 | 2-1 |
| ZKS STAL RZESZOW | 2-2 | 0-0 | 1-1 | 2-0 | 1-1 | 1-1 | | 2-1 | 0-1 | 2-0 | 1-1 | 2-0 | 3-1 | 2-0 | 2-2 | 1-0 | 0-0 | 5-1 | 0-2 | 0-2 |
| KS GORNIK WALBRZYCH | 0-1 | 1-1 | 2-1 | 1-1 | 0-0 | 2-0 | 2-1 | | 1-1 | 2-1 | 0-0 | 3-0 | 1-0 | 3-0 | 2-0 | 0-0 | 1-1 | 3-1 | 0-0 | 2-1 |
| ZKS STILON GORZOW W | 1-0 | 0-0 | 0-0 | 2-0 | 2-0 | 2-0 | 1-2 | 3-0 | | 2-1 | 2-0 | 3-0 | 1-1 | 0-1 | 2-2 | 1-1 | 3-0 | 3-0 | 2-0 | 2-0 |
| GKS ODRA WODZISLAW | 1-3 | 1-3 | 1-1 | 2-1 | 2-2 | 1-1 | 2-2 | 0-0 | 1-1 | | 3-1 | 2-2 | 2-0 | 1-0 | 1-2 | 1-1 | 6-0 | 1-1 | 2-1 | 2-0 |
| BKS LECHIA GDANSK | 0-0 | 3-0 | 0-0 | 2-1 | 2-1 | 2-0 | 1-0 | 0-0 | 0-2 | 3-2 | | 0-1 | 2-1 | 3-1 | 3-1 | 4-0 | 3-1 | 2-0 | 0-0 | 0-1 |
| KS SIARKA TARNOBRZEG | 1-0 | 1-1 | 4-1 | 1-1 | 1-0 | 2-1 | 3-1 | 2-0 | 0-0 | 4-0 | 1-1 | | 0-0 | 3-1 | 1-1 | 2-0 | 2-0 | 1-1 | 1-0 | 1-1 |
| GKS SZOMBIERKI BYTOM | 3-2 | 1-1 | 0-1 | 0-1 | 4-2 | 2-1 | 2-0 | 1-0 | 1-0 | 2-0 | 0-0 | 2-1 | | 2-1 | 1-1 | 0-0 | 0-0 | 1-0 | 2-0 | 0-1 |
| KS MIEDZ LEGNICA | 4-1 | 0-0 | 1-1 | 0-0 | 1-0 | 2-0 | 3-1 | 2-0 | 3-1 | 2-1 | 1-0 | 1-1 | 1-1 | | 0-0 | 3-0 | 3-0 | 2-0 | 1-1 | 1-0 |
| MKS POGON SZCZECIN | 1-0 | 0-1 | 2-1 | 0-0 | 2-0 | 4-2 | 2-2 | 3-1 | 0-0 | 1-1 | 0-1 | 2-1 | 4-1 | 1-2 | | 0-0 | 4-0 | 2-2 | 1-3 | 3-0 |
| C-WKS RESOVIA RZESZOW | 0-0 | 2-1 | 0-0 | 1-1 | 1-0 | 1-0 | 0-0 | 4-2 | 1-1 | 1-1 | 2-1 | 2-0 | 0-0 | 2-3 | 0-0 | | 4-0 | 4-1 | 1-1 | 2-0 |
| KKS OSTROVIA OSTROW | 1-2 | 0-2 | 1-1 | 1-2 | 0-0 | 0-0 | 2-2 | 3-5 | 1-1 | 1-1 | 0-0 | 4-2 | 1-0 | 0-4 | 2-1 | 2-0 | | 0-1 | 0-2 | 1-2 |
| HKS HUTNIK WARSZAWA | 0-1 | 1-0 | 1-2 | 2-1 | 1-2 | 0-0 | 1-2 | 0-2 | 0-1 | 3-3 | 4-2 | 1-1 | 0-1 | 0-3 | 2-1 | 2-1 | 2-0 | | 0-1 | 0-1 |
| RKS RAK.CZESTOCHOWA | 1-0 | 1-0 | 0-0 | 0-0 | 1-3 | 2-0 | 0-0 | 2-1 | 1-1 | 0-2 | 3-2 | 0-0 | 3-1 | 2-2 | 1-0 | 2-0 | 5-1 | 2-0 | | 4-2 |
| MKS KORONA KIELCE | 1-1 | 1-3 | 0-3 | 2-1 | 1-0 | 0-0 | 0-0 | 1-1 | 0-1 | 1-0 | 4-0 | 1-1 | 1-3 | 0-0 | 1-1 | 2-1 | 1-1 | 1-1 | 1-0 | |

## POLAND : All Time Records as at 31/12/90 - CAPS

1. Grzegorz Lato (Stal Mielec/SC Lokeren/Atlanta) — 104
2. Kazimierz Deyna (Legia Warszawa) — 102
3. Wladyslaw Zmuda (Gwardia Warszawa/Slask Wroclaw/Widzew Lodz/Hellas/Verona/New York Cosmos/ US Cremonese) — 92
4. Antoni Szymanowski (Wisla Krakow/Gwardia Warszawa) — 87
5. Wlodzimierz Lubanski (Gornik Zabrze/SC Lokeren) — 80
   Zbigniew Boniek (Widzew Lodz/Juventus FC/AS Roma) — 80
7. Robert Gadocha (Legia Warszawa/FC Nantes) — 65
   Jan Tomaszewski (Legia Warszawa/LKS Lodz/Beerschot VAV/Hercules Alicante) — 65
9. Henryk Kasperczak (Stal Mielec) — 63
10. Dariusz Dziekanowski (Gwardia Warszawa/Widzew Lodz/Legia Warszawa/Celtic) — 62

## POLAND : All Time Records as at 31/12/90 - GOALS

1. Wlodzimierz Lubanski (Gornik Zabrze/SC Lokeren) — (80) 50
2. Kazimierz Deyna (Legia Warszawa) — (102) 45
   Grzegorz Lato (Stal Mielec/SC Lokeren/Atlanta) — (104) 45
4. Ernest Pol (Legia Warszawa/Gornik Zabrze) — (49) 40
5. Andrzej Szarmach (Gornik Zabrze/Stal Mielec/AJ Auxerre) — (61) 33
6. Gerard Cieslik (Ruch Chorzow) — (46) 27
7. Zbigniew Boniek (Widzew Lodz/Juventus FC/AS Roma) — (80) 24
8. Ernest Wilimowski (Ruch Chorzow) — (22) 21
9. Robert Gadocha (Legia Warszawa/FC Nantes) — (65) 20
10. Dariusz Dziekanowski (Gwardia Warszawa/Widzew Lodz/Legia Warszawa/Celtic) — (62) 19

# POLAND 3RD DIVISION 1990/91

## WARSZAWA LEAGUE TABLE FINAL

| | P | W | D | L | F | A | Pts |
|---|---|---|---|---|---|---|---|
| Polonia Warszawa | 26 | 20 | 4 | 2 | 64 | 13 | 44 |
| Stomil Olsztyn | 26 | 19 | 5 | 2 | 61 | 15 | 43 |
| Ursus Warszawa | 26 | 14 | 9 | 3 | 48 | 16 | 37 |
| Bug Wyszkow | 26 | 10 | 11 | 5 | 33 | 21 | 31 |
| Jeziorak Ilawa | 26 | 9 | 11 | 6 | 28 | 20 | 29 |
| Wigry Suwalki | 26 | 11 | 6 | 9 | 31 | 28 | 28 |
| Narew Ostroleka | 26 | 8 | 10 | 8 | 29 | 29 | 26 |
| Gwardia Szczytno | 26 | 8 | 10 | 8 | 28 | 28 | 26 |
| Orleta Reszel | 26 | 10 | 4 | 12 | 43 | 34 | 24 |
| Polkolor Piaseczno | 26 | 7 | 10 | 9 | 27 | 33 | 24 |
| Mlawianka Mlawa | 26 | 6 | 8 | 12 | 24 | 45 | 20 |
| Olimpia Zambrow | 26 | 5 | 6 | 15 | 18 | 27 | 16 |
| Jagiellonia II Bialystok | 26 | 3 | 5 | 18 | 17 | 61 | 11 |
| Mazur Elk | 26 | 3 | 2 | 21 | 17 | 59 | 8 |

Promoted :- Polonia Warszawa and Stomil Olsztyn

## POZNAN-SOUTH LEAGUE TABLE FINAL

| | P | W | D | L | F | A | Pts |
|---|---|---|---|---|---|---|---|
| Warta Poznan | 26 | 15 | 9 | 2 | 46 | 18 | 39 |
| Lubuszanin Drzedenko | 26 | 18 | 3 | 5 | 44 | 19 | 39 |
| Lech II Poznan | 26 | 16 | 6 | 4 | 53 | 27 | 38 |
| Orzel Bialy Walcz | 26 | 12 | 6 | 8 | 44 | 27 | 30 |
| Warta Gorzow Wielkopolski | 26 | 11 | 7 | 8 | 34 | 30 | 29 |
| Lubuszanin Trzcianka | 26 | 10 | 5 | 11 | 33 | 41 | 25 |
| Mieszko Gniezno | 26 | 7 | 10 | 9 | 32 | 31 | 24 |
| Victoria Wrzesnia | 26 | 8 | 8 | 10 | 33 | 40 | 24 |
| Zjednoczeni Przytoczna | 26 | 11 | 1 | 14 | 43 | 46 | 23 |
| Kotwica Kornik | 26 | 8 | 6 | 12 | 24 | 42 | 22 |
| Meprozet Stare Kurowo | 26 | 7 | 8 | 11 | 31 | 31 | 22 |
| Olimpia II Poznan | 26 | 7 | 7 | 12 | 24 | 42 | 21 |
| Orzel Miedzyrzecz | 26 | 7 | 4 | 15 | 28 | 48 | 18 |
| Polonia/Polam Pila | 26 | 3 | 6 | 17 | 23 | 54 | 12 |

Promoted :- Warta Poznan

## POZNAN-NORTH LEAGUE TABLE FINAL

| | P | W | D | L | F | A | Pts |
|---|---|---|---|---|---|---|---|
| Chemik Police | 26 | 17 | 7 | 2 | 82 | 14 | 41 |
| Bleikitni Strd Szczecinski | 26 | 16 | 7 | 3 | 81 | 25 | 39 |
| Stoczniowiec Barlinek | 26 | 16 | 6 | 4 | 48 | 29 | 38 |
| Celuloza Kostrzyn | 26 | 14 | 6 | 6 | 42 | 30 | 34 |
| Pogon II Szczecin | 26 | 12 | 6 | 8 | 37 | 27 | 30 |
| Gwardia Koszalin | 26 | 10 | 10 | 6 | 36 | 34 | 30 |
| Dariovia Darlowo | 26 | 12 | 5 | 9 | 34 | 36 | 29 |
| Lucznik Strzelce Krajensk. | 26 | 6 | 12 | 8 | 39 | 47 | 24 |
| Energetyk Gryfino | 26 | 9 | 6 | 11 | 39 | 39 | 24 |
| Flota Swinoujscie | 26 | 8 | 7 | 11 | 31 | 41 | 23 |
| Arkonia Szczecin | 26 | 7 | 6 | 13 | 30 | 45 | 20 |
| Ina Goleniow | 26 | 4 | 7 | 15 | 28 | 47 | 15 |
| Odra Chojna | 26 | 4 | 7 | 15 | 24 | 64 | 15 |
| Mechanik Bobolice | 26 | 3 | 6 | 17 | 19 | 60 | 12 |

Promoted :- GKS Belchatow, Boruta Zgierz and Wisla Plock

## GDANSK LEAGUE TABLE FINAL

| | P | W | D | L | F | A | Pts |
|---|---|---|---|---|---|---|---|
| Weltinex/Chem. Byd'zcz | 30 | 20 | 7 | 3 | 73 | 14 | 47 |
| Baltyk Gdynia | 30 | 21 | 5 | 4 | 81 | 25 | 47 |
| Olimpia Elblag | 30 | 18 | 7 | 5 | 69 | 24 | 43 |
| Stoczniowiec Gdansk | 30 | 16 | 5 | 9 | 62 | 35 | 37 |
| Wisla Tczew | 30 | 14 | 8 | 8 | 43 | 34 | 36 |
| Elana Torun | 30 | 14 | 7 | 9 | 52 | 35 | 35 |
| Goplania Inowroclaw | 30 | 12 | 11 | 7 | 53 | 39 | 35 |
| Wierzyca St'gard Gdanski | 30 | 12 | 8 | 10 | 37 | 37 | 32 |
| Gryf Slupsk | 30 | 10 | 11 | 9 | 24 | 29 | 31 |
| Arka Gdynia | 30 | 10 | 8 | 12 | 36 | 36 | 28 |
| Brda Bydgoszcz | 30 | 10 | 6 | 14 | 36 | 50 | 26 |
| Cormidex Damnica | 30 | 9 | 8 | 13 | 37 | 70 | 26 |
| Polonia Bydgoszcz | 30 | 6 | 8 | 16 | 18 | 37 | 20 |
| Wda Swiecie n/Wisla | 30 | 5 | 5 | 21 | 26 | 65 | 13 |
| Unia Wabrzezno | 30 | 3 | 6 | 21 | 26 | 85 | 12 |
| Cujava Inowroclaw | 30 | 3 | 4 | 23 | 18 | 84 | 10 |

Promoted :- Weltinex/Chem Bydgoszcz, Baltyk Gdynia and Olimpia Elblag

## LODZ LEAGUE TABLE FINAL

| | P | W | D | L | F | A | Pts |
|---|---|---|---|---|---|---|---|
| GKS Belchatow | 30 | 21 | 7 | 2 | 63 | 18 | 49 |
| Boruta Zgierz | 30 | 19 | 10 | 1 | 56 | 11 | 48 |
| Wisla Plock | 30 | 19 | 7 | 4 | 55 | 16 | 45 |
| Terpol Sieradz | 30 | 13 | 14 | 3 | 52 | 19 | 40 |
| Wlokniarz Pabianice | 30 | 12 | 7 | 11 | 44 | 39 | 31 |
| LKS Jankowy | 30 | 11 | 9 | 10 | 41 | 44 | 31 |
| Mazovia Rawa Mazowiecka | 30 | 12 | 7 | 11 | 43 | 56 | 31 |
| Gornik Konin | 30 | 10 | 8 | 12 | 38 | 27 | 30 |
| Pilica Tomaszow Mazowiecki | 30 | 9 | 11 | 10 | 38 | 34 | 29 |
| Victoria Ostrzeszow | 30 | 12 | 4 | 14 | 39 | 28 | 28 |
| Wlokniarz Aleks. Lodzki | 30 | 9 | 10 | 11 | 34 | 34 | 27 |
| Mien Lipno | 30 | 7 | 10 | 13 | 41 | 41 | 24 |
| Orzel Lodz | 30 | 10 | 3 | 17 | 41 | 50 | 23 |
| Pelikan Lowicz | 30 | 5 | 12 | 13 | 18 | 33 | 12 |
| Stal Kutno | 30 | 2 | 1 | 27 | 19 | 108 | 5 |

Promoted :- GKS Belchatow, Boruta Zgierz and Wisla Plock

## KRAKOW LEAGUE TABLE FINAL

| | P | W | D | L | F | A | Pts |
|---|---|---|---|---|---|---|---|
| Stomil-Wisloka Debica | 24 | 15 | 4 | 5 | 40 | 13 | 35 |
| Sandecja Nowy Sacz | 24 | 14 | 6 | 4 | 41 | 22 | 34 |
| Cracovia Krakow | 24 | 14 | 6 | 4 | 38 | 23 | 34 |
| Unia Tarnow | 24 | 9 | 9 | 6 | 31 | 26 | 27 |
| Zelmer Rzeszow | 24 | 9 | 7 | 8 | 26 | 27 | 25 |
| Stal Sanok | 24 | 9 | 7 | 8 | 29 | 21 | 25 |
| Glinik Gorlice | 24 | 8 | 8 | 8 | 22 | 22 | 23 |
| Karpaty Krosno | 24 | 8 | 7 | 9 | 21 | 22 | 22 |
| Garbarnia Krakow | 24 | 8 | 5 | 11 | 29 | 28 | 21 |
| Czarni Jaslo | 24 | 6 | 7 | 11 | 26 | 45 | 19 |
| Wawel Krakow | 24 | 7 | 4 | 13 | 23 | 42 | 18 |
| Stal II Mielec | 24 | 4 | 10 | 10 | 11 | 26 | ... |
| Swit Krzeszowice | 24 | 1 | 8 | 15 | 7 | 34 | 10 |

Promoted :- Stomil-Wisloka Debica, Sandecja Nowy Sacz and Cracovia Krakow

## LUBLIN LEAGUE TABLE FINAL

| | P | W | D | L | F | A | Pts |
|---|---|---|---|---|---|---|---|
| Avia Swidnik | 30 | 20 | 8 | 2 | 72 | 18 | 48 |
| Bleikitni Kielce | 30 | 19 | 9 | 2 | 54 | 20 | 47 |
| Radomiak Radom | 30 | 15 | 11 | 4 | 55 | 16 | 41 |
| Stal Gorzyce | 30 | 16 | 7 | 7 | 57 | 38 | 39 |
| Wislan Pulawy | 30 | 15 | 7 | 8 | 47 | 34 | 37 |
| Hetman Zamosc | 30 | 12 | 7 | 11 | 37 | 27 | 31 |
| Bron Radom | 30 | 13 | 5 | 12 | 37 | 33 | 31 |
| Gornik Leczna | 30 | 8 | 13 | 9 | 25 | 28 | 29 |
| Lubinianka Lublin | 30 | 9 | 9 | 12 | 33 | 42 | 27 |
| AZS AWF Biala Podlaska | 30 | 8 | 11 | 13 | 34 | 56 | 27 |
| Orleta Lukow | 30 | 10 | 5 | 15 | 26 | 37 | 25 |
| Granat Skarzysko-K. | 30 | 9 | 7 | 15 | 29 | 45 | 25 |
| Bucovia Bukowa | 30 | 8 | 7 | 15 | 26 | 37 | 23 |
| KSZO Ostrowiec | 30 | 6 | 6 | 16 | 31 | 52 | 22 |
| Gwardia Chelm | 30 | 8 | 5 | 17 | 26 | 42 | 21 |
| Stadion Kielce | 30 | 2 | 4 | 24 | 19 | 84 | 8 |

Promoted :- Avia Swidnik and Bleikitni Kielce

## WROCLAW LEAGUE TABLE FINAL

| | P | W | D | L | F | A | Pts |
|---|---|---|---|---|---|---|---|
| Chrobry Glogow | 30 | 21 | 5 | 4 | 68 | 17 | 47 |
| Sleza Wroclaw | 30 | 18 | 9 | 3 | 69 | 21 | 45 |
| Moto Jelcz Olawa | 30 | 18 | 8 | 4 | 49 | 26 | 44 |
| Dozamet Nowa Sol | 30 | 17 | 7 | 6 | 49 | 26 | 41 |
| Piast Nowa Ruda | 30 | 14 | 9 | 7 | 55 | 26 | 37 |
| Bielawianka Bielawa | 30 | 15 | 5 | 10 | 59 | 38 | 35 |
| Lechia Zielona Gora | 30 | 11 | 12 | 7 | 38 | 30 | 34 |
| Lechia Dzierzoniow | 30 | 12 | 8 | 10 | 44 | 29 | 32 |
| Kuznia Jawor | 30 | 10 | 8 | 12 | 48 | 35 | 28 |
| Pogon Swiebodzin | 30 | 8 | 11 | 11 | 36 | 37 | 27 |
| Pogon Olesnica | 30 | 11 | 4 | 15 | 38 | 68 | 26 |
| Gornik Polkowice | 30 | 7 | 8 | 15 | 36 | 46 | 22 |
| Piast Zlawa | 30 | 6 | 9 | 15 | 38 | 46 | 21 |
| Stal Chocianow | 30 | 5 | 10 | 15 | 20 | 46 | 20 |
| Victoria Bogatynia | 30 | 2 | 4 | 24 | 18 | 95 | 9 |

Prom :- Chrobry Glogow, Sleza Wroclaw & Moto Jelcz Olawa

## KATOWICE LEAGUE TABLE FINAL

| | P | W | D | L | F | A | Pts |
|---|---|---|---|---|---|---|---|
| Gornik Pszow | 30 | 17 | 8 | 5 | 54 | 25 | 42 |
| Naprzod Rydultowy | 30 | 14 | 11 | 5 | 44 | 25 | 39 |
| GKS Jastrzebie | 30 | 15 | 8 | 7 | 34 | 21 | 38 |
| GKS Czeladz | 30 | 12 | 12 | 6 | 47 | 30 | 36 |
| GKS Tychy | 30 | 14 | 6 | 10 | 47 | 34 | 34 |
| Metal Kluczbork | 30 | 14 | 6 | 10 | 34 | 28 | 34 |
| Carbo Gliwice | 30 | 11 | 11 | 8 | 34 | 33 | 33 |
| Piast Gliwice | 30 | 10 | 12 | 8 | 51 | 41 | 32 |
| Odra Opole | 30 | 11 | 8 | 11 | 40 | 34 | 30 |
| MK Gornik Katowice | 30 | 13 | 3 | 14 | 38 | 32 | 29 |
| Concordia Knurow | 30 | 10 | 8 | 12 | 29 | 34 | 28 |
| AKS Chorzow | 30 | 7 | 10 | 13 | 17 | 33 | 24 |
| Ruch Radzionkow | 30 | 9 | 5 | 16 | 37 | 53 | 21 |
| BKS St. Bielsko-Biala | 30 | 5 | 6 | 17 | 33 | 53 | 17 |
| ROW Rybnik | 30 | 4 | 3 | 23 | 22 | 85 | 11 |

Prom :- Gornik Pszow and Naprzod Rydultowy

## CHAMPIONSHIP PLAY-OFF

Warta Poznan v Chemik Police

| | 1ST LEG | 2ND LEG | AGG. |
|---|---|---|---|
| | 0-0 | 2-1 | 2-1 |

Promoted :- Chemik Police

## 3RD PLACE PLAY-OFF :-

Lubuszanin Drzedenko......0   Bleikitni Stargard Szczecinski......0

Bleikitni Stargard Szczecinski win 3-4 on penalties

## PLAY-OFFS FOR 4 2ND DIVISION PLACES

| | 1ST LEG | 2ND LEG | AGG. |
|---|---|---|---|
| Ursus Warszawa v Olimpia Elblag | 1-0 | 0-2 | 1-2 |
| Bleikitni Stargard Szczecinski v Wisla Plock | 0-2 | 0-2 | 0-2 |
| Radomiak Radom v Cracovia Krakow | 0-0 | 1-1 | 1-3 |
| GKS Jastrzebie v Moto Jelcz Olawa | 0-2 | 0-2 | 0-2 |

# POLAND CUP 1990/91

## 1/16 FINALS

| | | | |
|---|---|---|---|
| Gwardia Warszawa....2 | Zaglebie Lubin ...........3 | Resovia Rzeszow.......1 | Gornik Zabrze............3 |
| Korona Kielce ...........0 | Ruch Chorzow ...........0 | Zaglebie Walbrzych ....3 | Wisla Krakow.............2 |
| Korona Kielce win 2-1 on penalties | | Sleza Wroclaw............1 | Legia Warszawa ........2 |
| Pogon Szczecin.........1 | Jagiellonia Bialystok ..3 | Wisla Plock ..............0 | LKS Lodz........ ........5 |
| Elana Torun ..............1 | Zawisza Bydgoszcz ...1 | Ostravia Ostrow...... ..0 | Motor Lublin...............2 |
| Zawisza Bydgoszcz win 2-3 on penalties | | Szombierki Bytom ......1 | GKS Katowice ...........2 |
| Polonia Bytom ...........0 | Widzew Lodz .............1 | Stal Stalowa Wola ......2 | Lech Poznan..............3 |
| Odra Wodzislaw ........2 | Slask Wroclaw ...........1 | Mazovia Rawa Mazo..0 | Stal Mielec................3 |
| Stal Rzeszow.............3 | Zaglebie Sosnowiec...0 | Stilon Gorzow ............0 | Olimpia Poznan .........1 |

## 1/8 FINALS

| | | | |
|---|---|---|---|
| Zaglebie Walbrzych ...0 | Legia Warszawa ........3 | LKS Lodz....................2 | Lech Poznan..............0 |
| Stal Rzeszow.............2 | Odra Wodzislaw.........0 | Jagiellonia Bialystok ...0 | Gornik Zabrze...........2 |
| Zaglebie Lubin ...........1 | Olimpia Poznan .........2 (aet.) | Zawisza Bydgrszcz.....2 | Motor Lublin...............0 |
| Widzew Lodz .............2 | Stal Mielec ................0 | Korona Kielce .............0 | GKS Katowice ...........2 |

## 1/4 FINALS

| | 1ST LEG | 2ND LEG | AGG. |
|---|---|---|---|
| Gornik Zabrze v GKS Katowice | 1-0 | 0-2 | 1-2 |
| Zawisza Bydgoszcz v Widzew Lodz (Zawisza win 3-1 on penalties) | 1-0 | 0-1 | 1-1 |
| Olimpia Poznan v Stal Rzeszow | 2-1 | 0-0 | 2-1 |
| Legia Warszawa v LKS Lodz (Legia win 6-5 on penalties) | 2-0 | 0-2 | 2-2 |

## SEMI-FINALS

| | 1ST LEG | 2ND LEG | AGG. |
|---|---|---|---|
| GKS Katowice v Zawisza Bydgoszcz | 3-1 | 1-0 | 4-1 |
| Olimpia Poznan v Legia Warszawa | 0-3 ⊗ | 0-1 | 0-4 |

⊗ Match awarded following Olimpia Poznan 2 Legia Warszawa 0. Olimpia Poznan fielded a player under suspension.

## FINAL   23/6/91 (at Piotrkow Trybunalski)

GKS Katowice ...........1   Legia Warszawa ........0

Katowice : Jojko, Macijewski, Szewczyk, Lesiak, M.Swierczewski, Nawrocki (Wolowicz 68), Grzesik, P.Swierczewski, **Rzezniczek**, Strojek, Walczak (Ksiazek 89).

Legia : Szczesny, Jozwiak (Gmur 71), Kubicki, Bak, Czykier, Pisz, Iwanicki, Czachowski, Sobczak (Sazonowicz 87), **Kowalczyk, Cyzio**.

1-0   Lesiak   77   Referee : Marek Kowalczyk (Lublin)
Attendance : 6,000

# INTERNATIONAL LINE-UPS 1990

## Matches

| Date | Result | Venue | Type | Referee | Scorers (Poland) |
|---|---|---|---|---|---|
| 2/2/90 | IRAN 0 POLAND 2 | Teheran | Friendly | Dezfuli (Iran) | (Ziober 2) |
| 4/2/90 | IRAN 0 POLAND 1 | Teheran | Friendly | Abamiroeri (Iran) | (Szewczyk) |
| 11/2/90 | KUWAIT 1 POLAND 1 | Cairo | Friendly | Ramadan (Egypt) | (Kosecki) |
| 28/3/90 | POLAND 0 YUGOSLAVIA 0 | Lodz | Friendly | Molnar (Hungary) | |
| 4/5/90 | COLUMBIA 2 POLAND 1 | Chicago | Friendly T | Bratis (USA) | (Kosecki) |
| 6/5/90 | COSTA RICA 0 POLAND 2 | Chicago | Friendly T | Bratis (USA) | (Pisz, Nowak) |
| 9/5/90 | USA 3 POLAND 1 | Hershey | Friendly | Purcell (Rep.Ireland) | (Ziober) |
| 19/5/90 | SCOTLAND 1 POLAND 1 | Glasgow | Friendly | Worrall (England) | (o.g.) |
| 21/5/90 | UAE 0 POLAND 4 | Marseille | Friendly | Batta (France) | (R.Warzycha 2, Dziekanowski, Kosecki) |
| 6/6/90 | BELGIUM 1 POLAND 1 | Brussels | Friendly | Philipi (Luxembourg) | (Ziober) |
| 15/8/90 | FRANCE 0 POLAND 0 | Paris | Friendly | | |
| 26/9/90 | RUMANIA 2 POLAND 1 | Bucuresti | Friendly | Midgeley (England) | (R.Warzycha) |
| 10/10/90 | POLAND 2 USA 3 | Warszawa | Friendly | Matusik (Czech.) | (Kosecki, Ziober) |
| 17/10/90 | ENGLAND 2 POLAND 0 | London | EuroCh.Q. | Föchler (Germany) | |
| 14/11/90 | TURKEY 0 POLAND 1 | Istanbul | EuroCh.Q. | Lanese (Italy) | (Dziekanowski) |
| 19/12/90 | GREECE 1 POLAND 2 | Volos | Friendly | Kefalas (Greece) | (Soczynski, Kosecki) |

## Line-ups (shirt numbers; substitutes in parentheses)

| Date | Wandzik | Kubicki | Szewczyk | Czachowski | Gora | R.Warzycha | Nawrocki | Kaczmarek | Ziober | Kosecki | Sliwowski | Bako | Soczynski | Fedoruk | Godlewski | Nowak | Duchowski | Lukasik | Wdowczyk | K.Warzycha | Tarasiewicz | Urban | Dziekanowski | Pisz | Moskal | Prusik | Furtok | Jakolcewicz | Jegor | Zejer | Cebula | Sidorczuk | Lesiak | Grzesik |
|---|---|---|---|---|---|---|---|---|---|---|---|---|---|---|---|---|---|---|---|---|---|---|---|---|---|---|---|---|---|---|---|---|---|---|
| 2/2/90 | 1 | 2 | 3 | 4 | 5 | 6 | 7 | 8 | 9 | 10 | 11 | (1) | (4) | (5) | (6) | (11) | | | | | | | | | | | | | | | | | | |
| 4/2/90 | 1 | (11) | 8 | (4) | | 2 | (4) | 3 | (10) | 10 | (11) | | (8) | | | | 2 | 5 | | 6 | 8 | 9 | 10 | | 11 | 7 | 11 | | (3) | 9 | 11 | (1) | (2) | (11) |
| 11/2/90 | 1 | 5 | 3 | 7 | | 2 | (6) | 7 | 11 | 10 | 1 | | 7 | 5 | 6 | 9 | | 4 | | | | | | | | | | | | | | | | |
| 28/3/90 | 1 | (2) | 3 | 2 | | (6) | (7) | 7 | 9 | 11 | (8) | (1) | 5 | | | | | 5 | 4 | | 8 | | 10 | (8) | | 7 | | | | | | | | |
| 4/5/90 | (1) | 2 | 4 | 4 | 5 | 2 | 8 | 7 | 9 | 10 | (9) | (1) | (7) | | 9 | | | (4) | 5 | | 8 | | 11 | 7 | | | | | | | | | | |
| 6/5/90 | (1) | 8 | 3 | 6 | 5 | 8 | 3 | 3 | 9 | 10 | (8) | (1) | | | (11) | | 4 | 4 | | 6 | 8 | | | 6 | | 7 | 10 | | | | | | | |
| 9/5/90 | 1 | 2 | 8 | 6 | 5 | | 8 | 3 | 11 | 10 | | 1 | 5 | | | | | 4 | | 10 | 8 | | 11 | | | 7 | 9 | | | | | | | |
| 19/5/90 | 1 | 2 | 3 | 4 | | 6 | 8 | 3 | 9 | 11 | (8) | (1) | (4) | | | (11) | | 5 | 5 | 10 | | | 10 | 7 | | 8 | | | | | | | | |
| 21/5/90 | 1 | (2) | 4 | 4 | 2 | 6 | (7) | 3 | 9 | 11 | | (2) | 5 | | 2 | | | 4 | 4 | | | | 10 | | | 7 | | | | | | | | |
| 6/6/90 | 1 | 2 | 2 | 4 | 6 | 6 | | 3 | 9 | 10 | | | | | | | | 11 | 5 | | | | | | | 8 | | | | | | | | |
| 15/8/90 | (1) | 5 | (7) | 2 | | 3 | (10) | 9 | | 11 | | 1 | | | | | | (11) | 5 | 10 | 7 | | | 1 | 11 | 7 | 9 | | | | | | | |
| 26/9/90 | (1) | 2 | 4 | 4 | | 5 | | 6 | 8 | 11 | | (1) | | | | | | (6) | | 10 | 8 | | 10 | 1 | (9) | | 10 | | | | | | | |
| 10/10/90 | (1) | | 2 | 3 | | 7 | (6) | 5 | 10 | 10 | | | 7 | | | | | 4 | 4 | 9 | | | | 1 | | 6 | | 3 | (3) | | | | | |
| 17/10/90 | 1 | | 4 | 4 | | 5 | | 5 | 9 | 11 | | 1 | | | | | | 11 | 4 | 4 | 8 | | 8 | | | | | | | 9 | | | | |
| 14/11/90 | 1 | 2 | | 2 | | 5 | 6 | 3 | 11 | 11 | | | | | | | | | | 9 | 8 | 9 | 10 | | | 7 | 10 | | | | 11 | (1) | (2) | (11) |
| 19/12/90 | 1 | 5 | 4 | 2 | | 6 | 8 | 3 | (10) | 10 | | | 7 | | | | | (6) | 4 | | 8 | | 8 | 7 | | | | 3 | | | | | | |
| **CAPS AT 31/12/90** | 38 | 38 | 13 | 21 | 6 | 28 | 16 | 28 | 30 | 35 | 6 | 20 | 19 | 2 | 3 | 4 | 1 | 27 | 47 | 31 | 52 | 50 | 62 | 6 | 2 | 47 | 25 | 10 | 3 | 3 | 1 | 1 | 1 | 1 |
| **GOALS AT 31/12/90** | | 1 | 1 | 2 | | 5 | | | 7 | 10 | | | 1 | | | 1 | | | 2 | 4 | 8 | 4 | 19 | 1 | | 5 | 8 | | | | | | | |

# PORTUGAL Correspondent : HUMBERTO PEREIRA SILVA

## PORTUGAL 1st Division Season 1990/91

| | PORTO | BENFICA | SPORTING | GUIMARAES | CHAVES | BELENENSES | SETUBAL | BOAVISTA | TIRSENSE | MARITIMO | BEIRA MAR | BRAGA | AMADORA | NACIONAL | PENAFIEL | UNIAO | GIL VICENTE | FAMALICAO | SALGUEIROS | FARENSE |
|---|---|---|---|---|---|---|---|---|---|---|---|---|---|---|---|---|---|---|---|---|
| FC PORTO | ■ | 0-2 | 2-0 | 5-0 | 3-1 | 0-0 | 4-1 | 3-1 | 2-1 | 3-1 | 2-1 | 2-0 | 2-0 | 1-2 | 2-0 | 5-0 | 2-0 | 2-0 | 3-0 | 1-0 |
| SL BENFICA | 2-2 | ■ | 1-1 | 2-0 | 1-0 | 2-0 | 2-0 | 1-1 | 5-0 | 3-1 | 3-0 | 2-0 | 4-0 | 3-0 | 2-0 | 4-1 | 3-0 | 1-0 | 4-0 | 2-0 |
| SPORTING CP | 0-2 | 0-2 | ■ | 3-0 | 1-1 | 1-0 | 1-0 | 2-1 | 1-0 | 0-0 | 2-0 | 3-0 | 1-0 | 3-0 | 2-0 | 2-0 | 2-0 | 2-0 | 5-1 | 0-1 |
| VITORIA SC (G'maraes) | 0-2 | 0-2 | 1-1 | ■ | 1-1 | 1-0 | 4-2 | 0-1 | 1-0 | 1-0 | 1-1 | 0-0 | 0-0 | 3-1 | 3-0 | 2-0 | 2-0 | 0-1 | 2-1 | 2-0 |
| GD CHAVES | 1-2 | 0-3 | 2-2 | 1-0 | ■ | 2-0 | 4-3 | 0-1 | 1-1 | 3-1 | 6-0 | 0-1 | 1-3 | 1-1 | 2-2 | 2-1 | 1-1 | 3-1 | 1-0 | 4-2 |
| CF "OS" BELENENSES | 0-1 | 0-2 | 0-1 | 1-0 | 2-0 | ■ | 2-1 | 2-0 | 1-1 | 1-2 | 2-2 | 1-1 | 2-1 | 2-3 | 1-0 | 0-1 | 3-0 | 0-0 | 2-0 | 1-0 |
| VITORIA FC (Setubal) | 0-2 | 2-0 | 3-3 | 2-3 | 1-1 | 2-0 | ■ | 2-0 | 3-0 | 5-2 | 1-1 | 0-1 | 1-1 | 2-0 | 3-0 | 0-1 | 3-1 | 0-0 | 3-1 | 2-1 |
| BOAVISTA FC | 1-1 | 1-2 | 0-3 | 0-0 | 2-0 | 1-0 | 2-1 | ■ | 1-1 | 1-0 | 1-1 | 2-0 | 3-0 | 4-0 | 5-0 | 1-1 | 2-1 | 2-2 | 0-0 | 2-0 |
| FC TIRSENSE | 1-2 | 1-3 | 0-0 | 1-0 | 0-2 | 1-0 | 1-1 | 4-4 | ■ | 1-0 | 2-0 | 1-0 | 1-1 | 3-1 | 2-2 | 0-1 | 1-2 | 2-0 | 2-1 | 3-2 |
| CS MARITIMO | 1-2 | 0-2 | 1-0 | 1-2 | 2-2 | 1-0 | 2-1 | 1-1 | 2-2 | ■ | 2-2 | 0-1 | 1-1 | 1-0 | 1-0 | 2-1 | 1-0 | 1-0 | 0-2 | 3-1 |
| SC BEIRA MAR | 1-2 | 0-1 | 0-1 | 1-0 | 2-1 | 1-1 | 1-0 | 2-0 | 3-2 | 1-0 | ■ | 1-0 | 2-1 | 1-0 | 3-0 | 4-1 | 0-0 | 1-0 | 1-1 | 0-0 |
| SC BRAGA | 0-1 | 1-3 | 0-1 | 0-0 | 1-1 | 2-0 | 2-3 | 5-2 | 1-2 | 3-1 | 2-1 | ■ | 1-0 | 6-2 | 2-0 | 1-2 | 1-2 | 1-0 | 3-0 | 4-2 |
| CF EST. DA AMADORA | 1-2 | 1-4 | 1-2 | 2-0 | 0-0 | 1-0 | 2-2 | 1-0 | 1-1 | 0-2 | 2-0 | 2-0 | ■ | 3-0 | 1-0 | 0-0 | 5-2 | 1-1 | 1-1 | 0-1 |
| CD NACIONAL | 2-3 | 0-2 | 0-2 | 3-1 | 2-0 | 0-1 | 1-1 | 1-1 | 0-0 | 0-0 | 0-0 | 1-0 | 0-0 | ■ | 1-1 | 1-2 | 2-1 | 1-3 | 1-1 | 3-1 |
| FC PENAFIEL | 0-0 | 1-1 | 2-5 | 1-0 | 2-0 | 1-0 | 2-1 | 2-1 | 1-0 | 1-1 | 3-0 | 2-0 | 2-1 | 1-2 | ■ | 3-0 | 0-2 | 0-0 | 1-0 | 4-1 |
| CF UNIAO (Madeira) | 1-3 | 0-2 | 0-2 | 0-0 | 1-1 | 1-1 | 1-1 | 0-2 | 2-0 | 1-1 | 2-2 | 1-1 | 0-0 | 1-0 | 3-0 | ■ | 1-0 | 2-1 | 2-2 | 0-0 |
| GIL VICENTE FC | 0-2 | 2-3 | 2-1 | 0-0 | 2-2 | 2-1 | 1-0 | 4-1 | 0-0 | 2-0 | 0-0 | 0-0 | 1-1 | 2-0 | 0-0 | 1-1 | ■ | 1-0 | 0-0 | 2-1 |
| FC FAMALICAO | 0-0 | 1-3 | 0-1 | 2-1 | 1-1 | 3-0 | 0-0 | 0-3 | 2-1 | 1-0 | 2-1 | 4-1 | 1-1 | 0-0 | 0-0 | 1-0 | 1-0 | ■ | 2-1 | 2-3 |
| SC SALGUEIROS | 1-3 | 0-3 | 0-0 | 0-0 | 1-0 | 0-0 | 1-0 | 2-0 | 1-0 | 0-0 | 2-1 | 0-0 | 2-1 | 1-1 | 1-0 | 3-0 | 1-0 | 3-1 | ■ | 1-0 |
| SC FARENSE | 0-1 | 2-2 | 0-1 | 2-0 | 2-0 | 0-0 | 2-0 | 1-2 | 2-0 | 1-2 | 3-2 | 0-0 | 3-0 | 2-1 | 2-0 | 0-0 | 2-0 | 1-0 | 5-0 | ■ |

The match Belenenses 0 Vitoria Guimaraes 1 was ordered to be replayed.

## PORTUGAL 1ST DIVISION 1990/91

### LEAGUE TABLE FINAL

| | | | | | | | |
|---|---|---|---|---|---|---|---|
| Benfica | 38 | 32 | 5 | 1 | 89 | 18 | 69 |
| FC Porto | 38 | 31 | 5 | 2 | 77 | 22 | 67 |
| Sporting | 38 | 24 | 8 | 6 | 58 | 23 | 56 |
| Boavista | 38 | 15 | 11 | 12 | 53 | 46 | 41 |
| Beira Mar | 38 | 12 | 12 | 14 | 40 | 49 | 36 |
| Salgueiros | 38 | 12 | 12 | 14 | 32 | 48 | 36 |
| Farense | 38 | 14 | 6 | 18 | 46 | 47 | 34 |
| Braga | 38 | 13 | 8 | 17 | 42 | 45 | 34 |
| Chaves | 38 | 10 | 14 | 14 | 49 | 52 | 34 |
| Vitoria Guimaraes | 38 | 12 | 10 | 16 | 31 | 40 | 34 |
| Maritimo | 38 | 12 | 10 | 16 | 37 | 48 | 34 |
| Famalicao | 38 | 11 | 11 | 16 | 33 | 41 | 33 |
| Gil Vicente | 38 | 11 | 11 | 16 | 34 | 46 | 33 |
| Penafiel | 38 | 12 | 9 | 17 | 34 | 51 | 33 |
| Uniao | 38 | 9 | 15 | 14 | 30 | 51 | 33 |
| Tirsense | 38 | 10 | 13 | 15 | 39 | 50 | 33 |
| Vitoria Setubal | 38 | 11 | 10 | 17 | 53 | 53 | 32 |
| Estrela Amadora | 38 | 9 | 14 | 15 | 37 | 46 | 32 |
| Belenenses | 38 | 10 | 9 | 19 | 27 | 38 | 29 |
| Nacional | 38 | 8 | 11 | 19 | 33 | 60 | 27 |

Champions : - Benfica
Relegated : - Tirsense, Vitoria Setubal, Estrela Amadora
Belenenses and Nacional

League reduced to 18 clubs for Season 1991/92

### TOP SCORERS

| | | |
|---|---|---|
| 1. | Rui Aguas (Benfica) | 25 |
| 2. | Domingos (FC Porto) | 24 |
| 3. | Fernando Gomes (Sporting) | 22 |
| 4. | Ricky (Estrela Amadora) | 15 |
| 5. | J.Andrade (Boavista) | 13 |
| | Yekini (Vitoria Setubal) | 13 |
| 7. | Curcic (Farense) | 12 |
| | Geraldao (FC Porto) | 12 |
| | Rudi (Chaves) | 12 |
| 10. | Tozé (Salgueiros) | 11 |
| | Marlon (Boavista) | 11 |
| 12. | Santos (Braga) | 10 |
| 13. | Edmilson (Nacional) | 9 |
| | P.Hinds (Maritimo) | 9 |
| | Mané (Farense) | 9 |
| | Moreira (Penafiel) | 9 |
| | V.Paneira (Benfica) | 9 |
| | Ricardo (Benfica) | 9 |
| | Zé Carlos (Gil Vicente) | 9 |
| | Mladenov (Vitoria Setubal) | 9 |
| | Ziad (Vitoria Guimaraes) | 9 |

| PORTUGAL 2nd Division Season 1990/91 | P'NENSE | FEIRENSE | AVES | PACOS DE FER | MAIA | FREAMUNDE | VARZIM | LEIXOES | ESPINHO | LEIRIA | COIMBRA | VISEU | AGUEDA | BENFICA CB | BARREIRENSE | LOULETANO | O ELVAS CAD | TORRIENSE | ESTORIL | LUSITANO |
|---|---|---|---|---|---|---|---|---|---|---|---|---|---|---|---|---|---|---|---|---|
| PORTIMONENSE SC | ■ | 2-0 | 3-0 | 0-1 | 2-0 | 3-1 | 1-2 | 0-0 | 0-1 | 1-0 | 2-3 | 3-1 | 4-2 | 0-0 | 4-1 | 1-2 | 1-1 | 3-0 | 2-0 | 3-1 |
| CD FEIRENSE | 1-0 | ■ | 3-0 | 1-1 | 2-1 | 3-2 | 1-0 | 1-0 | 1-0 | 2-0 | 2-2 | 3-1 | 3-1 | 0-0 | 2-2 | 1-0 | 1-4 | 1-0 | 1-0 | 3-0 |
| CD AVES | 2-1 | 1-0 | ■ | 3-2 | 2-1 | 1-1 | 2-2 | 5-0 | 1-1 | 0-0 | 0-1 | 0-2 | 3-1 | 3-0 | 1-0 | 0-1 | 2-0 | 3-2 | 0-0 | 1-0 |
| FC PACOS DE F'REIRA | 0-1 | 1-0 | 2-1 | ■ | 2-1 | 3-2 | 2-1 | 0-0 | 0-0 | 1-0 | 1-0 | 0-0 | 4-2 | 1-0 | 6-0 | 1-0 | 2-0 | 3-0 | 1-2 | 1-0 |
| FC MAIA | 2-0 | 1-0 | 1-0 | 1-1 | ■ | 2-3 | 2-1 | 1-0 | 0-3 | 3-2 | 3-2 | 0-0 | 4-0 | 2-0 | 5-0 | 1-3 | 1-2 | 2-3 | 0-1 | 2-1 |
| SC FREAMUNDE | 1-2 | 1-1 | 1-0 | 1-2 | 3-1 | ■ | 2-1 | 1-2 | 0-0 | 1-2 | 4-0 | 2-1 | 1-0 | 2-1 | 3-1 | 1-3 | 0-1 | 2-2 | 4-1 | 2-1 |
| VARZIM SC | 1-0 | 4-0 | 1-1 | 1-2 | 1-2 | 2-2 | ■ | 1-1 | 0-1 | 1-1 | 0-0 | 2-0 | 2-0 | 0-1 | 2-1 | 0-0 | 2-1 | 1-2 | 0-0 | 3-0 |
| LEIXOES SC | 0-1 | 1-1 | 1-0 | 1-0 | 3-2 | 3-1 | 0-2 | ■ | 2-0 | 1-0 | 2-0 | 1-2 | 5-0 | 4-1 | 1-1 | 3-2 | 3-2 | 1-1 | 0-0 | 4-0 |
| SC ESPINHO | 1-2 | 1-1 | 0-0 | 1-2 | 1-1 | 0-1 | 2-1 | 3-0 | ■ | 2-1 | 3-0 | 0-0 | 4-1 | 0-0 | 5-1 | 1-2 | 3-2 | 1-1 | 1-0 | 4-0 |
| UNIAO LEIRIA | 3-0 | 2-0 | 1-1 | 1-1 | 3-3 | 4-1 | 1-0 | 2-1 | 1-0 | ■ | 1-0 | 1-1 | 3-1 | 2-0 | 1-1 | 2-0 | 2-2 | 2-0 | 2-2 | 0-0 |
| ACADEMICA COIMBRA | 0-0 | 1-0 | 0-0 | 0-1 | 3-1 | 3-0 | 0-0 | 2-1 | 1-0 | 1-0 | ■ | 1-0 | 2-0 | 0-0 | 4-0 | 3-1 | 0-2 | 1-0 | 3-0 | 1-1 |
| CF ACADEMICO VISEU | 1-0 | 3-0 | 1-1 | 3-1 | 1-2 | 1-0 | 0-0 | 1-1 | 0-0 | 1-0 | 2-0 | ■ | 2-0 | 1-1 | 1-0 | 0-0 | 1-0 | 1-1 | 2-1 | 0-0 |
| RD AGUEDA | 1-0 | 2-0 | 1-3 | 0-1 | 3-1 | 7-4 | 2-0 | 1-1 | 1-0 | 0-1 | 0-3 | 4-3 | ■ | 0-1 | 2-0 | 1-2 | 1-1 | 1-1 | 0-0 | 1-0 |
| BEN. CAST. BRANCO | 1-0 | 0-0 | 2-1 | 1-1 | 2-1 | 2-0 | 1-0 | 0-2 | 1-1 | 1-1 | 2-0 | 3-2 | 1-0 | ■ | 2-0 | 2-0 | 1-0 | 3-3 | 1-0 | 3-1 |
| FC BARREIRENSE | 0-9 | 1-0 | 1-0 | 2-2 | 2-0 | 2-1 | 0-2 | 1-1 | 1-1 | 0-0 | 1-1 | 0-1 | 0-0 | 1-1 | ■ | 1-2 | 1-3 | 1-2 | 1-1 | 0-0 |
| LOULETANO DC | 2-0 | 1-2 | 1-2 | 3-1 | 1-1 | 0-0 | 0-0 | 2-3 | 0-1 | 0-0 | 0-0 | 1-2 | 3-1 | 1-0 | 4-2 | ■ | 2-1 | 0-0 | 0-1 | 1-1 |
| O ELVAS CAD | 0-0 | 0-0 | 3-1 | 1-0 | 1-0 | 3-1 | 3-2 | 0-0 | 0-0 | 2-1 | 1-0 | 1-2 | 3-0 | 0-0 | 1-0 | 1-5 | ■ | 1-2 | 0-2 | 1-1 |
| SCU TORRIENSE | 0-3 | 0-0 | 2-0 | 1-1 | 3-0 | 2-2 | 3-3 | 4-0 | 1-1 | 2-0 | 0-1 | 3-1 | 3-2 | 0-0 | 3-0 | 5-1 | 1-0 | ■ | 1-0 | 2-1 |
| GD ESTORIL PRAIA | 1-1 | 2-0 | 2-2 | 3-0 | 2-0 | 6-0 | 2-1 | 0-0 | 1-1 | 1-0 | 1-2 | 1-1 | 4-1 | 1-0 | 2-0 | 1-1 | 3-0 | 1-0 | ■ | 1-0 |
| LUSITANO FC (V. Real) | 1-2 | 1-0 | 0-1 | 0-1 | 2-1 | 0-1 | 0-0 | 0-0 | 0-1 | 1-2 | 0-0 | 0-1 | 0-1 | 1-0 | 0-0 | 1-0 | 1-1 | 0-0 | 0-0 | ■ |

The matches Espinho 1 Torriense 1 and Estoril 1 Esphino 1 were later awarded Esphino 0 Torriense 3 and Estoril 3 Esphino 0.

## PORTUGAL 2ND DIVISION 1990/91

### LEAGUE TABLE FINAL

| | | | | | | | |
|---|---|---|---|---|---|---|---|
| Pacos de Ferreira | 38 | 21 | 9 | 8 | 52 | 34 | 51 |
| Estoril | 38 | 17 | 12 | 9 | 48 | 28 | 46 |
| Torreense | 38 | 16 | 13 | 9 | 58 | 43 | 45 |
| Academico Viseu | 38 | 16 | 13 | 9 | 43 | 34 | 45 |
| Academica Coimbra | 38 | 17 | 10 | 11 | 41 | 32 | 44 |
| Benfica Castel.Branco | 38 | 16 | 12 | 10 | 35 | 31 | 44 |
| Leixoes | 38 | 15 | 13 | 10 | 49 | 41 | 43 |
| Portimonense | 38 | 18 | 6 | 14 | 57 | 34 | 42 |
| Uniao Leiria | 38 | 14 | 13 | 11 | 45 | 35 | 41 |
| Espinho | 38 | 14 | 12 | 12 | 42 | 31 | 40 |
| Feirense | 38 | 15 | 10 | 13 | 37 | 39 | 40 |
| Aves | 38 | 14 | 11 | 13 | 44 | 41 | 39 |
| Louletano | 38 | 14 | 10 | 14 | 47 | 44 | 38 |
| O Elvas | 38 | 14 | 10 | 14 | 45 | 45 | 38 |
| Varzim | 38 | 10 | 13 | 15 | 42 | 39 | 33 |
| Freamunde | 38 | 13 | 7 | 18 | 55 | 69 | 33 |
| Maia | 38 | 13 | 5 | 20 | 52 | 61 | 31 |
| Agueda | 38 | 10 | 5 | 23 | 41 | 73 | 25 |
| Lusitano (VRSA) | 38 | 4 | 13 | 21 | 16 | 45 | 21 |
| Barreirense | 38 | 4 | 13 | 21 | 26 | 76 | 21 |

Promoted : - Pacos de Ferreira, Estoril and Torriense
Relegated : - O Elvas, Varzim, Freamunde, Maia, Agueda, Lusitano and Barreirense.

League Reduced to 18 clubs for Season 1991/92

## PORTUGAL 3RD DIV. NORTH 1990/91

### LEAGUE TABLE FINAL

| | | | | | | | |
|---|---|---|---|---|---|---|---|
| Rio Ave | 38 | 23 | 10 | 5 | 79 | 21 | 56 |
| Fafe | 38 | 23 | 8 | 7 | 66 | 29 | 54 |
| Marco | 38 | 18 | 10 | 10 | 48 | 46 | 46 |
| Infesta | 38 | 18 | 7 | 13 | 68 | 54 | 43 |
| Moreirense | 38 | 14 | 14 | 10 | 66 | 49 | 42 |
| Vila Real | 38 | 17 | 8 | 13 | 52 | 39 | 42 |
| Joane | 38 | 16 | 10 | 12 | 49 | 37 | 42 |
| Uniao Lamas | 38 | 16 | 10 | 12 | 61 | 57 | 42 |
| Felgueiras | 38 | 18 | 5 | 15 | 54 | 41 | 41 |
| Vizela | 38 | 17 | 7 | 14 | 59 | 49 | 41 |
| Lousada | 38 | 17 | 7 | 14 | 54 | 49 | 41 |
| Paredes | 38 | 15 | 10 | 13 | 60 | 56 | 40 |
| Esposende | 38 | 14 | 11 | 13 | 46 | 49 | 39 |
| Amarante | 38 | 15 | 8 | 15 | 51 | 50 | 38 |
| Trofense | 38 | 13 | 12 | 13 | 45 | 46 | 38 |
| Braganca | 38 | 11 | 7 | 20 | 40 | 61 | 29 |
| Leca | 38 | 8 | 12 | 18 | 45 | 55 | 28 |
| Mirandela | 38 | 5 | 11 | 22 | 21 | 68 | 21 |
| Delaes | 38 | 7 | 6 | 25 | 35 | 90 | 20 |
| Valpacos | 38 | 6 | 5 | 27 | 40 | 93 | 17 |

Promoted : - Rio Ave
Relegated : - Amarante, Trofense, Braganca, Leca Mirandela, Delaes and Valpacos

## PORTUGAL 3RD DIV.CENTRE 1990/91

### LEAGUE TABLE FINAL

| | | | | | | | |
|---|---|---|---|---|---|---|---|
| Ovarense | 38 | 26 | 7 | 5 | 80 | 24 | 59 |
| Lousanense | 38 | 20 | 10 | 8 | 50 | 23 | 50 |
| Caldas | 38 | 21 | 6 | 11 | 51 | 30 | 48 |
| Sanjoanense | 38 | 18 | 11 | 9 | 57 | 30 | 47 |
| Mirandense | 38 | 15 | 16 | 7 | 36 | 21 | 46 |
| Oliveirense | 38 | 19 | 7 | 12 | 52 | 32 | 45 |
| Mirense | 38 | 15 | 14 | 9 | 60 | 47 | 44 |
| Oliveira Hospital | 38 | 14 | 14 | 10 | 47 | 44 | 42 |
| Covilha | 38 | 14 | 11 | 13 | 42 | 38 | 39 |
| Uniao Santarem | 38 | 15 | 8 | 15 | 44 | 41 | 38 |
| Naval | 38 | 13 | 12 | 13 | 40 | 47 | 38 |
| Uniao Tomar | 38 | 13 | 11 | 14 | 38 | 37 | 37 |
| Estarreja | 38 | 12 | 12 | 14 | 49 | 51 | 36 |
| Santacombadense | 38 | 11 | 11 | 16 | 32 | 39 | 33 |
| Os Marialvas | 38 | 10 | 12 | 16 | 39 | 49 | 32 |
| Uniao Coimbra | 38 | 11 | 6 | 21 | 36 | 61 | 28 |
| Mangualde | 38 | 10 | 7 | 21 | 25 | 50 | 27 |
| Anadia | 38 | 7 | 13 | 18 | 38 | 58 | 27 |
| Alcobaca | 38 | 7 | 11 | 20 | 25 | 63 | 25 |
| Guarda | 38 | 7 | 5 | 26 | 35 | 91 | 19 |

Promoted : - Ovarense
Releg. : - Estarreja, Santacombadense, Os Marialvas, Uniao Coimbra, Mangualde, Anadia, Aicobaca and Guarda

## PORTUGAL 3RD DIV. SOUTH 1990/91
### LEAGUE TABLE FINAL

| | | | | | | | |
|---|---|---|---|---|---|---|---|
| Olhanense | 38 | 18 | 13 | 7 | 58 | 34 | 49 |
| Campomaiorense | 38 | 21 | 6 | 11 | 53 | 37 | 48 |
| Sacavenense | 38 | 16 | 14 | 8 | 54 | 34 | 46 |
| Lusitano (Evora) | 38 | 18 | 10 | 10 | 47 | 36 | 46 |
| Atlético | 38 | 17 | 11 | 10 | 41 | 34 | 45 |
| Amora | 38 | 12 | 19 | 7 | 52 | 33 | 43 |
| Quarteirense | 38 | 16 | 11 | 11 | 42 | 37 | 43 |
| Montijo | 38 | 16 | 10 | 12 | 47 | 32 | 42 |
| Alverca | 38 | 16 | 7 | 15 | 54 | 38 | 39 |
| Silves | 38 | 12 | 15 | 11 | 39 | 32 | 39 |
| Esperanca de Lagos | 38 | 13 | 12 | 13 | 38 | 38 | 38 |
| Uniao Santiago | 38 | 13 | 12 | 13 | 46 | 46 | 38 |
| Juventude | 38 | 11 | 14 | 13 | 47 | 46 | 36 |
| Santa Clara | 38 | 12 | 9 | 17 | 40 | 56 | 33 |
| Oriental | 38 | 12 | 9 | 17 | 40 | 51 | 33 |
| Sintrense | 38 | 11 | 9 | 18 | 45 | 64 | 31 |
| Seixal | 38 | 10 | 11 | 17 | 34 | 46 | 31 |
| Uniao Almeirim | 38 | 9 | 11 | 18 | 39 | 71 | 29 |
| Olivais Moscavide | 38 | 8 | 10 | 20 | 37 | 05 | 26 |
| Loures | 38 | 7 | 11 | 20 | 34 | 57 | 25 |

Promoted : - Olhanense
Relegated : - Santa Clara, Oriental, Sintrense, Seixal
Uniao Almeirim, Olivais Moscavide and Loures.

Leagues to be reduced to 18 clubs each for Season 1991/92

## 3RD DIV. CHAMPIONSHIP PLAY-OFFS
### LEAGUE TABLE FINAL

| | | | | | | | |
|---|---|---|---|---|---|---|---|
| Ovarense | 4 | 3 | 0 | 1 | 10 | 4 | 6 |
| Rio Ave | 4 | 2 | 1 | 1 | 9 | 7 | 5 |
| Olhanense | 4 | 0 | 1 | 3 | 6 | 14 | 1 |

## 4TH DIV. CHAMPIONSHIP PLAY-OFFS
### NORTH LEAGUE TABLE FINAL

| | | | | | | | |
|---|---|---|---|---|---|---|---|
| Lourosa | 4 | 3 | 0 | 1 | 7 | 7 | 6 |
| Pedroucos | 4 | 1 | 1 | 2 | 5 | 4 | 3 |
| Arsenal Braga | 4 | 1 | 1 | 2 | 3 | 4 | 3 |

### SOUTH LEAGUE TABLE FINAL

| | | | | | | | |
|---|---|---|---|---|---|---|---|
| Vasco da Gama | 4 | 2 | 1 | 1 | 7 | 5 | 5 |
| Lusitania | 4 | 1 | 2 | 1 | 5 | 4 | 4 |
| Fatima | 4 | 1 | 1 | 2 | 8 | 11 | 3 |

### FINAL   (at Torres Novas)
Lourosa ..................... 2    Vasco da Gama ......... 4

## PORTUGAL 4TH DIVISION A 1990/91
### LEAGUE TABLE FINAL

| | | | | | | | |
|---|---|---|---|---|---|---|---|
| Arsenal de Braga | 34 | 22 | 8 | 4 | 58 | 20 | 52 |
| Neves | 34 | 20 | 9 | 5 | 58 | 24 | 49 |
| Maria Fonte | 34 | 17 | 9 | 8 | 40 | 19 | 43 |
| Vianense | 34 | 15 | 10 | 9 | 42 | 20 | 40 |
| Vieira | 34 | 14 | 11 | 9 | 34 | 26 | 39 |
| Valdevez | 34 | 15 | 8 | 11 | 42 | 23 | 38 |
| Santa Maria | 34 | 15 | 8 | 11 | 46 | 43 | 38 |
| P. Salgadas | 34 | 15 | 8 | 11 | 36 | 32 | 38 |
| C. Talpas | 34 | 13 | 12 | 9 | 33 | 32 | 38 |
| Moncao | 34 | 11 | 12 | 11 | 35 | 35 | 34 |
| Vila Pouca | 34 | 14 | 6 | 14 | 51 | 50 | 34 |
| Amares | 34 | 13 | 6 | 15 | 37 | 37 | 32 |
| Mac. Cavaleiros | 34 | 10 | 12 | 12 | 36 | 42 | 32 |
| Ponte da Barca | 34 | 10 | 11 | 13 | 32 | 44 | 31 |
| Ronfe | 34 | 7 | 13 | 14 | 36 | 50 | 27 |
| Maximinense | 34 | 5 | 10 | 19 | 19 | 47 | 20 |
| Amad. Caminha | 34 | 4 | 6 | 24 | 30 | 68 | 14 |
| Mondinense | 34 | 4 | 5 | 25 | 25 | 78 | 13 |

Promoted : - Arsenal de Braga and Neves

## PORTUGAL 4TH DIVISION C 1990/91
### LEAGUE TABLE FINAL

| | | | | | | | |
|---|---|---|---|---|---|---|---|
| Lourosa | 34 | 19 | 9 | 6 | 43 | 21 | 47 |
| Mealhada | 34 | 19 | 8 | 7 | 58 | 27 | 46 |
| Oliveirinha | 34 | 16 | 11 | 7 | 59 | 36 | 43 |
| Mortagua | 34 | 15 | 11 | 8 | 49 | 51 | 41 |
| Oliveira do Bairro | 34 | 17 | 5 | 12 | 46 | 38 | 39 |
| Avanca | 34 | 15 | 8 | 11 | 40 | 34 | 38 |
| Viseu FC | 34 | 14 | 8 | 12 | 46 | 32 | 36 |
| Argus | 34 | 14 | 8 | 12 | 56 | 44 | 36 |
| Alba | 34 | 13 | 9 | 12 | 41 | 33 | 35 |
| Nelas | 34 | 13 | 9 | 12 | 34 | 36 | 35 |
| Gouvela | 34 | 15 | 5 | 14 | 51 | 50 | 35 |
| Ala Arriba | 34 | 12 | 9 | 13 | 47 | 44 | 33 |
| P.Castelo | 34 | 10 | 12 | 12 | 36 | 29 | 32 |
| Tabuense | 34 | 11 | 7 | 16 | 32 | 49 | 29 |
| Brasfemes | 34 | 8 | 13 | 13 | 32 | 43 | 29 |
| AD Valonguense | 34 | 11 | 6 | 17 | 45 | 54 | 28 |
| Pinhelense | 34 | 7 | 6 | 21 | 29 | 51 | 20 |
| Luso | 34 | 2 | 6 | 26 | 19 | 91 | 10 |

Promoted : - Lourosa and Mealhada

## PORTUGAL 4TH DIV. B 1990/91
### LEAGUE TABLE FINAL

| | | | | | | | |
|---|---|---|---|---|---|---|---|
| Pedroucos | 34 | 21 | 8 | 5 | 61 | 32 | 50 |
| Ermesinde | 34 | 17 | 10 | 7 | 39 | 15 | 44 |
| Sandinenses | 34 | 13 | 15 | 6 | 45 | 35 | 41 |
| Mogadourense | 34 | 12 | 15 | 7 | 48 | 32 | 39 |
| Régua | 34 | 13 | 13 | 8 | 63 | 46 | 39 |
| V.N. Foz Coa | 34 | 17 | 3 | 14 | 49 | 37 | 37 |
| C. Maia | 34 | 12 | 12 | 10 | 46 | 41 | 36 |
| Valonguense | 34 | 13 | 9 | 12 | 41 | 47 | 35 |
| Rio Tinto | 34 | 14 | 7 | 13 | 31 | 40 | 35 |
| Rebordosa | 34 | 12 | 10 | 12 | 37 | 34 | 34 |
| S. Martinho | 34 | 9 | 15 | 10 | 40 | 36 | 33 |
| Lixa | 34 | 12 | 7 | 15 | 43 | 52 | 31 |
| Flaes | 34 | 12 | 7 | 15 | 36 | 39 | 31 |
| Paivense | 34 | 13 | 5 | 16 | 45 | 61 | 31 |
| Arsenal do Bessa | 34 | 9 | 11 | 14 | 41 | 49 | 29 |
| Celoricense | 34 | 10 | 7 | 17 | 38 | 52 | 27 |
| Valadares | 34 | 6 | 10 | 18 | 30 | 49 | 22 |
| Oliv Douro | 34 | 5 | 8 | 21 | 21 | 57 | 18 |

Promoted : - Pedroucos and Ermesinde

## PORTUGAL 4TH DIV. D 1990/91
### LEAGUE TABLE FINAL

| | | | | | | | |
|---|---|---|---|---|---|---|---|
| Torres Novas | 34 | 20 | 11 | 3 | 66 | 16 | 51 |
| C.D. Fátima | 34 | 22 | 6 | 6 | 63 | 17 | 50 |
| Marinhense | 34 | 21 | 8 | 5 | 62 | 14 | 50 |
| Lourinhanense | 34 | 18 | 11 | 5 | 53 | 27 | 47 |
| Peniche | 34 | 18 | 10 | 6 | 53 | 25 | 46 |
| Sertanense | 34 | 19 | 6 | 9 | 41 | 24 | 44 |
| Alcanenense | 34 | 17 | 8 | 9 | 46 | 23 | 42 |
| Portalegrense | 34 | 13 | 11 | 10 | 38 | 24 | 37 |
| Estrela Portalegre | 34 | 11 | 14 | 9 | 36 | 27 | 36 |
| Beneditense | 34 | 10 | 11 | 13 | 31 | 46 | 31 |
| Pombal | 34 | 11 | 7 | 16 | 33 | 51 | 29 |
| Alcains | 34 | 9 | 9 | 16 | 37 | 51 | 27 |
| Marrazes | 34 | 9 | 9 | 16 | 32 | 46 | 27 |
| V.C Fatima | 34 | 7 | 10 | 17 | 30 | 53 | 24 |
| Polares | 34 | 7 | 9 | 18 | 31 | 61 | 23 |
| Bombarralense | 34 | 7 | 6 | 21 | 21 | 52 | 20 |
| Fundao | 34 | 4 | 8 | 22 | 25 | 76 | 16 |
| Os Nazarenos | 34 | 3 | 6 | 25 | 22 | 87 | 12 |

Promoted : - Torres Novas and C.D. Fátima

## PORTUGAL 4TH DIVISION E 1990/91
### LEAGUE TABLE FINAL

| | | | | | | | |
|---|---|---|---|---|---|---|---|
| Lusitania | 34 | 20 | 7 | 7 | 47 | 19 | 47 |
| Fanhoes | 34 | 17 | 11 | 6 | 53 | 28 | 45 |
| Praiense | 34 | 16 | 10 | 8 | 44 | 23 | 42 |
| Samora Correira | 34 | 16 | 10 | 8 | 49 | 27 | 42 |
| Camara de Lobos | 34 | 17 | 6 | 11 | 42 | 21 | 40 |
| Odivelas | 34 | 12 | 14 | 8 | 34 | 32 | 38 |
| Vilafranquense | 34 | 15 | 7 | 12 | 45 | 33 | 37 |
| Portosantense | 34 | 12 | 13 | 9 | 37 | 25 | 37 |
| A. Musqueira | 34 | 14 | 9 | 11 | 33 | 40 | 37 |
| Malveira | 34 | 14 | 8 | 12 | 35 | 29 | 36 |
| Machico | 34 | 14 | 8 | 12 | 28 | 29 | 36 |
| Futebol Benfica | 34 | 11 | 9 | 14 | 35 | 36 | 31 |
| SL Cartaxo | 34 | 11 | 8 | 15 | 40 | 46 | 30 |
| Marinhais | 34 | 9 | 9 | 16 | 26 | 48 | 27 |
| Borbense | 34 | 9 | 7 | 18 | 25 | 47 | 25 |
| Vilanovense | 34 | 6 | 11 | 17 | 23 | 53 | 23 |
| Estremoz | 34 | 6 | 11 | 17 | 21 | 46 | 23 |
| Arronchense | 34 | 4 | 8 | 22 | 34 | 69 | 16 |

Promoted : - Lusitania and Fanhoes

## PORTUGAL 4TH DIVISION F 1990/91
### LEAGUE TABLE FINAL

| | | | | | | | |
|---|---|---|---|---|---|---|---|
| Vasco de Gama | 34 | 21 | 7 | 6 | 72 | 37 | 49 |
| Imortal | 34 | 18 | 11 | 5 | 49 | 23 | 47 |
| Moura | 34 | 15 | 15 | 4 | 48 | 25 | 45 |
| Uniao Montemor | 34 | 16 | 12 | 6 | 59 | 24 | 44 |
| Beja | 34 | 16 | 9 | 9 | 53 | 33 | 41 |
| Almada | 34 | 16 | 8 | 10 | 51 | 37 | 40 |
| Leoes Tavira | 34 | 14 | 9 | 11 | 51 | 34 | 37 |
| Aljustrelense | 34 | 13 | 11 | 10 | 40 | 32 | 37 |
| Juventude Belem | 34 | 13 | 9 | 12 | 36 | 41 | 35 |
| Quimigal | 34 | 13 | 7 | 14 | 48 | 41 | 33 |
| Almansilense | 34 | 13 | 7 | 14 | 38 | 43 | 33 |
| Lagoa | 34 | 11 | 11 | 12 | 28 | 38 | 33 |
| Alcacerense | 34 | 11 | 6 | 17 | 29 | 56 | 28 |
| Alvorense | 34 | 9 | 7 | 18 | 32 | 57 | 25 |
| Piense | 34 | 8 | 9 | 17 | 38 | 61 | 25 |
| Costa da Caparica | 34 | 8 | 8 | 18 | 26 | 57 | 24 |
| Estrela V'ndas Novas | 34 | 6 | 8 | 20 | 26 | 49 | 20 |
| Palmelense | 34 | 3 | 10 | 21 | 22 | 58 | 16 |

Promoted : - Vasco de Gama and Imortal

# PORTUGAL CUP 1990/91

## 5TH ROUND

| | | | | | | | | |
|---|---|---|---|---|---|---|---|---|
| Braga | 2 | Chaves | 1 | Vizela | 5 | Palmelense | 1 | |
| Farense | 3 | Belenenses | 2 | Tirsense | 5 | Viseu FC | 0 | |
| Silves | 0 | Maritimo | 2 | Boavista | 1 | Salgueiros | 0 | |
| Alcains | 1 | Academica Coimbra | 3 | Uniao de Leiria | 1 | Vitoria Guimaraes | 2 | |
| Penafiel | 0 | Atletico CP | 1 | Feirense | 1 | Moreirense | 0 | |
| Rio Ave | 2 | Academico Viseu | 0 | Pedroucos | 1 | Olhanense | 2 | |
| Portimonense | 3 | Oliveirense | 0 | Nacional | 0 | Vila Real | 1 | |
| Pacos de Ferreira | 1 | Uniao de Madeira | 1 (aet.) | Loures | 1 | Ovarense | 2 (aet.) |
| Benfica Cast. Branc. | 0 | Lusitano Evora | 1 | Varzim | 1 | Felgueiras | 0 (aet.) |
| FC Porto | 5 | O Elvas | 0 | Juventude de Belem | 1 | Gil Vicente | 3 | |
| Mirandense | 1 | Lourinhanense | 0 (aet.) | Beira Mar | 2 | Fafe | 0 | |
| Estrela Amadora | 6 | Sanjoanense | 0 | Agueda | 3 | Torreense | 1 | |
| Sporting CP | 6 | Peniche | 0 | Lousada | 4 | Estarreja | 0 | |
| Estoril | 2 | Arsenal de Braga | 4 (aet.) | Trofense | 1 | Leca | 0 | |
| Espinho | 2 | Vitoria Setubal | 2 (aet.) | Olivais e Moscavide | 0 | Arsenal do Bessa | 0 (aet.) |
| Campomaiorense | 1 | Famalicao | 2 | Abandoned after 58 minutes, later awarded to Famalicao | | | |
| Benfica | 4 | Uniao Tomar | 1 | | | | | |

## REPLAYS

| | | | | | | | |
|---|---|---|---|---|---|---|---|
| Uniao de Madeira | 1 | Pacos de Ferreira | 0 | Vitoria Setubal | 1 | Esphino | 0 |
| Arsenal do Bessa | 1 | Olivais e Moscavide | 0 | | | | |

5th round following disciplinary measures - Uniao de Montemor.....0   Gil Vicente.........2

## 6TH ROUND

| | | | | | | | | |
|---|---|---|---|---|---|---|---|---|
| Vitoria Setubal | 2 | SL Benfica | 3 | Arsenal do Bessa | 0 | Famalicao | 3 | |
| Braga | 2 | Lousada | 0 | Tirsense | 2 | Varzim | 0 | |
| Agueda | 2 | Vitoria Guimaraes | 3 | Academica Coimbra | 1 | Boavista | 3 | |
| Beira Mar | 2 | Uniao de Madeira | 0 | Maritimo | 3 | Trofense | 2 (aet.) |
| Vila Real | 0 | FC Porto | 1 | Sporting CP | 2 | Farense | 0 | |
| Vizela | 3 | Atletico CP | 2 | Olhanense | 2 | Ovarense | 4 (aet.) |
| Portimonense | 1 | Lusitano Evora | 0 | Feirense | 1 | Rio Ave | 0 (aet.) |
| Arsenal de Braga | 2 | Mirandense | 0 | Estrela Amadora | 2 | Gil Vicente | 2 (aet.) |

## REPLAY

| | | | | |
|---|---|---|---|---|
| Gil Vicente | 1 | Estrela Amadora | 1 (aet.) | Estrela Amadora win 3-4 on penalties |

## 7TH ROUND

| | | | | | | | |
|---|---|---|---|---|---|---|---|
| Ovarense | 1 | Arsenal de Braga | 1 (aet.) | Braga | 3 | Vizela | 0 |
| Boavista | 2 | Sporting CP | 0 | Tirsense | 2 | Portimonense | 1 |
| Famalicao | 0 | FC Porto | 1 | Feirense | 1 | Vitoria Guimaraes | 0 |
| Beira MAr | 1 | Estrela Amadora | 0 | Maritimo | 1 | Benfica | 2 |

## REPLAY

| | | | |
|---|---|---|---|
| Arsenal de Braga | 1 | Ovarense | 2 |

## 1/4 FINALS

| | | | | | | | |
|---|---|---|---|---|---|---|---|
| Feirense | 1 | Tirsense | 0 (aet.) | Boavista | 1 | Braga | 0 |
| Beira Mar | 3 | Ovarense | 0 | FC Porto | 2 | Benfica | 1 |

## SEMI-FINALS

| | | | | | | | |
|---|---|---|---|---|---|---|---|
| Feirense | 1 | FC Porto | 1 (aet.) | Beira Mar | 2 | Boavista | 0 |

## REPLAY

| | | | |
|---|---|---|---|
| FC Porto | 2 | Feirense | 0 |

## FINAL   2/6/91 (at Estadio Nacional, Lisboa)

FC Porto ............ 3   Beira Mar ............ 1 (aet.)

Porto : Vitor Baia, Joao Pinto, Fernando Couto, Aloisio, Paulo Pereira, Jaime Magalhaes, Semedo, André, Vlk (Abilio 90), Domingos, Jorge Couto (Kostadinov 73).

Beira Mar : Helder,Ze Ribeiro,Redondo, Oliveira, Petrov, China, Mito (Jarbas 77), Sousa (Penteado 99), Abdelghany, Jorge Silverio, Dino.

| | | | |
|---|---|---|---|
| 1-0 | Domingos | 5 | Referee : Vitor Correira |
| 1-1 | Abdelghany | 30 | |
| 2-1 | Kostadinov | 92 | |
| 3-1 | Jaime Magalhaes | 100 | |

# PORTUGAL INTERNATIONAL REVIEW 1990

## INTERNATIONAL LINE-UPS 1990

| Match | Louro Silvino | Antonio Veloso | Joao Antonio Galo | Hernani Neves | Pedro Venancio | Antonio Fonseca | Vitor Araujo "Paneira" | Antonio André | José Semedo | Rui Aguas | Jorge Paulo Cadete | José Carlos | Antonio Pacheco | Joao Pinto | Jorge Ferreira | Jaime Pacheco | Rui Barros | José Martins Leal | Oceano Cruz | Manuel Antonio Couto "Nelo" | Carlos Xavier | Fernando Couto | Domingos Oliveira | Paulo Futre | Vitor Baia | Jorge Couto |
|---|---|---|---|---|---|---|---|---|---|---|---|---|---|---|---|---|---|---|---|---|---|---|---|---|---|---|
| 28/8/90 PORTUGAL 1 GERMANY 1 Lisboa — Friendly — Ref.: Lo Bello (Italy) (Rui Aguas) | 1 | 2 | 3 | 4 | 5 | 6 | 7 | 8 | 9 | 10 | 11 | (3) | (9) | | | | | | | | | | | | | |
| 12/9/90 FINLAND 0 PORTUGAL 0 Helsinki — EuroCh.Q. — Ref.: Marko (Czechoslovakia) | 1 | 2 | | 4 | 5 | | 7 | 8 | | 11 | (11) | | (5) | 3 | 6 | 9 | 10 | | | | | | | | | |
| 17/10/90 PORTUGAL 1 HOLLAND 0 Porto — EuroCh.Q. — Ref.: Kirschen (DDR) (Rui Aguas) | 1 | 3 | | | 4 | | 7 | | | 10 | 11 | | | 2 | (8) | | 8 | 5 | 6 | 9 | | | | | | |
| 18/12/90 PORTUGAL 1 USA 0 Maia — Friendly — Ref.: Marcos (Spain) (Domingos) | 1 | | | | | | 6 | 9 | 7 | | | | | 2 | | | 8 | | 5 | (6) | (9) | 3 | 10 | 11 | (1) | (10) |
| CAPS AT 31/12/90 | 18 | 28 | 1 | 2 | 15 | 4 | 17 | 17 | 7 | 16 | 3 | 1 | 5 | 38 | 4 | 25 | 15 | 2 | 5 | 2 | 5 | 1 | 2 | 21 | 1 | 1 |
| GOALS AT 31/12/90 | | | | | | | 3 | 1 | 1 | 6 | | | | 1 | | | 1 | | | | | | 1 | 2 | | |

## PORTUGAL : All Time Records as at 31/12/90 - CAPS

1. Tamagnini Nené (SL Benfica) — 66
2. Eusebio Ferreira (SL Benfica) — 64
3. Humberto Coelho (SL Benfica/Paris St.Germain FC) — 64
4. Manuel Bento (SL Benfica) — 63
5. Mario Coluna (SL Benfica) — 57
6. Fernando Gomes (FC Porto) — 48
7. Antonio Simoes (SL Benfica) — 46
8. José Augusto (FC Barrierense/SL Benfica) — 45
9. Rui Jordao (SL Benfica/Sporting CP/Vitoria Setubal) — 43
10. Carlos Manuel (SI Benfica) — 42

## PORTUGAL : All Time Records as at 31/12/90 - GOALS

1. Eusebio Ferreira (SL Benfica) — (64) 41
2. Tamagnini Nené (SL Benfica) — (66) 22
3. Fernando Peyroteo (Sporting CP) — (20) 15
4. Rui Jordao (SL Benfica/Sporting CP/Vitoria Setubal) — (43) 15
5. José Torres (SL Benfica/Vitoria Setubal) — (33) 14
6. Lucas da Fonseca "Matateu" (CF OS Belenenses) — (27) 13
7. Fernando Gomes (FC Porto) — (48) 13
8. José Aguas (SL Benfica) — (25) 11
9. Artur de Sousa "Pinga" (CS Maritimo/FC Porto) — (21) 9
   José Augusto (FC Barreirense/SL Benfica) — (45) 9

# RUMANIA Correspondent : ROMEO IONESCU

RUMANIA Divizia A — Season 1990/91

| | DINAMO | STEAUA | UNIV. CR. | P TEHNICA | PETROLUL | FC INTER | BRASOV | CORVINUL | FC FARUL | FC BIHOR | SPORTUL ST. | FC ARGES | JIUL | UNIV. CLUJ. | BACAU | PROGRESUL | RAPID | GLORIA |
|---|---|---|---|---|---|---|---|---|---|---|---|---|---|---|---|---|---|---|
| DINAMO BUCURESTI | | 1-0 | 1-1 | 0-0 | 3-1 | 2-1 | 4-0 | 2-0 | 4-0 | 5-0 | 0-0 | 2-0 | 2-0 | 7-2 | 2-1 | 0-0 | 1-0 | 2-1 |
| STEAUA BUCURESTI | 1-0 | | 1-0 | 2-1 | 2-1 | 3-1 | 4-1 | 6-2 | 4-1 | 4-0 | 3-1 | 2-1 | 5-1 | 3-1 | 2-0 | 6-0 | 0-0 | 0-0 |
| UNIVERSITATEA CRAIOVA | 1-0 | 1-1 | | 3-0 | 3-0 | 5-1 | 3-0 | 8-1 | 2-2 | 4-0 | 3-1 | 4-0 | 1-1 | 4-0 | 3-1 | 2-0 | 3-1 | 5-2 |
| POLITEHNICA TIMISOARA | 3-1 | 3-2 | 0-2 | | 3-0 | 2-1 | 2-0 | 2-1 | 2-4 | 2-2 | 0-0 | 2-0 | 1-0 | 4-0 | 1-0 | 3-0 | 2-2 | 1-1 |
| PETROLUL PLOESTI | 2-0 | 2-1 | 1-0 | 6-2 | | 1-2 | 2-1 | 4-1 | 1-0 | 2-0 | 4-1 | 1-1 | 3-2 | 1-1 | 2-0 | 1-1 | 1-0 | 1-0 |
| FC INTER SIBIU | 2-0 | 1-2 | 3-0 | 3-0 | 4-2 | | 2-0 | 5-2 | 2-1 | 2-3 | 0-0 | 3-1 | 3-2 | 2-0 | 2-0 | 4-0 | 1-0 | 2-1 |
| FCM BRASOV | 1-1 | 1-1 | 1-1 | 4-1 | 1-0 | 3-0 | | 2-0 | 4-0 | 2-1 | 3-0 | 1-0 | 4-1 | 2-1 | 2-0 | 3-0 | 1-1 | 2-1 |
| CORVINUL HUNEDOARA | 2-1 | 0-0 | 0-2 | 1-0 | 0-1 | 2-1 | 1-0 | | 1-0 | ⊗ | 7-0 | 5-1 | 3-2 | 1-0 | 3-1 | 2-1 | 2-0 | 1-0 |
| FC FARUL CONSTANTA | 0-0 | 0-0 | 1-2 | 1-0 | 3-0 | 2-0 | 0-0 | 3-0 | | 3-1 | 2-1 | 3-1 | 0-0 | 1-0 | 0-0 | 3-1 | 2-1 | 1-1 |
| FC BIHOR ORADEA | 2-2 | 1-3 | 0-2 | 0-1 | 2-2 | 3-1 | 1-1 | 2-3 | 0-0 | | 2-2 | 2-1 | 1-3 | 3-1 | 4-1 | 0-0 | 3-2 | 1-1 |
| SPORTUL STUDENTESC BUC. | 1-3 | 1-2 | 2-2 | 0-2 | 3-0 | 1-1 | 1-0 | 1-1 | 2-2 | 2-0 | | 1-0 | 3-0 | 3-1 | 3-1 | 0-0 | 4-1 | 4-1 |
| FC ARGES PITESTI | 1-1 | 1-1 | 2-0 | 2-0 | 1-1 | 0-1 | 3-0 | 2-1 | 3-1 | 4-1 | 3-1 | | 5-1 | 3-0 | 1-0 | 4-0 | 2-1 | 2-0 |
| JIUL PETROSANI | 1-2 | 1-1 | 0-1 | 1-1 | 3-1 | 2-1 | 4-0 | 2-0 | 1-0 | 1-0 | 3-1 | 2-2 | | 3-0 | 2-1 | 3-1 | 1-2 | 1-3 |
| UNIVERSITATEA CLUJ-NAP. | 0-3 | 2-0 | 0-1 | 1-0 | 1-2 | 0-2 | 2-1 | 2-0 | ⊗ | 5-1 | 1-1 | 0-0 | 0-0 | | 2-2 | 0-1 | 0-0 | 0-3 |
| FC BACAU | 0-0 | 0-0 | 1-0 | 0-0 | 2-0 | 3-1 | 1-0 | 2-0 | 0-1 | 3-1 | 1-1 | 2-0 | 2-1 | | | 2-1 | 2-1 | 1-0 |
| FCM PROGRESUL BRAILA | 2-1 | 1-1 | 0-1 | 0-1 | 1-0 | 2-0 | 1-3 | 3-0 | 1-1 | 3-2 | 0-1 | 2-1 | 4-1 | 3-1 | 1-0 | | 1-0 | 1-0 |
| RAPID BUCURESTI | 0-0 | 0-2 | 1-4 | 2-1 | 2-1 | 0-1 | 2-1 | 0-0 | 2-0 | 4-0 | 2-2 | 1-0 | 6-1 | 3-0 | 3-1 | 1-0 | | 1-0 |
| GLORIA BISTRITA | 1-1 | 1-2 | 1-0 | 3-2 | 2-1 | 1-0 | 3-2 | 4-1 | 2-0 | 3-1 | 0-0 | 0-0 | 5-0 | 2-1 | 2-1 | 1-0 | 5-0 | |

⊗ FC Bihor Oradea were suspended for the Season's first round, the match Corvinul Hunedoara v FC Bihor Oradea being awarded Corvinul 3 FC Bihor 0.

The match Universitatea Cluj-Napoca 3 FC Farul Constanta 1 was later awarded Universitatea Cluj-Napoca 0 FC Farul Constanta 3.

## RUMANIA 1ST DIVISION 1990/91

### LEAGUE TABLE FINAL

| | | | | | | | | |
|---|---|---|---|---|---|---|---|---|
| Universitatea Craiova | 34 | 22 | 6 | 6 | 74 | 26 | 50 |
| Steaua Bucuresti | 34 | 20 | 10 | 4 | 67 | 28 | 50 |
| Dinamo Bucuresti | 34 | 16 | 11 | 7 | 54 | 27 | 43 |
| FC Inter Sibiu | 34 | 18 | 2 | 14 | 56 | 46 | 38 |
| Gloria Bistrita | 34 | 15 | 7 | 12 | 51 | 38 | 37 |
| Politehnica Timisoara | 34 | 14 | 7 | 13 | 45 | 45 | 35 |
| Petrolul Ploesti | 34 | 15 | 5 | 14 | 48 | 49 | 35 |
| FC Arges Pitesti | 34 | 13 | 8 | 13 | 49 | 42 | 34 |
| FCM Brasov | 34 | 14 | 6 | 14 | 47 | 45 | 34 |
| FC Farul Constanta | 34 | 12 | 10 | 12 | 40 | 40 | 34 |
| Rapid Bucuresti | 34 | 13 | 6 | 15 | 44 | 45 | 32 |
| Sportul Studentesc B'resti | 34 | 10 | 12 | 12 | 45 | 53 | 32 |
| FCM Progresul Braila | 34 | 13 | 5 | 16 | 33 | 49 | 32 |
| Corvinul Hunedoara | 34 | 15 | 2 | 17 | 47 | 62 | 30 |
| FC Bacau | 34 | 11 | 7 | 16 | 32 | 42 | 29 |
| Jiul Petrosani | 34 | 11 | 6 | 17 | 46 | 65 | 28 |
| FC Bihor Oradea | 34 | 7 | 8 | 19 | 40 | 75 | 18 |
| Universitatea Cluj-Napoca | 34 | 5 | 6 | 23 | 26 | 67 | 16 |

Cornivul Hunedoara had 2 points deducted
FC Bihor Oradea had 4 points deducted

Champions : - Universitatea Craiova
Relegated : - Jiul Petrosani, FC Bihor Oradea and Universitatea Cluj-Napoca

NAME CHANGE : -
SC Bacau to FC Bacau

### TOP SCORERS

1. Ovidiu Hanganu (Corvinul) — 24
2. Marian Bicu (Jiul) — 17
3. Marian Damaschin (Dinamo) — 15
   Gabor Gerstenmajer (Brasov) — 15
5. Ion Vladoiu (FC Arges/Steaua) — 14
6. Gheorghe Ciurea (Univ. Craiova) — 13
   Dan Petrescu (Steaua) — 13
   Emil Sandoi (Univ. Craiova) — 13
   Eusebiu Ion Suvagau (Gloria) — 13
   Adrian Vasii (FC Inter) — 13
11. Ovidiu Lazar (Steaua/FC Bihor) — 12
    Adrian Pigulea (Univ. Craiova) — 12
13. Burchel (FC Inter) — 11
    Daniel Iflodi (Gloria) — 11
    Costel Lazar (Petrolul) — 11
16. Pavel Badea (Univ. Craiova) — 10
    Vasile Caciureac (Rapid) — 10
    Ionel Dragoi (FCM Progresul) — 10
    Gabriel Marian Raduta (Sportul St.) — 10
    Ilie Stan (Steaua) — 10
    Ion Timofte (Politehnica) — 10
    Constantin Varga (Politehnica) — 10

## RUMANIA 2ND DIVISION SERIA I 1990/91

### LEAGUE TABLE FINAL

| | | | | | | | | |
|---|---|---|---|---|---|---|---|---|
| Otelul Galati | 34 | 21 | 5 | 8 | 65 | 30 | 47 |
| Gloria Buzau | 34 | 17 | 7 | 10 | 63 | 42 | 41 |
| Ceahlaul Piatra Neamt | 34 | 16 | 6 | 12 | 51 | 39 | 38 |
| Politehnica Iasi | 34 | 16 | 6 | 12 | 51 | 43 | 38 |
| Steaua Mizil | 34 | 17 | 4 | 13 | 39 | 38 | 38 |
| Gloria CFR Galati | 34 | 16 | 4 | 14 | 68 | 41 | 36 |
| Foresta Falticeni | 34 | 17 | 2 | 15 | 71 | 59 | 36 |
| Unirea Slobozia | 34 | 17 | 2 | 15 | 60 | 50 | 36 |
| Unirea Focsani | 34 | 16 | 4 | 14 | 48 | 41 | 36 |
| CSM Suceava | 34 | 14 | 7 | 13 | 46 | 38 | 35 |
| Callatis Mangalia | 34 | 15 | 5 | 14 | 48 | 45 | 35 |
| Olimpia Rimnicu Sarat | 34 | 14 | 5 | 15 | 35 | 51 | 33 |
| Aripile Victoria Bacau | 34 | 13 | 6 | 15 | 47 | 45 | 32 |
| CSM Borzesti | 34 | 13 | 5 | 16 | 49 | 58 | 31 |
| Siretul Pascani | 34 | 12 | 3 | 19 | 34 | 69 | 27 |
| Prahova Ploesti | 34 | 11 | 4 | 19 | 37 | 62 | 26 |
| Poiana Cimpina | 34 | 10 | 6 | 18 | 35 | 66 | 26 |
| Fortus Iasi | 34 | 10 | 1 | 23 | 48 | 78 | 21 |

Promoted : - Otelul Galati
Relegated : - Siretul Pascani, Prahova Ploesti, Poiana Cimpina and Fortus Iasi.

| RUMANIA Divizia B Seria I Season 1990/91 | GLORIA B | OTELUL | P'TEHNICA | STEAUA | OLIMPIA | SUCEAVA | ARIPILE | FORESTA | UNIREA F | PRAHOVA | UNIREA S | POIANA | CEAHLAUL | SIRETUL | GLORIA G | CALLATIS | BORZESTI | FORTUS |
|---|---|---|---|---|---|---|---|---|---|---|---|---|---|---|---|---|---|---|
| GLORIA BUZAU | ■ | 2-0 | 1-0 | 1-1 | 3-0 | 0-1 | 2-0 | 6-4 | 2-2 | 3-0 | 2-0 | 4-0 | 2-0 | 5-0 | 1-1 | 4-1 | 4-1 | 1-0 |
| OTELUL GALATI | 2-1 | ■ | 2-0 | 4-0 | 2-0 | 3-0 | 0-1 | 6-0 | 2-1 | 2-0 | 3-1 | 3-0 | 1-3 | 5-0 | 2-1 | 2-1 | 1-0 | 6-1 |
| POLITEHNICA IASI | 1-1 | 1-2 | ■ | 3-0 | 2-0 | 2-0 | 0-0 | 7-2 | 1-0 | 2-0 | 4-1 | 3-0 | 1-0 | 3-1 | 3-0 | 2-0 | 2-0 | 2-1 |
| STEAUA MIZIL | 1-2 | 1-1 | 1-1 | ■ | 1-0 | 3-0 | 2-2 | 1-0 | 1-0 | 1-0 | 0-1 | 1-0 | 1-0 | 2-0 | 2-0 | 2-1 | 2-0 | ⊗ |
| OLIMPIA RIMNICU SARAT | 0-0 | 0-1 | 2-0 | 0-1 | ■ | 1-0 | 3-2 | 1-0 | 2-0 | 3-0 | 2-1 | 0-0 | 0-0 | 4-0 | 3-1 | 2-1 | 2-0 | 2-1 |
| CSM SUCEAVA | 2-1 | 1-0 | 0-0 | 1-0 | 6-1 | ■ | 1-0 | 0-0 | 2-0 | 3-1 | 2-1 | 4-0 | 0-0 | 6-1 | 4-0 | 3-0 | 1-1 | 1-2 |
| ARIPILE BACAU | 1-2 | 0-2 | 5-0 | 0-1 | 2-0 | 2-1 | ■ | 3-0 | 2-1 | 4-0 | 3-1 | 3-1 | 4-2 | 4-1 | 0-0 | 0-0 | 1-1 | 2-1 |
| FORESTA FALTICENI | 3-2 | 0-0 | 4-0 | 2-0 | 3-0 | 4-1 | 3-0 | ■ | 5-0 | 3-2 | 5-1 | 4-1 | 4-2 | 5-0 | 1-0 | 3-0 | 3-0 | 1-0 |
| UNIREA FOCSANI | 4-2 | 0-0 | 2-0 | 3-0 | 2-0 | 0-0 | 2-0 | 1-0 | ■ | 2-0 | 1-0 | 5-0 | 3-1 | 2-0 | 1-0 | 1-0 | 2-0 | 2-1 |
| PRAHOVA PLOESTI | 1-1 | 2-3 | 1-0 | 0-1 | 1-1 | 2-0 | 0-0 | 2-0 | 3-2 | ■ | 3-1 | 2-1 | 2-0 | 1-1 | 2-1 | 3-1 | 1-0 | 3-0 |
| UNIREA SLOBOZIA | 3-3 | 1-0 | 3-1 | 2-0 | 5-0 | 3-0 | 1-0 | 5-2 | 2-0 | 2-1 | ■ | 2-0 | 3-1 | 4-0 | 0-2 | 2-1 | 4-1 | 4-1 |
| POIANA CIMPINA | 2-1 | 2-2 | 2-3 | 3-1 | 1-2 | 2-1 | 1-0 | 2-1 | 0-1 | 3-0 | 0-0 | ■ | 0-1 | 2-0 | 1-1 | 0-0 | 3-1 | 2-0 |
| CEAHLAUL PIATRA NEAMT | 1-0 | ⊗ | 2-0 | 3-1 | 1-1 | 1-1 | 2-0 | 4-2 | 1-1 | 5-1 | 1-0 | 4-1 | ■ | 1-1 | 1-0 | 1-0 | 4-0 | 2-0 |
| SIRETUL PASCANI | 2-1 | 1-0 | 1-2 | 1-0 | 4-0 | 1-0 | 2-3 | 1-0 | 3-2 | 1-0 | 2-1 | 3-0 | ⊗ | ■ | 1-0 | 0-2 | 2-2 | 2-0 |
| GLORIA CFR GALATI | 5-0 | 2-4 | 1-1 | 1-0 | 4-0 | 2-1 | 5-0 | 6-2 | 3-1 | 3-2 | 3-1 | 8-0 | 2-0 | 4-1 | ■ | 4-2 | 4-1 | 4-0 |
| CALLATIS MANGALIA | 0-1 | 1-1 | 2-0 | 3-0 | 1-0 | 3-1 | 2-1 | 2-0 | 3-2 | 2-0 | 1-0 | 1-1 | 3-0 | 1-0 | 1-0 | ■ | 5-0 | 4-1 |
| CSM BORZESTI | 3-1 | 2-1 | 2-0 | 1-3 | 5-0 | 0-0 | 1-0 | 1-0 | 2-1 | 7-0 | 3-1 | 1-3 | 1-0 | 2-1 | 1-0 | 3-3 | ■ | 5-0 |
| FORTUS IASI | 0-1 | 1-2 | 4-4 | 2-5 | 0-3 | 1-2 | 4-2 | 2-5 | 3-1 | 3-1 | 2-3 | 3-1 | 3-1 | 2-0 | 1-0 | 5-0 | 3-1 | ■ |

⊗ The match Steaua Mizil v Fortus Iasi was awarded Steaua 3 Fortus 0.
The match Ceahlaul Piatra Neamt 0 Otelul Galati 0 was later awarded Ceahlaul 3 Otelul 0.
The match Siretul Pascani 3 Ceahlaul Piatra Neamt 2 was later awarded Siretul Pascani 0 Ceahlaul Piatra Neamt 3.

## RUMANIA 2ND DIVISION SERIA II-a 1990/91

### LEAGUE TABLE FINAL

| | | | | | | | |
|---|---|---|---|---|---|---|---|
| Electroputere Craiova | 34 | 21 | 6 | 7 | 93 | 38 | 46 |
| Chimia Rimnicu Vilcea | 34 | 20 | 6 | 8 | 69 | 27 | 46 |
| CS Tirgoviste | 34 | 17 | 4 | 13 | 52 | 48 | 38 |
| Sportul 30 Decembrie | 34 | 15 | 7 | 12 | 57 | 37 | 37 |
| Soimii IPA Sibiu | 34 | 17 | 3 | 14 | 52 | 46 | 37 |
| Tractorul Brasov | 34 | 15 | 5 | 14 | 58 | 54 | 35 |
| Metalurgistul Slatina | 34 | 16 | 3 | 15 | 53 | 52 | 35 |
| Flacara Moreni | 34 | 12 | 10 | 12 | 47 | 34 | 34 |
| CF Drobeta Turnu Severin | 34 | 15 | 4 | 15 | 62 | 54 | 34 |
| FCM Caracal | 34 | 13 | 7 | 14 | 59 | 61 | 33 |
| Gaz Metan Medias | 34 | 15 | 3 | 16 | 57 | 60 | 33 |
| ICIM Brasov | 34 | 15 | 3 | 16 | 40 | 43 | 33 |
| Autobuzul Bucuresti | 34 | 14 | 5 | 15 | 48 | 56 | 33 |
| Progresul Soimii Bucuresti | 34 | 13 | 6 | 15 | 45 | 48 | 32 |
| Mecanica Fina Bucuresti | 34 | 12 | 7 | 15 | 40 | 50 | 31 |
| Pandurii Tirgu Jiu | 34 | 13 | 3 | 18 | 32 | 63 | 29 |
| Minerul Motru | 34 | 10 | 5 | 19 | 30 | 72 | 25 |
| M'tana Caraimanul Busteni | 34 | 7 | 5 | 22 | 26 | 77 | 19 |

Electroputere Craiova had 2 points deducted

Promoted : - Electroputere Craiova
Relegated : - Mecanica Fina Bucuresti, Pandurii Tirgu Jiu, Minerul Motru
And Montana Caraimanul Busteni.

### NAME CHANGES

IPA Sibiu to Soimii IPA Sibiu
Progresul Bucuresti to Progresul Soimii Bucuresti
Montana Sinaia to Montana Caraimanul Busteni

## RUMANIA 2ND DIVISION SERIA III-a 1990/91

### LEAGUE TABLE FINAL

| | | | | | | | |
|---|---|---|---|---|---|---|---|
| ASA Electro.Tirgu Mures | 34 | 18 | 9 | 7 | 54 | 38 | 45 |
| CFR Timisoara | 34 | 19 | 5 | 10 | 60 | 35 | 43 |
| Olimpia Satu Mare | 34 | 17 | 7 | 10 | 47 | 29 | 41 |
| FC Maramures Baia Mare | 34 | 18 | 4 | 12 | 84 | 42 | 40 |
| FCM UT Arad | 34 | 18 | 4 | 12 | 68 | 32 | 40 |
| Gloria Resita | 34 | 16 | 8 | 10 | 47 | 29 | 40 |
| Unirea Alba Iulia | 34 | 18 | 3 | 13 | 53 | 43 | 39 |
| Armatura Zalau | 34 | 16 | 4 | 14 | 49 | 43 | 36 |
| CS Astra Arad | 34 | 17 | 2 | 15 | 61 | 56 | 36 |
| FC Aris Arad | 34 | 14 | 8 | 12 | 51 | 46 | 36 |
| CSM Resita | 34 | 13 | 8 | 13 | 42 | 48 | 34 |
| Metalul Bocsa | 34 | 15 | 3 | 16 | 36 | 47 | 33 |
| Metalurgistul Cugir | 34 | 13 | 5 | 16 | 47 | 47 | 31 |
| Chimica Tirnaveni | 34 | 14 | 2 | 18 | 37 | 56 | 30 |
| Vulturii Textila Lugoj | 34 | 13 | 3 | 18 | 38 | 61 | 29 |
| CIL Sighet | 34 | 8 | 8 | 18 | 32 | 62 | 24 |
| Aurul Brad | 34 | 8 | 6 | 20 | 33 | 67 | 22 |
| ASA Progresul Timisoara | 34 | 6 | 1 | 27 | 29 | 87 | 13 |

Promoted : - ASA Electromures Tirgu Mures
Relegated : - Vulturii Textila Lugoj, CIL Sighet, Aurul Brad and ASA Progresul Timisoara

### NAME CHANGES

CS Vagonul Arad to CS Astra Arad
Strungul Arad to FC Aris Arad

## RUMANIA — Divizia B Seria II-a — Season 1990/91

| | FLACARA | AS DROBETA | CHIMIA | SP.30 DEC. | TIRGOVISTE | CARACAL | MEC. FINA | MINERUL | GAZ METAN | AUTOBUZUL | M'GISTUL | ICIM | PANDURII | TRACTORUL | E'PUTERE | IPA | PROGRESUL | MONTANA |
|---|---|---|---|---|---|---|---|---|---|---|---|---|---|---|---|---|---|---|
| FLACARA MORENI | ■ | 5-1 | 0-2 | 2-0 | 2-1 | 5-0 | 0-0 | 1-1 | 1-1 | 3-1 | 3-0 | 4-2 | 2-0 | 1-0 | 2-4 | 2-0 | 2-0 | 6-0 |
| CF DROBETA TURNU SEVERIN | 4-0 | ■ | 2-2 | 5-2 | 3-0 | 5-2 | 1-0 | 1-0 | 2-1 | 1-2 | 7-0 | 1-1 | 1-0 | 6-0 | 0-0 | 3-0 | 2-0 | 6-1 |
| CHIMIA RIMNICU VILCEA | 0-0 | 2-0 | ■ | 1-0 | 3-0 | 3-0 | 2-1 | 4-0 | 4-1 | 2-0 | 3-0 | 2-0 | 5-0 | 3-0 | 2-3 | 4-0 | 4-2 | 5-1 |
| SPORTUL 30 DECEMBRIE | 2-0 | 2-0 | 1-1 | ■ | 3-1 | 3-0 | 1-1 | 10-1 | 4-1 | 3-0 | 1-0 | 1-0 | 3-0 | 2-0 | 2-3 | 2-0 | 1-0 | 5-1 |
| CS TIRGOVISTE | 1-0 | 3-1 | 3-1 | 2-0 | ■ | 0-0 | 2-1 | 3-0 | 4-1 | 1-0 | 2-0 | 1-0 | 4-0 | 2-0 | 1-0 | 2-0 | 2-1 | 3-0 |
| FCM CARACAL | 1-0 | 4-1 | 1-1 | 0-0 | 1-1 | ■ | 4-1 | 6-2 | 2-0 | 2-0 | 2-0 | 4-0 | 3-0 | 4-3 | 2-2 | 3-0 | 2-0 | 3-1 |
| MECANICA FINA BUCURESTI | 1-0 | 3-2 | 2-1 | 0-3 | 2-0 | 2-1 | ■ | 3-0 | 2-1 | 0-1 | 2-1 | 2-0 | 4-0 | 1-1 | 3-2 | 2-0 | 2-2 | 1-1 |
| MINERUL MOTRU | 0-0 | 2-3 | 0-3 | 2-1 | 0-0 | 2-1 | 1-0 | ■ | 2-1 | 4-0 | 0-2 | 2-0 | 2-0 | 1-0 | 2-4 | 0-1 | 2-0 | 1-0 |
| GAZ METAN MEDIAS | 1-1 | 1-1 | 1-0 | 1-0 | 5-2 | 3-0 | 4-3 | 2-0 | ■ | 1-0 | 3-0 | 4-1 | 5-2 | 4-0 | 3-0 | 1-0 | 2-1 | 2-1 |
| AUTOBUZUL BUCURESTI | 1-1 | 1-0 | 2-5 | 1-1 | 4-1 | 3-1 | 1-0 | 1-0 | 4-1 | ■ | 2-1 | 1-0 | 3-0 | 2-1 | 1-1 | 3-1 | 2-2 | 3-1 |
| METALURGISTUL SLATINA | 1-1 | 1-0 | 1-1 | 3-1 | 3-0 | 4-2 | 4-1 | 4-0 | 3-1 | 3-2 | ■ | 2-0 | 4-0 | 4-1 | 0-0 | 2-0 | 1-0 | 4-1 |
| ICIM BRASOV | 2-0 | 2-0 | 1-0 | 3-2 | 0-1 | 1-0 | 4-0 | 3-0 | 2-0 | 1-0 | 2-0 | ■ | 2-0 | 1-1 | 2-1 | 4-2 | 3-1 | 2-1 |
| PANDURII TIRGU JIU | 1-0 | 1-2 | 1-0 | 0-0 | 2-1 | 3-2 | 2-0 | 1-1 | 3-2 | 3-1 | 2-0 | 1-0 | ■ | 2-1 | 1-0 | 0-0 | 2-0 | 3-0 |
| TRACTORUL BRASOV | 1-0 | 4-0 | 1-0 | 3-0 | 3-1 | 1-1 | 2-0 | 6-0 | 3-1 | 6-3 | 2-0 | 0-0 | 3-1 | ■ | 1-1 | 1-0 | 2-1 | 4-0 |
| ELECTROPUTERE CRAIOVA | 1-1 | 5-1 | 2-0 | 4-1 | 5-2 | 4-0 | 4-0 | 5-0 | 5-1 | 4-0 | 4-2 | 3-0 | 7-0 | 6-4 | ■ | 3-1 | 3-0 | 5-1 |
| SOIMII IPA SIBIU | 2-2 | 5-0 | 0-0 | 1-0 | 3-2 | 5-1 | 2-0 | 1-0 | 2-0 | 2-1 | 3-1 | 2-0 | 1-0 | 4-1 | 1-0 | ■ | 4-1 | 4-0 |
| PROGRESUL SOIMII BUCUREST | 1-0 | 1-0 | 1-2 | 0-0 | 1-0 | 3-3 | 0-0 | 4-0 | 3-0 | 2-2 | 3-1 | 3-1 | 2-0 | 2-1 | 1-0 | 3-1 | ■ | 3-0 |
| MONTANA CAR'MANUL BUSTEN | 1-0 | 1-0 | 0-1 | 0-0 | 3-3 | 2-1 | 0-0 | 1-1 | 2-1 | 1-0 | 0-1 | 1-0 | 2-1 | 0-1 | 0-2 | 2-4 | 0-1 | ■ |

The match Minerul Motru 2 Progresul Soimii Bucuresti 0 was later awarded Minerul Motra 3 Progresul Soimii Bucuresti 0.

## RUMANIA — Divizia B Seria III-a — Season 1990/91

| | UNIREA | UTA | MARAMURES | CSM | CFR | CHIMICA | ASA ELEC. | ARMATURA | GLORIA | ASTRA | ARIS | OLIMPIA | METALUL | PROGRESUL | M'STUL | VULTURII T | CIL | AURUL |
|---|---|---|---|---|---|---|---|---|---|---|---|---|---|---|---|---|---|---|
| UNIREA ALBA IULIA | ■ | 2-1 | 2-1 | 3-2 | 4-1 | 2-0 | 4-1 | 3-0 | 2-0 | 4-2 | 1-1 | 2-1 | 1-0 | 3-1 | 3-1 | 2-0 | 2-0 | 2-0 |
| FCM UT ARAD | 3-0 | ■ | 2-1 | 2-1 | 6-0 | 3-1 | 2-0 | 0-0 | 1-0 | 8-3 | 4-0 | 0-1 | 2-1 | 3-0 | 3-0 | 4-0 | 2-0 | 6-0 |
| FC MARAMURES BAIA MARE | 4-1 | 3-0 | ■ | 2-0 | 3-1 | 4-0 | 2-3 | 3-0 | 1-0 | 4-0 | 0-0 | 3-0 | 5-0 | 12-1 | 4-2 | 6-1 | 5-3 | 6-3 |
| CSM RESITA | 1-0 | 3-1 | 1-1 | ■ | 1-1 | 3-1 | 0-0 | 3-1 | 1-0 | 2-1 | 1-0 | 3-3 | 3-2 | 3-2 | 0-0 | 2-1 | 2-1 | 1-0 |
| CFR TIMISOARA | 2-0 | 0-0 | 1-1 | 4-0 | ■ | 3-1 | 3-1 | 4-0 | 4-0 | 2-0 | 2-0 | 2-0 | 2-0 | 3-1 | 1-0 | 1-0 | 4-2 | 3-0 |
| CHIMICA TIRNAVENI | 1-0 | 3-2 | 2-0 | 2-0 | 1-0 | ■ | 1-2 | 3-2 | 1-0 | 3-0 | 0-0 | 2-0 | 3-0 | ⊗ | 1-0 | 2-1 | 3-1 | 2-1 |
| ASA ELECT' MURES TG. MURES | 2-1 | 2-0 | 2-0 | 0-0 | 2-1 | 1-0 | ■ | 2-1 | 1-0 | 3-0 | 1-1 | 4-2 | 3-0 | 4-2 | 4-1 | 3-0 | 1-0 | |
| ARMATURA ZALAU | 2-0 | 0-1 | 2-2 | 3-0 | 1-0 | 2-0 | 3-0 | ■ | 0-0 | 2-1 | 5-3 | 1-0 | 3-0 | 4-0 | 2-0 | 2-0 | 3-0 | 2-0 |
| GLORIA RESITA | 3-0 | 1-0 | 2-1 | 1-1 | 1-1 | 3-1 | 1-0 | 2-1 | ■ | 3-1 | 4-1 | 0-0 | 1-0 | 6-0 | 2-0 | 5-1 | 2-0 | 1-0 |
| CS ASTRA ARAD | 2-0 | 2-4 | 3-1 | 2-0 | 1-1 | 6-0 | 1-0 | 1-1 | | ■ | 4-1 | 1-0 | 1-2 | 3-0 | 3-2 | 6-0 | 1-0 | 5-0 |
| FC ARIS ARAD | 1-1 | 2-1 | 2-1 | 1-0 | 3-0 | 1-0 | 1-1 | 5-0 | 1-1 | 1-0 | ■ | 1-1 | 2-0 | 4-2 | 5-0 | 3-1 | 5-1 | 2-0 |
| OLIMPIA SATU MARE | 1-0 | 1-1 | 1-0 | 0-0 | 2-1 | 3-0 | 4-0 | 1-0 | 2-1 | 4-0 | 2-0 | ■ | 5-0 | 1-0 | 3-0 | 2-1 | 2-0 | 2-1 |
| METALUL BOCSA | 4-1 | 1-0 | 1-0 | 1-0 | 0-1 | 3-1 | 0-0 | 2-0 | 0-2 | 1-2 | 2-0 | 1-0 | ■ | 2-0 | 3-0 | 4-1 | 1-1 | 2-0 |
| ASA PROGRESUL TIMISOARA | 0-2 | 0-6 | 1-2 | 4-2 | 1-3 | 1-0 | 0-2 | 1-4 | 1-3 | 0-1 | 1-2 | 0-1 | 0-1 | ■ | 2-0 | 1-0 | 0-0 | 4-0 |
| METALURGISTUL CUGIR | 2-1 | 0-0 | 0-2 | 3-1 | 0-4 | 2-0 | 1-1 | 3-0 | 3-0 | 2-0 | 3-0 | 1-0 | 3-0 | 4-0 | ■ | 5-0 | 3-0 | 4-0 |
| VULTURII TEXTILA LUGOJ | 1-1 | 1-0 | 3-1 | 1-3 | 1-0 | 5-1 | 0-0 | 1-0 | 1-0 | 0-2 | 1-0 | 2-1 | 3-0 | 3-0 | 0-0 | ■ | 2-0 | 1-0 |
| CIL SIGHET | 2-0 | 1-0 | 1-0 | 2-1 | 0-3 | 2-1 | 2-2 | 1-1 | 0-0 | 4-2 | 2-0 | 0-0 | 1-2 | 2-0 | 1-1 | 1-3 | ■ | 1-1 |
| AURUL BRAD | 0-3 | 2-0 | 1-3 | 2-1 | 2-1 | 0-0 | 3-3 | 1-2 | 1-1 | 1-3 | 3-2 | 1-1 | 0-0 | 2-1 | 1-0 | 2-1 | 5-0 | ■ |

⊗ The match Chimica Tirnaveni v ASA Progresul Timisoara did not take place and was awarded Chimica Tirnaveni 0 ASA Progresul

1. Ladislau Bölöni (ASA Tirgu Mures/Steaua Bucuresti/Racing Jette) — 108
2. Michael Klein (Corvinul Hunedoara/Dinamo Bucuresti/Bayer Uerdingen) — 86
3. Mircea Rednic (Corvinul Hunedoara/Dinamo Bucuresti) — 81
4. Cornel Dinu (Dinamo Bucuresti) — 75
   Rodion Camataru (Universitatea Craiova/Dinamo Bucuresti/Charleroi SC) — 75
6. Mircea Lucescu (Stiinta Bucuresti/Dinamo Bucuresti/Corvinul Hunedoara) — 70
   Silviu Lung (Universitatea Craiova/Steaua Bucuresti/CD Logrones) — 70
8. Ilie Balaci (Universitatea Craiova/FC Olt/Dinamo Bucuresti) — 69
9. Costica Stefanescu (Steaua Bucuresti/Universitatea Craiova/FCM Brasov) — 66
10. Anghel Iordanescu (Steaua Bucuresti) — 64
    Gheorghe Hagi (FC Constanta/Sportul Studentsc Bucuresti/Steaua Bucuresti/Real Madrid) — 64

## RUMANIA 3RD DIVISION SERIA I 1990/91

### LEAGUE TABLE FINAL

| | | | | | | | | |
|---|---|---|---|---|---|---|---|---|
| Relonul Savinesti | 28 | 19 | 4 | 5 | 53 | 19 | 42 |
| CS Botosani | 28 | 17 | 6 | 5 | 56 | 23 | 40 |
| CFR Pascani | 28 | 17 | 4 | 7 | 67 | 41 | 38 |
| Bucovina Radauti | 28 | 17 | 3 | 8 | 53 | 29 | 37 |
| Constructorul Iasi | 28 | 15 | 2 | 11 | 44 | 32 | 32 |
| Vointa Roman | 28 | 15 | 1 | 12 | 63 | 42 | 31 |
| ASA Explorari Cimpulung | 28 | 15 | 1 | 12 | 38 | 36 | 31 |
| Minerul Gura Humorului | 28 | 13 | 0 | 15 | 41 | 51 | 26 |
| Steaua Minerul V.Dornei | 28 | 10 | 3 | 15 | 45 | 49 | 23 |
| Carpati Galanesti | 28 | 10 | 3 | 15 | 32 | 47 | 23 |
| Cristalul Dorohoi | 28 | 10 | 2 | 16 | 41 | 44 | 22 |
| Aurora Tirgu Frumos | 28 | 9 | 4 | 15 | 34 | 43 | 22 |
| Metalul Roman | 28 | 9 | 4 | 15 | 22 | 45 | 22 |
| CSM Bucecea | 28 | 9 | 2 | 17 | 33 | 56 | 20 |
| Avintul Frasin | 28 | 5 | 1 | 22 | 13 | 78 | 11 |
| Zimbrui Siret expelled | | | | | | | |

Promoted : - Relonul Savinesti
Relegated :- Avintul Frasin and Zimbru Siret

## RUMANIA 3RD DIV. SERIA A III-a 1990/91

### LEAGUE TABLE FINAL

| | | | | | | | | |
|---|---|---|---|---|---|---|---|---|
| Petrolul Ianca | 28 | 19 | 4 | 5 | 78 | 20 | 42 |
| Petrolul Berca | 28 | 14 | 3 | 11 | 51 | 33 | 31 |
| Hidrotehnica Buzau | 28 | 14 | 2 | 12 | 51 | 37 | 30 |
| Metalul Buzau | 28 | 13 | 3 | 12 | 41 | 40 | 29 |
| Chimia Braila | 28 | 12 | 4 | 12 | 43 | 44 | 28 |
| IMASA Sfantu Gheorghe | 28 | 13 | 1 | 14 | 48 | 42 | 27 |
| Metalul Tirgu Secuiesc | 28 | 13 | 1 | 14 | 59 | 53 | 27 |
| Foresta Gugesti | 28 | 13 | 1 | 14 | 47 | 42 | 27 |
| Autobuzul Marasesti | 28 | 12 | 3 | 13 | 40 | 60 | 27 |
| Chimia Buzau | 28 | 11 | 4 | 13 | 41 | 35 | 26 |
| Celuloza Adjud | 28 | 12 | 2 | 14 | 36 | 49 | 26 |
| Unirea Faurei | 28 | 12 | 2 | 14 | 46 | 74 | 26 |
| Tricotex Panciu | 28 | 11 | 4 | 13 | 31 | 70 | 26 |
| Electro Sfantu Gheorghe | 28 | 11 | 3 | 14 | 46 | 47 | 25 |
| Minerul Baraolt | 28 | 11 | 1 | 16 | 34 | 46 | 23 |
| Carpati Covasna expelled | | | | | | | |

Promoted : - Petrolul Ianca
Relegated :- Minerul Baraolt and Carpati Covasna

## RUMANIA 3RD DIV. SERIA A II-a 1990/91

### LEAGUE TABLE FINAL

| | | | | | | | | |
|---|---|---|---|---|---|---|---|---|
| FEPA 74 Birlad | 28 | 21 | 1 | 6 | 74 | 27 | 43 |
| Textila Burlusi | 28 | 17 | 3 | 8 | 70 | 27 | 37 |
| Victoria Galati | 28 | 18 | 1 | 9 | 74 | 35 | 37 |
| Partizanul Bacau | 28 | 16 | 1 | 11 | 58 | 32 | 33 |
| Stiinta NAVROM Galati | 28 | 14 | 4 | 10 | 42 | 28 | 32 |
| Metalurgistul Tecuci | 28 | 15 | 1 | 12 | 53 | 45 | 31 |
| Minerul Comanesti | 28 | 13 | 4 | 11 | 46 | 36 | 30 |
| Steaua Mecanica Husi | 28 | 15 | 0 | 13 | 53 | 45 | 30 |
| Petrolul Monesti | 28 | 12 | 2 | 14 | 35 | 44 | 26 |
| MECON Onesti | 28 | 12 | 1 | 15 | 50 | 50 | 25 |
| Mecanica Vaslui | 28 | 10 | 3 | 15 | 52 | 46 | 23 |
| Proletarul Bě.cau | 28 | 10 | 2 | 16 | 35 | 61 | 22 |
| Unirea Birlad | 28 | 10 | 1 | 17 | 38 | 82 | 21 |
| Gloria Ivesti | 28 | 7 | 5 | 16 | 29 | 80 | 19 |
| Unirea Negresti | 28 | 4 | 3 | 21 | 17 | 88 | 11 |
| Prutul 90 Falciu expelled | | | | | | | |

Promoted :- FEPA 74 Birlad
Relegated :- Unirea Negresti and Prutul 90 Falciu

## RUMANIA 3RD DIV. SERIA A IV-a 1990/91

### LEAGUE TABLE FINAL

| | | | | | | | | |
|---|---|---|---|---|---|---|---|---|
| Portul Constanta | 26 | 18 | 5 | 3 | 78 | 19 | 41 |
| Dunarea Calarasi | 26 | 16 | 5 | 5 | 52 | 17 | 37 |
| Progresul CSS Medgidia | 26 | 17 | 3 | 6 | 58 | 24 | 37 |
| Victoria Lehliu | 26 | 12 | 4 | 10 | 43 | 41 | 28 |
| ISCIP Ulmeni | 26 | 11 | 5 | 10 | 61 | 35 | 27 |
| Santierul N.Oltenita | 26 | 12 | 3 | 11 | 48 | 36 | 27 |
| Muscelul Campulung | 26 | 11 | 3 | 12 | 35 | 39 | 25 |
| Dunarea Zimnicea | 26 | 9 | 6 | 11 | 44 | 43 | 24 |
| Unirea Pitesti | 26 | 10 | 2 | 14 | 52 | 41 | 22 |
| Unirea Urziceni | 26 | 10 | 2 | 14 | 42 | 50 | 22 |
| Rapid Fetesti | 26 | 8 | 5 | 13 | 37 | 54 | 21 |
| Arrubium Macin | 26 | 9 | 3 | 14 | 29 | 58 | 21 |
| Viitorul Chirnogi | 26 | 8 | 3 | 15 | 40 | 51 | 19 |
| Olimpia Slobozia | 26 | 5 | 1 | 20 | 21 | 132 | 11 |
| Progresul Isaccea expelled | | | | | | | |
| Fortuna Tulcea expelled | | | | | | | |

Promoted : - Portul Constanta
Relegated :- Progresul Isaccea and Fortuna Tulcea

1. Iuliu Bodola (CAO Oradea/Venus Bucuresti) — 108
2. Anghel Iordanescu (Steaua Bucuresti) — 86
3. Ladislau Bölöni (ASA Tirgu Mures/Steaua Bucuresti/Racing Jette) — 81
4. Rodion Camataru (Universitatea Craiova/Dinamo Bucuresti/Charleroi SC) — 75
5. Dudu Georgescu (Dinamo Bucuresti) — 75
6. Stefan Dobai (Ripensia Timisoara) — 70
7. Florea Dumitrache (Dinamo Bucuresti/Corvinul Hunedoara) — 70
8. Gratian Sepi (Politehnica Timisoara/Banatul Timisoara/Romania Cluj/Venus Bucuresti/Ripensia Timisoara) — 69
   Gheorghe Hagi (FC Constanta/Sportul Studensc Bucuresti/Steaua Bucuresti/Real Madrid) — 64

## RUMANIA 3RD DIV. SERIA A V-a 1990/91

### LEAGUE TABLE FINAL

| | | | | | | | | |
|---|---|---|---|---|---|---|---|---|
| Metalul Bucuresti | 28 | 20 | 5 | 3 | 83 | 28 | 45 |
| IMG Bucuresti | 28 | 20 | 3 | 5 | 73 | 24 | 43 |
| Mecos Bucuresti | 28 | 12 | 4 | 12 | 51 | 44 | 28 |
| MECON Bucuresti | 28 | 12 | 4 | 12 | 41 | 40 | 28 |
| Electrica Titu | 28 | 12 | 3 | 13 | 53 | 47 | 27 |
| Automatica Bucuresti | 28 | 12 | 2 | 14 | 39 | 34 | 26 |
| Danubiana Bucuresti | 28 | 13 | 4 | 13 | 38 | 46 | 26 |
| Tehnometal Bucuresti | 28 | 11 | 4 | 13 | 33 | 45 | 26 |
| Victoria Giurgiu | 28 | 12 | 2 | 14 | 28 | 55 | 26 |
| IUPS Chitila | 28 | 11 | 3 | 14 | 41 | 61 | 25 |
| Vointa Bucuresti | 28 | 9 | 6 | 13 | 48 | 45 | 24 |
| Viscofil Bucuresti | 28 | 10 | 4 | 14 | 40 | 40 | 24 |
| Dunarea Giurgiu | 28 | 10 | 4 | 14 | 36 | 48 | 24 |
| CFR BTA Bucuresti | 28 | 11 | 2 | 15 | 44 | 58 | 24 |
| Avicola Crevedia | 28 | 11 | 2 | 15 | 39 | 72 | 24 |
| Stiinta Baneasa expelled | | | | | | | |

Promoted :- Metalul Bucuresti
Relegated :- Avicola Crevedia and Stiinta Baneasa

## RUMANIA 3RD DIV. SERIA A VI-a 1990/91

### LEAGUE TABLE FINAL

| | | | | | | | | |
|---|---|---|---|---|---|---|---|---|
| Metrom Brasov | 30 | 19 | 2 | 9 | 61 | 24 | 40 |
| Metalul Plopeni | 30 | 15 | 3 | 12 | 62 | 39 | 33 |
| Victoria Floresti | 30 | 16 | 1 | 13 | 44 | 36 | 33 |
| Torpedo Zarnesti | 30 | 15 | 3 | 12 | 45 | 43 | 33 |
| Chimia Ploiesti | 30 | 15 | 2 | 13 | 43 | 36 | 32 |
| Precizia Sacele | 30 | 13 | 5 | 12 | 50 | 50 | 31 |
| Carpati Sinaia | 30 | 14 | 3 | 13 | 52 | 53 | 31 |
| Metalul Filipesti | 30 | 14 | 2 | 14 | 40 | 37 | 30 |
| Metalul Mija | 30 | 14 | 2 | 14 | 49 | 49 | 30 |
| Minerul Filipesti | 30 | 14 | 1 | 15 | 47 | 45 | 29 |
| Nitramonia Fagaras | 30 | 13 | 3 | 14 | 41 | 45 | 29 |
| Cimentul Fieni | 30 | 13 | 2 | 15 | 45 | 45 | 28 |
| Chimia Gaesti | 30 | 12 | 3 | 15 | 49 | 45 | 27 |
| Petrolul Tirgoviste | 30 | 12 | 3 | 15 | 31 | 50 | 27 |
| Minerul Sotinga | 30 | 12 | 3 | 15 | 32 | 69 | 27 |
| Electromotor Cimpina | 30 | 8 | 4 | 18 | 29 | 54 | 20 |

Promoted :- Metrom Brasov
Relegated :- Minerul Sotinga and Electromotor Cimpina

## RUMANIA 3RD DIV. SERIA A VII-a 1990/91

### LEAGUE TABLE FINAL

| | | | | | | | | |
|---|---|---|---|---|---|---|---|---|
| CS Olt 90 | 30 | 23 | 2 | 5 | 64 | 17 | 48 |
| Unirea Alexandria | 30 | 21 | 3 | 6 | 61 | 23 | 45 |
| Dacia Pitesti | 30 | 15 | 5 | 10 | 53 | 27 | 35 |
| Chimia Tarnu Magurele | 30 | 15 | 4 | 11 | 51 | 37 | 34 |
| Rova Rosiori | 30 | 13 | 6 | 11 | 45 | 35 | 32 |
| Electronistul C. Arges | 30 | 13 | 6 | 11 | 50 | 46 | 32 |
| Muscelul Campulung | 30 | 13 | 5 | 12 | 45 | 35 | 31 |
| Dunarea Zimnicea | 30 | 12 | 6 | 12 | 40 | 50 | 30 |
| Unirea Pitesti | 30 | 13 | 2 | 15 | 45 | 38 | 28 |
| Metalul Rimnicu Vilcea | 30 | 12 | 4 | 14 | 44 | 53 | 28 |
| Viitorul Dragasani | 30 | 11 | 5 | 14 | 36 | 52 | 27 |
| Rulmentul Alexandria | 30 | 12 | 1 | 17 | 43 | 41 | 25 |
| Minerul Matasari | 30 | 12 | 1 | 17 | 43 | 72 | 25 |
| Dierna Orsova | 30 | 11 | 4 | 15 | 39 | 55 | 26 |
| Dacia Cozia Calimanesti | 30 | 11 | 3 | 16 | 50 | 57 | 25 |
| Progresul Bailesti | 30 | 11 | 3 | 16 | 44 | 53 | 25 |
| Armatura Strehaia | 30 | 4 | 1 | 25 | 13 | 94 | 9 |

Promoted : - Jiul IEELIF Craiova
Relegated : - Progresul Bailesti and Armatura Strehaia

## RUMANIA 3RD DIV.SERIA A VIII-a 1990/91

### LEAGUE TABLE FINAL

| | | | | | | | | |
|---|---|---|---|---|---|---|---|---|
| Jiul Craiova | 30 | 19 | 4 | 7 | 55 | 31 | 42 |
| Minerul Uricani | 30 | 17 | 3 | 10 | 53 | 30 | 37 |
| Arsenal Resita | 30 | 16 | 4 | 10 | 64 | 35 | 36 |
| Minerul Moldova Noua | 30 | 16 | 3 | 11 | 57 | 37 | 35 |
| CSM Caransebes | 30 | 16 | 3 | 11 | 48 | 35 | 35 |
| Minerul Berbesti | 30 | 17 | 1 | 12 | 35 | 43 | 35 |
| SUCPI Craiova | 30 | 13 | 6 | 11 | 55 | 49 | 32 |
| Petrolul Stoina | 30 | 13 | 4 | 12 | 46 | 49 | 32 |
| Minerul Anina | 30 | 13 | 3 | 14 | 57 | 45 | 29 |
| TCI Craiova | 30 | 11 | 5 | 14 | 54 | 48 | 27 |
| Petrolul Ticleni | 30 | 11 | 5 | 14 | 35 | 40 | 27 |
| Minerul Matasari | 30 | 12 | 3 | 15 | 38 | 44 | 27 |
| Dierna Orsova | 30 | 11 | 4 | 15 | 39 | 55 | 26 |
| Dacia Cozia Calimanesti | 30 | 11 | 3 | 16 | 50 | 57 | 25 |
| Progresul Bailesti | 30 | 11 | 3 | 16 | 44 | 53 | 25 |
| Armatura Strehaia | 30 | 4 | 1 | 25 | 13 | 94 | 9 |

Promoted : - Jiul IEELIF Craiova
Relegated : - Sportul Muncitoresc Dragaesti Olt and IO3 Bals

## RUMANIA 3RD DIV. SERIA A IX-a 1990/91

### LEAGUE TABLE FINAL

| | P | W | D | L | F | A | Pts |
|---|---|---|---|---|---|---|---|
| Electromures T.Mures | 30 | 19 | 5 | 6 | 82 | 31 | 43 |
| Avintul Reghin | 30 | 18 | 3 | 9 | 69 | 27 | 39 |
| Muresul Toplita | 30 | 18 | 3 | 9 | 60 | 30 | 39 |
| Progresul Odorhei | 30 | 15 | 4 | 11 | 49 | 37 | 34 |
| Unirea Cristur | 30 | 14 | 2 | 14 | 47 | 55 | 30 |
| Progresul Nasaud | 30 | 14 | 2 | 14 | 39 | 52 | 29 |
| Rapid Mercurea Ciuc. | 30 | 13 | 2 | 15 | 49 | 28 | |
| Mecanica Bistrita | 30 | 13 | 2 | 15 | 44 | 50 | 28 |
| Minerul Balan | 30 | 12 | 3 | 15 | 42 | 27 | 27 |
| Muresul Ludus | 30 | 11 | 5 | 14 | 42 | 50 | 27 |
| Cetatea Tirgu Neamt | 30 | 11 | 5 | 14 | 38 | 49 | 27 |
| Laminorul Beclean | 30 | 11 | 5 | 14 | 40 | 57 | 27 |
| Metalotehnica T.Mures | 30 | 13 | 0 | 17 | 52 | 59 | 27 |
| Viitorul Gheorgheni | 30 | 13 | 0 | 17 | 52 | 58 | 26 |
| Metalul Reghin | 30 | 10 | 5 | 15 | 28 | 52 | 25 |
| Textila Cisnadie | 30 | 11 | 2 | 17 | 36 | 52 | 24 |

Promoted :- Electromures Tirgu Mures
Relegated :- Metalul Reghin and Textila 91 Cisnadie

## RUMANIA 3RD DIV. SERIA A X-a 1990/91

### LEAGUE TABLE FINAL

| | P | W | D | L | F | A | Pts |
|---|---|---|---|---|---|---|---|
| Minerul Cavnic | 30 | 17 | 3 | 10 | 56 | 33 | 37 |
| Somesul Satu Mare | 30 | 16 | 2 | 12 | 59 | 42 | 34 |
| Laminorul Zalau | 30 | 14 | 5 | 11 | 46 | 32 | 33 |
| Victoria Carei | 30 | 14 | 5 | 11 | 51 | 39 | 33 |
| Caval. Negresti | 30 | 14 | 5 | 11 | 39 | 45 | 33 |
| CUPROM Baia Mare | 30 | 13 | 4 | 13 | 48 | 37 | 30 |
| Mobila Simleu | 30 | 14 | 2 | 14 | 55 | 48 | 30 |
| Minerul Baia Sprie | 30 | 15 | 0 | 15 | 42 | 30 | 30 |
| Minerul Turt | 30 | 14 | 2 | 14 | 41 | 48 | 30 |
| Bradul Viseu | 30 | 14 | 2 | 14 | 42 | 54 | 30 |
| Minerul Sarmasag | 30 | 13 | 3 | 14 | 46 | 39 | 29 |
| Minerul Baia Borsa | 30 | 13 | 3 | 14 | 42 | 56 | 29 |
| Vointa Negresti | 30 | 13 | 3 | 14 | 42 | 53 | 29 |
| Chimia Tasnad | 30 | 12 | 3 | 15 | 45 | 49 | 27 |
| Minerul Baita | 30 | 11 | 5 | 14 | 35 | 51 | 27 |
| Unirea Seini | 30 | 8 | 3 | 19 | 32 | 64 | 19 |

Promoted :- Minerul Cavnic
Relegated :- Minerul Baita and Unirea Seini

## RUMANIA 3RD DIV. SERIA A XI-a 1990/91

### LEAGUE TABLE FINAL

| | P | W | D | L | F | A | Pts |
|---|---|---|---|---|---|---|---|
| CFR Cluj | 30 | 20 | 6 | 4 | 77 | 27 | 46 |
| Metalul Aiud | 30 | 16 | 5 | 9 | 44 | 29 | 37 |
| Ind.sirmii C.Turzii | 30 | 14 | 6 | 11 | 48 | 25 | 34 |
| Minerul Stiinta Vulc. | 30 | 14 | 4 | 12 | 48 | 43 | 32 |
| Minerul Lupeni | 30 | 15 | 1 | 14 | 59 | 45 | 31 |
| AS Paroseni | 30 | 12 | 7 | 11 | 44 | 37 | 31 |
| CFR Simeria | 30 | 13 | 5 | 12 | 46 | 49 | 31 |
| Soda Ocna Mures | 30 | 14 | 2 | 14 | 50 | 45 | 30 |
| CUG Cluj | 30 | 13 | 4 | 13 | 36 | 39 | 30 |
| Mecanica Alba Iulia | 30 | 13 | 4 | 13 | 44 | 44 | 30 |
| Muresul Deva | 30 | 11 | 7 | 12 | 45 | 44 | 29 |
| Retezatul Hateg | 30 | 13 | 2 | 15 | 37 | 53 | 28 |
| Unirea Dej | 30 | 13 | 2 | 15 | 48 | 63 | 28 |
| Carpati Agnita | 30 | 12 | 4 | 14 | 51 | 67 | 28 |
| Mecanica Sibiu | 30 | 9 | 6 | 15 | 36 | 52 | 24 |
| Electrometal Cluj | 30 | 3 | 5 | 22 | 20 | 73 | 11 |

Promoted :- CFR Cluj
Relegated :- CSU Mecanica Sibiu and Electrometal Cluj

## RUMANIA 3RD DIV. SERIA A XII-a 1990/91

### LEAGUE TABLE FINAL

| | P | W | D | L | F | A | Pts |
|---|---|---|---|---|---|---|---|
| UM Timisoara | 30 | 20 | 1 | 9 | 77 | 38 | 41 |
| Otelul Stei | 30 | 18 | 2 | 10 | 60 | 38 | 38 |
| Motorul Arad | 30 | 18 | 2 | 10 | 50 | 39 | 38 |
| Unirea Tomnatic | 30 | 14 | 4 | 12 | 55 | 65 | 32 |
| Metaloplastica Orastie | 30 | 14 | 3 | 13 | 61 | 42 | 31 |
| Infratirea Oradea | 30 | 15 | 1 | 14 | 50 | 38 | 31 |
| Somti Lipova | 30 | 12 | 4 | 14 | 57 | 54 | 28 |
| Energia Timisoara | 30 | 13 | 2 | 15 | 43 | 43 | 28 |
| Minerul Stei | 30 | 13 | 2 | 15 | 48 | 47 | 28 |
| Unirea Sinnicolau | 30 | 14 | 0 | 16 | 62 | 74 | 28 |
| Obilici Sinmartin | 30 | 12 | 4 | 14 | 48 | 56 | 28 |
| Victoria Caian | 30 | 12 | 4 | 14 | 52 | 58 | 28 |
| Ceramica Jimbolia | 30 | 13 | 2 | 15 | 48 | 63 | 28 |
| Petrolul Arad | 30 | 13 | 1 | 16 | 50 | 58 | 27 |
| Strungul Chisinau Cris | 30 | 11 | 5 | 14 | 39 | 70 | 27 |
| CFR Arad | 30 | 10 | 5 | 15 | 31 | 50 | 25 |

Promoted :- UM Timisoara
Relegated :- Metaloplastica Orastie (for disciplinary reasons) and CFR Arad

Promoted to 3rd Division for Season 1991/92 :- CSM Drobeta Turnu Severin, Universitatea Sibiu, Granitul Babadag, Petrolul Roata de Jos, Contructorul Slatina, Minerul Crucea, TEPRO Iasi, SN Galati, CFR Constanta, Calculatorul Bucuresti, Sportul IACMRS Calarasi, Laminorul Roman, CPL Bacau, Carpati Brasov, Unirea Uriati, Electrica Fieni, Autobuzul IJTL Craiova, Auto FZB Timisoara, Petrolul Carbunesti, Paringul Petrila Lonea, Sticla Ariesul Turda, Rapid Jibou, Ardeleana Ardud Satu Mare and CPL Arad.

## RUMANIA CUP 1990/91

### 1/16 FINALS

| | | |
|---|---|---|
| Automec. Resita .....1 | Corvinul Hunedoara....1 | Dinamo Bucuresti....1 |
| Otelul Galati .......0 | Universitat. Craiova ...1 (aet.) | FC Arges Pitesti...2 |
| Minerul Baita .......0 | FC Inter Sibiu.......1 | Jiul Petrosan.....0 |
| Universitatea Cluj...2 | Gloria Bistrita ......1 | FCM Bacau.......0 |
| Carpati Agnita .....0 | Muresul Toplita ......3 | FC Bacau......1 |
| Caval. Fiuier. Bistria..2 | Unirea Alba Iulia ....0 | FCM Progresul Braila 0 |
| CFR Progresul Braila 0 | Politehnic. Timisoara. 2 | Unirea Alba Iulia ...0 |
| Foresta Gugesti .....1 | C'ment.Voint.Medgid.. 0 | Sport.Stud'nt. Bucur.. 0 |
| Metrom Brasov .......0 | FEPA '74 Birlad ......0 | Petrolul Ploiesti .....0 |
| Rapid Bucuresti ......0 (aet.) | FC Farul Constanta ...2 | Petrolul Ploiesti .....0 (aet.) |
| Rapid Bucuresti win 4-5 on penalties | Petrolul Ploiesti win 6-7 on penalties | Steaua Bucuresti......1 (aet.) |
| | | FC Bihor Oradea .....1 |
| | | Steaua Bucuresti.....1 |
| | | Steaua Bucuresti win 2-3 on penalties. |

### 1/8 FINALS

| | | | |
|---|---|---|---|
| FC Inter Sibiu.......2 | Sportul Studentsc. ...1 | FC Farul Constanta ...4 | Arsenal Resita ......0 |
| Unirea Alba Iulia ...1 | Cavaleri Flueriul ...0 | FC Arges Pitesti....1 | Universitatea Cluj...0 |
| Muresul Toplita ....0 | FC Bacau......1 | Steaua Bucuresti....1 | Petrolul Ploiesti ....0 |
| Politehnic. Timisoara . 1 | Dinamo Bucuresti....3 | Rapid Bucuresti....2 | Universitat. Craiova ...3 (aet.) |

### 1/4 FINALS

Dinamo Bucuresti v Universitatea Craiova
FC Arges Pitesti v FC Bacau
FC Farul Constanta v FC Inter Sibiu (FC Inter win on the away goals rule)
Steaua Bucuresti v Unirea Alba Iulia

⊗ match awarded, Steaua fielded an unregistered player

| | 1ST LEG | 2ND LEG | AGG. |
|---|---|---|---|
| Dinamo Bucuresti v Universitatea Craiova | 1-0 | 0-2 | 1-2 |
| FC Arges Pitesti v FC Bacau | 2-1 | 0-2 | 2-3 |
| FC Farul Constanta v FC Inter Sibiu (FC Inter win on the away goals rule) | 0-3 ⊗ | 2-1 | 2-4 |

### SEMI-FINALS

| | 1ST LEG | 2ND LEG | AGG. |
|---|---|---|---|
| Universitatea Craiova v FC Bacau | 0-0 | 0-1 | 0-1 |
| Universitatea Craiova v Unirea Alba Iulia | 4-0 | 0-3 | 4-3 |

### FINAL

Universitatea Craiova.......2    FC Bacau....1

Craiova : Prunea, Manaila, Sandoi, A.Popescu, Mogosanu, Ciurea, Olaru, Zamfir, Badea, Pigulea (Craioveanu 87), Agaliu
Bacau : Alexa, Jercalau, Arteni, Fisic, Ionescu, Burleanu, Condurache (Postolache 81), Gireada (Popa 78), Hodina, Capusa, Haidau.

| | | |
|---|---|---|
| 1-0 | Zamfir | 48 |
| 1-1 | Jercalau pen | 51 |
| 2-1 | Zamfir | 64 |

Referee : Craciunescu

# RUMANIA INTERNATIONAL REVIEW 1990

## INTERNATIONAL LINE-UPS 1990

| Date | Match | Venue / Ref. / Type | Silviu Lung | Dan Petrescu | Ioan Andone | Stefan Iovan | Iosif Rotariu | Ioan Ovidiu Sabau | Gheorghe Hagi | Gheorghe Popescu | Danut Lupu | Marius Lacatus | Pele Gavril Balint | Marius Cheregi | Stefan Stoica | Gheorghe Liliac | Mircea Rednic | Tudorel Cristea | Daniel Timofte | Ilie Dumitrescu | Dorin Mateut | Emil Sandoi | Zsolt Muzsnay | Michael Klein | Florin Radu Raducioiu | Bogdan Stelea | Marian Popa | Rodion Camataru | Adrian Popescu | Ionut Lupescu | Pavel Badea | Ovidiu Lazar | Florin Prunea | Constantin Stanici |
|---|---|---|---|---|---|---|---|---|---|---|---|---|---|---|---|---|---|---|---|---|---|---|---|---|---|---|---|---|---|---|---|---|---|---|
| 4/2/90 | ALGERIA 0 RUMANIA 0 | Algiers — Ref: Medjiba (Algeria) — Friendly | 1 | 2 | 3 | 4 | 5 | 6 | 7 | 8 | 9 | 10 | 11 | (9) | (11) | | | | | | | | | | | | | | | | | | | |
| 28/3/90 | EGYPT 1 RUMANIA 3 | Cairo — Ref: Kevalas (Greece) — Friendly (D.Timofte, Balint 2) | | 2 | 3 | | | | 8 | 7 | 6 | 10 | | | | 1 | 4 | | 9 | (6) | (8) | | | | 11 | | | | | | | | | |
| 3/4/90 | SWITZERLAND 2 RUMANIA 1 | Luzern — Ref: Steindl (Austria) — Friendly (Hagi) | | 2 | | | 9 | | 7 | 3 | | 10 | 11 | | | | | 5 | | | | 4 | 6 | | | | | | | | | | | |
| 25/4/90 | ISRAEL 1 RUMANIA 4 | Haifa — Ref: Jakov (Israel) — Friendly (o.g., Hagi, Sabau, Balint) | 1 | | 3 | | (8) | 6 | 7 | 4 | 9 | 10 | (11) | | (10) | | | 5 | 8 | (7) | | | (9) | 5 | (11) | (1) | (5) | | | | | | | |
| 21/5/90 | RUMANIA 1 EGYPT 0 | Bucuresti — Ref: Rudy (Poland) — Friendly (Camataru) | 1 | | 3 | | 8 | 6 | 9 | 4 | 7 | 10 | (11) | | | | 2 | | (9) | (7) | | | | 5 | (11) | | | 11 | (2) | | | | | |
| 26/5/90 | BELGIUM 2 RUMANIA 2 | Brussels — Ref: Delmer (France) — Friendly (Rednic, Lacatus) | 1 | | 4 | | 7 | 6 | 8 | 3 | 9 | 10 | (10) | | | | 2 | | (8) | (9) | (6) | | | 5 | (11) | | | 11 | | | | | | |
| 9/6/90 | USSR 0 RUMANIA 2 | Bari — World Cup — Ref: Cardellino (Uruguay) (Lacatus 2) | 1 | | 3 | | 7 | 6 | | 4 | | 10 | (11) | | | | 2 | | 9 | (10) | | | | 5 | 11 | | | | | 8 | | | | |
| 14/6/90 | CAMEROON 2 RUMANIA 1 | Bari — World Cup — Ref: Silva Arce (Chile) (Balint) | 1 | | 3 | | 7 | 6 | 8 | 4 | | 10 | (11) | | | | 2 | | 9 | | | | | 5 | 11 | | | | | | | | | |
| 18/6/90 | ARGENTINA 1 RUMANIA 1 | Napoli — World Cup — Ref: Silva Valente (Portugal) (Balint) | 1 | | 3 | | 7 | 6 | 9 | 4 | (11) | 10 | 11 | | | | 2 | | | | (6) | | | 5 | 11 | | | | | 8 | | | | |
| 25/6/90 | REPUBLIC OF IRELAND 0 RUMANIA 0 (aet.) | Genova — World Cup — Ref: Wright (Brazil) — REPUBLIC OF IRELAND WIN 5-4 ON PENALTIES | 1 | | 3 | | 7 | 6 | 9 | 4 | (11) | 10 | 10 | | | | 2 | | (6) | (8) | | | | 5 | 11 | | | | | 8 | | | | |
| 29/8/90 | USSR 1 RUMANIA 2 | Moskva — Friendly — Ref: Listkiewicz (Poland) (Lacatus, Lupescu) | | 2 | | | 7 | | | | | 10 | | 2 | | | 3 | | | 8 | 6 | 4 | | 5 | 11 | 1 | | | | 9 | (8) | | | |
| 12/9/90 | SCOTLAND 2 RUMANIA 1 | Glasgow — EuroCh.Q. — Ref: Urizar (Spain) (Camataru) | 1 | 2 | | | 7 | (6) | 8 | | | 10 | | | | | | | | | 6 | 3 | | 5 | (11) | | | 11 | | 9 | | | | |
| 26/9/90 | RUMANIA 2 POLAND 1 | Bucuresti — Friendly — Ref: Matusik (Czechoslovakia) (Lazar, Rotariu) | | 2 | 3 | 4 | 7 | 6 | | 8 | | 10 | (11) | | | | (8) | | | (9) | 9 | | | 5 | 11 | 1 | | | | | (11) | 11 | | |
| 17/10/90 | RUMANIA 0 BULGARIA 3 | Bucuresti — EuroCh.Q. — Ref: Dos Santos (Portugal) | | 2 | 3 | | | 6 | 8 | 4 | | 10 | | | | | | | | | | (5) | | 5 | 11 | 1 | | | | 9 | | | | |
| 5/12/90 | RUMANIA 6 SAN MARINO 0 | Bucuresti — EuroCh.Q. — Ref: Rossner (Germany) (Sabau, Mateut, Raducioiu, Lupescu, Badea, Petrescu) | | 2 | | 4 | | | | 3 | | 10 | | | | | 5 | | | 8 | 7 | | | | 11 | | | | | 9 | (8) | | 1 | (9) |
| **CAPS AT 31/12/90** | | | 70 | 13 | 55 | 35 | 23 | 29 | 64 | 26 | 9 | 46 | 29 | 2 | 2 | 4 | 81 | 8 | 7 | 14 | 50 | 12 | 6 | 86 | 10 | 6 | 1 | 75 | 1 | 11 | 3 | 1 | 1 | 1 |
| **GOALS AT 31/12/90** | | | | 1 | 2 | 3 | 1 | 7 | 14 | 1 | | 8 | 9 | | | | 2 | | 1 | | 9 | | | 5 | 1 | | | 22 | | 2 | 1 | 1 | | |

# SAN MARINO Correspondent : MARCO ZUNINO

| SAN MARINO Serie A1 Season 1990/91 | COSMOS | DOMAGNANO | FAETANO | FOLGORE | LA FIORITA | LIBERTAS | MONTEVITO | MURATA | TRE FIORI | VIRTUS |
|---|---|---|---|---|---|---|---|---|---|---|
| COSMOS | | 1-1 | 0-1 | 3-0 | 2-1 | 1-1 | 4-1 | 1-1 | 0-0 | 4-0 |
| DOMAGNANO | 7-1 | | 2-1 | 1-0 | 1-2 | 3-0 | 2-0 | 0-1 | 3-1 | 1-1 |
| FAETANO | 4-3 | 1-0 | | 3-0 | 3-2 | 3-0 | 1-2 | 5-1 | 0-2 | 1-1 |
| FOLGORE | 1-0 | 3-1 | 1-1 | | 3-0 | 2-2 | 0-0 | 2-0 | 0-0 | 3-0 |
| LA FIORITA | 1-3 | 0-2 | 0-2 | 0-2 | | 0-2 | 0-2 | 1-1 | 2-6 | 3-2 |
| LIBERTAS | 0-0 | 0-0 | 1-1 | 0-1 | 3-0 | | 1-3 | 1-1 | 2-2 | 1-1 |
| MONTEVITO | 1-2 | 2-2 | 2-1 | 1-1 | 7-1 | 0-0 | | 1-1 | 0-1 | 4-2 |
| MURATA | 2-2 | 2-2 | 1-1 | 1-1 | 1-1 | 1-3 | 1-2 | | 3-4 | 0-2 |
| TRE FIORI | 4-2 | 3-1 | 2-1 | 2-0 | 2-0 | 1-0 | 0-1 | 0-1 | | 1-1 |
| VIRTUS | 0-1 | 0-6 | 2-6 | 2-3 | 2-2 | 2-4 | 2-3 | 1-3 | 1-3 | |

## SAN MARINO SERIE A1 1990/91
### LEAGUE TABLE FINAL

| | | | | | | | |
|---|---|---|---|---|---|---|---|
| Tre Fiori | 18 | 11 | 4 | 3 | 34 | 18 | 26 |
| Montevito | 18 | 9 | 5 | 4 | 32 | 22 | 23 |
| Faetano | 18 | 9 | 4 | 5 | 36 | 22 | 22 |
| Folgore | 18 | 8 | 6 | 4 | 23 | 17 | 22 |
| Domagnano | 18 | 8 | 5 | 5 | 35 | 19 | 21 |
| Cosmos | 18 | 7 | 6 | 5 | 30 | 26 | 20 |
| Libertas | 18 | 4 | 9 | 5 | 21 | 22 | 17 |
| Murata | 18 | 3 | 9 | 6 | 22 | 30 | 15 |
| Virtus | 18 | 1 | 5 | 12 | 22 | 49 | 7 |
| La Fiorita | 18 | 2 | 3 | 13 | 16 | 46 | 7 |

Relegated : - Virtus and La Fiorita

### TOP SCORERS

| | | |
|---|---|---|
| 1. | De Luigi (Faetano) | 13 |
| 2. | Mina (Virtus) | 12 |
| 3. | Giancecchi (Faetano) | 11 |
| 4. | Aversa (Montevito) | 10 |
| 5. | Riccardi (Faetano) | 9 |

| SAN MARINO Serie A2 Season 1990/91 | CAILUNGO | DOGANA | JUVENES | PENNA ROSSA | S. GIOVANNI | TRE PENNE |
|---|---|---|---|---|---|---|
| CAILUNGO | | 2-2 | 1-4 | 3-1 | 1-0 | 1-1 |
| | | 2-1 | 0-0 | | | |
| DOGANA | 3-3 | | 1-1 | 4-1 | 1-0 | 2-0 |
| | 0-1 | | 1-2 | 2-2 | | |
| JUVENES | 3-1 | 2-0 | | 4-1 | 1-0 | 0-2 |
| | 2-3 | | | 2-0 | | 0-1 |
| PENNA ROSSA | 1-4 | 1-2 | 2-8 | | 2-1 | 1-3 |
| | 1-6 | | | | 1-1 | |
| SAN GIOVANNI | 1-1 | 0-1 | 3-4 | 1-3 | | 0-1 |
| | | 1-3 | 0-2 | | | |
| TRE PENNE | 3-3 | 0-0 | 2-2 | 1-1 | 1-0 | |
| | 1-1 | | | 1-0 | 1-2 | |

## CHAMPIONSHIP PLAY-OFFS
Top 4 clubs of Serie A1 and Champions of serie A2 qualify for the Championship Play-Offs. Winners of Serie A1 are exempted until the Semi-finals. Clubs are drawn to play against one another and are eliminated following 2 defeats. Drawn matches are followed by extra-time and when necessary, penalty shoot-outs. The last 2 surviving clubs qualify fo the Championship Final.

### 1ST ROUND
| | | | | |
|---|---|---|---|---|
| Faetano....................3 | Folgore .................... 0 | | Juvenes .................... 4 | Montevito ................. 2 |
| Faetano....................2 | Juvenes .................... 1 | | Folgore ...................... 0 | Montevito ................. 1 |
| | | | Folgore eliminated | |

### SEMI-FINALS
| | | | | |
|---|---|---|---|---|
| Tre Fiori....................4 | Faetano .................... 1 | | Juvenes .................... 2 | Montevito ................. 1 |
| Faetano....................3 | Juvenes .................... 1 | | Montevito eliminated | |
| Juvenes eliminated | | | | |

### FINAL
Tre Fiori....................0    Faetano .................... 1

Champions : - Faetano

## SAN MARINO SERIE A2 1990/91
### LEAGUE TABLE FINAL

| | | | | | | | |
|---|---|---|---|---|---|---|---|
| Juvenes | 15 | 10 | 2 | 3 | 37 | 18 | 22 |
| Cailungo | 15 | 7 | 6 | 2 | 32 | 23 | 20 |
| Tre Penne | 15 | 6 | 7 | 2 | 18 | 13 | 19 |
| Dogana | 15 | 6 | 6 | 3 | 23 | 17 | 18 |
| Penna Rossa | 15 | 2 | 3 | 10 | 18 | 43 | 7 |
| San Giovanni | 15 | 1 | 2 | 12 | 11 | 25 | 4 |

Promoted : - Juvenes and Cailungo

## SAN MARINO : All Time Records as at 31/12/90 - CAPS

| | | |
|---|---|---|
| 1. | Pierluigi Benedettini | 6 |
| | Marco Montironi | 6 |
| | Valdes Pasolini | 6 |
| 4. | Giancarlo Bacciocchi | 5 |
| | Bruno Muccioli | 5 |
| 6. | Tirziano Giacobbi | 4 |
| | William Guerra | 4 |
| | Gianpaolo Mazza | 4 |
| | Massimo Zanotti | 4 |

No goals scored by San Marino as at 31/12/90

# SAN MARINO INTERNATIONAL REVIEW 1990

## INTERNATIONAL LINE-UPS 1990

| Date | Result | Venue | Competition | Referee |
|---|---|---|---|---|
| 14/11/90 | SAN MARINO 0 SWITZERLAND 4 | Serravalle | EuroCh.Q. | Kapsos (Cyprus) |
| 5/12/90 | RUMANIA 6 SAN MARINO 0 | Bucuresti | EuroCh.Q. | Rössner (Germany) |

| Player | 14/11/90 | 5/12/90 |
|---|---|---|
| Pierluigi Benedettini | 1 | 1 |
| Marco Montironi | 2 | 2 |
| William Guerra | 3 | 4 |
| Luca Gobbi | 4 | |
| Bruno Mucciol | 5 | 5 |
| Loris Zanotti | 6 | 8 |
| Massimo Ceccoli | 7 | 9 |
| Valdes Pasolini | 8 | 10 |
| Massimo Bonini | 9 | 11 |
| Fabio Francini | 10 | 7 |
| Marco Macina | 11 | 6 |
| Ivan Matteoni | (5) | 3 |
| Ivano Toccaceli | (9) | |
| Paulo Canti | | |
| Paulo Daniele Zanotti | | (9) |
| Giancarlo Bacciocchi | | (11) |

Note : Clubs of Paulo Daniele Zanotti and Giancarlo Bacciocchi take part in the League of San Marino, clubs of all the other players appear in Italian competitions.

## SAN MARINO TITANO CUP 1990/91

### 1ST ROUND

**GROUP A**

| | |
|---|---|
| Domagnano ...... 3 | Libertas ...... 3 |
| Montevito ...... 2 | Folgore ...... 0 |
| Folgore ...... 0 | Domagnano ...... 2 |
| Libertas ...... 2 | Montevito ...... 0 |
| Domagnano ...... 1 | Montevito ...... 0 |
| Folgore ...... 1 | Libertas ...... 6 |

**LEAGUE TABLE FINAL**

| | | | | | | | |
|---|---|---|---|---|---|---|---|
| Libertas | 3 | 2 | 1 | 0 | 11 | 4 | 5 |
| Domagnano | 3 | 2 | 1 | 0 | 6 | 4 | 5 |
| Montevito | 3 | 1 | 0 | 2 | 2 | 3 | 2 |
| Folgore | 3 | 0 | 0 | 3 | 2 | 10 | 0 |

**GROUP B**

| | |
|---|---|
| Tre Penne ...... 0 | Faetano ...... 0 |
| San Giovanni ...... 1 | La Fiorita ...... 4 |
| La Fiorita ...... 0 | Tre Penne ...... 0 |
| Faetano ...... 2 | San Giovanni ...... 1 |
| Tre Penne ...... 7 | San Giovanni ...... 1 |
| La Fiorita ...... 0 | Faetano ...... 3 |

**LEAGUE TABLE FINAL**

| | | | | | | | |
|---|---|---|---|---|---|---|---|
| Faetano | 3 | 2 | 1 | 0 | 5 | 1 | 5 |
| Tre Penne | 3 | 1 | 2 | 0 | 7 | 1 | 4 |
| La Fiorita | 3 | 1 | 1 | 1 | 4 | 4 | 3 |
| San Giovanni | 3 | 0 | 0 | 3 | 3 | 13 | 0 |

**GROUP C**

| | |
|---|---|
| Juvenes ...... 2 | Tre Fiori ...... 2 |
| Cosmos ...... 4 | Cailungo ...... 1 |
| Cailungo ...... 0 | Juvenes ...... 2 |
| Tre Fiori ...... 2 | Cosmos ...... 2 |
| Juvenes ...... 2 | Cosmos ...... 1 |
| Cailungo ...... 0 | Tre Fiori ...... 8 |

**LEAGUE TABLE FINAL**

| | | | | | | | |
|---|---|---|---|---|---|---|---|
| Juvenes | 3 | 2 | 1 | 0 | 6 | 3 | 5 |
| Tre Fiori | 3 | 1 | 1 | 1 | 12 | 4 | 4 |
| Cosmos | 3 | 1 | 1 | 1 | 7 | 5 | 3 |
| Cailungo | 3 | 0 | 0 | 3 | 1 | 14 | 0 |

**GROUP D**

| | |
|---|---|
| Murata ...... 1 | Dogana ...... 1 |
| Pennarossa ...... 0 | Virtus ...... 2 |
| Virtus ...... 1 | Murata ...... 2 |
| Dogana ...... 3 | Pennarossa ...... 1 |
| Murata ...... 5 | Pennarossa ...... 0 |
| Virtus ...... 1 | Dogana ...... 0 |

**LEAGUE TABLE FINAL**

| | | | | | | | |
|---|---|---|---|---|---|---|---|
| Murata | 3 | 2 | 1 | 0 | 8 | 2 | 5 |
| Virtus | 3 | 2 | 0 | 1 | 4 | 2 | 4 |
| Dogana | 3 | 1 | 1 | 1 | 4 | 3 | 3 |
| Pennarossa | 3 | 0 | 0 | 3 | 1 | 10 | 0 |

Winners and Runners-Up of each group qualify for the 2nd Round, clubs are eliminated following 2 defeats.

### 2ND ROUND
| | |
|---|---|
| Faetano ...... 1 | Juvenes ...... 0 |
| Murata ...... 1 | Domagnano ...... 3 |
| Libertas ...... 2 | Tre Penne ...... 0 |

### 3RD ROUND
| | |
|---|---|
| Faetano ...... 1 | Tre Fiori ...... 0 |
| Virtus ...... 2 | Murata ...... 2 |
| Domagnano ...... 3 | Tre Penne ...... 3 |

Virtus eliminated

### 4TH ROUND
| | |
|---|---|
| Juvenes ...... 1 | Tre Penne ...... 2 |
| Libertas ...... 3 | |

Tre Fiori eliminated   Tre Penne eliminated

### 5TH ROUND
| | |
|---|---|
| Libertas ...... 1 | Faetano ...... 1 |
| Domagnano ...... 0 | |

Juvenes eliminated

### SEMI-FINAL
| | |
|---|---|
| Domagnano ...... 2 | Libertas ...... 3 |

Domagnano eliminated

### FINAL   26/6/91 (at Serravalle)

Faetano ...... 0   Libertas ...... 2

Faetano : Ceci, Celli, Valentini, P.M.Della Valle, Gasperoni (S.Riccardi 65), P.D.Della Valle, Bizzocchi, Casadei, De Luigi, L.Riccardi, Gianni (Massari 81).

Libertas : Selva, I.Toccaceli, Rossi, Francini, S.Agarici, Moroni, Ghiotti, F.Agarici, Bartoletti, V.Toccaceli (Bernardi 26), Bernardini.

0-1  Bernardini  72 pen.
0-2  F.Agarici  83

Referee : Bruno Albani

# SCOTLAND Correspondent : JAN BUITENGA

**SCOTLAND Premier Division Season 1990/91**

| | RANGERS | ABERDEEN | HEARTS | DUNDEE UTD. | CELTIC | MOTHERWELL | HIBS | D'LINE ATH. | ST.MIRREN | ST.JOHNSTONE |
|---|---|---|---|---|---|---|---|---|---|---|
| RANGERS | | 2-2 | 4-0 | 1-2 | 1-1 | 1-0 | 4-0 | 3-1 | 5-0 | 4-1 |
| | | 2-0 | 2-1 | 1-0 | 2-0 | 2-0 | 0-0 | 2-0 | 1-0 | 3-0 |
| ABERDEEN | 0-0 | | 3-0 | 1-1 | 3-0 | 1-1 | 2-0 | 3-2 | 2-1 | 0-0 |
| | 1-0 | | 5-0 | 0-1 | 1-0 | 3-0 | 2-0 | 0-0 | 1-0 | 2-1 |
| HEART OF MIDLOTHIAN | 1-3 | 1-0 | | 1-0 | 1-0 | 3-2 | 1-1 | 1-1 | 1-1 | 2-3 |
| | 0-1 | 1-4 | | 2-1 | 0-1 | 2-1 | 3-1 | 4-1 | 2-0 | 2-1 |
| DUNDEE UNITED | 2-1 | 2-3 | 1-1 | | 3-1 | 1-0 | 1-0 | 3-0 | 1-0 | 1-2 |
| | 1-2 | 1-2 | 2-1 | | 2-1 | 3-0 | 0-0 | 1-0 | 3-2 | 0-0 |
| CELTIC | 1-2 | 0-3 | 3-0 | 0-0 | | 2-1 | 2-0 | 1-2 | 4-1 | 0-0 |
| | 3-0 | 1-0 | 1-1 | 1-0 | | 1-2 | 1-1 | 5-1 | 1-0 | 3-0 |
| MOTHERWELL | 2-4 | 0-0 | 1-1 | 0-2 | 2-0 | | 4-1 | 2-0 | 1-1 | 3-0 |
| | 3-0 | 0-2 | 1-3 | 1-0 | 1-1 | | 1-0 | 0-0 | 3-1 | 2-2 |
| HIBERNIAN | 0-0 | 1-1 | 0-3 | 0-0 | 0-3 | 1-0 | | 1-1 | 1-0 | 1-0 |
| | 0-2 | 2-4 | 1-4 | 1-0 | 0-2 | 1-1 | | 3-0 | 4-3 | 0-1 |
| DUNFERMLINE ATHLETIC | 0-1 | 1-1 | 2-0 | 1-0 | 1-1 | 3-3 | 1-1 | | 0-0 | 1-2 |
| | 0-1 | 1-4 | 3-1 | 1-0 | 0-1 | 2-5 | 1-1 | | 2-2 | 3-2 |
| ST.MIRREN | 0-3 | 0-4 | 2-1 | 1-1 | 2-3 | 1-0 | 1-0 | 0-1 | | 2-2 |
| | 0-1 | 0-1 | 0-0 | 0-1 | 0-2 | 2-2 | 1-0 | 2-2 | | 0-1 |
| ST.JOHNSTONE | 0-0 | 5-0 | 2-1 | 1-3 | 3-2 | 2-1 | 1-1 | 3-2 | 0-1 | |
| | 1-1 | 0-1 | 0-2 | 0-1 | 2-3 | 1-4 | 0-0 | 0-1 | 2-1 | |

## SCOTLAND PREMIER DIVISION SEASON 1990/91
### LEAGUE TABLE FINAL

| | | | | | | | |
|---|---|---|---|---|---|---|---|
| Rangers | 36 | 24 | 7 | 5 | 62 | 23 | 55 |
| Aberdeen | 36 | 22 | 9 | 5 | 62 | 27 | 53 |
| Celtic | 36 | 17 | 7 | 12 | 52 | 38 | 41 |
| Dundee United | 36 | 17 | 7 | 12 | 41 | 29 | 41 |
| Heart of Midlothian | 36 | 14 | 7 | 15 | 48 | 55 | 35 |
| Motherwell | 36 | 12 | 9 | 15 | 51 | 50 | 33 |
| St.Johnstone | 36 | 11 | 9 | 16 | 41 | 54 | 31 |
| Dunfermline Athletic | 36 | 8 | 11 | 17 | 38 | 61 | 27 |
| Hibernian | 36 | 6 | 13 | 17 | 24 | 51 | 25 |
| St.Mirren | 36 | 5 | 9 | 22 | 28 | 59 | 19 |

Champions : - Rangers

League increased to 12 clubs for season 1991/92

### TOP SCORERS
1. Tommy Coyne (Celtic) — 18
2. Dougie Arnott (Motherwell) — 14
   Hans Gillhaus (Aberdeen) — 14
4. Eoin Jess (Aberdeen) — 13
5. Darren Jackson (Dundee United) — 12
   John Robertson (Hearts) — 12
   Mark Walters (Rangers) — 12
8. Maurice Johnston (Rangers) — 11
   Ally McCoist (Rangers) — 11
10. Mark Hateley (Rangers) — 10

## SCOTLAND 1ST DIV. SEASON 1990/91
### LEAGUE TABLE FINAL

| | | | | | | | |
|---|---|---|---|---|---|---|---|
| Falkirk | 39 | 21 | 12 | 6 | 70 | 35 | 54 |
| Airdrieonians | 39 | 21 | 11 | 7 | 69 | 43 | 53 |
| Dundee | 39 | 22 | 8 | 9 | 59 | 33 | 52 |
| Partick Thistle | 39 | 16 | 13 | 10 | 56 | 53 | 45 |
| Kilmarnock | 39 | 15 | 13 | 11 | 58 | 48 | 43 |
| Hamilton Academical | 39 | 16 | 10 | 13 | 50 | 41 | 42 |
| Raith Rovers | 39 | 14 | 9 | 16 | 54 | 64 | 37 |
| Clydebank | 39 | 13 | 10 | 16 | 65 | 70 | 36 |
| Morton | 39 | 11 | 13 | 15 | 48 | 55 | 35 |
| Forfar Athletic | 39 | 9 | 15 | 15 | 50 | 57 | 33 |
| Meadowbank Thistle | 39 | 10 | 13 | 16 | 56 | 68 | 33 |
| Ayr United | 39 | 10 | 12 | 17 | 47 | 59 | 32 |
| Clyde | 39 | 9 | 9 | 21 | 41 | 61 | 27 |
| Brechin City | 39 | 7 | 10 | 22 | 44 | 80 | 24 |

Promoted : - Falkirk and Airdrieonians
Relegated : - Clyde and Brechin City

League reduced to 12 clubs for Season 1991/92

## SCOTLAND 2ND DIVISION SEASON 1990/91
### LEAGUE TABLE FINAL

| | | | | | | | |
|---|---|---|---|---|---|---|---|
| Stirling Albion | 39 | 20 | 14 | 5 | 62 | 24 | 54 |
| Montrose | 39 | 20 | 6 | 13 | 54 | 34 | 46 |
| Cowdenbeath | 39 | 18 | 9 | 12 | 64 | 50 | 45 |
| Stenhousemuir | 39 | 16 | 12 | 11 | 56 | 42 | 44 |
| Queen's Park | 39 | 17 | 8 | 14 | 48 | 42 | 42 |
| Stranraer | 39 | 18 | 4 | 17 | 61 | 60 | 40 |
| Dumbarton | 39 | 15 | 10 | 14 | 49 | 49 | 40 |
| Berwick Rangers | 39 | 15 | 10 | 14 | 51 | 57 | 40 |
| Alloa Athletic | 39 | 13 | 11 | 15 | 51 | 46 | 37 |
| East Fife | 39 | 14 | 9 | 16 | 57 | 65 | 37 |
| Albion Rovers | 39 | 11 | 13 | 15 | 48 | 63 | 35 |
| Queen of the South | 39 | 9 | 12 | 18 | 46 | 62 | 30 |
| East Stirlingshire | 39 | 9 | 11 | 19 | 36 | 71 | 29 |
| Arbroath | 39 | 8 | 11 | 20 | 41 | 59 | 27 |

Promoted : - Stirling Albion and Montrose

# SCOTLAND
## 1st Division
### Season 1990/91

| | DUNDEE | AIRDRIE | CLYDEBANK | FALKIRK | RAITH RVRS | HAMILTON ATH. | M'BANK T. | PARTICK T. | CLYDE | AYR UTD. | MORTON | FORFAR ATH. | BRECHIN CITY | KILMARNOCK |
|---|---|---|---|---|---|---|---|---|---|---|---|---|---|---|
| DUNDEE | | 0-1 | 1-0 | 2-2 | 2-1 | 3-2 | 1-2 | 1-1 | 3-1 | 1-0 | 1-0 | 1-0 | 1-2 | 1-1 |
| | | | | | 2-0 | | 4-0 | | | 4-0 | 1-0 | 4-1 | 0-1 | |
| AIRDRIEONIANS | 0-1 | | 2-2 | 1-3 | 1-5 | 2-1 | 2-0 | 0-0 | 2-2 | 4-0 | 4-0 | 1-1 | 3-0 | 2-0 |
| | 0-1 | | | 0-3 | | | | | 1-1 | | 3-0 | 2-1 | | 2-0 |
| CLYDEBANK | 1-3 | 5-2 | | 3-1 | 1-1 | 3-1 | 2-2 | 2-3 | 2-1 | 0-2 | 2-4 | 2-2 | 3-4 | 1-3 |
| | 1-1 | 1-3 | | 2-2 | | 1-3 | | 7-1 | | | | | 1-0 | 0-0 |
| FALKIRK | 1-0 | 1-1 | 5-1 | | 7-1 | 0-1 | 2-2 | 0-2 | 2-0 | 1-2 | 2-1 | 1-0 | 3-0 | 1-1 |
| | 0-0 | | | | 0-2 | 3-0 | 4-2 | | 1-0 | 4-1 | | | 2-1 | |
| RAITH ROVERS | 1-1 | 1-1 | 2-0 | 1-4 | | 1-0 | 1-3 | 0-0 | 1-1 | 3-0 | 1-0 | 2-1 | 1-2 | 1-1 |
| | | 0-1 | 1-2 | | | | 1-5 | 1-0 | | | 1-2 | 1-0 | 1-2 | |
| HAMILTON ACADEMICAL | 1-0 | 0-1 | 2-0 | 0-2 | 2-2 | | 2-1 | 2-2 | 1-0 | 0-0 | 1-1 | 2-0 | 2-1 | 3-1 |
| | 1-2 | 1-1 | | 1-2 | | | 1-1 | 0-1 | 3-1 | | 0-1 | | | |
| MEADOWBANK THISTLE | 0-1 | 2-4 | 0-3 | 0-1 | 1-1 | 1-1 | | 1-1 | 0-2 | 1-0 | 1-1 | 2-2 | 6-1 | 1-0 |
| | 0-1 | 2-3 | | 4-1 | | | | | 1-1 | | | 1-1 | 1-8 | |
| PARTICK THISTLE | 1-3 | 1-1 | 0-1 | 2-0 | 0-3 | 0-1 | 1-1 | | 2-0 | 2-0 | 2-2 | 3-2 | 3-3 | 2-0 |
| | 1-0 | 0-2 | | 1-1 | | | 2-4 | | | 0-0 | 2-0 | | | |
| CLYDE | 0-1 | 1-4 | 0-1 | 1-3 | 1-2 | 0-2 | 1-0 | 2-4 | | 2-2 | 1-3 | 1-1 | 1-1 | 1-1 |
| | 4-2 | | 3-1 | | | | | 2-1 | | 1-0 | 0-1 | 0-1 | | 2-1 |
| AYR UNITED | 2-4 | 2-2 | 1-1 | 1-1 | 2-0 | 2-2 | 1-1 | 0-1 | 4-1 | | 1-0 | 1-1 | 4-0 | 1-2 |
| | | 0-1 | 0-1 | 5-3 | 1-2 | 2-0 | | | | | 1-1 | | | 1-0 |
| MORTON | 0-1 | 1-0 | 2-0 | 0-0 | 1-2 | 0-2 | 0-3 | 4-0 | 0-0 | 2-1 | | 1-1 | 3-3 | 3-0 |
| | | 2-2 | 0-1 | 4-0 | 0-4 | 1-1 | 1-1 | | | | | | | |
| FORFAR ATHLETIC | 1-1 | 1-4 | 0-3 | 1-2 | 3-1 | 0-0 | 3-2 | 0-1 | 1-3 | 3-1 | 5-1 | | 0-0 | 2-2 |
| | | 2-2 | 0-0 | | 2-0 | | | | 1-1 | 2-2 | | | 4-1 | 1-1 |
| BRECHIN CITY | 1-3 | 1-2 | 3-2 | 0-2 | 0-4 | 0-1 | 1-3 | 2-2 | 0-2 | 1-2 | 0-1 | 2-1 | | 0-2 |
| | | 1-1 | | | 2-2 | | 1-2 | 2-0 | 2-2 | 1-3 | | | | |
| KILMARNOCK | 2-1 | 3-4 | 3-0 | 1-1 | 1-1 | 1-0 | 2-3 | 2-3 | 2-1 | 3-1 | 3-1 | 1-0 | 2-1 | |
| | 0-0 | | | 1-1 | | 1-0 | | 1-0 | | | 1-1 | | 2-2 | |

## HIGHLAND LEAGUE SEASON 1990/91
### LEAGUE TABLE FINAL

| | | | | | | | |
|---|---|---|---|---|---|---|---|
| Ross County | 34 | 24 | 4 | 6 | 91 | 37 | 76 |
| Inverness Caledonian | 34 | 23 | 4 | 7 | 87 | 40 | 73 |
| Cove Rangers | 34 | 23 | 2 | 9 | 95 | 52 | 71 |
| Forres Mechanics | 34 | 22 | 3 | 9 | 77 | 40 | 69 |
| Inverness Thistle | 34 | 20 | 5 | 9 | 55 | 38 | 65 |
| Huntly | 34 | 17 | 10 | 7 | 79 | 52 | 61 |
| Elgin City | 34 | 17 | 6 | 11 | 84 | 53 | 57 |
| Peterhead | 34 | 13 | 11 | 10 | 50 | 45 | 50 |
| Brora Rangers | 34 | 13 | 10 | 11 | 66 | 54 | 49 |
| Lossiemouth | 34 | 14 | 5 | 15 | 69 | 61 | 47 |
| Buckie Thistle | 34 | 12 | 7 | 15 | 47 | 52 | 43 |
| Fort William | 34 | 11 | 10 | 13 | 76 | 85 | 43 |
| Fraserburgh | 34 | 11 | 8 | 15 | 54 | 56 | 41 |
| Keith | 34 | 11 | 4 | 19 | 37 | 55 | 37 |
| Deveronvale | 34 | 7 | 9 | 18 | 37 | 91 | 30 |
| Invern. Clachnacuddin | 34 | 8 | 2 | 24 | 42 | 92 | 26 |
| Nairn County | 34 | 4 | 3 | 27 | 36 | 104 | 15 |
| Rothes | 34 | 2 | 5 | 27 | 36 | 102 | 11 |

## EAST OF SCOTLAND LEAGUE SEASON 1990/91

### PREMIER DIV. LEAGUE TABLE FINAL

| | | | | | | | |
|---|---|---|---|---|---|---|---|
| Gala Fairydean | 18 | 12 | 5 | 1 | 43 | 26 | 29 |
| Whitehill Welfare | 18 | 11 | 3 | 4 | 44 | 27 | 25 |
| Edinburgh City | 18 | 9 | 5 | 4 | 34 | 21 | 23 |
| Spartans | 18 | 6 | 6 | 6 | 23 | 19 | 18 |
| Berwick Rangers 'A' | 18 | 6 | 6 | 6 | 32 | 31 | 18 |
| Coldstream | 18 | 7 | 2 | 9 | 32 | 26 | 16 |
| Annan Athletic | 18 | 5 | 5 | 8 | 35 | 35 | 15 |
| Craigroyston | 18 | 5 | 5 | 8 | 29 | 43 | 15 |
| Civil Service Strollers | 18 | 5 | 4 | 9 | 24 | 35 | 14 |
| Peebles Rovers | 18 | 2 | 3 | 13 | 20 | 53 | 7 |

Champions : - Gala Fairydean
Relegated : - Civil Service Strollers and Peebles Rovers

### 1ST DIVISION LEAGUE TABLE FINAL

| | | | | | | | |
|---|---|---|---|---|---|---|---|
| Easthouses Lily | 18 | 12 | 6 | 0 | 48 | 18 | 30 |
| Vale of Leithen | 18 | 11 | 2 | 5 | 50 | 28 | 24 |
| Eyemouth United | 18 | 9 | 6 | 3 | 37 | 26 | 24 |
| Hawick Royal Albert | 18 | 9 | 5 | 4 | 42 | 35 | 23 |
| Pencaitland | 18 | 8 | 6 | 4 | 31 | 20 | 22 |
| Selkirk | 18 | 9 | 4 | 5 | 36 | 34 | 22 |
| Kelso United | 18 | 5 | 2 | 11 | 18 | 45 | 12 |
| Tollcross United | 18 | 5 | 1 | 12 | 33 | 34 | 11 |
| Edinburgh University | 18 | 5 | 1 | 12 | 27 | 39 | 11 |
| Heriot-Watt Univ'sity | 18 | 0 | 1 | 17 | 7 | 50 | 1 |

Promoted : - Easthouses Lily and Vale of Leithen

# SCOTLAND LEAGUE CUP 1990/91

**1ST ROUND**

| | | | |
|---|---|---|---|
| East Stirlingshire | 2 | Dumbarton | 3 (aet) |
| East Stirlingshire win 4-1 on penalties | | | |
| Stenhousemuir | 0 | Cowdenbeath | 2 |
| Stirling Albion | 1 | Arbroath | 2 |
| Queen's Park | 3 | East Fife | 3 (aet) |
| Queen's Park win 5-4 on penalties | | | |
| Montrose | 2 | Queen of the South | 2 (aet) |
| Stranraer | 4 | Berwick Rangers | 3 (aet) |

**2ND ROUND**

| | | | |
|---|---|---|---|
| Airdrieonians | 1 | Stranraer | 2 |
| Brechin City | 0 | Hamilton Academ. | 2 |
| Cowdenbeath | 0 | Heart of Midlothian | 4 |
| Falkirk | 1 | Partick Thistle | 1 (aet) |
| Partick Thistle win 1-4 on penalties | | | |
| Meadowbank Thistle | 0 | Kilmarnock | 3 |
| Queen of the South | 2 | Hibernian | 1 (aet) |
| Queen of the South win 4-1 on penalties | | | |
| St.Johnstone | 0 | Clyde | 2 |

**3RD ROUND**

| | | | |
|---|---|---|---|
| Aberdeen | 4 | Stranraer | 0 |
| Hamilton Academ. | 0 | Celtic | 1 |
| Partick Thistle | 1 | Dundee United | 3 |
| Rangers | 1 | Kilmarnock | 0 |

**1/4 FINALS**

| | | | |
|---|---|---|---|
| Aberdeen | 3 | Heart of Midlothian | 0 |
| Dundee United | 2 | Motherwell | 0 |
| Celtic | 2 | St.Mirren | 1 |

**SEMI-FINALS**

| | | | |
|---|---|---|---|
| Celtic | 2 | Dundee United | 0 |
| Rangers | 1 | Aberdeen | 0 |

## FINAL

28/10/90 at Hampden Park, Glasgow

Rangers ..... 2    Celtic ..... 1 (aet)

Rangers : Woods, Stevens, Gough, Brown, Munro, Steven, Hurlock (Huistra 63), Spackman, Walters, McCoist (Ferguson 95), Hateley.

Celtic : Bonner, Grant, Elliott, Wdowczyk, Rogan, McStay, Collins, Fulton (Hewitt 45), Miller (Morris 58), Dziekanowski, Creaney.

| 0-1 | Elliott | 51 |
|---|---|---|
| 1-1 | Walters | 64 |
| 2-1 | Gough | 95 |

Referee : J.McCluskey
Attendance : 62,817

---

# SCOTLAND CUP 1990/91

**1ST ROUND**

| | | | |
|---|---|---|---|
| East Stirlingshire | 1 | Fraserburgh | 3 |
| Ross County | 1 | Alloa Athletic | 1 |
| Whitehill Welfare | 0 | East Fife | 4 |

**REPLAYS**

| | | | |
|---|---|---|---|
| Alloa Athletic | 1 | Ross County | 3 |

**2ND ROUND**

| | | | |
|---|---|---|---|
| Berwick Rangers | 1 | Albion Rovers | 0 |
| Montrose | 0 | Arbroath | 2 |
| Stirling Albion | 2 | Stenhousemuir | 0 |
| Spartans | 0 | Cowdenbeath | 0 |

**REPLAYS**

| | | | |
|---|---|---|---|
| East Fife | 1 | Inverness Thistle | 0 |
| Queen of the South | 2 | Ross County | 6 |
| Cowdenbeath | 2 | Spartans | 0 |

**3RD ROUND**

| | | | |
|---|---|---|---|
| Aberdeen | 0 | Heart of Midlothian | 1 |
| Airdrieonians | 2 | Cowdenbeath | 2 |
| Cove Rangers | 1 | Dundee United | 1 |
| East Fife | 1 | Arbroath | 2 |
| Kilmarnock | 3 | Raith Rovers | 1 |
| Forfar Athletic | 0 | Celtic | 2 |
| Hamilton Academ. | 1 | Morton | 1 |
| Meadowbank Thistle | 0 | Dundee United | 1 |
| St.Johnstone | 4 | Stirling Albion | 0 |
| Clyde | 0 | Falkirk | 2 |
| Hibernian | 2 | Meadowbank Thistle | 0 |
| Morton | 0 | Rangers | 0 |

**4TH ROUND**

| | | | |
|---|---|---|---|
| Ayr United | 2 | Hamilton Academ. | 0 |
| Dundee | 1 | Dundee United | 2 |
| Forfar Athletic | 0 | Celtic | 3 |
| Kilmarnock | 0 | St.Johnstone | 2 |

**REPLAYS**

| | | | |
|---|---|---|---|
| Morton | 1 | Motherwell | 1 (aet) |
| Motherwell win 4-5 on penalties | | | |

**1/4 FINALS**

| | | | |
|---|---|---|---|
| Dundee United | 3 | Airdrieonians | 2 |
| St.Johnstone | 5 | Cowdenbeath | 0 |
| Celtic | 2 | Rangers | 0 |
| Morton | 1 | Motherwell | 1 (aet) |

**SEMI-FINALS**

| | | | |
|---|---|---|---|
| Motherwell | 0 | Celtic | 0 |
| Dundee United | 2 | St.Johnstone | 1 |

**REPLAY**

| | | | |
|---|---|---|---|
| Celtic | 2 | Motherwell | 4 |

## FINAL

18/5/91 (at Hampden Park, Glasgow)

Motherwell ..... 4    Dundee United ..... 3 (aet)

Motherwell : Maxwell, Nijholt, Boyd, Griffin, Paterson, McCart, Arnott, Angus, Ferguson (Kirk 62), O'Donnell, Cooper (O'Neill 118).

Dundee U : Main, Clark, Malpas, McInally, Krivokapic, Bowman, van der Hoorn, McKinnon (McKinlay 67), French, Ferguson (O'Neil 46), Jackson.

| 1-0 | Ferguson | 32 |
|---|---|---|
| 1-1 | Bowman | 55 |
| 2-1 | O'Donnell | 58 |
| 3-1 | Angus | 65 |
| 3-2 | O'Neil | 67 |
| 3-3 | Jackson | 89 |
| 4-3 | Kirk | 94 |

Referee : D Syme
Attendance : 57,319

# SCOTLAND INTERNATIONAL REVIEW 1990

## INTERNATIONAL LINE-UPS 1990

| Fixture | Jim Leighton | Richard Gough | Stewart McKimmie | Craig Levein | Alex McLeish | Murdo MacLeod | Jim Bett | Stuart McCall | Alan McInally | Paul McStay | Robert Fleck | Roy Aitken | Brian McClair | Andy Goram | Gary Gillespie | Gary McAllister | Gordon Durie | Maurice Johnston | John Collins | Ally McCoist | Bryan Gunn | Maurice Malpas | Davie Cooper | Dave McPherson | Brian Irvine | John Robertson | Robert Connor | Pat Nevin | Tommy Boyd | Steve Nicol | Jim McInally |
|---|---|---|---|---|---|---|---|---|---|---|---|---|---|---|---|---|---|---|---|---|---|---|---|---|---|---|---|---|---|---|---|
| 28/3/90 SCOTLAND 1 ARGENTINA 0 Glasgow — Ref: Houben (Holland) — Friendly (McKimmie) | 1 | 2 | 3 | 4 | 5 | 6 | 7 | 8 | 9 | 10 | 11 | (7) | (9) | | | | | | | | | | | | | | | | | | |
| 25/4/90 SCOTLAND 0 DDR 1 Glasgow — Ref: Midgeley (England) — Friendly | | 6 | 2 | 4 | 5 | 3 | | 8 | | (2) | 11 | | | 1 | 2 | 7 | 9 | 10 | 11 | (9) | | 6 | 9 | | | | | | | | |
| 16/5/90 SCOTLAND 1 EGYPT 3 Aberdeen — Ref: Pedersen (Norway) — Friendly (McCoist) | | 3 | | (5) | | | 7 | (2) | (10) | 8 | | | | | 4 | | 10 | 11 | | 11 | | 6 | | | | | | | | | |
| 19/5/90 SCOTLAND 1 POLAND 1 Glasgow — Ref: Worrall (England) — Friendly (Johnston) | | 2 | | 4 | | 9 | | 6 | 11 | (8) | | 7 | | 1 | 3 | 8 | | 10 | (9) | 11 | 1 | 5 | | | | | | | | | |
| 28/5/90 MALTA 1 SCOTLAND 2 Ta Qali — Ref: Longhi (Italy) — Friendly (A.McInally 2) | (1) | 2 | | (5) | 4 | | 8 | 7 | 11 | 6 | | 3 | | | 5 | (8) | | 10 | (6) | (10) | | 9 | | 4 | | | | | | | |
| 11/6/90 COSTA RICA 1 SCOTLAND 0 Genova — Ref: Lousta (Argentina) — World Cup | 1 | 2 | (2) | | 4 | | 9 | 8 | 11 | 6 | 9 | 7 | | 1 | | | | 10 | | 9 | | 5 | | 3 | | | | | | | |
| 16/6/90 SWEDEN 1 SCOTLAND 2 Genova — Ref: Maciel (Paraguay) — World Cup (McCall, Johnston) | 1 | | 2 | 3 | 4 | 7 | 8 | 7 | | (10) | (11) | 6 | | 1 | (9) | | 10 | | | 9 | | 5 | | 2 | | | | | | | |
| 20/6/90 BRAZIL 1 SCOTLAND 0 Torino — Ref: Kohl (Austria) — World Cup | 1 | | | | 5 | 9 | 9 | | | 8 | | 4 | | | | | 11 | 11 | | 11 | | 6 | | 3 | | | | | | | |
| 12/9/90 SCOTLAND 2 RUMANIA 1 Glasgow — Ref: Urizar (Spain) — EuroCh.Q. (Robertson, McCoist) | | | 2 | | 6 | 10 | | 4 | | 8 | | | 10 | 1 | 6 | 4 | | | | 9 | | 3 | | | 5 | 7 | 11 | (4) | (11) | | |
| 17/10/90 SCOTLAND 2 SWITZERLAND 1 Glasgow — Ref: Palsi (Finland) — EuroCh.Q. (Robertson, McAllister) | | | 2 | | 6 | 10 | | | | | | | | 1 | | 8 | (11) | | (8) | 9 | | 3 | | 5 | | 7 | (11) | | 11 | 3 | |
| 14/11/90 BULGARIA 1 SCOTLAND 1 Sofia — Ref: Kaupe (Austria) — EuroCh.Q. (McCoist) | | | 2 | | | | | | | | | | 10 | 1 | | 8 | 7 | | 5 | 9 | | 3 | | 5 | 1 | | | (7) | 11 | | 4 |
| **CAPS AT 31/12/90** | 58 | 50 | 9 | 6 | 74 | 19 | 26 | 9 | 8 | 49 | 3 | 56 | 15 | 12 | 13 | 6 | 9 | 36 | 5 | 29 | 1 | 39 | 22 | 9 | 1 | 2 | 4 | 10 | 3 | 24 | 4 |
| **GOALS AT 31/12/90** | | 5 | 1 | 1 | | 1 | 1 | 1 | 3 | 6 | | 1 | 1 | | | 1 | 1 | 14 | 1 | 8 | | | 6 | | | | | | | | |

## SCOTLAND : All Time Records as at 31/12/90 - CAPS

1. Kenny Dalglish (Celtic/Liverpool) — 102
2. Alex McLeish (Aberdeen) — 74
3. Willie Miller (Aberdeen) — 65
4. Danny McGrain (Celtic) — 62
5. Jim Leighton (Aberdeen/Manchester United) — 58
6. Roy Aitken (Celtic/Newcastle United) — 56
7. Denis Law (Huddersfield Town/Manchester City/Torino/Manchester United) — 55
8. Billy Bremner (Leeds United) — 54
9. Graeme Souness (Middlesbrough/Liverpool/Sampdoria) — 54
10. Alan Rough (Partick Thistle/Hibernian) — 53
    George Young (Rangers) — 53

## SCOTLAND : All Time Records as at 31/12/90 - GOALS

1. Dennis Law (Huddersfield Town/Manchester City/Torino/Manchester United) — (55) 30
   Kenny Dalglish (Celtic/Liverpool) — (102) 30
3. Hughie Gallacher (Airdrieonians/Newcastle United/Chelsea/Derby County) — (20) 23
4. Lawrie Reilly (Hibernian) — (38) 22
5. Robert Hamilton (Rangers/Dundee) — (11) 14
   Maurice Johnston (Celtic/FC Nantes/Rangers) — (36) 14
7. Andrew Wilson (Dunfermline Athletic/Middlesbrough) — (12) 13
   Robert McColl (Queen's Park/Newcastle United) — (13) 13
9. John Smith (Mauchline/Edinburgh University/Queen's Park) — (10) 12
   Billy Steel (Morton/Derby County/Dundee) — (30) 12

# SPAIN Correspondent : JOSE DEL OLMO

## SPAIN 1st Division Season 1990/91

| | R. MADRID | VALENCIA | BARCELONA | ATLÉT.MADRID | R. SOCIEDAD | SEVILLA | LOGRONES | OSASUNA | ZARAGOZA | MALLORCA | OVIEDO | ATHLETIC | SPORTING | CASTELLON | CADIZ | VALLADOLID | TENERIFE | BURGOS | BETIS | ESPANOL |
|---|---|---|---|---|---|---|---|---|---|---|---|---|---|---|---|---|---|---|---|---|
| REAL MADRID CF | | 4-0 | 1-0 | 0-3 | 2-3 | 7-0 | 0-0 | 0-4 | 2-0 | 3-0 | 1-1 | 4-1 | 2-1 | 1-0 | 2-1 | 1-0 | 3-0 | 0-1 | 3-0 | 2-1 |
| VALENCIA CF | 2-1 | | 2-2 | 1-1 | 0-1 | 2-1 | 0-1 | 1-1 | 2-0 | 1-0 | 1-1 | 2-1 | 0-1 | 1-0 | 2-1 | 2-0 | 4-2 | 0-1 | 3-1 | 2-0 |
| FC BARCELONA | 2-1 | 3-1 | | 1-1 | 1-3 | 3-0 | 2-1 | 2-0 | 2-1 | 2-1 | 0-0 | 4-1 | 3-2 | 6-0 | 2-0 | 1-0 | 1-0 | 0-0 | 4-2 | 5-2 |
| ATLÉTICO MADRID | 0-3 | 2-0 | 2-1 | | 4-0 | 1-0 | 3-0 | 2-2 | 4-0 | 0-1 | 0-0 | 2-0 | 3-1 | 3-1 | 0-0 | 2-0 | 1-1 | 0-0 | 2-1 | 4-0 |
| REAL SOCIEDAD | 1-1 | 1-0 | 1-1 | 2-1 | | 1-1 | 2-0 | 1-1 | 1-0 | 0-0 | 3-1 | 0-1 | 1-0 | 1-1 | 0-0 | 1-1 | 1-3 | 3-1 | 1-0 | 0-0 |
| SEVILLA FC | 2-0 | 2-1 | 0-1 | 1-1 | 1-0 | | 1-0 | 2-1 | 1-2 | 1-0 | 3-0 | 3-0 | 1-0 | 3-0 | 2-1 | 1-0 | 2-2 | 1-2 | 3-2 | 1-1 |
| CD LOGRONES | 1-0 | 1-0 | 0-2 | 0-1 | 0-0 | 2-1 | | 2-0 | 1-1 | 1-2 | 1-0 | 1-1 | 1-2 | 2-1 | 1-1 | 1-2 | 1-0 | 0-0 | 1-0 | 1-0 |
| CA OSASUNA | 3-3 | 0-2 | 0-0 | 0-3 | 3-1 | 1-0 | 1-1 | | 1-0 | 1-0 | 0-0 | 1-0 | 2-1 | 2-0 | 1-1 | 2-1 | 3-1 | 1-0 | 3-0 | 1-0 |
| REAL ZARAGOZA CD | 1-3 | 2-1 | 0-2 | 1-0 | 1-1 | 2-0 | 0-1 | 0-0 | | 2-2 | 0-1 | 1-0 | 4-0 | 2-0 | 3-0 | 2-2 | 2-0 | 1-0 | 0-0 | 1-1 |
| RCD MALLORCA | 1-1 | 0-1 | 1-1 | 1-0 | 2-1 | 1-1 | 2-0 | 1-1 | 3-2 | | 1-1 | 0-0 | 1-1 | 1-0 | 0-0 | 0-0 | 0-1 | 0-0 | 1-0 | 4-0 |
| REAL OVIEDO CF | 0-0 | 2-1 | 1-0 | 3-0 | 2-1 | 0-0 | 0-0 | 0-0 | 2-1 | 1-0 | | 1-1 | 0-0 | 3-0 | 1-1 | 1-0 | 3-1 | 1-1 | 1-0 | 4-1 |
| ATHLETIC BILBAO | 1-0 | 0-2 | 0-6 | 2-1 | 2-1 | 2-0 | 1-1 | 2-0 | 2-0 | 2-0 | 2-1 | | 1-2 | 1-1 | 1-0 | 0-1 | 2-0 | 2-1 | 4-0 | 1-1 |
| SPORTING GIJON | 0-2 | 1-1 | 1-0 | 1-2 | 2-1 | 2-0 | 1-0 | 1-1 | 1-0 | 1-1 | 0-0 | 3-1 | | 1-0 | 3-1 | 4-0 | 2-1 | 0-0 | 4-0 | 3-0 |
| CD CASTELLON | 0-3 | 0-2 | 0-1 | 0-0 | 1-1 | 0-0 | 0-0 | 1-0 | 0-0 | 0-1 | 1-0 | 2-0 | 3-2 | | 2-0 | 4-2 | 5-1 | 0-0 | 3-1 | 1-1 |
| CADIZ CF | 1-0 | 0-0 | 4-0 | 0-1 | 1-1 | 2-1 | 2-0 | 1-1 | 2-1 | 1-0 | 2-1 | 2-3 | 1-1 | 0-0 | | 0-0 | 1-2 | 0-0 | 1-2 | 0-0 |
| REAL VALLADOLID | 0-1 | 3-1 | 1-5 | 0-0 | 4-2 | 2-1 | 0-0 | 1-1 | 0-0 | 5-1 | 1-0 | 1-0 | 0-0 | 0-0 | 0-0 | | 6-2 | 1-0 | 1-1 | 2-0 |
| CD TENERIFE | 0-1 | 1-1 | 0-1 | 0-0 | 2-0 | 0-4 | 2-0 | 2-1 | 0-2 | 2-1 | 1-2 | 1-0 | 0-0 | 1-0 | 1-0 | 1-0 | | 1-0 | 1-1 | 2-0 |
| REAL BURGOS CF | 2-1 | 0-0 | 1-3 | 1-1 | 2-0 | 1-1 | 1-2 | 1-1 | 0-1 | 1-1 | 4-0 | 2-1 | 1-1 | 4-0 | 1-0 | 0-1 | 2-0 | | 1-2 | 0-0 |
| REAL BETIS BALOMPIÉ | 1-3 | 2-2 | 2-3 | 0-0 | 1-1 | 0-3 | 3-2 | 0-1 | 1-1 | 2-2 | 1-1 | 1-0 | 2-2 | 1-0 | 3-0 | 0-0 | 1-1 | 0-0 | | 1-2 |
| RCD ESPANOL | 3-1 | 0-0 | 0-1 | 3-1 | 1-0 | 4-0 | 0-1 | 0-1 | 0-0 | 3-0 | 5-0 | 1-2 | 0-2 | 1-0 | 2-1 | 2-0 | 1-0 | 1-0 | 2-2 | |

## SPAIN 1ST DIVISION SEASON 1990/91

### LEAGUE TABLE FINAL

| | | | | | | | |
|---|---|---|---|---|---|---|---|
| FC Barcelona | 38 | 25 | 7 | 6 | 74 | 33 | 57 |
| Atlético Madrid | 38 | 17 | 13 | 8 | 52 | 28 | 47 |
| Real Madrid CF | 38 | 20 | 6 | 12 | 63 | 37 | 46 |
| CA Osasuna | 38 | 15 | 15 | 8 | 43 | 34 | 45 |
| Sporting Gijon | 38 | 16 | 12 | 10 | 50 | 37 | 44 |
| Real Oviedo CF | 38 | 13 | 16 | 9 | 36 | 35 | 42 |
| Valencia CF | 38 | 15 | 10 | 13 | 44 | 40 | 40 |
| Sevilla FC | 38 | 15 | 8 | 15 | 45 | 47 | 38 |
| Real Valladolid | 38 | 12 | 13 | 13 | 38 | 40 | 37 |
| CD Logrones | 38 | 13 | 11 | 14 | 28 | 35 | 37 |
| Real Burgos CF | 38 | 10 | 17 | 11 | 32 | 27 | 37 |
| Athletic Bilbao | 38 | 15 | 6 | 17 | 41 | 50 | 36 |
| Real Sociedad | 38 | 11 | 14 | 13 | 39 | 45 | 36 |
| CD Tenerife | 38 | 14 | 7 | 17 | 37 | 53 | 35 |
| RCD Mallorca | 38 | 9 | 16 | 13 | 32 | 40 | 34 |
| RCD Espanol | 38 | 12 | 10 | 16 | 39 | 47 | 34 |
| Real Zaragoza CD | 38 | 11 | 11 | 16 | 36 | 40 | 33 |
| Cadiz CF | 38 | 7 | 15 | 16 | 29 | 41 | 29 |
| CD Castellon | 38 | 8 | 12 | 18 | 27 | 48 | 28 |
| Real Betis Balompié | 38 | 6 | 13 | 19 | 37 | 65 | 25 |

Champions : - FC Barcelona
Relegated : - CD Castellon and Real Betis Balompié

### TOP SCORERS

1. Butragueno (Real Madrid) 19
2. Aldridge (Real Sociedad) 17
3. Manolo (Atlético Madrid) 16
4. Luhovy (Sporting Gijon) 15
   Luis Enrique (Sporting Gijon) 15
6. Fonesca (Real Valladolid) 14
   Mel (Real Betis) 14
   Stoichkov (FC Barcelona) 14
9. Bakero (FC Barcelona) 13
   Fernandez (Tenerife) 13
   Pardeza (Real Zaragoza) 13
   Polster (Sevilla FC) 13
   Urban (CA Osasuna) 13
   Valverde (Athletic Bilbao) 13
15. Atkinson (Real Sociedad) 12
    Carlos (Real Oviedo) 12
    Hugo Sanchez (Real Madrid) 12
18. Alcaniz (CD Castellon) 11
    Bango (Real Oviedo) 11
    Ciganda (CA Osasuna) 11
    Julio Salinas (FC Barcelona) 11

## SPAIN 2ND DIVISION SEASON 1990/91

### LEAGUE TABLE FINAL

| | | | | | | | |
|---|---|---|---|---|---|---|---|
| Albacete Balompié | 38 | 18 | 13 | 7 | 56 | 31 | 49 |
| RC Deportivo La Coruna | 38 | 20 | 8 | 10 | 60 | 32 | 48 |
| Real Murcia | 38 | 18 | 12 | 8 | 56 | 36 | 48 |
| CD Málaga | 38 | 16 | 14 | 8 | 52 | 35 | 46 |
| Orihuela DVA | 38 | 12 | 19 | 7 | 46 | 39 | 43 |
| UE Lérida | 38 | 16 | 11 | 11 | 41 | 36 | 43 |
| UE Figueras | 38 | 14 | 11 | 13 | 44 | 42 | 39 |
| Sestao Sport | 38 | 9 | 20 | 9 | 29 | 27 | 38 |
| Real Avilés Industrial | 38 | 10 | 18 | 10 | 35 | 37 | 38 |
| SD Eibar | 38 | 9 | 19 | 10 | 35 | 34 | 37 |
| AD Rayo Vallecano | 38 | 8 | 20 | 10 | 44 | 50 | 36 |
| CE Sabadell FC | 38 | 11 | 14 | 13 | 32 | 45 | 36 |
| Bilbao Athletic | 38 | 11 | 14 | 13 | 35 | 43 | 36 |
| RC Celta Vigo | 38 | 8 | 20 | 10 | 31 | 38 | 36 |
| UD Las Palmas | 38 | 10 | 16 | 12 | 38 | 43 | 36 |
| Palamós CF | 38 | 9 | 17 | 12 | 33 | 46 | 35 |
| Elche CF | 38 | 12 | 10 | 16 | 39 | 45 | 34 |
| UD Salamanca | 38 | 9 | 13 | 16 | 41 | 40 | 31 |
| Levante UD | 38 | 6 | 15 | 17 | 27 | 51 | 27 |
| Jerez CD | 38 | 6 | 12 | 20 | 37 | 61 | 24 |

Promoted : - Albecete Balompié & RC Deportivo La Coruna
Relegated : - Elche CF, UD Salamanca, Levante UD and Jerez CD

### PROMOTION/RELEGATION PLAY-OFFS

| | 1ST LEG | 2ND LEG | AGG. |
|---|---|---|---|
| Real Murcia v Real Zaragoza | 0-0 | 2-5 | 2-5 |
| CD Málaga v Cádiz CF | 1-0 | 0-1 (aet.) | 1-1 |

Cádiz CF win 5-4 on penalties.

| SPAIN 2nd Division Season 1990/91 | MALAGA | CELTA | RAYO V | BILBAO A | DEPORTIVO | LAS PALMAS | SABADELL | PALAMOS | MURCIA | JEREZ | SALAMANCA | SESTAO | ELCHE | LEVANTE | FIGUERAS | EIBAR | AVILÉS | LÉRIDA | ALBACETE | ORIHUELA |
|---|---|---|---|---|---|---|---|---|---|---|---|---|---|---|---|---|---|---|---|---|
| CD MALAGA | ■ | 1-1 | 1-0 | 1-0 | 1-2 | 1-1 | 4-2 | 5-0 | 1-1 | 3-0 | 1-0 | 1-0 | 2-0 | 4-1 | 0-0 | 0-0 | 1-0 | 0-1 | 3-2 | 2-2 |
| RC CELTA VIGO | 0-0 | ■ | 2-2 | 1-1 | 0-0 | 1-0 | 0-0 | 1-2 | 0-2 | 1-0 | 1-0 | 1-1 | 1-1 | 2-1 | 2-0 | 2-1 | 0-0 | 1-1 | 0-2 | 2-0 |
| AD RAYO VALLECANO | 1-1 | 2-1 | ■ | 0-0 | 0-3 | 4-0 | 0-0 | 0-0 | 2-0 | 1-0 | 2-0 | 2-0 | 1-2 | 2-2 | 1-1 | 0-0 | 0-2 | 1-4 | 1-1 | 0-0 |
| BILBAO ATHLETIC | 1-2 | 1-1 | 1-1 | ■ | 3-1 | 2-1 | 1-0 | 2-0 | 2-1 | 0-0 | 1-1 | 0-2 | 3-0 | 0-1 | 2-0 | 1-1 | 2-0 | 1-0 | 2-0 | 1-1 |
| RC DEP. LA CORUNA | 1-0 | 3-0 | 3-0 | 2-1 | ■ | 0-0 | 4-2 | 3-0 | 2-0 | 2-0 | 2-1 | 1-0 | 2-0 | 5-0 | 2-1 | 2-3 | 1-0 | 5-0 | 2-1 | 1-0 |
| UD LAS PALMAS | 3-0 | 1-1 | 2-2 | 1-1 | 2-1 | ■ | 0-0 | 1-1 | 2-0 | 3-1 | 2-0 | 0-1 | 0-1 | 1-0 | 0-2 | 1-0 | 2-0 | 2-0 | 0-1 | 0-0 |
| CE SABADELL FC | 1-0 | 3-0 | 2-2 | 2-0 | 1-0 | 0-0 | ■ | 0-0 | 1-2 | 3-2 | 1-0 | 1-1 | 0-2 | 1-1 | 2-1 | 1-2 | 1-0 | 2-3 | 0-4 | 1-1 |
| PALAMOS CF | 0-0 | 3-2 | 1-1 | 0-0 | 1-1 | 2-0 | 0-0 | ■ | 0-1 | 3-2 | 0-3 | 1-1 | 1-0 | 0-0 | 3-2 | 1-1 | 0-1 | 1-0 | 1-1 | 4-1 |
| REAL MURCIA | 1-1 | 1-1 | 6-1 | 1-0 | 3-2 | 2-1 | 4-0 | 1-1 | ■ | 0-0 | 2-1 | 3-1 | 2-1 | 2-0 | 3-0 | 1-0 | 1-1 | 1-0 | 2-0 | 3-0 |
| JEREZ CD | 1-4 | 1-1 | 2-2 | 1-0 | 3-0 | 0-0 | 1-2 | 3-0 | 1-1 | ■ | 1-1 | 0-0 | 1-2 | 2-0 | 0-2 | 0-0 | 1-2 | 0-0 | 1-2 | 4-1 |
| UD SALAMANCA | 1-1 | 1-1 | 2-2 | 3-0 | 1-0 | 4-1 | 0-1 | 4-0 | 3-0 | 3-0 | ■ | 1-0 | 2-2 | 0-0 | 2-0 | 2-2 | 0-0 | 1-1 | 0-1 | 0-2 |
| SESTAO SPORT | 2-0 | 0-0 | 2-1 | 1-1 | 0-0 | 1-1 | 0-0 | 1-0 | 0-0 | 4-1 | 1-1 | ■ | 2-1 | 0-1 | 0-0 | 0-0 | 2-0 | 1-1 | 0-0 | 1-1 |
| ELCHE CF | 0-1 | 0-1 | 1-3 | 6-0 | 0-0 | 0-0 | 2-0 | 1-4 | 3-2 | 1-0 | 0-0 | 1-1 | ■ | 0-0 | 2-1 | 0-0 | 2-0 | 0-0 | 2-0 | 0-1 |
| LEVANTE UD | 1-3 | 1-1 | 0-0 | 1-1 | 0-2 | 2-3 | 0-0 | 0-0 | 1-1 | 2-3 | 1-0 | 1-0 | 3-1 | ■ | 0-1 | 0-0 | 0-0 | 2-0 | 0-2 | 0-0 |
| UE FIGUERAS | 0-1 | 1-0 | 2-0 | 5-1 | 1-0 | 1-1 | 3-0 | 0-0 | 2-1 | 3-1 | 3-2 | 2-0 | 0-1 | 2-1 | ■ | 1-1 | 0-2 | 0-2 | 3-1 | 1-1 |
| SD EIBAR | 1-0 | 0-0 | 1-1 | 0-1 | 2-2 | 2-2 | 3-0 | 1-0 | 1-0 | 1-1 | 2-0 | 0-1 | 1-1 | 3-1 | 0-0 | ■ | 0-0 | 3-0 | 0-3 | 1-1 |
| REAL AVILES INDUST. | 3-3 | 0-0 | 1-1 | 0-0 | 1-1 | 2-0 | 1-0 | 3-3 | 0-0 | 5-0 | 1-1 | 1-1 | 3-2 | 1-1 | 0-0 | 2-1 | ■ | 1-0 | 1-2 | 1-1 |
| UE LÉRIDA | 2-0 | 2-1 | 1-0 | 1-0 | 2-1 | 1-1 | 0-1 | 0-0 | 1-1 | 3-1 | 1-0 | 1-1 | 2-0 | 2-1 | 1-1 | 2-0 | 3-0 | ■ | 1-0 | 2-2 |
| ALBACETE BALOMPIÉ | 2-2 | 2-0 | 1-1 | 1-1 | 2-1 | 4-1 | 0-0 | 2-0 | 2-2 | 0-0 | 2-0 | 0-0 | 2-1 | 3-1 | 5-1 | 3-1 | 0-0 | 2-0 | ■ | 0-0 |
| ORIHUELA DVA | 1-1 | 1-1 | 2-4 | 3-1 | 0-0 | 2-2 | 1-1 | 1-0 | 1-2 | 3-2 | 2-0 | 1-0 | 3-0 | 3-0 | 1-1 | 1-0 | 4-0 | 1-0 | 0-0 | ■ |

## SPAIN : All Time International Records as at 31/12/90 - CAPS

1. Jose Antonio Camacho (Real Madrid) — 81
2. Rafael Gordillo (Real Betis Balompie/Real Madrid) — 75
3. Luis Arconada (Real Sociedad) — 68
4. Victor Munoz (Real Zaragoza/FC Barcelona) — 60
5. Andoni Zubizarreta (Athletic Bilbao/FC Barcelona) — 57
   Emilio Butragueno (Real Madrid) — 57
7. Carlos Alonso "Santillana" (Real Madrid) — 56
8. Miguel Gonzalez Michel (Real Madrid) — 52
9. Jose Angel Iribar (Athletic Bilbao) — 49
10. Ricardo Zamora (FC Barcelona/RCD Espanol/Madrid FC) — 46

## SPAIN : All Time International Records as at 31/12/90 - GOALS

1. Emilio Butragueno (Real Madrid) — (57) 26
2. Alfredo Di Stefano (Real Madrid) — (31) 23
3. Telmo Zarraonandia "Zarra" (Athletico Bilbao) — (20) 20
4. Miguel Gonzalez "Michel" (Real Madrid) — (52) 18
5. Isidro Langara (Oviedo FC) — (12) 17
6. Luis Regueiro (Real Union Irun/Madrid FC) — (25) 16
   Jose Martinez "Pirri" (Real Madrid) — (41) 16
8. Carlos Alonso "Santillana" (Real Madrid) — (56) 15
9. Luis Suarez (CF Barcelona/Internazionale/Sampdoria) — (32) 14
10. Estanislao Basora (CF Barcelona) — (22) 13

## SPAIN 3RD DIVISION GROUP 1 1990/91

### LEAGUE TABLE FINAL

| | P | W | D | L | F | A | Pts |
|---|---|---|---|---|---|---|---|
| Real Madrid Deportivo | 38 | 20 | 13 | 5 | 44 | 25 | 53 |
| CD Lugo | 38 | 16 | 15 | 7 | 38 | 23 | 47 |
| SD Compostela | 38 | 18 | 11 | 9 | 44 | 31 | 47 |
| Getafe CF | 38 | 16 | 13 | 9 | 45 | 24 | 45 |
| CD Leganés | 38 | 12 | 19 | 7 | 38 | 27 | 43 |
| Palencia CF | 38 | 15 | 13 | 10 | 34 | 28 | 43 |
| Atlético Madrileno CF | 38 | 16 | 9 | 13 | 51 | 44 | 41 |
| CD Orense | 38 | 12 | 17 | 9 | 44 | 41 | 41 |
| CD Leonesa | 38 | 11 | 18 | 9 | 40 | 36 | 40 |
| Real Avila CF | 38 | 14 | 11 | 13 | 42 | 42 | 39 |
| SD Vetusta Oviedo | 38 | 9 | 21 | 8 | 32 | 26 | 39 |
| CD Endesa As Pontes | 38 | 12 | 14 | 12 | 42 | 36 | 38 |
| Sporting Atlético Gijon | 38 | 9 | 17 | 12 | 28 | 33 | 35 |
| Pontevedra CF | 38 | 10 | 15 | 13 | 42 | 42 | 35 |
| SD Ponferradina | 38 | 10 | 13 | 15 | 32 | 42 | 33 |
| CJ Cambados | 38 | 9 | 15 | 14 | 34 | 47 | 33 |
| CD Pegaso Madrid | 38 | 6 | 18 | 14 | 29 | 47 | 30 |
| UP Langreo | 38 | 9 | 11 | 18 | 41 | 43 | 29 |
| CD Móstoles | 38 | 7 | 14 | 17 | 26 | 41 | 28 |
| RSD Alcalá de Henares | 38 | 6 | 5 | 27 | 22 | 57 | 17 |

## SPAIN 3RD DIVISION GROUP 2 1990/91

### LEAGUE TABLE FINAL

| | P | W | D | L | F | A | Pts |
|---|---|---|---|---|---|---|---|
| Racing Santander | 38 | 22 | 10 | 6 | 67 | 32 | 54 |
| Deportivo Alavés Vitoria | 38 | 21 | 10 | 7 | 61 | 28 | 52 |
| Atlético Osasuna | 38 | 18 | 12 | 8 | 61 | 31 | 48 |
| San Sebastián CF | 38 | 18 | 11 | 9 | 52 | 31 | 47 |
| CD Aragón | 38 | 17 | 10 | 11 | 59 | 36 | 44 |
| SD Lemona | 38 | 13 | 15 | 10 | 38 | 31 | 41 |
| FC Andorra | 38 | 15 | 11 | 12 | 43 | 32 | 41 |
| Baracaldo CF | 38 | 12 | 16 | 10 | 36 | 36 | 40 |
| CD Baskonia Basauri | 38 | 12 | 16 | 10 | 37 | 35 | 40 |
| CFJ Mollerussa | 38 | 14 | 10 | 14 | 45 | 41 | 38 |
| CD Numancia | 38 | 12 | 14 | 12 | 49 | 48 | 38 |
| CD Binéfar | 38 | 12 | 12 | 14 | 33 | 40 | 36 |
| SD Huesca | 38 | 12 | 11 | 15 | 39 | 48 | 35 |
| RS Gimnást. Torrelavega | 38 | 14 | 6 | 18 | 40 | 51 | 34 |
| CD Santurtzi | 38 | 9 | 13 | 16 | 34 | 43 | 31 |
| CD Izarra Estella | 38 | 10 | 10 | 18 | 29 | 43 | 30 |
| Club Endesa Andorra | 38 | 8 | 14 | 16 | 24 | 43 | 30 |
| CD Cultural Durango | 38 | 10 | 9 | 19 | 43 | 56 | 29 |
| CD Mirandés | 38 | 8 | 12 | 18 | 21 | 43 | 28 |
| CD Teruel | 38 | 5 | 10 | 23 | 29 | 82 | 20 |

## SPAIN 3RD DIVISION GROUP 3 1990/91

### LEAGUE TABLE FINAL

| | P | W | D | L | F | A | Pts |
|---|---|---|---|---|---|---|---|
| CD Badajoz | 38 | 22 | 12 | 4 | 72 | 23 | 56 |
| RC Recreativo Huelva | 38 | 21 | 9 | 8 | 50 | 22 | 51 |
| Córdoba CF | 38 | 21 | 9 | 8 | 52 | 30 | 51 |
| Mérida CF | 38 | 18 | 13 | 7 | 49 | 29 | 49 |
| Granada CF | 38 | 15 | 17 | 6 | 49 | 28 | 47 |
| UD Melilla | 38 | 17 | 10 | 11 | 39 | 44 | 44 |
| AD Ceuta | 38 | 14 | 10 | 14 | 37 | 47 | 38 |
| CD Fuengirola | 38 | 13 | 12 | 13 | 26 | 34 | 38 |
| CD Estepona | 38 | 13 | 11 | 14 | 24 | 33 | 37 |
| CD Valdepeñas | 38 | 12 | 11 | 15 | 38 | 44 | 35 |
| Real Betis Deportivo | 38 | 12 | 11 | 15 | 49 | 49 | 35 |
| CD Marino Los Christianos | 38 | 11 | 12 | 15 | 37 | 50 | 34 |
| Atlético Sanluqueno CF | 38 | 12 | 9 | 17 | 30 | 42 | 33 |
| CF Extremadura | 38 | 10 | 13 | 15 | 30 | 42 | 33 |
| CD Los Boliches | 38 | 10 | 13 | 15 | 48 | 61 | 33 |
| Real Balompédica Linense | 38 | 12 | 9 | 17 | 39 | 46 | 33 |
| CD Toledo | 38 | 10 | 11 | 17 | 32 | 47 | 31 |
| Sevilla Atlético Club | 38 | 8 | 13 | 17 | 38 | 50 | 29 |
| UD Teide | 38 | 11 | 6 | 21 | 38 | 58 | 28 |
| US Las Palmas Atlético | 38 | 6 | 16 | 16 | 34 | 44 | 28 |

## SPAIN 3RD DIVISION GROUP 4 1990/91

### LEAGUE TABLE FINAL

| | P | W | D | L | F | A | Pts |
|---|---|---|---|---|---|---|---|
| ADC Manlleu | 38 | 18 | 13 | 7 | 55 | 39 | 49 |
| Barcelona Atlétic | 38 | 20 | 9 | 9 | 65 | 35 | 49 |
| Cartagena FC | 38 | 18 | 13 | 7 | 48 | 29 | 49 |
| CD Alcoyano | 38 | 18 | 12 | 8 | 43 | 29 | 48 |
| Hércules CF Alicante | 38 | 19 | 10 | 9 | 66 | 39 | 48 |
| CE Hospitalet | 38 | 15 | 17 | 6 | 47 | 34 | 47 |
| Girona FC | 38 | 16 | 15 | 7 | 47 | 32 | 47 |
| UD Alzira | 38 | 15 | 12 | 11 | 34 | 30 | 42 |
| CF Gandia | 38 | 16 | 10 | 12 | 47 | 42 | 42 |
| Benidorm CD | 38 | 15 | 11 | 12 | 45 | 41 | 41 |
| CD Torrevieja | 38 | 13 | 15 | 10 | 46 | 45 | 41 |
| CF Sporting Mahonés | 38 | 14 | 12 | 12 | 45 | 50 | 40 |
| UE S'nt Andreu Barcelona | 38 | 11 | 15 | 12 | 43 | 44 | 37 |
| Torrent CF | 38 | 11 | 12 | 15 | 34 | 44 | 34 |
| Yeclano CF | 38 | 13 | 8 | 17 | 40 | 50 | 34 |
| Atlético Tomelloso | 38 | 11 | 10 | 17 | 44 | 64 | 32 |
| RCD Mallorca Atlético | 38 | 10 | 12 | 16 | 31 | 44 | 32 |
| CD Eldense | 38 | 7 | 15 | 16 | 29 | 44 | 29 |
| CD Manacor | 38 | 6 | 6 | 26 | 30 | 97 | 18 |
| CD Olímpic Xátiva | 38 | 5 | 6 | 27 | 27 | 77 | 16 |

## PROMOTION PLAY-OFFS

### GROUP A LEAGUE TABLE FINAL

| | P | W | D | L | F | A | Pts |
|---|---|---|---|---|---|---|---|
| Racing Santander | 6 | 2 | 4 | 0 | 14 | 9 | 8 |
| Cartagena FC | 6 | 2 | 2 | 2 | 9 | 8 | 6 |
| Getafe CF | 6 | 1 | 4 | 1 | 6 | 6 | 6 |
| Córdoba CF | 6 | 0 | 2 | 4 | 4 | 13 | 2 |

### GROUP B LEAGUE TABLE FINAL

| | P | W | D | L | F | A | Pts |
|---|---|---|---|---|---|---|---|
| CP Mérida | 6 | 4 | 1 | 1 | 10 | 4 | 9 |
| FC Barcelona | 6 | 2 | 2 | 2 | 9 | 8 | 6 |
| Recreativo Huelva | 6 | 2 | 1 | 3 | 4 | 8 | 5 |
| CA Osasuna | 6 | 1 | 2 | 4 | 2 | 12 | 3 |

### GROUP C LEAGUE TABLE FINAL

| | P | W | D | L | F | A | Pts |
|---|---|---|---|---|---|---|---|
| SD Compostela | 6 | 3 | 2 | 1 | 7 | 6 | 8 |
| CD Badajoz | 6 | 3 | 1 | 2 | 9 | 6 | 7 |
| Getafe CF | 6 | 2 | 2 | 2 | 9 | 9 | 6 |
| CD Alcoyano | 6 | 1 | 2 | 3 | 10 | 11 | 4 |

### GROUP D LEAGUE TABLE FINAL

| | P | W | D | L | F | A | Pts |
|---|---|---|---|---|---|---|---|
| Real Madrid Deportivo | 6 | 2 | 2 | 2 | 7 | 4 | 8 |
| Real Sociedad | 6 | 2 | 2 | 2 | 2 | 3 | 6 |
| FC Barcelona | 6 | 2 | 2 | 2 | 3 | 5 | 9 |
| Atlético Madrid | 6 | 1 | 2 | 3 | 2 | 4 | 4 |

Promoted :- Racing Santander, CP Mérida, SD Compostela and Real Madrid Deportivo.

## SPAIN COPA DEL REY 1990/91

### 1ST ROUND

| | 1ST LEG | 2ND LEG | AGG. |
|---|---|---|---|
| SD Huesca v Cadiz CF (Cadiz CF win on penalties) | 0-0 | 1-1 | 1-1 |
| CD San Roque v Orihuela DVA | 0-1 | 0-1 | 0-2 |
| CD Badajoz v Real Betis Balompié | 1-0 | 1-4 | 2-4 |
| CD Benidorm v Real Valladolid | 1-1 | 0-7 | 1-8 |
| Racing Santander v Athletic Bilbao | 1-2 | 0-0 | 1-2 |
| Real Avila v Real Oviedo | 1-2 | 0-3 | 1-5 |
| Aguilas Atlético v AD Rayo Vallecano | 2-2 | 0-1 | 2-3 |
| Sporting Mahonés v CD Logrones | 1-2 | 0-1 | 1-3 |
| Atlético Baleares v RC Deportivo La Coruna | 0-0 | 0-3 | 0-3 |
| FC Andorra v CD Malaga | 1-2 | 2-2 | 3-4 |
| RSG Alcala v CF Palamos | 0-1 | 0-5 | 0-6 |
| CE Sabadell v RCD Mallorca | 0-3 | 1-4 | 1-7 |
| CD Tenerife v CA Osasuna | 3-0 | 1-2 | 4-2 |

European Cup participants, Real Madrid, FC Barcelona, Valencia CF, Atlético Madrid, Real Sociedad and Sevilla FC, were all awarded byes until the 1/8 Finals.

### 2ND ROUND

| | 1ST LEG | 2ND LEG | AGG. |
|---|---|---|---|
| Cadiz CF v Athletic Bilbao | 1-0 | 2-1 | 3-1 |
| Deportivo La Coruna v CD Malaga | 2-1 | 0-0 | 2-1 |
| Elche CF v Palamos CF | 2-0 | 2-1 | 4-1 |
| UD Las Palmas v RC Celta Vigo | 2-0 | 0-3 | 2-3 |
| Real Murcia v CD Logrones | 1-0 | 0-6 | 1-6 |
| SD Ponferradina v Real Zaragoza | 1-2 | 0-2 | 1-4 |
| Cultural Durango v Sporting Gijon | 0-1 | 1-3 | 1-4 |
| CD Castellon v RCD Espanol | 2-2 | 0-1 | 2-3 |

### 1/8 FINALS

| | 1ST LEG | 2ND LEG | AGG. |
|---|---|---|---|
| Deportivo La Coruna v Valencia CF | 2-3 | 0-4 | 2-7 |
| Elche CF v FC Barcelona | 2-1 | 1-3 (aet) | 3-4 |
| RCD Espanol v Real Valladolid | 2-1 | 0-2 | 2-3 |
| UD Las Palmas v Real Zaragoza | 1-0 | 0-6 | 1-6 |
| CD Logrones v Real Betis Balompié | 1-0 | 0-6 | 1-6 |
| RCD Mallorca v Atlético Madrid | 1-1 | 0-1 | 1-2 |
| Real Sociedad v Real Madrid | 0-0 | 0-2 | 2-0 |
| Sevilla FC v Cadiz CF | 3-0 | 3-0 | 6-0 |

### 1/4 FINALS

| | 1ST LEG | 2ND LEG | AGG. |
|---|---|---|---|
| Deportivo La Coruna v Valencia CF | 2-3 | 0-4 | 2-7 |
| CD Logrones v Sporting Gijon | 2-0 | 0-3 (aet) | 3-4 |
| Sevilla FC v FC Barcelona | 2-1 | 0-6 | 2-3 |
| Valencia CF v RCD Mallorca | 1-1 | 0-1 | 1-2 |

### SEMI-FINALS

| | 1ST LEG | 2ND LEG | AGG. |
|---|---|---|---|
| Sporting Gijon v RCD Mallorca | 0-1 | 0-1 | 0-2 |
| FC Barcelona v Atlético Madrid | 0-2 | 3-2 | 3-4 |

# SPAIN INTERNATIONAL REVIEW 1990

## INTERNATIONAL LINE-UPS 1990

| | A. Zubizarreta | M. Chendo | G. Andrinua | A. Gorriz | F. Perez Villarro | M. Gonzalez Michel | M. Sanchis | R. Fernandez | R. Martin Vazquez | M. Sanchez Manolo | E. Butragueno | J. Rodriguez Juanito | Rafa Paz | Luis Milla | J. Salinas Fernandez | M. Pardeza Pichardo | M. Jimenez | E. Sanchez Quique | R. Alcorta | F. Gomez | J.M. Bakero | F. Munoz Nando | R. Serna | C.A. Munoz | J.A. Goicoechea | J.C. Iglesias Ablanedo | R. Gonzalez Bango | Olaya Eloy | A. Mujica Beguiristain | E. Valverde | G. Amor Martinez | F. Ruiz Hierro III |
|---|---|---|---|---|---|---|---|---|---|---|---|---|---|---|---|---|---|---|---|---|---|---|---|---|---|---|---|---|---|---|---|---|
| **21/2/90** SPAIN 1 CZECHOSLOVAKIA 0 — Alicante — Ref: Philippoz (Switzerland) — Friendly (Manolo) | 1 | 2 | 3 | 4 | 5 | 6 | 7 | 8 | 9 | 10 | 11 | (3) | (6) | (8) | (10) | (11) | | | | | | | | | | | | | | | | |
| **28/3/90** SPAIN 2 AUSTRIA 3 — Malaga — Ref: D'Elia (Italy) — Friendly (Manolo, Butragueno) | 1 | 2 | 4 | (7) | 9 | 6 | 3 | 7 | 8 | 10 | 11 | | (8) | | (10) | (11) | 5 | (2) | | | | | | | | | | | | | | |
| **26/5/90** YUGOSLAVIA 0 SPAIN 1 — Ljubljana — Ref: Lo Bello (Italy) — Friendly (Butragueno) | 1 | 2 | 3 | (4) | 9 | 6 | 4 | 7 | 8 | 10 | 11 | | (9) | | | | 5 | | (2) | | | | | | | | | | | | | |
| **13/6/90** URUGUAY 0 SPAIN 0 — Udine — Ref: Kohl (Austria) — World Cup | 1 | 5 | 2 | | 9 | 6 | 4 | 7 | 8 | 10 | 11 | | (9) | 3 | | (10) | | | | | | | | | | | | | | | | |
| **17/6/90** SOUTH KOREA 1 SPAIN 3 — Udine — Ref: Guerrero (Ecuador) — World Cup (Michel 3) | 1 | 5 | 2 | | 9 | 6 | 4 | 7 | 8 | | 10 | | | | 11 | | 3 | | | (10) | | | | | | | | | | | | |
| **21/6/90** BELGIUM 1 SPAIN 2 — Verona — Ref: Lousteau (Argentina) — World Cup (Michel, Gorriz) | 1 | 3 | 2 | 5 | 7 | 6 | 4 | 9 | 8 | | 10 | | | | 11 | (11) | | | | (10) | | | | | | | | | | | | |
| **26/6/90** YUGOSLAVIA 2 SPAIN 1 (aet.) — Verona — Ref: Schmidhuber (W.Germany) — World Cup (Julio Salinas) | 1 | 3 | 2 | 5 | 9 | 6 | 4 | 7 | 8 | | 11 | | (11) | (2) | 10 | | | | | | | | | | | | | | | | | |
| **12/9/90** SPAIN 3 BRAZIL 0 — Gijon — Ref: D'Elia (Italy) — Friendly (Carlos, Fernando, Michel) | 1 | | | | | 8 | 5 | 6 | | (9) | 9 | | 4 | | | | | | (6) | 10 | (11) | 2 | 3 | 7 | 11 | (1) | (4) | (7) | | | | |
| **10/10/90** SPAIN 2 ICELAND 1 — Sevilla — Ref: Mintoff (Malta) — EuroCh.Q (Butragueno, Carlos) | 1 | | | | | 8 | 5 | | 9 | | 11 | | | | | | | | 4 | 6 | | 2 | 3 | 10 | 7 | | | | (4) | (10) | | |
| **14/11/90** CZECHOSLOVAKIA 3 SPAIN 2 — Praha — Ref: Trischler (Germany) — EuroCh.Q (Roberto, Carlos) | 1 | | | | | 7 | 5 | 9 | | 8 | 10 | | | | | | | | | (11) | | 2 | 3 | 11 | 6 | | | | 4 | | (7) | |
| **19/12/90** SPAIN 9 ALBANIA 0 — Sevilla — Ref: Constantin (Belgium) — EuroCh.Q (Amor, Carlos 2, Butragueno 4, Hierro, Bakero) | 1 | | | | | 7 | 5 | | 9 | 8 | 10 | | | | | | | | 3 | | (2) | | | 11 | 2 | | | | (10) | | 6 | 4 |
| **CAPS AT 31/12/90** | 57 | 26 | 28 | 12 | 11 | 52 | 38 | 28 | 29 | 16 | 57 | 2 | 7 | 3 | 29 | 5 | 15 | 13 | 4 | 5 | 14 | 3 | 6 | 4 | 4 | 3 | 1 | 15 | 9 | 1 | 6 | 4 |
| **GOALS AT 31/12/90** | | | 2 | 1 | | 18 | 1 | 1 | | 7 | 26 | 1 | 1 | | 8 | | | | | 2 | 3 | | | 5 | | | | 3 | 1 | 1 | 1 | 1 |

**FINAL** 29/6/91 (at Madrid)

Atlético de Madrid......1    RCD Mallorca.........0    (aet)

At.Madrid : Mejías, Tomás, Ferreira, Juanito, Vizcaino, Toni, Vizcaino, Schuster, Orejuela (Alfredo 62), Manolo, Futre (Sabas 87).

Mallorca : Ezaki, Pedraza, Del Campo, Fradera, Serer, Armando, Parra, Soler, Nadal, Marcos (Alvaro 52), Hassan (Claudio 80).

1-0 Alfredo 111    Referee : Ramos Marcos    Attendance : 60,000

# SWEDEN Correspondent : JANNE STARK

## SWEDEN PREMIER DIVISION 1990
### LEAGUE TABLE FINAL

| | | | | | | | |
|---|---|---|---|---|---|---|---|
| IFK Göteborg | 22 | 14 | 3 | 5 | 39 | 22 | 45 |
| IFK Norrköping | 22 | 12 | 4 | 6 | 41 | 23 | 40 |
| Örebro SK | 22 | 10 | 6 | 6 | 23 | 17 | 36 |
| Östers IF | 22 | 10 | 6 | 6 | 28 | 27 | 36 |
| Djurgardens IF | 22 | 9 | 6 | 7 | 37 | 23 | 33 |
| Malmö FF | 22 | 6 | 10 | 6 | 20 | 15 | 28 |
| GAIS | 22 | 7 | 7 | 8 | 17 | 17 | 28 |
| AIK | 22 | 8 | 3 | 11 | 25 | 39 | 27 |
| Halmstads BK | 22 | 7 | 5 | 10 | 27 | 34 | 26 |
| IK Brage | 22 | 5 | 9 | 8 | 23 | 26 | 24 |
| Örgryte IS | 22 | 6 | 3 | 13 | 22 | 40 | 21 |
| Hammarby IF | 22 | 5 | 4 | 13 | 32 | 51 | 19 |

Champions : - IFK Göteborg
Relegated : - IK Brage, Örgryte IS and Hammarby IF

Note : League reduced to 10 clubs for Season 1991.

### SWEDEN Premier Division Season 1990

| | MALMÖ | NORRKÖPING | GAIS | ÖREBRO | HALMSTAD | DJURGARDEN | GÖTEBORG | AIK | ÖRGRYTE | BRAGE | HAMMARBY | ÖSTER |
|---|---|---|---|---|---|---|---|---|---|---|---|---|
| MALMÖ FF | ■ | 2-0 | 0-0 | 0-0 | 5-0 | 0-0 | 0-2 | 2-3 | 0-2 | 0-1 | 0-0 | 1-1 |
| IFK NORRKÖPING | 1-0 | ■ | 3-0 | 2-2 | 3-1 | 3-2 | 6-0 | 4-1 | 1-2 | 2-1 | 3-1 | 2-2 |
| GAIS (Västra Frölunda) | 0-0 | 2-0 | ■ | 0-1 | 0-0 | 0-0 | 0-1 | 1-0 | 2-0 | 2-0 | 1-0 | 3-0 |
| ÖREBRO SK | 0-0 | 1-0 | 1-0 | ■ | 1-0 | 0-1 | 2-6 | 3-0 | 0-1 | 1-1 | 4-1 | 0-0 |
| HALMSTADS BK | 1-2 | 0-2 | 3-0 | 3-0 | ■ | 0-0 | 1-0 | 2-2 | 0-1 | 2-1 | 4-3 | 2-0 |
| DJURGARDENS IF (St'holm) | 2-2 | 0-2 | 2-1 | 0-2 | 2-0 | ■ | 2-0 | 2-1 | 7-1 | 1-1 | 9-1 | 4-0 |
| IFK GÖTEBORG | 0-0 | 1-0 | 0-0 | 1-0 | 3-1 | 2-1 | ■ | 5-0 | 3-0 | 1-0 | 2-2 | 2-0 |
| AIK (Solna) | 1-1 | 1-3 | 2-2 | 1-0 | 2-1 | 1-0 | 1-2 | ■ | 1-0 | 1-0 | 2-0 | 1-2 |
| ÖRGRYTE IS (Göteborg) | 0-3 | 1-1 | 2-0 | 0-2 | 3-3 | 0-1 | 0-3 | 0-1 | ■ | 1-3 | 3-0 | 2-3 |
| IK BRAGE (Borlänge) | 0-1 | 1-1 | 1-1 | 0-1 | 1-1 | 0-0 | 2-1 | 4-2 | 1-1 | ■ | 1-1 | 1-1 |
| HAMMARBY IF (Stockholm) | 0-1 | 2-0 | 0-2 | 0-2 | 1-2 | 3-0 | 2-4 | 4-1 | 4-2 | 3-1 | ■ | 2-2 |
| ÖSTERS IF (Växjö) | 1-0 | 0-2 | 1-0 | 0-0 | 2-0 | 3-1 | 2-0 | 1-0 | 1-0 | 1-2 | 5-2 | ■ |

## SWEDEN PREMIER DIVISION CHAMPIONSHIP PLAY-OFFS 1990

| SEMI-FINALS | 1ST LEG | 2ND LEG | AGG. |
|---|---|---|---|
| Östers IF v IFK Norrköping (IFK Norrköping win on away goals) | 4-3 | 1-2 | 5-5 |
| Örebro SK v IFK Göteborg | 1-1 | 1-2 | 2-3 |

## FINAL

**1ST LEG** 28/10/90

IFK Norrköping ......... 0    IFK Göteborg ............ 3

Norrköping : L.Eriksson, J.Kalén (J.Rödlund 67), S.Vaattovaara, M.Almgren, J.Hedén, T-A.Fredheim, Y.Kuznetsov, J.Lind, G.Holter, P.Andersson (R.Ericsson 56), J.Hellström.
Göteborg : T.Ravelli, T.Pedersen, M.Nilsson (T.Andersson 88), O.Svensson, M.Johansson, M.Johansson, S.Rehn, H.Mild, P.Eriksson, K.Andersson, K.Eskelinen (L.Nilsson 85).

| | | | |
|---|---|---|---|
| 0-1 | K.Eskelinen | 21 | |
| 0-2 | O.Svensson | 60 | |
| 0-3 | K.Eskelinen pen. 75 | | |

Referee : Bo Persson (Gävle)
Attendance : 9,086

**2ND LEG** 3/11/90

IFK Göteborg ............ 0    IFK Norrköping ......... 0

Göteborg : T.Ravelli, T.Pedersen, M.Nilsson, O.Svensson, M.Johansson, M.Johansson, S.Rehn, H.Mild, P.Eriksson, K.Eskelinen (T.Andersson 78), K.Andersson.
Norrköping : L.Eriksson, J.Kalén, S.Vaattovaara, M.Almgren, J.Hedén (R.Ericsson 72), T-A.Fredheim, Y.Kuznetsov, J.Lind, G.Holter (M.Karlsson 54), J.Hellström, J.Rödlund.

Referee : Bo Karlsson (Jönköping)
Attendance : 10, 079

**IFK GÖTEBORG WIN 3-0 ON AGGREGATE**

### TOP SCORERS

| | | |
|---|---|---|
| 1. Kaj Eskelinen (IFK Göteborg) | | 10 |
| 2. Kenneth Andersson (IFK Göteborg) | | 8 |
| Patrik Andersson (IFK Norrköping) | | 8 |
| Jan Hellström (IFK Norrköping) | | 8 |
| Niclas Jönsson (Hammarby IF) | | 8 |
| Niklas Karlström (Djurgardens IF) | | 8 |
| Mikael Martinsson (Djurgardens IF) | | 8 |
| 8. Lasse Asp (Hammarby IF) | | 7 |
| Tomas Brolin (IFK Norrköping) | | 7 |
| Martin Dahlin (Malmö FF) | | 7 |
| Hans Eklund (Östers IF) | | 7 |
| Tor-Arne Fredheim (IFK Norrköping) | | 7 |
| Magnus Gustafsson (GAIS) | | 7 |
| Steve Whitton (Halmstads BK) | | 7 |

## SWEDEN 1ST DIVISION NORTH 1990
### LEAGUE TABLE FINAL

| | | | | | | | |
|---|---|---|---|---|---|---|---|
| GIF Sundsvall | 26 | 19 | 4 | 3 | 69 | 27 | 61 |
| Vasalunds IF | 26 | 15 | 4 | 7 | 45 | 21 | 49 |
| IF Brommapojkarna | 26 | 15 | 4 | 7 | 46 | 29 | 49 |
| Sparvägens GolF | 26 | 13 | 6 | 7 | 55 | 37 | 45 |
| Västeras SK | 26 | 12 | 5 | 9 | 46 | 31 | 41 |
| Kiruna FF | 26 | 11 | 5 | 10 | 50 | 39 | 38 |
| IFK Lulea | 26 | 10 | 8 | 8 | 37 | 28 | 38 |
| Gefle IF | 26 | 12 | 2 | 12 | 35 | 38 | 38 |
| BK Forward | 26 | 8 | 11 | 7 | 33 | 29 | 35 |
| Motala AIF | 26 | 9 | 7 | 10 | 41 | 44 | 34 |
| Väsby IK FK | 26 | 9 | 5 | 12 | 33 | 44 | 32 |
| IFK Eskilstuna | 26 | 7 | 7 | 12 | 34 | 45 | 28 |
| IFK Holmsund | 26 | 2 | 6 | 18 | 16 | 68 | 12 |
| Tyresö FF | 26 | 1 | 4 | 21 | 18 | 78 | 7 |

Promoted : - GIF Sundsvall
Relegated : - IFK Holmsund and Tyresö FF

IFK Holmsund was declared bankrupt at the end of the season.
1st Division to consist of 4 groups of 8 clubs for Season 1991.

**PROMOTION PLAY-OFFS**

| | 1ST LEG | 2ND LEG | AGG. |
|---|---|---|---|
| BK Häcken v GIF Sundsvall | 4-2 | 1-4 | 5-6 |

## SWEDEN 1ST DIVISION SOUTH 1990
### LEAGUE TABLE FINAL

| | | | | | | | |
|---|---|---|---|---|---|---|---|
| BK Häcken | 26 | 14 | 9 | 3 | 53 | 23 | 51 |
| Helsingborgs IF | 26 | 14 | 8 | 4 | 37 | 19 | 50 |
| Västra Frölunda IF | 26 | 15 | 4 | 7 | 38 | 27 | 49 |
| Trelleborgs FF | 26 | 13 | 3 | 10 | 41 | 33 | 42 |
| Jonsereds IF | 26 | 10 | 8 | 8 | 38 | 30 | 38 |
| Kalmar AIK | 26 | 10 | 6 | 10 | 35 | 41 | 36 |
| IK Oddevold | 26 | 9 | 6 | 11 | 33 | 34 | 33 |
| Kalmar FF | 26 | 9 | 5 | 12 | 32 | 34 | 32 |
| Markaryds IF | 26 | 8 | 7 | 11 | 30 | 43 | 31 |
| IF Elfsborg | 26 | 7 | 9 | 10 | 30 | 35 | 30 |
| Gunnilse IS | 26 | 7 | 8 | 11 | 31 | 34 | 29 |
| Landskrona BoIS | 26 | 7 | 8 | 11 | 30 | 39 | 29 |
| Mjällby AIF | 26 | 7 | 7 | 12 | 27 | 37 | 28 |
| Karlskrona AIF | 26 | 5 | 6 | 15 | 22 | 48 | 21 |

Relegated : - Mjällby AIF and Karlskrona AIF

## SWEDEN — 1st Division North — Season 1990

| | SUNDSVALL | VASALUND | KIRUNA | FORWARD | MOTALA | LULEA | VASTERAS | GEFLE | ESKILSTUNA | B'POJKARNA | VÄSBY | HOLMSUND | SPARVÅGEN | TYRESÖ |
|---|---|---|---|---|---|---|---|---|---|---|---|---|---|---|
| GIF SUNDSVALL | | 1-0 | 4-3 | 2-2 | 3-2 | 1-1 | 2-1 | 3-1 | 3-2 | 1-0 | 2-3 | 2-1 | 1-0 | 3-0 |
| VASALUNDS IF (Solna) | 4-2 | | 2-0 | 2-0 | 5-1 | 0-1 | 1-2 | 2-1 | 3-1 | 0-0 | 2-0 | 7-0 | 0-2 | 4-0 |
| KIRUNA FF | 1-7 | 0-0 | | 1-3 | 4-1 | 4-1 | 4-1 | 2-2 | 3-2 | 2-0 | 4-1 | 1-0 | 1-2 | 6-1 |
| BK FORWARD (Örebro) | 1-1 | 0-1 | 2-1 | | 2-2 | 2-2 | 1-0 | 2-0 | 0-0 | 1-1 | 0-1 | 4-0 | 1-2 | 1-0 |
| MOTALA AIF | 1-0 | 1-1 | 2-1 | 0-0 | | 1-0 | 2-0 | 0-2 | 1-1 | 0-3 | 1-1 | 6-0 | 5-1 | 3-2 |
| IFK LULEA | 0-1 | 0-1 | 2-0 | 1-1 | 3-0 | | 2-1 | 2-0 | 1-1 | 4-5 | 0-0 | 0-0 | 2-2 | 2-0 |
| VASTERAS SK | 2-2 | 2-0 | 0-0 | 0-0 | 2-1 | 1-2 | | 3-1 | 0-1 | 4-0 | 1-2 | 3-2 | 1-1 | 3-0 |
| GEFLE IF (Gävle) | 0-2 | 0-1 | 1-0 | 3-0 | 1-1 | 1-0 | 1-2 | | 2-0 | 2-0 | 1-0 | 2-0 | 2-6 | 1-0 |
| IFK ESKILSTUNA | 0-5 | 1-2 | 0-0 | 4-0 | 1-1 | 1-3 | 1-6 | 4-2 | | 1-2 | 2-1 | 4-1 | 0-0 | 3-2 |
| IFK BROMMAPOJKARNA | 1-2 | 2-1 | 1-1 | 2-0 | 2-1 | 2-1 | 0-2 | 1-2 | 2-0 | | 3-1 | 3-0 | 3-0 | 4-0 |
| VÄSBY IK FK | 0-2 | 2-0 | 0-3 | 1-6 | 4-1 | 1-3 | 1-3 | 4-1 | 1-0 | 0-0 | | 2-2 | 2-2 | 2-0 |
| IFK HOLMSUND | 0-5 | 1-4 | 1-4 | 1-3 | 0-2 | 0-0 | 0-0 | 0-3 | 1-0 | 1-3 | 0-1 | | 1-0 | 2-2 |
| SPARVÄGENS GOIF (Ensk.) | 1-2 | 1-1 | 3-2 | 1-1 | 3-2 | 2-0 | 4-2 | 3-2 | 1-2 | 1-3 | 2-0 | 5-0 | | 5-1 |
| TYRESÖ FF | 0-10 | 0-1 | 0-2 | 0-0 | 2-3 | 0-4 | 0-4 | 0-1 | 2-2 | 1-3 | 3-2 | 2-2 | 0-5 | |

## SWEDEN — 1st Division South — Season 1990

| | V FRÖLUNDA | TRELLEBORG | ELFSBORG | ODDEVOLD | KALMAR FF | MJÄLLBY | HÄCKEN | LANDSKRONA | MARKARYD | JONSERED | KARLSKRONA | KALMAR AIK | GUNNILSE | H'SINGBORG |
|---|---|---|---|---|---|---|---|---|---|---|---|---|---|---|
| VÄSTRA FRÖLUNDA IF | | 2-3 | 1-0 | 1-1 | 2-1 | 1-0 | 1-3 | 3-0 | 0-0 | 1-0 | 0-2 | 3-1 | 2-0 | 1-1 |
| TRELLEBORGS FF | 1-0 | | 6-0 | 0-1 | 1-0 | 2-3 | 0-2 | 3-1 | 2-0 | 1-1 | 2-3 | 1-0 | 0-2 | 1-1 |
| IF ELFSBORG (Boras) | 1-2 | 0-2 | | 1-1 | 1-0 | 1-2 | 4-3 | 2-1 | 3-0 | 1-1 | 0-0 | 4-1 | 1-1 | 0-1 |
| IK ODDEVOLD (Uddevalla) | 0-1 | 1-2 | 1-2 | | 1-2 | 2-0 | 3-3 | 4-0 | 1-2 | 1-1 | 1-0 | 2-3 | 3-1 | 2-0 |
| KALMAR FF | 0-2 | 1-4 | 0-3 | 2-0 | | 2-2 | 1-0 | 2-2 | 1-0 | 2-0 | 2-0 | 4-0 | 0-1 | 0-3 |
| MJÄLLBY AIF (Sölvesborg) | 0-2 | 0-1 | 1-0 | 1-2 | 2-1 | | 1-2 | 0-2 | 0-1 | 3-6 | 3-0 | 0-0 | 0-1 | 1-1 |
| BK HÄCKEN (Göteborg) | 4-1 | 3-0 | 0-0 | 3-1 | 1-1 | 3-0 | | 3-2 | 5-0 | 1-0 | 5-0 | 1-1 | 2-0 | 0-0 |
| LANDSKRONA BOIS | 3-0 | 1-3 | 0-0 | 0-0 | 1-0 | 2-2 | 1-1 | | 4-0 | 3-2 | 0-0 | 0-4 | 1-1 | 3-1 |
| MARKARYDS IF | 0-5 | 2-2 | 2-1 | 1-2 | 1-0 | 1-1 | 0-2 | 2-1 | | 1-0 | 2-2 | 4-0 | 2-2 | 1-2 |
| JONSEREDS IF (Partille) | 3-0 | 3-1 | 0-0 | 1-0 | 5-3 | 0-1 | 2-2 | 3-1 | 0-0 | | 2-1 | 0-0 | 4-1 | 0-2 |
| KARLSKRONA AIF | 0-2 | 2-0 | 2-2 | 1-0 | 2-5 | 0-0 | 0-2 | 0-1 | 2-5 | 0-1 | | 3-5 | 0-4 | 0-2 |
| KALMAR AIK | 0-1 | 0-3 | 1-1 | 1-2 | 0-2 | 3-2 | 1-1 | 1-0 | 2-1 | 3-0 | 0-0 | | 3-0 | 3-0 |
| GUNNILSE IS (Angered) | 2-3 | 3-0 | 4-1 | 4-0 | 0-0 | 1-1 | 1-1 | 0-0 | 1-1 | 0-2 | 0-1 | 1-2 | | 0-2 |
| HELSINGBORGS IF | 1-1 | 1-0 | 2-1 | 1-1 | 0-0 | 0-1 | 2-0 | 2-0 | 2-1 | 1-1 | 2-1 | 5-0 | 2-0 | |

## SWEDEN : All Time Internat. Records as at 31/12/90 - CAPS

1. Björn Nordqvist (IFK Nörrkoping/PSV/IFK Göteborg) — 115
2. Orvar Bergmark (Örebro SK/AIK/AS Roma) — 94
3. Thomas Ravelli (Östers IF/IFK Göteborg) — 78
4. Ronnie Hellström (Hammarby IF/1FC Kaiserslautern) — 77
5. Karl Svensson (Helsingborgs IF) — 73
6. Bo Larsson (Malmö FF/VfB Stuttgart) — 70
7. Ingemar Erlandsson (Malmö FF) — 69
8. Glenn Hysén (IFK Göteborg/PSV/AC Fiorentina/Liverpool) — 68
9. Stig Fredriksson (Västeras SK/IFK Göteborg) — 53
10. Gunnar Gren (Garda BK/IFK Göteborg/Örgryte IS) — 57
   Bengt Gustavsson (IFK Norrköping/Atvidabergs FF/Atalanta BC) — 57
   Erik Nilsson (Malmö FF) — 57

## SWEDEN : All Time Internat. Records as at 31/12/90 - GOALS

1. Sven Rydell (Örgryte IS/Redberglids IK) — (43) 49
2. Gunnar Nordahl (Degerfors IF/IFK Norrköping) — (33) 43
3. Gunnar Gren (Garda BK/IFK Göteborg/Örgryte IS) — (57) 32
4. Agne Simonsson (Örgryte IS/Real Madrid/Real Sociedad) — (51) 27
5. Per Kaufeldt (AIK) — (33) 23
6. Karl Gustafsson (IFK Köping/Köpings IS/Djurgardens IF) — (32) 22
7. Albin Dahl (Landskrona BoIS/Helsingborgs IF) — (29) 21
8. Nils-Ake Sandell (Malmö FF/Lunds BK) — (20) 20
   Erik Persson (AIK) — (32) 20
   Sven Johansson (IF Elfsborg) — (42) 20

Name Change for Season 1991 :- Raslatts SK to FC Jönköping

Promoted from 3rd Division :- Sunnana SK (Skelleftea), Notvikens IK (Lulea), Alnö IF, IF Älgarna (Härnösand), Ludvika FK, Sandvikens AIK-FK, Gimo IF, IFK Österaker FK (Akersberga), FK Sumarice (Johanneshov), Assyriska Föreningen (Södertälje), Hertzöga Bk (Karlstad), Västeras IK, Gullringens GolF, Lerums IS, Askims IK, Ulvakers IF (Skövde), Raslatts SK (Jönköping), Horna Fure IF (Ahus), Yngsjö IF, IF Norvalla (Väröbacka), Kungsbacka BI, FBK Balkan (Malmö) and BK Astrio (Halmstad).

## SWEDEN 2ND DIVISION NORTH 1990
### LEAGUE TABLE FINAL

| Team | P | W | D | L | F | A | Pts |
| --- | --- | --- | --- | --- | --- | --- | --- |
| IFK Sundsvall | 26 | 19 | 5 | 2 | 68 | 18 | 62 |
| IK Sirius (Uppsala) | 26 | 19 | 5 | 2 | 71 | 22 | 62 |
| IFK Östersund | 26 | 14 | 5 | 7 | 53 | 32 | 49 |
| Umea FC | 26 | 12 | 6 | 8 | 50 | 32 | 42 |
| Sandvikens IF | 26 | 13 | 1 | 12 | 44 | 38 | 40 |
| Morön BK (Skelleftea) | 26 | 11 | 4 | 11 | 36 | 34 | 37 |
| Hudiksvalls ABK | 26 | 9 | 10 | 7 | 38 | 38 | 37 |
| Forssa BK (Borlänge) | 26 | 9 | 11 | 6 | 37 | 49 | 29 |
| Kvarnsvedens IK (Borlänge) | 26 | 7 | 8 | 11 | 32 | 55 | 29 |
| Ope IF (Östersund) | 26 | 5 | 11 | 10 | 27 | 35 | 26 |
| Skelleftea AIK | 26 | 7 | 7 | 12 | 29 | 42 | 23 |
| Ömsköldsviks FF | 26 | 7 | 7 | 12 | 29 | 62 | 23 |
| Gimonäs CK (Umea) | 26 | 5 | 7 | 14 | 28 | 56 | 22 |
| IFK Mora FK | 26 | 4 | 7 | 15 | 23 | 62 | 19 |

Promoted :- IFK Sundsvall and IK Sirius
Relegated :- Ömsköldsviks FF, Gimonas CK and IFK Mora FK

## SWEDEN 2ND DIVISION WEST 1990
### LEAGUE TABLE FINAL

| Team | P | W | D | L | F | A | Pts |
| --- | --- | --- | --- | --- | --- | --- | --- |
| Degerfors IF | 26 | 17 | 7 | 2 | 56 | 17 | 58 |
| Skövde AIK | 26 | 17 | 6 | 3 | 65 | 29 | 57 |
| Tidaholms GIF | 26 | 14 | 7 | 5 | 47 | 30 | 49 |
| Asa IF | 26 | 9 | 9 | 8 | 33 | 34 | 36 |
| KB Karlskoga | 26 | 9 | 7 | 10 | 36 | 31 | 34 |
| Norrby IF (Boras) | 26 | 10 | 3 | 13 | 35 | 41 | 33 |
| IFK Uddevalla | 26 | 7 | 11 | 8 | 39 | 49 | 32 |
| Holmalunds IF (Alingsas) | 26 | 9 | 4 | 13 | 49 | 49 | 31 |
| IF Warta (Göteborg) | 26 | 7 | 10 | 9 | 34 | 41 | 31 |
| IFK Strömstad | 26 | 8 | 7 | 11 | 28 | 39 | 31 |
| Grimsas IF | 26 | 8 | 6 | 12 | 39 | 55 | 30 |
| Säffle FF | 26 | 8 | 5 | 13 | 45 | 49 | 29 |
| Norrstrands IF (Karlstad) | 26 | 6 | 7 | 13 | 36 | 45 | 25 |
| Karlstads BK | 26 | 6 | 5 | 15 | 37 | 52 | 23 |

Promoted :- Degerfors IF
Relegated :- Säffle FF, Norrstrands IF and Karlstads BK

2nd Division to consist of 8 groups of 8 clubs for Season 1991

## SWEDEN 2ND DIVISION EAST 1990
### LEAGUE TABLE FINAL

| Team | P | W | D | L | F | A | Pts |
| --- | --- | --- | --- | --- | --- | --- | --- |
| Mjölby AI | 26 | 12 | 10 | 4 | 47 | 28 | 46 |
| Enköpings SK | 26 | 13 | 6 | 7 | 41 | 30 | 45 |
| Nyköpings BIS | 26 | 12 | 6 | 8 | 38 | 30 | 42 |
| IFK Västeras | 26 | 11 | 8 | 7 | 45 | 32 | 41 |
| Vik Fotboll | 26 | 12 | 5 | 9 | 33 | 39 | 41 |
| Karlslunds IF (Örebro) | 26 | 10 | 7 | 9 | 42 | 39 | 37 |
| Spanga IS | 26 | 10 | 7 | 9 | 42 | 39 | 37 |
| IK City (Eskilstuna) | 26 | 10 | 6 | 10 | 35 | 42 | 36 |
| Söderkoping FF | 26 | 9 | 7 | 10 | 35 | 42 | 34 |
| IK Sleipner (Norrköping) | 26 | 10 | 4 | 12 | 51 | 47 | 34 |
| Älvsjö AIK | 26 | 9 | 8 | 9 | 32 | 42 | 33 |
| Films SK (Österbybruk) | 26 | 8 | 4 | 14 | 36 | 59 | 28 |
| Linköpings FF | 26 | 8 | 3 | 15 | 19 | 43 | 27 |
| Visby IF Gute | 26 | 6 | 8 | 12 | 27 | 38 | 26 |

Promoted :- Mjölby AI and Enköpings SK
Relegated :- Linköpings FF, Films SK and Visby IF Gute

## SWEDEN 2ND DIVISION SOUTH 1990
### LEAGUE TABLE FINAL

| Team | P | W | D | L | F | A | Pts |
| --- | --- | --- | --- | --- | --- | --- | --- |
| Myresjö IF (Landsbro) | 26 | 16 | 6 | 4 | 55 | 28 | 54 |
| Varbergs BoIS | 26 | 15 | 6 | 5 | 36 | 28 | 51 |
| IFK Hässleholm | 26 | 14 | 8 | 4 | 58 | 32 | 50 |
| Falkenbergs FF | 26 | 13 | 8 | 5 | 50 | 27 | 47 |
| IFK Värnamo | 26 | 13 | 6 | 7 | 50 | 43 | 45 |
| IF Leikin (Halmstad) | 26 | 10 | 7 | 9 | 50 | 47 | 35 |
| Nybro IF | 26 | 8 | 11 | 7 | 25 | 24 | 31 |
| BK Olympic (Malmö) | 26 | 8 | 7 | 11 | 25 | 30 | 30 |
| Lunds BK | 26 | 8 | 6 | 12 | 29 | 35 | 30 |
| Tomelilla IF | 26 | 6 | 11 | 9 | 22 | 30 | 29 |
| Waggeryds IK (Vaggeryd) | 26 | 9 | 2 | 15 | 37 | 63 | 29 |
| Kirsebergs IF (Malmö) | 26 | 7 | 7 | 12 | 25 | 30 | 28 |
| IFÖ/Bromölla IF | 26 | 6 | 7 | 13 | 20 | 38 | 27 |
| NK Croatia (Malmö) | 26 | 4 | 5 | 17 | 17 | 63 | 17 |

Promoted :- Myresjö IF
Relegated :- Kirsebergs IF, IFÖ/Bromölla IF and NK Croatia

## PROMOTION PLAY-OFFS

Skövde AIK v Enköpings SK
Varbergs BolS v IK Sirius

| | 1ST LEG | 2ND LEG | AGG. |
| --- | --- | --- | --- |
| | 1-1 | 0-1 | 1-2 |
| | 1-3 | 1-1 | 2-4 |

## SWEDEN CUP 1990

### 5TH ROUND

| | | | |
| --- | --- | --- | --- |
| Boras AIK | 0 | FBK Balkan | 4 |
| Kaverös BK | 2 | Raslätts SK | 2 |
| Sösdala IF | 2 | Helsingborgs IF | 3 |
| Tidaholms GolF | 0 | Trelleborgs FF | 6 |
| BK Forward | 1 | Kungsbacka BI | 2 |
| Kallereds SK | 2 | Hertzöga BK | 0 |
| Askerods SK | 2 | Kalmar AIK | 1 |
| BK Forward | 10 | Hertzöga BK | 0 |
| Myresjö IF | 7 | Kalmar FF | 1 |
| IFÖ/Bromölla IF | 8 ⊗ | Spanga IS | 2 |
| Norrstrands IF | 2 | BK Sport | 4 |
| IF Brommapojkarna | 2 | Kalmar FF | 14 |
| Hammarby IF | 8 | IFK Västeras | 1 |
| Fanna BK | 2 | IK Spleiner | 14 |
| Arvika Fotboll | 2 | IFK Västeras | 6 |
| Östers IF | 1 | IK Brage | 6 |
| GAIS | 2 | Karlskrona AIF | 2 |
| Rasunda IS | 2 | Vasby IK | 1 |
| Matfors IF | 3 | Lycksele IF | 1 |
| Rimforsa IF | 2 | Lulea FF/IFK Lulea | 6 |
| Morön BK | 1 | Vasby IK | 2 ⊗ |
| Umea IK | 2 | Gefle IF | 3 |

Landskrona BolS | 2

### 6TH ROUND

| | | | |
| --- | --- | --- | --- |
| Kungsbacka BI | 1 | Malmö FF | 0 |
| IK Sleipner | 8 | Karlskrona AIF | 2 |
| Spanga IS | 0 | Östers IF | 2 |
| Umea IK | 1 | Örebro SK | 8 |
| Djurgardens IF | 7 | IK Brage | |
| Gunnlise IS | 2 | GAIS | |
| Lulea FF/IFK Lulea | 2 | IF Älgarna | 6 |
| BK Häcken | 3 | IF Brommapojkarna | |
| Sandvikens IF | 0 | Gefle IF | |
| Askerods IF | | Kaliskrona AIF | |
| Alnö IF | 0 | | |

### 7TH ROUND

| | | | |
| --- | --- | --- | --- |
| IF Elfsborg | 1 | Örgryte IS | 0 |
| Karlskrona AIF | 1 | IFK Göteborg | 2 |
| Lulea FF/IFK Lulea | 3 | Djurgardens IF | 6 ⊗ |
| BK Häcken | 3 | IF Brommapojkarna | 0 |

### 1/4 FINALS

| | | | |
| --- | --- | --- | --- |
| IF Elfsborg | 1 | Gunnlise IS | 0 |
| Karlskrona AIF | 1 | Helsingborgs IF | 2 |
| Lulea FF/IFK Lulea | 6 | Sandvikens IF | 3 |
| BK Häcken | 1 | BK Häcken | 2 |
| | | Vasby IK | 2 |
| | | IK Brage | |

### SEMI-FINALS

| | | | |
| --- | --- | --- | --- |
| BK Häcken | 4 | IK Brage | 1 |
| IK Brage win 4-3 on penalties | | Djurgardens IF | 3 |
| Sandvikens IF | 0 | Trelleborgs FF | 1 |
| IFK Göteborg | 2 | | |

IFK Göteborg ... 2
Djurgardens IF ... 2 (aet)
Djurgardens IF win 4-5 on penalties

### FINAL  22/5/90 at Rasunda Stadion, Solna

Djurgardens IF ..... 3  BK Häcken ..... 0

Djurgarden : A.Almgren, G.Schiller, J.Andersson, S.Kjellberg, L.Nilsson, K.Nordin, N.Karlström, K.Burwall (P.Mörk 75), P.Skoog (T.Lundmark 75), M.Martinsson.
Häcken : M.Sehlström, J.Hellström, P.Lessmark, T.Olausson, M.Carlsson, S.Bjur, M.Källström, P.Granqvist, H.Palmqvist, S.Karlsson (J.Fortes 56), A.Kiel (J.Magnusson 70).

Referee : Lars Carlsson
Attendance : 3,357

1-0 M.Martinsson 42
2-0 K.Nordin 56
3-0 M.Martinsson 74

⊗ After extra time and penalties.

# SWEDEN INTERNATIONAL REVIEW 1990

## INTERNATIONAL LINE-UPS 1990

| Match | Sven Andersson | Niclas Larsson-Nylén | Jean-Paul Vonderburg | Sulo Vaattovaara | Pontus Kamark | Stefan Rehn | Jonny Rödlund | Leif Engkvist | Magnus Erlingmark | Hans Eskilsson | Stefan Lindqvist | Stefan Schwarz | Lars Eriksson | Jan Eriksson | Klas Ingesson | Joakim Nilsson | Kennet Andersson | Johnny Ekström | Thomas Ravelli | Roland Nilsson | Glenn Hysén | Peter Larsson | Roger Ljung | Stefan Pettersson | Mats Magnusson | Anders Limpár | Glenn Strömberg | Tomas Brolin | Jonas Thern | Mats Gren | Ulrik Jansson | Jens Fjellström | Hans Eklund | Dan Corneliusson | Patrick Andersson | Per Blohm |
|---|---|---|---|---|---|---|---|---|---|---|---|---|---|---|---|---|---|---|---|---|---|---|---|---|---|---|---|---|---|---|---|---|---|---|---|---|
| 14/2/90 UAE 2 SWEDEN 1 — Dubai — Ref: Al Mulla (UAE) — Friendly (Schwarz) | 1 | 2 | 3 | 4 | 5 | 6 | 7 | 8 | 9 | 10 | 11 | (5) | | | | | | | | | | | | | | | | | | | | | | | | |
| 17/2/90 UAE 0 SWEDEN 2 — Dubai — Ref: Ali Boujsaim (UAE) — Friendly (Rehn, Ingesson) | | | | | 2 | 7 | | 6 | 3 | (11) | | 5 | 1 | 4 | 8 | 9 | 10 | 11 | | | | | | | | | | | | | | | | | | |
| 21/2/90 BELGIUM 0 SWEDEN 0 — Brussels — Ref: Kaupe (Austria) — Friendly | | (7) | | | | 7 | | 6 | | | | (3) | | | 8 | 9 | | (11) | 1 | 2 | 3 | 4 | | 10 | 11 | | | | | | | | | | | |
| 11/4/90 ALGERIA 1 SWEDEN 1 — Algiers — Ref: Medjiba (Algeria) — Friendly (Schwarz) | | | | | | | | | | | 11 | 5 | | | 7 | 9 | 10 | (11) | 1 | 2 | 3 | 4 | | 10 | (10) | 6 | | | | | | | | | | |
| 25/4/90 SWEDEN 4 WALES 2 — Solna — Ref: Ruokonen (Finland) — Friendly (Brolin 2, Ingesson 2) | | | | | | | | 6 | | | | 9 | | | 8 | | | | 1 | 2 | 3 | 4 | 5 | (10) | 10 | 7 | | 11 | | | | | | | | |
| 27/5/90 SWEDEN 6 FINLAND 0 — Solna — Ref: Presberg (Norway) — Friendly (Magnusson, Limpár, Brolin 2, Larsson, Thern) | | (2) | | | | | | | | | | 5 | | | 8 | 9 | | (10) | 1 | 2 | 3 | 4 | | (11) | 10 | 6 | (8) | 11 | 7 | | | | | | | |
| 10/6/90 BRAZIL 2 SWEDEN 1 — Torino — Ref: Lanese (Italy) — World Cup (Brolin) | | | | | | | | | | | | 5 | | | 8 | 9 | | | 1 | 2 | 3 | | 4 | (10) | 10 | 6 | (4) | 11 | 7 | | | | | | | |
| 16/6/90 SCOTLAND 2 SWEDEN 1 — Genova — Ref: Maciel (Paraguay) — World Cup (Strömberg) | | | | | | | | | | | | 5 | | | 8 | 9 | | (11) | 1 | 2 | 3 | | 4 | 11 | | 6 | (4) | 10 | 7 | | | | | | | |
| 20/6/90 COSTA RICA 2 SWEDEN 1 — Genova — Ref: Petrovic (Yugo.) — World Cup (Ekström) | | | | | | | | (6) | | | | 4 | | | 8 | 9 | | 11 | 1 | 2 | 3 | | | | | | 6 | 10 | | (10) | | | | | | |
| 22/8/90 NORWAY 1 SWEDEN 2 — Stavanger — Ref: Nielsen (Denmark) — Friendly (Engkvist, Fjellström) | | | | (7) | | 6 | | 5 | 2 | | | | | 4 | | | 10 | 11 | 1 | | | | 3 | | | | | 11 | | 8 | 7 | 9 | (11) | | | |
| 5/9/90 SWEDEN 0 DENMARK 1 — Västeras — Ref: Hope (Scotland) — Friendly | | | 2 | (8) | | 6 | | (5) | (5) | | | 9 | 1 | 4 | | | 10 | | | | 3 | | | 11 | | | | | 7 | | 8 | | (10) | | | |
| 26/6/90 SWEDEN 2 BULGARIA 0 — Solna — Ref: Damgaard (Denmark) — Friendly (Corneliusson, K.Andersson) | | | | (7) | | 6 | | | (8) | | | 10 | | 2 | 7 | 9 | 11 | | | 5 | 3 | 3 | 4 | 11 | 9 | 8 | | | | 7 | 5 | | | (10) | (11) | |
| 10/10/90 SWEDEN 1 GERMANY 3 — Solna — Ref: Worrall (England) — Friendly (Rehn) | | | | 2 | | 6 | | | | | | 11 | | 4 | | 9 | | | 1 | 5 | 3 | | | 11 | | | | 10 | | 8 | 8 | | | (9) | | (7) |
| **CAPS AT 31/12/90** | 1 | 8 | 2 | 6 | 2 | 12 | 1 | 18 | 5 | 8 | 5 | 11 | 4 | 5 | 15 | 24 | 4 | 34 | 78 | 37 | 68 | 40 | 22 | 24 | 30 | 24 | 52 | 7 | 24 | 13 | 4 | 1 | 4 | 22 | 1 | 1 |
| **GOALS AT 31/12/90** | | 1 | 2 | 2 | 4 | 4 | | 2 | | 2 | 1 | 2 | 1 | | 6 | 1 | 1 | 11 | | | 6 | 4 | 2 | 1 | 9 | 2 | 7 | 5 | 5 | | | 1 | | 12 | | |

# SWITZERLAND Correspondent : JAN ALSSEMA

| SWITZERLAND 1st Division Autumn 1990 | GC | LAUSANNE | XAMAX | LUZERN | ST.GALLEN | LUGANO | YOUNG BOYS | SION | SERVETTE | ZÜRICH | AARAU | WETTINGEN |
|---|---|---|---|---|---|---|---|---|---|---|---|---|
| GRASSHOPPER CLUB | ■ | 1-1 | 1-0 | 0-0 | 2-0 | 2-0 | 0-0 | 2-2 | 1-1 | 1-2 | 0-0 | 2-2 |
| LAUSANNE-SPORTS | 0-0 | ■ | 1-0 | 3-3 | 3-1 | 3-0 | 1-4 | 3-4 | 2-0 | 4-2 | 1-0 | 4-0 |
| XAMAX FC | 0-0 | 5-1 | ■ | 1-1 | 1-0 | 1-1 | 0-0 | 1-1 | 0-0 | 0-1 | 2-0 | 2-0 |
| FC LUZERN | 0-2 | 2-2 | 0-1 | ■ | 3-1 | 0-1 | 3-2 | 0-0 | 1-3 | 5-1 | 2-0 | 0-0 |
| FC SANKT GALLEN | 0-3 | 1-1 | 1-1 | 0-1 | ■ | 3-0 | 1-1 | 2-1 | 1-4 | 3-0 | 2-1 | 2-0 |
| FC LUGANO | 3-1 | 3-2 | 3-0 | 1-2 | 0-0 | ■ | 0-0 | 0-0 | 0-0 | 3-0 | 0-0 | 3-1 |
| BSC YOUNG BOYS | 2-0 | 1-1 | 1-1 | 3-0 | 0-0 | 2-2 | ■ | 0-0 | 2-2 | 5-1 | 2-2 | 6-1 |
| FC SION | 2-1 | 2-1 | 2-2 | 1-0 | 1-1 | 3-0 | 2-0 | ■ | 2-1 | 1-0 | 2-1 | 3-2 |
| SERVETTE FC | 1-3 | 0-3 | 0-0 | 2-3 | 0-2 | 0-1 | 3-0 | 2-1 | ■ | 3-2 | 1-0 | 1-0 |
| FC ZÜRICH | 1-2 | 0-0 | 0-1 | 1-0 | 1-1 | 1-1 | 0-3 | 1-1 | 1-2 | ■ | 1-1 | 2-4 |
| FC AARAU | 0-2 | 0-1 | 1-3 | 2-2 | 1-1 | 1-1 | 2-1 | 0-0 | 1-1 | 2-1 | ■ | 1-0 |
| FC WETTINGEN | 0-3 | 1-1 | 0-3 | 1-2 | 1-3 | 0-4 | 4-0 | 0-0 | 1-3 | 2-2 | 4-3 | ■ |

| SWITZERLAND 1st Division Championship Play Offs Spring 1991 | SION | GC | XAMAX | LAUSANNE | LUGANO | SERVETTE | YOUNG BOYS | LUZERN |
|---|---|---|---|---|---|---|---|---|
| FC SION | ■ | 1-0 | 0-0 | 1-0 | 1-0 | 1-1 | 1-1 | 2-3 |
| GRASSHOPPER CLUB | 3-2 | ■ | 1-1 | 0-1 | 2-0 | 1-1 | 2-2 | 3-2 |
| XAMAX FC | 1-1 | 0-2 | ■ | 1-1 | 1-0 | 1-0 | 2-1 | 2-0 |
| LAUSANNE-SPORTS | 1-1 | 0-0 | 1-1 | ■ | 2-0 | 1-3 | 1-3 | 3-1 |
| FC LUGANO | 1-1 | 3-3 | 2-1 | 0-1 | ■ | 1-1 | 4-0 | 1-0 |
| SERVETTE FC | 0-0 | 1-5 | 1-4 | 1-1 | 2-2 | ■ | 2-4 | 1-1 |
| BSC YOUNG BOYS | 2-2 | 1-2 | 2-0 | 1-1 | 0-1 | 2-2 | ■ | 1-5 |
| FC LUZERN | 2-0 | 0-3 | 1-1 | 0-1 | 0-1 | 0-0 | 1-1 | ■ |

## SWITZERLAND 1ST DIVISION
### LEAGUE TABLE 1ST STAGE FINAL
| | | | | | | | |
|---|---|---|---|---|---|---|---|
| FC Sion | 22 | 10 | 10 | 2 | 31 | 20 | 30 |
| Grasshopper Club | 22 | 9 | 9 | 4 | 29 | 17 | 27 |
| Xamax FC | 22 | 8 | 10 | 4 | 25 | 15 | 26 |
| Lausanne-Sports | 22 | 9 | 8 | 5 | 39 | 30 | 26 |
| FC Lugano | 22 | 8 | 9 | 5 | 27 | 22 | 25 |
| Servette FC - | 22 | 9 | 6 | 7 | 30 | 27 | 24 |
| BSC Young Boys | 22 | 6 | 11 | 5 | 35 | 26 | 23 |
| FC Luzern | 22 | 8 | 7 | 7 | 30 | 28 | 23 |
| FC St.Gallen | 22 | 7 | 8 | 7 | 26 | 26 | 22 |
| FC Aarau | 22 | 3 | 9 | 10 | 19 | 30 | 15 |
| FC Zürich | 22 | 3 | 6 | 13 | 21 | 45 | 12 |
| FC Wettingen | 22 | 3 | 5 | 14 | 24 | 50 | 11 |

## SWITZERLAND 1ST DIVISION
### LEAGUE TABLE 2ND STAGE FINAL
| | | | | | | | | |
|---|---|---|---|---|---|---|---|---|
| Grasshopper Club | 14 | 7 | 5 | 2 | 27 | 15 | (14) | 33 |
| FC Sion | 14 | 3 | 8 | 3 | 14 | 15 | (15) | 29 |
| Xamax FC | 14 | 5 | 6 | 3 | 16 | 13 | (13) | 29 |
| Lausanne-Sports | 14 | 5 | 6 | 3 | 15 | 13 | (13) | 29 |
| FC Lugano | 14 | 5 | 4 | 5 | 16 | 15 | (13) | 27 |
| BSC Young Boys | 14 | 3 | 6 | 5 | 21 | 26 | (12) | 24 |
| Servette FC | 14 | 1 | 9 | 4 | 16 | 24 | (12) | 23 |
| FC Luzern | 14 | 3 | 4 | 7 | 16 | 20 | (12) | 22 |

Note : - Clubs level on points are separated by the final first stage standings. Bonus points carried forward from the 1st Stage are shown in brackets.

Champions : - Grasshopper Club (Zürich)

| SWITZERLAND 2nd Division East Autumn 1990 | BASEL | BELLINZONA | CHUR | SCHAFFHAUSEN | BADEN | LOCARNO | WINTERTHUR | GLARUS | E'BRÜCKE | CHIASSO | SC ZUG | KRIENS |
|---|---|---|---|---|---|---|---|---|---|---|---|---|
| FC BASEL | ■ | 2-1 | 0-3 | 6-2 | 1-3 | 1-2 | 1-1 | 3-0 | 2-1 | 2-2 | 2-2 | 2-1 |
| AC BELLINZONA | 0-0 | ■ | 2-0 | 3-1 | 0-0 | 1-2 | 3-4 | 4-1 | 1-1 | 2-0 | 3-0 | 4-1 |
| FC CHUR | 1-1 | 1-1 | ■ | 0-0 | 1-2 | 0-2 | 1-2 | 1-1 | 1-1 | 1-1 | 0-1 | 3-0 |
| FC SCHAFFHAUSEN | 3-2 | 5-1 | 4-1 | ■ | 2-0 | 2-0 | 2-1 | 7-0 | 2-0 | 2-1 | 0-3 | 4-2 |
| FC BADEN | 2-0 | 3-0 | 1-0 | 0-0 | ■ | 1-1 | 3-0 | 6-3 | 4-0 | 1-0 | 1-2 | 3-1 |
| FC LOCARNO | 2-3 | 2-1 | 2-0 | 2-0 | 1-0 | ■ | 0-0 | 5-0 | 3-2 | 2-1 | 2-2 | 4-0 |
| FC WINTERTHUR | 2-2 | 1-1 | 0-2 | 0-2 | 3-1 | 1-1 | ■ | 1-3 | 1-0 | 0-1 | 3-1 | 2-1 |
| FC GLARUS | 0-0 | 0-0 | 0-1 | 0-5 | 0-2 | 2-6 | 1-1 | ■ | 2-1 | 1-3 | 3-1 | 2-0 |
| FC EMMENBRÜCKE | 0-3 | 1-2 | 2-1 | 2-1 | 1-1 | 0-0 | 3-2 | 1-1 | ■ | 0-0 | 0-2 | 1-2 |
| FC CHIASSO | 2-2 | 2-1 | 0-1 | 4-0 | 3-5 | 4-0 | 2-0 | 7-2 | 4-0 | ■ | 0-0 | 2-1 |
| SC ZUG | 0-2 | 2-1 | 0-0 | 1-1 | 0-0 | 1-1 | 4-0 | 0-0 | 3-0 | 2-1 | ■ | 1-1 |
| SC KRIENS | 0-3 | 3-2 | 2-1 | 0-0 | 0-2 | 1-4 | 0-1 | 3-1 | 1-1 | 1-3 | 1-1 | ■ |

### TOP SCORERS
1. Dario Zuffi (BSC Young Boys) (12) 17
2. John Eriksen (FC Luzern) (10) 16
3. Adrian De Vicente (Grasshopper Club) (10) 15
4. Stéphane Chaupisat (Lausanne) (13) 13
   Maurizio Jacobacci (Servette FC) (5) 13
6. Peter Nadig (FC Luzern) (6) 12
7. Edwin Gorter (FC Lugano) (6) 11
8. Andy Löbmann (BSC Young Boys) (6) 10
   Marc Strudal (Grasshopper Club) (4) 10

Note : - The above list only includes players whose clubs qualified for the Season's 2nd Stage. Goals totals are over the whole season, 1st Stage totals are in brackets.

Note : - The 1st Stage matches were played during the Autumn Season of 1990. The top 8 clubs of the 1st Stage formed the 1st Division Championship Play-Off section whose matches were played during the Spring Season 1991. These clubs commenced the 2nd Stage with half the total points gained in the Autumn Season 1990 (half points were rounded up). Each clubs' points are shown in brackets in the 2nd Stage Final League Table. At the end of the second stage, Clubs level on points are separated by their final 1st Stage standings.
The Bottom 4 clubs: St.Gallen, Aarau, Zürich & Wettingen join 12 2nd Division clubs to form 2 groups of 8 clubs during the Spring Season 1991 to decide the remaining 4 places in the 1st Division for the Season 1991/92. 1st Stage records of these clubs are not carried forward in any way to the 2nd Stage.

## SWITZERLAND 2nd Division West — Autumn 1990

| | YVERDON | FRIBOURG | BULLE | GRENCHEN | CHENOIS | E CAROUGE | MALLEY | MONTREUX | CH-DE-FONDS | OLD BOYS | URANIA | BURGDORF |
|---|---|---|---|---|---|---|---|---|---|---|---|---|
| YVERDON-SPORTS | | 3-2 | 3-0 | 2-0 | 3-0 | 4-2 | 0-0 | 3-0 | 4-0 | 4-1 | 0-0 | 3-0 |
| FC FRIBOURG | 0-3 | | 3-0 | 5-2 | 5-0 | 4-1 | 0-0 | 7-0 | 1-1 | 0-0 | 2-2 | 4-0 |
| FC BULLE | 1-1 | 1-1 | | 1-2 | 4-3 | 0-2 | 3-1 | 2-0 | 2-2 | 4-2 | 0-0 | 0-1 |
| FC GRENCHEN | 1-1 | 1-1 | 1-2 | | 3-0 | 4-0 | 1-1 | 3-0 | 0-1 | 2-3 | 5-1 | 3-0 |
| CS CHENOIS | 1-4 | 0-4 | 0-6 | 2-1 | | 0-2 | 0-0 | 1-1 | 4-4 | 1-3 | 0-3 | 0-0 |
| ETOILE CAROUGE FC | 1-3 | 5-3 | 1-0 | 1-1 | 2-1 | | 0-0 | 3-3 | 0-0 | 1-1 | 4-2 | 2-0 |
| FC MALLEY | 1-1 | 1-3 | 0-0 | 1-5 | 1-0 | 2-3 | | 1-4 | 3-3 | 2-3 | 1-2 | 0-0 |
| MONTREUX-SPORTS | 0-0 | 0-0 | 0-0 | 2-0 | 2-2 | 1-3 | 0-1 | | 2-4 | 0-1 | 3-1 | 5-1 |
| LA CH.-DE-FONDS FC | 7-2 | 4-2 | 2-0 | 0-1 | 2-2 | 1-1 | 2-2 | 3-0 | | 2-6 | 2-0 | 5-0 |
| BSC OLD BOYS | 4-2 | 5-2 | 4-3 | 3-2 | 1-1 | 0-1 | 1-2 | 5-2 | 2-2 | | 4-2 | 4-0 |
| URANIA GE | 0-2 | 5-3 | 5-0 | 0-0 | 2-0 | 0-2 | 1-1 | 5-1 | 3-1 | 2-2 | | 4-0 |
| SC BURGDORF | 0-1 | 2-2 | 1-2 | 0-4 | 0-1 | 1-1 | 1-1 | 1-1 | 0-4 | 1-1 | 0-5 | |

## SWITZERLAND 2nd Division — Promotion Section A — Spring 1991

| | ST.GALLEN | WETTINGEN | BADEN | BASEL | CHIASSO | YVERDON | CAROUGE | FRIBOURG |
|---|---|---|---|---|---|---|---|---|
| FC SANKT GALLEN | | 3-0 | 2-0 | 1-0 | 1-1 | 1-1 | 2-3 | 6-1 |
| FC WETTINGEN | 2-1 | | 5-1 | 1-3 | 1-1 | 1-0 | 1-0 | 2-0 |
| FC BADEN | 0-1 | 1-3 | | 1-1 | 1-1 | 2-1 | 2-0 | 2-2 |
| FC BASEL | 0-1 | 1-2 | 1-4 | | 3-0 | 3-0 | 3-1 | 0-0 |
| FC CHIASSO | 0-3 | 1-5 | 3-2 | 0-0 | | 2-0 | 1-0 | 2-0 |
| YVERDON-SPORTS | 1-4 | 1-1 | 4-1 | 2-0 | 2-1 | | 3-1 | 1-3 |
| ETOILE CAROUGE FC | 1-5 | 0-1 | 2-1 | 2-1 | 2-3 | 0-5 | | 3-2 |
| FC FRIBOURG | 1-2 | 2-0 | 0-1 | 2-2 | 1-3 | 2-0 | 2-1 | |

## SWITZERLAND 2nd Division — Promotion Section B — Spring 1991

| | AARAU | ZÜRICH | LOCARNO | S'HAUSEN | SC ZUG | OLD BOYS | CHAUX DE F. | URANIA |
|---|---|---|---|---|---|---|---|---|
| FC AARAU | | 2-2 | 1-2 | 2-1 | 2-0 | 4-0 | 3-1 | 2-2 |
| FC ZÜRICH | 0-0 | | 3-1 | 2-0 | 4-0 | 0-0 | 2-1 | 6-3 |
| FC LOCARNO | 0-0 | 0-0 | | 1-0 | 3-0 | 1-0 | 1-1 | 1-1 |
| FC SCHAFFHAUSEN | 0-1 | 0-0 | 1-0 | | 2-1 | 3-0 | 1-0 | 4-1 |
| SC ZUG | 1-4 | 1-1 | 0-2 | 1-2 | | 2-0 | 2-3 | 0-0 |
| BSC OLD BOYS | 2-6 | 2-2 | 0-4 | 0-1 | 0-3 | | 2-3 | 2-1 |
| LA CH.-DE-FONDS FC | 0-0 | 0-4 | 5-1 | 2-3 | 5-2 | 0-3 | | 6-0 |
| URANIA GENEVE | 1-1 | 0-2 | 1-1 | 1-1 | 1-1 | 2-0 | 2-0 | |

## SWITZERLAND 2nd Division — Relegation Section A — Spring 1991

| | WINTERTHUR | GLARUS | KRIENS | GRENCHEN | MALLEY | CHENOIS |
|---|---|---|---|---|---|---|
| FC WINTERTHUR | | 2-0 | 4-0 | 2-1 | 1-0 | 1-1 |
| FC GLARUS | 1-1 | | 2-2 | 1-1 | 0-1 | 3-1 |
| SC KRIENS | 0-1 | 4-1 | | 3-1 | 2-0 | 2-1 |
| FC GRENCHEN | 2-1 | 3-1 | 2-1 | | 0-0 | 2-4 |
| FC MALLEY | 0-0 | 1-3 | 1-2 | 0-2 | | 3-0 |
| CS CHENOIS | 1-1 | 1-1 | 0-1 | 1-2 | 0-2 | |

## SWITZERLAND 2nd Division — Relegation Section B — Spring 1991

| | BELLINZONA | CHUR | E' BRÜCKE | BULLE | MONTREUX | BURGDORF |
|---|---|---|---|---|---|---|
| AC BELLINZONA | | 3-1 | 2-4 | 1-3 | 3-0 | 0-0 |
| FC CHUR | 0-1 | | 3-0 | 0-0 | 3-1 | 1-1 |
| FC EMMENBRÜCKE | 3-0 | 1-2 | | 0-2 | 2-0 | 2-1 |
| FC BULLE | 2-2 | 0-0 | 3-1 | | 1-2 | 4-1 |
| MONTREUX-SPORTS | 0-0 | 0-0 | 0-0 | 0-6 | | 1-1 |
| SC BURGDORF | 2-2 | 0-0 | 2-0 | 0-5 | 0-0 | |

## SWITZERLAND 2ND DIVISION EAST

### LEAGUE TABLE 1ST STAGE FINAL

| | P | W | D | L | F | A | Pts |
|---|---|---|---|---|---|---|---|
| FC Locarno | 22 | 13 | 6 | 3 | 44 | 23 | 32 |
| FC Baden | 22 | 13 | 5 | 4 | 41 | 19 | 31 |
| FC Schaffhausen | 22 | 12 | 4 | 6 | 45 | 29 | 28 |
| FC Basel | 22 | 8 | 6 | 8 | 40 | 30 | 26 |
| SC Zug | 22 | 8 | 10 | 4 | 29 | 22 | 26 |
| FC Chiasso | 22 | 10 | 5 | 7 | 43 | 26 | 25 |
| AC Bellinzona | 22 | 7 | 9 | 6 | 34 | 32 | 20 |
| FC Winterthur | 22 | 7 | 6 | 9 | 26 | 35 | 20 |
| FC Glarus | 22 | 5 | 7 | 10 | 22 | 35 | 17 |
| FC Chur | 22 | 6 | 5 | 11 | 25 | 58 | 17 |
| FC Emmenbrücke | 22 | 3 | 7 | 12 | 18 | 39 | 13 |
| SC Kriens | 22 | 4 | 4 | 14 | 22 | 47 | 12 |

Note :- The top 6 clubs :- Locarno, Baden, Schaffhausen, Basel, SC Zug and Chiasso, joined the bottom 4 clubs of the 1st Division together with the top 6 clubs of the 2nd Division West to form 2 groups of 8 clubs for the 2nd Stage, played in the Spring Season of 1991. The top 2 clubs of each group gain 1st Division status for Season 1991/92. The 1st Stage results of these clubs are not carried forward in any way to the 2nd Stage.

The bottom 6 clubs join the bottom 6 clubs of 2nd Division West to play in the Spring Season of 1991 in order to decide 3 relegation places. Bonus points are carried on from the 1st Stage together with the top 6 clubs of the 2nd Division appropriate tables. Clubs level on points during the 2nd Stage are separated by goal difference gained from the 2nd Stage matches only.

## SWITZERLAND 2ND DIV. PROMOTION A

### LEAGUE TABLE 2ND STAGE FINAL

| | P | W | D | L | F | A | Pts |
|---|---|---|---|---|---|---|---|
| FC St.Gallen | 14 | 10 | 2 | 2 | 33 | 11 | 22 |
| FC Wettingen | 14 | 9 | 2 | 3 | 25 | 15 | 20 |
| FC Chiasso | 14 | 6 | 4 | 4 | 19 | 21 | 16 |
| FC Basel | 14 | 4 | 6 | 4 | 18 | 17 | 12 |
| Yverdon-Sports | 14 | 5 | 2 | 7 | 21 | 22 | 12 |
| FC Fribourg | 14 | 4 | 3 | 7 | 18 | 25 | 11 |
| SC Zug | 14 | 3 | 5 | 6 | 19 | 26 | 11 |
| BSC Old Boys | 14 | 2 | 2 | 10 | 11 | 32 | 6 |

Note :- FC St.Gallen and FC Wettingen retain their 1st Division status.

## SWITZERLAND 2ND DIV. RELEGATION A

### LEAGUE TABLE 2ND STAGE FINAL

| | P | W | D | L | F | A | (Bonus) | Pts |
|---|---|---|---|---|---|---|---|---|
| FC Winterthur | 10 | 5 | 2 | 3 | 14 | 6 | (5) | 19 |
| FC Grenchen | 10 | 5 | 3 | 2 | 16 | 14 | (6) | 18 |
| SC Kriens | 10 | 6 | 1 | 3 | 17 | 13 | (1) | 14 |
| FC Malley | 10 | 4 | 4 | 2 | 10 | 7 | (4) | 12 |
| FC Glarus | 10 | 2 | 4 | 4 | 13 | 16 | (3) | 11 |
| CS Chenois | 10 | 1 | 3 | 6 | 8 | 15 | (1) | 9 |

Note :- Bonus points carried forward from the 1st Stage are shown in brackets.

Relegated :- FC Glarus & CS Chenois

### PLAY OFF

| | 1ST LEG | 2ND LEG | AGG. |
|---|---|---|---|
| FC Glarus v Montreux-Sports | 2-1 | 1-3 | 3-4 |

Relegated :- SC Burgdorf

## SWITZERLAND 2ND DIVISION WEST

### LEAGUE TABLE 1ST STAGE FINAL

| | P | W | D | L | F | A | Pts |
|---|---|---|---|---|---|---|---|
| Yverdon-Sports | 22 | 14 | 6 | 2 | 49 | 21 | 34 |
| BSC Old Boys | 22 | 12 | 6 | 4 | 56 | 38 | 30 |
| Etoile Carouge | 22 | 11 | 7 | 4 | 38 | 31 | 29 |
| Chaux-de-Fonds | 22 | 9 | 9 | 4 | 52 | 37 | 27 |
| FC Fribourg | 22 | 8 | 8 | 6 | 54 | 36 | 24 |
| Urania Genève | 22 | 8 | 8 | 6 | 45 | 33 | 24 |
| FC Grenchen | 22 | 9 | 5 | 8 | 42 | 37 | 23 |
| FC Bulle | 22 | 9 | 5 | 8 | 31 | 35 | 23 |
| FC Malley | 22 | 7 | 6 | 9 | 27 | 47 | 20 |
| Montreux-Sports | 22 | 4 | 5 | 13 | 19 | 53 | 13 |
| CS Chenois | 22 | 2 | 7 | 13 | 18 | 53 | 11 |
| SC Burgdorf | 22 | 1 | 7 | 14 | 9 | — | 9 |

Note :- The top 6 clubs :- Yverdon, Old Boys, Carouge, Chaux-de-Fonds, Fribourg and Urania joined the bottom 4 clubs of the 1st Division together with the top 6 clubs of the 2nd Division East to form 2 groups of 8 clubs for the 2nd Stage, played in the Spring Season of 1991. The top 2 clubs of each group gain 1st Division status for Season 1991/92. The 1st Stage results of these clubs are not carried forward in any way to the 2nd Stage.

The bottom 6 clubs join the bottom 6 clubs of 2nd Division East to play in the Spring Season of 1991 in order to decide 3 relegation places. Bonus points are carried on from the 1st Stage and are shown in brackets in the appropriate tables. Clubs level on points during the 2nd Stage are separated by goal difference gained from the 2nd Stage matches only.

## SWITZERLAND 2ND DIV. PROMOTION B

### LEAGUE TABLE 2ND STAGE FINAL

| | P | W | D | L | F | A | Pts |
|---|---|---|---|---|---|---|---|
| FC Zürich | 14 | 7 | 7 | 0 | 28 | 10 | 21 |
| FC Aarau | 14 | 7 | 6 | 1 | 28 | 12 | 20 |
| AC Bellinzona | 14 | 8 | 2 | 4 | 19 | 12 | 18 |
| FC Schaffhausen | 14 | 8 | 2 | 4 | 18 | 13 | 18 |
| FC Locarno | 14 | 5 | 2 | 7 | 27 | 26 | 12 |
| La Chaux-de-Fonds | 14 | 5 | 2 | 7 | 18 | 27 | 12 |
| Urania Genève | 14 | 4 | 2 | 8 | 16 | 27 | 11 |
| BSC Old Boys | 14 | 2 | 2 | 10 | 11 | 32 | 6 |

Note :- FC Zürich and FC Aarau retain their 1st Division status.

## SWITZERLAND 2ND DIV. RELEGATION B

### LEAGUE TABLE 2ND STAGE FINAL

| | P | W | D | L | F | A | (Bonus) | Pts |
|---|---|---|---|---|---|---|---|---|
| FC Bulle | 10 | 6 | 1 | 3 | 26 | 7 | (5) | 20 |
| AC Bellinzona | 10 | 3 | 4 | 3 | 14 | 15 | (6) | 16 |
| FC Chur | 10 | 3 | 4 | 3 | 12 | 10 | (7) | 15 |
| FC Emmenbrücke | 10 | 3 | 5 | 2 | 13 | 16 | (4) | 15 |
| Montreux-Sports | 10 | 1 | 4 | 5 | 4 | 16 | (3) | 11 |
| SC Burgdorf | 10 | 1 | 6 | 3 | 8 | 15 | (1) | 9 |

Note :- Bonus points carried forward from the 1st Stage are shown in brackets.

### 3RD PLACE PLAY-OFF

Brühl St.Gallen .......0    Brüttisellen .......0 (aet)

Brüttisellen win 3-5 on penalties.

Promoted :- Chatel-St.Denis, Delémont and Brüttisellen.

### PROMOTION PLAY-OFFS

| | 1ST LEG | 2ND LEG | AGG. |
|---|---|---|---|
| Delémont v Martigny | 5-0 | 3-2 | 8-2 |
| Brühl v Solothurn | 0-0 | 1-0 | 1-0 |
| Pratteln v Brüttisellen | 2-0 | 0-3 | 2-3 |
| Chatel-St.Denis v Colombier | 3-1 | 2-1 | 5-2 |

### 2ND ROUND

| | 1ST LEG | 2ND LEG | AGG. |
|---|---|---|---|
| Brühl v Chatel-St.Denis | 0-1 | 1-1 | 1-2 |
| Brüttisellen v Delémont | 1-5 | 0-3 | 1-8 |

## SWITZERLAND 3RD DIVISION GROUP 1

### LEAGUE TABLE FINAL

| | P | W | D | L | F | A | Pts |
|---|---|---|---|---|---|---|---|
| FC Martigny-Sports | 26 | 16 | 5 | 5 | 66 | 39 | 37 |
| FC Monthey | 26 | 14 | 8 | 4 | 57 | 26 | 36 |
| FC Chatel-St.Denis | 26 | 15 | 6 | 5 | 53 | 24 | 36 |
| FC Savièse | 26 | 12 | 7 | 7 | 51 | 41 | 31 |
| FC Fully | 26 | 10 | 9 | 7 | 43 | 28 | 29 |
| FC Echallens | 26 | 11 | 5 | 10 | 44 | 49 | 27 |
| SC Bümpliz 78 | 26 | 9 | 9 | 8 | 45 | 40 | 27 |
| FC Versoix | 26 | 9 | 7 | 10 | 43 | 38 | 25 |
| FC Collex-Bossy | 26 | 9 | 7 | 10 | 41 | 39 | 25 |
| FC Moutier | 26 | 10 | 4 | 12 | 40 | 40 | 24 |
| FC Renens | 26 | 6 | 11 | 9 | 40 | 44 | 23 |
| FC Aigle | 26 | 7 | 9 | 10 | 32 | 39 | 23 |
| FC Raron | 26 | 7 | 7 | 12 | 45 | 47 | 21 |
| Vevey-Sports | 26 | 7 | 7 | 12 | 40 | 53 | 21 |
| FC Jorat-Mézières | 26 | 3 | 3 | 20 | 26 | 84 | 9 |

### PLAY-OFFS

FC Monthey ......0    FC Chatel-St.Denis .....1

Concordia/Folgore .....1    Vevey-Sports .....0 (aet)

## SWITZERLAND 3RD DIVISION GROUP 3

### LEAGUE TABLE FINAL

| | P | W | D | L | F | A | Pts |
|---|---|---|---|---|---|---|---|
| FC Solothurn | 26 | 14 | 4 | 8 | 48 | 23 | 36 |
| FC Pratteln | 26 | 12 | 10 | 4 | 39 | 23 | 34 |
| SC Buochs | 26 | 13 | 8 | 5 | 53 | 24 | 34 |
| FC Riehen | 26 | 12 | 7 | 7 | 51 | 41 | 31 |
| FC Mendrisio | 26 | 10 | 9 | 7 | 36 | 22 | 29 |
| FC Klus-Baisthal | 26 | 11 | 7 | 8 | 45 | 35 | 29 |
| FC Sursee | 26 | 9 | 9 | 8 | 32 | 34 | 27 |
| FC Ascona | 26 | 8 | 10 | 8 | 25 | 23 | 26 |
| FC Altstetten | 26 | 8 | 9 | 9 | 28 | 30 | 26 |
| FC Tresa | 26 | 7 | 11 | 8 | 39 | 45 | 25 |
| FC Zug | 26 | 8 | 7 | 11 | 29 | 42 | 23 |
| FC Suhr | 26 | 5 | 13 | 8 | 25 | 32 | 23 |
| FC Brugg | 26 | 6 | 10 | 14 | 42 | 45 | 14 |
| FC Nordstern | 26 | 4 | 7 | 17 | 30 | 60 | 14 |

### PLAY-OFF

Buochs .......0    Pratteln .......3

## SWITZERLAND 3RD DIVISION GROUP 2

### LEAGUE TABLE FINAL

| | P | W | D | L | F | A | Pts |
|---|---|---|---|---|---|---|---|
| FC Colombier | 26 | 17 | 6 | 3 | 63 | 23 | 40 |
| SR Delémont | 26 | 18 | 2 | 6 | 68 | 26 | 39 |
| FC Müsingen | 26 | 12 | 8 | 6 | 40 | 30 | 32 |
| FC Laufen | 26 | 10 | 9 | 7 | 41 | 36 | 29 |
| SV Lyss | 26 | 9 | 10 | 7 | 42 | 28 | 28 |
| SC Bümpliz 78 | 26 | 11 | 6 | 9 | 45 | 40 | 28 |
| FC Leichenfeld | 26 | 9 | 10 | 7 | 44 | 40 | 28 |
| FC Moutier | 26 | 7 | 13 | 6 | 43 | 38 | 27 |
| FC Dornidier | 26 | 9 | 6 | 11 | 41 | 44 | 24 |
| FC Thun | 26 | 8 | 7 | 11 | 39 | 50 | 23 |
| FC Bern | 26 | 6 | 11 | 9 | 35 | 34 | 23 |
| FC Beauregard FR | 26 | 7 | 9 | 10 | 37 | 44 | 23 |
| Le Locle-Sports | 26 | 6 | 13 | 7 | 27 | 20 | 20 |
| FC Breitenbach | 26 | 2 | 3 | 21 | 27 | 95 | 7 |

## SWITZERLAND 3RD DIVISION GROUP 4

### LEAGUE TABLE FINAL

| | P | W | D | L | F | A | Pts |
|---|---|---|---|---|---|---|---|
| FC Brüttisellen | 26 | 17 | 6 | 3 | 55 | 18 | 40 |
| SC Brühl | 26 | 15 | 10 | 1 | 39 | 14 | 40 |
| FC Young Fellows | 26 | 16 | 1 | 9 | 43 | 29 | 32 |
| FC Rorschach | 26 | 10 | 12 | 4 | 40 | 33 | 32 |
| FC Red Star | 26 | 11 | 7 | 8 | 33 | 29 | 29 |
| FC Tuggen | 26 | 8 | 8 | 10 | 48 | 39 | 28 |
| FC Herisau | 26 | 10 | 8 | 8 | 42 | 36 | 28 |
| FC Frauenfeld | 26 | 10 | 8 | 8 | 36 | 28 | 28 |
| FC Kreuzlingen | 26 | 9 | 5 | 12 | 35 | 53 | 21 |
| FC Altstätten | 26 | 8 | 7 | 11 | 26 | 38 | 20 |
| FC Balzers | 26 | 7 | 6 | 13 | 33 | 48 | 20 |
| FC Einsiedeln | 26 | 6 | 6 | 14 | 35 | 43 | 18 |
| SC Veltheim | 26 | 6 | 6 | 14 | 27 | 45 | 18 |
| FC Kilchberg | 26 | 3 | 3 | 20 | 20 | 52 | 9 |

### PLAY-OFF

Einsiedeln .......1    Veltheim .......2

## RELEGATION PLAY-OFFS

Concordia/Folgore .....2    Beauregard ...............2  (aet.)
Concordia/Folgore win 3-1 on penalties

Veltheim ...................1    Suhr ...........................1  (aet.)
Suhr win 3-0 on penalties

| LAST PLACE PLAY-OFF | 1ST LEG | 2ND LEG | AGG. |
|---|---|---|---|
| Beauregard v Veltheim | | 2-21-23-4 | |

Relegated : - Vevey, Jorat-Mézières, Beauregard, Le Locle, Breitenbach, Brugg, Nordstern, Einsiedeln and Kilchberg.

Promoted to 3rd Division for Season 1991/92 : - Kölliken, Stäfa, Stabio, Wil, Wangen, Freienbach, Grand-Lancy, Stade Lausanne and Serrières.

# SWITZERLAND CUP 1990/91

## 1/32 FINALS

| | | | |
|---|---|---|---|
| Chenois...................0 | Servette ...................4 | Yverdon .....................1 | Xamax......................2 |
| Grenchen........ .....1 | Aarau .......................0 | Emmenbrücke ...........0 | Luzern......................2 |
| Old Boys ...................1 | Wettingen..................2 | Locarno.....................2 | Lugano.....................0 |
| Rorschach................0 | St.Gallen ...................2 | Fully ..........................1 | Sion..........................3 |
| Stade Nyonnais ........0 | Lausanne ..................5 | Bassecourt................0 | Young Boys...............7 |
| Fehraltorf .................0 | Zürich .......................7 | Malley .......................3 | Urania ......................0 |
| Kriens.......................2 | Bellinzona .................1 | Baden .......................0 | Glarus ......................2 |
| Chaux-de-Fonds........4 | Bulle .........................1 | Collex-Bossy..............2 | Etoile Carouge ..........8 |
| Vevey.......................1 | Montreux...................4 | Thun .........................2 | Fribourg ...................4  (aet.) |
| FC Zug.....................0 | SC Zug......................3 | Münsingen.................0 | Burgdorf ...................0  (aet.) |
| Beringen ..................3 | Schaffhausen ...........11 | Burgdorf win 2-3 on penalties | |
| Maggia ....................0 | Chiasso.....................3 | Solothurn ..................0 | Pratteln ....................1 |
| Raron .......................3 | Monthey ...................2 | Laufen.......................1 | Suhr .........................2 |
| Kreuzlingen...............1 | Frauenfeld.................5 | Brühl ........................1 | Tuggen......................2 |
| Moutier.....................5 | Lyss ..........................0 | Cortaillod ..................2 | Colombier .................1 |
| Wohlen.....................0 | Sursee ......................1 | Bülach.......................3 | Spreitenbach.............0 |
| Winterthur ................1 | Grasshoppers ............3 | | |

## 1/16 FINALS

| | | | |
|---|---|---|---|
| Chaux-de-Fonds........3 | Servette ...................0 | Raron ........................0 | Sion..........................2 |
| Moutier.....................0 | Xamax.......................7 | Cortaillod ..................0 | Lausanne ..................4 |
| Fribourg ...................0 | Young Boys...............1 | Malley .......................3 | Burgdorf ...................0 |
| Etoile Carouge ..........5 | Montreux...................2 | Tuggen......................1 | Suhr .........................1  (aet.) |
| Locarno.....................1 | Grenchen ..................0 | Tuggen win 3-2 on penalties | |
| Bülach......................0 | Grasshoppers ............3 | Frauenfeld .................0 | St.Gallen ..................1 |
| Chiasso....................2 | Luzern.......................1 | Pratteln .....................0 | Zürich .......................1 |
| Kriens.......................0 | Wettingen..................1 | Sursee ......................0 | Glarus ......................0  (aet.) |
| Schaffhausen.............2 | SC Zug......................0  (aet.) | Sursee win 6-5 on penalties | |

## 1/8 FINALS

| | | | |
|---|---|---|---|
| Young Boys...............3 | Schaffhausen .............0 | Grasshoppers .............1 | Lausanne ..................0  (aet.) |
| Locarno.....................0 | Sion...........................1  (aet.) | Chaux-de-Fonds.........1 | Xamax......................0 |
| Etoile Carouge ..........1 | Zürich .......................3  (aet.) | Wettingen ..................1 | St.Gallen ..................5 |
| Chiasso....................2 | Malley........................1  (aet.) | Tuggon......................1 | Sursee .....................0 |

## 1/4 FINALS

| | | | |
|---|---|---|---|
| Sion..........................1 | St.Gallen ...................0  (aet.) | Tuggen......................0 | Chiasso.....................4 |
| Young Boys...............2 | Grasshoppers ............0 | Zürich .......................4 | Chaux-de-Fonds........1  (aet.) |

## SEMI-FINALS

| | | | |
|---|---|---|---|
| BSC Young Boys .......5 | FC Zürich ..................1 | FC Sion......................2 | FC Chiasso ...............1 |

## FINAL    20/5/91 (at Wankdorf Stadion, Bern)

FC Sion.....................3    BSC Young Boys .......2

FC Sion : - Lehmann, Geiger, **Clausen**, Brigger, Sauthier, Piffaretti, Lopez (Orlando 46), Gertschen, Calderon, Baljic, Tudor (Rey 46).

BSC Young Boys : - Pulver, **Baumann**, Wittwer, Weber, Gottardi, Bohinen, Bregy, Hänzi, Zuffi, Löbmann, Jakobsen.

| | | |
|---|---|---|
| 0-1 Lopez  o.g. | 4 | **Referee** : Röthlisberger (Suhr) |
| 0-2 Zuffi | 45 | **Attendance** : 50000 |
| 1-2 Orlando | 51 | |
| 2-2 Orlando | 79 | |
| 3-2 Rey | 80 | |

# SWITZERLAND INTERNATIONAL REVIEW 1990

## INTERNATIONAL LINE-UPS 1990

| | Martin Brunner | Marc Hottiger | Dominique Herr | Urs Fischer | Herbert Baumann | Blaise Piffaretti | Marcel Koller | Heinz Hermann | Alain Sutter | Adrian Knup | Stephane Chapuisat | Frederic Chassot | Philipp Walker | Philippe Hertig | Peter Schepull | Didier Gigon | Alain Geiger | Kubilay Türkyilmaz | Patrick Sylvestre | Reto Gertschen | Christian Colombo | Thomas Bickel | Beat Sutter | André Egli | Christophe Bonvin |
|---|---|---|---|---|---|---|---|---|---|---|---|---|---|---|---|---|---|---|---|---|---|---|---|---|---|
| **31/3/90** SWITZERLAND 0 ITALY 1 — Basel — Ref: Assenmacher (W.Germany) — Friendly | 1 | 2 | 3 | 4 | 5 | | 7 | 8 | 9 | 10 | 11 | (6) | | | | | | 11 | | | | | | | |
| **3/4/90** SWITZERLAND 2 RUMANIA 1 — Luzern — Ref: Steindl (Austria) — Friendly (Hermann, Chassot) | | 2 | 3 | | 5 | 6 | 7 | 8 | 9 | 10 | (9) | 11 | 1 | | | | 4 | 10 | | | | | 7 | | |
| **8/5/90** SWITZERLAND 1 ARGENTINA 1 — Bern — Ref: Kelly (Rep.Ireland) — Friendly (Türkyilmaz) | | 2 | 3 | (4) | 5 | 6 | 4 | 8 | 9 | 10 | 11 | (3) | 1 | | (5) | | 4 | 10 | | | | | (5) | | |
| **2/6/90** SWITZERLAND 2 USA 1 — St.Gallen — Ref: Cooper (Wales) — Friendly (Schepull, Knup) | | 2 | 3 | (6) | 5 | 7 | 7 | 9 | 11 | 10 | (7) | (9) | 1 | | 5 | 6 | 4 | 9 | | | | | | | |
| **21/8/90** AUSTRIA 1 SWITZERLAND 3 — Wien — Ref: Longhi (Italy) — Friendly (Türkyilmaz 2, Knup) | (1) | | 3 | | | (9) | 8 | 6 | 9 | (9) | 11 | | 1 | 6 | 3 | | | 4 | 2 | | | 8 | 9 | | |
| **12/9/90** SWITZERLAND 2 BULGARIA 0 — Genève — Ref: Goethals (Belgium) — EuroCh.Q. (Hottiger, Bickel) | 1 | 2 | 3 | | | | 6 | 9 | (9) | 10 | (10) | | | 3 | (4) | (6) | | 4 | 6 | | 5 | 6 | 9 | | (8) |
| **17/10/90** SCOTLAND 2 SWITZERLAND 1 — Glasgow — Ref: Palsi (Finland) — EuroCh.Q. (Knup) | 1 | 2 | | | | (5) | 7 | 8 | 8 | 10 | 11 | | (1) | 8 | (5) | | | 4 | (10) | | | 6 | 9 | | |
| **14/11/90** SAN MARINO 0 SWITZERLAND 4 — Serravalle — Ref: Kapsos (Cyprus) — EuroCh.Q. (A.Sutter, Chapuisat, Knup, Chassot) | 1 | 2 | 2 | | | | | 5 | 5 | 7 | 8 | 11 | (11) | | (6) | | 9 | | | | 2 | 6 | (11) | 4 | 4 |
| **19/12/90** GERMANY 4 SWITZERLAND 0 — Stuttgart — Ref: Longhi (Italy) — Friendly | 1 | | 3 | | | | | 7 | | | | | | | | (10) | 3 | | | 1 | | 7 | | 5 | |
| **CAPS AT 31/12/90** | 30 | 10 | 13 | 4 | 11 | 15 | 41 | 107 | 19 | 12 | 12 | 6 | 8 | 3 | 11 | 1 | 66 | 24 | 2 | 1 | 2 | 21 | 43 | 61 | 17 |
| **GOALS AT 31/12/90** | | 1 | | | | | 1 | 11 | 2 | 6 | 2 | | 1 | | | 1 | 4 | 9 | 2 | | | 9 | 8 | 8 | 4 |

# TURKEY Correspondent : DAVE CLAYTON

**TURKEY 1st Division Season 1990/91**

| | BESIKTAS | FENERBAHCE | TRABZON | G'SARAY | SARIYER | BURSA | KONYA | KARSIYAKA | ANKARAGÜCÜ | Z.BURNU | G'BIRLIGI | ADANA | BOLU | BAKIRKOY | AYDIN | GAZIANTEP |
|---|---|---|---|---|---|---|---|---|---|---|---|---|---|---|---|---|
| BESIKTAS | | 1-1 | 3-2 | 1-1 | 1-0 | 2-0 | 3-0 | 1-1 | 3-0 | 5-0 | 0-0 | 1-1 | 1-0 | 2-0 | 4-2 | 3-0 |
| FENERBAHCE | 0-2 | | 3-5 | 1-2 | 0-0 | 0-0 | 1-0 | 3-3 | 1-1 | 0-0 | 2-1 | 2-0 | 2-1 | 1-0 | 1-6 | 2-0 |
| TRABZONSPOR | 3-3 | 3-0 | | 3-0 | 1-0 | 0-0 | 3-1 | 3-2 | 0-1 | 1-1 | 2-1 | 1-1 | 1-1 | 4-1 | 0-0 | 4-2 |
| GALATASARAY | 2-3 | 4-1 | 3-1 | | 5-1 | 2-1 | 2-1 | 6-1 | 0-0 | 2-2 | 2-0 | 5-2 | 1-1 | 2-1 | 6-2 | 1-0 |
| SARIYER | 0-1 | 2-1 | 1-1 | 2-2 | | 1-2 | 1-1 | 3-2 | 1-0 | 3-1 | 4-1 | 2-1 | 2-0 | 2-2 | 1-1 | 2-1 |
| BURSASPOR | 0-1 | 2-0 | 1-3 | 0-1 | 0-2 | | 2-1 | 2-1 | 1-0 | 0-1 | 2-2 | 3-1 | 1-0 | 1-4 | 2-2 | 0-1 |
| KONYASPOR | 1-4 | 2-3 | 3-1 | 1-1 | 1-0 | 1-0 | | 1-0 | 3-2 | 1-0 | 1-2 | 2-0 | 0-1 | 1-0 | 1-1 | 2-1 |
| KARSIYAKA | 0-3 | 2-6 | 0-2 | 1-2 | 2-2 | 0-1 | 0-1 | | 0-2 | 0-0 | 2-1 | 0-0 | 0-0 | 2-1 | 2-0 | 1-0 |
| MKE ANKARAGÜCÜ | 2-2 | 3-3 | 1-0 | 0-1 | 0-1 | 3-0 | 3-0 | 1-0 | | 2-2 | 7-2 | 2-0 | 1-1 | 0-2 | 3-1 | 1-2 |
| ZEYTINBURNU | 0-0 | 0-1 | 1-3 | 0-1 | 1-1 | 2-1 | 2-2 | 1-2 | 1-2 | | 1-0 | 2-3 | 2-2 | 1-3 | 1-0 | 1-0 |
| GENCLERBIRLIGI | 2-0 | 3-0 | 2-1 | 0-3 | 1-2 | 2-1 | 1-0 | 1-0 | 2-2 | 2-0 | | 2-1 | 0-0 | 1-1 | 1-1 | 2-2 |
| ADANASPOR | 0-0 | 3-2 | 0-1 | 2-2 | 0-0 | 0-4 | 2-1 | 3-2 | 3-5 | 1-3 | 1-1 | | 2-2 | 1-1 | 2-2 | 3-0 |
| BOLUSPOR | 1-3 | 2-4 | 2-0 | 1-0 | 1-1 | 0-0 | 2-1 | 1-4 | 0-0 | 0-0 | 2-0 | 4-1 | | 2-0 | 2-2 | 2-0 |
| BAKIRKOYSPOR | 2-4 | 2-2 | 1-4 | 0-2 | 2-0 | 1-2 | 2-0 | 1-1 | 7-1 | 0-0 | 2-1 | 3-0 | 3-1 | | 3-1 | 7-2 |
| AYDINSPOR | 3-5 | 1-5 | 2-2 | 1-2 | 1-1 | 1-0 | 2-1 | 1-0 | 3-1 | 1-0 | 1-1 | 3-0 | 3-3 | 0-0 | | 0-0 |
| GAZIANTEPSPOR | 0-1 | 2-5 | 0-0 | 1-0 | 1-1 | 1-2 | 3-2 | 1-1 | 1-0 | 1-0 | 4-1 | 0-0 | 2-0 | 0-1 | 1-0 | |

## TURKEY 1ST DIVISION 1990/91
### LEAGUE TABLE FINAL

| | | | | | | | |
|---|---|---|---|---|---|---|---|
| Besiktas | 30 | 20 | 9 | 1 | 63 | 24 | 69 |
| Galatasaray | 30 | 19 | 7 | 4 | 63 | 31 | 64 |
| Trabzonspor | 30 | 14 | 9 | 7 | 55 | 37 | 51 |
| Sariyer | 30 | 11 | 12 | 7 | 39 | 34 | 45 |
| Fenerbahce | 30 | 12 | 8 | 10 | 53 | 53 | 44 |
| Bakirköyspor | 30 | 12 | 7 | 11 | 53 | 41 | 43 |
| Ankaragücü | 30 | 11 | 8 | 11 | 46 | 43 | 41 |
| Bursaspor | 30 | 11 | 5 | 14 | 31 | 36 | 38 |
| Boluspor | 30 | 8 | 13 | 9 | 35 | 37 | 37 |
| Genclerbirligi | 30 | 9 | 9 | 12 | 36 | 47 | 36 |
| Aydinspor | 30 | 7 | 13 | 10 | 44 | 51 | 34 |
| Konyaspor | 30 | 10 | 4 | 16 | 33 | 45 | 34 |
| Gaziantepspor | 30 | 9 | 6 | 15 | 29 | 45 | 33 |
| Zeytinburnu | 30 | 6 | 11 | 13 | 26 | 40 | 29 |
| Karsiyaka | 30 | 6 | 8 | 16 | 32 | 50 | 26 |
| Adanaspor | 30 | 5 | 11 | 14 | 34 | 58 | 26 |

Champions : - Besiktas
Relegated : - Zeytinburnu, Karsiyaka & Adanaspor

## TURKEY 2ND DIVISION GROUP A 1990/91
### LEAGUE TABLE FINAL

| | | | | | | | |
|---|---|---|---|---|---|---|---|
| Samsunspor | 34 | 23 | 9 | 2 | 74 | 24 | 78 |
| Kocaelispor | 34 | 22 | 7 | 5 | 49 | 18 | 73 |
| Eskisehirspor | 34 | 15 | 8 | 11 | 46 | 36 | 53 |
| Yalovaspor | 34 | 13 | 9 | 12 | 46 | 42 | 48 |
| Sakaryaspor | 34 | 12 | 12 | 10 | 32 | 31 | 48 |
| Fatih Karagümrük | 34 | 12 | 9 | 13 | 42 | 38 | 45 |
| Rizespor | 34 | 10 | 14 | 10 | 48 | 45 | 44 |
| Gaziosmanpasa | 34 | 11 | 11 | 12 | 31 | 31 | 44 |
| Emlak Bankasi Eyüpspor | 34 | 11 | 9 | 14 | 27 | 30 | 42 |
| Ünyespor | 34 | 11 | 9 | 14 | 28 | 47 | 42 |
| Kartalspor | 34 | 12 | 5 | 17 | 35 | 35 | 41 |
| Düzce Dogsanspor | 34 | 9 | 13 | 12 | 32 | 38 | 40 |
| Orduspor | 34 | 10 | 10 | 14 | 36 | 43 | 40 |
| Demir-Celik Karabükspor | 34 | 10 | 10 | 14 | 28 | 39 | 40 |
| Kasimpasa | 34 | 9 | 13 | 12 | 26 | 39 | 40 |
| Giresunspor | 34 | 10 | 9 | 15 | 34 | 39 | 39 |
| Sümerbank Beykoz | 34 | 7 | 14 | 13 | 30 | 43 | 35 |
| Akcaabat Sebatspor | 34 | 8 | 11 | 15 | 30 | 56 | 35 |

Promoted : - Samsunspor
Relegated : - Giresunspor, Sümerbank Beykoz & Akcaabat Sebatspor.

### TOP SCORERS

| | | |
|---|---|---|
| 1. | Tanju Colak (Galatasaray) | 31 |
| 2. | Feyyaz Ucar (Besiktas) | 16 |
| | Sead Sabotic (Ankaragücü) | 16 |
| 4. | Hamdi Aslan (Trabzonspor) | 15 |
| | Kemal Yildirim (Genclerbirligi) | 15 |
| 6. | Ali Gultiken (Besiktas) | 14 |
| | Faruk Yilgit (Boluspor) | 14 |
| 8. | Jaroslaw Araskiewicz (Bakirkoyspor) | 13 |
| | Aykut Kocaman (Fenerbahce) | 13 |
| | Erhan Kiremitci (Bursaspor) | 13 |
| | Hami Mandirali (Trabzonspor) | 13 |
| | Jerabek (Adanaspor) | 13 |
| 13. | Zafer Tuzun (Bakirkoyspor) | 11 |
| 14. | Mehmet Ozdilek (Besiktas) | 10 |
| | Recep Umut (Karsiyaka) | 10 |
| | Ziya Yildiz (Ankaragücü) | 10 |

**TURKEY**
**2nd Division Group A**
**Season 1990/91**

| | SAMSUN | SAKARYA | EYÜP | RIZE | ORDU | KARTAL | A. SEBAT | KARABÜK | ESKISEHIR | KARAGÜMRÜK | BEYKOZ | GIRESUN | KASIMPASA | KOCAELI | ÜNYE | D DOGSAN | G. PASA | YALOVA |
|---|---|---|---|---|---|---|---|---|---|---|---|---|---|---|---|---|---|---|
| SAMSUNSPOR | ■ | 1-1 | 1-1 | 1-1 | 3-1 | 3-2 | 5-0 | 0-0 | 5-1 | 2-2 | 2-0 | 3-0 | 7-0 | 1-0 | 4-0 | 2-0 | 2-0 | 2-0 |
| SAKARYASPOR | 0-3 | ■ | 0-0 | 2-1 | 2-0 | 1-0 | 3-0 | 1-0 | 1-1 | 4-2 | 0-0 | 0-0 | 0-0 | 2-1 | 1-1 | 1-0 | 2-0 | 1-0 |
| EYÜPSPOR | 0-0 | 1-0 | ■ | 3-2 | 1-1 | 0-2 | 0-3 | 3-1 | 2-1 | 0-0 | 1-0 | 1-0 | 1-2 | 0-1 | 0-0 | 0-0 | 1-1 | 5-0 |
| RIZESPOR | 3-5 | 3-2 | 1-0 | ■ | 1-1 | 1-0 | 3-1 | 0-0 | 2-0 | 2-2 | 2-0 | 2-2 | 2-0 | 4-2 | 3-0 | 2-3 | 3-1 | 0-0 |
| ORDUSPOR | 0-1 | 1-1 | 0-0 | 1-1 | ■ | 3-1 | 2-1 | 2-0 | 2-2 | 1-0 | 1-1 | 1-0 | 3-2 | 0-1 | 0-0 | 0-1 | 1-1 | 3-1 |
| KARTALSPOR | 2-3 | 3-1 | 2-0 | 2-0 | 0-2 | ■ | 1-2 | 0-1 | 0-1 | 1-0 | 2-0 | 1-0 | 3-1 | 0-0 | 2-0 | 3-1 | 0-0 | 0-1 |
| AKCAABAT SEBATSPOR | 0-2 | 1-1 | 0-1 | 2-1 | 0-2 | 1-2 | ■ | 1-1 | 1-1 | 2-0 | 1-1 | 0-0 | 2-1 | 1-0 | 1-1 | 2-1 | 3-3 | 1-1 |
| DC KARABÜKSPOR | 1-0 | 1-1 | 0-1 | 3-0 | 2-1 | 2-1 | 2-0 | ■ | 3-1 | 0-2 | 1-1 | 1-2 | 1-0 | 1-1 | 1-0 | 2-0 | 0-0 | 2-2 |
| ESKISEHIRSPOR | 2-0 | 1-0 | 2-1 | 1-0 | 4-1 | 1-1 | 0-1 | 1-0 | ■ | 1-1 | 0-1 | 3-0 | 3-1 | 0-1 | 4-1 | 1-1 | 2-0 | 3-1 |
| FATIH KARAGÜMRÜK | 1-2 | 1-0 | 1-2 | 1-1 | 3-0 | 2-1 | 0-0 | 0-0 | 1-0 | ■ | 5-2 | 2-1 | 1-0 | 1-3 | 3-0 | 1-1 | 1-0 | 2-2 |
| SÜMERBANK BEYKOZ | 0-2 | 2-0 | 1-0 | 1-1 | 2-1 | 0-2 | 4-0 | 2-2 | 2-2 | 3-2 | ■ | 0-0 | 0-1 | 0-2 | 1-0 | 0-0 | 1-1 | 0-1 |
| GIRESUNSPOR | 1-1 | 2-0 | 1-0 | 1-1 | 0-0 | 2-0 | 2-0 | 2-0 | 0-3 | 0-1 | 1-1 | ■ | 0-2 | 0-1 | 4-0 | 5-1 | 1-0 | 3-2 |
| KASIMPASA | 0-2 | 0-0 | 1-2 | 1-1 | 2-1 | 0-0 | 1-1 | 1-0 | 2-1 | 1-0 | 1-1 | 2-1 | ■ | 0-0 | 0-0 | 0-0 | 0-0 | 2-1 |
| KOCAELISPOR | 1-1 | 1-0 | 1-0 | 2-0 | 3-2 | 2-1 | 3-0 | 5-0 | 1-0 | 2-1 | 2-0 | 3-0 | 2-0 | ■ | 3-0 | 1-0 | 0-0 | 1-0 |
| ÜNYESPOR | 1-1 | 0-1 | 2-0 | 1-1 | 1-2 | 1-0 | 3-1 | 1-0 | 0-1 | 1-0 | 1-1 | 3-1 | 1-0 | 1-0 | ■ | 1-0 | 2-1 | 2-2 |
| DÜZCE DOGSANSPOR | 1-3 | 0-0 | 1-0 | 0-0 | 2-0 | 1-0 | 5-0 | 1-0 | 0-0 | 0-2 | 2-2 | 0-0 | 1-1 | 1-1 | 2-3 | ■ | 2-1 | 2-2 |
| GAZIOSMANPASA | 1-2 | 1-2 | 1-0 | 2-1 | 2-0 | 0-0 | 1-1 | 1-0 | 3-1 | 1-0 | 2-0 | 2-1 | 0-0 | 0-0 | 3-0 | 1-0 | ■ | 1-0 |
| YALOVASPOR | 1-2 | 3-1 | 1-0 | 2-2 | 1-0 | 2-0 | 2-0 | 5-0 | 0-1 | 2-1 | 2-0 | 2-1 | 1-1 | 1-1 | 3-0 | 1-2 | 1-0 | ■ |

**TURKEY**
**2nd Division Group B**
**Season 1990/91**

| | ALTAY | KÜTAHYA | GÖZTEPE | ANTALYA | DENIZLI | ALANYA | SÖKE | AYVALIK | KUSADASI | BANDIRMA | IZMIR | ALTINORDU | INEGÖL | Y SALIHLI | MUGLA | Y AFYON | BUCA | GÖNEN |
|---|---|---|---|---|---|---|---|---|---|---|---|---|---|---|---|---|---|---|
| ALTAY | ■ | 4-1 | 2-1 | 3-0 | 0-0 | 2-1 | 2-0 | 1-1 | 4-2 | 1-0 | 2-0 | 2-1 | 5-2 | 3-0 | 5-0 | 1-0 | 1-0 | 3-1 |
| KÜTAHYASPOR | 0-1 | ■ | 1-4 | 2-0 | 0-2 | 3-2 | 3-2 | 1-0 | 2-4 | 0-0 | 3-1 | 4-0 | 1-1 | 0-0 | 3-1 | 0-0 | 1-1 | 5-3 |
| GÖZTEPE | 2-2 | 4-0 | ■ | 2-0 | 0-1 | 1-0 | 3-1 | 1-0 | 4-1 | 4-0 | 5-3 | 2-1 | 2-1 | 8-0 | 3-1 | 2-0 | 2-0 | 2-2 |
| ANTALYASPOR | 0-3 | 2-1 | 1-4 | ■ | 0-2 | 1-0 | 0-2 | 1-0 | 1-0 | 3-2 | 2-7 | 2-1 | 1-3 | 7-3 | 2-0 | 0-1 | 1-0 | 1-1 |
| DENIZLISPOR | 3-2 | 1-0 | 2-0 | 1-2 | ■ | 0-0 | 0-1 | 4-1 | 5-0 | 5-0 | 3-0 | 1-2 | 0-0 | 1-0 | 0-0 | 5-0 | 2-2 | 4-0 |
| ALANYASPOR | 2-1 | 2-0 | 1-2 | 3-2 | 1-0 | ■ | 2-1 | 3-3 | 3-0 | 2-2 | 3-3 | 4-1 | 2-0 | 1-1 | 3-2 | 1-2 | 1-0 | 1-2 |
| SÖKESPOR | 1-5 | 1-0 | 0-2 | 0-1 | 1-4 | 3-2 | ■ | 2-1 | 1-2 | 2-1 | 2-0 | 1-4 | 0-1 | 3-5 | 1-0 | 1-2 | 1-0 | |
| AYVALIKGÜCÜ | 1-6 | 1-1 | 0-1 | 2-0 | 3-1 | 1-1 | 0-0 | ■ | 1-0 | 0-2 | 2-2 | 1-0 | 2-0 | 2-0 | 1-0 | 0-3 | 1-0 | 1-0 |
| KUSADASI GENCLIK | 0-1 | 0-3 | 1-3 | 2-2 | 2-0 | 1-1 | 2-1 | 3-4 | ■ | 3-0 | 1-4 | 1-2 | 1-3 | 2-2 | 1-1 | 3-1 | 4-1 | 3-0 |
| BANDIRMASPOR | 0-1 | 2-1 | 1-0 | 2-1 | 2-0 | 3-2 | 2-1 | 1-1 | 2-1 | ■ | 0-0 | 2-0 | 0-0 | 0-3 | 0-0 | 1-0 | 1-0 | 2-3 |
| IZMIRSPOR | 2-3 | 4-1 | 2-3 | 2-1 | 4-2 | 4-1 | 3-0 | 2-1 | 2-1 | 3-0 | ■ | 2-1 | 1-1 | 1-1 | 3-4 | 2-2 | 0-6 | 1-3 |
| ALTINORDU | 0-2 | 4-1 | 2-6 | 2-0 | 0-1 | 2-1 | 1-0 | 4-1 | 0-0 | 2-1 | 1-1 | ■ | 3-1 | 1-0 | 0-0 | 3-1 | 1-1 | 1-1 |
| INEGÖLSPOR | 0-1 | 3-1 | 0-1 | 5-0 | 1-1 | 2-0 | 0-0 | 3-4 | 2-1 | 1-3 | 1-0 | 2-0 | ■ | 3-0 | 0-1 | 3-1 | 1-0 | 2-2 |
| YENI SALIHLISPOR | 0-4 | 1-3 | 0-3 | 2-1 | 1-0 | 1-2 | 0-1 | 3-1 | 3-0 | 1-2 | 2-1 | 2-1 | 1-0 | ■ | 2-3 | 4-0 | 1-3 | 2-1 |
| MUGLASPOR | 1-2 | 4-1 | 0-1 | 4-2 | 0-1 | 1-1 | 4-2 | 2-3 | 3-2 | 4-3 | 1-2 | 2-1 | 6-2 | 0-1 | ■ | 1-1 | 5-0 | 4-1 |
| YENI AFYONSPOR | 1-1 | 1-1 | 1-1 | 0-1 | 1-2 | 2-1 | 0-3 | 1-0 | 0-3 | 1-4 | 2-0 | 1-0 | 2-2 | 1-2 | 1-1 | ■ | 2-0 | 1-0 |
| BUCASPOR | 0-0 | 0-0 | 2-1 | 2-0 | 1-2 | 2-2 | 0-0 | 1-2 | 0-0 | 1-1 | 1-0 | 1-1 | 4-1 | 1-0 | 3-0 | | ■ | 2-2 |
| GÖNENSPOR | 0-0 | 2-0 | 1-1 | 1-1 | 0-0 | 2-2 | 4-1 | 2-2 | 1-3 | 1-3 | 1-2 | 1-1 | 3-1 | 1-1 | 2-1 | 0-0 | 1-0 | ■ |

| TURKEY 2nd Division Group C Season 1990/91 | MALATYA | AD DEMIR | PETROLOFIS | MERSIN IY | KECIÖREN | SIIRT | DIYARBAKIR | POLATLI | NIGDE | PTT | SEKER | NEVSEHIR | VAN | ERZURUM | K MARAS | ELAZIG | HATAY |
|---|---|---|---|---|---|---|---|---|---|---|---|---|---|---|---|---|---|
| MALATYASPOR | | 2-0 | 6-2 | 4-1 | 3-1 | 1-2 | 4-0 | 1-0 | 2-1 | 1-2 | 1-0 | 3-0 | 1-0 | 3-0 | 1-0 | 1-0 | 6-0 |
| ADANA DEMIRSPOR | 2-1 | | 3-2 | 3-2 | 6-1 | 2-0 | 7-0 | 6-2 | 2-2 | 4-1 | 1-0 | 3-1 | 4-1 | 2-1 | 4-0 | 2-0 | 6-0 |
| PETROLOFISI | 2-2 | 2-0 | | 1-0 | 2-1 | 2-5 | 2-1 | 1-0 | 2-1 | 5-1 | 4-1 | 0-0 | 0-1 | 1-0 | 1-0 | 3-1 | 2-2 |
| MERSIN IDMANYURDU | 1-1 | 3-2 | 1-0 | | 4-4 | 4-0 | 3-1 | 3-1 | 1-0 | 2-0 | 3-0 | 7-1 | 3-1 | 3-1 | 2-1 | 5-3 | 1-1 |
| KECIÖRENGÜCÜ | 0-0 | 2-0 | 1-2 | 1-1 | | 5-2 | 1-1 | 4-0 | 1-0 | 4-1 | 2-0 | 2-1 | 1-1 | 1-4 | 6-1 | 0-1 | 3-1 |
| SIIRT KOYHIZMETLERI/YSE | 0-1 | 2-3 | 2-2 | 1-0 | 2-0 | | 0-0 | 1-0 | 0-1 | 0-1 | 1-1 | 2-0 | 2-1 | 0-1 | 2-1 | 1-0 | 1-0 |
| DIYARBAKIRSPOR | 1-1 | 1-2 | 0-1 | 1-3 | 1-0 | 0-0 | | 3-2 | 2-0 | 2-0 | 1-4 | 1-0 | 2-0 | 1-3 | 1-1 | 2-0 | 1-1 |
| POLATLISPOR | 0-3 | 1-5 | 0-2 | 0-3 | 0-3 | 0-2 | 0-3 | | 1-1 | 0-0 | 0-0 | 2-0 | 0-1 | 1-0 | 3-1 | 0-2 | 0-0 |
| NIGDESPOR | 2-5 | 0-6 | 1-2 | 2-2 | 2-1 | 0-3 | 1-2 | 1-2 | | 3-1 | 2-3 | 0-3 | 1-0 | 2-0 | 2-0 | 3-0 | 1-4 |
| PTT | 1-1 | 0-1 | 1-3 | 2-1 | 1-3 | 0-1 | 3-2 | 2-2 | 3-3 | | 2-0 | 0-1 | 2-0 | 2-0 | 1-1 | 0-1 | 1-1 |
| SEKERSPOR | 0-0 | 2-0 | 0-1 | 1-2 | 1-1 | 2-1 | 1-1 | 2-1 | 0-1 | 0-1 | | 1-0 | 2-1 | 0-1 | 1-0 | 2-0 | 0-1 |
| NEVSEHIRSPOR | 1-1 | 0-0 | 4-1 | 0-3 | 4-2 | 1-0 | 2-0 | 1-1 | 0-1 | 0-3 | 0-0 | | 1-1 | 2-0 | 0-0 | 1-1 | 2-1 |
| VANSPOR | 1-0 | 1-1 | 1-2 | 1-1 | 0-0 | 1-2 | 1-1 | 1-0 | 3-0 | 3-1 | 3-2 | 1-0 | | 0-0 | 3-1 | 3-2 | 3-0 |
| ERZURUMSPOR | 1-0 | 0-0 | 1-1 | 1-0 | 1-1 | 0-1 | 1-3 | 0-0 | 1-0 | 2-1 | 0-0 | 2-1 | 1-0 | | 2-3 | 1-0 | 2-0 |
| KAHRAMANMARASSPOR | 1-2 | 0-2 | 0-0 | 0-2 | 2-3 | 1-2 | 2-0 | 2-1 | 2-0 | 1-4 | 0-1 | 1-0 | 1-0 | 3-0 | | 4-0 | 3-0 |
| ELAZIGSPOR | 1-2 | 1-2 | 1-0 | 1-2 | 2-1 | 1-2 | 3-3 | 2-0 | 2-1 | 3-1 | 1-0 | 0-0 | 2-1 | 2-1 | 0-0 | | 2-1 |
| HATAYSPOR | 1-1 | 0-1 | 2-2 | 0-0 | 3-2 | 2-1 | 3-0 | 4-1 | 2-0 | 1-2 | 0-1 | 3-1 | 3-1 | 1-1 | 0-0 | 1-0 | |

## TURKEY 2ND DIVISION GROUP B 1990/91
### LEAGUE TABLE FINAL

| | | | | | | | |
|---|---|---|---|---|---|---|---|
| Altay | 34 | 26 | 6 | 2 | 76 | 23 | 84 |
| Göztepe | 34 | 25 | 4 | 5 | 81 | 30 | 79 |
| Denizlispor | 34 | 18 | 7 | 9 | 56 | 27 | 61 |
| Bandirmaspor | 34 | 15 | 6 | 13 | 44 | 48 | 51 |
| Ayvalikgücü | 34 | 13 | 9 | 12 | 45 | 52 | 48 |
| Izmirspor | 34 | 13 | 8 | 13 | 66 | 63 | 47 |
| Inegölspor | 34 | 12 | 10 | 12 | 51 | 47 | 46 |
| Muglaspor | 34 | 12 | 8 | 14 | 61 | 56 | 44 |
| Yeni Salihlispor | 34 | 13 | 5 | 16 | 42 | 61 | 44 |
| Alanyaspor | 34 | 11 | 10 | 13 | 54 | 53 | 43 |
| Bucaspor | 34 | 10 | 11 | 13 | 38 | 38 | 41 |
| Altinordu | 34 | 11 | 6 | 17 | 39 | 50 | 39 |
| Sökespor | 34 | 12 | 3 | 19 | 38 | 57 | 39 |
| Antalyaspor | 34 | 12 | 3 | 19 | 39 | 65 | 39 |
| Gönenspor | 34 | 8 | 14 | 12 | 45 | 55 | 38 |
| Kütahyaspor | 34 | 10 | 8 | 16 | 44 | 58 | 38 |
| Kusadasi Genclik | 34 | 10 | 6 | 18 | 50 | 63 | 36 |
| Yeni Afyonspor | 34 | 8 | 10 | 16 | 30 | 53 | 34 |

Promoted : - Altay
Relegated : - Kütahyaspor, Kusadasi & Yeni Afyonspor.

## TURKEY 2ND DIVISION GROUP C 1990/91
### LEAGUE TABLE FINAL

| | | | | | | | |
|---|---|---|---|---|---|---|---|
| Adana Demirspor | 32 | 23 | 4 | 5 | 82 | 31 | 73 |
| Malatyaspor | 32 | 19 | 8 | 5 | 61 | 24 | 65 |
| Mersin Idmanyurdu | 32 | 19 | 7 | 6 | 69 | 36 | 64 |
| Petrolofisi | 32 | 10 | 7 | 7 | 53 | 40 | 61 |
| Siirt Köyhizmetleri/YSE | 32 | 17 | 4 | 11 | 41 | 34 | 55 |
| Keciörengücü | 32 | 12 | 8 | 12 | 58 | 50 | 44 |
| Erzurumspor | 32 | 12 | 7 | 13 | 29 | 35 | 43 |
| Vanspor | 32 | 11 | 7 | 14 | 36 | 39 | 40 |
| Sekerspor | 32 | 11 | 7 | 14 | 28 | 33 | 40 |
| Hatayspor | 32 | 10 | 10 | 12 | 39 | 48 | 40 |
| Elazigspor | 32 | 12 | 4 | 16 | 35 | 46 | 40 |
| PTT | 32 | 11 | 6 | 15 | 41 | 52 | 39 |
| Diyarbakirspor | 32 | 10 | 9 | 13 | 38 | 52 | 39 |
| Kahramanmarasspor | 32 | 9 | 6 | 17 | 33 | 46 | 33 |
| Nevsehirspor | 32 | 8 | 9 | 15 | 28 | 43 | 33 |
| Nigdespor | 32 | 9 | 4 | 19 | 35 | 58 | 31 |
| Polatlispor | 32 | 4 | 7 | 21 | 21 | 60 | 19 |

Promoted : - Adana Demirspor
Relegated : - Nevsehirspor, Nigdespor & Polatlispor.

## TURKEY 3RD DIV. GROUP 1 - 1990/91
**LEAGUE TABLE FINAL**

| Team | P | W | D | L | F | A | Pts |
|---|---|---|---|---|---|---|---|
| Bafraspor | 32 | 28 | 2 | 2 | 85 | 12 | 86 |
| Merzifonspor | 32 | 17 | 6 | 9 | 41 | 29 | 57 |
| Bulancakspor | 32 | 14 | 10 | 8 | 40 | 28 | 52 |
| Hopaspor | 32 | 13 | 10 | 9 | 37 | 27 | 49 |
| Bayburtspor | 32 | 12 | 9 | 11 | 38 | 39 | 45 |
| Erbaaspor | 32 | 12 | 9 | 11 | 37 | 37 | 45 |
| Artvinspor | 32 | 11 | 11 | 10 | 37 | 43 | 44 |
| Tek 12 Martspor | 32 | 11 | 9 | 12 | 35 | 38 | 42 |
| Trabzon PTT | 32 | 11 | 8 | 13 | 42 | 45 | 41 |
| Yalispor | 32 | 10 | 11 | 11 | 26 | 33 | 41 |
| Fatsaspor | 32 | 10 | 9 | 13 | 32 | 38 | 39 |
| Gümüshane K.Hizm. | 32 | 10 | 8 | 14 | 32 | 39 | 38 |
| Carsambaspor | 32 | 9 | 8 | 15 | 31 | 44 | 35 |
| Suluovaspor | 32 | 9 | 8 | 15 | 31 | 44 | 35 |
| Sinop K. Hizmetleri | 32 | 9 | 7 | 16 | 42 | 53 | 34 |
| Cayelispor | 32 | 8 | 7 | 17 | 37 | 56 | 31 |
| Görelespor | 32 | 7 | 8 | 17 | 20 | 35 | 29 |

Promoted : - Bafraspor

## TURKEY 3RD DIV. GROUP 2 - 1990/91
**LEAGUE TABLE FINAL**

| Team | P | W | D | L | F | A | Pts |
|---|---|---|---|---|---|---|---|
| Musspor | 34 | 25 | 5 | 4 | 68 | 24 | 80 |
| Sanliurfaspor | 34 | 22 | 4 | 8 | 56 | 36 | 70 |
| Erzincanspor | 34 | 21 | 4 | 9 | 63 | 28 | 67 |
| Batman Belediyespor | 34 | 16 | 7 | 11 | 44 | 32 | 55 |
| Agrispor | 34 | 15 | 7 | 12 | 49 | 53 | 52 |
| Bingölspor | 34 | 14 | 8 | 12 | 52 | 52 | 50 |
| Mardinspor | 34 | 12 | 14 | 8 | 37 | 30 | 50 |
| Yüksekova Belediyespor | 34 | 13 | 11 | 10 | 40 | 46 | 50 |
| Kars Köy Hizmetleri | 34 | 15 | 3 | 16 | 47 | 48 | 48 |
| Tatvanspor | 34 | 11 | 7 | 16 | 26 | 39 | 40 |
| Tuncelispor | 34 | 9 | 11 | 14 | 36 | 39 | 38 |
| Kiziltepespor | 34 | 11 | 5 | 18 | 37 | 57 | 38 |
| Karamanspor | 34 | 10 | 7 | 17 | 45 | 47 | 37 |
| Silvanspor | 34 | 10 | 7 | 17 | 30 | 44 | 37 |
| Ercisspor | 34 | 11 | 4 | 19 | 34 | 52 | 37 |
| Bitlisspor | 34 | 9 | 9 | 16 | 29 | 39 | 36 |
| Cizrespor | 34 | 9 | 8 | 17 | 28 | 48 | 35 |
| Igdirspor | 34 | 9 | 7 | 18 | 25 | 48 | 34 |

Promoted : - Musspor

## TURKEY 3RD DIV. GROUP 3 - 1990/91
**LEAGUE TABLE FINAL**

| Team | P | W | D | L | F | A | Pts |
|---|---|---|---|---|---|---|---|
| Tarsus Idmanyurdu | 34 | 24 | 10 | 0 | 77 | 12 | 82 |
| Iskenderunspor | 34 | 22 | 7 | 5 | 69 | 27 | 73 |
| Aksarayspor | 34 | 20 | 6 | 8 | 57 | 26 | 66 |
| Adana Genclerbirligi | 34 | 15 | 11 | 8 | 61 | 27 | 56 |
| Adana Polisgücü | 34 | 16 | 6 | 12 | 46 | 32 | 54 |
| Osmaniyespor | 34 | 15 | 5 | 14 | 46 | 40 | 50 |
| Elbistanspor | 34 | 14 | 8 | 12 | 47 | 50 | 50 |
| Kadirli Idmanyurdu | 34 | 13 | 7 | 14 | 58 | 47 | 46 |
| Adiyamanspor | 34 | 13 | 7 | 14 | 40 | 53 | 46 |
| Sahilspor | 34 | 12 | 7 | 15 | 37 | 39 | 43 |
| Nizipspor | 34 | 12 | 4 | 18 | 36 | 60 | 40 |
| Reyhanlispor | 34 | 11 | 7 | 16 | 39 | 58 | 40 |
| Islahiyespor | 34 | 11 | 6 | 17 | 35 | 43 | 39 |
| Kozanspor | 34 | 10 | 8 | 16 | 34 | 43 | 38 |
| Besnispor | 34 | 9 | 10 | 15 | 35 | 64 | 37 |
| Ceyhan Belediyespor | 34 | 8 | 10 | 16 | 34 | 62 | 34 |
| Kilisspor | 34 | 9 | 7 | 18 | 29 | 56 | 34 |
| Atsinspor | 34 | 4 | 13 | 17 | 23 | 57 | 25 |

Promoted : - Tarsus Idmanyurdu

## TURKEY 3RD DIV. GROUP 4 - 1990/91
**LEAGUE TABLE FINAL**

| Team | P | W | D | L | F | A | Pts |
|---|---|---|---|---|---|---|---|
| Kayserispor | 34 | 25 | 7 | 2 | 81 | 24 | 82 |
| Cubukspor | 34 | 21 | 7 | 6 | 64 | 28 | 70 |
| Kirikkalespor | 34 | 20 | 7 | 7 | 47 | 25 | 67 |
| Yeni Yozgatspor | 34 | 19 | 5 | 10 | 76 | 43 | 62 |
| Beypazari Belediyespor | 34 | 18 | 3 | 13 | 51 | 35 | 57 |
| Amasyaspor | 34 | 17 | 6 | 11 | 51 | 35 | 57 |
| Corumspor | 34 | 15 | 5 | 14 | 46 | 32 | 50 |
| Turhalspor | 34 | 15 | 5 | 14 | 44 | 30 | 50 |
| Erciyesspor | 34 | 11 | 9 | 14 | 39 | 51 | 42 |
| Ankara Demirspor | 34 | 10 | 9 | 15 | 37 | 39 | 39 |
| Sivasspor | 34 | 10 | 9 | 15 | 42 | 48 | 39 |
| Kastamonuspor | 34 | 11 | 6 | 17 | 47 | 72 | 39 |
| Tokatspor | 34 | 8 | 11 | 15 | 35 | 55 | 35 |
| Yeni Sincanspor | 34 | 8 | 9 | 17 | 34 | 82 | 33 |
| Kirsehirspor | 34 | 8 | 8 | 18 | 35 | 64 | 32 |
| Ankara Emniyet | 34 | 7 | 10 | 17 | 41 | 63 | 31 |
| Cankirispor | 34 | 6 | 11 | 17 | 27 | 54 | 29 |
| Sivas Demirspor | 34 | 5 | 7 | 22 | 31 | 63 | 22 |

Promoted : - Kayserispor

## TURKEY 3RD DIV. GROUP 5 - 1990/91
**LEAGUE TABLE FINAL**

| Team | P | W | D | L | F | A | Pts |
|---|---|---|---|---|---|---|---|
| Ispartaspor | 34 | 28 | 5 | 1 | 84 | 21 | 89 |
| Yeni Nazillispor | 34 | 28 | 2 | 4 | 107 | 25 | 86 |
| Etibank SAS. | 34 | 19 | 9 | 6 | 58 | 38 | 66 |
| Marmarisspor | 34 | 17 | 6 | 11 | 65 | 36 | 57 |
| Tiresspor | 34 | 16 | 8 | 10 | 60 | 47 | 56 |
| Kemer Belediyespor | 34 | 14 | 6 | 14 | 59 | 52 | 48 |
| Yeni Milasspor | 34 | 13 | 9 | 12 | 37 | 35 | 48 |
| Antalya Koy Hizmetleri | 34 | 13 | 8 | 13 | 48 | 44 | 47 |
| Buldanspor | 34 | 12 | 8 | 14 | 51 | 63 | 44 |
| Konya Ereglispor | 34 | 12 | 7 | 15 | 39 | 43 | 43 |
| Yeni Sandiklispor | 34 | 11 | 7 | 16 | 43 | 70 | 40 |
| Karamanspor | 34 | 10 | 6 | 18 | 33 | 47 | 36 |
| Yeni Aksehirspor | 34 | 10 | 6 | 18 | 37 | 60 | 36 |
| Burdurgücü | 34 | 8 | 10 | 16 | 28 | 62 | 34 |
| Antalya Yolspor | 34 | 8 | 7 | 19 | 41 | 62 | 31 |
| Fethiyespor | 34 | 7 | 10 | 17 | 19 | 55 | 31 |
| Yeni Dinarspor | 34 | 7 | 9 | 18 | 27 | 51 | 30 |
| Sarayköyspor | 34 | 6 | 12 | 16 | 40 | 70 | 30 |

Promoted : - Ispartaspor

## TURKEY 3RD DIV. GROUP 6 - 1990/91
**LEAGUE TABLE FINAL**

| Team | P | W | D | L | F | A | Pts |
|---|---|---|---|---|---|---|---|
| Manisaspor | 34 | 24 | 7 | 3 | 66 | 22 | 79 |
| Tarisspor | 34 | 19 | 13 | 2 | 52 | 21 | 70 |
| Bergamaspor | 34 | 17 | 11 | 6 | 51 | 29 | 62 |
| Yeni Bergamaspor | 34 | 18 | 6 | 10 | 61 | 32 | 60 |
| Tavsanli Linyitspor | 34 | 15 | 9 | 10 | 60 | 47 | 54 |
| Alpelspor | 34 | 13 | 8 | 13 | 46 | 49 | 47 |
| Akhisarspor | 34 | 11 | 12 | 11 | 53 | 45 | 45 |
| Torbalispor | 34 | 12 | 8 | 14 | 40 | 40 | 44 |
| Ödemisspor | 34 | 12 | 8 | 14 | 33 | 63 | 44 |
| Soma Sotesspor | 34 | 10 | 9 | 15 | 46 | 40 | 39 |
| Yesilova | 34 | 9 | 12 | 13 | 38 | 44 | 39 |
| Soma Linyitspor | 34 | 8 | 14 | 12 | 42 | 51 | 38 |
| Usakspor | 34 | 10 | 8 | 16 | 35 | 55 | 38 |
| Burhaniyespor | 34 | 11 | 5 | 18 | 46 | 56 | 38 |
| Alasehirspor | 34 | 10 | 8 | 16 | 46 | 56 | 38 |
| Cesmespor | 34 | 9 | 7 | 18 | 39 | 57 | 34 |
| Selcuk Efesspor | 34 | 10 | 5 | 19 | 31 | 52 | 37 |
| Menemenspor | 34 | 9 | 7 | 18 | 32 | 52 | 34 |

Promoted : - Manisaspor

## TURKEY 3RD DIV. GROUP 7 - 1990/91
**LEAGUE TABLE FINAL**

| Team | P | W | D | L | F | A | Pts |
|---|---|---|---|---|---|---|---|
| Bozüyükspor | 34 | 20 | 7 | 7 | 57 | 37 | 67 |
| Mustafakemalpasa | 34 | 19 | 8 | 7 | 74 | 37 | 65 |
| Mudanyaspor | 34 | 17 | 6 | 11 | 56 | 39 | 57 |
| Sönmez Filament | 34 | 15 | 12 | 7 | 42 | 25 | 57 |
| Canakkalespor | 34 | 16 | 4 | 14 | 46 | 39 | 52 |
| Anadoluhisari Idman. | 34 | 14 | 9 | 11 | 46 | 36 | 51 |
| Balikesirspor | 34 | 14 | 9 | 11 | 33 | 31 | 51 |
| Edremitspor | 34 | 13 | 11 | 10 | 31 | 30 | 50 |
| Eskisehir Sekerspor | 34 | 11 | 9 | 14 | 32 | 38 | 42 |
| Babaeskispor | 34 | 10 | 9 | 15 | 38 | 39 | 39 |
| Karacabeyspor | 34 | 10 | 9 | 15 | 46 | 47 | 39 |
| THY | 34 | 11 | 6 | 17 | 47 | 72 | 39 |
| Bayrampasa | 34 | 10 | 7 | 17 | 33 | 46 | 37 |
| Bileckspor | 34 | 10 | 5 | 19 | 35 | 46 | 35 |
| Sümerbank Merinos | 34 | 9 | 8 | 17 | 35 | 46 | 35 |
| Bigaspor | 34 | 9 | 7 | 18 | 27 | 44 | 34 |
| Canspor | 34 | 8 | 10 | 16 | 31 | 47 | 34 |
| Izrikspor | 34 | 3 | 14 | 17 | 22 | 63 | 23 |

Promoted : - Bozüyükspor

## TURKEY 3RD DIV. GROUP 8 - 1990/91
**LEAGUE TABLE FINAL**

| Team | P | W | D | L | F | A | Pts |
|---|---|---|---|---|---|---|---|
| Süleymaniye Kücükcek. | 34 | 22 | 9 | 3 | 57 | 24 | 75 |
| Galata | 34 | 18 | 8 | 8 | 42 | 24 | 62 |
| Lüleburgazspor | 34 | 15 | 15 | 4 | 52 | 28 | 60 |
| Silivrispor | 34 | 18 | 6 | 10 | 46 | 29 | 60 |
| Istanbulspor | 34 | 17 | 8 | 9 | 39 | 29 | 59 |
| Feriköy | 34 | 14 | 10 | 10 | 39 | 29 | 52 |
| Nisantasi | 34 | 12 | 12 | 10 | 35 | 27 | 48 |
| Corluspor | 34 | 13 | 8 | 13 | 36 | 45 | 47 |
| TB Edirnespor | 34 | 8 | 16 | 10 | 39 | 35 | 40 |
| Kesanspor | 34 | 9 | 12 | 13 | 36 | 37 | 39 |
| Kapalicarsi | 34 | 11 | 6 | 17 | 31 | 37 | 39 |
| Kirklarelispor | 34 | 11 | 6 | 17 | 52 | 43 | 39 |
| Uzunköprüspor | 34 | 8 | 13 | 13 | 40 | 61 | 37 |
| Vefa | 34 | 8 | 12 | 14 | 32 | 43 | 36 |
| Tekirdagspor | 34 | 8 | 11 | 15 | 24 | 35 | 35 |
| Beylerbeyi | 34 | 8 | 10 | 16 | 27 | 42 | 34 |
| Malkaraspor | 34 | 9 | 7 | 18 | 35 | 52 | 34 |
| Erdekspor | 34 | 8 | 9 | 17 | 27 | 52 | 33 |

Promoted : - Süleymaniye Kücükcekmece

## TURKEY 3RD DIVISION GROUP 9 - 1990/91

### LEAGUE TABLE FINAL

| | | | | | | | |
|---|---|---|---|---|---|---|---|
| Üsküdar Anadolu | 34 | 23 | 6 | 5 | 56 | 23 | 75 |
| Cengelköy | 34 | 22 | 7 | 5 | 59 | 15 | 73 |
| Yücespor | 34 | 16 | 9 | 9 | 42 | 28 | 57 |
| Bartinspor | 34 | 14 | 13 | 7 | 40 | 29 | 55 |
| Erdemir Ereglispor | 34 | 15 | 7 | 12 | 49 | 39 | 52 |
| Gebzespor | 34 | 13 | 9 | 12 | 43 | 42 | 48 |
| Gölcükspor | 34 | 11 | 14 | 9 | 30 | 29 | 47 |
| Maltepespor | 34 | 11 | 12 | 11 | 33 | 31 | 45 |
| Pendikspor | 34 | 12 | 7 | 15 | 32 | 35 | 43 |
| Ayazispor | 34 | 10 | 12 | 12 | 27 | 40 | 42 |
| Küçükköy | 34 | 10 | 11 | 13 | 35 | 41 | 41 |
| Zonguldakspor | 34 | 11 | 8 | 15 | 35 | 50 | 41 |
| Ümraniyespor | 34 | 9 | 13 | 12 | 30 | 36 | 40 |
| Darica Genclerbirligi | 34 | 10 | 10 | 14 | 31 | 51 | 40 |
| Düzcespor | 34 | 11 | 6 | 17 | 39 | 42 | 39 |
| Kilimlispor | 34 | 7 | 13 | 14 | 29 | 43 | 34 |
| Adapazarispor | 34 | 9 | 6 | 19 | 46 | 61 | 33 |
| Petkimspor | 34 | 6 | 9 | 19 | 25 | 46 | 27 |

Promoted : - Üsküdar Anadolu

# TURKEY CUP 1990/91

### 1/8 FINALS

| | | | |
|---|---|---|---|
| Bursaspor ................. 3 | Trabzonspor ............. 5 | Sariyer ........................ 3 | Karsiyaka .................. 0 |
| Fenerbahce ............. 2 | Gaziantepspor .......... 1 | Samsunspor ............... 0 | Besiktas .................... 1 |
| Ankaragücü ............. 2 | Altay .......................... 0 | Genclerbirligi ............. 2 | Bakirköyspor ............. 5 |
| Konyaspor ............... 0 | Galatasaray .............. 1 | Zeytinburnu ............... 2 | Aydinspor ................. 4 |

### 1/4 FINALS

| | | | |
|---|---|---|---|
| Besiktas .................... 2 | Galatasaray .............. 2 (aet.) | Fenerbahce ............... 2 | Sariyer ..................... 2 (aet.) |
| Galatasaray win 5-4 on penalties | | Fenerbahce win 4-3 on penalties | |
| Ankaragücü ............. 4 | Aydinspor ................. 0 | Trabzonspor ............. 2 | Bakirköyspor ............ 1 |

### SEMI FINALS

| | | | |
|---|---|---|---|
| Fenerbahce ............. 1 | Ankaragücü ............. 3 | Galatasaray ............... 2 | Trabzonspor ............. 1 (aet.) |

## FINAL    8/5/91

Galatasaray .............. 3   Ankaragücü .............. 1 (aet.)

Galatasaray : - Hayrettin, Bülent, Yusuf, Cüneyt, Muhammet, Erdal, Ugur (Rotariu 114), Tugay, Metin, Hasan (Prekazi 54), Tanju.

Ankaragücü : - Zalad, Hayati, Bahattin, Serhat, Erhan, Hayrettin, Abdullah, Ergun (Tarik13), Sinan, Sabotic, Cengiz.

| | |
|---|---|
| 0-1 Cengiz   16 | Referee : Hasan Ceylan |
| 1-1 Tanju    18 | Attendance : 20240 |
| 2-1 Ugur    107 | |
| 3-1 Tugay   119 | |

## TURKEY SUPER CUP (PRESIDENT'S CUP) 1990/91    26/5/91

Galatasaray .............. 1   Besiktas .................... 0

Galatasaray : - Hayrettin, Cüneyt, Yusuf, Bülent, Muhammet, Tugay, Rotariu (Prekazi 66), Ugur, Metin, Tanju, Kosecki

Besiktas : - Engin, Recep, Gökhan, Ulvi, Kadir, Ali, Riza, Mehmet, Walsh, Feyyaz, Metin.

| | |
|---|---|
| 1-0 Kosecki 77 | Referee : Ahmet Cakar |
| | Attendance : 14650 |

## TURKEY SUPER CUP CONSOLATION (PRIME MINISTER'S CUP) 1990/91    22/5/91

Ankaragücü .............. 3   Trabzonspor .............. 1

Ankaragücü : - Zalad, Hayati, Bahattin, Serhat, Erhan, Hayrettin (Isa 89), Abdullah, Ergün, Cengiz, Ziya (Behzat 85), Sinan.

Trabzonspor : - Petranovic, Ismail, Ogün, Kemal, Mehmet, Lemi (Turgut 72), Abdullah (Sehmuz 33), Ünal, Orhan, Hamdi, Hami.

| |
|---|
| 0-1 Ünal |
| 1-1 Ziya |
| 2-1 Ziya |
| 3-1 Ergün |

Referee : Yüksel Okcuoglu

# TURKEY INTERNATIONAL REVIEW 1990

## INTERNATIONAL LINE-UPS 1990

**Matches:**

| Date | Result | Venue | Referee | Type |
|---|---|---|---|---|
| 11/4/90 | DENMARK 1 TURKEY 0 | København | Ref: Van Langenhove (Belgium) | Friendly |
| 27/5/90 | TURKEY 0 REPUBLIC OF IRELAND 0 | Izmir | Ref: Kirkov (USSR) | Friendly |
| 5/9/90 | HUNGARY 4 TURKEY 1 | Budapest | Ref: Listkiewicz (Poland) | Friendly (Tanju) |
| 17/10/90 | REPUBLIC OF IRELAND 5 TURKEY 0 | Dublin | Ref: Fredriksson (Sweden) | EuroCh.Q. |
| 14/11/90 | TURKEY 0 POLAND 1 | Istanbul | Ref: Spirin (USSR) | EuroCh.Q. |

**Appearances (shirt numbers; substitutes in parentheses):**

| Player | 11/4/90 | 27/5/90 | 5/9/90 | 17/10/90 | 14/11/90 | CAPS at 31/12/90 | GOALS at 31/12/90 |
|---|---|---|---|---|---|---|---|
| Engin Ipekoglu | 1 | 1 | 1 | 1 | 1 | 11 | |
| Riza Calimbay | 2 | 3 | 5 | 5 | 5 | 19 | |
| Gökhan Keskin | 3 | 2 | 3 | 3 | | 15 | |
| Yusuf Altintas | | | 2 | 2 | 3 | 27 | 2 |
| Semih Yuvakuran | 5 | | | | | 21 | |
| Ugur Tutuneker | | | | | | 13 | |
| Ünal Karaman | 7 | 8 | 8 | | 8 | 18 | |
| Oguz Cetin | 8 | 6 | 6 | 7 | 7 | 14 | 2 |
| Gökhan Gedikali | 9 | (2) | 7 | | 9 | 8 | |
| Metin Tekin | 10 | 10 | 7 | (4) | 10 | 31 | 2 |
| Feyyaz Ucar | 11 | 11 | | | 11 | 11 | 4 |
| Mustafa Yucedag | 6 | 7 | (6) | | | 9 | |
| Osman Yildirim | (9) | (11) | | | | 1 | |
| Hami Mandirali | (11) | 10 | 10 | | | 5 | |
| Kemal Serdar | 2 | 3 | | | | 9 | |
| Ogün Temizkanoglu | 4 | 9 | | | | 1 | |
| Tugay Kerimoglu | 9 | 9 | | | | 3 | |
| Savas Demiral | (7) | (3) | | | | 14 | |
| Mehmet Ozdilek | (8) | (10) | 8 | (6) | | 4 | |
| Hasan Vezir | 4 | 10 | 4 | | | 16 | |
| Hakan Tecimer | 10 | 11 | | | | 3 | |
| Tanju Colak | 11 | (11) | 11 | | | 25 | 10 |
| Ümit Kale | (6) | | | | | 1 | |
| Ercan Kol | 4 | | | | | 1 | |
| Bülent Korkmaz | 6 | 4 | | | | 2 | |
| Sercan Gogulu | 11 | (9) | 4 | | | 2 | |
| Muhammet Altintas | 9 | 6 | | | | 1 | |
| Ülken Turek | 9 | 1 | | | | 1 | |

## TURKEY : All Time Records as at 31/12/90 - CAPS

1. Fatih Terim (Galatasaray) — 51
2. Turgay Seren (Galatasaray) — 47
3. Lefter Kücükandonyadis (Fenerbahce) — 46
4. Cemil Turan (Istanbulspor/Fenerbahce) — 44
5. Seref Has (Fenerbahce) — 39
6. Metin Oktay (Galatasaray) — 36
7. Turgay Semercioglu (Trabzonspor) — 35
8. Sedat Özden (Bursaspor) — 34
9. Ogün Altiparmak (Karsiyaka/Fenerbahce) — 32
10. Metin Tekin (Besiktas) — 31

## TURKEY : All Time Records as at 31/12/90 - GOALS

1. Lefter Kücükandonyadis (Fenerbahce) — (46) 21
2. Metin Oktay (Galatasaray) — (36) 19
3. Cemil Turan (Istanbulspor/Fenerbahce) — (44) 19
4. Zeki-Riza Sporel (Fenerbahce) — (16) 15
5. Tanju Colak (Samsunspor/Galatasaray) — (25) 10
6. Burhan Sargin (Fenerbahce) — (8) 7
7. Sedat Özden (Bursaspor) — (34) 7
8. Reha Eken (Galatasaray) — (4) 6
   Ilyas Tüfekci (VfB Stuttgart/Fenerbahce/Galatasaray) — (18) 6
   Fevzi Zemzem (Göztepe) — (18) 6
   Can Bartu (Fenerbahce/Lazio) — (26) 6
   Ogün Altiparmak (Karsiyaka/Fenerbahce) — (32) 6

# USSR Correspondent : ALGIRDAS JASINSKAS

| USSR Supreme League Season 1990 | SPARTAK | DNEPR | DINAMO K | ZALGIRIS | TORPEDO | CHRETS | METALLIST | DINAMO MO | DINAMO MI | ROTOR | ARARAT | PAMIR | SHAKHTYOR | TSKA |
|---|---|---|---|---|---|---|---|---|---|---|---|---|---|---|
| SPARTAK MOSKVA | | 2-0 | 1-3 | | 2-0 | 3-1 | 6-0 | 1-2 | 2-1 | 0-0 | 4-0 | 1-0 | 0-0 | 5-4 |
| DNEPR DNEPROPETROVSK | 1-1 | | 1-0 | | 1-0 | 2-0 | 3-0 | 5-1 | 3-1 | 3-1 | 1-1 | 4-1 | 4-2 | 2-2 |
| DINAMO KIEV | 3-1 | 2-1 | | | 4-3 | 2-1 | 2-0 | 0-1 | 3-0 | 3-0 | 1-0 | 3-1 | 2-0 | 4-1 |
| ZALGIRIS VILNIUS | | ⊗ | | | | | ⊗ | | | | | | | · |
| TORPEDO MOSKVA | 1-0 | 1-0 | 0-0 | | | 1-0 | 0-0 | 3-1 | 2-1 | 1-0 | 2-1 | 1-0 | 1-1 | 0-2 |
| CHERNOMORETS ODESSA | 1-0 | 1-0 | 0-3 | 1-0 | 0-1 | | 1-0 | 2-3 | 3-1 | 0-0 | 1-0 | 3-1 | 4-2 | 0-0 |
| METALLIST KHARKOV | 0-1 | 0-0 | 0-2 | | 2-1 | 1-0 | | 0 1 | 1-0 | 1-0 | 0-0 | 1-1 | 1-1 | 0-1 |
| DINAMO MOSKVA | 1-1 | 1-0 | 0 0 | | 1-2 | 3-2 | 1-0 | | 1-0 | 1-1 | 1-2 | 2-1 | 2-0 | 0-0 |
| DINAMO MINSK | 0-1 | 2-0 | 3-2 | | 1-2 | 2-1 | 0-0 | 0-0 | | 3-1 | 0-0 | 1-0 | 2-0 | 1-2 |
| ROTOR VOLGOGRAD | 0-2 | 2-1 | 0-0 | | 2-2 | 0-2 | 1-2 | 0-1 | 2-0 | | 0-0 | 1-0 | 3-2 | 0-1 |
| ARARAT YEREVAN | 1-3 | 2-2 | 2-1 | | 0-1 | 1-0 | 0-0 | 1-2 | 3-0 | 3-0 | | 1-0 | 0-0 | 4-0 |
| PAMIR DUSHANBE | 5-1 | 2-3 | 1-1 | | 0-1 | 0-0 | 1-0 | 2-0 | 3-1 | 1-0 | 3-2 | | 2-1 | 0-2 |
| SHAKHTYOR DONETSK | 0-0 | 0-0 | 2-2 | | 2-1 | 1-0 | 2-2 | 1-1 | 1-0 | 3-0 | 1-0 | 0-0 | | 1-0 |
| TSKA MOSKVA | 2-1 | 1-2 | 1-1 | | 3-1 | 2-0 | 3-2 | 0-0 | 1-0 | 7-0 | 0-1 | 4-1 | 4-0 | |

Note: Georgian clubs, Dinamo Tbilisi and Guriya Lanchkhuti, withdrew from the league prior to the commencement of the season.

⊗ Zalgiris Vilnius failed to appear for home matches against Dnepr and Dinamo Moskva, matches being awarded 0-3. Zalgiris then withdrew from the league however, and results of matches played and forfeited were declared void.

Scorecharts compiled on home and away basis, contrary to those produced in the Soviet Union, which use distinction of matches played in the first and second halves of the season.

## USSR SUPREME LEAGUE 1990

### LEAGUE TABLE FINAL

| | | | | | | | |
|---|---|---|---|---|---|---|---|
| Dinamo Kiev | 24 | 14 | 6 | 4 | 44 | 20 | 34 |
| TSKA Moskva | 24 | 13 | 5 | 6 | 43 | 26 | 31 |
| Dinamo Moskva | 24 | 12 | 7 | 5 | 27 | 24 | 31 |
| Torpedo Moskva | 24 | 13 | 4 | 7 | 28 | 24 | 30 |
| Spartak Moskva | 24 | 12 | 5 | 7 | 39 | 26 | 29 |
| Dnepr Dnepropetrovsk | 24 | 11 | 6 | 7 | 39 | 26 | 28 |
| Ararat Yerevan | 24 | 8 | 7 | 9 | 25 | 23 | 23 |
| Shakhtyor Donetsk | 24 | 6 | 10 | 8 | 23 | 31 | 22 |
| Chernomorets Odessa | 24 | 8 | 3 | 13 | 23 | 29 | 19 |
| Pamir Dushanbe | 24 | 7 | 4 | 13 | 26 | 34 | 18 |
| Metallist Kharkov | 24 | 5 | 8 | 11 | 13 | 28 | 18 |
| Dinamo Minsk | 24 | 6 | 3 | 15 | 20 | 34 | 15 |
| Rotor Volgograd | 24 | 4 | 6 | 14 | 14 | 39 | 14 |

Champions : - Dinamo Kiev
Relegated : - Rotor Volgograd

League to be increased again to 16 clubs for Season 1991. Bottom club obliged to play off against the 4th club in the 1st Division for one Supreme league place.

### TOP SCORERS

| | |
|---|---|
| 1. Oleg Protasov (Dinamo Kiev) | 12 |
| Valery Shmarov (Spartak Moskva) | 12 |
| 3. Eduard Son (Dnepr Dnepropetrovsk) | 10 |
| 4. Nikolai Kudritsky (Dnepr Dnepropetrovsk) | 9 |
| Aleksandr Mostovoy (Spartak Moskva) | 9 |
| Mukhsin Mukhamadiev (Pamir Dushanbe) | 9 |
| Sergei Yuran (Dinamo Kiev) | 9 |
| 8. Igor Korneyev (TSKA Moskva) | 8 |
| Valery Masalitin (TSKA Moskva) | 8 |
| Yuri Savichev (Torpedo Moskva) | 8 |

Note : Clubs finishing level on points in the Soviet Union are separated by the following list of priorities : -
1. Most victories
2. Results of Mutual Matches
3. Most Goals
4. Goal Difference

### PROMOTION/RELEGATION TEST MATCHES

| | 1ST LEG | 2ND LEG | AGG. |
|---|---|---|---|
| Lokomotiv Moskva v Rotor Volgograd | 3-1 | 0-1 | 3-2 |

| USSR 1st Division Season 1990 | LOK M. | ZENIT | KAIRAT | DINAMO ST. | FAKEL | TAVRIYA | METALLURG | NEFTCHI | KOTAIK | NISTRU | GEOLOG | PAKHTAKOR | R' MASH | KUZBASS | SHINNIK | SPARTAK | KUBAN | LOK G | TIRAS | DINAMO SU |
|---|---|---|---|---|---|---|---|---|---|---|---|---|---|---|---|---|---|---|---|---|
| LOKOMOTIV MOSKVA | ■ | 1-0 | 1-0 | 3-2 | 2-0 | 1-1 | 2-1 | 2-1 | 1-2 | 3-1 | 2-1 | 1-0 | 2-1 | 5-0 | 2-1 | 0-1 | 1-0 | 0-0 | 4-0 | 0-0 |
| ZENIT LENINGRAD | 1-1 | ■ | 0-1 | 0-0 | 3-0 | 0-0 | 0-0 | 2-2 | 2-1 | 1-2 | 1-2 | 1-1 | 4-1 | 2-0 | 0-1 | 1-1 | 1-0 | 1-1 | 0-0 | 2-0 |
| KAIRAT ALMA ATA | 1-0 | 1-1 | ■ | 4-1 | 0-1 | 1-2 | 0-2 | 2-0 | 1-1 | 1-1 | 2-0 | 0-1 | 3-1 | 2-1 | 1-1 | 0-3 | 0-0 | 1-0 | 2-2 | 0-2 |
| DINAMO STAVROPOL | 2-1 | 1-0 | 2-1 | ■ | 2-1 | 1-0 | 2-3 | 3-0 | 3-0 | 1-1 | 2-0 | 1-0 | 4-1 | 3-1 | 3-1 | 0-3 | 1-0 | 2-0 | 2-0 | 2-0 |
| FAKEL VORONEZH | 1-2 | 0-0 | 1-2 | 2-2 | ■ | 0-1 | 1-0 | 2-1 | 2-1 | 0-2 | 1-1 | 3-1 | 3-0 | 4-0 | 3-0 | 1-1 | 3-0 | 2-0 | 0-0 | 0-1 |
| TAVRIYA SIMFEROPOL | 1-1 | 0-0 | 1-0 | 3-2 | 1-2 | ■ | 2-2 | 2-2 | 2-1 | 0-0 | 0-1 | 3-3 | 2-1 | 2-0 | 0-0 | 1-1 | 5-1 | 3-1 | 3-1 | 1-0 |
| METALLURG ZAPOROZHE | 0-0 | 3-2 | 4-1 | 2-0 | 5-1 | 0-0 | ■ | 3-1 | 1-0 | 1-1 | 2-0 | 1-0 | 2-0 | 2-1 | 1-1 | 0-0 | 2-0 | 6-1 | 2-0 | 2-1 |
| NEFTCHI BAKU | 0-0 | 1-0 | 0-0 | 1-0 | 3-1 | 2-1 | 2-0 | ■ | ⊗ | 1-0 | 6-0 | 3-0 | 2-0 | 3-0 | 3-0 | 1-2 | 3-0 | 2-2 | 1-1 | 1-0 |
| KOTAIK ABOVYAN | 4-1 | 0-0 | 2-1 | 2-3 | 1-1 | 0-0 | 2-3 | ⊗ | ■ | 2-1 | 1-1 | 1-0 | 3-1 | 2-0 | 0-3 | 2-2 | 2-1 | 1-0 | 3-0 | 2-1 |
| NISTRU KISHINEV | 2-2 | 2-1 | 0-0 | 0-0 | 1-0 | 1-0 | 2-2 | 1-0 | 1-1 | ■ | 4-1 | 2-3 | 3-3 | 2-0 | 1-2 | 0-2 | 3-1 | 1-0 | 0-0 | 4-0 |
| GEOLOG TYUMEN | 0-0 | 1-0 | 2-0 | 0-1 | 0-1 | 2-0 | 0-0 | 4-1 | 2-0 | 3-1 | ■ | 0-0 | 0-1 | 1-1 | 1-0 | 2-1 | 3-0 | 2-1 | 1-0 | 2-0 |
| PAKHTAKOR TASHKENT | 3-1 | 2-1 | 2-1 | 2-2 | 2-0 | 2-0 | 2-1 | 2-2 | 6-2 | 3-0 | 2-0 | ■ | 2-1 | 3-3 | 3-0 | 2-1 | 6-2 | 7-2 | 2-0 | 3-0 |
| ROSTSELMASH ROSTOV | 0-1 | 2-0 | 2-0 | 1-3 | 0-0 | 2-1 | 1-1 | 1-1 | 1-0 | 1-0 | 2-2 | 1-2 | ■ | 2-0 | 2-0 | 1-1 | 0-1 | 2-0 | 1-0 | 1-2 |
| KUZBASS KEMEROVO | 0-1 | 1-2 | 0-1 | 0-1 | 0-1 | 1-0 | 0-1 | 0-0 | 0-0 | 0-3 | 2-1 | 1-2 | 0-1 | ■ | 1-2 | 1-1 | 1-2 | 0-0 | 1-0 | 3-1 |
| SHINNIK YAROSLAVL | 3-2 | 3-1 | 2-0 | 0-0 | 2-2 | 1-0 | 0-0 | 4-0 | 2-0 | 4-1 | 2-1 | 1-1 | 5-0 | 2-1 | ■ | 0-2 | 3-0 | 1-0 | 2-0 | 1-0 |
| SPARTAK ORDZHONIKIDZE | 1-0 | 5-2 | 6-2 | 4-1 | 2-0 | 1-1 | 2-0 | 4-0 | 1-0 | 1-0 | 3-1 | 3-4 | 2-1 | 1-0 | 2-1 | ■ | 2-1 | 3-0 | 3-0 | 3-2 |
| KUBAN KRASNODAR | 0-3 | 2-1 | 1-0 | 2-1 | 0-0 | 0-0 | 0-0 | 4-1 | 1-1 | 0-1 | 4-0 | 0-1 | 1-1 | 1-0 | 2-0 | 0-2 | ■ | 3-1 | 1-3 | 3-2 |
| LOKOMOTIV GORKYI | 0-2 | 2-0 | 3-2 | 1-0 | 1-3 | 4-1 | 0-0 | 1-0 | 2-1 | 1-3 | 0-0 | 2-2 | 2-1 | 2-0 | 2-0 | 0-0 | 2-0 | ■ | 1-1 | 0-0 |
| TIRAS TIRASPOL | 1-0 | 0-2 | 1-1 | 1-0 | 2-0 | 0-0 | 2-2 | 2-2 | 1-0 | 1-1 | 0-0 | 0-3 | 0-0 | 3-1 | 1-1 | 1-0 | 3-0 | 3-2 | ■ | 2-1 |
| DINAMO SUKHUMI | 2-1 | 0-0 | 0-0 | 1-0 | 3-0 | 0-0 | 0-1 | 2-0 | 1-0 | 2-1 | 1-0 | 2-0 | 1-1 | 4-0 | 0-3 | 1-0 | 1-0 | 2-2 | 0-0 | ■ |

⊗ Due to civil unrest, the matches between Neftchi Baku and Kotaik Abovyan were forbidden to take place. In both cases, the home club were awarded a 3-0 victory. For the same reason, Kotaik were not allowed to play throughout the season in Abovyan and obliged to arrange all home fixtures in Yerevan.

## USSR 1ST LEAGUE 1990

### LEAGUE TABLE FINAL

| | | | | | | | |
|---|---|---|---|---|---|---|---|
| Spartak Vladikavkaz | 38 | 24 | 9 | 5 | 73 | 30 | 57 |
| Pakhtakor Tashkent | 38 | 23 | 8 | 7 | 80 | 45 | 54 |
| Metallurg Zaporozhe | 38 | 19 | 14 | 5 | 58 | 30 | 52 |
| Lokomotiv Moskva | 38 | 19 | 9 | 10 | 52 | 34 | 47 |
| Dinamo Stavropol | 38 | 20 | 6 | 12 | 56 | 42 | 46 |
| Shinnik Yaroslavl | 38 | 19 | 8 | 11. | 55 | 39 | 46 |
| Nistru Kishinev | 38 | 14 | 12 | 12 | 50 | 44 | 40 |
| Neftchi Baku | 38 | 14 | 10 | 14 | 52 | 51 | 38 |
| Tavriya Simferopol | 38 | 11 | 16 | 11 | 40 | 38 | 38 |
| Fakel Voronezh | 38 | 14 | 9 | 15 | 43 | 45 | 37 |
| Geolog Tyumen | 38 | 14 | 9 | 15 | 38 | 45 | 37 |
| Dinamo Sukhumi | 38 | 14 | 8 | 16 | 36 | 41 | 36 |
| Tiras Tiraspol | 38 | 10 | 15 | 13 | 32 | 45 | 35 |
| Kotaik Abovyan | 38 | 12 | 9 | 17 | 44 | 52 | 33 |
| R'selmash Rostov-na-Donu | 38 | 11 | 9 | 18 | 39 | 56 | 31 |
| Loko. Nizhny Novgorod | 38 | 10 | 11 | 17 | 39 | 58 | 31 |
| Kairat Alma Ata | 38 | 10 | 10 | 18 | 35 | 50 | 30 |
| Zenit Leningrad | 38 | 8 | 14 | 16 | 35 | 41 | 30 |
| Kuban Krasnodar | 38 | 11 | 6 | 21 | 34 | 60 | 28 |
| Kuzbass Kemerovo | 38 | 4 | 6 | 28 | 21 | 66 | 14 |

Promoted : - Spartak Vladikavkaz, Pakhtakor Tashkent, Metallurg Zaporozhe and Lokomotiv Moskva.

**NAME CHANGE PRE-SEASON : -**
Tekstilschik Tiraspol to Tiras Tiraspol
**NAME CHANGES DURING SEASON : -**
Spartak Ordzhonikidze to Spartak Vladikavkaz
Lokomotiv Gorkyi to Lokomotiv Nizhny Novgorod

Georgian clubs Torpedo Kutaisi and Dinamo Batumi withdrew from the league prior to commencement of the season. Dinamo Sukhumi lost the bulk of their players due to the Georgian independence issue, and were granted a late start to the season in order to allow them time to replenish their staff.

Soccer in the Soviet Union during Season 1990 has of course been affected by the political situation, particularly regarding the strong nationalistic tendencies and developments in the state of Georgia and the declaration of independence issue in Lithuania. In order to substantiate these claims, Dinamo Tbilisi, Guriya Lanchkhuti, Zalgiris Vilnius, Torpedo Kutaisi and Dinamo Batumi withdrew from the Soviet Supreme and 1st Leagues. These clubs then proceeded to join the Georgian Supreme League and Baltic League, both competitions in fact belonging to the local league structure below the various zones of the Soviet 3rd League. Nevertheless we feel that the final tables of these local leagues should appear as they contain clubs from the 1989 Soviet Supreme and 1st Leagues. Dinamo Tbil si, Torpedo Kutaisi and Dinamo Batumi had in fact changed their names to Iberya, Kutaisi and Batumi respectively, prior to Season 1990.
Naturally, these clubs in taking their action, are reliant on the future independence of the republics of Georgia and Lithuania from the Soviet Union. Whatever the future may hold in this respect, any re-entry in to the Soviet League will entail re-joining at the lowest level.

# USSR 2ND LEAGUE ZONE 1 1990

## LEAGUE TABLE FINAL

| | P | W | D | L | F | A | Pts |
|---|---|---|---|---|---|---|---|
| Neftyanik Fergana | 42 | 28 | 8 | 6 | 84 | 26 | 64 |
| Novbakhor Namangan | 42 | 25 | 8 | 9 | 67 | 36 | 58 |
| Okean Nakhodka | 42 | 23 | 11 | 8 | 64 | 34 | 57 |
| Amur Blagoveschensk | 42 | 23 | 6 | 13 | 53 | 37 | 52 |
| Meliorator Chimkent | 42 | 23 | 5 | 14 | 72 | 43 | 51 |
| Khimik Dzhambul | 42 | 23 | 5 | 14 | 53 | 40 | 51 |
| Avtomobilist Kokand | 42 | 19 | 5 | 18 | 56 | 48 | 43 |
| Kopetdag Ashkhabad | 42 | 17 | 9 | 16 | 61 | 43 | 43 |
| Alga Frunze | 42 | 18 | 6 | 18 | 58 | 57 | 42 |
| Traktor Pavlodar | 42 | 19 | 3 | 20 | 58 | 55 | 41 |
| Zvezda Irkutsk | 42 | 16 | 9 | 17 | 49 | 48 | 41 |
| Sogdiana Dzhizak | 42 | 16 | 8 | 18 | 48 | 55 | 40 |
| Dinamo Barnaul | 42 | 18 | 3 | 21 | 51 | 56 | 39 |
| Shakhtyor Karanganda | 42 | 15 | 9 | 18 | 44 | 47 | 39 |
| Vakhsh Kurgan-Tyube | 42 | 16 | 6 | 20 | 57 | 75 | 38 |
| Tselinnik Tselinograd | 42 | 14 | 10 | 18 | 36 | 40 | 38 |
| Ekibastuzets Ekibastuz | 42 | 15 | 7 | 20 | 48 | 59 | 37 |
| Surkhan Termez | 42 | 13 | 9 | 20 | 39 | 65 | 35 |
| Kaysar Kzyl-Orda | 42 | 12 | 11 | 19 | 30 | 46 | 35 |
| Irtysh Omsk | 42 | 13 | 8 | 21 | 48 | 60 | 34 |
| Zarafshan Navoi | 42 | 11 | 11 | 20 | 43 | 68 | 33 |
| Spartak Andizhan | 42 | 4 | 5 | 33 | 32 | 113 | 13 |

# USSR 2ND LEAGUE ZONE 2 1990

## LEAGUE TABLE FINAL

| | P | W | D | L | F | A | Pts |
|---|---|---|---|---|---|---|---|
| Uralmash Sverdlovsk | 42 | 23 | 13 | 6 | 62 | 22 | 59 |
| Tekstilschik Kamyshin | 42 | 22 | 8 | 12 | 73 | 49 | 52 |
| Krilya Scvetov Kuybyshev | 42 | 20 | 11 | 11 | 56 | 35 | 49 |
| Metallurg Lipetsk | 42 | 18 | 13 | 11 | 56 | 43 | 49 |
| Kyapaz Gyandzha | 42 | 21 | 9 | 16 | 66 | 65 | 47 |
| Tsement Novorossysk | 42 | 19 | 9 | 14 | 67 | 55 | 47 |
| Druzhba Maykop | 42 | 19 | 7 | 16 | 56 | 56 | 45 |
| Torpedo Ryazan | 42 | 15 | 15 | 12 | 41 | 44 | 45 |
| Zvezda Perm | 42 | 18 | 8 | 16 | 59 | 51 | 44 |
| Goyazan Kazakh | 42 | 15 | 14 | 13 | 68 | 45 | 44 |
| Torpedo Vladimir | 42 | 19 | 4 | 19 | 55 | 55 | 42 |
| Terek Grozny | 42 | 18 | 5 | 19 | 55 | 51 | 41 |
| Gastello Ufa | 42 | 17 | 7 | 18 | 40 | 50 | 41 |
| Zenit Izhevsk | 42 | 16 | 9 | 17 | 47 | 52 | 41 |
| Nart Cherkessk | 42 | 16 | 8 | 18 | 46 | 52 | 40 |
| Torpedo Volzhsky | 42 | 16 | 7 | 19 | 48 | 61 | 39 |
| Sokol Saratov | 42 | 15 | 9 | 18 | 53 | 58 | 39 |
| Mashuk Pyatigorsk | 42 | 15 | 6 | 21 | 48 | 64 | 36 |
| SKA Rostov-na-Donu | 42 | 14 | 5 | 23 | 47 | 63 | 33 |
| Zarya Kaluga | 42 | 10 | 8 | 24 | 39 | 74 | 28 |
| Volgar Astrakhan | 42 | 6 | 10 | 26 | 32 | 65 | 22 |

# USSR 2ND LEAGUE ZONE 3 1990

## LEAGUE TABLE FINAL

| | P | W | D | L | F | A | Pts |
|---|---|---|---|---|---|---|---|
| Bukovina Chernovtsy | 42 | 23 | 12 | 7 | 69 | 27 | 58 |
| Daugava Riga | 42 | 22 | 12 | 8 | 67 | 37 | 56 |
| Karpaty Lvov | 42 | 23 | 9 | 10 | 61 | 36 | 55 |
| Niva Ternopol | 42 | 22 | 11 | 9 | 70 | 51 | 55 |
| Niva Vinnitsa | 42 | 17 | 16 | 9 | 56 | 29 | 50 |
| SKA Odessa | 42 | 21 | 7 | 14 | 59 | 32 | 49 |
| Zarya Lugansk | 42 | 20 | 9 | 13 | 72 | 44 | 49 |
| Spartak Nalchik | 42 | 20 | 7 | 15 | 55 | 46 | 47 |
| Dinamo Brest | 42 | 15 | 15 | 12 | 49 | 39 | 45 |
| Kremen Kremenchug | 42 | 16 | 11 | 15 | 49 | 45 | 43 |
| Zarya Beltsy | 42 | 15 | 12 | 15 | 52 | 52 | 42 |
| Vorskla Poltava | 42 | 15 | 11 | 16 | 47 | 51 | 41 |
| Dnepr Mogilev | 42 | 17 | 6 | 19 | 58 | 54 | 40 |
| Galichina Drogobich | 42 | 12 | 15 | 15 | 52 | 50 | 39 |
| Khimik Grodno | 42 | 16 | 6 | 20 | 46 | 52 | 38 |
| Start Ulyanovsk | 42 | 12 | 13 | 17 | 34 | 45 | 37 |
| Volyn Lutsk | 42 | 14 | 7 | 21 | 42 | 61 | 35 |
| Lori Kirovakan | 42 | 14 | 5 | 23 | 39 | 79 | 33 |
| Iskra Smolensk | 42 | 11 | 10 | 21 | 45 | 65 | 32 |
| Zakarpate Uzhgorod | 42 | 12 | 7 | 23 | 41 | 69 | 31 |
| Baltika Kaliningrad | 42 | 7 | 13 | 22 | 32 | 64 | 27 |
| Shirak Leninakan | 42 | 10 | 2 | 30 | 37 | 104 | 22 |

Note : SKA Karpaty Lvov, relegated from the 1st league at the end of Season 1989, no longer existed for Season 1990. Karpaty Lvov already played in the 2nd League during Season 1989.

## NAME CHANGES DURING SEASON : - ZONE 1

Eshlik Dzhizak to Sogdiana Dzhizak
Meliorator Kzyl-Orda to Kaysar Kzyl-Orda

## NAME CHANGES DURING SEASON : - ZONE 3

Zarya Voroshilovgrad to Zarya Lugansk
Drogobich Drogobich to Galichina Drogobich

# GEORGIA SUPREME LEAGUE 1990

## LEAGUE TABLE FINAL

| | P | W | D | L | F | A | Pts |
|---|---|---|---|---|---|---|---|
| Iberya Tbilisi | 34 | 24 | 6 | 4 | 91 | 23 | 78 |
| Guriya Lanchkhuti | 34 | 22 | 6 | 6 | 73 | 33 | 72 |
| Gorda Rustavi | 34 | 22 | 3 | 9 | 63 | 33 | 69 |
| Kutaisi Kutaisi | 34 | 20 | 5 | 9 | 62 | 33 | 65 |
| Kolkheti 1913 Poti | 34 | 19 | 5 | 10 | 53 | 31 | 62 |
| Batumi Batumi | 34 | 18 | 7 | 9 | 56 | 28 | 61 |
| Tskhumi Sukhumi | 34 | 13 | 10 | 11 | 50 | 36 | 49 |
| Odishi Zugdidi | 34 | 12 | 10 | 12 | 47 | 36 | 46 |
| Mertskhali Ozurgeti | 34 | 11 | 10 | 13 | 49 | 47 | 43 |
| Dila Gori | 34 | 12 | 6 | 16 | 52 | 58 | 42 |
| Kolkheti Khobi | 34 | 11 | 8 | 15 | 42 | 43 | 41 |
| Sanavardo Samtredia | 34 | 11 | 7 | 16 | 35 | 50 | 40 |
| Mziuri Gali | 34 | 11 | 6 | 17 | 47 | 69 | 40 |
| Samgurali Tskhaltubo | 34 | 11 | 4 | 19 | 42 | 57 | 39 |
| Iverya Khashuri | 34 | 11 | 5 | 18 | 33 | 61 | 38 |
| Shevardeni 1906 Tbil. | 34 | 10 | 7 | 17 | 36 | 64 | 38 |
| Amirani Ochamchire | 34 | 8 | 7 | 17 | 36 | 55 | 37 |
| Liakhvi Tskhinvali | 34 | 0 | 0 | 34 | 11 | 135 | 0 |

Champions :- Iberya Tbilisi

CUP FINAL : -

Guriya Lanchkhuti......1    Tskhumi Sukhumi......0

# BALTIC LEAGUE 1990

## LEAGUE TABLE FINAL

| | P | W | D | L | F | A | Pts |
|---|---|---|---|---|---|---|---|
| Zalgiris Vilnius | 32 | 27 | 4 | 1 | 104 | 11 | 58 |
| Sirijus Klaipeda | 32 | 19 | 9 | 4 | 47 | 19 | 47 |
| Ekranas Panevezys | 32 | 19 | 8 | 5 | 62 | 24 | 46 |
| Progress Chernyakhovsk | 32 | 19 | 4 | 9 | 46 | 33 | 42 |
| Jovaras Mazeikiai | 32 | 16 | 8 | 8 | 40 | 25 | 40 |
| Inkaras Kaunas | 32 | 15 | 9 | 8 | 54 | 25 | 39 |
| Banga Kaunas | 32 | 13 | 11 | 8 | 45 | 30 | 37 |
| RAF Jelgava 2 | 32 | 13 | 10 | 9 | 44 | 37 | 36 |
| Sakalas Siauliai | 32 | 12 | 10 | 10 | 41 | 32 | 34 |
| Sport Tallinn | 32 | 11 | 11 | 10 | 43 | 39 | 33 |
| Neris Vilnius | 32 | 10 | 8 | 14 | 27 | 47 | 28 |
| Stroitel Daugavpils | 32 | 8 | 7 | 17 | 29 | 45 | 23 |
| Torpedo Riga | 32 | 6 | 10 | 16 | 29 | 49 | 22 |
| LVFKI Riga | 32 | 4 | 13 | 15 | 16 | 49 | 21 |
| Pardaugava Riga | 32 | 5 | 8 | 19 | 24 | 53 | 18 |
| Metalurg Liepaja | 32 | 5 | 5 | 23 | 20 | 97 | 13 |
| Suduva Marijampole | 32 | 1 | 5 | 26 | 13 | 69 | 7 |
| SKA Fosfarit Tallinn withdrew | | | | | | | |

## TOP SCORER

Baranauskas (Zalgiris) 18

Note : The Baltic League was disbanded at the end of Season 1990.
Lithuanian clubs to form their own national championship for Season 1991.

## NAME CHANGE

Atlantas Klaipeda to Sirijus Klaipeda

## NAME CHANGES

Dinamo Tbilisi to Iberya Tbilisi
Metallurg Rustavi to Gorda Rustavi
Torpedo Kutaisi to Kutaisi Kutaisi
Dinamo Batumi to Batumi Batumi
Lokomotiv Samtredia to Sanavardo Samtredia

27/5/90 at Tbilisi National Stadium

Georgia......2   Lithuania......2

Georgia : Aslan Baladze (Batumi), Gela Ketashvili (Iberya), Kakhi Tskadadze (Iberya) (Kakhi Kacharava (Iberya) 70), Dmitri Kudinov (Gorda), Giya Piritskhalava (Gorda), Georgi Nadiradze (Kutaisi), Temur Ketsbaya (Iberya), Zaza Revishvili (Iberya) (Melor Bigvava (Odishi) 46), Otar Korgalidze (Guriya), 'Rostom Torgashvili (Kutaisi) 46), Giya Guruli (Iberya), Mamuka Pantsulaya (Gorda) (Gocha Togrigyani (Tskhumi) 46).

Lithuania : Valdemaras Martinkenas (Alvydas Koncevicius 85), Vladimir Buzmakov, Rytis Narusevicius, Rimas Mazeikis, Arvydas Janonis (Virginijus Baltusnikas 17), Robertas Tautkus, Romas Cirba, Valdas Ivanauskas, Robertas Fridrikas, Vyacheslav Sukristov, Arminas Narbekovas (all Za giris Vilnius).

| | | |
|---|---|---|
| 0-1 | Narbekovas pen. | 12 |
| 1-1 | Guruli | 62 |
| 1-2 | Baltusnikas | 66 |
| 2-2 | Kacharava | 81 |

Referee : Mevlud Muminoshvili

The existence of the Baltic League was as things turned out extremely shortlived, following the decision of the Lithuanian clubs to form their own national championship in 1991. The clubs have chosen for an autumn-spring season and a shortened championship has therefore been played during Spring 1991. The 1991/92 Championship will commence on the 15th August 1991. Algirdas Jasinskas informs us that he is in possession of detailed information covering the Spring 1991 Season, and we are pleased to announce that we hope to produce the publication FOOTBALL IN LITHUANIA Spring Season 1991 during the coming months.

## LITHUANIAN CHAMPIONSHIP SPRING 1991

### LEAGUE TABLE FINAL

| Team | P | Pts |
|---|---|---|
| Zalgiris Vilnius | 14 | 24 |
| Banga Kaunas | 14 | 22 |
| Neris Vilnius | 14 | 21 |
| Ekranas Panevezys | 14 | 21 |
| Sirijus Klaipeda | 14 | 20 |
| Vilija Kaunas | 14 | 14 |
| Granitas Klaipeda | 14 | 14 |
| Panerys Vilnius | 14 | 14 |
| Sakalas Siauliai | 14 | 13 |
| Elektronas Tauragé | 14 | 10 |
| Vienybe Ukmergé | 14 | 10 |
| Jovaras Mazeikiai | 14 | 9 |
| Tauras Siauliai | 14 | 8 |
| Vytis-Inkaras Kaunas | 14 | 8 |
| Suduva Marijampole | 14 | 2 |

## CHAMPIONSHIP PLAY-OFFS

### SEMI-FINALS

| | 1ST LEG | 2ND LEG | AGG. |
|---|---|---|---|
| Ekranas Panevezys v Zalgiris Vilnius | 1-0 | 1-4 | 2-4 |
| Lietuvos Makabi Vilnius v Banga Kaunas | 2-1 | 2-1 | 4-2 |

### 3RD PLACE

Ekranas Panevezys .. 1   Banga Kaunas ...... 3   (at Ukmerge)

### FINAL

Zalgiris Vilnius ........ 3   Lietuvos Makabi Vilnius ....... 1   (at Vilnius)

Name Change 1/6/91 - Neris Vilnius to Lietuvos Makabi Vilnius

## USSR CUP 1989/90

### 1ST ROUND

| | | | |
|---|---|---|---|
| Alga Frunze ............ 3 | Metal.Novokuznetsk .. 0 | Dinamo Vologda ....... 1 | Saturn Ramenskoe... 0 |
| Khimik Grodno .......... 1 | SKA Karpaty Lvov... 0 | Traktor Pavlodar..... 0 | Kairat Alma Ata ... 2 |
| Tekstilschik Tiraspol.. 1 | Nistru Kishinev ... 1 (aet) | Meliorator Chimkent.. 1 | SKA Rostov ....... 1 (aet) |
| Tekstilschik win 5-3 on penalties | | Meliorator win 5-4 on penalties | |
| Atlantas Klaipeda...... 2 | Metall. Zaporozhe ... 2 | Sokhibkor Khalkabad..1 | Geolog Tyumen ..... 1 (aet) |
| P'dolye Khmelnitskyi.. 0 | Okean Kerch ....... 2 | Sokhibkor win 4-2 on penalties | |
| Vorskla Poltava........ 3 | Tavriya Simferopol... 0 | Novbak. Namangan... 3 | Energetik Kustanay.. 0 |
| SKA Odessa ............ 2 | Chaika Sevastopol... 0 | K'nsaets Kasansay... 1 | Pakhtakor Tashkent.. 4 |
| Krivbass Krivoj Rog .. 2 | Daugava Riga....... 0 | Lokomotiv Chita..... 0 | Kuzbass Kemerovo... 0 |
| Dnepr Mogilev......... 1 | Bukovina Chernovt... 0 | Amur Blagovesch... 2 | Neftyanik Fergana .. 0 |
| Zarya V'shilovgrad.... 1 | Kuban Krasnodar ... 0 | Kyapaz Kirovabad.... 0 | TSKA Moskva....... 1 |
| Torpedo Taganrog..... 1 | Shinnik Yaroslavi... 2 | Shinnik Yaroslavi.... 3 | Torpedo Kutaisi.... 0 |
| Tsement Nov'ssyisk.. 2 | Sokol Saratov .... 1 (aet) | Zenit Izhevsk....... 0 | Neftchi Baku ..... 3 |
| Torpedo Ryazan....... 1 | Spartak Nalchik ... 3 | Gastello Ufa........ 1 | Goyazan Kazakh ... 2 |
| Kolos Nikopol......... 1 | Fakel Voronezh ... 0 | Metall. Rustavi..... 3 | Dinamo Batumi .... 2 |
| Dinamo Stavropol..... 3 | Zarya Kaluga ...... 2 | Kriya Stov Kuybysh.. 1 | Sp'tk Ordzhonikidze .. 2 |
| Druzhba Maikop....... 1 | Rosselmash Rostov.. 2 | Zvezda Perm ........ 2 | Guriya Lanchkhuti... 3 (aet) |
| Irtysh Omsk.......... 1 | Uralm'sh Sverdlovsk .0 | | |

### 2ND ROUND

| | | | |
|---|---|---|---|
| Tekstilschik Tiraspol...3 | Khimik Grodno...... 0 | Okean Kerch....... 0 | Metall. Zaporozhe... 4 |
| Vorskla Poltava....... 0 | SKA Odessa........ 0 | Dnepr Mogilev..... 0 | Krivbass Krivoj Rog.. 4 |
| Shinnik Yaroslavi.... 1 | Zarya V'shilovgrad... 0 | Dinamo Stavropol.. 0 | Kolos Nikopol .... 0 |
| Rosselmash Rostov.. 1 | Dinamo Vologda.... 2 | Kairat Alma Ata.... 2 | Meliorator Chimkent..0 |
| N'bakhor Namangan.. 3 | Sokhibkor Khalkabad.0 | Pakhtakor Tashkent.. 0 | Alga Frunze ..... 0 |
| Amur Blagovesch... 2 | Lokomotiv Chita... 0 | TSKA Moskva...... 4 | Sokol Saratov .... 2 |
| Goyazan Kazakh .... 1 | Neitchi Baku ..... 2 | Kriya Stov Kuybysh.. 2 | Metall. Rustavi ... 0 |
| Guriya Lanchkhuti w.o. Irtysh Omsk | | Spartak Naichik .... 0 | Tsement Nov'ssyisk.. 4 |
| | | Abandoned, crowd violence, awarded to Tsement. | |

### 1/16 FINALS

| | 1ST LEG | 2ND LEG | AGG. |
|---|---|---|---|
| Shinnik Yaroslavi v Spartak Moskva | 0-1 | 1-2 | 1-3 |
| Metallurg Zaporozhe v Chernomorets Odessa | 2-1 | 1-1 | 3-2 |
| Neftchi Baku v Rotor Volgograd | 2-1 | 0-3 | 2-4 |
| Dinamo Stavropol v Dinamo Moskva | 1-3 | 2-2 | 3-5 |
| Tekstilschik Tiraspol v Torpedo Moskva | 2-2 | 0-4 | 2-6 |
| Vorskla Poltava v Zalgiris Vilnius | 1-0 | 1-5 | 2-5 |
| Amur Blagoveschensk v Metallist Kharkov | 2-3 | ⊗ | |
| TSKA Moskva v Dnepr Dnepropetrovsk (TSKA win on away goals) | 1-1 | 2-2 | 3-3 |
| Guriya Lanchkhuti v Shakhtyor Donetsk | 1-0 | 2-4 | 3-4 |
| Krivbass Krivoj Rog v Lokomotiv Moskva | 0-1 | 0-5 | 0-6 |
| Tsement Novorossyisk v Dinamo Minsk | 2-4 | 2-0 | 4-4 |
| Dinamo Vologda v Ararat Yerevan (Ararat win on away goals) | 0-1 | 1-3 | 1-4 |
| Kairat Alma Ata v Dinamo Kiev | 3-2 | 3-0 | 6-2 |
| Pakhtakor Tashkent v Pamir Dushanbe | 2-5 | 0-4 | 2-9 |
| Zenit Leningrad v Krilya Sovetov Kuybyshev | 0-5 | 0-2 | 0-7 |
| Novbakhor Namangan v Dinamo Tbilisi | | | |

⊗ Amur withdrew, tie awarded to Metallist Kharkov

### 1/8 FINALS

| | 1ST LEG | 2ND LEG | AGG. |
|---|---|---|---|
| Dinamo Moskva v Ararat Yerevan | 1-0 | 1-0 | 2-0 |
| Dinamo Kiev v Dinamo Tbilisi | 1-0 | ⊗ | 1-2 |
| Spartak Moskva v Dinamo Minsk (Dinamo win on away goals) | 2-1 | 0-1 | 2-2 |
| Rotor Volgograd v TSKA Moskva | 3-2 | 0-2 | 3-4 |

Chernomorets Odessa v Torpedo Moskva  1-0  0-3  1-3
Zalgiris Vilnius v Lokomotiv Moskva  1-1  0-3  1-4
Pakhtakor Tashkent v Metallist Kharkov  0-3  2-0  2-3
Shakhtyor Donetsk v Krilya Sovetov Kuybyshev  0-0  0-1  0-1
⊗ Dinamo Tbilisi withdrew, tie awarded to Dinamo Kiev

## 1/4 FINALS

TSKA Moskva .......... 3    Krilya S'tov Kuyby ..... 1
Dinamo Minsk .......... 0    Dinamo Moskva .......... 0 (aet.)
Dinamo Moskva win 4-5 on penalties

Lokomotiv Moskva ........ 2    Torpedo Moskva ........ 0
Metallist Kharkov ........ 0    Dinamo Kiev ............. 1

## SEMI-FINALS

Dinamo Moskva ........ 0    Lokomotiv Moskva ....0 (aet.)
Lokomotiv win 2-4 on penalties

Dinamo Kiev ............ 4    TSKA Moskva............ 2

## FINAL   2/5/90 at Lenin Stadium, Moskva

Dinamo Kiev ............. 6    Lokomotiv Moskva ....... 1

Dinamo : Chanov, Shmatovalenko, Tsveyba, Kuznetsov, Demianenko (Luzhny 87), Rats, Mikhailichenko (Bal 87), Litovchenko, Salenko, Protasov, Zayets (Kovalets 51).

Lokomotiv : Bidzhiev, Nesterov, Mileshkin, Arifullin, Solovtsov, Gorkov, Rybakov (Plotnikov 60), Gallakberov, Samarov (Pronichev 60), Sukhov (Fedin 72), Chugaynov.

| | | | |
|---|---|---|---|
| 1-0 | Mikhailichenko | 19 | Referee : I.Timoshenko |
| 2-0 | Rats | 30 | Attendance : 15,000 |
| 3-0 | Salenko | 43 | |
| 3-1 | Mileshkin pen. | 52 | |
| 4-1 | Salenko | 65 | |
| 5-1 | Litovchenko | 71 | |
| 6-1 | Salenko | 90 | |

## USSR : All Time International Records as at 31/12/90 - CAPS

1. Oleg Blokhin (Dinamo Kiev/SK Vorwärts Steyr) — 109
2. Rinav Dasayev (Spartak Moskva/Sevilla FC) — 94
3. Albert Shesternev (TSKA Moskva) — 89
4. Vladimir Bessonov (Dinamo Kiev) — 82
5. Anatoly Demyanenko (Dinamo Kiev) — 80
6. Lev Yashin (Dinamo Moskva) — 75
7. Murtaz Khurtsilava (Dinamo Tbilisi) — 67
8. Oleg Protasov (Dnepr Dnepropetrovsk/Dinamo Kiev/Olympiakos Piraeus) — 66
9. Valery Voronin (Torpedo Moskva) — 65
   Sergei Aleinikov (Dinamo Minsk/Juventus FC/US Lecce) — 65

## USSR : All Time International Records as at 31/12/90 - GOALS

1. Oleg Blokhin (Dinamo Kiev/SK Vorwärts Steyr) — (109) 39
2. Oleg Protasov (Dnepr Dnepropetrovsk/Dinamo Kiev/Olympiakos Piraeus) — (66) 28
3. Valentin Ivanov (Torpedo Moskva) — (59) 25
4. Eduard Streltsov (Torpedo Moskva) — (38) 24
5. Viktor Kolotov (Rubin Kazan/Dinamo Kiev) — (53) 22
6. Viktor Ponedelnik (SKA Rostov-na-Donu/Spartak Moskva) — (29) 20
7. Anatoly Banishevsky (Neftyanik/Neftchi Baku) — (49) 19
   Igor Chislenko (Dinamo Moskva) — (51) 19
9. Anatoly Ilyin (Spartak Moskva) — (32) 15
   Fyodor Cherenkov (Spartak Moskva) — (37) 15
   Anatoly Byshovets (Dinamo Kiev) — (39) 15

# USSR INTERNATIONAL REVIEW 1990

## INTERNATIONAL LINE-UPS 1990

### Matches

| Date | Result | Venue | Referee | Competition | Scorers |
|---|---|---|---|---|---|
| 20/2/90 | COLOMBIA 0 USSR 0 | Los Angeles | Ref: Bratsis (USA) | Friendly | |
| 22/2/90 | COSTA RICA 1 USSR 2 | Los Angeles | Ref: Bratsis (USA) | Friendly | |
| 24/2/90 | USA 1 USSR 3 | Palo Alto | Ref: Mauro (USA) | Friendly | |
| 28/3/90 | USSR 2 HOLLAND 0 | Kiev | Ref: Puhl (Hungary) | Friendly | (Bessonov, Cherenkov, Protasov) |
| 25/4/90 | REPUBLIC OF IRELAND 1 USSR 0 | Dublin | Ref: Kleinaitis (USA) | Friendly | |
| 16/5/90 | ISRAEL 3 USSR 2 | Tel Aviv | Ref: v/d Wijngaert (Belgium) | Friendly | (Litovchenko, Mikhailichenko) |
| 9/6/90 | RUMANIA 2 USSR 0 | Bari | Ref: Cardellino (Uruguay) | World Cup | |
| 13/6/90 | ARGENTINA 2 USSR 0 | Napoli | Ref: Fredriksson (Sweden) | World Cup | |
| 18/6/90 | CAMEROON 0 USSR 4 | Bari | Ref: Wright (Brazil) | World Cup | (Protassov, Zygmantovich, Zavarov, Dobrovolsky) |
| 29/8/90 | USSR 1 RUMANIA 2 | Moskva | Ref: Listkewicz (Poland) | Friendly | |
| 12/9/90 | USSR 2 NORWAY 0 | Moskva | Ref: Förstinger (Austria) | EuroCh.Q. | (Mikhailichenko) |
| 3/11/90 | ITALY 0 USSR 0 | Roma | Ref: Van Langenhove (Belgium) | EuroCh.Q. | |
| 21/11/90 | USA 0 USSR 0 | Port of Spain | Ref: Stewart (Trinidad & Tobago) | Friendly | |
| 23/11/90 | TRINIDAD & TOBAGO 0 USSR 2 | Port of Spain | Ref: Singh (Trinidad) | Friendly | |
| 30/11/90 | GUATEMALA 0 USSR 3 | Guatemala City | Ref: Chinchilla (Guatemala) | Friendly | (Mostovoy, Dobrovolsky, Kolivanov) |

### Caps and goals at 31/12/90

| Player | Caps at 31/12/90 | Goals at 31/12/90 |
|---|---|---|
| V.Chanov | 21 | |
| V.Bessonov | 82 | 5 |
| O.Kuznetsov | 54 | 1 |
| A.Zygmantovich | 36 | 3 |
| O.Luzhny | 8 | |
| V.Rats | 47 | 4 |
| F.Cherenkov | 37 | 15 |
| G.Litovchenko | 57 | 14 |
| I.Yaremchuk | 18 | 2 |
| O.Protasov | 66 | 28 |
| S.Rodionov | 37 | 8 |
| V.Tischenko | 8 | |
| I.Kolivanov | 9 | 1 |
| V.Tatarchuk | 8 | |
| A.Tsveyba | 7 | |
| R.Dasayev | 94 | |
| S.Gorlukovich | 19 | 1 |
| V.Khidyatulin | 61 | 1 |
| S.Aleinikov | 65 | 6 |
| A.Borodyuk | 6 | 1 |
| P.Yakovenko | 19 | 1 |
| V.Lyuty | 3 | 1 |
| A.Uvarov | 6 | |
| S.Fokin | 3 | |
| V.Broshin | 3 | |
| I.Belanov | 33 | 8 |
| Y.Savichev | 8 | |
| S.Shmatovalenko | 2 | |
| A.Demyanenko | 80 | 6 |
| A.Mikhailichenko | 27 | 7 |
| V.Shmarov | 3 | |
| A.Zavarov | 41 | 6 |
| I.Dobrovolsky | 22 | 6 |
| I.Shalimov | 8 | 1 |
| M.Yeremin | 1 | |
| A.Chernishov | 6 | |
| V.Kulkov | 8 | |
| E.Dolgov | 1 | |
| A.Konchelskis | 5 | |
| I.Getsko | 5 | |
| A.Mostovoy | 4 | 1 |
| S.Yuran | 10 | |
| A.Mokh | 7 | |
| D.Kuznetsov | 8 | |
| G.Perepadenko | 8 | |
| D.Radchenko | 2 | |
| S.Cherchesov | 2 | |
| D.Galyamin | 2 | |
| A.Sidelnikov | 2 | |

Note : On 3rd April 1991 the USSR Football Federation decided to recognize 12 matches previously played by the country's Olympic XI, as full internationals. This decision has an important bearing on the information appearing on this page, e.g. caps totals of Oleg Blokhin and Rinat Dasayev become 112 & 97 respectively. Furthermore one of the matches concerned is USSR 3 Israel 0 played 9/10/90 in Moscow. It is felt however that the published International Review does not reflect the position as it stood on 31/12/90. We will therefore be providing full details of the belatedly recognized matches with our 1991 International Review .

# WALES Correspondent : ANDY MILLAR

## WELSH CUP 1990/91

### 1ST ROUND

| | | | |
|---|---|---|---|
| Ammanford Town .......1 | Skewen Athletic......... 1 | Fflint Town United ...... 2 | Ruthin Town ............. 1 |
| BP Llandarcy.............1 | South Wales Police ... 0 | Knighton Town ........... 3 | Llanidloes Town ........ 1 |
| Bala Town ................5 | Rub.owen Rockwell... 0 | Llandudno ................. 4 | Llanfairpwll .............. 1 |
| Brecon Corinthians ....1 | Carmarthen Town...... 2 | Llangefni Town........... 5 | Pwllheli Borough ....... 1 |
| Bridgend Town ..........4 | Seven Sisters............ 1 | Locomotive Llanberis. 1 | CPD Porthmadog...... 1 |
| British Aerospace.......1 | Mochdre .................. 8 | Morda United ............. 0 | Hednesford Town ...... 2 |
| Briton Ferry Athletic ...1 | Afan Lido Port Talbot. 0 | Mostyn .................... 4 | Rhyl Victory Club ...... 2 |
| Brymbo Steelworks ....2 | Llay Welfare ............. 0 | Newport YMCA .......... 2 | Inter Cardiff ............. 2 |
| Buckley .....................1 | Lex XI Wrexham........ 1 | Newtown .................... 5 | CPD Penrhyncoch ... 0 |
| Builth Wells ..............2 | Llansantffraid............ 1 | Penycae..................... 1 | Gresford Athletic ....... 1 |
| Caerleon ..................0 | Caldicot Town............ 1 | Pontardawe Athletic... 1 | Pembroke Borough ... 2 |
| Caersws ...................2 | Tywyn/Bryncrug........ 1 | Pontlottyn Blst Fnce.. 0 | Newport AFC ............ 9 |
| CIHE Cardiff..............0 | Pontllanfraith ............ 3 | Pontyclun .................. 1 | Morriston Town.......... 2 |
| Carno ......................0 | Worcester City........... 1 | Port Talbot Athletic.... 2 | Caerau .................... 0 |
| Chirk AAA ................1 | New Broughton .......... 1 | Rhos Aelwyd.............. 3 | Cefn Albion ............. 5 |
| Colwyn Bay ..............2 | Bethesda Athletic ...... 0 | Rhyl........................... 9 | Holywell Town ........... 0 |
| Connah's Qy.Nmds....5 | Pilkingtons SA ........... 2 | Risca United .............. 1 | Cardiff Civil Service... 1 |
| Conwy United...........3 | Llanrwst United ......... 2 | Stourbridge ............... 4 | Welshpool ................ 1 |
| Corwen Amateurs .....1 | Llay RBL .................. 2 | Stroud ....................... 3 | Llanwern ................. 0 |
| Ebbw Vale ................3 | Tonyrefail Welfare ..... 0 | Taffs Well ................. 8 | Abercynon Athletic ... 0 |
| Ferndale Athletic........1 | Cheltenham Town ..... 1 | Trelewis Welfare ........ 0 | Cardiff Corinthians ... 2 |

#### REPLAYS

| | | | |
|---|---|---|---|
| Skewen Athletic .........3 | Ammanford Town ...... 3 (aet.) | Lex XI Wrexham ........ 3 | Buckley .................... 0 |
| Ammanford Town win 3-4 on penalties | | New Broughton .......... 0 | Chirk AAA ................ 1 |
| Cheltenham Town ......4 | Ferndale Athletic ....... 0 | Llanfairpwll................. 1 | Llandudno ................ 0 |
| CPD Porthmadog.......4 | Locomotive Llanberis 1 (aet.) | Inter Cardiff ............... 4 | Newport YMCA ........ 2 |
| Gresford Athletic ........2 | Penycae ................... 1 | Cardiff Civil Service ... 7 | Risca United............. 3 |

### 2ND ROUND

| | | | |
|---|---|---|---|
| Abergavenny Thurs....4 | Carmarthen Town...... 0 | Aberystwyth Town...... 5 | Knighton Town .......... 1 |
| Ammanford Town .......3 | Cardiff Civil Service... 0 | Builth Wells ............... 1 | Cheltenham Town ..... 5 |
| Caldicot Town............0 | Cardiff Corinthians .... 0 | Chirk AAA ................. 5 | Brymbo Steelworks.... 0 |
| Connah's Qy.Nmds....0 | Colwyn Bay .............. 1 | Conwy Town ............. 0 | Llangefni Town ......... 3 |
| Cwmbran Town ..........1 | Maesteg Park ........... 1 | Haverfordwest Cnty. .. 3 | Ebbw Vale ............... 0 |
| Hednesford Town .......1 | Stourbridge ............... 3 | Inter Cardiff ............... 0 | Ton Pentre................ 2 |
| Lex XI Wrexham ........3 | Bala Town ................ 0 | Llanelli....................... 2 | Morriston Town.......... 1 |
| Llanfairpwll.................1 | Caernarfon Town....... 4 | Llay RBL .................. 2 | Gresford Athletic ...... 0 |
| Mochdre....................0 | Fflint Town United...... 3 | Newport AFC ............ 3 | Pembroke Borough ... 0 |
| Newtown ...................6 | Cefn Albion .............. 2 | Pontllanfraith............. 0 | Bridgend Town ......... 3 |
| Port Talbot Athletic.....1 | Britton Ferry Athletic.. 1 | CPD Porthmadog....... 0 | Bangor City ............. 4 |
| Rhyl..........................2 | Mostyn ..................... 0 | Stroud ....................... 3 | Kidderminst.Harriers . 3 |
| Taffs Well .................0 | BP Llandarcy............ 2 | Worcester City .......... 4 | Caersws ................... 1 |

#### REPLAYS

| | | | |
|---|---|---|---|
| Cardiff Corinthians .....2 | Caldicot Town............ 0 | Maesteg Park............ 0 | Cwmbran Town ........ 1 |
| Briton Ferry Athletic ...0 | Port Talbot Athletic .... 0 (aet.) | Kidderminst.Harriers .. 2 | Stroud ...................... 3 |
| Briton Ferry Athletic win 7-6 on penalties | | | |

### 3RD ROUND

| | | | |
|---|---|---|---|
| Ammanford Town .......2 | Haverfordwest Cnty... 1 | Bangor City ............... 2 | Stourbridge .............. 1 |
| Bridgend Town ..........1 | Abergavenny Thurs... 1 | Briton Ferry Athletic ... 0 | BP Llandarcy............ 1 |
| Cardiff City ...............1 | Merthyr Tydfil............ 4 | Cardiff Corinthians ..... 0 | Newport AFC ............ 3 |
| Chirk AAA .................0 | Stroud ...................... 3 | Colwyn Bay............... 3 | Rhyl.......................... 1 |
| Cwmbran Town .........1 | Cheltenham Town ...... 7 | Fflint Town United ...... 1 | Aberystwyth Town ..... 2 |
| Hereford United.........1 | Newtown .................. 1 | Lex XI Wrexham ........ 4 | Llangefni Town ......... 3 |
| Llay RBL ...................0 | Caernarfon Town....... 2 | Swansea City............ 8 | Llanelli...................... 1 |
| Ton Pentre................0 | Barry Town ............... 1 | Wrexham .................. 3 | Worcester City .......... 1 |

#### REPLAYS

| | | |
|---|---|---|
| Newtown ...................1 | Hereford United......... 1 (aet.) | Abergavenny Thursdays w.o. Bridgend Town withdrew |
| Hereford United win 3-4 on penalties | | |

### 4TH ROUND

| | | | |
|---|---|---|---|
| Merthyr Tydfil ............1 | Swansea City ............ 2 | Newport AFC ............ 0 | Colwyn Bay .............. 1 |
| Ammanford Town .......0 | Wrexham.................. 5 | BP Llandarcy ............ 0 | Stroud ...................... 3 |
| Aberystwyth Town ......1 | Hereford United......... 3 | Caernarfon Town ....... 1 | Abergavenny Thurs... 2 |
| Bangor City ..............4 | Lex XI Wrexham........ 1 | Barry Town ............... 3 | Cheltenham Town ..... 1 |

### 1/4 FINALS

| | | | |
|---|---|---|---|
| Stroud ......................1 | Wrexham................... 2 | Colwyn Bay............... 1 | Swansea City ........... 1 |
| Barry Town ...............1 | Abergavenny Thurs... 1 | Hereford United ......... 1 | Bangor City ............. 1 |

#### REPLAYS

| | | | |
|---|---|---|---|
| Swansea City ............2 | Colwyn Bay .............. 1 | Bangor City .............. 0 | Hereford United......... 0 (aet.) |
| Abergavenny Thurs....0 | Barry Town ............... 1 | Hereford United win 4-5 on penalties | |

## INTERNATIONAL LINE-UPS 1990

| Date | Match | Venue | Type | Southall | Hall | Phillips | Nicholas | Aizlewood | Melville | Maguire | Horne | Rush | Allen | A. Davies | Bowen | Law | Hodges | Saunders | Blackmore | Bodin | Young | Hopkins | Hughes | Speed | Ratcliffe |
|---|---|---|---|---|---|---|---|---|---|---|---|---|---|---|---|---|---|---|---|---|---|---|---|---|---|
| 28/3/90 REPUBLIC OF IRELAND 1 WALES 0 | Dublin | Friendly | Ref: Gunn (England) | 1 | 2 | 3 | 4 | 5 | 6 | 7 | 8 | 9 | 10 | 11 | | | | | | | | | | | |
| 25/4/90 SWEDEN 4 WALES 2 (Saunders 2) | Stockholm | Friendly | Ref: Ruokonen (Finland) | 1 | | 3 | 7 | 4 | 5 | 2 | 8 | 9 | (10) | | 4 | 6 | 9 | 11 | 2 | 3 | 5 | | | | |
| 20/5/90 WALES 1 COSTA RICA 0 (Saunders) | Cardiff | Friendly | Ref: Martino (Switzerland) | 1 | | 7 | 8 | 4 | 5 | | 7 | 9 | (11) | | 11 | | 10 | 11 | 3 | 5 | 5 | 6 | 10 | (9) | 6 |
| 11/9/90 DENMARK 1 WALES 0 | København | Friendly | Ref: Palsi (Finland) | 1 | | | 4 | | | | 9 | | | | 11 | | | 10 | 3 | 5 | 6 | | 10 | 3 | 6 |
| 17/10/90 WALES 3 BELGIUM 1 (Rush, Saunders, Hughes) | Cardiff | EuroCh.Q. | Ref: Rothlisberger (Switzerland) | 1 | | 3 | 8 | | | | | 9 | (11) | | 11 | | | 7 | 5 | 5 | | | 10 | | |
| 14/11/90 LUXEMBOURG 0 WALES 1 (Rush) | Luxembourg | EuroCh.Q. | Ref: Ulrich (Czechoslovakia) | 1 | | 2 | 8 | | | | | 9 | | | 11 | | | 7 | 2 | 3 | 5 | | 10 | 3 | 6 |
| GOALS AT 31/12/90 | | | | – | – | 1 | 2 | | | | | 18 | | | | | | 8 | | | | | 9 | | |
| CAPS AT 31/12/90 | | | | 47 | 8 | 28 | 68 | 20 | 4 | 5 | 17 | 47 | 3 | 11 | | | | 22 | 27 | | | | 31 | | 51 |

**SEMI-FINALS**

Barry Town v Swansea City
Wrexham v Hereford United

**FINAL**   19/5/91 (at Arms Park, Cardiff)

Swansea City .......... 2   Wrexham .......... 0

Swansea : Kendall, Williams, Coleman, Hough, Trick, Legg, Watson (Chalmers 75), Raynor, Coughlin, Connor, Penney.

Wrexham : Morris, Thackeray (Owen 45), Hardy, Sertori, Phillips, J.Jones, Bowden, Murray (Beaumont 71), L.Jones, Preece, Griffiths.

| | | | 1ST LEG | 2ND LEG | AGG. |
|---|---|---|---|---|---|
| 1-0 | Penney | 61 pen. | 2-2 | 0-1 | 2-3 |
| 2-0 | Raynor | 79 | 1-1 | 2-1 | 3-2 |

Referee : K.Burge
Attendance : 5,046

## WALES : All Time Records as at 31/12/90 - GOALS

1. Trevor Ford (Swansea Town/Aston Villa/Sunderland/Cardiff City) — (38) 23
2. Ivor Allchurch (Swansea Town/Newcastle United/Cardiff City) — (68) 23
3. Ian Rush (Liverpool/Juventus) — (47) 18
4. John Charles (Leeds United/Juventus/Cardiff City) — (38) 15
5. Cliff Jones (Swansea Town/Tottenham Hotspur/Fulham) — (59) 15
6. John Toshack (Cardiff City/Liverpool/Swansea City) — (40) 13
7. Dai Astley (Charlton Athletic/Aston Villa/Derby County/Blackpool) — (13) 12
8. William Lewis (Bangor City/Crewe Alexandra/Chester/Manchester United) — (30) 11
9. Billy Meredith (Manchester City/Manchester United) — (46) 11
10. Leighton James (Burnley/Derby County/Manchester City/Swansea City/Sunderland) — (54) 10

## WALES : All Time Records as at 31/12/90 - CAPS

1. Joey Jones (Liverpool/Wrexham/Chelsea/Huddersfield Town) — 72
2. Ivor Allchurch (Swansea Town/Newcastle United/Cardiff City) — 68
3. Peter Nicholas (Crystal Palace/Arsenal/Luton Town/Aberdeen/Chelsea) — 66
4. Brian Flynn (Burnley/Leeds United) — 66
5. Cliff Jones (Swansea Town/Tottenham Hotspur/Fulham) — 59
6. Terry Yorath (Leeds United/Coventry City/Tottenham Hotspur/Vancouver Whitecaps) — 59
7. Leighton Phillips (Cardiff City/Aston Villa/Swansea City/Charlton Athletic) — 58
8. Leighton James (Burnley/Derby County/Queen's Park Rangers/Swansea City/Sunderland) — 54
9. Dai Davies (Everton/Wrexham/Swansea City) — 52
10. John Mahoney (Stoke City/Middlesbrough/Swansea City) — 51
    Mickey Thomas (Wrexham/Manchester United/Everton/Brighton & Hove Albion/Stoke City/Chelsea/West Bromwich Albion) — 51
    Kevin Ratcliffe (Everton) — 51

# YUGOSLAVIA Correspondent : DAVE CLAYTON

## YUGOSLAVIA 1st Division Season 1990/91

| | C ZVEZDA | DINAMO | HAJDUK | PARTIZAN | RAD | RIJEKA | ZNICAR | OLIMPIJA | SLOBODA | BUDUCNOST | VOJVODINA | SPARTAK | SARAJEVO | BORAC | RADNICKI | OSIJEK | VELEZ | ZEMUN | PROLETER |
|---|---|---|---|---|---|---|---|---|---|---|---|---|---|---|---|---|---|---|---|
| CR. ZVEZDA BEOGRAD | | 3-1 | 1-0 | 3-1 | 2-0 | 2-1 | 3-1 | 2-1 | 4-3 | 4-1 | 2-1 | 4-0 | 4-1 | 2-0 | 6-0 | 5-1 | 2-0 | 5-1 | 1-2 |
| DINAMO ZAGREB | 3-2 | | 1-1 | 0-0 | 2-1 | 3-1 | 2-1 | 3-0 | 3-1 | 6-0 | 2-2 | 3-1 | 8-1 | 2-1 | 2-0 | 1-1 | 2-1 | 2-0 | 4-1 |
| HAJDUK SPLIT | 1-1 | 1-2 | | ⊗ | 4-2 | 1-1 | 1-1 | 2-0 | 1-0 | 1-0 | 1-1 | 3-0 | 2-0 | 1-1 | 3-0 | 3-0 | 1-1 | 2-1 | 3-0 |
| PARTIZAN BEOGRAD | 1-1 | 2-1 | 4-0 | | 0-0 | 1-2 | 3-0 | 1-0 | 3-1 | 2-1 | 3-0 | 1-1 | 2-0 | 2-2 | 3-1 | 4-0 | 5-0 | 4-1 | 0-2 |
| RAD BEOGRAD | 0-1 | 0-2 | 1-0 | 2-1 | | 0-1 | 2-0 | 2-0 | 3-0 | 1-1 | 2-0 | 2-1 | 0-0 | 1-0 | 1-0 | 4-0 | 1-0 | 2-1 | 0-1 |
| NK RIJEKA | 0-0 | 0-0 | 0-0 | 3-0 | 0-0 | | 1-1 | 1-0 | 0-1 | 1-0 | 3-0 | 3-0 | 2-0 | 0-0 | 3-0 | 2-0 | 1-0 | 0-1 | 3-0 |
| ZELJEZNICAR SARAJEVO | 0-2 | 1-3 | 3-2 | 1-0 | 1-0 | 2-0 | | 3-0 | 1-1 | 0-0 | 3-1 | 0-0 | 1-1 | 1-1 | 1-0 | 1-1 | 1-0 | 1-1 | 2-0 |
| OLIMPIJA LJUBLJANA | 0-6 | 1-3 | 2-1 | 0-1 | 1-0 | 2-1 | 3-0 | | 1-3 | 2-1 | 4-2 | 5-0 | 1-0 | 1-2 | 1-1 | 1-0 | 1-3 | 2-1 | 1-0 |
| SLOBODA TUZLA | 0-1 | 0-3 | 2-1 | 3-1 | 2-1 | 1-0 | 1-0 | 0-1 | | 2-1 | 1-2 | 2-2 | 0-4 | 0-0 | 1-0 | 0-5 | 0-0 | 1-1 | 1-2 |
| BUDUCNOST TITOGRAD | 2-0 | 1-0 | 1-0 | 2-1 | 1-4 | 2-0 | 1-2 | 1-1 | 3-1 | | 0-1 | 2-0 | 4-0 | 3-0 | 2-0 | 1-1 | 2-3 | 1-1 | 1-0 |
| VOJVODINA NOVI SAD | 1-1 | 3-1 | 0-2 | 1-2 | 2-1 | 1-1 | 0-0 | 4-3 | 2-0 | 2-0 | | 3-0 | 4-3 | 1-1 | 1-0 | 1-0 | 1-1 | 4-3 | 0-0 |
| SPARTAK SUBOTICA | 1-2 | 0-0 | 0-1 | 0-1 | 0-0 | 0-1 | 1-2 | 0-2 | 1-3 | 2-3 | 1-2 | | 1-1 | 1-1 | 1-2 | 3-3 | 1-1 | 0-0 | 0-1 |
| FK SARAJEVO | 3-2 | 0-0 | 1-1 | 1-0 | 1-1 | 1-0 | 1-1 | 2-0 | 0-0 | 1-0 | 1-0 | 4-1 | | 1-0 | 3-0 | 2-0 | 0-0 | 1-0 | 3-1 |
| BORAC BANJA LUKA | 2-2 | 1-1 | 0-2 | 0-0 | 2-1 | 0-0 | 2-1 | 2-0 | 3-2 | 3-1 | 1-0 | 2-0 | 3-0 | | 0-2 | 3-0 | 1-0 | 2-0 | 2-0 |
| RADNICKI NIS | 0-4 | 1-1 | 1-0 | 0-3 | 0-0 | 1-0 | 1-0 | 1-2 | 1-1 | 1-0 | 3-0 | 2-0 | 2-0 | 2-0 | | 3-0 | 4-2 | 1-0 | 2-1 |
| NK OSIJEK | 2-0 | 2-1 | 0-1 | 3-2 | 0-3 | 2-0 | 1-1 | 4-0 | 1-2 | 1-1 | 3-1 | 5-2 | 1-0 | 2-0 | 2-1 | | 2-1 | 4-1 | 4-1 |
| VELEZ MOSTAR | 3-3 | 1-2 | 4-3 | 0-1 | 3-2 | 1-0 | 1-1 | 3-1 | 1-0 | 2-0 | 0-1 | 5-2 | 0-0 | 2-4 | 2-0 | 1-0 | | 2-2 | 5-2 |
| FK ZEMUN | 1-3 | 1-1 | 1-0 | 2-2 | 2-1 | 0-0 | 1-0 | 2-0 | 1-0 | 0-2 | 2-1 | 2-1 | 1-0 | 1-0 | 2-2 | 2-1 | 3-3 | | 1-0 |
| PROLETER ZRENJANIN | 0-2 | 3-1 | 2-3 | 2-2 | 2-1 | 2-1 | 3-0 | 1-1 | 2-0 | 2-1 | 1-1 | 0-1 | 5-0 | 3-0 | 1-0 | 2-0 | 3-2 | 2-0 | |

⊗ The match Hajduk v Partizan was abndoned due to a crowd disturbance after 72 minutes. The score at the time was Hajduk 0 Partizan 2. The match was later awarded Hajduk 0 Partizan 3.

## YUGOSLAVIA 1ST DIVISION SEASON 1990/91

### LEAGUE TABLE FINAL

| | | | | | | | | |
|---|---|---|---|---|---|---|---|---|
| Crvena Zvezda Beograd | 36 | 25 | 6/4 | 5 | 88 | 35 | (26/22) | 54 |
| Dinamo Zagreb | 36 | 20 | 10/6 | 6 | 72 | 36 | (47/45) | 46 |
| Partizan Beograd | 36 | 18 | 8/5 | 10 | 62 | 36 | (28/27) | 41 |
| Borac Banja Luka | 36 | 14 | 11/7 | 11 | 42 | 38 | (63/60) | 35 |
| Proleter Zrenjanin | 36 | 17 | 4/1 | 15 | 50 | 49 | (14/17) | 35 |
| Hajduk Split | 36 | 15 | 9/3 | 12 | 49 | 38 | (28/31) | 33 |
| Vojvodina Novi Sad | 36 | 14 | 9/5 | 13 | 47 | 52 | (40/37) | 33 |
| Rad Beograd | 36 | 14 | 7/4 | 15 | 42 | 34 | (30/28) | 32 |
| NK Osijek | 36 | 14 | 6/4 | 16 | 52 | 57 | (21/16) | 32 |
| Radnicki Nis | 36 | 14 | 5/4 | 17 | 35 | 49 | (21/16) | 32 |
| FK Sarajevo | 36 | 13 | 10/5 | 13 | 37 | 48 | (38/38) | 31 |
| Velez Mostar | 36 | 12 | 10/6 | 14 | 54 | 55 | (42/39) | 30 |
| FK Zemun | 36 | 12 | 10/6 | 14 | 40 | 53 | (40/36) | 30 |
| Olimpija Ljubljana | 36 | 14 | 3/2 | 19 | 41 | 59 | (12/10) | 30 |
| NK Rijeka | 36 | 13 | 10/3 | 13 | 33 | 25 | (33/42) | 29 |
| Zeljeznicar Sarajevo | 36 | 11 | 13/7 | 12 | 35 | 41 | (40/37) | 29 |
| Buducnost Titograd | 36 | 13 | 6/2 | 17 | 43 | 48 | (14/18) | 28 |
| Sloboda Tuzla | 36 | 11 | 7/1 | 18 | 36 | 56 | (34/40) | 23 |
| Spartak Subotica | 36 | 1 | 10/2 | 25 | 25 | 74 | (30/42) | 4 |

Champions : - Crvena Zvezda Beograd
Relegated : - Buducnost Titograd, Sloboda Tuzla and Spartak Subotica
Clubs later retained 1st Division status for Season 1991/92 following withdrawal of Croatian and Slovenian clubs.
League to be reduced to 18 clubs for Season 1991/92

### NAME CHANGE FOR SEASON 1991/92
Dinamo Zagreb to HASK Gradanski Zagreb

### TOP SCORERS

| | | |
|---|---|---|
| 1. | Darko Pancev (C.Zvezda) | 34 |
| 2. | Davor Suker (Dinamo) | 22 |
| 3. | Zvonimir Boban (Dinamo) | 15 |
| 4. | Predrag Mijatovic (Partizan) | 14 |
| | Ljubomir Vorkapic (Vojvodina) | 14 |
| 6. | Dragisa Binic (C.Zvezda) | 13 |
| | Anto Drobnjak (Buducnost) | 13 |
| | Meho Kodro (Velez) | 13 |
| 9. | Vladimir Gudelj (Velez) | 12 |
| 10. | Zoran Kuntic (Spartak) | 11 |
| | Robert Prosinecki (C.Zvezda) | 11 |
| | Zoran Sliskovic (Zeljeznicar) | 11 |
| | Goran Vlaovic (Osijek) | 11 |
| 14. | Ljubinko Drulovic (Rad) | 10 |
| | Ilija Ivic (Proleter) | 10 |
| | Dejan Lukic (Borac) | 10 |
| | Vesko Mihajlovic (Proleter) | 10 |
| | Emir Music (Osijek) | 10 |
| | Goran Stojljkovic (Radnicki) | 10 |
| | Josip Visnjic (Partizan) | 10 |

| YUGOSLAVIA 2nd Division Season 1990/91 | VARDAR | PRISTINA | SUTJESKA | SIBENIK | SLOBODA | KIKINDA | CIBALIA | PELISTER | GOSK JUG | LEOTAR | MACVA | NAPREDAK | ISKRA | BEOGRAD | BORAC | RADNICKI | ZAGREB | BOR | BUDVA |
|---|---|---|---|---|---|---|---|---|---|---|---|---|---|---|---|---|---|---|---|
| VARDAR SKOPLJE | ■ | 2-0 | 2-0 | 1-0 | 4-2 | 3-2 | 6-0 | 1-0 | 2-1 | 2-0 | 3-0 | 1-0 | 2-1 | 3-3 | 4-1 | 2-0 | 2-0 | 2-1 | 1-0 |
| FK PRISTINA | 2-0 | ■ | 1-0 | 1-0 | 3-1 | 3-2 | 1-1 | 4-0 | 1-0 | 3-0 | 1-1 | 2-0 | 4-1 | 1-0 | 5-0 | 3-1 | 2-1 | 3-0 | 2-0 |
| SUTJESKA NIKSIC | 1-0 | 2-0 | ■ | 4-2 | 0-0 | 3-0 | 2-0 | 2-1 | 1-0 | 4-0 | 1-0 | 4-1 | 2-0 | 1-0 | 1-0 | 5-1 | 1-0 | 2-0 | 1-1 |
| NK SIBENIK | 1-0 | 4-0 | 1-0 | ■ | 1-0 | 2-1 | 3-0 | 0-0 | 0-0 | 3-0 | 1-1 | 3-0 | 4-1 | 1-0 | 2-0 | 2-0 | 2-1 | 2-3 | 3-1 |
| SLOBODA TITIVO UZICE | 2-1 | 1-0 | 2-0 | 2-2 | ■ | 0-1 | 3-0 | 1-0 | 4-0 | 2-0 | 0-0 | 2-0 | 3-0 | 1-0 | 3-1 | 0-0 | 0-1 | 1-0 | 1-0 |
| OFK KIKINDA | 1-0 | 3-0 | 1-0 | 1-1 | 1-1 | ■ | 1-0 | 5-2 | 3-0 | 2-0 | 1-0 | 1-0 | 1-0 | 1-1 | 1-0 | 2-0 | 0-3 | 1-0 | 0-1 |
| CIBALIA VINKOVCI | 2-0 | 2-1 | 1-2 | 4-1 | 4-1 | 1-0 | ■ | 4-2 | 2-0 | 4-0 | 6-0 | 0-0 | 4-2 | 1-0 | 3-0 | 3-0 | 2-0 | 1-0 | 3-0 |
| PELISTER BITOLJ | 1-1 | 2-0 | 1-0 | 3-0 | 2-1 | 2-0 | 0-0 | ■ | 2-0 | 1-1 | 3-1 | 2-1 | 5-1 | 3-1 | 5-1 | 5-1 | 2-1 | 3-0 | 2-0 |
| GOSK JUG DUBROVNIK | 0-1 | 2-0 | 1-1 | 2-0 | 2-0 | 0-2 | 2-0 | 3-0 | ■ | 3-1 | 1-0 | 0-0 | 1-0 | 2-1 | 2-1 | 2-0 | 0-0 | 1-0 | 2-0 |
| LEOTAR TREBINJE | 3-3 | 2-1 | 2-1 | 3-1 | 3-0 | 1-3 | 2-0 | 2-0 | 1-0 | ■ | 4-1 | 2-1 | 2-0 | 1-1 | 2-1 | 1-0 | 2-3 | 1-2 | 3-1 |
| MACVA SABAC | 2-0 | 1-0 | 2-1 | 1-0 | 1-0 | 2-0 | 2-0 | 1-3 | 0-0 | 2-1 | ■ | 1-0 | 1-0 | 0-0 | 2-1 | 1-0 | 0-0 | 0-0 | 1-1 |
| NAPREDAK KRUSEVAC | 1-1 | 4-0 | 1-0 | 3-0 | 1-1 | 2-0 | 3-1 | 2-1 | 1-0 | 4-1 | 1-0 | ■ | 2-0 | 0-0 | 5-0 | 3-1 | 1-1 | 2-1 | 3-1 |
| ISKRA BUGOJNO | 3-2 | 0-0 | 2-0 | 3-0 | 2-1 | 0-1 | 0-0 | 1-0 | 3-1 | 0-0 | 1-0 | 1-0 | ■ | 1-0 | 1-0 | 2-1 | 0-1 | 0-0 | 1-0 |
| OFK BEOGRAD | 2-2 | 2-1 | 1-0 | 1-0 | 2-1 | 3-0 | 7-0 | 1-0 | 3-0 | 1-0 | 2-0 | 4-3 | 1-1 | ■ | 4-1 | 1-1 | 2-0 | 1-0 | 1-0 |
| BORAC CACAK | 0-2 | 2-1 | 1-0 | 3-0 | 0-0 | 2-1 | 0-0 | 0-1 | 0-0 | 3-2 | 1-1 | 1-1 | 4-0 | 1-1 | ■ | 0-2 | 2-3 | 1-1 | 0-1 |
| RADNICKI BEOGRAD | 2-0 | 2-1 | 1-0 | 2-1 | 1-0 | 1-1 | 4-1 | 4-0 | 1-2 | 4-0 | 2-0 | 1-1 | 4-0 | 2-1 | 3-1 | ■ | 1-0 | 4-0 | 0-2 |
| NK ZAGREB | 3-1 | 3-1 | 1-1 | 1-0 | 1-0 | 1-1 | 5-0 | 1-0 | 3-1 | 4-0 | 4-0 | 0-1 | 1-0 | 3-0 | 1-0 | 2-0 | ■ | 1-0 | 7-0 |
| FK BOR | 0-0 | 1-0 | 2-0 | 2-1 | 1-1 | 2-0 | 1-0 | 3-0 | 2-0 | 2-0 | 0-0 | 1-1 | 0-3 | 0-2 | 1-0 | 2-1 | 1-0 | ■ | 3-0 |
| FK BUDVA | 1-1 | 1-0 | 0-0 | 0-0 | 1-0 | 1-1 | 2-0 | 1-0 | 5-0 | 2-1 | 1-2 | 4-1 | 1-0 | 1-0 | 1-0 | 1-0 | 2-1 | 3-1 | ■ |

**European Cup Winners Fk Crvena Zvezda Beograd with the trophy.**

# YUGOSLAVIA 2ND DIVISION SEASON 1990/91

## LEAGUE TABLE FINAL

| | | | | | | | | |
|---|---|---|---|---|---|---|---|---|
| NK Zagreb | 36 | 20 | 5/2 | 11 | 58 | 28 | (23/24) | 42 |
| Vardar Skoplje | 36 | 19 | 7/4 | 10 | 58 | 38 | (24/23) | 42 |
| OFK Beograd | 36 | 16 | 9/6 | 11 | 50 | 33 | (37/31) | 38 |
| Sutjeska Niksic | 36 | 17 | 5/4 | 14 | 43 | 29 | (31/27) | 38 |
| OFK Kikinda | 36 | 17 | 6/3 | 13 | 42 | 38 | (29/30) | 37 |
| Pelister Bitolj | 36 | 17 | 4/1 | 15 | 54 | 46 | (13/17) | 35 |
| Napredak Krusevac | 36 | 15 | 9/4 | 12 | 50 | 39 | (31/33) | 34 |
| FK Pristina | 36 | 16 | 3/1 | 17 | 48 | 44 | (10/14) | 33 |
| Radnicki Novi Beograd | 36 | 15 | 4/3 | 17 | 48 | 48 | (16/14) | 33 |
| Cibalia Vinkovci | 36 | 16 | 5/1 | 15 | 50 | 53 | (18/22) | 33 |
| Mogren Budva | 36 | 16 | 6/1 | 14 | 37 | 42 | (28/33) | 33 |
| NK Sibenik | 36 | 14 | 6/4 | 16 | 44 | 45 | (25/20) | 32 |
| FK Bor | 36 | 14 | 7/4 | 15 | 33 | 38 | (26/25) | 32 |
| Macva Sabac | 36 | 13 | 10/6 | 13 | 27 | 40 | (35/33) | 32 |
| Sloboda Titovo Uzice | 36 | 13 | 8/5 | 15 | 38 | 36 | (31/27) | 31 |
| GOSK Jug Dubrovnik | 36 | 14 | 6/3 | 16 | 31 | 41 | (19/22) | 31 |
| Iskra Bugojno | 36 | 13 | 5/3 | 18 | 31 | 49 | (18/13) | 29 |
| Leotar Trebinje | 36 | 13 | 4/1 | 19 | 44 | 65 | (17/19) | 27 |
| Borac Cacak | 36 | 6 | 7/2 | 23 | 29 | 63 | (19/23) | 14 |

Promoted : - NK Zagreb and Vardar Skoplje

Relegated : - GOSK Jug Dubrovnik, Iskra Bugojno, Leotar Trebinje and Borac Cacak

**NAME CHANGES DURING SEASON : -**

Oct.90 - Dinamo Vinkovci to Cibalia Vinkovci

Mar.91 - FK Budva to Mogren Budva

Note : Due to the withdrawal of Croatian and Slovenian clubs, OFK Beograd, Sutjeska Niksic and Pelister Bitolj were promoted to the 1st Division and Iskra Bugojno, Leotar Trebinje and Borac Cacak reta ned 2nd Division status for Season 1990/91.

# YUGOSLAVIA 3RD DIV. NORTH 1990/91

## LEAGUE TABLE FINAL

| | | | | | | | |
|---|---|---|---|---|---|---|---|
| NK Zadar | 34 | 20 | 5/2 | 9 | 63 | 23 | 42 |
| Jugokeramika Zapres. | 34 | 19 | 4/4 | 11 | 48 | 35 | 42 |
| Rudar Ljubija | 34 | 15 | 5/2 | 14 | 48 | 44 | 32 |
| Jedinstvo Bihac | 34 | 14 | 5/4 | 15 | 27 | 50 | 32 |
| Varteks Varazdin | 34 | 14 | 6/3 | 14 | 41 | 42 | 31 |
| FK Izola | 34 | 14 | 4/1 | 15 | 40 | 42 | 31 |
| Maribor Branik | 34 | 14 | 5/3 | 15 | 34 | 37 | 31 |
| Tresnjevka Zagreb | 34 | 14 | 3/2 | 17 | 52 | 50 | 30 |
| Radnik Velika Gorica | 33 | 13 | 6/4 | 14 | 39 | 39 | 30 |
| Krajina Cazin | 34 | 14 | 5/2 | 15 | 34 | 39 | 30 |
| Orijent Rijeka | 34 | 13 | 5/4 | 16 | 31 | 45 | 30 |
| NK Koper | 34 | 13 | 11/3 | 10 | 39 | 23 | 29 |
| Segesta Sisak | 34 | 12 | 10/5 | 12 | 42 | 29 | 29 |
| Junak Sinj | 34 | 14 | 5/1 | 15 | 50 | 51 | 29 |
| OFK Prijedor | 34 | 13 | 6/3 | 15 | 29 | 40 | 29 |
| Primorac Stobrec | 34 | 10 | 12/7 | 12 | 23 | 36 | 27 |
| NK Split | 33 | 11 | 9/2 | 13 | 44 | 43 | 24 |
| Mladost Petrinja | 32 | 11 | 4/2 | 17 | 32 | 48 | 24 |

Promoted : - NK Zadar

# YUGOSLAVIA 3RD DIV. EAST 1990/91

## LEAGUE TABLE FINAL

| | | | | | | | |
|---|---|---|---|---|---|---|---|
| FK Becej | 34 | 26 | 4/2 | 4 | 83 | 22 | 54 |
| Vrbas Titov Vrbas | 34 | 16 | 9/7 | 9 | 60 | 36 | 39 |
| Hajduk Kula | 34 | 16 | 10/6 | 8 | 39 | 29 | 38 |
| Drina Zvornik | 34 | 16 | 7/1 | 11 | 40 | 26 | 33 |
| AIK Backa Topola | 34 | 14 | 10/4 | 10 | 42 | 33 | 32 |
| Metalac OLT Osijek | 34 | 15 | 7/2 | 12 | 48 | 42 | 32 |
| Obilic Beograd | 34 | 13 | 7/6 | 14 | 46 | 48 | 32 |
| Jedinstvo Brcko | 34 | 14 | 7/3 | 13 | 39 | 41 | 31 |
| Olimpija Osijek | 34 | 14 | 5/2 | 15 | 41 | 39 | 30 |
| FK Novi Sad | 34 | 12 | 6/6 | 16 | 44 | 45 | 30 |
| Kabel Novi Sad | 34 | 13 | 7/3 | 14 | 52 | 57 | 29 |
| Sloga Doboj | 34 | 13 | 7/3 | 14 | 35 | 45 | 29 |
| IEK Rudar Kostolac | 34 | 13 | 5/3 | 16 | 47 | 59 | 29 |
| FK Belisce | 34 | 13 | 7/2 | 14 | 55 | 52 | 28 |
| BSK Beograd | 34 | 13 | 4/2 | 17 | 48 | 51 | 28 |
| Radnicki Lukevac | 34 | 12 | 6/4 | 16 | 32 | 47 | 28 |
| Kolubara Lazarevac | 34 | 8 | 3/1 | 23 | 27 | 63 | 17 |
| BSK Slavonski Brod | 34 | 6 | 7/2 | 21 | 25 | 68 | 14 |

Promoted : - FK Becej

# YUGOSLAVIA 3RD DIV. WEST 1990/91

## LEAGUE TABLE FINAL

| | | | | | | | |
|---|---|---|---|---|---|---|---|
| Celik Zenica | 34 | 19 | 4/4 | 11 | 54 | 27 | 42 |
| Jedinstvo Bijelo Polje | 34 | 17 | 4/3 | 13 | 55 | 33 | 37 |
| Neretva Metkovic | 33 | 17 | 5/2 | 11 | 41 | 27 | 36 |
| Radnicki Gorazde | 33 | 17 | 4/2 | 13 | 46 | 41 | 36 |
| Mornar Bar | 34 | 16 | 3/2 | 15 | 41 | 27 | 34 |
| Rudar Kakanj | 34 | 14 | 6/3 | 14 | 45 | 40 | 31 |
| Krijava Zavidovici | 34 | 14 | 7/3 | 13 | 49 | 48 | 31 |
| FK Vitez | 34 | 15 | 1/1 | 18 | 40 | 43 | 31 |
| Slaven Grude | 34 | 15 | 2/1 | 17 | 42 | 53 | 31 |
| Famos Hrasnica | 34 | 13 | 7/4 | 14 | 55 | 45 | 30 |
| Neretvanac Opuzen | 33 | 15 | 1/0 | 17 | 48 | 43 | 30 |
| FK Ivangrad | 34 | 14 | 5/2 | 15 | 36 | 35 | 30 |
| Bosna Visoko | 34 | 14 | 6/2 | 14 | 38 | 41 | 30 |
| Borac Travnik | 33 | 14 | 4/2 | 15 | 31 | 47 | 30 |
| Bokelj Kotor | 33 | 14 | 3/1 | 16 | 34 | 46 | 29 |
| Loveen Cetinje | 33 | 14 | 3/0 | 16 | 36 | 50 | 28 |
| Borac Capljina | 33 | 12 | 4/3 | 17 | 37 | 65 | 27 |
| ZSK Metalno Zenica | 34 | 11 | 7/3 | 16 | 46 | 44 | 25 |

Promoted : - Celik Zenica

# YUGOSLAVIA 3RD DIV. SOUTH 1990/91

## LEAGUE TABLE FINAL

| | | | | | | | |
|---|---|---|---|---|---|---|---|
| Balkanstok. Skoplje | 34 | 19 | 8/5 | 7 | 51 | 25 | 43 |
| Radnicki Kragujevac | 34 | 18 | 8/1 | 8 | 60 | 32 | 37 |
| Teteks Tetovo | 34 | 17 | 5/3 | 12 | 49 | 37 | 37 |
| Sileks Kratovo | 34 | 16 | 4/4 | 14 | 58 | 44 | 36 |
| FAP Priboj na Limu | 34 | 14 | 9/7 | 11 | 54 | 38 | 35 |
| Dubicica Leskovac | 34 | 15 | 6/3 | 13 | 48 | 46 | 33 |
| Radnicki Pirot | 34 | 15 | 4/2 | 15 | 58 | 51 | 32 |
| Bregalnica Strumica | 34 | 15 | 5/2 | 14 | 44 | 48 | 32 |
| Pobeda Prilep | 34 | 15 | 3/2 | 16 | 52 | 60 | 32 |
| Crv'na Zvez. Gnjilane | 34 | 15 | 5/2 | 14 | 48 | 54 | 32 |
| Sloga Kraljevo | 34 | 14 | 6/2 | 14 | 41 | 37 | 30 |
| FK Majdanpek | 34 | 13 | 6/4 | 15 | 34 | 38 | 30 |
| Mladost Lucani | 33 | 15 | 1/0 | 17 | 36 | 43 | 30 |
| FK Novi Pazar | 34 | 13 | 6/2 | 15 | 42 | 40 | 28 |
| Borac Titov Veles | 33 | 13 | 5/1 | 16 | 34 | 37 | 27 |
| Vlaznimi Dakovica | 34 | 11 | 10/4 | 13 | 33 | 43 | 26 |
| Liria Prizren | 34 | 9 | 7/5 | 18 | 33 | 58 | 23 |
| Trepca Mitrovica | 33 | 7 | 3/0 | 23 | 35 | 78 | 14 |

Promoted : - Balkanstokokomerc Skoplje

Note : - Due to civil unrest in Yugoslavia, it is not known whether outstanding matches were in fact played.

# YUGOSLAVIA CUP 1990/91

## 1/16 FINALS

| | | | | |
|---|---|---|---|---|
| NK Koper...................3 | Spartak Subotica........0 | | Borac B'ski Samac .....0 | Dinamo Zagreb..........7 |
| Trepca Titova Mit........1 | Vojvodina Novi Sad....7 | | Pelister Bitolj .............2 | Rad Beograd .............1 |
| NK Zadar..................0 | NK Rijeka ..................0 (aet.) | | Vratnik Sarajevo.........1 | Zeljeznicar Sarajevo.. 5 |
| NK Rijeka win 2-4 on penalties | | | NK Belisce.................2 | Crvena Zvez. B'grad.. 4 |
| NK Osijek ..................3 | Velez Mostar ..............2 | | FK Novi Sad ...............0 | Sloboda Tuzla............1 |
| Vrapce Zagreb ..........0 | Hajduk Split................6 | | Partizan Beograd .......2 | Sutjeska Niksic ..........0 |
| Borac Banja Luka.......1 (aet.) | Vardar Skoplje............0 | | Buducnost Titograd ....1 | Sloboda Titovo Uzice. 0 |
| FK Sarajevo ..............6 (aet.) | Borac Cacak ..............1 | | Olimpija Ljubljana.......1 | Proleter Zrenjanin ......1 |
| Radnicki Nis ..............1 | OFK Beograd .............2 (aet.) | | Proleter Zrenjanin win 2-4 on penalties | |

## 1/8 FINALS

| | 1ST LEG | 2ND LEG | AGG. |
|---|---|---|---|
| Proleter Zrenjanin v NK Koper | 2-0 | 0-0 | 2-0 |
| OFK Beograd v Zeljeznicar Sarajevo | 2-1 | 1-1 | 3-2 |
| Borac Banja Luka v NK Osijek | 2-0 | 0-1 | 2-1 |
| Sloboda Tuzla v NK Rijeka | 2-0 | 1-4 | 3-4 |
| Hajduk Split v Pelister Bitolj ⊗ | 1-1 | 2-2 | 3-3 |
| Buducnost Titograd v Partizan Beograd | 2-0 | 0-1 | 2-1 |
| Vojvodina Novi Sad v Crvena Zvezda Beograd | 0-2 | 1-2 | 1-4 |
| Dinamo Zagreb v FK Sarajevo | 1-0 | 4-1 | 5-1 |

⊗ Hajduk win on the away goals rule.

## 1/4 FINALS

| | 1ST LEG | 2ND LEG | AGG. |
|---|---|---|---|
| NK Rijeka v Hajduk Split | 0-1 | 1-1 | 1-2 |
| Borac Banja Luka v Dinamo Zagreb | 3-2 | 0-0 | 3-2 |
| Crvena Zvezda Beograd v Proleter Zrenjanin | 4-1 | 0-1 | 4-2 |
| Buducnost Titograd v OFK Beograd | 1-2 | 1-1 | 2-3 |

## SEMI-FINALS

| | 1ST LEG | 2ND LEG | AGG. |
|---|---|---|---|
| Crvena Zvezda Beograd v OFK Beograd | 3-0 | 3-3 | 6-3 |
| Hajduk Split v Borac Banja Luka | 1-0 | 1-0 | 2-0 |

## FINAL   8/5/91 (at Stadion JNA, Beograd)

Hajduk Split ...............1    Crvena Zvezda Beograd........0

Hajduk : Mihacic, Hadziabdic, Kovac (Osibov 70), Stimac, Setinov, Bilic, Kozniku (Jelicic 80), Mise, Boksic, Vucevic, Jarni.
C.Zvezda : Stojanovic, Radinovic (Stosic 82), Marovic, Jugovic, Belodedic, Najdoski, Prosinecki, Mihajlovic, Pancev, Savicevic, Binic.

1-0  Boksic    66
Referee : Adem Fazlagic (Capljina)
Attendance : 7,000

# DEVELOPMENTS IN YUGOSLAVIA

The political upheavals and civil unrest during the Summer of 1991 have at the time of going to press alrady had an important influence on Yugoslav football. Soon after the troubles began Dinamo Zagreb changed its' name to HASK Gradanski Zagreb reverting to the names of the clubs from whence it originated. The name change is of course political dynamite as HASK Zagreb prior to and during the 2nd world war were known as the club portraying strong Croatian nationalistic feeling.

Also in June an International match was arranged between Croatia and Slovenia. At the time the question of Yugoslavia's borders was of great political importance and it is no doubt deliberate provocation that the match was held at Murska Sobota, a spot very close to the point where the borders of Yugoslavia, Hungary and Austria meet. No effort was spared to acquire the strongest possible representation, Croatia even making use of foreign based stars, Bogdan (Karlsruher SC), Asanovic (AS Cannes) and Cvjetkovic (St.Truiden VV). A similar invitation afforded to Srecko Katanec was however declined. For their part, Slovenia selected the Partizan Beograd player, Dzoni Novak.

19/6/91 (at Murska Sobota)
Slovenia ................... 0    Croatia ...................... 1

Slovenia : Simeunovic, Jancic, Englaro, Galic, Jermanis (Cvikl 68), Zulic, Zidan, Ceh (Lorger 80), Pate, Novak, Gliha (Vidovic 80).

Croatia : Ladic, Vulic (Vukovic 30), Drazic, Zupetic, Bogdan, Istvanic, Jurcevic (Komljenovic 45), Mladenovic (Kalapac 80), Asanovic (Biskup 80), Boban, Cvjetkovic (Separovic 45).

0-1  Komljenovic    65          Referee : Bucar
                                Attendance : 4,000

The Yugoslav Football Federation could only follow these events with dismay, and reacted by promptly publishing the 1st and 2nd Division fixtures for Season 1991/92. The season was to open on the 3rd of August with the following 1st Division fixtures : -

Zeljeznicar v Zemun, Vardar v C.Zvezda, Rijeka v Borac, Proleter v HASK Gradanski, Osijek v Radnicki, Zagreb v Vojvodina, Hajduk v Velez, Partizan v Olimpija and Rad v Sarajevo.

As time passed the chances of these matches taking place diminished day by day, leading the Federation to postpone them until the 10th of August, at the same time issuing an ultimatum to the Croatian and Slovenian clubs that if they did not declare their intention of taking part prior to the 7th of August they would be excluded and their places taken by other clubs. In the event only Olimpija Ljubljana heeded the ultimatum, however, they withdrew at the last minute following pressure from the Slovenia Federation insisting that they should take part in the Slovenian Championship to be formed shortly. The draw for the 1st round of the Yugoslavian Cup was allowed to stand, with the stipulation that clubs drawn against opponents that failed to appear would be awarded a 3-0 victory. Particularly amusing here was the planned match between The Yugoslavian Army XI and HASK Gradanski. It is of course impossible to predict events in the coming months, however we do feel that we should clarify the position of FOOTBALL IN EUROPE concerning political developments in Yugoslavia and the Soviet Union. It is felt that it is of great interest to record the formation of new leagues set up in republics striving for independence. We will however not create separate sections for these republics until they are recognised as separate entities by UEFA.

# COMPOSTITION OF LEAGUES FOR SEASON 1990/91

| YUGOSLAVIA 1ST DIVISION | YUGOSLAVIA 2ND DIVISION | SLOVENIA 1ST DIVISION |
| --- | --- | --- |
| Crvena Zvezda Beograd | OFK Kikinda | Olimpija Ljubljana |
| Partizan Beograd | Napredak Krusevac | Svoboda LM Ljubljana |
| Borac Banja Luka | FK Pristina | Slovan Mavrica Ljubljana |
| Poleter Zrenjanin | Radnicki Novi Beograd | Eurospektar Ljubljana |
| Vojvodina Novi Sad | Mogren Budva | Potrosnik Beltinci |
| Rad Beograd | FK Bor | Steklar Rogaska Slatina |
| Radnicki Nis | Macva Sabac | Domzale LEK |
| FK Sarajevo | Sloboda Titovo Uzice | Vozila Nova Gorica |
| Velez Mostar | Iskra Bugojno | Rudar Velnje |
| FK Zemun | Leotar Trebinje | Ingrad Kladivar Celje |
| Zeljeznicar Sarajevo | Borak Cacak | Rudar Trbovlje |
| Buducnost Titograd | Rudar Ljubija | NK Koper |
| Sloboda Tuzla | FK Becej | Proletarac Zagorje |
| Spartak Subotica | Vrbas Titov Vrbas | Zivila Naklo |
| Vardar Skoplje | Hajduk Kula | Jadran Lama Dekani |
| OFK Beograd | Celik Zenica | Nafta Lendava |
| Sutjeska Niksic | Jedinstvo Bijelo Polje | Mura Murska Sobota |
| Pelister Bitolj | Balkan Skoplje | FK Izola |
|  | Radnicki Kragujevac | Maribor Branik |
|  | Teteks Tetovo | Primorje Ajdovscina |
|  |  | FK Medvode |

| CROATIA 1ST DIVISION | CROATIA 2ND DIVISION EAST | CROATIA 2ND DIVISION WEST |
| --- | --- | --- |
| HASK Gradanski Zagreb | Tresnjevka Zagreb | Neretva Metkovic |
| Hajduk Split | Radnik Velica Gorica | Primorac Stobrec |
| NK Osijek | NK Samobor | MAR Solin |
| NK Rijeka | Spansko CB Zagreb | NK Split |
| NK Zagreb | NK Karlovac | Slaven Gruda |
| Cibalia Vinkovci | Metalac Sisak | Junak Sinj |
| NK Sibenik | Segesta Sisak | Jadran Ploce |
| GOSK Jug Dubrovnik | Metalac OLT Osijek | Neretvanac Opuzen |
| NK Zadar | Olimpija Osijek | Orijent Rijeka |
| INKER Zapresic | Croatia Bogdanovci | Pazinka Pazin |
| Varteks Varazdin | NK Belisce | Rudar Labin |
| Istra Pula | HSK Marsonia Slavonski Brod | NK Kraljevica |

Name Change : - Jugokeramica Zapresic to INKER Zapresic

## INTERNATIONAL LINE-UPS 1990

| Date | Match | Venue | Competition | Referee | Scorers |
|---|---|---|---|---|---|
| 28/3/90 | POLAND 0 YUGOSLAVIA 0 | Lodz | Friendly | Ref: Molnar (Hungary) | |
| 26/5/90 | YUGOSLAVIA 0 SPAIN 1 | Ljubljana | Friendly | Ref: Lo Bello (Italy) | |
| 3/6/90 | YUGOSLAVIA 0 HOLLAND 2 | Zagreb | Friendly | Ref: Kupe (Austria) | |
| 10/6/90 | WESTERN GERMANY 4 YUGOSLAVIA 1 | Milano | World Cup | Ref: Mikkelsen (Austria) | (Jozic) |
| 14/6/90 | COLUMBIA 0 YUGOSLAVIA 1 | Bologna | World Cup | Ref: Agnolin (Italy) | (Jozic) |
| 19/6/90 | UAE 1 YUGOSLAVIA 4 | Bologna | World Cup | Ref: Takada (Japan) | (Susic, Pancev 2, Prosinecki) |
| 26/6/90 | SPAIN 1 YUGOSLAVIA 2 (aet.) | Verona | World Cup | Ref: Schmidhuber (W.Germany) | (Stojkovic 2) |
| 30/6/90 | ARGENTINA 0 YUGOSLAVIA 0 (aet.) ARGENTINA WIN 3-2 ON PENALTIES | Firenze | World Cup | Ref: Röthlisberger (Switzerland) | |
| 12/9/90 | NORTHERN IRELAND 0 YUGOSLAVIA 0 (aet.) | Belfast | EuroCh.Q. | Ref: Uilenberg (Holland) | (Pancev, Prosinecki) |
| 31/10/90 | YUGOSLAVIA 4 AUSTRIA 1 | Beograd | EuroCh.Q. | Ref: Schmidhuber (W.Germany) | (Pancev 3, Katanec) |
| 14/11/90 | DENMARK 0 YUGOSLAVIA 2 | København | EuroCh.Q. | Ref: Migdley (England) | (Bazdarevic, Jarni) |

### CAPS AT 31/12/90 and GOALS AT 31/12/90

| Player | CAPS | GOALS |
|---|---|---|
| Tomislav Ivkovic | 34 | |
| Zoran Vulic | 22 | 2 |
| Vujadin Stanojkovic | 18 | 1 |
| Faruk Hadzibegic | 53 | 6 |
| Davor Jozic | 25 | 2 |
| Predrag Spasic | 26 | 1 |
| Dragoljub | 26 | 1 |
| Dragan Stojkovic | 39 | 9 |
| Safet Susic | 54 | 21 |
| Darko Pancev | 20 | 11 |
| Zlatko Vujovic | 70 | 24 |
| Dragan Kanatlarovski | 1 | |
| Mirsad Baljic | 29 | 3 |
| Robert Prosinecki | 12 | 3 |
| Refik Sabanadzovic | 8 | |
| Robert Jarni | 4 | 1 |
| Srecko Katanec | 31 | 5 |
| Dejan Savicevic | 17 | 5 |
| Ilija Najdoski | 2 | |
| Dragisa Binic | 1 | |
| Zeljko Petrovic | 1 | |
| Vlada Stosic | 1 | |
| Mehmed Bazdarevic | 47 | 4 |
| Zvonimir Boban | 5 | |

## YUGOSLAVIA : All Time Records as at 31/12/90 - CAPS

1. Dragan Dzajic (Crvena Zvezda Beograd/SEC Bastia) — 85
2. Zlatko Vujovic (Hajduk Split/Girondins Bordeaux/AS Cannes/Paris St.Germain FC) — 70
3. Branko Zebec (Borac Zagreb/Partizan Beograd/Crvena Zvezda Beograd) — 65
4. Stjepan Bobek (Partizan Beograd) — 63
5. Branko Stankovic (Crvena Zvezda Beograd) — 61
6. Ivan Horvat (Dinamo Zagreb) — 60
7. Bernard Vukas (Hajduk Split) — 59
7. Rajko Mitic (Crvena Zvezda Beograd) — 59
9. Vladimir Beara (Hajduk Split/Crvena Zvezda Beograd) — 59
10. Blagoje Marjanovic (Beogradski SK) — 57
    Vujadin Boskov (Vojvodina Novi Sad) — 57

## YUGOSLAVIA : All Time Records as at 31/12/90 - GOALS

1. Stjepan Bobek (Patizan Beograd) — (63) 38
2. Milan Galic (Partizan Beograd) — (51) 37
3. Blagoje Marjanovic (Beogradski SK) — (57) 36
4. Rajko Mitic (Crvena Zvezda Beograd) — (59) 32
5. Dusan Bajevic (Velez Mostar) — (37) 29
6. Todor Veselinovic (Vojvodina Novi Sad) — (37) 28
7. Borivoje Kostic (Crvena Zvezda Beograd) — (33) 26
7. Zlatko Vujovic (Hajduk Split/Girondins Bordeaux/AS Cannes/Paris St.Germain) — (70) 24
9. Dragan Dzajic (Crvena Zvezda Beograd/SEC Bastia) — (85) 23
10. Bernard Vukas (Hajduk Split) — (59) 22

# EUROPEAN CUP 1990/91

### 1ST ROUND

| | 1ST LEG | 2ND LEG | AGG. |
|---|---|---|---|
| APOEL Nicosia v FC Bayern München | 2-3 | 0-4 | 2-7 |
| Crvena Zvezda Beograd v Grasshopper Club | 1-1 | 4-1 | 5-2 |
| Dinamo Bucuresti v St.Patrick's Athletic | 4-0 | 1-1 | 5-1 |
| KA v CSKA Sofia | 1-0 | 0-3 | 1-3 |
| Lech Poznan v Panathinaikos AO | 3-0 | 2-1 | 5-1 |
| Lillestrøm SK v FC Brugge | 1-1 | 0-2 | 1-3 |
| Malmö FF v Besiktas JK | 3-2 | 2-2 | 5-4 |
| Napoli SSC v Ujpesti Dózsa SC | 3-0 | 2-0 | 5-0 |
| OB v Real Madrid CF | 1-4 | 0-6 | 1-10 |
| Olympique Marseille v Dinamo Tiranë | 5-1 | 0-0 | 5-1 |
| FC Porto v Portadown | 5-0 | 8-1 | 13-1 |
| Sparta Praha v Spartak Moskva | 0-2 | 0-2 | 0-4 |
| FC Tirol v FC Kuusysi | 5-0 | 2-1 | 7-1 |
| Union Luxembourg v 1FC Dynamo Dresden | 1-3 | 0-3 | 1-6 |
| Valletta FC v Rangers | 0-4 | 0-6 | 0-10 |
| Bye - Milan AC | | | |

### 2ND ROUND

| | 1ST LEG | 2ND LEG | AGG. |
|---|---|---|---|
| FC Bayern München v CSKA Sofia | 4-0 | 3-0 | 7-0 |
| Crvena Zvezda Beograd v Rangers | 3-0 | 1-1 | 4-1 |
| Dinamo Bucuresti v FC Porto | 0-0 | 0-4 | 0-4 |
| Dynamo Dresden v Malmö FF (Dynamo Dresden win 5-4 on penalties) | 1-1 | 1-1 (aet.) | 2-2 |
| Lech Poznan v Olympique Marseille | 3-2 | 1-6 | 4-8 |
| Milan AC v FC Brugge | 0-0 | 1-0 | 1-0 |
| Napoli SSC v Spartak Moskva (Spartak Moskva win 5-3 on penalties) | 0-0 | 0-0 (aet.) | 0-0 |
| Real Madrid CF v FC Tirol | 9-1 | 2-2 | 11-3 |

### 1/4 FINALS

| | 1ST LEG | 2ND LEG | AGG. |
|---|---|---|---|
| FC Bayern München v FC Porto | 1-1 | 2-0 | 3-1 |
| Crvena Zvezda Beograd v Dynamo Dresden | 3-0 | 3-0 ⊗ | 6-0 |
| Milan AC v Olympique Marseille | 1-1 | 0-3 ⊗ | 1-4 |
| Spartak Moskva v Real Madrid CF | 0-0 | 3-1 | 3-1 |

⊗ Matches awarded following Dynamo Dresden 1 Crvena Zvezda Beograd 2 abandoned after 78 minutes, crowd disturbance, and Olympique Marseille 1 Milan AC 0 abandoned after 90 minutes, Milan refused to play on following floodlight failure.

### SEMI-FINALS

| | 1ST LEG | 2ND LEG | AGG. |
|---|---|---|---|
| FC Bayern München v Crvena Zvezda Beograd | 1-2 | 2-2 | 3-4 |
| Spartak Moskva v Olympique Marseille | 1-3 | 1-2 | 2-5 |

### FINAL   29/5/91 at Stadio Nuovo Comunale, Bari

FK Crvena Zvezda Beograd......0   Olympique Marseille......0  (aet.)

C.Zvezda : S.Stojanovic, V.Jugovic, M.Belodedic, I.Najdoski, S.Marovic, R.Sabanadzovic, R.Prosinecki, S.Mihajlovic, D.Savicevic (V.Stosic 85), D.Pancev, D.Binic.
Marseille : P.Olmeta, M.Amoros, B.Boli, C.Mozer, B.Casoni, E.Di Meco (D.Stojkovic 110), B.Germain, L.Fournier (P.Vercruysse 75), C.Waddle, J-P.Papin, A.Pele.
Referee : Lanese (Italy)
Attendance : 51,000

**FK CRVENA ZVEZDA BEOGRAD WIN 5-3 ON PENALTIES.**

**Chris Waddle gets in a cross in the 1991 European Cup Final**

# EUROPEAN CUP-WINNERS CUP 1990/91

## PRELIMINARY ROUND

| | 1ST LEG | 2ND LEG | AGG. |
|---|---|---|---|
| Bray Wanderers v Trabzonspor | 1-1 | 0-2 | 1-3 |

## 1ST ROUND

| | 1ST LEG | 2ND LEG | AGG. |
|---|---|---|---|
| Estrela Amadora v Xamax FC (Estrela Amadora win 4-3 on penalties) | 1-1 | 1-1 (aet.) | 2-2 |
| Fram v Djurgardens IF | 3-0 | 1-1 | 4-1 |
| Glentoran v Steaua Bucuresti | 1-1 | 0-5 | 1-6 |
| 1FC Kaiserslautern v UC Sampdoria | 1-0 | 0-2 | 1-2 |
| KuPS v Dinamo Kiev | 2-2 | 0-4 | 2-6 |
| Legia Warszawa v Swift Hesperange | 3-0 | 3-0 | 6-0 |
| Manchester United v Pecsi MSC | 2-0 | 1-0 | 3-0 |
| Montpellier HSC v PSV | 1-0 | 0-0 | 1-0 |
| NEA Salamina v Aberdeen | 0-2 | 0-3 | 0-5 |
| Olympiakos Piraeus v Flamurtari Vlorë | 3-1 | 2-0 | 5-1 |
| PSV Schwerin v FK Austria Wien | 0-2 | 0-0 | 0-2 |
| Sliema Wanderers v Dukla Praha | 1-2 | 0-2 | 1-4 |
| FK Sliven v Juventus FC | 0-2 | 1-6 | 1-8 |
| Trabzonspor v FC Barcelona | 1-0 | 2-7 | 3-7 |
| Viking FK v FC Liégeois | 0-2 | 0-3 | 0-5 |
| Wrexham v Lyngby BK | 0-0 | 1-0 | 1-0 |

## 2ND ROUND

| | 1ST LEG | 2ND LEG | AGG. |
|---|---|---|---|
| Aberdeen v Legia Warszawa | 0-0 | 0-1 | 0-1 |
| FK Austria Wien v Juventus FC | 0-4 | 0-4 | 0-8 |
| Dinamo Kiev v Dukla Praha | 1-0 | 2-2 | 3-2 |
| Fram v FC Barcelona | 1-2 | 0-3 | 1-5 |
| FC Liégeois v Estrela Amadora | 2-0 | 0-1 | 2-1 |
| Manchester United v Wrexham | 3-0 | 2-0 | 5-0 |
| Montpellier HSC v Steaua Bucuresti | 5-0 | 3-0 | 8-0 |
| Olympiakos Piraeus v UC Sampdoria | 0-1 | 1-3 | 1-4 |

## 1/4 FINALS

| | 1ST LEG | 2ND LEG | AGG. |
|---|---|---|---|
| Dinamo Kiev v FC Barcelona | 2-3 | 1-1 | 3-4 |
| Legia Warszawa v Juventus FC | 1-0 | 2-2 | 3-2 |
| FC Liégeois v UC Sampdoria | 1-3 | 0-3 | 1-6 |
| Manchester United v Montpellier HSC | 1-1 | 2-0 | 3-1 |

## SEMI-FINALS

| | 1ST LEG | 2ND LEG | AGG. |
|---|---|---|---|
| Legia Warszawa v Manchester United | 1-3 | 1-1 | 2-4 |
| FC Barcelona v Juventus FC | 3-1 | 0-1 | 3-2 |

## FINAL   15/5/91   at Feyenoord Stadion, Rotterdam

Manchester United ....2     FC Barcelona ..........1

Man. Utd. : L.Sealey, D.Irwin, S.Bruce, G.Pallister, C.Blackmore, M.Phelan, B.Robson, P.Ince, B.McClair, M.Hughes, L.Sharpe.

Barcelona : Busquets,Nando,Alesanco (Pinilla 71), R.Koeman,Ferrer,Eusebio,Bakero,Beguiristain,Goicoechea,Julio Salinas,M.Laudrup.

| 1-0 | Hughes | 68 |
|---|---|---|
| 2-0 | Hughes | 75 |
| 2-1 | Koeman | 80 |

Referee : Karlsson (Sweden)
Attendance : 46,000

**Manchester United's captain Bryan Robson holds aloft the European Cup-Winner's Cup trophy**

# UEFA CUP 1990/91

| 1ST ROUND | 1ST LEG | 2ND LEG | | AGG. |
|---|---|---|---|---|
| RSC Anderlecht v Petrolul Ploesti | 2-0 | 2-0 | | 4-0 |
| Royal Antwerp FC v Ferencvárosi TC | 0-0 | 1-3 | (aet.) | 1-3 |
| Aston Villa v Banik Ostrava | 3-1 | 2-1 | | 5-2 |
| Atalanta BC v Dinamo Zagreb (Atalanta BC win on away goals rule) | 0-0 | 1-1 | | 1-1 |
| Avenir Beggen v Inter Bratislava | 2-1 | 0-5 | | 2-6 |
| Bayer Leverkusen v FC Twente | 1-0 | 1-1 | (aet.) | 2-1 |
| Borussia Dortmund v Chemnitzer FC | 2-0 | 2-0 | | 4-0 |
| Brøndbyernes IF v SG Eintracht Frankfurt | 5-0 | 1-4 | | 6-4 |
| Chernomorets Odessa v Rosenborg BK | 3-1 | 1-2 | | 4-3 |
| Derry City v Vitesse | 0-1 | 0-0 | | 0-1 |
| Dnepr Dnepropetrovsk v Heart of Midlothian | 1-1 | 1-3 | | 2-4 |
| Fenerbahce v Vitoria SC Guimaraes | 3-0 | 3-2 | | 6-2 |
| FH v Dundee United | 1-3 | 2-2 | | 3-5 |
| Glenavon v Girondins Bordeaux | 0-0 | 0-2 | | 0-2 |
| Hibernians Pawla v Partizan Beograd | 0-3 | 0-2 | | 0-5 |
| Iraklis v Valencia CF | 0-0 | 0-2 | (aet.) | 0-2 |
| GKS Katowice v TPS | 3-0 | 1-0 | | 4-0 |
| Lausanne Sports v Real Sociedad (Real Sociedad win on away goals rule) | 3-2 | 0-1 | | 3-3 |
| 1FC Magdeburg v RoPS | 0-0 | 1-0 | | 1-0 |
| MTK-VM v FC Luzern | 1-1 | 1-2 | | 2-3 |
| IFK Norrköping v 1FC Köln | 0-0 | 1-3 | | 1-3 |
| Partizani Tiranë v Universitatea Craiova | 0-1 | 0-1 | | 0-2 |
| Politehnica Timisoara v Atlético Madrid | 2-0 | 0-1 | | 2-1 |
| SK Rapid Wien v Internazionale FC | 2-1 | 1-3 | (aet.) | 3-4 |
| Roda JC v AS Monaco | 1-3 | 1-3 | | 2-6 |
| AS Roma v SL Benfica | 1-0 | 1-0 | | 2-0 |
| Sevilla FC v PAOK (Sevilla FC win 4-3 on penalties) | 0-0 | 0-0 | (aet.) | 0-0 |
| Slavia Sofia v Omonia Nicosia | 2-1 | 2-4 | (aet.) | 4-5 |
| Sporting CP v KV Mechelen | 1-0 | 2-2 | | 3-2 |
| Torpedo Moskva v GAIS | 4-1 | 1-1 | | 5-2 |
| Vejle BK v FC Admira-Wacker | 0-1 | 0-3 | | 0-4 |
| Zaglebie Lubin v Bologna FC | 0-1 | 0-1 | | 0-2 |

| 2ND ROUND | 1ST LEG | 2ND LEG | | AGG. |
|---|---|---|---|---|
| Aston Villa v Internazionale FC | 2-0 | 0-3 | | 2-3 |
| Brøndbyernes IF v Ferencvárosi TC | 3-0 | 1-0 | | 4-0 |
| Chernomorets Odessa v AS Monaco | 0-0 | 0-1 | | 0-1 |
| Fenerbahce v Atalanta BC | 0-1 | 1-4 | | 1-5 |
| Heart of Midlothian v Bologna FC | 3-1 | 0-3 | | 3-4 |
| GKS Katowice v Bayer Leverkusen | 1-2 | 0-4 | | 1-6 |
| 1FC Köln v Inter Bratislava | 0-1 | 2-0 | | 2-1 |
| FC Luzern v FC Admira-Wacker | 0-1 | 1-1 | | 1-2 |
| 1FC Magdeburg v Girondins Bordeaux | 0-1 | 0-1 | | 0-2 |
| Omonia Nicosia v RSC Anderlecht | 1-1 | 0-3 | | 1-4 |
| Real Sociedad v Partizan Beograd (Partizan win 3-4 on penalties) | 1-0 | 0-1 | (aet.) | 1-1 |
| Sporting CP v Politehnica Timisoara | 7-0 | 0-2 | | 7-2 |
| Torpedo Moskva v Sevilla FC | 3-1 | 1-2 | | 4-3 |
| Universitatea Craiova v Borussia Dortmund | 0-3 | 0-1 | | 0-4 |
| Valencia CF v AS Roma | 1-1 | 1-2 | | 2-3 |
| Vitesse v Dundee United | 1-0 | 4-0 | | 5-0 |

| 3RD ROUND | 1ST LEG | 2ND LEG | | AGG. |
|---|---|---|---|---|
| FC Admira-Wacker v Bologna FC (Bologna FC win 6-5 on penalties) | 3-0 | 0-3 | (aet.) | 3-3 |
| RSC Anderlecht v Borussia Dortmund (Anderlecht win on away goals) | 1-0 | 1-2 | | 2-2 |
| Brøndbyernes IF v Bayer Leverkusen | 3-0 | 0-0 | | 3-0 |
| Internazionale FC v Partizan Beograd | 3-0 | 1-1 | | 4-1 |
| 1FC Köln v Atalanta BC | 1-1 | 0-1 | | 1-2 |
| AS Roma v Girondins Bordeaux | 5-0 | 2-0 | | 7-0 |
| Torpedo Moskva v AS Monaco | 2-1 | 2-1 | | 4-2 |
| Vitesse v Sporting CP | 0-2 | 1-2 | | 1-4 |

| 1/4 FINALS | 1ST LEG | 2ND LEG | | AGG. |
|---|---|---|---|---|
| Atalanta BC v Internazionale FC | 0-0 | 0-2 | | 0-2 |
| Bologna FC v Sporting CP | 1-1 | 0-2 | | 1-3 |
| Brøndbyernes IF v Torpedo Moskva (Brøndby win 4-2 on penalties) | 1-0 | 0-1 | (aet.) | 1-1 |
| AS Roma v RSC Anderlecht | 3-0 | 3-2 | | 6-2 |

| SEMI-FINALS | 1ST LEG | 2ND LEG | AGG. |
|---|---|---|---|
| Brøndbyernes IF v AS Roma | 0-0 | 1-2 | 1-2 |
| Sporting CP v Internazionale FC | 0-0 | 0-2 | 0-2 |

## FINAL

**1ST LEG**  8/5/91 at Stadio Giuseppe Meazza (San Siro), Milano
Internazionale FC...... 2    AS Roma.................. 0

Inter : W.Zenga, G.Bergomi, A.Brehme, S.Battistini, R.Ferri, A.Paganin (G.Baresi 65), A.Bianchi, N.Berti, L.Matthäus, J.Klinsmann, A.Serena (F.Pizzi 89).
Roma : G.Cervone, A. Tempestilli, S.Nela, T.Berthold, Aldair (A.Carboni 72), A.Comi (R.Muzzi 75), M.Gerolin, F.Di Mauro, G.Giannini, R.Völler, R.Rizzitelli.

| | | | |
|---|---|---|---|
| 1-0 | Matthäus pen. | 56 | Referee : Spirin (USSR) |
| 2-0 | Berti | 65 | Attendance : 68,887 |


**2ND LEG**  22/5/91 at Stadio Olimpico, Roma
AS Roma.................. 1    Internazionale FC...... 0

Roma : G.Cervone, A.Tempestilli (F.Salsano 58), S.Nela, Aldair, T.Berthold, M.Gerolin, S.Desideri (R.Muzzi 69), F.Di Mauro, G.Giannini, R.Völler, R.Rizzitelli.
Inter : W.Zenga, A.Paganin, G.Bergomi, R.Ferri, A.Brehme, A.Bianchi, L.Matthäus, S.Battistini, N.Berti, J.Klinsmann, F.Pizzi (A.Mandorlini 67).

| | | | |
|---|---|---|---|
| 1-0 | Rizzitelli | 81 | Referee : Quiniou (France) |
| | | | Attendance : 70,901 |


**INTERNAZIONALE FC WIN 2-1 ON AGGREGATE.**

**Matthäus and Brehme with the UEFA trophy**

# INTERTOTO 1991

The Intertoto competition is played each summer, primarily during the month of July, solely for the purpose of providing matches for the coupons of European football pools. The competition provides 10 group winners and no further matches are played. For 1991 the competition was affected by withdrawals, particularly in respect of Yugoslavian clubs caught up in the country's political upheavals.

## INTERTOTO GROUP 1

| | | | |
|---|---|---|---|
| Slovan Bratislava | 0 | Xamax | 2 |
| Tatabanya | 1 | Malmö FF | 1 |
| Slovan Bratislava | 1 | Malmö FF | 1 |
| Tatabanya | 0 | Xamax | 3 |
| Malmö FF | 1 | Xamax | 2 |
| Slovan Bratislava | 4 | Tatabanya | 2 |
| Malmö FF | 2 | Slovan Bratislava | 2 |
| Xamax | 5 | Tatabanya | 0 |
| Malmö FF | 0 | Tatabanya | 0 |
| Xamax | 2 | Slovan Bratislava | 2 |
| Xamax | 0 | Malmö FF | 0 |
| Tatabanya | 2 | Slovan Bratislava | 1 |

### LEAGUE TABLE FINAL

| | | | | | | | |
|---|---|---|---|---|---|---|---|
| Xamax FC | 6 | 4 | 2 | 0 | 14 | 3 | 10 |
| Slovan Bratislava | 6 | 1 | 3 | 2 | 10 | 11 | 5 |
| Malmö FF | 6 | 0 | 5 | 1 | 5 | 6 | 5 |
| Tatabanya | 6 | 1 | 2 | 3 | 5 | 14 | 4 |

## INTERTOTO GROUP 2

| | | | |
|---|---|---|---|
| Lausanne Sports | 4 | Lyngby BK | 1 |
| Zaglebie Lubin | 2 | IFK Norrköping | 1 |
| Lausanne Sports | 3 | IFK Norrköping | 1 |
| Zaglebie Lubin | 3 | Lyngby BK | 0 |
| IFK Norrköping | 3 | Lyngby BK | 6 |
| Zaglebie Lubin | 1 | Lausanne Sports | 3 |
| Lyngby BK | 3 | Lausanne Sports | 1 |
| IFK Norrköping | 2 | Zaglebie Lubin | 2 |
| Lyngby BK | 3 | Zaglebie Lubin | 0 |
| IFK Norrköping | 0 | Lausanne Sports | 3 |
| Lyngby BK | 3 | IFK Norrköping | 1 |
| Lausanne Sports | 8 | Zaglebie Lubin | 1 |

### LEAGUE TABLE FINAL

| | | | | | | | |
|---|---|---|---|---|---|---|---|
| Lausanne Sports | 6 | 5 | 0 | 1 | 22 | 7 | 10 |
| Lyngby BK | 6 | 4 | 0 | 2 | 16 | 12 | 8 |
| Zaglebie Lubin | 6 | 2 | 1 | 3 | 9 | 17 | 5 |
| IFK Norrköping | 6 | 0 | 1 | 5 | 8 | 19 | 1 |

## INTERTOTO GROUP 3

| | | | |
|---|---|---|---|
| Hallescher FC | 0 | Austria Salzburg | 1 |
| Ikast FS | 0 | Austria Salzburg | 1 |
| Vác | 2 | Hallescher FC | 1 |
| Hallescher FC | 5 | Ikast FS | 2 |
| Vác | 1 | Austria Salzburg | 2 |
| Austria Salzburg | 0 | Hallescher FC | 0 |
| Vác | 2 | Ikast FS | 0 |
| Hallescher FC | 5 | Vác | 1 |
| Austria Salzburg | 2 | Ikast FS | 0 |
| Ikast FS | 2 | Vác | 1 |
| Austria Salzburg | 1 | Vác | 1 |
| Ikast FS | 0 | Hallescher FC | 2 |

### LEAGUE TABLE FINAL

| | | | | | | | |
|---|---|---|---|---|---|---|---|
| Austria Salzburg | 6 | 4 | 2 | 0 | 7 | 2 | 10 |
| Hallescher FC | 6 | 3 | 1 | 2 | 13 | 6 | 7 |
| Vác | 6 | 2 | 1 | 3 | 8 | 11 | 5 |
| Ikast FS | 6 | 1 | 0 | 5 | 4 | 13 | 2 |

## INTERTOTO GROUP 4

| | | | |
|---|---|---|---|
| Silkeborg IF | 4 | Hammarby IF | 1 |
| Hammarby IF | 1 | Dukla Banska B'rica | 2 |
| Energie Cottbus | 0 | Slikeborg IF | 1 |
| Energie Cottbus | 3 | Hammarby IF | 1 |
| Silkeborg IF | 1 | Dukla Banska B'rica | 4 |
| Dukla Banska B'rica | 1 | Energie Cottbus | 0 |
| Hammarby IF | 1 | Silkeborg IF | 3 |
| Silkeborg IF | 4 | Energie Cottbus | 1 |
| Dukla Banska B'rica | 0 | Hammarby IF | 1 |
| Hammarby IF | 3 | Energie Cottbus | 0 |
| Dukla Banska B'rica | 2 | Silkeborg IF | 0 |
| Energie Cottbus | 0 | Dukla Banska B'rica | 2 |

### LEAGUE TABLE FINAL

| | | | | | | | |
|---|---|---|---|---|---|---|---|
| Dukla Banska B'rica | 6 | 5 | 0 | 1 | 11 | 3 | 10 |
| Silkeborg IF | 6 | 4 | 0 | 2 | 13 | 9 | 8 |
| Hammarby IF | 6 | 2 | 0 | 4 | 8 | 12 | 4 |
| Energie Cottbus | 6 | 1 | 0 | 5 | 4 | 12 | 2 |

## INTERTOTO GROUP 5

| | | | |
|---|---|---|---|
| FK Austria Wien | 1 | Djurgardens IF | 0 |
| FK Austria Wien | 1 | B 1903 | 3 |
| Djurgardens IF | 0 | SKP Union Cheb | 0 |
| FK Austria Wien | 4 | SKP Union Cheb | 1 |
| Djurgardens IF | 1 | B 1903 | 2 |
| B 1903 | 1 | FK Austria Wien | 0 |
| SKP Union Cheb | 1 | Djurgardens IF | 0 |
| B 1903 | 2 | Djurgardens IF | 3 |
| SKP Union Cheb | 0 | FK Austria Wien | 1 |
| Djurgardens IF | 1 | FK Austria Wien | 2 |
| SKP Union Cheb | 0 | B 1903 | 2 |
| B 1903 | 3 | SKP Union Cheb | 0 |

### LEAGUE TABLE FINAL

| | | | | | | | |
|---|---|---|---|---|---|---|---|
| B1903 | 6 | 5 | 0 | 1 | 13 | 5 | 10 |
| FK Austria Wien | 6 | 4 | 0 | 2 | 9 | 6 | 8 |
| Djurgardens IF | 6 | 1 | 1 | 4 | 5 | 8 | 3 |
| SKP Union Cheb | 6 | 1 | 1 | 4 | 2 | 10 | 3 |

## INTERTOTO GROUP 6

| | | | |
|---|---|---|---|
| Siófok | 1 | Grasshoppers | 1 |
| BK Frem | 1 | Siófok | 4 |
| BK Frem | 2 | Grasshoppers | 0 |
| Grasshoppers | 3 | BK Frem | 2 |
| Grasshoppers | 1 | Siófok | 0 |
| Siófok | 3 | BK Frem | 3 |

### LEAGUE TABLE FINAL

| | | | | | | | |
|---|---|---|---|---|---|---|---|
| Grasshoppers | 4 | 2 | 1 | 1 | 5 | 5 | 5 |
| Siófok | 4 | 1 | 2 | 1 | 8 | 6 | 4 |
| BK Frem | 4 | 1 | 1 | 2 | 8 | 10 | 3 |

Olimpija Ljubljana did not take part.

## INTERTOTO GROUP 7

| | | | |
|---|---|---|---|
| Bayer Uerdingen ....... 2 | Östers IF ................... 1 |
| Pirin Blagoevgrad ..... 2 | Sturm Graz ............... 0 |
| Pirin Blagoevgrad ...... 2 | Bayer Uerdingen ....... 0 |
| Sturm Graz ............... 1 | Östers IF ................... 1 |
| Bayer Uerdingen ...... 3 | Sturm Graz ............... 1 |
| Pirin Blagoevgrad ..... 1 | Östers IF ................... 1 |
| Bayer Uerdingen ....... 1 | Pirin Blagoevgrad ..... 0 |
| Östers IF .................. 2 | Sturm Graz ............... 0 |
| Sturm Graz ............... 2 | Pirin Blagoevgrad ..... 1 |
| Östers IF .................. 1 | Bayer Uerdingen ....... 1 |
| Östers IF .................. 0 | Pirin Blagoevgrad ..... 0 |
| Sturm Graz ............... 1 | Bayer Uerdingen ....... 0 |

### LEAGUE TABLE FINAL

| | | | | | | | |
|---|---|---|---|---|---|---|---|
| Bayer Uerdingen | 6 | 3 | 1 | 2 | 7 | 6 | 7 |
| Pirin Blagoevgrad | 6 | 2 | 2 | 2 | 6 | 4 | 6 |
| Östers IF | 6 | 1 | 4 | 1 | 6 | 5 | 6 |
| SK Sturm Graz | 6 | 2 | 1 | 3 | 5 | 9 | 5 |

## INTERTOTO GROUP 8

| | | | |
|---|---|---|---|
| Rapid Bucuresti ......... 2 | Botev Plovdiv ............. 1 |
| Botev Plovdiv ............. 1 | DAC Dunajsk.Streda . 3 |
| Rapid Bucuresti ......... 1 | DAC Dunajsk.Streda . 0 |
| DAC Dunajsk.Streda 4 | Botev Plovdiv ............. 0 |
| DAC Dunajsk.Streda .. 3 | Rapid Bucuresti ......... 0 |
| Botev Plovdiv ............. 5 | Rapid Bucuresti ......... 0 |

### LEAGUE TABLE FINAL

| | | | | | | | |
|---|---|---|---|---|---|---|---|
| DAC Dunajska Streda | 4 | 3 | 0 | 1 | 10 | 3 | 6 |
| Rapid Bucuresti | 4 | 2 | 0 | 2 | 3 | 9 | 4 |
| Botev Plovdiv | 4 | 1 | 0 | 3 | 8 | 9 | 2 |
| Rot-Weiss Essen did not take part | | | | | | | |

## INTERTOTO GROUP 9

| | | | |
|---|---|---|---|
| FC Lugano ............... 0 | Buducnost Titograd ... 1 |
| FC Tirol..................... 6 | Sportul Stud'sc B'sti... 0 |
| FC Lugano ............... 4 | Sportul Stud'sc B'sti... 1 |
| FC Tirol..................... 5 | Buducnost Titograd ... 0 |
| FC Tirol..................... 2 | FC Lugano................ 1 |
| Sportul Stud'sc B'sti .. 1 | FC Tirol..................... 2 |
| Sportul Stud'sc B'sti .. 2 | FC Lugano................ 0 |
| FC Lugano ............... 2 | FC Tirol..................... 1 |

### LEAGUE TABLE FINAL

| | | | | | | | |
|---|---|---|---|---|---|---|---|
| FC Tirol | 5 | 4 | 0 | 1 | 16 | 4 | 8 |
| FC Lugano | 5 | 2 | 0 | 3 | 7 | 7 | 4 |
| Buducnost Titograd | 2 | 1 | 0 | 1 | 1 | 5 | 2 |
| Sportul Studensc Bucuresti | 4 | 1 | 0 | 3 | 4 | 12 | 2 |

## INTERTOTO GROUP 10

| | | | |
|---|---|---|---|
| Hapoel P.Tikva ........... 1 | Örebro SK ................. 2 |
| Maccabi Haifa ........... 0 | 1FC Saarbrücken ...... 6 |
| Hapoel P.Tikva ........... 2 | 1FC Saarbrücken ...... 2 |
| Maccabi Haifa ........... 0 | Örebro SK ................. 3 |
| Örebro SK ................. 1 | Hapoel P.Tikva........... 0 |
| 1FC Saarbrücken ....... 5 | Maccabi Haifa............. 1 |
| Örebro SK ................. 1 | Maccabi Haifa............. 0 |
| 1FC Saarbrücken ....... 7 | Hapoel P.Tikva........... 3 |
| Örebro SK ................. 2 | 1FC Saarbrücken ...... 2 |
| Hapoel P.Tikva ........... 2 | Maccabi Haifa............. 3 |
| 1FC Saarbrücken ...... 1 | Örebro SK ................. 2 |
| Maccabi Haifa ........... 2 | Hapoel P.Tikva........... 0 |

### LEAGUE TABLE FINAL

| | | | | | | | |
|---|---|---|---|---|---|---|---|
| Örebro SK | 6 | 5 | 1 | 0 | 11 | 4 | 11 |
| 1FC Saarbrücken | 6 | 3 | 2 | 1 | 23 | 10 | 8 |
| Maccabi Haifa | 6 | 2 | 0 | 4 | 6 | 17 | 4 |
| Hapoel P.Tikva | 6 | 0 | 1 | 5 | 8 | 17 | 1 |

# MITROPA CUP 1991

## GROUP A

| | | | |
|---|---|---|---|
| Torino........................1 | Vorwärts Steyr ...........0 |
| Vorwärts Steyr ...........2 | Veszprem...................2 |
| Veszprem...................0 | Torino ........................1 |

### LEAGUE TABLE FINAL

| | | | | | | | |
|---|---|---|---|---|---|---|---|
| Torino | 2 | 2 | 0 | 0 | 2 | 0 | 4 |
| Veszprem | 2 | 0 | 1 | 1 | 2 | 3 | 1 |
| Vorwärts Steyr | 2 | 0 | 1 | 1 | 2 | 3 | 1 |

## GROUP B

| | | | |
|---|---|---|---|
| Pisa ..........................4 | Rad Beograd .............1 |
| Bohemians Praha.......0 | Pisa...........................0 |
| Rad Beograd .............2 | Bohemians Praha ......4 |

### LEAGUE TABLE FINAL

| | | | | | | | |
|---|---|---|---|---|---|---|---|
| Pisa | 2 | 1 | 1 | 0 | 4 | 1 | 3 |
| Bohemians Praha | 2 | 1 | 1 | 0 | 4 | 2 | 3 |
| Rad Beograd | 2 | 0 | 0 | 2 | 3 | 8 | 0 |

## FINAL

| | | |
|---|---|---|
| Torino........................2 | Pisa...........................1 (aet.) |